Turbo Pascal
Programming and Problem Solving

Turbo Pascal
Programming and Problem Solving

Mickey Settle
Pensacola Junior College

Michel Boillot
Pensacola Junior College

West Publishing Company
St. Paul   New York   Los Angeles   San Francisco

Production Credits

Copyediting:	Mary Peterson Berry, Naples Editing Service; Chris Thillen; and Janet M. Hunter
Text Design:	David J. Farr, *Imagesmythe, Inc.*
Composition:	Carlisle Communications
Technical Art:	Carlisle Communications
Cover Design:	David J. Farr, *Imagesmythe, Inc.*
Cover Art:	Pix*Elation/Fran Heyl Associates

COPYRIGHT © 1988 By WEST PUBLISHING COMPANY
50 W. Kellogg Boulevard
P.O. Box 64526
St. Paul, MN 55164-1003

Printed in the United States of America

Library of Congress Cataloging-in-Publication Data

Settle, Mickey
    Turbo Pascal: programming and problem solving/Mickey Settle, Michel Boillot.
        p. cm.
    Includes index.
    ISBN 0-314-62309-4, ISBN 0-314-62308-8 (soft)
    1. PASCAL (Computer program language)   2. Turbo Pascal (Computer
program)   I. Boillot, Michel H.   II. Title.
QA76.73.P2863   1988
005.265—dc 19

                                                        87-29519
                                                        CIP

Contents

Preface

This text presents an approach to problem solving and programming using micro-computers and the Pascal language. The material, designed for students who are taking a first course in programming, is presented in a clear, concise, and interesting fashion. The examples and their solutions illustrate the top down problem-solving approach and the modular approach to programming.

Top down design

The book is designed to be used with the Turbo Pascal language. The major feature of the language emphasized is its ability to produce readable programs that can be altered and expanded. The key to the production of these programs is solution design. Each example problem presented is followed by a design of its solution and refinement of the steps in the design. Additionally, a set of style rules that enhance readability is presented in Chapter 1 and is used in all programs throughout the book.

Readability

The learner's background was taken into account in selecting the order of the topics. First, the essentials of problem solution design and of Pascal programs are discussed. Next, decision control and repetition control are covered. Procedures and functions are then presented. Since procedures and functions are the essence of the Pascal approach to programming, its presentation is carefully developed. The last half of the text is devoted to data, data structures, and examples of problem solving; this portion begins with an in-depth discussion of strings (which are introduced in Chapter 1 and used throughout the book) and TEXT files.

Organization

Learning Features

We use appropriate pedagogical techniques to optimize student learning. This starts with readability—the material is easy to read. Do It Now exercises and their answers are interspersed throughout each chapter to provide the student with immediate feedback. Problem examples and their solutions (complete with design, refinement, discussion, and actual Pascal code) are presented in nearly every section of the book to insure that concept and application fuse into a whole. Comments, programming points, and warnings are strategically positioned throughout the book to capture the student's attention. A vocabulary list—essentially a mini-glossary—is included at the end of each section. Also included at the end of each section is an instructional unit in question and answer format; in it, we anticipate commonly asked questions and provide informally phrased answers. The questions represent a compilation of predictable pitfalls for novice programmers.

Do It Now
Comments
Mini-glossary
Glad You Asked

Exercise Sets

Finally, and often of great importance to students and instructors, each section concludes with a complete set of exercises. These exercises consist of objective questions, outlines of programs to be completed, and programming problems graduated in order of difficulty. Each chapter includes a comprehensive chapter test. Chapters 4 through 9 each conclude with two major programming projects.

Disk

Source diskette

A major innovative feature is the diskette Source available with the book. This diskette contains TEXT files for all the programming examples in the book. The book's user can experiment with these programs without having to spend long hours keying in the programs. The diskette also includes the tutorial NumFun on numeric operations, format, and functions and the tutorial BOOL on BOOLEAN expressions and operations. At least one problem in each exercise set refers to files from the Source diskette. These problems are flagged with a diskette icon.

Student Information Processor

The Source diskette also contains a Student Information Processor (SIP). This application program allows users to study the vocabulary of the text through use of multiple choice, matching, true-or-false, and completion (spelling) quizzes. A ten-item quiz is selected randomly, with random ordering of the items. Thus, users can work with a lesson until they achieve mastery. Data files containing the vocabulary terms from the first five chapters are already on the Source diskette. The program allows full interaction with existing lessons and provides the ability to create new lessons. This application can be accessed from the system prompt by entering A:SIP (provided the Source diskette is in disk drive A).

Additional Materials

Complete coverage of Turbo editor

Instruction on the Turbo Editor begins in Chapter 1 with a section on the copy command; in Chapter 2, the Search and Replace applications are covered; later chapters discuss debugging. This information allows students to use the full power of the editor to create Pascal programs. It is supplemented by Appendix A, a tutorial on the Turbo Editor.

Graphics

Another extra is the appendix on graphics. This appendix provides (in tutorial form) information on the graphics features of Turbo Pascal. Additionally, the Source diskette contains programs that produce attractive graphics and games (see the DesignRe and LifeGo files). Overviews of the Turbo Editor commands, copy applications, and reminders of such features as error messages are included for easy reference on the inside back cover.

Supplements

The solutions to **all** the exercises in the text are set forth in an instructor's manual, available separately. This manual also contains teaching suggestions, discussion questions, and a test bank. Both the test bank and the solutions are available on diskette for PC systems. Through the use of this software, many interesting exercises can be developed. First, tests and practice tests can be composed from the test bank. Some exercises developed from the solutions diskette include completion exercises for programming problems that are not assigned. That is, the instructor can clip a program from the diskette, make deletions to the program, and present it to students as a completion exercise. Another possible exercise, to teach debugging and program testing, is to alter a program from the diskette and have the students debug the altered version. Finally, programs from the diskette can be given to the students to alter or expand to meet instructor-stated objectives. These activities increase student understanding and are time efficient. A set of 50 transparency masters is available to adopters.

Also available is a student lab manual Turbo Pascal IS. This manual contains a series of computer lab experiments involving the programs listed in the book. These experiments demonstrate the ability to alter and expand Pascal programs. Additionally, special features of the Pascal language (such as the Include option) and of the Turbo Editor are explored. An experiment is provided for each section from the book. Each experiment is followed by a lab report, which allows for ready feedback on the learning activity.

The idea behind the approach to programming instruction used in the lab manual is to allow students to experiment with the programs presented in the book without expending the time and effort to key in the programs. Finally, and of utmost importance, the concept of converting programs to modules for use in other programs is fully developed in the manual. This major topic of modular programming, so difficult to develop in a text book, is a natural in a lab experiment environment. Through the lab experiments, the students build diskettes of utilities (modules) that are then used in other programs (including the programming exercises in the book).

Instructor's package
• Solutions to all exercises
• Test bank
• Transparency masters
• Turbo 4.0 tutorials
• Two disks containing all solutions plus test bank
• SIP tutorial

Turbo Pascal IS
Student independent study, computer lab manual, works with Source disk.

Acknowledgments

The authors would like to thank editor Peter Marshall for his support and insight. Special acknowledgment is extended to Becky Tollerson for her assistance throughout the project and to Beth Wickum, production editor. Rab Ceka is to be commended for the pen and ink drawings found in the book.

The many reviewers who helped shape and define this book are listed here. Our thanks go to all of them.

Wilna Ates	Central Piedmont Community College
Rayford Ball	Odessa College
Al Cripps	Middle Tennessee State University
Phillip Gabrini	New Mexico State University
Don Goulet	University of Wisconsin—Stevens Point
Ann Heard	Georgetown College
Jacquelyn Jarboe	University of Wisconsin—Milwaukee
Christine Kay	DeVry Institute of Technology—Chicago
George Kung	University of Wisconsin—Stevens Point
Jack Lin	Northern Virginia Community College
Jack Lloyd	Montgomery College—Rockville
Woody Martin	Chaffey College
Malik Rahman	Massachusetts Bay Community College
Fred Scott	Broward Community College
James Aman	St. Pius X High School—Houston, Texas
Tom Cuthbertson	Rochester High School—Rochester, Michigan
Jeff Gold	Tuxedo Union Free High School—Tuxedo Park, New York
Linda Hardman	Judson High School—Converse, Texas
Hugh Harris	Orange High School—Pepper Pike, Ohio
Bob Hartman	Kent Meridian High School—Kent, Washington
Bronson Hokuf	Perryville High School—Perryville, Maryland
David Martin	Jericho Public Schools—Jericho, New York
Wayne Merckling	Mt. Olive Schools—Budd Lake, New Jersey
Don Newsted	Ann Arbor Huron High School—Ann Arbor, Michigan
James Smith	Central High School—Elkhart, Indiana
Jim Villman	Palm Springs High School—Palm Springs, California

Linda Hardman deserves special note both for her input into the project and for her work on the instructor's manual developed for the text.

Author Mickey G. Settle would like to extend special thanks to his family for their support in this project. Thank you Robin, Joshua, Gary, and David.

Turbo Pascal
Programming and Problem Solving

Chapter One

Introduction to Problem Solving

Introduction

In this chapter, you will be introduced to the process of solving problems on the computer. The main steps of problem solving with the computer will be discussed. This problem-solving process will be used throughout the textbook. You will be introduced to the general function of the computer: input data, work on the data, and output results. In particular, you will study the Pascal instructions READ, READLN, WRITE, and WRITELN. You will also study some of the types of data available in Pascal: CHAR, STRING, INTEGER, and REAL. Of major importance, you will see the building blocks of a Pascal program and the punctuation required for the computer to understand the program. Also, you will be introduced to a writing style to be used in writing Pascal programs.

```
PROGRAM Chapter1 ;                              {page 14}
CONST Greet = 'Hello ' ;                        {page 25}
VAR Name : STRING [20] ;                        {page 15}
    Ans : CHAR ;                                {page 15}
    Age : INTEGER ;                             {page 34}
    Weight : REAL ;                             {page 45}
BEGIN                                           {page 16}
  WRITE ('Enter your name: ') ;                 {page 17}
  READLN (Name) ;                               {page 19}
  WRITELN (Greet, Name) ;                       {page 17}
  WRITE (Name) ;
  WRITE (' enter age: ') ;
  READLN (Age) ;                                {page 38}
  Age := Age + 2 ;                              {page 36}
  WRITE ('Enter weight: ') ;
  READLN (Weight) ;                             {page 46}
  WRITELN (LST,Name) ;                          {page 18}
  WRITELN (LST,'Age:', Age:10) ;                {page 37}
  WRITELN (LST,'Weight:',Weight:10:2) ;         {page 49}
  WRITE ('Press Q to quit- ') ;
  READ (Ans)                                    {page 19}
END .                                           {page 16}
```

Problem Solving and the Computer

In the coming weeks, you will experience an introduction to computer programming with the computer language Pascal. Computer programming consists of writing programs (solutions to problems) in a language that can be understood by a computer. The major goal of this textbook is to provide you with guidance and instruction in a method of solving problems. The computer and the Pascal computer language will be very supportive in this endeavor.

For the purpose of this introduction, the process you will encounter in solving problems with the computer can be divided into two parts: the physical process and the mental process.

1-1.1 The Physical Process

The physical process you will encounter in this course involves a computer system and the Pascal language. We will start with a short discussion of a **computer system.** A computer system can be thought of as a system composed of five components: input devices, memory, control, arithmetic/logic, and output devices. A typical personal computer system is shown in Figure 1-1.

Figure 1-1

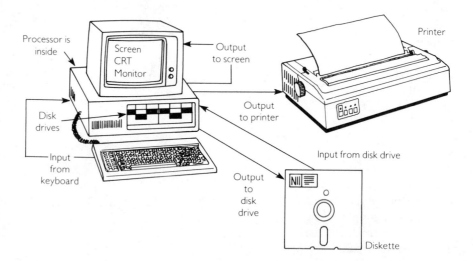

For the system in Figure 1-1, there are two **input devices:** the **disk drives** and the **keyboard.** Through these devices, information enters the computer. The information is usually in the form of instructions (your program) or data (information on which a program will operate).

The memory, control, and arithmetic/logic units are all grouped together under the label *processor.* (See Figure 1-2.)

1. **Memory.** This is divided into cells. Each cell has an address. In these cells, instructions and data are stored.

2. **Control.** This unit is used to obtain and execute the instructions of a program. It is also used to get data needed by the program and to store the data generated by the program.

3. **Arithmetic/logic.** This unit is used to perform operations such as addition, subtraction, multiplication, and division. It also performs logical operations such as comparing two numbers or two names.

The last two components (the control unit and the arithmetic/logic unit) are often referred to as the **central processing unit (CPU).**

The computer system pictured in Figure 1–1 contains three **output devices**: the disk drives, the **monitor** (TV screen or cathode-ray tube, also called CRT), and the **printer.** Information generated by the computer program might be displayed on the screen, printed on paper, or stored on a diskette. When information is printed out on paper, it is called a **hard copy** of the information.

All of these devices (disk drives, CRT, keyboard, CPU, and printer) are referred to as **hardware.** That is, hardware consists of physical components. But a computer is much more than just hardware. Its other major part is the **software.** Software includes the language used by the programmer and the programs written by the programmer. Of course, the language you will be using in this course is Pascal. To obtain a feel for how hardware and software combine and interact, consider the following example.

The computer user runs a program that requests the user to type in a name. The user types in a name. The name is then printed out on the printer.

1. At the start, let us assume the program instructions are already stored on a diskette in a disk drive. When the user runs the program, the computer inputs (reads) these instructions into its main memory:

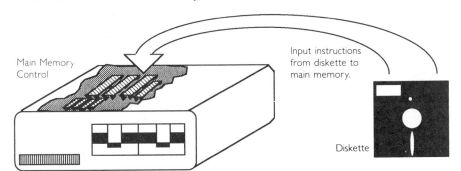

Main Memory
Control

Input instructions from diskette to main memory.

Diskette

2. As the instructions are executed, a program instruction causes the computer's CPU to output (print) a message such as the one here to the screen (CRT).

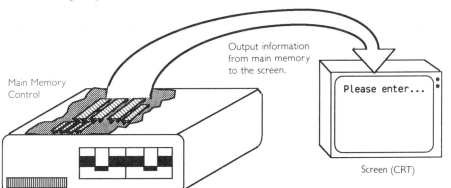

Main Memory
Control

Output information from main memory to the screen.

Please enter...

Screen (CRT)

Figure 1–2

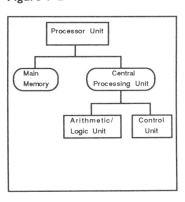

Sample Execution

Please enter your name:

3. The user types in his/her name on the keyboard to input the data. An instruction in the computer program causes the characters typed by the user to be stored in memory.

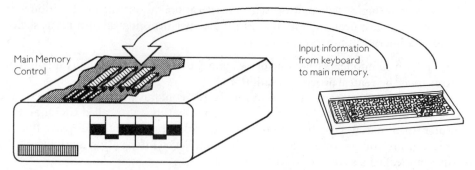

4. An instruction in the computer program causes the CPU to look up the memory location of the characters entered and to output a copy of these characters to the printer.

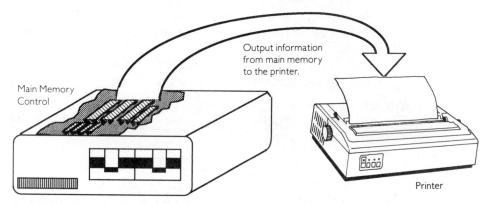

The physical process you will encounter also involves the **Pascal** language, which was written by Niklaus Wirth in 1970 and 1971 and named for the French mathematician and philosopher Blaise Pascal (1623–1662). This language is referred to as Standard Pascal. In 1975 and 1976, under the supervision of Kenneth Bowles, a version of the Pascal language was developed for the personal computer environment. This language is referred to as UCSD Pascal. Philippe Kahn and Borland International released Turbo Pascal in 1983. This book is concerned mainly with Turbo Pascal. Some of the major differences between Turbo Pascal and Standard Pascal are presented in Appendix C.

The process you will encounter in using Turbo Pascal is essentially as shown in Figure 1–3.

Figure 1–3

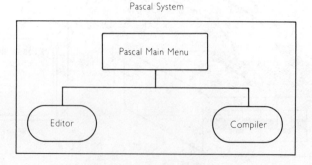

1. You will boot up the Pascal system. That is, you will load the Pascal language from a diskette in the disk drive into the computer's memory. You will be greeted by a screen displaying the various built-in programs of the Pascal language. This screen is referred to as the Pascal main menu.

Turbo Pascal Main Menu

```
Logged drive: A
Active directory: \

Work file :
Main file :

Edit  Compile     Run    Save

Dir   Quit      compiler Options

  ext :       0 bytes
  ree :  62024 bytes

  >
```

2. From the Pascal main menu, you will enter the **editor**. In the editor, you will type in the text of the program you have written.

Turbo Pascal Editor   status line

```
      Line 1  Col 1  Insert  Indent  A:MyFile.PAS
  _
```

3. You will return to the main menu and have the compiler convert the text of your program to code.
4. The code will then be executed. The code may cause information to be written to the screen, to a diskette in a disk drive, or to the printer.

Steps 3 and 4 are combined when the Run application is selected from the main menu. For a much more detailed explanation (refinement) of this process, see Appendix A.

1-1.2 The Mental Process/Top Down Design

The main focus of this book is on the mental process. Essentially, the mental process is solve the problem, then convert your solution to the Pascal language. The refinement of this mental process will be discussed throughout this book. Essential to the mental process is a procedure for solving problems. An outline of the problem-solving procedure presented in this book is as follows:

1. Obtain a problem to be solved.
2. Outline a solution to the problem.
3. Fill in the outline with details.
4. Write a program; that is, convert the solution to a language that the computer can understand.

5. Enter the program into the computer.
6. Have the computer execute the program.
7. Verify that the program solves the original problem.

This problem-solving approach is known as a top down approach with stepwise refinement. The major steps required to solve the problem are listed (Step 2). These major steps are successively refined until only simple instructions remain (Step 3).

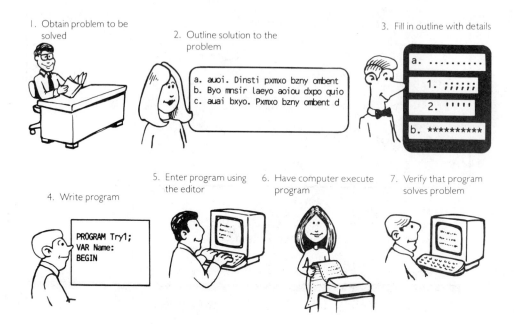

1. Obtain problem to be solved

2. Outline solution to the problem

   a. auoi. Dinsti pxmxo bzny ombent
   b. Byo mnsir laeyo aoiou dxpo quio
   c. auai bxyo. Pxmxo bzny ombent d

3. Fill in outline with details

4. Write program

PROGRAM Try1;
VAR Name:
BEGIN

5. Enter program using the editor

6. Have computer execute program

7. Verify that program solves problem

Obtain a Problem to Be Solved The text material (or your instructor) will provide the problems.

COMMENT
If you cannot reason how to solve the problem by hand, then you cannot write instructions to tell the computer how to solve the problem.

Outline a Solution to the Problem This is the "thinking" part of the process. The text material will help with illustrations and discussions. However, this phase draws largely on *your* knowledge and *your* past experiences. Inherent in this phase is testing your proposed solution.

Testing a proposed solution is usually done by "a hand simulation" or "a walk through" of the design. This testing involves knowing the situation in which your program is to work. To get a feel for this phase, consider the following story.

Jody is to solve the problem, "Find the arithmetic average of three numbers." Jody reasons as follows: "The average of 5, 6, and 7 is 6; the average of 8, 12, and 16 is 12; the average of 45, 65, and 85 is 65." Jody proposes this design:

    READ in the three numbers
    Order the three numbers from smallest to largest
    Select the middle number
    WRITE the value of the middle number

Jody tests the design using the above examples.

Jody's solution works in all the above situations. But it does not work for *any* three numbers. Suppose Jody were given the numbers 3, 4, and 20. This method would produce an average of 4. However, the arithmetic average of 3, 4, and 20 is 9. Jody did not fully test the design. This is an extreme example, but it does illustrate this critical phase of solving problems. Failure to test a design fully is the major cause of program failures and rewrites.

Fill in the Outline with Details This phase simply expands the outline of the solution. In the outline, you stated the steps needed to solve the problem. Here, you state how each step can be performed. This phase is often referred to as **stepwise refinement** of the solution design. Of course, you will test the refinement of a step by "hand simulation." Also, at this stage you begin to consider translating your solution into a language the computer can understand, such as Pascal.

COMMENT
At this point, all you have is an outline of the solution. If it does not test out, you have not lost much work. If you wait until later to test your solution, you will have invested considerable time and effort that might end up being wasted.

Write a Program (Convert the Solution to a Language the Computer Can Understand) This phase involves knowledge of a computer language. In this text, the computer language will be Pascal. Your solution, called an **algorithm,** will be converted to a collection of instructions that the compiler can understand. This collection of instructions is called a **computer program.**

Enter the Program into the Computer In a computer system using Pascal, this is accomplished by running a program called the editor. This program allows you to type in text material, move lines, delete lines, and insert lines. When you have typed in your program, the editor keeps a copy of your work. This copy is held in a "file" and is known as the **source code.** Different computer systems have different editors. Your instructor will discuss the editor used on your system, or you can use the tutorial in Appendix A.

Have the Computer Execute the Program In a computer system using Pascal, this is accomplished by first running a program called the **compiler.** The compiler takes the text you typed in during the last phase (the source code) and converts it to a language that is more natural (machinelike) to the computer. The converted program is called the **object code.** After the program has been converted to object code, the object code can be "executed" by the computer.

Verify That the Program Solves the Original Problem This stage is often referred to as "debugging" the program. A "bug" (error) is a part of the program that does not perform as the programmer intended. Most of these errors have their source in the design of the solution. Often they originate in situations overlooked by the programmer at the design stage. Sometimes they arise from situations unknown to the programmer during the design stage. Only through program testing (debugging) can these errors be identified and ultimately corrected.

If you don't fully understand all this information at this point, do not worry. The problem-solving approach will be illustrated over and over in the material that follows. A major goal of this textbook is to teach you to approach problem solving by following the steps just explained.

In summary, a computer program is a list of instructions to be carried out by the computer. In solving a problem, you compose a list of instructions (algorithm) on paper. You make every effort to obtain a list of instructions that will solve the problem prior to sitting down at the computer. Once the problem has been solved, the solution design is converted to a Pascal program, which is then executed. In most situations, the computer does not enter the problem-solving process until the problem has been solved.

COMMENT

A major mistake made by beginning students is attempting to solve a problem while sitting at a computer terminal. Most often, this results in frustration caused by forgetting to include critical parts of the solution. When a program is produced in this manner, it is often disorganized and unreadable. This is contrary to the goals of the Pascal approach to programming. Sitting at a computer terminal is not a good environment for the critical activity in problem solving: *thinking*.

1-1.3 Structured Programming

Before heading off into the material that lies ahead, take this time to get your bearings on where you are going. To obtain this view, consider the following problem.

PROBLEM

Convert a numeric grade input by the user to a letter grade (based on the following grading scale), then write the letter grade to the screen. Do this until the user requests to quit.

Numeric Grade	Letter Grade
93–100	A
85–92	B
75–84	C
65–74	D
Below 65	F

Sample Execution

```
Enter number grade (0..100): 88
Your letter grade is: B
Press RETURN to continue, enter Q to quit: Q
```

SOLUTION

The place to start in solving a problem is with a **design** of the solution. That is, compose an outline of the major steps that will solve the problem. Here, the idea is to get an overall or global view of the problem's solution. The details of the major steps are put off until later.

Design: REPEAT
          Get numeric grade from user
          Look up numeric grade in scale and get letter grade
          Write letter grade to the screen
          Check with user about quitting
        UNTIL user wants to quit

The next step is to test the design by walking through it with several examples. Walking through the design with examples will not only test the design; it also will give you an idea of how to refine a given step in the design. After testing the design, the steps are refined.

Refinement of *Get numeric grade from user*
          WRITE ('Enter number grade (0 .. 100): ')
          READLN (NumGrade)

Refinement of *Look up numeric grade in scale and get letter grade*
          IF (NumGrade > = 93) AND (NumGrade < = 100)
            THEN LetGrade : = 'A'
          IF (NumGrade > = 85) AND (NumGrade < = 92)
            THEN LetGrade : = 'B'
          IF (NumGrade > = 75) AND (NumGrade < = 84)
            THEN LetGrade : = 'C'
          IF (NumGrade > = 65) AND (NumGrade < = 74)
            THEN LetGrade : = 'D'
          IF NumGrade < 65
            THEN LetGrade : = 'F'

Refinement of *Write letter grade to the screen*
          WRITE ('Your letter grade is: ')
          WRITE (LetGrade)

Refinement of *Check with user about quitting*
          WRITE ('Press RETURN to continue, ')
          WRITE ('enter Q to quit- ')
          READ (Ans)

At this point, the design and its refinements are tested by walking through the design with several sample inputs. That is, you want to make every effort to assert that you have solved the problem.

The next step is to convert the design to a Pascal program. You enter the editor and type in the Pascal program. The program text would then be converted to code. The final phase would be to test the program. This would be accomplished by executing the code. Several different numeric grades would be entered and the corresponding output observed.

To accomplish the conversion to a Pascal program you must know the following:

1. The general layout of a Pascal program. This will be covered in Chapter 1.
2. How to work with character and numeric data. This will be covered in Chapter 1.
3. How to make a decision as to whether or not to execute an instruction (as in the IF-THEN instruction above). This will be covered in Chapter 2.
4. How to repeat the execution of an instruction (as in the REPEAT-UNTIL instruction above). This will be covered in Chapter 3.
5. How to construct a subprogram to do a complex step in the design (that is, how to make the program reflect the solution design). This will be covered in Chapter 4.

From Chapter 5 on, you will enter the next major phase of constructing a computer program. This phase involves data and its various structures (that is, how the data can be arranged). These structures include sets, text files, arrays, and records.

The programming approach just described is known as **structured programming.** The idea is to produce a top down design of the problem's solution, then convert the design to a program that parallels the design. The objectives of using this approach are to produce programs that are: readable; easily tested and corrected; reliable (they solve the problem); and easily altered and/or expanded.

Vocabulary

Page		
7	**Algorithm**	A step-by-step procedure for solving a problem. In computer programming, the algorithm yields the computer program.
3	**Arithmetic/logic**	The unit of the computer that performs arithmetic and logic operations on data.
3	**Central processing unit (CPU)**	A part of the computer's processor unit that executes the instructions of a computer program.
7	**Compiler**	A program that converts the text of a program (the source code) to machine code (object code).
7	**Computer program**	A list of instructions to be performed by the computer. These instructions must be written in a language that the computer understands (such as Pascal).
2	**Computer system**	A collection of components typically containing input devices, output devices, and a processor unit.
3	**Control**	The unit of the computer used to obtain and execute the instructions of a program. It also gets data needed by the program and stores the data generated by the program.
9	**Design**	The process of producing an outline containing the main steps in a problem's solution. The main steps are then refined into smaller, more manageable steps.
2	**Disk drive**	A physical component of a computer system that serves as both an input device and an output device.
5	**Editor**	A computer program that aids the programmer in composing a program. This program provides the ability to insert and delete text.
3	**Hard copy**	A printed copy (on paper) of information output by the computer.
3	**Hardware**	The physical components of a computer system.
3	**Input**	The process of getting information to the processor. This process is most often accomplished by use of the keyboard or the disk drive.

Input device   One of the physical components of a computer system. Such a device allows information (data) to be entered into the computer's main memory. A disk drive and the keyboard are input devices.   2

Keyboard   A physical component of a computer system that allows the user to input information by pressing typewriter-like keys.   2

Memory   The internal data storage unit of a computer system.   2

Monitor   A physical component of a computer system that serves as an output device. Also known as the CRT and the screen.   3

Object code   The results of the compiler's operating on the source code of a Pascal program. This code can be executed by the computer's CPU.   7

Output   The process of getting information from the processor. The results of this process are usually displayed on the screen or printed out on the printer. However, the results could be stored on a diskette in the disk drive.   3

Output device   One of the physical components of a computer system. Such a device allows information (data) to be output from the computer's main memory. A disk drive and the screen are output devices.   3

Pascal   A language the computer can understand. This language can be used to write a computer program that reflects the design of a problem's solution.   4

Printer   A physical component of a computer system that outputs information by printing it on paper.   3

Problem solving   A process of obtaining (through thinking) a list of instructions needed to solve a selected problem.   6

Software   The collection of all computer programs used by the computer system. These programs include the language used by the programmer and the programs produced using the language.   3

Source code   The text of a Pascal program. This text is entered into the computer by use of the editor.   7

Stepwise refinement   One of the phases of top down approach to problem solving. In this phase, the major steps required to solve the problem are broken down into even smaller tasks.   7

Structured programming   An approach to producing a computer program by first producing a top down design of a problem's solution. Once the design is developed, it is converted to a computer program that parallels the design.   10

Section 1-1 Exercises

1. Match the following items on the left with the letter of the correct description on the right.

   _____ **1.** CPU   **a.** the results produced by the compiler
   _____ **2.** source code   **b.** a program used to enter the text of a Pascal program
   _____ **3.** disk drive   **c.** central processing unit
   _____ **4.** keyboard   **d.** a device that can be used for both input and output
   _____ **5.** algorithm   **e.** the text form of a Pascal program
   _____ **6.** object code   **f.** a device used to input data
   _____ **7.** printer   **g.** a device used to produce a hard copy of the output of
   _____ **8.** editor   a computer program
                         h. a list of instructions that solve a problem

2. When you type in the contents of a computer program you have written, which of the following do you use?

   a. CPU   **b.** editor   **c.** printer   **d.** compiler

3. The text of a Pascal program is called the
   a. CRT.   **b.** object code.   **c.** debugger.   **d.** source code.

4. To solve a problem by the process discussed in this section, you should start by
   a. sitting down at the computer and typing in a program.
   b. thinking about the problem and writing an outline of the solution.
   c. running a program called the editor.
   d. running a program called the compiler.

5. Which of the following is an output device?
   a. CRT   **b.** compiler   **c.** CPU   **d.** keyboard

6. Which of the following is an input device?
   a. printer   **b.** CRT   **c.** disk drive   **d.** monitor

7. After an outline is made for a problem's solution, the next step is to
   a. have the computer execute the outline.
   b. fill in the outline with details.
   c. use the editor to compile the outline.
   d. convert the outline to a Pascal program.
   e. use the compiler to convert the outline to object code.

8. Which of the following is used to convert source code to object code?
   a. compiler   **b.** CRT   **c.** editor   **d.** the disk drive

9. After an outline has been made of a problem's solution and the details of the outline have been filled in, the next step is to
   a. convert the outline and its details to a Pascal program.
   b. have the compiler convert the outline to object code.
   c. execute the outline and its details.
   d. have the CPU process the outline.

10. One of the major steps in the problem-solving process discussed in this section is "outline a solution to the problem." Complete the outline of the solution to the following problems.
   a. Problem: Find the sum of two fractions.
      1. Find a common denominator for the two denominators.
      2. Rename each fraction such that the denominator is the common denominator.
      3. . . .
      4. . . .
   b. Problem: Find the volume of a box.
      1. Find the measurements of the length, width, and height.
      2. . . .
   c. Problem: Solve a first-degree equation in one variable.
      1. Remove parentheses from the equation.
      2. Simplify the polynomial on the left side of the equation.
      3. . . .
   d. Problem: Teach a friend how to subtract integers.
      1. . . .
         . . .
   e. Problem: Buy a car.
      1. . . .
         . . .
   f. Problem: Raise money for a charitable cause.
      1. . . .
         . . .

11. Suppose you were assigned the problem of writing a ten-page term paper on the life of Blaise Pascal (1623–1662). Outline a solution to this problem.

12. (Difficult) Suppose you wanted to write a program to solve a second-degree equation in one variable. A possible design would be

Design: Rewrite the equation to standard form
          Identify the values a, b, and c
          Compute the discriminant
          Report the solution to the equation

Walk through this design for the equation $x^2 - 3x = 2x + 6$.

Using the actions you took in your walk through, give a refinement of each of the steps in the design. Test your design and the refinements of each step with the equation $2x^2 - 5 = x^2 - 2x + 3$.

13. Use the knowledge you have obtained and the skills you have developed in working with the Pascal system (from Appendix A) to
    a. use the editor to enter the program text below.
    b. save the material to a TEXT file on a diskette.
    c. write to the printer the contents of the TEXT file.

```
PROGRAM APascalSample ;

VAR Count : INTEGER ;
    Name : STRING [80] ;

BEGIN
  WRITE ('Please enter your name: ') ;
  READLN (Name) ;
  FOR Count := 1 TO 10 DO
    WRITELN ('Welcome to Pascal ', Name) ;
  WRITELN ('We will work together soon. Goodbye')
END .
```

14. The material in problem 13 is a valid Pascal program. Use the knowledge you have obtained and the skills you have developed in working with the Pascal system to
    a. convert the text material to code.
    b. execute the code.
15. Referring to the code of the Pascal program you executed in problem 14,
    a. what was the input for the program?
    b. what was the output of the program?
16. Use the Pascal editor to write a short paper on the topic "A Human as a Computer System." Discuss the input devices, output devices, and processor unit. Use the Pascal system to produce a hard copy of your paper.

Section 1–2

READ and WRITE

In Section 1–1, you were presented the "big picture" of solving problems with Pascal. In this section, you will study some of the pieces that make up the big picture. You will study the general form of a Pascal program; identifiers; the Pascal reserved word VAR and the concept of variables; the data types CHAR and STRING; and the Pascal predefined procedures WRITE, WRITELN, READ, and READLN.

1-2.1 The Program Form

A Pascal program is constructed in blocks. Each major part of a Pascal program is thought of as a block of the program. The mental image suggested is that of taking the blocks and building a Pascal program.

Each block of a Pascal program can be decomposed into a header section and various other sections. For now, you will only be concerned with the main program block. Later, you will study other program blocks (such as procedure blocks and function blocks). Consider the following Pascal program:

COMMENT
The material enclosed in braces (the symbols { and }) is referred to as program comments. Any material enclosed in braces is ignored by the Pascal compiler.

```
PROGRAM TryIt ;                              {Program header}

VAR Name : String [80] ;                     {VAR section}
    Ch   : CHAR ;

BEGIN                                        {Execution section}
  WRITE ('Please enter your name- ') ;
  READLN (Name) ;
  WRITELN ('Thank you ' , Name) ;
  WRITE ('Press RETURN key to quit ') ;
  READ (Ch)
END .
```

The first line, `PROGRAM TryIt`, is called the **program header.** This line contains the Pascal reserved word PROGRAM and the name (identifier) of the program. Every Pascal program must start with the word PROGRAM. Following the word PROGRAM comes the name of the program. In the above program, the name is `TryIt`. The name of the program is made up by the programmer.

1-2.2 Identifiers

COMMENT
The Pascal compiler accepts either uppercase or lowercase letters. That is, `Name, NAME,` and `name` are all the same identifier.

In Pascal, names made up by the programmer are called **identifiers.** In making up these names (identifiers), the programmer must follow these rules:

1. The identifier may contain *only* **alphanumeric** characters (A, B, C, . . . , Y, Z; a, b, c, . . . , y, z; 0, 1, 2, . . . , 8, 9) and the *underscore* (the character __) character.
2. The identifier must *start* with a letter of the alphabet.
3. A word reserved by the Pascal language cannot be used as an identifier (these words, called **reserved words,** are listed in Appendix B).
4. Blank spaces are not allowed in an identifier.
5. An identifier can be up to 127 characters long.

PROGRAMMING POINT
In writing a Pascal program, the Pascal reserved words should be written in capital letters. This enables the reader to see quickly which words are from the Pascal language and which words are made up by the programmer. Also, since blank spaces are not allowed, names such as `TryIt` and `Try_It` are used.

PROGRAMMING POINT
In choosing an identifier (name), the programmer should select one that describes the object being named! That is, stay away from names like `KT4, RedDog,` or `PitPat`.

The following identifiers (names) are valid:

```
Data2      LastLine   Answer
Data3      X3         In_Word
SquareIt   J          In_Line
```

The following are not valid identifiers:

```
$word   #two   2words    (these start with a nonalphabetic character)
BEGIN   end    Program   (these are Pascal reserved words)
See It                   (this one contains a blank space)
```

DO IT NOW

Which of the following are valid identifiers?

1. `PasCow`
2. `3rdProg`
3. `Prog03`
4. `Program`
5. `Draw Square`
6. `drawAsquare`

1-2.3 The VAR Section

The next section of the program `TryIt` is the **VAR section.** In this section, variables are declared and the variable's **type** is listed. In mathematics, a variable is something that holds the place for a number. In the Pascal language, a variable references a memory location. The content of the memory location can be a number; however, it could also be other types of data, such as a character or a string of characters. For this reason, each variable listed in the VAR section must be given a data type. The variable identifier and its type are separated by a colon.

A good visual image of a variable in Pascal is that of a group of memory cells, as shown in Figure 1–4. In these cells, the variable's value is stored. When the Pascal program encounters a variable identifier, the computer looks up the memory cells to obtain the value of the variable. Also, the value in these cells can be changed by an instruction of the Pascal program.

Consider the VAR section for the program `TryIt`:

```
VAR Name : STRING [80] ;
    Ch   : CHAR ;
```

The first variable declared has an identifier of `Name`. The variable's type is listed as `STRING [80]`. That is, there will be a group of memory cells referenced by the identifier `Name`. The number in brackets (`80`) indicates that there will be 80 cells set aside for the STRING variable `Name`. In these cells, a string of characters will be stored. The

Figure 1–4

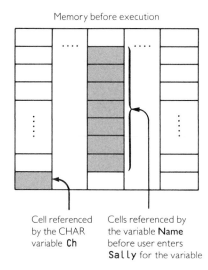

Memory before execution

Cell referenced by the CHAR variable **Ch**

Cells referenced by the variable **Name** before user enters **Sally** for the variable

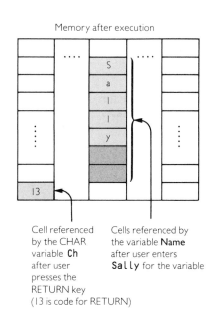

Memory after execution

Cell referenced by the CHAR variable **Ch** after user presses the RETURN key (13 is code for RETURN)

Cells referenced by the variable **Name** after user enters **Sally** for the variable number in the brackets can be any whole number from 1 to 255 inclusive. When the program TryIt is executed, the person at the keyboard enters a name. The characters in that name are stored in the computer's memory. When the computer needs to find these characters, it looks to the area of memory referenced by the variable identifier Name.

The second variable declared in the VAR section has the identifier Ch. The variable's type is listed as **CHAR** (rhymes with car). The variable Ch will reference one memory cell, and in this cell a character will be stored. When the program TryIt is executed, the person at the keyboard presses the RETURN key to end the program (recall the message Press RETURN key to quit). The character that the RETURN key represented is stored in the memory cell referenced by the variable Ch.

1-2.4 The Execution Section

The last section of the program TryIt is the **execution section.** This section holds the instructions for the program—that is, the statements that will be executed. The execution section always starts with the Pascal reserved word BEGIN and always ends with the Pascal reserved word END. Any collection of instructions bracketed by the reserved words BEGIN and END is called a **compound instruction.** The execution section for the Pascal program TryIt is

```
BEGIN
  WRITE ('Please enter your name- ') ;
  READLN (Name) ;
  WRITELN ('Thank you ', Name) ;
  WRITE ('Press RETURN key to quit ') ;
  READ (Ch)
END .
```

Every Pascal program ends with a **period.** The period marks the end of the complete Pascal program.

Next we will discuss the statements to be executed—that is, the instructions listed in the execution section. These statements involve the Pascal built-in procedures READ, READLN, WRITE, and WRITELN.

1-2.5 The WRITE Procedure

The **WRITE** procedure is an instruction to the computer to write something on the screen. The material to be written is enclosed in parentheses. Consider the following instruction:

```
WRITE ('Please enter your name- ')
```

Any material enclosed in single quotation marks will be written to the screen exactly as it appears. Thus, when this instruction executes, the computer outputs to the screen (writes to the screen) the following string of characters:

```
Please enter your name-
```

Next, consider this instruction:

```
WRITELN ('Thank you ', Name)
```

Sample Execution

```
Please enter your name- Sally
Thank you Sally
Press RETURN to quit
```

COMMENT

A variable of type CHAR is used to store a single character.

The Pascal built-in procedure **WRITELN** is just like WRITE, with the added feature of causing the cursor to advance to the next line on the screen after the writing is done. That is, WRITELN does a WRITE, then issues a line feed. In the parentheses for the instruction just given are the following items:

'Thank you ' and Name.

These items are separated by a comma. When this instruction is executed, the following actions will take place:

1. Thank you will be printed on the screen (a blank will be printed at the end, since a blank space was enclosed in the single quotes).
2. The computer will look to the memory location referenced by the variable Name, get the string of characters stored there, and print the string of characters.
3. Finally, the instruction will cause the cursor to move to the start of the next line on the screen.

A sample execution of WRITELN ('Thank you ' , Name) where the variable Name contains Sally is

Thank you Sally

Following are some examples of WRITE. Assume the CHAR variable Ch contains the character B and the STRING variable Name contains the string of characters Joshua.

Instruction	Results (□ indicates a blank space)
WRITE (' Hello ')	□□Hello□
WRITE (' Hello', Name)	□HelloJoshua
WRITE ('Hello ', Name, Ch)	Hello□JoshuaB
WRITE ('Hello ', Name, ' ', Ch)	Hello□Joshua□B
WRITE ('Hello ', Name, ' ', Ch, '.')	Hello□Joshua□B.

To understand the difference between WRITE and WRITELN, consider the following (the ■ indicates the location of the cursor). The instructions

WRITE ('Hello ') ;   yield an
WRITE ('Robin. ') ;   output of
WRITE ('How are you?')

```
Hello Robin. How are you?■
```

whereas the instructions

WRITE ('Hello ') ;   yield an
WRITELN ('Robin. ') ;   output
WRITE (' How are you?') of

```
Hello Robin.
  How are you?■
```

Finally, the Pascal instruction WRITELN can be used to print a blank line. The following instructions

WRITE ('Hello ') ;   yield an
WRITELN ('Robin. ') ;   output
WRITELN ;   of
WRITELN ('How are you?')

```
Hello Robin.

How are you?
■
```

Consider outputting this string of characters: John's. The fact that this string contains the single quotation character makes the string a special case. This is because

Sample Execution

```
Please enter your name- Sally
Thank you Sally
Press RETURN to quit
```

the single quotation character is used to mark the beginning and ending of the characters to be written by the WRITE and WRITELN procedures. To write this string to the screen, the following is used:

```
WRITE ('John''s')
```

That is, *two* single quotation marks are used (not a double quotation mark).

1-2.6 The Printer

One additional feature of the built-in procedures WRITE and WRITELN needs to be discussed. This feature allows the programmer to specify where the material output by WRITE and WRITELN will be written. Normally, the material is written to the screen. However, the material can be written to other devices, such as a printer. That is, a hard copy can be made of the output. Consider the following instruction:

```
WRITE (LST , 'Hello')
```

This instruction will write the string of characters He llo to the printer device. The following program, PrinterDemo, will write to the printer the string of characters stored in the STRING variable Name:

```
PROGRAM PrinterDemo ;

VAR Name : STRING [30] ;

BEGIN
  WRITE ('Enter Name: ') ;
  READLN (Name) ;
  WRITELN (LST , Name) ;
  WRITELN ('That is it!')
END .
```

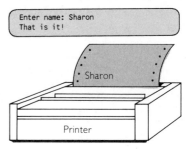

DO IT NOW

1. Give the output of the following instructions (use ▌ to indicate the location of the cursor):

   a. WRITE ('What is your age?');
   WRITE ('Thank you. ')

   b. WRITELN ('What is your age?');
   WRITELN ('Thank you. ')

2. If the variable Ch is of type CHAR and contains the value Q, and the variable Str is of type STRING and contains the value John, give the output of the following (use ▌ to indicate the location of the cursor):

   a. WRITE (Str) ;
   WRITE (Ch)

   b. WRITE (Str, ' ') ;
   WRITELN (Ch, '.')

   c. WRITELN (Str) ;
   WRITE (Ch, '. Public')

   d. WRITELN (Str, ' ', Ch, '. Public') ;
   WRITELN ;
   WRITE ('Main Street, USA')

DO IT NOW ANSWERS

```
1a. What is your age?Thank you. ▌
 b. What is your age?
    Thank you.
    ▌
```

```
2a. JohnQ▌          b. John Q.          c. John          d. John Q. Public
                       ▌                   Q. Public▌         Main Street, USA▌
```

1-2.7 The READ Procedure

The built-in procedure **READ** is used to input data to be stored in (assigned to) a memory location referenced by a variable. For now, the data will be input (read in) from the keyboard. Consider the following READ instruction, where Ch is of type CHAR:

    READ (Ch)

When this instruction is executed, the cursor pauses to wait for the user to enter a value. The user types a character, then presses the RETURN key. The execution of the READ instruction is completed.

When the user presses a key on the keyboard, the corresponding internal code for that key is stored in a buffer. A **buffer** is an area of memory used to store (hold) data being input (or output) from the computer program. When the user presses the RETURN key, the first character in the buffer is stored in the memory location Ch. If the user enters more than one character in response to the instruction READ (Ch), the extra characters are ignored, since Ch is of type CHAR.

COMMENT

By using a buffer, the information input from the keyboard can be corrected before it is stored in main memory. That is, if you make a mistake in striking a key, you can use the backspace key to erase the characters you have typed and then type the correct value. After the input is correct, press the RETURN key, and the information is stored in main memory.

The closely related built-in Pascal procedure **READLN** is also used to input a value for a variable. Consider the READLN instruction from the Pascal program TryIt (see page 14):

    READLN (Name)

When this instruction is executed, the following actions will take place:

1. The cursor pauses and waits for input from the keyboard.
2. The user presses several keys on the keyboard. This information is stored in the buffer.
3. Once the user presses the RETURN key, the information in the buffer is stored in the memory location Name.
4. The READLN instruction causes the cursor to move to the start of the next line on the screen.

That is, the READLN instruction does a READ, then advances the cursor to the start of the next screen line.

Sample Execution

    Please enter your name- Sally
    ▮

WARNING

To input a value for a variable of type STRING, the READLN procedure should be used.

COMMENT

Since Name was declared to be a variable of type STRING and the length was specified as 80, any characters in the buffer beyond 80 would be ignored.

Vocabulary

	Page
Alphanumeric A member of the collection of characters consisting of the letters of the alphabet and the digits.	14
Buffer An area of main memory used to hold information (data) being input and/or output to devices.	19
CHAR A Pascal reserved word used to state that the memory location referenced by a variable will be used to store a single character.	16

16 **Compound instruction** A collection of instructions that are bracketed by the reserved words BEGIN and END. The execution section is an example of a compound instruction.

16 **Execution section** An area of a Pascal program where the instructions to be executed are placed. This section must start with the reserved word BEGIN and end with the reserved word END.

14 **Identifiers** Names composed by the programmer that are used to name (identify) the program, the program variables, etc.

16 **Period** A punctuation mark used to indicate the end of a Pascal program.

14 **Program header** The first line of a Pascal program. The line contains the program's identifier (name). This line must begin with the reserved word PROGRAM.

19 **READ** A Pascal predefined procedure that is used to input information into a program variable. Example: READ (DogName).

19 **READLN** A Pascal predefined procedure that does a READ, then advances the cursor to the next line. Example: READLN (NameOne).

14 **Reserved words** A collection of words that are predefined by the Pascal system. These words cannot be used as identifiers by the programmer. Examples: PROGRAM, BEGIN, END, VAR.

15 **STRING [n]** A Pascal reserved word used to state that the memory locations referenced by a variable will be used to store a string of characters. The value in *n* indicates the number of memory cells to be used and must be from 1 to 255.

15 **Type** A description of the kind of data (information) to be stored in a memory location referenced by a variable.

15 **VAR section** The section of a Pascal program in which variables are declared and the type of the variable is stated. This section must begin with the reserved word VAR.

16 **WRITE** A Pascal predefined procedure that is used to output information to a device such as the screen or printer.
Example: WRITE ('My dog is named ' ,DogName).

17 **WRITELN** A Pascal predefined procedure that does a WRITE, then sends the cursor to the start of the next line.
Example: WRITELN ('Pascal is a GREAT language!').

Glad You Asked

Q What is a data file?

A First, the word *data* means information. The information might be a collection of numbers, or it might be a collection of characters. Second, to understand the word *file,* you must know that at one time, the data in most computers was input from cards. These cards had holes punched in them. The computer read the cards to obtain the data for the program. A stack of these cards looked very much like a file in a file cabinet. Of course, today most of the data entered into a computer program comes from the keyboard or from a diskette in a disk drive. However, the word *file* is still used to refer to the source of the data.

Q I really don't understand the difference between READ and READLN. Can you explain it further?

A I would be glad to try. However, first read the answer to the previous question. Now, back to the cards. When the computer received a card to read, this card might contain several pieces of data. That is, it might contain several names or several numbers. Using the READ instruction, the computer would read a name on the card; then using the READ instruction, it again would read the next name on the same card; and so forth. Using the instruction READLN, the computer would read a name on the card, then move to the next card. That is, after the READ, it would look for the end of the card. When the Pascal language was developed, it had to be able to handle card input. For now, working with the keyboard, it is hard to see the need for both instructions. Later, when data is entered from a diskette in the disk drive, you will see the need for READ and READLN.

Q How do you get the computer to work with numbers?

A This area will be covered later in the chapter.

Q What is information processing?

A Information processing, or data processing, means taking in information, working on the information (processing it), then outputting the results. A very simple example is input two numbers, add them together (process the data), and output the sum. A very complex example is read an algebra word problem (input the information); think about the problem, write an equation, and solve the equation (process the information); and write the answer (output the results).

Q How can I print my Pascal program on the printer without transferring out of the Pascal system to the disk operating system (DOS)?

A From the Pascal main menu, press D for Directory. Respond to the `Dir Mask:` prompt by entering `A:` Read the list of files present. If the file `LISTER.PAS` is on the diskette, you can use it to obtain a hard copy of your program. If not, you must quit the Turbo system to DOS to obtain a printed copy.

Assuming `LISTER.PAS` is on the diskette, save the material currently in the workfile (if it is of any value). Set the workfile to `LISTER.PAS` by pressing W for Workfile, then entering `LISTER.PAS`. After the `LISTER` program is loaded into the workfile, press R for Run. The source code for the program `LISTER` is converted to object code, and the object code is executed. The screen clears, and the prompt

        `Enter filename:_`

appears on the screen.

Make sure the printer is ready and the paper is positioned correctly:

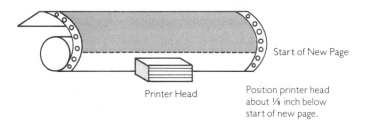

Printer Head

Start of New Page

Position printer head about ⅛ inch below start of new page.

If the paper is not properly positioned, position the paper by using the LF (line feed) button on the printer.

Respond to the `Enter filename:` prompt by entering the name of the file containing the program you wish to print. When printing is finished, you are returned to the Pascal prompt.

Instructions

`READ (Name1);`
`READ (Name2)`

Results

Name1 assigned value of **Alice**
Name2 assigned value of **Sue**

Data File

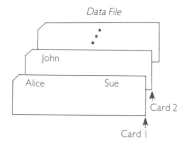

John

Alice   Sue

Card 2

Card 1

Instructions

`READLN (Name1);`
`READLN (Name2)`

Results

Name1 assigned value of **Alice**
Name2 assigned value of **John**

COMMENT
See Appendix A for DOS approach to sending output to the printer.

Section 1-2 Exercises

1. Use the Pascal editor and the printer to make a copy of the following Pascal program:

```
PROGRAM LeaveMess;

VAR Name : STRING [15] ;
    PhoneN : STRING [9] ;
    Ans : CHAR ;

BEGIN
  WRITELN ('Hello, who''s calling? ') ;
  READLN (Name) ;
  WRITE (Name) ;
  WRITE (' should we call back?(y/n) ') ;
  READLN (Ans) ;
  WRITE (' Please enter phone number- ') ;
  READLN (PhoneN) ;
  WRITELN (Name, ' thanks for calling.')
END .
```

   a. Draw a box around the program header.
   b. Draw a box around the VAR section.
   c. Draw a box around the execution section.
   d. List the STRING variable(s): _____ .
   e. List the CHAR variable(s): _____ .
   f. Write down what the screen looks like after executing the program and responding to the prompts.
   g. What is the output if the program user types Johnny B. Extraordinary in response to the following prompt?

```
     Hello, who's calling?
```

2. The section of a Pascal program that contains the instructions to be executed is called
   a. the program header.   d. the execution section.
   b. the VAR section.   e. the housing block.
   c. the STRING section.

3. Which of the following is *not* a Pascal reserved word?
   a. CHARACTER   b. BEGIN   c. PROGRAM   d. VAR   e. END

4. The section of a Pascal program in which variables are declared and their types are listed is called
   a. the VARIABLE section.   d. the STRING section.
   b. the execution section.   e. the compound section.
   c. the VAR section.

5. Which of the following is a Pascal built-in procedure used to output data?
   a. READ   b. WRITE   c. TYPE   d. OUTPUT   e. PRINT

6. Which of the following is a Pascal built-in procedure used to input data?
   a. WRITELN   b. INPUT   c. BEGIN   d. READLN   e. GET IT

7. The first word of a Pascal program is _____ , and the last word is _____ .

8. A collection of instructions bracketed by the reserved words BEGIN and END is called a _____ instruction.

9. To declare the identifier NameOne to be a variable and to state its type as a string of 12 characters, which of the following would be used?
   a. NameOne : CHAR [12]   d. NameOne : STRING [12]
   b. Name One : STRING   e. NameOne : STRING (12)
   c. WRITE (NameOne)

10. Which of the following could be used to write the string of characters `Robin's house`?

    a. `WRITE ('Robin's house')`   **d.** `WRITE ['Robin''s house']`

    b. `WRITE ('Robin''s house')`   **e.** `WRITE ('Robin's');`

    c. `WRITE (''Robin''s house'')`   `WRITE ('house')`

11. Give the output of the following Pascal instructions.

    a. `WRITE ('Pascal is a') ;`
        `WRITELN (' structured language.') ;`
        `WRITELN;`
        `WRITE ('This language promotes good ') ;`
        `WRITELN ('programming habits.')`

    b. `WRITE ('The Pascal language ', 'is named') ;`
        `WRITELN ('for Blaise Pascal.') ;`
        `WRITELN (' Pascal was a French ') ;`
        `WRITELN ('mathematician.')`

12. Given the following STRING and CHAR variables and their values, give the output of the program instructions.

Variable Identifier	Type	Value
Word1	STRING [20]	mind
Word2	STRING [20]	imagination
Word3	STRING [20]	matter
Ch	CHAR	s

    a. `WRITELN ('The ', Word1, Ch, ' of some') ;`
        `WRITELN (' boggle the ', Word2, Ch, ' of others') ;`
        `WRITELN ('The ', Word2, Ch, ' of some') ;`
        `WRITELN (' boggle the ', Word1, Ch, ' of others.')`

    b. `WRITE ('What is ', Word1, '?') ;`
        `WRITELN (' Never ', Word3, '!') ;`
        `WRITE ('What is ', Word3, '?') ;`
        `WRITELN (' Oh, never ', Word1, '.')`

13. Insert *Valid* for a valid identifier. Insert *Invalid* for an invalid identifier.

    a. _____ `PhoneCalls`   **d.** _____ `*Walk`

    b. _____ `3Numbers`   **e.** _____ `Numbers3`

    c. _____ `Begin`   **f.** _____ `A + B`

14. Write output instructions to produce the following outputs.

    a. `The Pascal language was`
        `written by Niklaus Wirth.`

    b. `The first word in every Pascal`
        `program is- PROGRAM`
        `The last word in every Pascal`
        `program is- END`
        `Every Pascal program ends with a period.`

15. Using the STRING variables `Name1`, whose content is `John Queue Public`, and `Address1`, whose content is `1987 October Street`, write a collection of Pascal output instructions to output

Sample Execution

```
I am John Queue Public and I
live at 1987 October Street in
Center Point, Kansas.
```

Assume the following VAR section for questions 16 and 17:

```
VAR Ch : CHAR;
    NameOne : STRING [8] ;
    NameTwo : STRING [15]
```

16. Which of the following will allow the user to enter the value Gary Joseph?
    a. READ (Ch)
    b. READLN (NameOne)
    c. READ (NameOne)
    d. READLN (NameTwo)
    e. INPUT (NameTwo)

17. Suppose the variable NameOne contains the value Hilda. Which of the following would output Hilda's car?
    a. WRITELN (NameOne, 's car')
    b. WRITE (NameOne,'s car')
    c. WRITELN (NameOne,'''s car')
    d. WRITE ('Hilda's car)
    e. WRITE ('Hilda','s car)

18. Boot up Pascal; set the workfile to the file TRYIT.PAS from the Source diskette. Enter the Turbo Pascal editor. Edit the program instructions to output the following:

Sample Execution

```
Please enter your name: Wilson
Please enter the name of your city: Albany

Thank you Wilson from Albany.

Press the ENTER key to quit.
```

19. Use the Pascal system to
    a. enter the text of the Pascal program in problem 1.
    b. produce a hard copy of the program text.
    c. convert the source code to object code.
    d. execute the object code.

20. Use the Pascal editor to alter the Pascal program in exercise 1 to write to the printer all information output by the program. Run this altered version.

21. Use the Pascal editor and compiler to alter the Pascal program in problem 1 to answer the following question: If you delete the period at the end of the program, what happens when you attempt to compile this altered version?

Section 1-3

Punctuation and Style

In this section, you will be introduced to some of the essentials of Pascal programs. Of utmost importance are the punctuation marks used in a Pascal program. Additionally, a new program section called the CONST section and a set of writing style rules will be introduced.

1-3.1 The CONST Section

Consider the following Pascal program:

```
PROGRAM BoxExample ;

CONST Message = 'Hello ' ;

VAR Name    : STRING [50] ;
    Address : STRING [80] ;
BEGIN
  WRITE (Message, 'what is your name? ') ;
  READLN (Name) ;
  WRITELN (Name, ' where are you from? ') ;
  READLN (Address) ;
  WRITELN (Message, Name, ' from ' , Address)
END .
```

```
Hello what is your name? Milo
Milo where are you from?
San Antonio
Hello Milo from San Antonio
```

As you can see, a new section has been introduced. This section is called a **CONST section** (CONST is short for constant, just as VAR is short for variable). The CONST section is always positioned *before* the VAR section. The reserved word CONST indicates the start of this section.

In the CONST section, identifiers are listed and their values are stated. In the program BoxExample, the identifier Message is listed and its value is stated as the string of characters Hello. When this program is executed, an area of the computer's memory is filled with the string of characters Hello. Anywhere the identifier Message is found in an execution section, the memory area referenced by Message is looked up, and the contents of that area are used. The contents of this area of memory cannot be changed (that is, they are **constant**) while the program is executing.

Consider the instruction from the execution section of the preceding program:

```
WRITE (Message, 'what is your name? ')
```

When this instruction is executed, the results will be

```
Hello what is your name? █
```

1-3.2 Punctuation

The **punctuation** marks in a Pascal program are essential! Without proper punctuation, the program cannot be compiled (converted to object code). The easiest punctuation mark to use is the **period.** Every Pascal program must end with a period. The reserved word END followed by a period indicates to the compiler that the program text has ended.

The most used (and often the most troublesome) punctuation mark in a Pascal program is the **semicolon.** The semicolon is used as a *separator.* The semicolon is used to separate two different items of a Pascal program.

1. A semicolon is used to separate the program sections.
2. A semicolon is used to separate statements within a program section.

Consider the program `BoxExample`:

```
PROGRAM BoxExample ;

CONST Message = 'Hello ' ;

VAR Name    : STRING [50] ;
    Address : STRING [80] ;

BEGIN
  WRITE (Message, 'what is your name? ') ;
  READLN (Name) ;
  WRITELN (Name, ' where are you from? ') ;
  READLN (Address) ;
  WRITELN (Message, Name, ' from ', Address)
END .
```

The semicolon after the identifier `BoxExample` is used to separate the program header from the CONST section. The semicolon after the value `'Hello '` is used to separate the CONST section from the VAR section. The semicolon after the line `Address : STRING [80]` is used to separate the VAR section from the execution section. The other semicolons in the program are used to separate statements within a program section.

Boxing   As the Pascal programs you study become more complicated, it is good to have a visual tool to help with the punctuation, especially the semicolons. Such a tool is **boxing.**

To box a Pascal program, start by drawing a box around the program sections. Consider the Pascal program `BoxExample`, which follows. Each program section has been boxed.

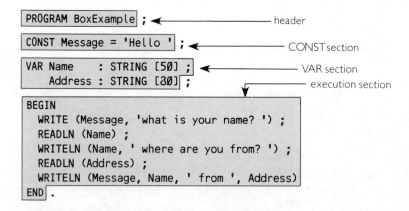

As you can see, a semicolon is used to separate each of the boxes. Also notice that the program ends with a period.

Next, each section of the program is boxed again, as follows. The header is further boxed by enclosing the identifier in a box. The CONST section is further boxed by enclosing each identifier and its declared value in a box. The VAR section is further boxed by enclosing each identifier and its declared type in a box. And the execution section is boxed by enclosing each instruction in a box.

When two boxes are next to each other (without one box containing the other), the boxes are called *adjacent* boxes. If one box is within another box, the boxes are said to be *nested*.

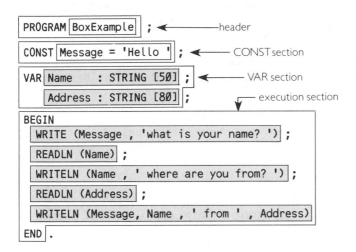

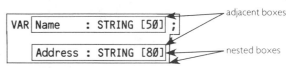

COMMENT
The words *adjacent* and *nested* refer to a relationship between boxes.

A semicolon is always required to separate adjacent boxes. A semicolon is not used to separate nested boxes. This is the case with the box containing the VAR section and the box containing the variable `Address` and its type.

Many beginning learners have trouble with the fact that there is no semicolon after the statement

```
WRITELN (Message, Name, ' from ' , Address)
```

Remember, the semicolon is used to separate two consecutive statements within the section.

Comma Your experience with the comma punctuation mark has been with the WRITE and WRITELN instructions, as in

```
WRITE (Name, ' from ', Address)
```

The comma is used to separate items within a list of items to be output. Much as a semicolon is used to separate program sections and to separate instructions within a program section, the comma is used to separate items in a list.

The comma can be used to separate a list of variables in the VAR section as follows:

```
VAR FName,                   VAR FName, MName, LName : STRING [40] ;
    MName,                       Sex : CHAR ;
    LName : STRING [40] ;
    Sex : CHAR ;
```

Also, the comma can be used in READ and READLN instructions. Consider the following instruction:

```
READLN (ChA, ChB, ChC)
```

When this instruction is executed, three input values will be requested. The comma in `READLN (ChA, ChB, ChC)` is used to separate the variables `ChA`, `ChB`, and `ChC`. The previously given instruction could be used as follows:

```
WRITE ('Enter 3 characters: ') ;
READLN (ChA, ChB, ChC)
```

1-3.3 Style

When a Pascal program is compiled, the compiler ignores extra spaces and does not differentiate between capital and lowercase letters (that is, P and p are the same). The program BoxExample could be written as follows:

```
program boxexample; const Message = 'Hello ' ;
var name : string [50] ; address : string [80] ; begin
write (Message,'what is your name? '); readln (name);
writeln(name,' where are you from? '); readln (address);
writeln (Message, name, ' from ', address) end.
```

Of course, the program is very hard to read in this form. The idea of a set of **style rules** is to help the programmer write a program that can be easily read, altered, extended, and/or corrected.

STYLE RULE 1 Write every Pascal reserved word in capital letters. Examples: PROGRAM, CONST, VAR.

STYLE RULE 2 Separate the program sections with a blank line. That is, there should be a blank line between the program header and the CONST section, etc.

STYLE RULE 3 Indent the contents of a section. That is, the instructions in the program execution section should all be indented at least two spaces under the reserved word BEGIN.

STYLE RULE 4 Never place more than one instruction on a line.

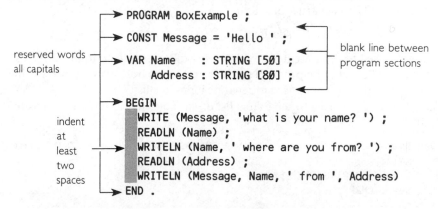

In addition to the writing style rules, there is a collection of **user rules** that aid the programmer in writing programs that are easy to use. The following user rules deal with prompts presented on the screen. As the course progresses, other user rules will be introduced.

USER RULE 1 Precede every request for information (READ or READLN instruction) from the program user with a prompt. The prompt should be in plain English and describe as much as possible the type of input expected from the user.

USER RULE 2 In most cases, the rightmost character in a prompt should be a blank space. That is, there should be at least one blank space between the prompt and the data input by the user.

Bad prompt

```
?█
```

Good prompt

```
Please enter name Jil
Please enter age (1..92): █
```

1-3.4 Documentation

A major theme of the Pascal approach to programming is to write programs that are readable. By writing readable programs, the programs are easier to alter, expand, and/or update. The use of meaningful identifiers and program style that has been discussed is designed to improve readability. Documentation is another way to improve the readability of a program.

Documentation is an effort to describe what the program or a part of the program is to accomplish. User Rule 1 just given concerns documenting a request for information. Often there is a need for inserting a comment (in plain English) describing the program or a part of the program. This is accomplished in Pascal through the use of the symbols { and }. That is, additional information can be enclosed in braces. This information does nothing to aid in solving a problem. The information is ignored by the compiler when the text of the program is converted to code. However, the information can aid a reader in understanding the program (and thus updating, expanding, and/or altering the program).

For now, only a *program comment section* will be considered. Later, as the programs get longer and subprograms are introduced, additional comments will be considered. A program comment section generally has the following form:

```
{***************************************************************}
{Programmer:                                                    }
{Date:                                                          }
{Purpose:                                                       }
{                                                               }
{***************************************************************}

PROGRAM
```

PROGRAMMING POINT

An easy way to place a comment section like the one just given in your programs is as follows:

1. From the Pascal main menu, set the workfile to the file **B:ProgForm**.
2. Enter the editor, and type in the form just presented.
3. Quit the editor, and save the text entered.
4. Set the workfile to any file name you wish (say, **B:MyProg.PAS**).
5. Enter the editor.
6. Use Ctrl-K R to enter the editor's *Read block from disk* application.
7. Respond to the **Read block from file:** prompt by entering **B:ProgForm.PAS**.

The comment section is read into the file. Fill out the form, then enter the text of your program. Once the form is created in Steps 1, 2, and 3, you simply copy the form into the program on which you are working.

Vocabulary   Page

Boxing   A visual tool that is a very useful aid in punctuating a Pascal program.   26
Comma   A punctuation mark used to separate items in a list, for example   27
   WRITELN (ChA, ChB, ChC).

Glad You Asked

Q I really do not see the need for a CONST section. In the program `BoxExample`, why not just include the message in the WRITE instruction? Is this not just busywork?

A The program `BoxExample` could have been done without the constant `Message` (whose value was `Hello`). In general, there is usually a way around the use of constants. However, using constants often makes the program easier to read. More importantly, the use of constants makes it easy to alter a program. In a long program, rather than your having to look through the program to change each occurrence of a value, you can simply change the value in the CONST section.

   As for your charge of busywork, often you will find a very simple example used in order to make a point. The price paid for this simplicity is that the concept presented often seems to be the hard way to do the example. You can be assured that the CONST section is necessary and very helpful in more complex Pascal programs. Have faith.

Q All this seems like a lot of work for nothing. I use the BASIC language on my computer at home and can do what the program `BoxExample` does in about three lines. Why go to all this trouble?

A There is an old saying: "The easy way can get harder; the hard way can get easier." With short programs, Pascal does seem like a lot of extra work. Of course, these short programs are used to make a point about a concept of the Pascal language or about a concept in programming. In computing, there is little need for short programs. As programs get longer, the value of the Pascal language becomes clearer. Also, the shortcomings of a language like BASIC become more evident.

   COMMENT

   One problem with languages like BASIC is that the programmer may become sloppy in presenting the program. Long programs in BASIC are often hard to read, alter, and repair. The Pascal language makes an effort to encourage the programmer to write a program that can be read and understood by other people (and the programmer).

Section 1-3 Exercises

1. Match the following items on the left with the letter of the correct definition on the right.

   _____ **1.** READ   **a.** a punctuation mark used to separate

   _____ **2.** WRITE   **b.** a set of rules that aid in making a program readable

   _____ **3.** PROGRAM   **c.** a word that marks the start of the program section

   _____ **4.** VAR   where variables are declared

   _____ **5.** CONST   **d.** a data type

   _____ **6.** style rules   **e.** an instruction used to input data

   _____ **7.** boxing   **f.** the first word of a Pascal program

   _____ **8.** semicolon   **g.** an instruction used to output data

   _____ **9.** CHAR   **h.** a word that marks the start of the program section

   _____ **10.** period   where constants are defined

                                 i. a tool used to aid in punctuating a program

                                 j. a punctuation mark used to incorporate

                                 k. a punctuation mark used to mark the end of a Pascal program

2. Given the following CONST section,

```
CONST FirstCoin = ' quarter' ;
      SecondCoin = ' dime' ;
      ThirdCoin = ' nickel'
```

give the output for the following.

a. WRITELN ('You get back one', SecondCoin)

b. WRITE ('John''s change was ') ;
   WRITELN ('3', FirstCoin, 's') ;
   WRITELN ('and 2', ThirdCoin, 's')

3. Identify the error(s) in the following.

a. CONST Name : ' John ' ;
      Name2 = 'Sue'

b. CONSTANT Line1 = 'Hello'

c. CONST ; User2 = 'Homer'
        Mess = Hi, Mom

d. CONST 2ndName = 'Ike'
      %Name = '12%'

4. **a.** Construct a CONST section that (1) declares the constant `Prompt1` and assigns it the value `Please enter your name-` and (2) declares the constant `Note` and assigns it the value `thank you!`.

   b. Construct a VAR section that declares the variable `UserName` and states its type to be STRING, to hold up to 30 characters.

   c. Using the CONST section constructed in part a and the VAR section constructed in part b, construct an execution section that will yield the following (`Mickey` is to be entered by the program's user for the variable `UserName`):

Sample Execution

```
Please enter your name- Mickey

Mickey, thank you!
```

5. Given the following Pascal program, make a copy of the program.

```
PROGRAM DescribeIt;

CONST Line1 = 'What was the suspect''s ';
      Line2 = 'Was the suspect wearing ';

VAR Ans : STRING [30];

BEGIN
  WRITE (Line1, 'height? ') ;
  READLN (Ans) ;
  WRITE (Line2, 'glasses? ') ;
  READLN (Ans) ;
  WRITE (Line1, 'age? ') ;
  READLN (Ans)
END .
```

   a. Enclose each program section in a box. Label each box with the name of the section.
   b. Enclose each identifier and its value in the CONST section in a box.
   c. Enclose each identifier and its type in the VAR section in a box.
   d. Enclose each instruction in the execution section in a box.
   e. Give the program's output (make up entries for Ans).

6. Insert the eight semicolons required in the following program (use boxing as an aid):

```
PROGRAM CarParts

CONST Make = 'Please enter model '
      Year = 'Please enter year '

VAR Answer : STRING [40]

BEGIN
  WRITE (Make)
  READLN (Answer)
  WRITELN
  WRITE (Year)
  READLN (Answer)
END .
```

7. Rewrite the following Pascal program using the style rules discussed in this section (that is, insert the blank lines needed, indent the sections, and use the proper capitalization).

```
program badstyle; const heading = 'Name  Hours  Rate';
heading2 = 'OT Hrs  Total'; var name : string [35] ;
hours : string [40] ; begin writeln (heading, heading2);
readln (name) end.
```

8. In the following program, fill in the execution section so as to construct a Pascal program that will take as input a person's first name and last name. The program's output should be the person's last name, first name.

```
PROGRAM ReverseIt;

CONST Comma = ', ';

VAR FirstN : STRING [50];
    LastN : STRING [50];

BEGIN
  :
  :
END .
```

Sample Execution

```
Please enter your first name: Katie
Please enter your last name: Greenberg
Name reversed is: Greenberg, Katie
```

9. Boot up Pascal; set the workfile to the file **BOXEX.PAS** from the **Source** diskette. Enter the Turbo Pascal editor. Insert the following declaration in the CONST section:

```
Message2 = 'What is your ' ;
```

Declare the variables **Height** and **Weight** of type **STRING [7]** in the VAR section. Use the constant **Message2** to edit the program instructions to output the following:

Sample Execution

```
Hello, what is your name? Julian
Julian, where are you from? England
Hello Julian from England
What is your height? 5' 11"
What is your weight? 156 pounds
```

10. Fill in the following program shell so as to
   a. declare Author a constant with value **'Enter author: '**.
   b. declare Title a constant with value **'Enter title: '**.
   c. declare Name a variable of type STRING with 20 characters.
   d. declare Book a variable of type STRING with 30 characters.
   e. allow the user to input a name and book title.
   f. produce an output of the book's title followed by the author's name.

```
PROGRAM Books;
CONST Author = _____;
          _____;
VAR Name : _____;
        _____;
BEGIN
  WRITE (Author) ;
  READLN (Name) ;
  _____;
  _____;
  WRITELN (Book, ' ', _____)
END .
```

11. Use the Pascal editor to enter the text of the program **Books** from problem 10. Use the compiler to convert the program to object code. Execute the object code. Test your program with the following data:

Name	Book
Pearl Buck	*The Good Earth*
Virginia Woolf	*The Waves*
Hermann Hesse	*Steppenwolf*

12. Use the Pascal editor to alter the program **Books** from problem 10 so as to write to the printer the line giving the book's title followed by its author. Compile and execute this altered version.

Type **INTEGER**

In this section, you will be introduced to a new data type: INTEGER. This data type deals with numbers. In addition, we will discuss the concept of assignment, operations on integer data, and order of operations rules.

1-4.1 INTEGER and Assignment

Up to this point, you have been exposed to two data types, CHAR and STRING. These data types dealt with characters and strings of characters. The next data type to be considered is INTEGER.

In mathematics, the numbers 0, 1, 2, 3, . . . , are called whole numbers. When this collection of numbers is combined with its additive opposites (0, -1, -2, -3, . . .), the resulting collection of numbers is called the **integers.** In Pascal, when a variable is declared to be of type **INTEGER,** the value the variable holds must be an integer. That is, the number must be in the collection

$$(-\text{MAXINT} - 1, \ldots, -2, -1, 0, 1, 2, \ldots, \text{MAXINT})$$

The identifier **MAXINT** is a predefined Pascal constant whose value is 32767.

Consider this VAR section:

```
VAR HoursWk : INTEGER
```

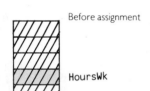

Before assignment

HoursWk

The variable HoursWk has been declared, and its type is stated as INTEGER. This means that any number placed in the memory location referenced by the variable HoursWk must be an integer (that is, a number like -6 or 18 or -56 or 913).

Assignment In the Pascal language, there is a special way of placing a value in a memory location referenced by a variable. This action is accomplished by using :=, the **assignment** symbol. Consider the following Pascal instruction:

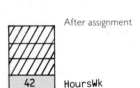

After assignment

42 HoursWk

```
HoursWk := 42
```

This Pascal instruction reads *"HoursWk is assigned (:=) the value 42."* When this instruction is executed, the integer 42 is placed in the memory location referenced by the identifier HoursWk.

WARNING
1. Until an assignment is made to a variable, it is impossible to know the value in the memory location referenced by the variable.
2. If the variable HoursWk is declared to be of type INTEGER, an integer must be assigned to HoursWk. That is, an instruction like HoursWk = 28.3 will produce an error (called a **type conflict**).
3. Assigning a value to HoursWk greater than **MAXINT** or less than **–MAXINT – 1** will not produce an error. However, such an assignment will lead to erroneous results. For example, HoursWk := 32768 will result in the value –32768 being stored in HoursWk. Likewise, HoursWk := 32769 will result in the value –32767 being stored in HoursWk.
4. Commas are not allowed in integer values. That is, HoursWk := 1,345 will result in an error.

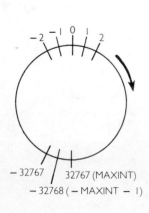

The assignment instruction can be used with any variable type. For example, if `Name` is declared a variable of type `STRING [9]`, then the statement `Name := 'Gary '` is a valid Pascal instruction. The Pascal reserved words READ and READLN also are used to assign a value to a variable. However, READ and READLN allow the program user to make the assignment by entering information from the keyboard during the execution of the program.

DO IT NOW

Given the VAR section   `VAR NumA : INTEGER ;`
                              `Name : STRING [8] ;`

1. Write a Pascal instruction to assign the value −12 to the variable `NumA`.
2. Write a Pascal instruction to assign the value `David` to the variable `Name`.
3. Discuss the error in each of the following instructions:
   a. `NumA := 'Michelle'`   **b.** `Name := 15`   **c.** `NumA = 13`

COMMENT
In `Name := 'Kathmandu'`, no error is generated. Also, in `READLN (Name)`, if `Kathmandu` is entered, no error is generated. In both cases, only `Kathmand` is assigned to `Name`.

1-4.2 Operations on INTEGER Data

The operations available for INTEGER data are addition, subtraction, multiplication, and division. The operations of addition, subtraction, and multiplication are indicated by use of the symbols + , − , and *, respectively. These operations require no further introduction. The last operation, division, does require explanation.

The operation of division can be indicated by the / symbol. However, a problem develops with the division performed by using this symbol (the **slash,** or /). Consider the following VAR section and execution section:

```
VAR NumA : INTEGER ;
    NumB : INTEGER ;
    NumC : INTEGER ;

BEGIN
  NumA := -18 ;
  NumB := 5 ;
  NumC := NumA / NumB
END .
```

COMMENT
There is no symbol for exponentiation (such as 3^5) in Pascal. This topic will be covered in Chapter 3.

When the instruction `NumC := NumA / NumB` is executed, the operation of division is performed on the data in the memory locations referenced by variables `NumA` and `NumB`. In this case, division will be performed on −18 and 5, producing a result of −3.6. An attempt is made to assign this value (−3.6) to the INTEGER variable `NumC`. At this point, an error (type conflict) is produced, since the value − 3.6 is not an integer.

To avoid this problem, another form of division is available in the Pascal language. This division is indicated by the Pascal reserved word **DIV** and is used with data of type INTEGER. This operation can best be explained by using an example.

Consider 23 divided by 5. In elementary school, you first solved this problem by doing the following:

COMMENT
The slash division always yields a decimal number. For example, `18 / 6` yields `3.0` (a non-integer).

DO IT NOW ANSWERS
1. `NumA := -12`
2. `Name := 'David'`
3a. `NumA` must be assigned a value of type INTEGER.
   b. `Name` cannot be assigned a number.
   c. To assign a value to `NumA`, the symbol `:=` must be used.

You reported an answer of 4 with a remainder of 3. The number 4 was called the **quotient.** The quotient is always an integer. The above division is indicated by the Pascal reserved word DIV. Thus,

> 23 DIV 5 yields 4

The **remainder** is indicated by the Pascal reserved word **MOD.** Thus,

> 23 MOD 5 yields 3

In general,

> Number = quotient * divisor + number MOD divisor

To better understand the operations /, DIV, and MOD, observe the following comparisons:

Computation	Results	Computation	Results	Computation	Results
$-7/2$	-3.5	-7 DIV 2	-3	-7 MOD 2	-1
$11/5$	2.2	11 DIV 5	2	11 MOD 5	1
$28/4$	7.0	28 DIV 4	7	28 MOD 4	0
$-55/8$	-6.875	-55 DIV 8	-6	-55 MOD 8	-7
$-17/-2$	8.5	-17 DIV -2	8	-17 MOD -2	-1

As you can see, the division operation DIV always yields an integer, and the operation MOD always yields an integer. The operation / always yields a decimal number.

Now, reconsider the VAR section and execution section presented earlier with the / operation replaced by the DIV operation:

```
VAR NumA, NumB, NumC : INTEGER ;

BEGIN
  NumA := -18 ;
  NumB := 5 ;
  NumC := NumA DIV NumB
END .
```

This time, when the Pascal instruction NumC := NumA DIV NumB is executed, the variable NumC is assigned the value −3. Now, since −3 is an integer, no error is generated.

1-4.3 Using READ and WRITE with Type INTEGER

The Pascal commands READ and READLN work the same with INTEGER variables as they do with CHAR or STRING variables. In the previous example, the Pascal instruction NumB := 5 could be replaced by WRITE ('Enter an integer: ') and READLN (NumB) to yield the following:

```
VAR NumA, NumB, NumC : INTEGER ;

BEGIN
  NumA := -18 ;
  WRITE ('Enter an integer: ') ;
  READLN (NumB) ;
  NumC := NumA DIV NumB
END .
```

When these instructions are executed, the prompt Enter an integer: will appear on the screen. The user types a string of characters, then presses the RETURN key. If the characters can be converted to an integer, then the integer will be assigned to the variable NumB. The only characters allowed when inputting an integer value are the digits (0, 1, 2, . . . , 9) and the plus (+) and minus (−) signs. Entering other characters will result in the program execution's stopping and issuing an error message.

Before execution

NumA

NumB
NumC

After execution

−18 NumA

5 NumB
−3 NumC

Outputting Numbers The Pascal instructions WRITE and WRITELN are used with INTEGER data to output numbers. The integer is output in a field whose width is specified in the output instruction. Consider the following Pascal instruction:

    WRITE (-13 : 5)

When this instruction is executed, the integer −13 is output in a field of width 5 that is **right justified.** That is, the output is as follows (the ☐ symbol represents a blank space):

    ☐☐-13

If the variable NumA is of type INTEGER and contains the value −6, then the instruction WRITELN (NumA : 5, 16 : 6, -23) will yield an output of

    ☐☐☐-6☐☐☐☐16-23

As you can see, if a field width is not specified (as in −23), the width is only as wide as required to print the integer. However, on some implementations of the Pascal language, if the field width is not specified, the field width of 5 is used by default. Thus, it is best to set the field width.

Field width specification is not restricted to integers. For example, the instruction WRITE ('Hello' : 8, -12 : 4) would yield an output of

    ☐☐☐Hello☐-12

COMMENT

If the field width is set to a value that is less than is needed, the extra spaces are provided by the Pascal system.

Examples: WRITE ('Hello' : 2)   outputs Hello
           WRITE (123 : 1 , 123 : 4) outputs 123☐123

DO IT NOW

Give the output of the following instructions (use a ☐ to indicate a blank space). The variable NumA is of type INTEGER and contains the value −19. The variable City is of type STRING [12] and contains the value Lusaka.

1. WRITE (-13 : 4 , 12 : 4)
2. WRITE (City : 8 , NumA : 5)
3. WRITE (City , -13) ;
   WRITELN (NumA : 1) ;
   WRITE (NumA : 6)

DO IT NOW ANSWERS
1. ☐-13☐☐12
2. ☐☐Lusaka☐☐-19
3. Lusaka-13-19
   ☐☐☐-19

1–4.4 Order of Operations

For the next topic on integers, we'll discuss **order-of-operations rules (precedence rules).** Consider this arithmetic expression:

160 DIV 20 − 5 * 2 + ⁻5

A person might do this computation using one of the two methods shown:

$$
\begin{array}{ll}
\underbrace{160\ \text{DIV}\ 20}\ -\ 5*2+{}^-5 & \qquad 160\ \text{DIV}\ 20\ -\ 5*\underbrace{2+{}^-5} \\
\underbrace{8\ -\ 5}*2+{}^-5 & \qquad 160\ \text{DIV}\ 20\ -\ \underbrace{5*{}^-3} \\
\underbrace{3*2}+{}^-5 & \qquad 160\ \text{DIV}\ \underbrace{20\ -\ {}^-15} \\
\underbrace{6+{}^-5} & \qquad \underbrace{160\ \text{DIV}\ 35} \\
1 & \qquad 4
\end{array}
$$

Obviously, one of these computations is incorrect (actually, they both are). To avoid this type of problem, an order in which to do the operations was decided upon. The order selected is as follows:

1. Start at the left and do *multiplication* and *division* operations in order (that is, these operations have the same level of precedence).
2. Start at the left and do *addition* and *subtraction* operations in order (that is, these operations have the same level of precedence).

   Applying the order-of-operation rules to the computation just given, the following result is obtained:

$$
\begin{aligned}
160\ \text{DIV}\ 20\ -\ 5*2+{}^-5 &= 8\ -\ 10\ +\ {}^-5 \\
&= {}^-2\ +\ {}^-5 \\
&= {}^-7
\end{aligned}
$$

   Thus, 160 DIV 20 − 5 * 2 + ⁻5 is ⁻7.

3. If a computation involves **parentheses,** the computations inside the parentheses are done first. In doing the computation inside the parentheses, the order-of-operation rules are applied. Consider this computation:

$$
\begin{aligned}
160\ \text{DIV}\ (20\ -\ 5*2)\ +\ -5 &= 160\ \text{DIV}\ (20\ -\ 10)\ +\ {}^-5 \\
&= 160\ \text{DIV}\ 10\ +\ {}^-5 \\
&= 16\ +\ {}^-5 \\
&= 11
\end{aligned}
$$

   Thus, 160 DIV (20 − 5 * 2) + ⁻5 is 11.

   The operation MOD has the same order of precedence as DIV. That is, in any computation using the operation MOD, the operation is done in the first pass through the computation. For example,

20 MOD 5 − 3 * 7 MOD 2 would yield 0 − 21 MOD 2 = 0 − 1 = ⁻1.

Likewise,

5 + 20 MOD 7 DIV 2 would yield 5 + 6 DIV 2 = 5 + 3 = 8.

The order-of-operations (precedence) rules are as shown in Table 1–1.

Table 1–1

Operation	Precedence
( )	Highest
*, /, DIV, MOD	↓
+, −	Lowest

1. Do the following computations.

   a. `17 DIV 5 + 2 = _____`   **d.** `20 * 5 - 6 = _____`

   b. `17 + 5 DIV 2 = _____`   **e.** `20 MOD 3 - 5 * 3 DIV 4 + -2 = _____`

   c. `20 - 5 * 6 = _____`

2. Do the following computations.

   a. `17 DIV (5 + 2) = _____`   **d.** `20 * (5 - 6) = _____`

   b. `(17 + 5) DIV 2 = _____`   **e.** `20 MOD (3 - 5) * 3 DIV (4 + -2) = _____`

   c. `(20 - 5) * 6 = _____`

1-4.5 RANDOM

Before ending this section, we will discuss an instruction that deals with integers. This instruction is named **RANDOM.** The instruction RANDOM can be used to obtain an integer between 0 and MAXINT − 1 (the value 32766) inclusive. This type of instruction is very useful in an area of problem solving known as **simulation** of an event (such as rolling a pair of dice). The number obtained by the instruction RANDOM does not follow an observable pattern. Consider the following short demonstration program:

```
PROGRAM DisOrder ;

VAR NumA : INTEGER ;
    NumB : INTEGER ;

BEGIN
  WRITELN ('Two random numbers are:') ;
  NumA := RANDOM (MAXINT) ;
  NumB := RANDOM (MAXINT) ;
  WRITELN (NumA , ' and ' , NumB)
END .
```

DO IT NOW ANSWERS

1a. 5	2a. 2
b. 19	b. 11
c. −10	c. 90
d. 94	d. −20
e. −3	e. 0

Sample Execution

```
Two random numbers are:
956 and 23782
```

COMMENT

The instruction `RANDOM (MAXINT)`, when executed, obtains an integer between 0 and 32766 inclusive and places this number in the memory location identified by the name `RANDOM` (such as instruction is called a function). When the assignment instruction `NumA := RANDOM (MAXINT)` is executed, the number in the location labeled `RANDOM` is assigned to the variable `NumA`.

To increase your understanding of RANDOM and to see an example of simulation, consider the following example.

EXAMPLE

Write a Pascal program that simulates rolling a pair of dice.

SOLUTION

Each die contains the numbers 1, 2, 3, 4, 5, and 6. When the die is rolled, one of these numbers appears on the top face in a random fashion. Thus, the program needs a random number from 1 to 6. Consider this instruction:

If the cheese is shaped like a die

Will we catch a mie?

Never, say die!

```
DieA := RANDOM (6)
```

RANDOM selects a number from 0 to the value in the parentheses minus 1 (0 to 5 in this case). Thus, the assignment instruction needed is

```
DieA := RANDOM (6) + 1
```

A number from 0 to 5 plus 1 yields a number from 1 to 6. A Turbo Pascal program to simulate rolling a pair of dice is given here:

Sample Execution

```
A pair of dice has been rolled.
The results are: a 4 and a 1
```

```
PROGRAM Dice ;

VAR DieA : INTEGER ;
    DieB : INTEGER ;

BEGIN
  WRITELN ('A pair of dice has been rolled.') ;
  WRITE ('The results are: ') ;
  DieA := RANDOM (6) + 1 ;
  DieB := RANDOM (6) + 1 ;
  WRITELN ('a ' , DieA , ' and a ' , DieB)
END .
```

DO IT NOW

1. Alter the program `Dice` to also output the sum of the numbers on each die.
2. Write an assignment instruction to assign to variable `NumRnd`
   a. a number from 0 to 20.
   b. a number from 1 to 52.
   c. a number from 5 to 15.

DO IT NOW ANSWERS

1. One such alteration would be to insert the instruction

```
WRITELN ('The sum of the dice is: ' , DieA + DieB)
```

as the last instruction in the execution section.

```
2a. NumRnd := RANDOM (21)
 b. NumRnd := RANDOM (52) + 1
 c. NumRnd := RANDOM (11) + 5
```

Vocabulary

Page		
34	**Assignment**	The act of placing a value in a variable. The symbol for assignment is `:=`. The Pascal instruction `NumA := -7 + NumB` is an assignment instruction.
35	**DIV**	A Pascal reserved word used to indicate division in the following sense: `12 DIV 5 = 2`. This form of division always yields an integer.
34	**INTEGER**	A Pascal reserved word used to indicate that a variable has been declared and that the value in the variable will be a number that is an integer. That is, the value will be in the collection `-MAXINT - 1, . . . ., -3, -2, -1, 0, 1, 2, 3, . . . , MAXINT`.
34	**Integers**	The collection of numbers consisting of the whole numbers and their additive opposites (. . . $-3, -2, -1, 0, 1, 2, 3, . . .$).

Glad You Asked

Q I just do not understand type. Could you explain it better?

A I would be glad to try. Often, an analogy is helpful with this type of explanation. Suppose you ran a food store. A delivery person comes with some goods. You must store the goods. You ask what kinds of goods they are. Aha, frozen foods; they must be put in the place created for them (the freezer). Oh, fresh fruit; it must be put in the place created for it (on a shelf up front for quick movement). The Pascal language is said to be strongly typed. That is, you, the programmer, must create a place for the data to be delivered to the program. Also, the data put in a place must be of the type the place was created to hold. (Back to the analogy: you do not want to put frozen foods on the shelf up front or, for that matter, put fresh fruit in the freezer.)

Q When do you use the symbol = and when do you use the symbols :=?

A First, `:=` is one symbol. Up to this point, the symbol = has only been used in the CONST section; for example, `Mess1 = 'Hello'`. Later, when the symbol = appears in the execution section, its purpose will be to indicate a comparison. The symbol `:=` is used to assign a value to a variable; for example, `NumB := 7`. This tells the computer to look up the memory cells referenced by `NumB` and place in those cells the number 7.

Q I tried the following execution block in a program and did not get past the compiler. The error message was "Error in variable."

```
BEGIN
  WRITE ('Please enter first number: ') ;
  READLN (NumA) ;
  WRITE ('Please enter second number: ') ;
  READLN (NumB) ;
  NumC = NumA + NumB ;
  WRITELN ('The sum is: ' , NumC)
END .
```

What is wrong?

A The line `NumC = NumA + NumB`. The computer expected the assignment operation `:=` in this context. That is, the line should be `NumC := NumA + NumB`. You want to assign the sum to the variable `NumC`. Later, you will see that = means "to compare."

Section 1-4 Exercises

1. Which of the following is a valid assignment of a value to the variable Age of type INTEGER?
   a. Age := 12/3
   b. Age = -13 MOD 5
   c. Age := 'Sixteen'
   d. Age := 3 DIV 5
   e. Age := (-12 - 5) / (6 * 3)

2. The value of 23 - 11 DIV 5 - 6 * 8 is
   a. -28.8 b. -59 c. -28 d. -27.2 e. none of these

3. The predefined constant that represents the largest value that a variable of type INTEGER can represent has the identifier _____ .

4. A Pascal instruction that places a value in the memory location referenced by a variable is called an _____ instruction.

5. The Pascal reserved word used to obtain the remainder of a division of two integers is _____ .

6. The set of rules that govern the order in which the operations of a computation are performed is called _____ rules.

7. In the instruction WRITE (-13 : 7), the field width specifier is _____ .

8. In the instruction WRITE (-13 : 7), the value -13 will be written to the screen in a field that is 7 spaces wide and is _____ justified.

9. Given the following VAR section and execution section:

```
VAR FirstN : INTEGER ;
    SecondN : INTEGER ;
    ThirdN : INTEGER ;

BEGIN
  FirstN := -15 ;
  WRITE ('Enter an integer: ') ;
  READLN (ThirdN ) ;
  SecondN := FirstN + ThirdN
END .
```

   a. If the program user enters the number 30, give the value in the variable SecondN.
   b. If the program user enters the number -40, give the value in the variable SecondN.

10. Given this VAR section:

```
VAR FirstN : INTEGER ;
    SecondN : INTEGER ;
    ThirdN : STRING [13] ;
```

   Explain why each of the following will yield an error.
   a. FirstN := 15 / 7
   b. SecondN := ThirdN
   c. -20 := SecondN
   d. FirstN := -18 * 3 ;
      SecondN = FirstN + 2

11. Insert the diskette Source in disk drive B. From the disk operating system (DOS) prompt, type B:NUMFUN, then press the RETURN key. Experiment with each of the options A, B, and C. Use the program to compute the following. (Press the CAPS LOCK key.)
   a. 34 MOD 4
   b. -13 * -4
   c. 137 DIV 7
   d. -28 - -3

12. Give the output of the following (use a ▯ to indicate a blank space):
   a. WRITE (-15 : 6)
   b. WRITE (20 DIV -4 : 3)
   c. WRITE (72 : 3 , 18 : 5)
   d. WRITELN (-3 , 64 : 1) ;
      WRITE (-156 : 8 , 13 : 2)
   e. WRITE (23 MOD 5 : 5, -13 : 5) ;
      WRITE (-164 DIV 10 : 3)

13. Complete the following table.

Expression	Results	Expression	Results	Expression	Results
23 / 4	_____	23 DIV 4	_____	23 MOD 4	_____
−45 / 9	_____	−45 DIV 9	_____	−45 MOD 9	_____
135 / 2	_____	135 DIV 2	_____	135 MOD 2	_____
95 / −10	_____	95 DIV −10	_____	95 MOD −10	_____
−42 / −5	_____	−42 DIV −5	_____	−42 MOD −5	_____

14. Insert *True* for a true statement. Insert *False* for a false statement.
_____ **a.** −156 DIV Ø is Ø.
_____ **b.** Any integer MOD 2 yields Ø or 1.
_____ **c.** If Amt is a variable of type INTEGER, then 12.3 would be a valid assignment to the variable Amt.
_____ **d.** 26.Ø8 DIV 3 is undefined.
_____ **e.** 28 + 4 DIV 8 is 4
_____ **f.** (28 + 4) DIV 8 is 4
_____ **g.** 28 + 4 DIV 8 is 3Ø

15. Compute the following.
a. −64 DIV 4 − 36 * 2
b. −64 DIV (4 − 36) * 2
c. 23 + −19 MOD 1Ø DIV 3
d. (23 + −19) MOD 1Ø DIV 3
e. 128 DIV 16 − 16 * 2 + −8
f. 128 DIV 16 − (16 * 2 − 8)
g. 128 DIV (16 − 16 * 2 − 8)
h. 128 DIV (16 − 16) * (2 − 8)

16. a. Given the formula $A = h(b1 + B2)/2$, rewrite it as a Pascal assignment instruction to assign to A an INTEGER value.
b. If h contains 18, b1 contains 1Ø, and B2 contains 5, then A will be assigned what value?

17. The screen on Jill's home computer has 40 character positions per line. The language she is using has a function called HTab to position the cursor on the screen. If HTab is larger than a multiple of 40, then the cursor is positioned on the next line at location HTab MOD 4Ø. If HTab is 732, then the cursor will be at what position on the line?

18. Given:

```
PROGRAM SwapEm ;

CONST MessA = 'first number: ' ;
      MessB = ' second number: ' ;

VAR NumA : INTEGER ;
    NumB : INTEGER ;
    Hold : INTEGER ;

BEGIN
  WRITE ('Enter ' , MessA) ;
  READLN (NumA) ;
     :
     :
  WRITE ('first number: ' , NumA) ;
  WRITELN (' and second number: ' , NumB)
END .
```

Sample Execution

```
Enter first number: 8
Enter second number: 15
The numbers switched are-
first number: 15 and second number: 8
```

Complete the execution section such that the program will take as input two numbers, switch the numbers, and then output the results. An example of the screen after executing the program is as shown.

19. Identify and explain each of the seven errors in the following program:

```
PROG SevenErr ;

VAR FirstN : INTEGER
    SecondN = -12 ;

BEIGN ;
  FirstN := 5 / 2 ;
  WRITELN ('ThirdN is ' , ThirdN : 8) ;
END
```

Problems with RANDOM

20. Give the range of numbers that would be assigned to the variable ANum by the following.
    a. ANum := RANDOM (8)   c. ANum := RANDOM (3) + 5
    b. ANum := RANDOM (50)   d. ANum := RANDOM (MAXINT) MOD 2

21. Write an assignment instruction to assign a random number to variable RNum in the following range:
    a. from 0 to 1000 inclusive.   c. from 6 to 23 inclusive.
    b. from 1 to 47 inclusive.   d. from 15 to 50 inclusive.

22. Boot up Pascal; set the workfile to the file DICEDEMO.PAS from the Source diskette. Enter the Turbo Pascal editor.
    a. Expand the program commands to output the sum of the dice. That is, the output should appear as follows:

Sample Execution

```
A pair of dice has been rolled.
The results are: a 3 and a 5
The sum is 8
```

    b. Alter the program commands to roll dice that are 12-sided (rather than 6-sided) and contain the numbers 1 through 12 on the faces.

23. Complete the following Pascal program. The program is to simulate randomly selecting a social security number. A social security number has the form ###-##-####. (The first digit of each section must be 1 or larger).

```
PROGRAM LuckySS ;

VAR FNum : INTEGER ;
    MNum : INTEGER ;
    LNum : INTEGER ;

BEGIN
  RANDOMIZE ;
  WRITELN ('Your Lucky Social Security Number is') ;
  FNum := RANDOM (900) + 100 ;
      :
      :
END .
```

Sample Execution

```
Your Lucky Social Security Number is
264-34-1129
```

COMMENT
The instruction RANDOMIZE results in a different sequence of random numbers each time the program is compiled and executed.

Programming Problems

24. Write a Pascal program that allows the user to enter an integer value for the variable NumDays. The program is to output the number of weeks in the input number of days and the days left over.

Sample Execution

```
Please enter number of days: 569
Number of weeks is: 81 with 2 days over.
```

(Follow the steps given in Section 1-1. That is, start by designing a solution to the problem, then hand simulating the design, and so on.)

25. Write a Pascal program similar to the one in problem 23 that generates a lucky phone number.

```
Your lucky phone number is 555-1223
```

Section 1–5

Type REAL

In this section, you will be introduced to another data type: REAL. This data type, like INTEGER, deals with numbers. The topic of scientific notation will be discussed and some of the built-in Pascal functions dealing with numbers will be introduced.

1-5.1 REAL Numbers

In mathematics, the collection of ratios of whole numbers is called the fractions (numbers like 0, 18/5, 123/512, etc.). If this collection of numbers is combined with their additive inverses ($-3/4$, $-13/3$, etc.), the resulting collection of numbers is called the rational numbers.

Every rational number has a decimal name. That is, 1/2 has the decimal name 0.5. The number 2/3 has the decimal name 0.6666 . . . (the . . . indicates that the pattern continues).

Some numbers are not rational numbers; that is, they do not have decimal names. The ratio of the circumference of a circle to the diameter of the circle is such a number (called π). Another number that is irrational (not rational) is the positive number whose square is 2 (called $\sqrt{2}$). If the collection of rational numbers is combined with the collection of irrational numbers, the resulting collection of numbers is called the **real numbers.**

In the Pascal language, any number written as a decimal is said to be of type **REAL.** A digital computer cannot store all real numbers in memory. For example, the number π and the number 1/3 cannot be stored in memory. A decimal approximation is used for real numbers that cannot be stored in memory. However, using approximations in computations with data of type REAL can lead to some surprises (as will be shown later).

Observe the following CONST and VAR sections:

```
CONST Angle = 0.56 ;

VAR SideA : REAL ;
    Perimeter : REAL ;
    NumSides : INTEGER
```

The constant `Angle` has been declared and its value stated as the real number `0.56`. The variables `SideA` and `Perimeter` have been declared and their type stated as `REAL`. Notice the form used with the decimal number in `Angle = 0.56`. The Pascal language is very strict about the form of the decimal name used. The name must have a digit on both sides of the decimal point. That is, the number 1/2 as a decimal must be written `0.5` (.5 will not work). Likewise, the number 7 as a decimal must be written `7.0` (7. will not work).

DO IT NOW

1. Identify and discuss the error(s) in the following:
   a. CONST Rate = .23 ;
   b. VAR Dist : REAL ;
       Time := 1.23 ;
2. Construct a VAR section that declares Height and Weight as variables and states their type as REAL.

Operations and Assignment The operations available for variables of type REAL are addition, subtraction, multiplication, and division. These operations are indicated in a Pascal program by use of the symbols $+$, $-$, $*$, and $/$. In computations involving more than one operation, the order-of-operations rules are followed (see Table). Consider the following:

$$3.2 - 5.1 * 6.0 = 3.2 - 30.6$$
$$= {}^-27.4$$
$$\text{and } (3.2 - 5.1) * 6.0 = {}^-1.9 * 6.0$$
$$= {}^-11.4$$

The operations of multiplication and division are done first; the operations of addition and subtraction are done second. If parentheses are present, the computation in the parentheses is done first.

Assignment of a value to a variable of type REAL is accomplished by use of READ, READLN, or the assignment instruction :=. Consider the following VAR section and execution section:

```
VAR SideA : REAL ;
    Perimeter : REAL ;
    NumSides : INTEGER ;

BEGIN
  WRITE ('Enter number of sides: ') ;
  READLN (NumSides) ;
  WRITE ('Enter length of side: ') ;
  READLN (SideA) ;
  Perimeter := NumSides * SideA ;
  WRITELN ('Perimeter is: ' , Perimeter)
END .
```

Here, assignment to the variables NumSides and SideA is accomplished with the READLN instruction. Assignment to the variable Perimeter is accomplished with the assignment operation, :=.

If an integer is assigned to a variable of type REAL, either by READ, READLN, or the assignment operation :=, the value is converted to a real number. That is, suppose the user enters 8 in response to the following prompt:

```
Enter length of side:
```

Although the program is requesting a real number, the integer 8 is accepted. Likewise, an assignment instruction like NumR := 8 will not yield an error. The integer 8 would be renamed to its real number name (8.0). This is because of the mathematical fact that every integer has a real name.

Operation	**Precedence**
( )	Highest
*, /, DIV, MOD	↓
+, −	Lowest

Sample Execution

```
Enter number of sides: 5
Enter length of side: 10.2
Perimeter is: 5.1000000000E+01
```

COMMENT
The number 5.1000000000E+01 is E notation for 51 and will be discussed shortly.

COMMENT
For NumR of type REAL, NumR := .5 yields an error. However, for READLN (NumR), entering .5 will not yield an error.

DO IT NOW

1. Do the following computations:
   a. `18 / 3 - 1.2 * 10`
   b. `18 / (3 - 1.2) * 10`
2. Given that variables `SideA` and `SideB` are of type REAL and variable `NumSides` is of type INTEGER, which of the following are valid Pascal instructions?
   a. `NumSides := 3.5`
   b. `SideA := 9`
   c. `SideB = 18.4`
   d. `NumSides := SideA DIV 3`

1-5.2 Scientific Notation

Consider the following Pascal instruction and its results:

Instruction	Output
`WRITE (12345.678)`	`1.2345780000E+04`

This output notation is called **E notation** (or **floating point notation**). It is based on a notation system developed by scientists for writing very large and very small numbers. The notation is called **scientific notation.** In scientific notation, the number 12345.678 is written

$$1.2345678 \times 10^4$$

The raised 4 is called an **exponent.** The exponent is used to indicate how many times the number (1.2345678, in this case) should be multiplied by 10. Exponent notation is hard to do on computers. Thus, E notation was substituted. The number following the E is the exponent for 10 (that is, E4 means 10^4).

Example   Write 2.34000E3 in decimal notation.

Solution   2.34000E3 means 2.34×10^3.
Now, $2.34 \times 10^3 = 2.34 \times 1000 = 2340$.

Example   Write $-1.45E - 3$ in decimal notation.

Solution $-1.45E - 3$ means -1.45×10^{-3}. The negative exponent (-3) means divide by 10 three times. Now, $-1.45 \times 10^{-3} = -1.45 / 1000 = -0.00145$

The general forms for scientific and Turbo Pascal E notation are

scientific notation form   Turbo E notation form

Thus, to write a number in scientific notation,

1. Select a number from 1 up to (but not including) 10.
2. Figure out the power of 10 needed to multiply or divide the number (selected in part 1) by to obtain the original number.

Example   Write 23000000 in scientific notation and in E notation.

Solution   First, select a number between 1 and 10. In this case, 2.3 is selected. Thus, 23000000 is $2.3 \times 10^?$.
Second, figure out the number of 10s needed. In this case, you need to multiply 2.3 by 10 seven times. Thus, the exponent is 7. So, 23000000 is 2.3×10^7 in scientific notation. In E notation, 23000000 would be 2.3000000000E + 07.

Example   Write 0.0000000000345 in scientific notation and E notation.

Solution   First, select a number between 1 and 10 (in this case, 3.45). Thus, 0.0000000000345 will be

$$3.45 \times 10^?$$

Second, figure out the exponent needed. In this case, you need to divide 3.45 by a number of 10s to get 0.0000000000345. *To indicate division by 10, a negative number is used for the exponent.* Here, 3.45 needs to be divided by 10 eleven times. Thus, $0.0000000000345 = 3.45 \times 10^{-11}$. The E notation name will be 3.4500000000E − 11.

DO IT NOW

1. Convert the following to decimal notation:
   a. 1.23×10^4 b. $-5.60000E - 3$
2. Convert the following to scientific notation and E notation:
   a. 1234.05   c. -15.01
   b. 0.000023   d. -0.12

1-5.3 *Output of Real Numbers*

In Turbo Pascal, when the WRITE or WRITELN instruction is used with data of type REAL, the number is output in E notation. Consider the following VAR and execution sections:

```
VAR SideA : REAL ;
    Perimeter : REAL ;
    NumSides : INTEGER ;

BEGIN
  WRITE ('Enter number of sides: ') ;
  READLN (NumSides) ;
  WRITE ('Enter length of side: ') ;
  READLN (SideA) ;
  Perimeter := NumSides * SideA ;
  WRITELN ('The perimeter is ' , Perimeter)
END .
```

Sample Execution

```
Enter number of sides: 5
Enter length of side: 1.5
The perimeter is 7.5000000000E+00
```

The field width can be specified in the output of data of type REAL. Consider this WRITE instruction:

```
WRITE (- 0.0001234 : 20 , 123.45 : 20)
```

When executed, this WRITE instruction yields an output of (the ☐ represents a blank space)

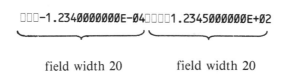

```
☐☐☐-1.2340000000E-04☐☐☐☐1.2345000000E+02
```

field width 20   field width 20

Each number is output in a field of width 20, right justified (that is, shifted to the right side of the field). The field width is the smallest number of spaces used. If more spaces are needed to output the number, they are allocated by the Pascal system.

In addition to specifying field width, the number of digits to the right of the decimal point can be specified. This is called **decimal specification.** Consider the following WRITE instruction:

```
WRITE ( -0.0001234 : 10 : 2 , 123.47 : 10 : 1 )
```

When executed, this WRITE instruction yields an output of (the ☐ represents a blank space)

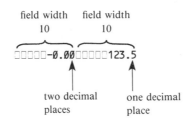

field width   field width
    10   10
```
☐☐☐☐☐-0.00☐☐☐☐☐123.5
```
two decimal   one decimal
places   place

For the number **-0.0001234**, a field width of 10 was specified. Also, two decimal places were specified. Thus, when **-0.0001234** is rounded off to two decimal places, the result is **-0.00**. For the number **123.47**, a field width of 10 was specified and one decimal place was specified. Thus, when **123.47** is rounded off to one decimal place, the result is **123.5**.

COMMENT

There are situations in which the programmer wishes to write an integer value but the value is outside the range **-MAXINT - 1** to **MAXINT**. For example, suppose the programmer wants NumA to hold a value like **4587912** and to write the value in NumA to the screen. In Turbo Pascal, by declaring NumA to be of type **REAL** then using the instruction **WRITE (NumA:7:0)**, the output of NumA will be written to appear as an integer.

Finally, consider the following VAR section and execution section:

```
VAR SideA : REAL ;
    Perimeter : REAL ;
    NumSides : INTEGER ;

BEGIN
  WRITE ('Enter number of sides: ') ;
  READLN (NumSides) ;
  WRITE ('Enter length of side: ') ;
  READLN (SideA) ;
  Perimeter := NumSides * SideA ;
  WRITELN ('The perimeter is ' , Perimeter : 1 : 2)
END .
```

Given an input of 5 for NumSides and 1.5 for SideA, the output will be

```
The perimeter is 7.50
```

Given an input of 1000 for NumSides and 18.2 for SideA, the output will be

```
The perimeter is 18200.00
```

Given an input of 1000 for NumSides and 3.2E37 for SideA, the output will be

```
Run-time error
```

COMMENT

The run-time error appears since 1000*3.2E37 is greater than 1.0E38 the upper limit for positive REAL data.

COMMENT

It is good programming practice always to specify the output form desired. With variables of type REAL, the field specification number is the minimal number of output spaces. If the number requires more spaces for output than the number specified, the spaces will be allotted. Thus, using a field width of 1 assures that the real value will be written in the minimal number of spaces.

DO IT NOW

1. Give the output of the following.
   a. WRITE (2.3)
   b. WRITE (12.3)
   c. WRITE (1.23 : 10)
   d. WRITE (0.00023)
   e. WRITE (16.35 : 1 : 2)
   f. WRITE (0.000236 : 1 : 2)
2. Given Mag, a variable of type REAL with a value of 24.0, and Pie, a variable of type INTEGER with a value of 4, give the output of the following.
   a. WRITE (Pie * 3)
   b. WRITE (Mag / 4)
   c. WRITE (Mag / 2)
   d. WRITE (Pie / 2)
   e. WRITE (Pie DIV 2)
   f. WRITE (Mag + Pie)
3. For the previously given VAR section and execution section, suppose an integer value is entered for NumSides and SideA. Alter the instruction

   ```
   WRITELN ('The perimeter is ' , Perimeter : 1 : 2)
   ```

   to output the perimeter to appear as an integer value.

DO IT NOW ANSWERS

1a. □□2.3000000000E+00
 b. □□1.2300000000E+01
2a. 12
 b. □□6.0000000000E+00
3. WRITELN ('The perimeter is ' , Perimeter : 1 : 0)

c. 1.2300E+00
d. □□2.3000000000E−04
c. □□1.2000000000E+01
d. □□2.0000000000E+00

e. 16.35
f. 0.00
e. 2
f. □□2.8000000000E+01

1–5.4 *Predefined Functions*

A **function** can be thought of as an operator such that when given an input value (or values), the value is operated on to yield an output value. The output value is stored in a memory location identified by the function name.

Consider the predefined Pascal function **SQR** (short for *square*) in the following instruction:

```
A := SQR (7)
```

The function SQR is given an input of the value 7. The function takes this value and multiplies it times itself. The result (49 in this case) is output by the function SQR. This output value is then assigned to the variable A.

Consider the following:

Instruction	Result
Hyp := SQR (4) + SQR (3) WRITE (SQR (0.3))	Hyp is assigned the value 25. The real number 0.09 is output as ▯▯9.0000000000E-02

If the input value to the Pascal function SQR is of type INTEGER, then the output value is of type INTEGER. Likewise, an input value of type REAL yields an output value of type REAL.

Another Pascal predefined function is **ROUND.** Consider this Pascal instruction:

```
A := ROUND (123.4567)
```

The function ROUND is given the input value 123.4567. The function takes this value and rounds it off to the nearest integer (123 in this case). The output value is then assigned to the variable A. Consider the following instructions and their results:

Instruction	Result
StepF := ROUND (9.67) WRITE (ROUND (-15.5) : 5)	The integer 10 is assigned to the variable StepF. The integer − 16 is output as ▯▯−16

The function ROUND takes a value of type REAL or INTEGER as an input value and outputs a value of type INTEGER.

A function closely related to ROUND is **TRUNC.** Consider the following instruction:

```
B := TRUNC (123.4567)
```

The predefined function TRUNC is given the input value 123.4567. The function TRUNC takes this value and truncates (cuts off or lops) the decimal part of the value. The output value (123 in this case) is then assigned to the variable B. Consider the following instructions and their results:

Instruction	Result
StepF := TRUNC (9.67) WRITE (TRUNC (-15.5) : 5)	The integer 9 is assigned to the variable StepF. The integer − 15 is output as ▯▯−15

The function TRUNC takes as input a value of type REAL or INTEGER and outputs a value of type INTEGER.

Yet another predefined (built-in) function that has input data of type INTEGER or REAL is **ABS.** Consider this instruction:

```
Number := ABS (-13)
```

When this instruction is executed, the variable `Number` will be assigned the absolute value of the number − 13. The absolute value is computed as follows:

1. If the number is greater than or equal to zero, then the absolute value of the number is the number.
2. If the number is less than zero, then the absolute value of the number is − 1 times the number.

Thus, `Number` will be assigned `-1*-13` (since − 13 is less than 0), or the value `13`.

One other predefined function dealing with data of type REAL is the **SQRT** function (SQRT is Pascal shorthand for *square root*). Consider this instruction:

```
Hyp := SQRT (16)
```

The result of this assignment instruction is that the variable `Hyp` will be assigned the input value `4.0`. The variable must be declared and its type stated as REAL since the function SQRT always returns a value of type REAL.

Consider the following instructions and their results:

Instruction	Result

`Discrim := SQRT (323.0)`
`Hyp := SQRT (SQR (4) + SQR (3))`
`WRITE (SQRT (100))`
	`Discrim` is assigned the value `17.9722`.
	`Hyp` is assigned the value `5.0`.
	The real number 10.0 is output as
	`⎕⎕1.0000000000E+01`

The function SQRT takes as input a *nonnegative* value (zero or larger) of type REAL or INTEGER. The function finds the positive number such that the number times itself yields the input value. The output of the function SQRT is always a value of type REAL.

WARNING
1. The input value for SQRT must be zero or larger. That is, `SQRT (-25)` yields an error.
2. A variable assigned the output of SQRT must be of type REAL. That is,
   `NumJ := SQRT (16)` will yield an error if the variable `NumJ` is of type INTEGER.

The preceding discussion gave you an introduction to Pascal functions shown in the table that follows. Several other functions that deal with data of type REAL, data of type INTEGER, data of type CHAR, and data of type STRING will be discussed as they are needed. Also, soon you will be defining your own functions to perform the various tasks needed to solve a problem.

Function	Purpose	Input Type	Output Type
SQR	Find square	INTEGER	INTEGER
		REAL	REAL
ROUND	Round off number	INTEGER	INTEGER
		REAL	INTEGER
TRUNC	Lop off decimal part	INTEGER	INTEGER
		REAL	INTEGER
ABS	Find absolute value	INTEGER	INTEGER
		REAL	REAL
SQRT	Find square root	INTEGER	REAL
		REAL	REAL

DO IT NOW

1. Give the output of the following instructions.
   a. WRITE (SQR (8) : 10)
   b. WRITE (ROUND (-2.3))
   c. WRITE (SQR (2.0))
   d. WRITE (ROUND (18.56))
   e. WRITE (SQR (ROUND (-2.8)) : 5)
   f. WRITE (SQRT (36))
   g. WRITE (SQR (SQRT (18)) : 1 : 2)
   h. WRITE (ABS (TRUNC (-34.67)))
   i. WRITE (TRUNC (SQR (3.2)))

2. Identify and discuss the error(s) in the following (NumA has been declared a REAL variable, and NumB has been declared an INTEGER variable).
   a. NumB := SQR (5.0)
   b. NumA := SQR 15.0
   c. WRITE (SQR (NumA)) : 6 : 2)
   d. WRITE (ROUND (NumA) : 6 : 2)
   e. NumB := SQRT (64)
   f. NumB := ROUND (SQRT (456.23))
   g. NumB := SQRT (ROUND (456.23))
   h. NumA := SQRT (16 - 25)

DO IT NOW ANSWERS

1a. □□□□□□□□64
 b. -2
 c. □□4.0000000000E+00
 d. 19
 e. □□□□9
 f. □□6.0000000000E+00
 g. 18.00
 h. 34
 i. 10

2a. SQR (5.0) yields a number of type REAL, and NumB is of type INTEGER. Thus, the error is a type conflict.
 b. Parentheses are missing in the SQR function.
 c. An extra parenthesis has been inserted after SQR (NumA).
 d. ROUND (NumA) yields an integer. A number of decimal places cannot be specified for integer data.
 e. SQRT yields a real number. NumB is of type INTEGER.
 f. There is no error.
 g. SQRT yields a real number. NumB is of type INTEGER.
 h. 16 - 25 yields -9. The function SQRT must have as input a number that is zero or larger.

1-5.5 A Top Down Design

As an example of the problem-solving process discussed in Section 1–1 and working with data of type REAL, consider the following example.

EXAMPLE

In the country of Zanadu, workers are paid at an hourly rate. The government deducts 7% of a worker's gross pay for retirement. Of the remaining pay, the government deducts 20% for taxes. The remaining pay after retirement and tax deductions is the worker's net pay (take-home pay). Write a Pascal program that allows the user to enter an employee's name, number of hours worked, and hourly pay rate. The program is to output to the screen the employee's name, followed by a column header line for Gross, Retirement, Taxes, and Net. Under this column header line, the values for each item are to be written.

Sample Execution

```
Please enter employee's name: Gaafar Nimeiri
Please enter hours worked: 56
Please enter hourly pay rate: 8.20

Employee: Gaafar Nimeiri
  Gross   Retirement      Taxes     Net
  459.20       32.14      85.41  341.64
```

SOLUTION

The place to start is by composing a design of the solution.

Design: Input employee information
Compute Gross
Compute Retirement
Compute Taxes
Compute Net
Output results

Next, the steps of the design are refined.

Refinement of: *Input employee information*
WRITE ('Please enter name: ')
READLN (Name)
WRITE ('Please enter hours worked: ')
READLN (Hours)
WRITE ('Please enter hourly pay rate: ')
READLN (Rate)

COMMENT
From this refinement, the variable needs can be determined. A STRING variable **Name** will be required. REAL variables **Hours** and **Rate** will be required.

Refinement of: *Compute Gross*
Gross := Hours * Rate

Refinement of: *Compute Retirement*
Retirement := 0.07 * Gross

Refinement of: *Compute Taxes*
Taxes : = 0.20 * (Gross − Retirement)

Refinement of: *Compute Net*
Net : = Gross − Retirement − Taxes

Refinement of: *Output results*
WRITELN
WRITELN ('Employee: ' , Name)
WRITE ('Gross' : 7 , 'Retirement' : 13)
WRITELN ('Taxes' : 11 , 'Net' : 8)
WRITE (Gross : 7 : 2 , Retirement : 13 : 2)
WRITELN (Taxes : 11 : 2 , Net : 8 : 2)

COMMENT
From the refinement of these four steps, the program will need REAL variables `Gross`, `Retirement`, `Taxes`, and `Net`.

The field width specifications are found by laying out the screen and desired outputs as follows:

```
          1         2         3         4         5
12345678901234567890123456789012345678901234567890
Employee: Gaafar Nimeiri
  Gross    Retirement      Taxes      Net
      7            20          31       39
```
7 − 0 = 7   20 − 7 = 13   31 − 20 = 11   39 − 31 = 8

The next step is to test the design. That is, a hand simulation is made with several sets of data. As an illustration of such a walk through, suppose the user enters `Desire Bouterse` for `Name`, `21.5` for `Hours`, and `17.32` for `Rate`.

The step *Compute Gross* yields `21.5 * 17.32`, or `372.38`, and assigns the value to the variable `Gross`.

The step *Compute Retirement* yields `0.07 * 372.38`, or `26.0666`, and assigns the value to the variable `Retirement`.

The step *Compute Taxes* yields `0.20 * (372.38 − 26.0666)`, or `69.26268`, and assigns the value to the variable `Taxes`.

The step *Compute Net* yields `372.38 − 26.0666 − 69.26268`, or `277.05072`, and assigns the value to the variable `Net`.

The step *Output Results* writes to the screen

```
Employee: Desire Bouterse
  Gross    Retirement      Taxes      Net
 372.38         26.07      69.26   277.05
```

Several other tests would be run on the design. Once the design has been tested (see Section 1–5, exercise 17), it is converted to a Pascal program (see Section 1–5, exercise 18). Next, the physical part of the problem-solving process begins.

Boot up the Pascal system (if it is not already available). From the Pascal command line, enter the editor. Type in the Pascal program. Make a return to the Pascal main menu. Use the compiler to convert the text of the Pascal program to code. If errors (like spelling errors and/or punctuation errors) are found during the compilation, reenter the editor and correct the errors. Once the compiler is successful in converting the Pascal program to code, execute the code. Execute the code over and over to find errors in the logic of the design that were not discovered during the hand simulations.

COMMENT
Soon (in Chapter 3) you will learn how to repeat the instructions of a program. At that point, the program can be tested without having to execute the code over and over.

Vocabulary

Glad You Asked

Q What is wrong with the assignment instruction where NumR is of type REAL and NumI is of type INTEGER?

```
NumR := NumI DIV 3.2
```

I thought you said that if a variable of type REAL was assigned an INTEGER value, everything would be all right.

A If a variable of type REAL is assigned an INTEGER value, the value is converted to a decimal. However, for the instruction

```
NumR := NumI DIV 3.2
```

the operation DIV (and MOD also) only works with INTEGER values. The number 3.2 is not an integer. Thus, an error was produced. An instruction such as NumR := NumI DIV 3 would not produce an error. Likewise, an instruction such as NUMR := NumI DIV ROUND (3.2) would not produce an error.

Q Why didn't they just call data type REAL type DECIMAL, since irrational numbers can't be represented on a digital computer anyhow?

A Maybe the next time they will. However, type DECIMAL wouldn't be quite accurate either, since nonterminating decimals like 1/3 can't be represented accurately on a digital computer.

Q How will I know when the output of a real number will be in decimal notation and when the output will be in E (floating point) notation?

A The best solution to this problem is to use field width and decimal specification in the WRITE or WRITELN instruction. That is, rather than use `WRITE (NumR)`, use `WRITE (NumR : 1 : 3)`. Since the field width is `1`, the number will take as many spaces as needed. Since the accuracy (or the number of decimal places you desire) is `3`, the number will be written as a decimal.

Q Why not just use numbers of type REAL and forget about numbers of type INTEGER?

A The use of integers provides for much faster computations and for much less storage space taken up by the number. In large programs and/or programs doing many computations, storage space and computation time can become problem areas. There might not be enough room in the computer's memory to execute the program. Likewise, the program's execution might be so slow that a user would not want to use the program. Finally, as mentioned earlier, computations with data of type REAL can produce errors due to inaccuracies in rounding off the data. Thus, if INTEGER data can be used, it is best to use it.

Q How can I round off a real value to 100s? That is, I want to output `89189.22` as `89200.00`.

A One approach is the following algorithm (assume `NumR` contains `89189.22`). First, divide `NumR` by 100 (to obtain `891.8922`). Second, round this value (to obtain `892`). Third, multiply by 100 (to obtain `89200`). Thus, the assignment instruction

```
NumR := 100.0 * ROUND (NumR/100)
```

would assign to `NumR` the value in `NumR` rounded off to 100s. To output the value to the screen, the instruction would be

```
WRITELN (NumR:1:2)
```

Q I had the following instructions in a Pascal program:

```
READLN (NumR) ;
NumR := 1000 * ROUND(NumR) ;
WRITELN ('A 1000 times number is ', NumR:1:0)
```

where `NumR` was of type REAL. When I entered `40`, the output was

```
A 1000 times number is -25536
```

What's going on with this language?

A Although `NumR` was of type REAL, `1000` and `ROUND(NumR)` are of type INTEGER. Thus, the multiplication was performed on integers. A value greater than `MAXINT (32767)` was obtained, and the number was an integer overflow (that is, an overflow into the negative values). If you had used `1000.0`, things would have gone as you planned. Any operation involving REAL data results in REAL results.

Q Why is MAXINT the value 32767? Also, why does `MAXINT + 1` yield `-32768`?

A A personal computer is based on the binary numbering system. This system uses the digits 0 and 1 and a place value of powers of 2. The powers of 2 are 1, 2, 4, 8, 16, 32, 64, 128, 256, 512, 1024, 2048, 4096, 8192, 16384, . . . A memory location designed to hold an integer has 16 placeholders: _ _ _ _ _ _ _ _ _ _ _ _ _ _ _ _

The leftmost placeholder represents the sign of the number (0 = positive, 1 = negative). When the remaining 15 places are filled with a 1, the number represents $1 + 2 + 4 + 8 + \ldots + 16384$, or 32767. When 1 is added, the leftmost placeholder becomes 1 (indicating a negative value), and the remaining placeholders become 0. Thus, the number is -32768. Adding 1 at this point would yield a 1, then 14 zeros, then a 1. This value would be $-32768 + 1$ or -32767.

Section 1–5 Exercises

1. Match the following items on the left with the letter of the correct description on the right.

   _____ 1. SQRT
   _____ 2. ROUND
   _____ 3. REAL
   _____ 4. SQR
   _____ 5. DIV
   _____ 6. 32767
   _____ 7. /
   _____ 8. 5
   _____ 9. scientific notation

   a. a division that always yields an INTEGER
   b. a notation for writing a very large or a very small number
   c. a function that yields the square of a number
   d. a function that yields the closest integer to a number
   e. a division that always yields a REAL
   f. the value of the decimal specification in
      `WRITE (Num : 2 : 5)`
   g. a data type for decimal numbers
   h. a function that yields the square root of a number
   i. the value of MAXINT

2. Construct a CONST section to declare `Factor` a constant with value `7.8` and `Coeff` a constant with value `4/5`.

3. Complete:

Scientic Notation	Decimal Notation
3.2×10^3	_____
5.145×10^1	_____
1.023×10^{-2}	_____
9.45×10^{-4}	_____

4. Complete:

Decimal Notation	E Notation
134.02	_____
22000000	_____
0.000023	_____
-0.00873	_____

5. Given variable `NumR` of type REAL and `NumI` of type INTEGER, state why the following are invalid. If valid, state *valid*.

   a. `CONST Coeff = .78`
   b. `CONST Coeff = 12,000.45`
   c. `NumR := 1923.`
   d. `NumI := 2.3`
   e. `NumI := 15/5`
   f. `NumI := NumR MOD 3`
   g. `WRITE (NumI : 6 : 2)`
   h. `NumR := NumI - 5.0`

6. Insert the diskette `Source` in disk drive **B**. From the disk operating system (DOS) prompt, type **B:NUMFUN**, then press the RETURN key. Experiment with option **D**. Use the program to give the output of the following. (Press the CAPS LOCK key.)
   a. `WRITE (2.83)`
   b. `WRITE (23.85)`
   c. `WRITE (0.0123)`
   d. `WRITE (18 : 4)`
   e. `WRITE (-234.67)`
   f. `WRITE (12.003 : 1 : 2)`
   g. `WRITE (-0.000238 : 1 : 5)`
   h. `WRITE (120000000)`

7. Given variable `NumR` of type REAL, `NumA` of type REAL with value `1.2`, and `NumB` of type REAL with value `2.0`, state the value in `NumR` after the following assignments.
   a. `NumR := NumB + NumA * 3`
   b. `NumR := (NumB + NumA) * 3`
   c. `NumR := NumA / 0.3 - NumB + NumA`
   d. `NumR := NumA / (0.3 - NumB) + NumA`
   e. `NumR := (NumA + 2) / (NumB - 1.5)`

8. Given the following partial Pascal program:

```
PROGRAM CentToFah ;

CONST Coeff = 1.8 ;

VAR
  :
  :
BEGIN
  WRITE ('Enter Centigrade measurement: ') ;
  READLN (Cent) ;
  Fah := Coeff * Cent + 32 ;
  WRITE ('The Fahrenheit measurement is ') ;
  WRITELN (Fah : 1 : 2)
END .
```

   a. Complete the program by declaring the variable(s) and their type(s) in the VAR section.
   b. If the number **38** is entered in response to the prompt
      `Enter Centigrade measurement:`
      give the output of the program.
   c. If the line `WRITELN (Fah : 1 : 2)` is changed to `WRITELN (Fah)` and **38** is entered in response to the prompt `Enter Centigrade measurement:`, give the output of the program.

9. Given that the formula to convert Fahrenheit (F) measurements to centigrade (C) is $C = (5/9)(F - 32)$, complete the following Pascal program:

```
PROGRAM FahToCent ;

VAR Fah : REAL ;
    Cent : REAL ;

BEGIN
  WRITE ('Enter Fahrenheit measurement: ') ;
  _____

  _____

  WRITE ('The Centigrade measurement is ') ;
  _____

END .
```

10. Complete the following Pascal program. The program is to have an input of three grades (all integers) and to output the arithmetic average accurate to two decimal places.

```
PROGRAM Average ;
VAR _____

     _____

BEGIN
  WRITE ('Enter first grade: ') ;

     _____

     _____

  WRITE ('The average is: ') ;
  WRITELN ( _____ )
END .
```

11. Identify and explain the errors in the following program:

```
PROGRAM ErrorALot

CONST InterestR := .0125 ;

VAR Amt : REAL ;
    Invest : INTEGER

BEGIN
  WRITE ('Enter investment amount: $') ;
  READLN (Invest ) ;
  Amt = (Invest )SQR(1 + InterestR) ;
  WRITE ('Amount is: $') ;
  WRITELN (Amt ; 1 : 2)
END .
```

12. Write an assignment statement that will assign to the variable NumR of type REAL the following expressions:
   a. $2\pi r$
   b. $((BB + SB)/2)Ht$
   c. $(1/ROne + 1/RTwo)$
   d. $\dfrac{a}{1 - r}$
   e. $SOne^2 + STwo^2$
   f. $ax^2 + bx + c$

13. Insert the diskette Source in disk drive B. From the disk operating system (DOS) prompt, type B:NUMFUN, then press the RETURN key. Experiment with option E. Use the program to give the output of the following. (Press the CAPS LOCK key.)
   a. WRITE (TRUNC (67.896))
   b. WRITE (ROUND (67.896))
   c. WRITE (SQR (-4))
   d. WRITE (SQRT (225))
   e. WRITE (ABS (-56))
   f. WRITE (SQR (SQRT (3.56)))

14. Give the value in variable RNum after the assignment instruction:
   a. RNum := SQRT (ROUND (64.16))
   b. RNum := ROUND (SQRT (64.16))

15. It appears from problem 14 that SQRT followed by ROUND always yields the same results as ROUND followed by SQRT. Find a counterexample to this statement. That is, find a number x such that SQRT (ROUND (x)) is not equal to ROUND (SQRT (x)). One such value for x is _____.

Programming Problems

For the following problems, follow the process presented in Section 1–1. Write a design for the solution, refine the design, test the design with hand simulations, convert the design to a Pascal program, enter the Pascal system, use the editor to create the text of the program, use the compiler to convert the text to code, execute the code, and debug the program. Turn in a copy of your design and its refinement. Turn in a hard copy of the text of the program and its output.

16. Write a Pascal program that will take as input a real number. The output is to be a table of values (to two decimal places for real values) for the functions ROUND, TRUNC, SQR, and SQRT.

Sample Execution

```
Please enter a number: 36.79
Rounded    Truncated    Squared    Square Root
    37           36      1353.50           6.07
```

17. In the example given on page 54, do a walk through of the design for the following input values.
  a. Mobutu Seko , 70.2 , 20.85
  b. David Kaunda , 80 , 500.25
  c. The test values in part b result in a design error. Should this design error be taken seriously? That is, should the design be altered to accommodate this type of data?
18. a. Convert the design given on page 54 to a Pascal program.
  b. In the design given, complete decimal accuracy is kept throughout the computations. Suppose the government of Zanadu requires that you redesign the program such that all computations are rounded off to the nearest hundredth. Give the alterations required to fulfill this request.
19. a. Write a Pascal program that allows the user to input a stock name, the number of shares bought, and the buying price per share. The program is to output the purchase price for the stock buy.

Sample Execution

```
Enter name of stock: AVX
Enter number of shares bought: 200
Enter buying price per share: $53.25

Price of 200 shares of AVX at
$53.25 per share is $10650.00
```

  b. Expand your program to add to the purchase price the stock broker's fee (2% of the purchase price). The expansion should add to the output two lines similar to the following.

```
Broker's fee is $213.00
Total price of buy is $10863.00
```

c. Further expand your program to allow the user to enter a selling price per share for the stock. The output should be expanded to show the return on the sale and the profit/loss. Both the purchase price and selling price should include the broker's fee of 2% of the transaction.

Sample Execution

```
Enter name of stock: AVX
Enter number of shares bought: 200
Enter buying price per share: $53.25

Price of 200 shares of AVX at
$53.25 per share is $10650.00
Broker's fee is $213.00
Total price of buy is $10863.00

Enter selling price per share: $55.00
Total for selling 200 shares of AVX
at $55.00 per share is $11000.00
Broker's fee is $220.00
Total return on sell is $10780.00

Profit/Loss is -$83.00
```

20. The speed of light is $1.86E5$ miles per second. The distance to the Andromeda galaxy is $2.0E6$ light-years. A light-year is the distance light travels in one year. Write a Pascal program to write to the screen

a. the distance to the Andromeda galaxy in miles.

b. the time (in years) to travel to the Andromeda galaxy, traveling at one-tenth the speed of light.

Sample Execution

```
The distance to the Andromeda galaxy is ..... miles.
The time for travel at one-tenth speed of light is ..... years.
```

Design: Convert 2.0E6 light-years to miles
          Report miles
          Convert 1.86E5 miles per second to miles per hour
          Compute 0.1 of miles per hour
          Compute Time in hours
          Convert Time to years
          Report years

CHAPTER TEST

1. Match the following items on the left with the correct definition on the right.

_____ **1.** disk drive
_____ **2.** READ
_____ **3.** SQR
_____ **4.** WRITELN
_____ **5.** compiler
_____ **6.** CONST
_____ **7.** period
_____ **8.** semicolon
_____ **9.** VAR
_____ **10.** compound instruction
_____ **11.** END

a. the program execution section
b. a program that converts source code to object code
c. an output device
d. a punctuation mark used to separate
e. a Pascal predefined function
f. a Pascal built-in procedure for inputting data
g. a program section where variables are declared
h. a Pascal built-in procedure for outputting data
i. a program section where constants are declared and their values stated
j. the last word in a Pascal program
k. the punctuation mark used to mark the end of a Pascal program

2. Give the output of each of the following.

   a.
   ```
   WRITE ('Pascal is a structured') ;
   WRITELN ('language developed by') ;
   WRITE ('Niklaus Wirth.')
   ```
   b.
   ```
   WRITE ('A number of type REAL is: ') ;
   WRITE (17/4 : 5 : 1)
   ```

3. To solve a problem, the first step is
   a. to sit down at the computer and use the compiler.
   b. to think about the problem and outline a solution.
   c. to use the editor to write a Pascal program.
   d. to convert the source code to object code.
   e. to panic and quit.

4. Rewrite the following program using the style rules.

   ```
   program style ; var numa : integer ; numb : real ;
   begin read (numa) ; numb := numa / 3 ; writeln (numb : 2) end .
   ```

5. Give the output after the execution of the following (all variables are of type INTEGER; use a ☐ to indicate a blank space).

   a.
   ```
   BEGIN
      NumA := 16 ;
      NumB := 3 ;
      NumC := -8 ;
      NumD := NumA DIV NumB ;
      WRITELN (NumD : 5)
   END .
   ```
   b.
   ```
   BEGIN
      NumA  = 12 MOD 5 - 3 ;
      NumB := 5*(13 - 8) ;
      NumA := NumA + NumB ;
      WRITE (NumA , NumB)
   END .
   ```

6. Identify the semicolons required in the following program:

```
PROGRAM Punctuation

CONST Message = 'Enter your name: '

VAR Name : STRING [18]
    Wage : REAL

BEGIN
  WRITE (Message)
  READLN (Name)
  WRITE ('Enter your hourly wage: ')
  READLN (Wage)
END .
```

7. Which of the following would *not* yield an error? Assume this VAR section.

```
VAR Age : INTEGER ;
    Wage : REAL ;
    Name : STRING [8]
```

a. Name := 'Australia'   e. Wage := Name
b. Age := 13/2   f. Wage := Age / 2
c. Wage = 5   g. Age := Wage DIV 2
d. Wage := 3 DIV 2   h. WRITE (Name : 5 : 2)

8. Complete the following program. It is to allow the user to input two numbers, then output the arithmetic average.

```
PROGRAM Average ;

VAR NumA, NumB, Aver : REAL ;

BEGIN
  WRITE ('Enter first number: ') ;
  READLN (NumA) ;
     :
     :
END .
```

9. Write a Pascal program that has as input the lengths of sides of a triangle. The program is to output the area measure of the triangle.

Sample Execution

```
Enter length of side A of the triangle: 18
Enter length of side B of the triangle: 12
Enter length of side C of the triangle: 8

The area measure is: 38.25
```

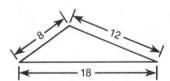

Hint: Use Heron's formula:

$$A = \sqrt{s(s - A)(s - B)(s - C)}$$

where $s = (1/2)(A + B + C)$ and A, B, and C are the lengths of the sides of the triangle.

The Turbo Editor

The Copy Command

The Turbo Pascal editor has several word processing features designed to make writing programs easier. One such feature is the copy commands. These commands allow the programmer to copy and/or move blocks of text from one point in the program to another point in the program. Also, they allow the blocks of text to be copied to and from a diskette TEXT file.

COMMENT
A block of text is a collection of characters ranging from a single character to several lines of text to an entire TEXT file.

Marking a Block of Text

To use the copy commands, you must first learn to mark a block of text. To do this, the cursor is moved to the start of the text. The keystrokes Ctrl-K B (or the F7 function key) place an invisible mark at the beginning of a text block. Next, the cursor is moved to the end of the block. The keystrokes Ctrl-K K (or the F8 function key) place an invisible mark at the end of the block of text. The material between the two marks inserted should change color (to blue) or appear dimmed. Once a block of text is marked, the block can be manipulated with the copy commands.

From the Turbo Pascal main menu, set the workfile to the file BoxEx from the Demos: diskette. Enter the Pascal editor. Move the cursor to the start of the line

```
WRITE (Message, 'what is your name? ') ;
```

Use Ctrl-K B (or the F7 key) to mark the beginning of the block. Move the cursor to the end of the line. Use Ctrl-K K (or the F8 key) to mark the end of the block. The text between the marks should now appear as dimmed or blue. You have marked a block of text.

COMMENT
To jump to the end of a line, use the END key. To jump to the start of a line, use the HOME key.

Move the cursor to the end of the line

```
READLN (Address) ;
```

Press the RETURN key to insert a blank line. Use Ctrl-K C, and the marked block is copied to the new location. Move the cursor to the end of the line

```
READLN (Name) ;
```

Press the RETURN key to insert a blank line. Use Ctrl-K V, and the block of text is moved to the new location. Finally, use Ctrl-K Y, and the block of text is deleted. When a block of text is moved, the begin/end markers are moved with it. When a block of text is deleted, the markers are deleted.

COMMENT
The blank lines that now appear in the program were inserted when the RETURN key was pressed. They were not part of the marked block. Thus, they were neither moved nor deleted when the block was moved and then deleted.

Marked Blocks and Files

Use the backspace key and Ctrl-Y to delete text from the workspace to achieve the following form:

```
PROGRAM ;

CONST ;

VAR ;

BEGIN

END .
```

Use Ctrl-K R to jump to the start of the TEXT file. Press the RETURN key to insert a blank line. Type the following comment section:

```
{************************************************************}
{Programmer:                                                }
{Date:                                                      }
{Purpose:                                                   }
{************************************************************}
```

Jump to the beginning of the text (use Ctrl-HOME), and mark the beginning of the block by using Ctrl-K B (or the F7 key). Jump to the end of the text (use Ctrl-END), and mark the end of the block by using Ctrl-K K (or the F8 function key).

Use Ctrl-K W to copy the marked block to a TEXT file. Respond to the `Write block to file:` prompt by typing `B:PROGFORM`, then pressing the RETURN key. After some disk drive activity, you are returned to the editor. Quit the editor. Press the RETURN key to see the main menu. Obtain a listing of the files on the diskette `Source`. One of the files should be `PROGFORM.PAS`. You have copied a block of text to a TEXT file on the diskette `Source`.

Set the workfile to the file `B:MyBlock` (a new file). Respond to the `Save workfile?` prompt by pressing the N key for no. Enter the editor. Use Ctrl-K R to read a TEXT file into the editor. Respond to the prompt `Read block from file:` by typing `B:PROGFORM`, then pressing the RETURN key. The contents of the file `PROGFORM.PAS` from the diskette `Source` are copied into the editor. You could now fill in the program form with the comments and instructions for a Pascal program. When you quit the editor and save its contents, the material will be saved to the file `MYBLOCK.PAS` on the diskette `Source`.

COMMENT

Although the prompt for the read block from a file application states *block,* the entire TEXT file will be copied into the editor.

Chapter Two

Decision Control

Introduction

In the previous chapter, you looked at how to get data into the computer, how to assign data to variables, and how to output data. These actions are fundamental to any computer language. In this chapter, you will study another fundamental feature of any computer language: the ability to make a *decision* as to whether or not to execute an instruction. To make a decision, the computer must be able to compare values. These comparisons are made by the logic unit of the computer's CPU.

The chapter starts by looking at the relational operators (=, >, >=, <, <=, and <>) and a new data type called BOOLEAN. Next, the decision control instruction IF-THEN-ELSE is discussed. Compound instructions and nested instructions are covered. Finally, another decision control instruction, the CASE-OF-END instruction, is considered. After finishing this chapter, you will be able to write a Pascal program that can decide whether or not to execute an instruction.

```
PROGRAM Chapter2 ;

VAR Divisible : BOOLEAN ;                {page 68}
    NumA, NumB : INTEGER ;

BEGIN
  WRITE ('Enter the divisor ') ;
  WRITE ('(2,3,5, or 7): ') ;
  READLN (NumA) ;
  WRITE ('Enter a number') ;
  WRITE ('(2 .. 1000): ') ;
  READLN (NumB) ;
  Divisible := (NumB MOD NumA = 0) ;     {page 70}
  CASE NumA OF                           {page 106}
    2 : IF Divisible                     {page 76}
          THEN WRITELN ('2 is a divisor')
          ELSE WRITELN ('Not 2') ;
    3 : IF Divisible                     {page 78}
          THEN WRITELN ('3 divides it.') ;
    5 : IF Divisible
          THEN BEGIN                     {page 91}
                 WRITE ('Five is a') ;
                 WRITE (' divisor of ') ;
                 WRITELN (NumB)
               END
    ELSE WRITELN ('7 divides it.')       {page 106}
  END ;
  WRITELN ('That is it.')
END .
```

Type **BOOLEAN**

In this section, you will study the relational operators in Pascal. You will be introduced to a new data type, BOOLEAN. Finally, you will study some of the operations available for this data type. The purpose of this material is to allow you to learn the decision control instructions that are presented later in this chapter and the repetition control instructions presented in Chapter 3.

2-1.1 BOOLEAN Expressions

In Chapter 1, you studied four data types: CHAR, STRING, INTEGER, and REAL. Each of these data types represented a collection of values. Also, each data type had a collection of operations available for values of the given type. For example, INTEGER represents the values . . . $-2, -1, 0, 1, 2, \ldots$ The collection of operations available for values of this data type were $+, -, *$, DIV, and MOD.

The values represented by type **BOOLEAN** are TRUE and FALSE. That's right: there are only two values. These values are used to give the truth value of a statement. For example, the statement $13 = 5 + 3$ has the truth value FALSE.

As simple a type as BOOLEAN is, it is essential to computer programming. In the next section of this chapter, you will see an instruction similar to this:

    IF BOOLEAN expression is true
       THEN InstructionA
       ELSE InstructionB

And, in the next chapter, you will see an instruction similar to this:

    WHILE BOOLEAN expression is true DO
       Instruction

To understand and use these instructions, it is essential that you understand BOOLEAN expressions. (BOOLEAN is named for George Boole, a nineteenth century English mathematician and the inventor of the calculus of logic.)

One source of BOOLEAN expressions is the relational operators, or relationals: $=, >, > =, <, < =$, and $< >$. These operators are read as shown in Table 2–1.

Table 2–1

Operator	Example	Read as
=	15 = 3(5)	15 is equal to 3(5).
>	13 > −5	13 is greater than −5.
> =	a > = b	a is greater than or equal to b.
<	x < −3	x is less than −3.
< =	a + b < = c	a + b is less than or equal to c.
< >	−3 < > 3	−3 is not equal to 3.

When these relational operators are applied to numbers (of type REAL or INTEGER), characters, or strings of characters, a **BOOLEAN expression** results. Consider the BOOLEAN expressions and their values shown in Table 2–2.

With numbers, the BOOLEAN value is arrived at through arithmetic. With characters, the BOOLEAN value is arrived at by comparing the character's *ASCII value* (a standardized value given to each keyboard character). Some of these values are listed in Table 2–3.

Table 2–2

BOOLEAN expression	Value
17 = 13 + 4	TRUE
17 < > 13 + 4	FALSE
−13 > 5	FALSE
2.3 <= 3 * 8 / 4	TRUE
'A' < 'B'	TRUE
'John' > 'Joan'	TRUE
'New' < 'New York'	TRUE

Character	ASCII Value	Character	ASCII Value	Character	ASCII Value	Character	ASCII Value	Table 2-3
RETURN	13	K	75	Y	89	m	109	
SPACE	32	L	76	Z	90	n	110	
0	48	M	77	a	97	o	111	
1	49	N	78	b	98	p	112	
A	65	O	79	c	99	q	113	
B	66	P	80	d	100	r	114	
C	67	Q	81	e	101	s	115	
D	68	R	82	f	102	t	116	
E	69	S	83	g	103	u	117	
F	70	T	84	h	104	v	118	
G	71	U	85	i	105	w	119	
H	72	V	86	j	106	x	120	
I	73	W	87	k	107	y	121	
J	74	X	88	l	108	z	122	

As you can see from Table 2-3, all the keyboard characters have ASCII values. (For a more complete listing, see Appendix E.) Note that character A and character a have different ASCII values.

With strings of characters, the comparison is made character by character. For example, with the strings 'John' and 'Joan', the BOOLEAN expression 'John' > 'Joan' has the BOOLEAN value TRUE. The first character (J) of the strings is the same; the second character (o) is also the same. In the case of the third character, h has a greater ASCII value than character a. Thus, 'John' > 'Joan' has the BOOLEAN value TRUE. The same argument applies to 'John' > 'Joanna', which has BOOLEAN value TRUE. In the case of the expression 'New' < 'New York', the first three characters are equal, but the length of the string 'New' is less than the length of the string 'New York'. Thus, 'New' < 'New York' has BOOLEAN value TRUE.

DO IT NOW

Given the following BOOLEAN expressions, give their truth value.

1. -12 >= -4 _____
2. -12 > -4 + 5 _____
3. 12 < -4 * 5 _____
4. 12 <= -4 * -5 _____
5. 'Z' >= 'F' _____

6. 'Z' >= 'a' _____
7. 'Thelma' > 'Tom' _____
8. '123' <= '78' _____
9. 'Susan' = 'susan' _____

(*Hint:* ASCII for '7' is 55.)

2-1.2 *Type BOOLEAN in Programs*

Consider the following program section:

```
VAR Ans : BOOLEAN ;
    Count : INTEGER ;
```

Here, the identifier Ans has been declared a variable, and its type is listed as BOOLEAN. This means a memory location is created and the value stored in memory location Ans will be one of the values TRUE or FALSE.

Of course, once a variable has been declared and its type stated as BOOLEAN, the variable can be assigned a value (by use of the assignment operator, :=). The value assigned the variable must be of type BOOLEAN. Consider the following:

DO IT NOW ANSWERS

1. FALSE	6. FALSE
2. FALSE	7. FALSE
3. FALSE	8. TRUE
4. TRUE	9. FALSE
5. TRUE	

```
READ (Count) ;
Ans := (Count DIV 3 = 0) ;
```

Suppose a value of 13 is assigned the variable Count by the READ instruction. Then the value assigned to the variable Ans would be FALSE. That is, the value FALSE would be stored in the memory location referenced by the **BOOLEAN variable** Ans. Variables of type BOOLEAN must be assigned a BOOLEAN value (just as variables of type CHAR must be assigned a character).

The READ and READLN procedures *cannot* be used to obtain a value for a variable of type BOOLEAN. That is, if Ans is of type BOOLEAN, then READ (Ans) will yield an error. A BOOLEAN value *can* be written to the screen. The instruction WRITELN (Ans) will write to the screen the value TRUE if the BOOLEAN variable Ans contains the value TRUE.

DO IT NOW

1. Given that variables KtDoor and FtDoor are of type BOOLEAN, which of the following are valid instructions?
   a. KtDoor := 13/2
   b. KtDoor := (13/2 < 7)
   c. FtDoor := 'J' < > 'Joe'
   d. FtDoor = 'TRUE'

2. Give the value assigned to BOOLEAN variable Ans.
   a. Ans := (12 >= 13)
   b. Ans := ('A < b')
   c. Ans := ('A' < 'b')
   d. Ans := ('Jo' <= 'Joe')

2-1.3 Operations for Type BOOLEAN

The operations available for data of type BOOLEAN (**BOOLEAN operations**) are the logic operations: NOT, AND, and OR. This is much like the operations available for data of type INTEGER are: +, −, *, DIV, and MOD. The operation **NOT** operates on one piece of BOOLEAN data; the operations of **AND** and **OR** operate on two pieces of BOOLEAN data. Consider the following BOOLEAN expression:

```
NOT (17 > 3)
```

The expression 17 > 3 has BOOLEAN value TRUE. Thus, the expression NOT (17 > 3) has BOOLEAN value FALSE. When NOT operates on a piece of BOOLEAN data, it simply yields the other piece of BOOLEAN data (remember, there are only two pieces of BOOLEAN data: TRUE and FALSE).

The BOOLEAN operation AND operates on two pieces of BOOLEAN data. Consider the following:

```
(17 > 3) AND (8 < 9)
```

When AND operates on two pieces of data, it yields the BOOLEAN value TRUE if both pieces of data are TRUE. Otherwise, it yields the BOOLEAN value FALSE. In the previous example, the expression (17 > 3) has BOOLEAN value TRUE. The expression (8 < 9) has BOOLEAN value TRUE. Thus, the operation yields a BOOLEAN value of TRUE. That is, the BOOLEAN expression (17 > 3) AND (8 < 9) has the BOOLEAN value TRUE. Consider Table 2–4. As you can see from the table, the only time the BOOLEAN operation AND yields a result of TRUE is when both pieces of data have BOOLEAN value TRUE.

DO IT NOW ANSWERS
1a. Invalid.
  b. Valid.
  c. Valid.
  d. Invalid.
2a. FALSE
  b. An error results, since 'A < b' is string data.
  c. TRUE
  d. TRUE

Expression 1	Value	Expression 2	Value	AND Expression	Value
'A' < 'H'	TRUE	17 > 8	TRUE	('A' < 'H') AND (17 > 8)	TRUE
23 < 15	FALSE	5 > 1	TRUE	(23 < 15) AND (5 > 1)	FALSE
9 > 2	TRUE	3 < 1	FALSE	(9 > 2) AND (3 < 1)	FALSE
8 = 3	FALSE	7 < > 7	FALSE	(8 = 3) AND (7 < > 7)	FALSE

Table 2–4

Table 2–5 is the truth value table for the BOOLEAN operator AND.

The BOOLEAN operation OR also operates on two pieces of BOOLEAN data. Consider the following:

Table 2–5

$$(17 > 3) \text{ OR } (5 > 2 + 3)$$

If both BOOLEAN expressions have BOOLEAN value FALSE, then the BOOLEAN operation OR yields the BOOLEAN value FALSE. Otherwise, the operation OR yields the value TRUE. In the BOOLEAN expression just given, the expression (17 > 3) has value TRUE. The expression (5 > 2 + 3) has BOOLEAN value FALSE. Thus, the BOOLEAN expression (17 > 3) OR (5 > 2 + 3) has BOOLEAN value TRUE. Consider Table 2–6.

AND	TRUE	FALSE
TRUE	TRUE	FALSE
FALSE	FALSE	FALSE

Expression 1	Value	Expression 2	Value	OR Expression	Value
'A' < 'H'	TRUE	17 > 8	TRUE	('A' < 'H') OR (17 > 8)	TRUE
23 < 15	FALSE	5 > 1	TRUE	(23 < 15) OR (5 > 1)	TRUE
9 > 2	TRUE	3 < 1	FALSE	(9 > 2) OR (3 < 1)	TRUE
8 = 3	FALSE	7 < > 7	FALSE	(8 = 3) OR (7 < > 7)	FALSE

Table 2–6

As you can see, the only time the BOOLEAN operation OR yields a value of FALSE is when both of the BOOLEAN values are FALSE. Table 2–7 is the truth value table for the operator OR.

The BOOLEAN operations NOT, AND, and OR have a set of precedence rules, just as +, −, *, and / have precedence rules (an order of operations). The order (precedence) is

Table 2–7

OR	TRUE	FALSE
TRUE	TRUE	TRUE
FALSE	TRUE	FALSE

NOT	Always done first
*, /, DIV, MOD, AND	Done next
+, −, OR	Done next
<, >, =, < =, > =, < >	Done last

Thus, 17 > 5 + 20 yields 17 < 25 yields TRUE.

However, 7 > 10 OR 15 < 20 yields an error. Since the operation OR is performed first, an attempt is made to OR the non-BOOLEAN values 10 and 15. To avoid this problem, parentheses are used. Remember, any operations in parentheses are done first.

WARNING
Any time BOOLEAN operations are used, use parentheses to be safe.

(15 < 20) OR (7 > 10)	is a valid BOOLEAN expression and has the value TRUE.
NOT (15 < 20) AND (7 > 10)	is a valid BOOLEAN expression and has the value FALSE.
NOT ((15 < 20) AND (7 > 10))	is a valid BOOLEAN expression and has the value TRUE.

DO IT NOW

Give the BOOLEAN value of the following.

1. NOT (-13 >= 10)
2. (8 MOD 3 = 2) AND (5 DIV 3 = 1)
3. (20 > 10) AND (5 = 3 + 7)
4. (-13 = 7 - 20) AND (10 > 20)
5. (16 MOD 5 = 2) OR (-3 > 5)
6. NOT (18 <= 4) AND (3 = 8 - 5)
7. NOT ((18 <= 4) AND (3 = 8 - 5))
8. NOT (18 <= 4) OR (3 = 8 - 5)
9. NOT ((18 <= 4) OR (3 = 8 - 5))

Vocabulary

Page		
70	**AND**	A BOOLEAN operation that operates on two pieces of BOOLEAN data to yield TRUE if and only if both pieces have value TRUE. Example: (17 >= -5) AND (12 MOD 3 = 0).
68	**BOOLEAN**	A Pascal data type used to indicate that a variable will assume one of the values, TRUE or FALSE.
68	**BOOLEAN expression**	An expression that, when evaluated, yields one of the BOOLEAN values, TRUE or FALSE.
70	**BOOLEAN operation**	An operation that operates on BOOLEAN data. There are three such operations: NOT, AND, and OR.
70	**BOOLEAN variable**	An identifier declared to be a variable and whose type is stated as BOOLEAN. The variable will assume (store) the value TRUE or FALSE.
68	FALSE	A BOOLEAN value.
70	**NOT**	A BOOLEAN operation that operates on one piece of BOOLEAN data to yield the other piece of BOOLEAN data. Example: NOT (17 >= -5).
70	**OR**	A BOOLEAN operation that operates on two pieces of BOOLEAN data to yield FALSE if and only if both pieces have value FALSE. Example: (17 >= -5) OR (12 MOD 3 = 0).
68	**Relationals**	The relational operators: =, >, >=, <, <=, and < >.
68	TRUE	A BOOLEAN value.

Glad You Asked

Q What would happen if I wrote CONST Value = (5 + 3 > 2) in a Pascal program?

A An error would occur, since constants cannot be computed.

Q I claim that NOT 7 = 3 + 2 has the BOOLEAN value TRUE, but a friend claims it is FALSE. Which one of us is right?

A Neither one of you. NOT 7 = 3 + 2 would yield an error, since the BOOLEAN operation NOT would try to operate on 7 (a non-BOOLEAN piece of data). Remember to use parentheses next time. That is, write NOT (7 = 3 + 2).

Q Suppose I have the variable Discrim of type REAL, and I want to write 5.3 < Discrim < 39.1. How would I do this?

A The key is in reading. It is read "Discrim is greater than 5.3 and Discrim is less than 39.1." Thus, you would write

        (Discrim > 5.3) AND (Discrim < 39.1)

Q What would be the output of `WRITE (Time >= 12 : 8)` if the variable `Time` contains the value `8`?

A The output would be □□□`FALSE`

Q How do you write a BOOLEAN expression for *x* is between 10 and 20 inclusive?

A `(x >= 10) AND (x <= 20)`

Q At the end of this section, you stated that `NOT ((15 < 20) AND (7 < 10))` is `TRUE`. Why is it?

A The operations in the parentheses are done first. `(15 < 20)` is `TRUE`. `(7 > 10)` is `FALSE`. Thus, `(15 < 20) AND (7 > 10)` is `FALSE`. Finally,

    NOT ((15 < 20) AND (7 > 10))

has the value `TRUE`.

Q I heard someone saying that DeMorgan's laws could be used to eliminate NOT from a BOOLEAN expression. What are DeMorgan's laws, and how are they used to remove the NOT?

A DeMorgan's laws are as follows:

1. NOT (a OR b) = NOT (a) AND NOT (b)
2. NOT (a AND b) = NOT (a) OR NOT (b)

DeMorgan's laws state a distributive property for NOT over OR and a distributive property for NOT over AND. Compare DeMorgan's laws with the distributive property for multiplication over addition:

$$a * (b + c) = a * b + a * c$$

The following examples show how to employ DeMorgan's laws to eliminate NOT from a BOOLEAN expression:

    NOT ((15 < 20) AND (7 > 10))

which can be rewritten as

    NOT (15 < 20) OR NOT (7 > 10)

Now, this last expression can be written

    (15 >= 20) OR (7 <= 10)

Thus, the NOT operation has been removed from the BOOLEAN expression. Next consider:

    NOT ((Num > 5) OR (Num < 20))

which can be rewritten

    NOT (Num > 5) AND NOT (Num < 20)

Now, this last expression can be written

    (Num <= 5) AND (Num >= 20)

Not only has the NOT operation been removed from the BOOLEAN expression, but doing so also reveals an expression that always has the value `FALSE`. That is, no matter which number the variable `Num` represents, the BOOLEAN expression is `FALSE`. This fact is not obvious from the original statement of the BOOLEAN expression.

Q Can more than one BOOLEAN operation be used in a BOOLEAN expression?

A Sure. The BOOLEAN expression `(5 <= 7) OR (16 > 13) AND (-4 > 2)` has the value `TRUE`. The AND operation is performed first.

Section 2–1 Exercises

1. In which of the following program sections could the word BOOLEAN appear?
   a. CONST   **b.** VAR   **c.** header   **d.** execution   **e.** none of these
2. Which of the following is a BOOLEAN value?
   a. AND   **b.** OR   **c.** NOT   **d.** TRUE   **e.** CONSTANT
3. Operators like $>$, $<$, $=$, $> =$, $< =$, and $< >$ are called _____.
4. Which of the following is a BOOLEAN operation?
   a. AND   **b.** TRUE   **c.** FALSE   **d.** VAR   **e.** +
5. If Ans is a variable of type BOOLEAN, which of the following is a valid Pascal instruction?
   a. READ (Ans)   **d.** Ans := 12 < 5 OR 7 > 17
   b. Ans := (7 <= 9)   **e.** WRITELN (Ans + 3 : 5)
   c. WRITE (Ans / 2)
6. The three operations available for data of type BOOLEAN are _____, _____, and _____.
7. In writing expressions involving BOOLEAN operations, to be safe, the programmer should use _____ to state how the operations are to be performed.
8. Give the BOOLEAN value of the following.
   a. 17 >= 30 + -10   **f.** 'Frank' <= 'Flow'
   b. 'A' <= 'j'   **g.** 34 MOD 2 = 0
   c. 4 * 5 = 4 * (3 + 2)   **h.** -13 DIV 2 - 3 <= -1
   d. -12 + 6 <= -6   **i.** 'Al' <= 'Alton'
   e. -12 + 6 < -6   **j.** 'pepsi' < > 'Pepsi'
9. Given the following CONST section and VAR section,

   ```
   CONST Value = TRUE ;

   VAR Ans : BOOLEAN ;
       Num : INTEGER
   ```

   give the value assigned to Ans by the following.
   a. Num := 15 ;   **c.** Num := -14 ;
        Ans := (Num MOD 7 = 2)   Ans := ((Num > 4) OR Value)
   b. Ans := (17 - 3 >= 8) ;   **d.** Num := -14 ;
        Ans := NOT Ans   Ans := ((Num > 4) AND Value)
10. Insert the diskette Source in disk drive B. From the disk operating system (DOS) prompt, type B:BOOL, then press the RETURN key. Experiment with option E. Use the program to give the truth value of the following.
    a. 'Jolly' <= 'Roger'
    b. '123' < '78'
    c. NOT (-4 = 5) OR NOT (5 < 7)
    d. (-4 < > 5) AND (5 >= 7)
    e. NOT(('Jack' > 'Jill') AND (4 < -3))
    f. NOT ('Jack' > 'Jill') OR NOT (4 < -3)
    g. ('Jack' <= 'Jill') OR (4 >= -3)
11. Write a BOOLEAN expression for the following.
    Example: *Time is between 3 and 11 exclusive* becomes:
           (Time > 3) AND (Time < 11)
    a. 13 is between -2 and 23 inclusive.
    b. Sound is not Hi.
    c. Sound is between Hi and Lo exclusive.
    d. Sound is neither 12 nor 20.

12. Find the errors in the following program:

```
PROGRAM Errors ;

CONST MyWord = (17 > 3) ;

VAR InNum : INTEGER ;
    Value : BOOLEAN ;

START
  Value := 17 - 3 ;
  READ (InNum)
  WRITE ((InNum - 6 > 8) + 3) ;
  WRITE ((17 = 3 OR 20 < 20), Value / 2)
END .
```

13. Write a Pascal program that allows the user to input a number from 10 to 30000 inclusive. The program should then allow the user to input a second number from the range 2 to first number minus 1 (inclusive). The program will determine whether the second number is a factor of the first number. Results will be printed as follows:

Sample Execution

```
Please enter number (10 .. 30000): 4567
Enter number to check as factor (2 .. 4566): 17
17 is a factor of 4567 is FALSE
```

Hint: If `FirstNum MOD SecondNum = 0` has BOOLEAN value `TRUE`, then `SecondNum` is a factor of `FirstNum`.

Section 2-2

IF-THEN-ELSE

In this section, you will be introduced to the first of a collection of Pascal instructions known as control instructions: the IF-THEN-ELSE decision control instruction. You will study how the instruction works, the style used in writing it, and how to construct it. Also, you will study a special case of the IF-THEN-ELSE known as an IF-THEN instruction.

2-2.1 *Control Instructions*

Fundamental to any computer language is the ability to alter the flow of execution of instructions in a program. Up to this point, the Pascal programs discussed have executed each instruction listed in the execution section from first to last (sequentially). You are now ready for an instruction that allows for skipping another instruction. That is, a decision can be made to specify which of two instructions to execute. Such an instruction is called a **decision control instruction.**

A Pascal instruction that allows for decision making is the **IF-THEN-ELSE** instruction. The form of this instruction, as well as its meaning, is shown in Figure 2-1.

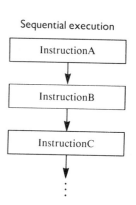

Sequential execution

Figure 2-1

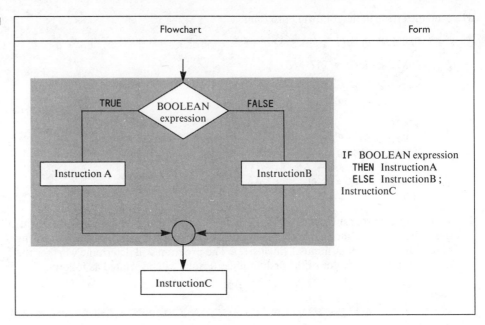

Consider the following IF-THEN-ELSE instruction:

```
IF NumA >= 0
   THEN WRITE (NumA , ' is good.')
   ELSE WRITE (NumA , ' is no good.')
```

Suppose the variable NumA contains the value 8. The BOOLEAN expression NumA >= 0 has BOOLEAN value TRUE. Thus, the output is 8 is good. Suppose the variable NumA contains the value −13. The BOOLEAN expression NumA >= 0 has BOOLEAN value FALSE. Thus, the output is −13 is no good.

In the program in Figure 2–2, the IF-THEN-ELSE instruction is used to make a decision about the size of two numbers. The program has for input two numbers. The program is to output the two numbers in order from smallest to largest.

Figure 2-2

Sample Execution

```
Enter first number: 23.7
Enter second number: 19.8
Numbers in order are:    19.80   23.70
Thank you!
```

```
PROGRAM Order ;

VAR NumA, NumB : REAL ;

BEGIN
  WRITE ('Enter first number: ') ;
  READLN (NumA) ;
  WRITE ('Enter second number: ') ;
  READLN (NumB) ;
  WRITE (Numbers in order are: ') ;
  IF NumA <= NumB
     THEN WRITELN (NumA : 8 : 2 , NumB : 8 : 2)
     ELSE WRITELN (NumB : 8 : 2 , NumA : 8 : 2) ;
  WRITELN ('Thank you!')
END .
```

As you can see from the sample input/output for program `Order`, the execution of the instructions was sequential until the IF-THEN-ELSE instruction was reached. At that point, a decision was made based on the value of the BOOLEAN expression `NumA <= NumB`. For the sample input (`23.7` and `19.8`), the value was `FALSE`. Thus, the instruction

```
WRITELN (NumA : 8 : 2 , NumB : 8 : 2)
```

was skipped, and the instruction `WRITELN (NumB : 8 : 2 , NumA : 8 : 2)`

was executed. After the IF-THEN-ELSE instruction was executed, the flow of the instruction execution returned to sequential execution (`Thank you!` was printed) and continued until the `END` was reached.

DO IT NOW

1. Give the output of the following instruction:

```
IF (-17 < 7 + -10)
   THEN WRITE (-17 , ' is smallest.')
   ELSE WRITE (7 + - 10 , ' is smallest.')
```

2. Give the output of the following instruction if

```
IF NumA MOD 3 = 0
   THEN WRITE (NumA, ' is divisible by 3.')
   ELSE WRITE ('3 is not a factor of ' , NumA)
```

   a. `NumA` contains 35   **b.** `NumA` contains 78

2-2.2 *Style and Punctuation*

The style for writing the IF-THEN-ELSE instruction follows (where ⬚ represents a blank space):

```
IF BOOLEAN expression
⬚⬚THEN < InstructionA >
⬚⬚ELSE < InstructionB >
```

The BOOLEAN expression should go on the same line as the IF. The words THEN and ELSE should be indented at least two spaces and should be followed by their instruction. The IF-THEN-ELSE instruction is boxed as follows:

1. The word IF starts the IF-THEN-ELSE box.
2. Following the word IF, a BOOLEAN expression is sought and enclosed in a box.
3. The word THEN is sought.
4. Following the word THEN, an instruction is sought and boxed.
5. The word ELSE is sought.
6. Following the word ELSE, an instruction is sought and boxed.
7. The IF-THEN-ELSE box is closed.

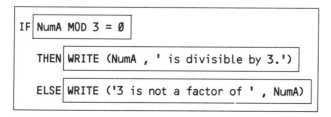

DO IT NOW ANSWERS

1. `-17 is smallest.`
2a. `3 is not a factor of 35`
   b. `78 is divisible by 3.`

COMMENT
The notation < InstructionA > represents a single valid Pascal instruction.

Figure 2-3

COMMENT
A common error is to place a semicolon after the THEN instruction.

As you can see in Figure 2–3, there are no adjacent boxes. The BOOLEAN expression box is separated from the THEN instruction box by the word THEN. The THEN instruction box is separated from the ELSE instruction box by the word ELSE. Thus, the IF-THEN-ELSE instruction requires no semicolons for separation. (Of course, if another Pascal instruction follows the IF-THEN-ELSE instruction, a semicolon will be needed to separate the two instructions.)

2-2.3 IF-THEN Instructions

The ELSE part of the IF-THEN-ELSE instruction can sometimes be left off, if desired by the programmer. A diagram of this situation is shown in Figure 2–4.

In Figure 2–4, the program's instructions are executed in order until the **IF-THEN** instruction is reached. At that point, the BOOLEAN expression is evaluated. If it has the value TRUE, InstructionA is executed. If it has the value FALSE, InstructionA is skipped. After the IF-THEN instruction, the flow of execution returns to sequential, and InstructionC is executed.

Figure 2–4

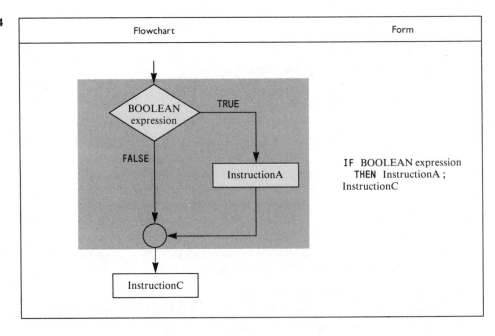

Sample Execution

```
Enter amount (quarter, dime): quarter
Change: 2 dimes, 1 nickel.
```

Sample Execution

```
Enter amount (quarter, dime): dime
Change: 2 nickels.
```

Consider the following instructions to output the change from a change machine for a quarter and/or a dime:

```
WRITE ('Enter amount (quarter, dime): ') ;
READLN (Amount) ;
IF Amount = 'quarter'
   THEN WRITELN ('Change: 2 dimes, 1 nickel.') ;
IF Amount = 'dime'
   THEN WRITELN ('Change: 2 nickels.')
```

When the user entered the string `quarter`, the BOOLEAN expression `Amount = 'quarter'` was evaluated as `TRUE`. Thus, the message

```
Change: 2 dimes, 1 nickel.
```

was written to the screen. When the user entered the string `dime`, the BOOLEAN expression `Amount = 'dime'` was evaluated as `TRUE`. Thus, the instruction `WRITELN ('Change: 2 nickels.')` was executed.

To increase your understanding of a series of IF-THEN instructions, study the following example.

EXAMPLE

Write a Pascal program that will act as a change machine. The program should take as input a value (dollar, quarter, dime, or nickel). The program will produce an output of the change based on the following:

dollar:	3 quarters, 2 dimes, 1 nickel
quarter:	2 dimes, 1 nickel
dime:	2 nickels
nickel:	no change

SOLUTION

Look over and think about the problem. Next, sketch out a design that will solve the problem:

Design: Get amount to be changed
      If dollar then write 3 quarters, 2 dimes, 1 nickel
      If quarter then write 2 dimes, 1 nickel
      If dime then write 2 nickels
      If nickel then write no change
      Stop

Your first sketch of a design portrays your thoughts and words as to how to solve the problem. Carefully walk through the design to make sure it will work. If the design does not work, discard it and start over. It is better to start over at the design stage than after time and effort have been invested in getting the program to the computer.

After the design has been tested (by hand simulation), convert it to the Pascal language:

Get amount to be changed
```
WRITE (Enter amount for change (dollar,quarter,dime,nickel): ')
READLN (Amount)
```
If dollar then write 3 quarters, 2 dimes, 1 nickel
```
IF Amount = 'dollar'
  THEN WRITELN ('Change is 3 quarters, 2 dimes, 1 nickel')
```
If quarter then write 2 dimes, 1 nickel
```
IF Amount = 'quarter'
  THEN WRITELN ('Change is 2 dimes, 1 nickel')
```
If dime then write 2 nickels
```
IF Amount = 'dime'
  THEN WRITELN ('Change is 2 nickels')
```
If nickel then write no change
```
IF Amount = 'nickel'
  THEN WRITELN ('Sorry, I don''t do nickels')
```

From the design, it can be seen that a variable of type STRING will be needed. The rest of the design can be handled in the execution section. The Pascal program is shown in Figure 2–5.

Figure 2–5

```
PROGRAM ChangeIt ;

VAR Amount : STRING [80] ;

BEGIN
  WRITE ('Enter amount for change ') ;
  WRITELN ('(dollar,quarter,dime,nickel): ') ;
  READLN (Amount) ;
  IF Amount = 'dollar'
    THEN WRITELN ('Change is 3 quarters, 2 dimes, 1 nickel') ;
  IF Amount = 'quarter'
    THEN WRITELN ('Change is 2 dimes, 1 nickel') ;
  IF Amount = 'dime'
    THEN WRITELN ('Change is 2 nickels') ;
  IF Amount = 'nickel'
    THEN WRITELN ('Sorry, I don''t do nickels')
END .
```

Sample Execution

```
Enter amount for change (dollar,quarter,dime,nickel): quarter
Change is 2 dimes, 1 nickel
```

DO IT NOW

1. For the program `ChangeIt` in Figure 2–5, what would be the results of the user's entering `Dime` to the prompt

        Enter amount for change (dollar,quarter,dime,nickel):

2. Determine the effect of replacing the instructions

        IF Amount = 'dime'
          THEN WRITELN ('Change is 2 nickels') ;
        IF Amount = 'nickel'
          THEN WRITELN ('Sorry, I don''t do nickels')

    with the instruction

        IF Amount = 'dime'
          THEN WRITELN ('Change is 2 nickels')
          ELSE WRITELN ('Sorry, I don''t do nickels')

DO IT NOW ANSWERS

1. There would be no output. If the value in the variable **Amount** were **Dime**, each of the BOOLEAN expressions would be evaluated as **FALSE**. The string **Dime** is not equal to the string **dime**.
2. If the variable **Amount** contained a value other than **dime**, the output would always include the message

        Sorry, I don't do nickels

A hand simulation of the altered version follows:
Input:
```
Enter amount for change (dollar,quarter,dime,nickel): quarter
```

```
Change is 2 dimes, 1 nickel
Sorry, I don't do nickels
```

Also,
Input:
```
    Enter amount for change (dollar,quarter,dime,nickel): dime
```

```
Change is 2 nickels
```

Finally,
Input:
```
    Enter amount for change (dollar,quarter,dime,nickel): Quarter
```

```
Sorry, I don't do nickels
```

2-2.4 *Decisions with REAL Data*

Before we end this discussion, we'll cover the topic of making decisions with data of type REAL. Consider these instructions:

```
A := 1 ;
B := 3 ;
IF (A/B + A/B + A/B = 1)
   THEN WRITELN ('1/3 + 1/3 + 1/3 = 1')
   ELSE WRITELN ('Error due to approximation')
```

The execution of these instructions yields `Error due to approximation`. The problem is with the BOOLEAN expression and the way the computer must use approximations for some real numbers. In the IF-THEN-ELSE instruction, the BOOLEAN expression is `1/3 + 1/3 + 1/3 = 1`. This expression should yield the value `TRUE`. However, since the computer converts `1/3` to a decimal, the expression is

```
0.333 . . . 3 + 0.333 . . . 3 + 0.333 . . . 3 = 1
```

This expression yields the value FALSE, since the computer compares 0.999...9 and 1.

When comparing real values for equality, we could ask if the two values are very close to one another. In this situation, we could write the BOOLEAN expression as

```
ABS ((A/B + A/B + A/B) - 1) < 0.001
```

That is, the difference between `A/B + A/B + A/B` and `1` is small, making the two values nearly equal.

Consider the following problem.

PROBLEM

Write a Pascal program that allows the user to enter a numerator and denominator for a fraction. The user will then enter a closeness factor. Finally, the user will enter an approximation for the fraction. The output of the program will be whether or not the approximation was close enough.

Sample Execution

```
Demonstration of REAL data in decisions.
Enter numerator of fraction: 2
Enter denominator of fraction: 3
Enter a small positive number for closeness: 0.001
Enter approximation of fraction: 0.67
Sorry, not close enough.
```

SOLUTION

Design: Get input data
IF (a/b − Approx) < CLOSE
   THEN WRITELN ('Close enough.')
   ELSE WRITELN ('Sorry, not close enough.')

COMMENT
The value ⅔ − 0.67 is
− 0.00333... in decimal notation.

Walking through the design with the data from the sample execution yields (2/3 − 0.67) < 0.001 for the BOOLEAN expression. This expression has the value TRUE, since 2/3 − 0.67 is negative. Thus, the output will be

```
Close enough.      <<<<<< design error! >>>>>>
```

In fact, a value entered for Approx like 7 or 143.6 would yield an output of Close enough. The design error is with the BOOLEAN expression. This expression needs to be

```
 ABS (a/b − Approx) < Close
```

After testing this alteration to the design, a Pascal program is written as shown in Figure 2–6. In working with values or variables of type REAL in a BOOLEAN expression, be careful with the use of the relational = . The reason for this is the approximations used by computers for most real numbers.

Figure 2–6

```
PROGRAM RealDemo ;

VAR a, b : INTEGER ;
    Close, Approx : REAL ;

BEGIN
  WRITELN ('Demonstration of REAL data in decisions.') ;
  WRITE ('Enter numerator of fraction: ') ;
  READLN (a) ;
  WRITE ('Enter denominator of fraction: ') ;
  READLN (b) ;
  WRITE ('Enter a small positive number for closeness: ') ;
  READLN (Close) ;
  WRITE ('Enter approximation of fraction: ') ;
  READLN (Approx) ;
  IF ABS (a/b − Approx) < Close
    THEN WRITELN ('Close enough.')
    ELSE WRITELN ('Sorry, not close enough.')
END .
```

DO IT NOW

1. For the program RealDemo in Figure 2–6, suppose the user entered 1 for **a**, 10 for **b**, 0 for Close, and 0.1 for Approx. What would the output be?
2. For the program RealDemo in Figure 2–6, suppose the user entered 1 for **a**, 3 for **b**, 0.000001 for Close, and 1/3 for Approx. What would the output be?

2-2.5 Design Testing versus Program Testing

In writing a computer program to solve a problem, two levels of testing are involved. The first level of testing is at the design stage. Testing the solution design is accomplished via hand simulation (walking through) of the design of the solution. Once the design has been tested and approved, it is converted to a Pascal program. When the program is compiled (converted from the Pascal language to code the CPU can understand), syntax errors in the program are detected by the compiler. Once these errors are corrected and the program is compiled, the next level of testing begins.

The testing at this level is called **program testing**. A program error can refer to a semantics error (an error in the meaning of an instruction). Also, a program error can refer to a missing feature of the program. Program testing involves executing the program in a wide variety of situations. If data is to be entered into the program, program testing would include entering test data to make sure the program solves the problem it was designed to solve. Program testing detects errors that simply were not foreseen at the design stage. Often these errors are not a reflection on your solution design (however, a good design can greatly reduce these errors). Once a program error is detected, it is "fixed" either by returning to the editor or by returning to the design stage of the problem-solving process. The process of removing a program error (or bug) is referred to as debugging.

DO IT NOW ANSWERS

1. Sorry, not close enough. To fix this error, replace the < relational with < = .
2. The program would stop and issue an Input/Output (IO) error message. The / is not part of the characters that make up a REAL value.

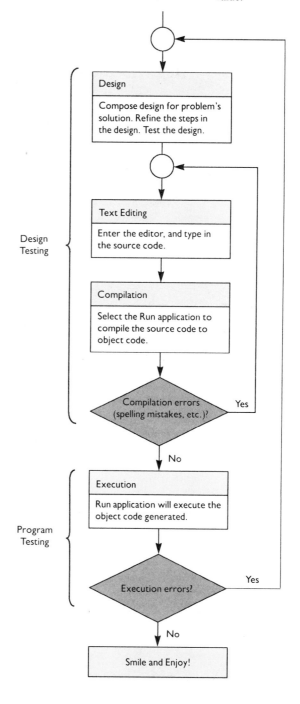

Vocabulary

Page

75 **Decision control instruction** An instruction that alters the normal flow in which instructions are executed. That is, a decision control instruction makes a decision as to whether an instruction will be executed or not.

78 **IF-THEN** A control instruction that allows a decision to be made whether or not to execute an instruction. The general form is

> IF BOOLEAN expression
> THEN < InstructionA >

InstructionA will be executed if the BOOLEAN expression has a value of TRUE. Otherwise, InstructionA will be skipped.

75 **IF-THEN-ELSE** A control instruction that allows a decision to be made as to which one of two instructions will be executed. The general form is

> IF BOOLEAN expression
> THEN < InstructionA >
> ELSE < InstructionB >

The decision to execute is based on the value of the BOOLEAN expression. Exactly one of the instructions will be executed.

83 **Program testing** The process of verifying that a program accomplishes the task(s) for which it was written.

Glad You Asked

Q I don't quite understand the idea of an IF-THEN-ELSE instruction and why it is called a flow control instruction. Can you explain it in another way? Perhaps with a picture?

A Consider the following picture:

```
Instruction A ;
IF BOOLEAN expression
   THEN Instruction B
   ELSE Instruction C ;
Instruction D
```

Imagine the instructions of a program being executed in order (like moving down a river). An IF-THEN-ELSE instruction is like coming to an island in the river; the flow is disrupted. When the BOOLEAN expression is evaluated, the flow of the program will go on one side of the island or the other (that is, execute InstructionB or InstructionC in the picture). Afterwards, the flow returns to normal (that is, the next instruction after the IF-THEN-ELSE is executed). You should make a similar drawing for the IF-THEN instruction.

Q I typed in the program ChangeIt from Figure 2–5, page 80 and had it execute. When I got the message Enter amount for change (dollar,quarter,dime,nickel):, I entered $1.00 and nothing happened. I ran the program again and entered 1.23 (a real number); still nothing happened. Each time, I was returned to the Pascal command line. What is going on?

A The program was looking for data of type STRING (that is, a collection of characters) since Amount was of type STRING. That is exactly what you provided it. There is a difference between 1.23 (the number) and '1.23' (the string). This provides a good way to protect against entry errors. It is hard for a program to yield an error from inputting string data. The reason nothing happened when the program executed the IF-THEN instructions is that your entries did not result in any of the BOOLEAN expressions' having a value of TRUE; that is, the string '1.23' was not equal to any of the strings ('dollar', etc.) in the IF-THEN instructions.

Q In the program ChangeIt, you showed that entering the string Dime resulted in no output. Could this not be fixed by using an OR expression in the BOOLEAN expression part?

A Yes, the following IF-THEN instruction would allow the user such a choice:

```
IF (Amount = 'dime') OR (Amount = 'Dime')
   THEN WRITELN ('Change is 2 nickels')
```

Q What is a conditional?

A The IF-THEN-ELSE and IF-THEN instructions are examples of conditional instructions. That is, the instruction part is executed or not, based on the condition of the BOOLEAN expression.

Q Can I write an IF-THEN-ELSE instruction like this?

```
IF NumA = 10
   THEN
   ELSE WRITE (NumA , ' is not equal to ten.')
```

That is, can I leave out the instruction for the THEN?

A Yes. The instruction after the THEN is called the *empty instruction*. However, it would be much more readable to write the instruction as

```
IF NumA < > 10
   THEN WRITE (NumA , ' is not equal to ten.')
```

Always look out for the program's reader; the reader might be you!

Q I tried to run the following IF-THEN-ELSE instruction:

```
IF Name <= 'James'
   THEN WRITELN ('James is larger') ;
   ELSE WRITELN (Name, ' is larger') ;
```

The compiler stopped with an unknown identifier or syntax error. What is wrong?

A The semicolon at the end of the THEN instruction is wrong. The IF-THEN-ELSE is one instruction. By placing the semicolon at the end of the THEN instruction, you caused the compiler to compile an IF-THEN instruction. When the ELSE was found, there was no THEN to match it with—thus, the error message.

Q What is wrong with this instruction?

```
IF TRUE
   THEN Sum := 0
```

My instructor marked it wrong.

A It can be replaced by Sum := 0, since the assignment instruction is always executed.

Q Is this stuff going to get much harder?

A *Hard* is relative to how well you are prepared when you begin the task. It is hard for a nonrunner to run five miles. However, if you run a little each day and always work on extending the distance, soon running five miles is not hard. Learning to solve problems with the computer is the same way.

Section 2–2 Exercises

1. For the THEN instruction of an IF-THEN-ELSE instruction to execute, the BOOLEAN expression must have the value _____ .

2. Which of the following could *not* be a BOOLEAN expression for an IF-THEN-ELSE instruction?
   a. 7 MOD 2   **b.** Ch = 'a'   **c.** Name < 'James'   **d.** Num = 0.35

3. Insert TRUE for a true statement. Insert FALSE for a false statement.
   _____ **a.** When an IF-THEN-ELSE instruction is executed, it is possible for both the THEN instruction and the ELSE instruction to execute.
   _____ **b.** The ELSE instruction of an IF-THEN-ELSE can be left out to form an IF-THEN instruction.
   _____ **c.** The BOOLEAN expression for an IF-THEN-ELSE instruction cannot involve values of type STRING.
   _____ **d.** The BOOLEAN expression Number = 1/7 should not be used in an IF-THEN-ELSE instruction because of the inaccuracy of real number representation on a digital computer.
   _____ **e.** In an IF-THEN-ELSE instruction, a semicolon should be used to separate the THEN instruction from the ELSE instruction.

4. Discuss why the following should never appear in a Pascal program:
   a. IF TRUE
   　　　THEN WRITELN (NumA)
   b. Num := 1 – InNumber ;
   　　　IF Num = 1/9
   　　　THEN WRITELN ('Hit it!')
   c. IF (Num < 9) AND (Num > 10)
   　　　THEN Num := Num + 1
   d. IF Num > 5
   　　　THEN Num := 1 ;
   　　　ELSE Num := Num + 2

5. Give the output of the following instructions (NumA contains 17, NumB contains –5, and NumC contains 4.)
   a. IF NumA < NumB
   　　　THEN WRITE (NumB , ' is largest.')
   　　　ELSE WRITE (NumA , ' is largest.')
   b. IF NumA MOD NumC = 0
   　　　THEN WRITE (NumC , ' is a factor of ' , NumA)
   　　　ELSE WRITE (NumA , ' is not divisible by ' , NumC)
   c. IF (NumA < NumB) AND (NumB < NumC)
   　　　THEN WRITE ('Order is: ' , NumA , NumB : 3 , NumC : 2)
   　　　ELSE WRITE ('Order of numbers is unknown.')

6. Complete the following Pascal program to write to the screen the message:

   　　　Send alarm note to student.

   if the variable Passing has value FALSE, and to write to the screen the message:

   　　　Send good work note to student.

   if the variable Passing has value TRUE.

   ```
   PROGRAM StudentCheck ;

   VAR Passing : BOOLEAN ;
       Average : REAL ;
   ```

```
BEGIN
  WRITE ('Please enter student''s average: ') ;
  READLN (Average) ;
  Passing := (Average >= 65) ;
  _____
END .
```

7. **a.** Complete the following program which is to take an integer as input. The output is to state if 7 is a factor or not.

```
PROGRAM Factor7 ;

VAR InNum : INTEGER ;

BEGIN
  WRITE ('Please enter an integer: ') ;
  READLN (InNum) ;
  IF _____
    THEN _____
    ELSE _____
END .
```

   b. What is the output of program Factor7 for an input of 79?

   c. What is the output of program Factor7 for an input of 147?

8. Replace the following two IF-THEN instructions with an IF-THEN-ELSE instruction:

```
IF CTemp >= 100
  THEN WRITE ('Boiling.') ;
IF CTemp < 100
  THEN WRITE ('Still liquid')
```

```
IF _____
  THEN _____
  ELSE _____
```

9. **a.** Rewrite the following Pascal program to conform to the style rules:

```
program max ; var NumA : integer ; NumB : integer ; NumC : integer ;
MaxN : integer ; begin write ('Please enter three numbers:') ;
readln ( NumA ) ; readln (NumB) ; readln (NumC) ;
if NumA >= NumB then MaxN := NumA else MaxN := NumB ;
if NumC >= MaxN then MaxN := NumC ; write ('Largest is ' , MaxN)
end .
```

   b. Give the output if 19 is entered for NumA, 35 for NumB, and 31 for NumC.

10. Boot up Pascal; set the workfile to the file CHANGEIT.PAS from the Source diskette. Enter the Turbo Pascal editor. Alter the program CHANGEIT by replacing the last two IF-THEN instructions with the following IF-THEN-ELSE instruction:

```
IF Amount = 'dime'
  THEN WRITELN ('Change is 2 nickels')
  ELSE WRITELN ('Sorry, I don''t do nickels')
```

Quit the editor, and execute the program commands. Give the output for the following inputs:

Input	Output
dime	_____
quarter	_____
DIME	_____
Ostrich	_____

11. Boot up Pascal; set the workfile to the file **REALDEMO.PAS** from the **Source** diskette. Enter the Turbo Pascal editor. Edit the program such that the condition for the IF-THEN-ELSE instruction is as follows:

```
ABS (a/b - Approx) <= Close
```

Quit the editor, and execute the program. Enter **2** for the numerator, **3** for the denominator, **0.001** for closeness, and **0.67** for the approximation. The output is _____ .

12. A number is called a perfect square if its square root is a whole number. Complete the Pascal program below. The input is a whole number. The output is whether or not the number is a perfect square.

```
PROGRAM PerfectSq ;

VAR NumIn : INTEGER ;
    Hold : INTEGER ;

BEGIN
  WRITE ('Please enter a whole number (0, 1, 2, ... ): ') ;
  READLN (NumIn) ;
  Hold := ROUND (SQRT (NumIn)) ;
  IF _____
     THEN _____
     ELSE _____
END .
```

13. The twenty-four-hour clock (or military) time can be given for any time traditionally stated as A.M. or P.M. That is,

8:43 A.M. 843 hours military time
9:15 P.M. 2115 hours military time
10:00 P.M. 2200 hours military time

Complete the pascal program below to convert traditional time to military time.

```
PROGRAM Military ;

VAR Hour : INTEGER ;
    Minute : INTEGER ;
    Half : STRING [2]

BEGIN
  WRITE ('Enter hour: ') ;
  _____

  _____
END .
```

Sample Execution

```
Enter hour: 3
Enter minute: 35
Enter AM or PM: PM
Military time is: 1535 hours
```

14. Identify the errors in the following program:

```
PROGRAM Errors ;

CONST ConNum := 17 ;

VAR InNum : INTEGER ;

BEGIN
  WRITE ('Enter First Number: ')
  READLN (FirstN) ;
  IF InNum MOD ConNum ;
    THEN WRITE (ConNum , ' not a factor') ;
    ELSE WRITE ('The end!')
STOP .
```

15. About 2500 years ago, the Pythagoreans concluded that if the longest side of a triangle squared equals the sum of the square of one leg and the square of the other leg, then the triangle must be a right triangle (it has an angle whose measure is 90 degrees). Use this fact to complete the following Pascal program.
Input: longest side, first leg, second leg.
Output: whether or not the triangle is a right triangle.

```
PROGRAM Pythagoras ;

VAR LSide : REAL ;
    LegA : REAL ;
    LegB : REAL ;

BEGIN
  WRITE ('Please enter longest side of triangle: ') ;
  READLN (LSide) ;
  WRITE ('Please enter second side of triangle: ') ;
  READLN (LegA) ;
  WRITE ('Please enter third side of triangle: ') ;
  READLN (LegB) ;
  IF _____
    THEN _____
    ELSE _____
END .
```

Sample Execution

```
Please enter longest side of triangle: 5
Please enter second side to triangle: 3
Please enter third side of triangle: 4
Triangle is a right triangle.
```

COMMENT
Use ABS function in constructing the BOOLEAN expression.

16. Write a Pascal program to take an input of a (whole) number grade, then output a letter grade. The letter grades are based on the following:

Above 89: A	60 to 69: D
80 to 89: B	Below 60: F
70 to 79: C	

Sample Execution

```
Please enter number grade: 86
Letter grade is: B
```

Use the following design:
```
WRITE ('Please enter number grade: ')
GetNumber
WRITE ('Letter grade is: ')
IF Number > 89
  THEN WRITELN ('A')
IF (Number > = 80) AND (Number < = 89)
  THEN WRITELN ('B')
IF (Number > = 70) AND (Number < = 79)
  THEN WRITELN ('C')
IF (Number > = 60) AND (Number < = 69)
  THEN WRITELN ('D')
IF Number < 60
  THEN WRITELN ('F')
```

Programming Problems

For the following problems, follow the process presented in Section 1-1. Write a design for the solution, refine the design, test the design with hand simulations, convert the design to a Pascal program, enter the Pascal system, use the editor to create the text of the program, use the compiler to convert the text to code, execute the code, and debug the program. Turn in a copy of your design and its refinement. Turn in a hard copy of the text of the program and its output.

Sample Execution

```
Enter grade for Test1: 70
Enter grade for Test2: 60
Enter grade for Test3: 90

Average is: 76.33
```

Sample Execution

```
Enter employee number: 718
Enter weekly pay rate: $432.00
Enter position code (1,2,3): 2
Enter years experience: 18

Bonus for year is: $770.00
```

Sample Execution

```
Please enter makeup test score: 92
Grade book score is: 77
```

17. Dr. Spandow is computing his students' class average for mid-term grade reports. He averages the numeric grades recorded for Test1, Test2, and Test3. If a student scored more than 85 on Test3, a three point bonus is added to the average. Write a Pascal program that has input three test scores. The program is to output the student's numeric average (accurate to two decimal places).

18. The employees at Sarah's Style Shop are to be paid an end of the year bonus based on the following table.

Position Code	Basis for Bonus
1	One week's pay
2	Two week's pay; maximum of $700
3	One and a half week's pay

If the employee has more than ten years' experience with the company, the bonus is increased by 10%. If the employee has less than 3 years' experience with the company, the maximum bonus is $300. Write a Pascal program that allows the user to input an employee number, weekly pay rate, position code, and number of years' experience. The program is to output the employee's bonus.

19. On a makeup test, Ms. Desmond scales all grades to be a C or less (where 70 up to 79 is a C). She does this based on the following:

> Amt = test score − 70
> ScaleAmt = Amt DIV 3
> Amt < = 0 : test score entered in grade book
> Amt > 0 : 70 + ScaleAmt entered in grade book

Write a Pascal program to take as input a makeup test score. The output will be a grade book score. Remember, start with a design of the solution.

20. The Broken Spirit is running a 30%-off sale on all items in the store. If a customer is a student at J.K.H.S., the customer gets an additional 20% off the discounted price for any item purchased for cash. Since it is also Guy Day, all males receive a $5.00 discount on any item purchased that has a marked price over $15.00. Write a Pascal program that allows the user to enter the required information on a purchase. The program is to write to the screen the list of each of the three possible deductions from the price, as well as the final price.

Sample Execution

```
Please enter tagged price: $85.78
Is customer a J.K.H.S. student? (Y/N): Y
Is this a cash sale? (Y/N) Y
Is customer male? (Y/N): Y
Sale discount is: $25.73
J.K.H.S. discount is: $12.01
Guy Day discount is: $5.00
Final price is: $43.04
```

21. Easter Sunday always falls between March 22 and April 25 inclusive. A procedure to compute the actual day is as follows. Let Year represent the desired year.

```
A := Year MOD 19
B := Year MOD 4
C := Year MOD 7
D := (19*A + 24) MOD 30
E := (2*B + 4*C + 6*D + 5) MOD 7
DayNum := 22 + D + E
Month := 'March'
IF DayNum > 31
   THEN Month := 'April'
IF Month = 'April'
   THEN DayNum := DayNum MOD 31
```

Sample Execution

```
Please enter year ( 0 ... 2200 ): 1998
Easter Sunday will be: April 12
```

Write a Pascal program that allows the user to input a positive integer value for Year less than 2201. The program is to write to the screen the month and day number for Easter Sunday.

Section 2–3

Nested and Compound Instructions

In this section, you will study two extensions to decision control instructions. The first is that of compound instructions; the second, that of nested control instructions.

2-3.1 Compound Instructions

A collection of instructions bracketed by the words BEGIN and END is called a **compound instruction.** For example,

```
BEGIN
  WRITE ('Please enter first side: ') ;
  READLN (SideA)
END
```

is a compound instruction. The program execution section is an example of a compound instruction. Another use of the concept of compound instructions is with control instructions.

Consider the general form of the IF-THEN-ELSE control instruction:

```
IF BOOLEAN expression
   THEN < InstructionA >
   ELSE < InstructionB >
```

Since a compound instruction is an instruction, InstructionA and/or InstructionB could be replaced by a compound instruction. For example,

```
IF Sales >= 6000
   THEN
      BEGIN
        Commission := 0.1*Sales ;
        WRITELN ('Your commission is: $', Commission : 1 : 2) ;
        WRITELN ('Salary is: $', Salary + Commission : 1 : 2)
      END
   ELSE WRITELN ('Salary is: $', Salary : 1 : 2)
```

Here, InstructionA has been replaced by the compound instruction

```
BEGIN
  Commission := 0.1*Sales ;
  WRITELN ('Your commission is: $', Commission : 1 : 2) ;
  WRITELN ('Salary is: $', Salary + Commission : 1 : 2)
END
```

Notice the slight change in style when a compound instruction is used. The compound instruction has been indented under the word THEN to show that it belongs to the THEN part of the IF-THEN-ELSE. This style change is optional (that is, the word BEGIN can be on the same line as the word THEN).

When this IF-THEN-ELSE instruction is executed, the BOOLEAN expression `Sales >= 6000` is evaluated. If the value is `TRUE`, the instruction

```
BEGIN
  Commission := 0.1*Sales ;
  WRITELN ('Your commission is: $', Commission : 1 : 2) ;
  WRITELN ('Salary is: $', Salary + Commission : 1 : 2)
END
```

is executed. If the value is `FALSE`, the instruction

```
WRITELN ('Salary is: $', Salary : 1 : 2)
```

is executed.

Suppose variable `Salary` contains the number `2000`, and the variable `Sales` contains the number `18000`. Since `Sales >= 6000` has value `TRUE`, the output of the IF-THEN-ELSE instruction would be as shown.

Suppose variable `Salary` contains the number `2000`, and variable `Sales` contains the number `3000`. Since `Sales >= 6000` has value `FALSE`, the output of the IF-THEN-ELSE instruction would be as shown.

Punctuation and Style   An IF-THEN-ELSE control instruction involving a compound instruction is boxed as follows:

1. The word IF starts the IF-THEN-ELSE box.
2. Following the word IF, a BOOLEAN expression is sought and enclosed in a box.
3. The word THEN is sought.
4. Following the word THEN, an instruction is sought and boxed. If the instruction is a compound instruction,
    a. The word BEGIN starts the compound instruction box.
    b. Following the word BEGIN,
        1. If an instruction is found, it is boxed.
        2. Step 1 is repeated until the word END is found.
    c. After the word END, the compound instruction box is closed.
5. The word ELSE is sought.
6. Following the word ELSE, an instruction is sought and boxed (if it is a compound instruction, Steps 4a, 4b, and 4c are executed).
7. The IF-THEN-ELSE box is closed.

From the boxed IF-THEN-ELSE instruction in Figure 2–7, you can see that the only adjacent boxes are in the compound instruction box. Thus, the only semicolons used are in the compound instruction box.

Sample Execution

```
Your commission is: $18000.00
Salary is: $3800.00
```

Sample Execution

```
Salary is: $2000.00
```

Figure 2–7

```
IF (C < (A + B)) AND (C > (A - B))
  THEN
    BEGIN
      S := (A + B + C ) / 2 ;
      Area := SQRT (S*(S-A)*(S-B)*(S-C)) ;
      WRITE ('Area is ' : Area : 1 : 2)
    END
  ELSE WRITE ('Triangle not possible!')
```

PROGRAMMING POINT

Boxing is a very good exercise. Not only does it provide an aid to punctuation, but boxing also can give you insight into how the compiler treats an instruction. When an IF is encountered, a BOOLEAN expression is sought. Next, the word THEN is sought. After the word THEN is found, an instruction is sought (it can be a simple instruction or a compound instruction). If the word ELSE is found, another instruction is sought (again, it can be a simple instruction or a compound instruction). The IF-THEN or IF-THEN-ELSE instruction (depending on whether an ELSE was found) is okayed.

DO IT NOW

1. Give the output of

```
IF NumA < 1Ø
  THEN
    BEGIN
      NumB := SQR (NumA) ;
      NumC := NumA + NumB
    END
  ELSE NumC := NumA - 1Ø ;
WRITE (NumA , NumC : 5)
```

   a. If NumA contains 8   **b.** If NumA contains 16

2. Consider the following instructions:

```
NumA := 13 ;
NumB := 3 ;
IF NumA MOD NumC < 1
  THEN
    BEGIN
      NumB := NumB + NumC ;
      NumA := NumA MOD NumC ;
      WRITE (NumA)
    END ;
WRITE (NumA + NumB)
```

   a. If NumC contains 4, give the output.
   b. If NumC contains 13, give the output.
   c. Remove the words BEGIN and END. Would the instructions still be valid? If so, rewrite to adjust the style, then give the output for NumC containing 4.

DO IT NOW ANSWERS

1a. 8□□□72   b. 16□□□□6
2a. 16   b. Ø16
  c. Yes, they would be valid.
     Adjusted for style:

```
NumA := 13 ;
NumB := 3 ;
IF NumA MOD NumC < 1
  THEN NumB := NumB + NumC ;
NumA := NumA MOD NumC ;
WRITE (NumA) ;
WRITE (NumA + NumB)
```

If NumC contains 4, the output is 14

2-3.2 Nested Control Instructions

The second adjustment to the control instructions is called a **nested control instruction.** A nested control instruction is a control instruction that itself contains a control instruction as one of its instructions. Again, consider the basic form of the IF-THEN-ELSE instruction:

```
IF BOOLEAN expression
  THEN < InstructionA >
  ELSE < InstructionB >
```

Now, an IF-THEN-ELSE instruction is an instruction. Thus, InstructionA and/or InstructionB could be replaced by an IF-THEN-ELSE instruction. Consider the following instruction:

```
IF NumA < Ø
  THEN WRITE ('Negative')
  ELSE IF NumA > Ø
          THEN WRITE ('Positive')
          ELSE WRITE ('Zero')
```

Here, InstructionB has been replaced by the IF-THEN-ELSE instruction

```
IF NumA > Ø
  THEN WRITE ('Positive')
  ELSE WRITE ('Zero')
```

This type of IF-THEN-ELSE instruction is called a nested IF-THEN-ELSE instruction.

Although nested IF-THEN-ELSE instructions are more complex, they are often very helpful in solving problems. Consider classifying homework papers as *ok, good,* or *very good,* depending on whether the value in Score is less than 90, between 90 and 94 (inclusive), or greater than 94. A nested IF-THEN-ELSE instruction that solves this problem is

```
IF Score < 9Ø
  THEN WRITE (Score , ' ok')
  ELSE IF Score > 94
          THEN WRITE (Score , ' very good!')
          ELSE WRITE (Score , ' good.')
```

Suppose Score contains the value 96. The BOOLEAN expression Score < 9Ø has value FALSE. Thus, the instruction

```
IF Score > 94
  THEN WRITE (Score , ' very good!')
  ELSE WRITE (Score , ' good.')
```

will be executed. Since Score contains 96, the BOOLEAN expression Score > 94 has value TRUE. Thus, the instruction WRITE (Score , ' very good!') will be executed. That is, the output will be 96 very good! Table 2–8 shows a walk through of the instruction for selected values in the variable Score.

Score	BOOLEAN Expression	Value	Results/Output	Table 2–8
96	Score < 90	FALSE	ELSE instruction executed	
96	Score > 94	TRUE	96 very good!	
93	Score < 90	FALSE	ELSE instruction is executed	
93	Score > 94	FALSE	93 good.	
87	Score < 90	TRUE	87 ok	

PROGRAMMING POINT

Note that the instruction WRITE (Score , ' very good!') is executed only if the condition Score < 90 is FALSE and the condition Score > 94 is TRUE. Often, for a deeply nested instruction, it is hard for the reader to see the conditions that must be satisfied for the nested instruction to execute. In such cases, a series of IF-THEN instructions can be used (as will be seen later).

Boxing Not only is boxing helpful with punctuation, but it can also aid you in analyzing a nested IF-THEN-ELSE instruction. Analyzing a nested IF-THEN-ELSE instruction is needed to make sure it is a valid Pascal instruction and to make sure it serves its intended purpose. Consider the boxed instruction in Figure 2–8.

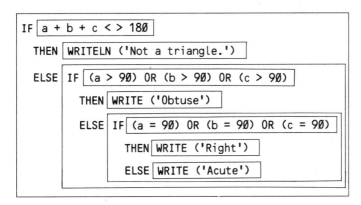

Figure 2–8

To box the nested IF-THEN-ELSE instruction,

1. The word IF starts the IF-THEN-ELSE instruction box.
2. After the word IF, a BOOLEAN expression is sought and boxed.
3. The word THEN is sought.
4. After the word THEN, if an instruction is found, it is boxed.
5. If the word ELSE is found and another instruction is found, it is boxed. (If the instruction is an IF-THEN-ELSE instruction, the previous steps starting with Step 1 are performed on the instruction).
6. The IF-THEN-ELSE instruction box is closed.

Looking at the boxed instruction in Figure 2–8, you can see three IF-THEN-ELSE instructions. Each has its needed parts. Also, you can see that for the instruction WRITE ('Right') to execute, the following must occur:

1. The BOOLEAN expression a + b + c < > 180 must have a value of FALSE.
2. The BOOLEAN expression (a > 90 OR (b > 90) OR (c > 90) must have a value of FALSE.
3. The BOOLEAN expression (a = 90) OR (b = 90) OR (c = 90) must be TRUE.

Consider the Pascal program shown in Figure 2–9 for finding the largest of three integers.

Figure 2–9

```
PROGRAM Max ;

VAR NumA , NumB , NumC , Max : INTEGER ;

BEGIN
  WRITE ('Please enter first integer: ') ;
  READLN (NumA) ;
  WRITE ('Please enter second integer: ') ;
  READLN (NumB) ;
  WRITE ('Please enter third integer: ') ;
  READLN (NumC) ;
  IF NumA > NumB
    THEN IF NumA >= NumC                    { largest is NumA or NumC }
            THEN Max := NumA
            ELSE Max := NumC
    ELSE IF NumB >= NumC                     { largest is NumB or NumC }
            THEN Max := NumB
            ELSE Max := NumC ;
  WRITELN ('Largest number is: ' , Max)
END .
```

Suppose the user enters the numbers 20, 13, and 30. First, variable NumA is assigned the value 20, variable NumB is assigned the value 13, and variable NumC is assigned the value 30. Next, the BOOLEAN expression (NumA > NumB) will have a value of TRUE. Thus, the instruction

```
IF NumA >= NumC
  THEN Max := NumA
  ELSE Max := NumC
```

will be executed. The BOOLEAN expression NumA >= NumC will have a value of FALSE. Thus, the instruction Max := NumC will be executed. Finally, the instruction WRITELN ('Largest number is: ', Max) is executed, producing an output of

```
Largest number is: 30
```

2-3.3 The Dangling ELSE

Consider the instruction where you would like to nest an IF-THEN as follows:

```
IF NumA > 5
  THEN IF NumA < 20
          THEN WRITE (NumA ,' is ok.')
  ELSE WRITE (NumA , ' is too small.')
```

The boxing of this instruction is shown in Figure 2–10.

Figure 2-10

```
    IF NumA > 5
       THEN IF NumA < 20
              THEN WRITE (NumA , ' is ok.')
       ELSE WRITE (NumA , ' is too small.')
```

IF NumA > 5

   THEN IF NumA < 20

           THEN WRITE (NumA , ' is ok.')

   ELSE WRITE (NumA , ' is too small.')

1. After this instruction is boxed, an ELSE is found.

2. Its instruction is boxed.

3. The IF-THEN-ELSE box is closed.

4. The IF-THEN box is closed.

Although the instruction is indented to indicate an IF-THEN-ELSE instruction (where InstructionA is an IF-THEN instruction), the compiler will *not* see it that way. The first ELSE encountered in the code will always be paired with the most recent THEN. Thus, the instruction will be compiled as follows:

```
IF NumA > 5
   THEN IF NumA < 20
           THEN WRITE (NumA ,' is ok.')
           ELSE WRITE (NumA ,' is too small.')
```

Thus, if the variable NumA contains the value 3, the BOOLEAN expression NumA > 5 will have a value FALSE. There will be *no* output. Likewise, if the variable NumA contains the value 33, the BOOLEAN expression NumA > 5 will have a value TRUE, and the instruction

```
IF NumA < 20
   THEN WRITE (NumA ,' is ok.')
   ELSE WRITE (NumA ,' is too small.')
```

will be executed. The BOOLEAN expression NumA < 20 has value FALSE, so the instruction WRITE (NumA, ' is too small.') is executed, and the output will be

    33 is too small.

The use of indentation (blank spaces), blank lines, and capitalization do not affect how the compiler will compile the source code to object code. Their use is for the benefit of the reader in terms of readability and clarity.

2-3.4 *Efficiency of Nested IF-THEN-ELSE*

Although the nested If-THEN-ELSE instruction is more complex than a series of IF-THEN instructions, it is a more efficient construct. Consider the following series of IF-THEN instructions, where it is desired to determine the largest of three integers:

```
IF (NumA >= NumB) AND (NumA >= NumC)
   THEN Max := NumA ;
IF (NumB >= NumA) AND (NumB >= NumC)
   THEN Max := NumB ;
IF (NumC >= NumA) AND (NumC >= NumB)
   THEN Max := NumC
```

The series of IF-THEN instructions always requires *six* comparisons when it is executed. An improvement in the efficiency of the instructions can be made by using a series of nested IF-THEN instructions:

```
IF NumA >= NumB
   THEN IF NumA >= NumC
           THEN Max := NumA ;
   IF NumB >= NumA
     THEN IF NumB >= NumC
             THEN Max := NumB ;
   IF NumC >= NumA
     THEN IF NumC >= NumB
             THEN Max := NumC ;
```

Here, a minimum of *four* and a maximum of *six* comparisons are made to assign a value to Max. The most efficient approach is the following nested instruction:

```
IF NumA >= NumB
   THEN IF NumA >= NumC
             THEN Max := NumA
             ELSE Max := NumC
   ELSE IF NumB >= NumC
             THEN Max := NumB
             ELSE Max := NumC
```

For this nested instruction, *two* comparisons are made before a value is assigned to Max.

Often in industry, nested instructions are frowned upon. Simplicity, clarity, and readability of a series of IF-THEN instructions are valued over the **efficiency** of nested instructions. When considered from the viewpoint of altering and maintaining the code of a program, writing the most efficient code is often not the most efficient approach.

DO IT NOW

1. Given the following instructions, state the conditions required for the instruction Max := NumC to execute.

```
IF (NumA >= NumB) AND (NumA >= NumC)
   THEN Max := NumA
   ELSE IF NumB >= NumC
             THEN Max := NumB
             ELSE Max := NumC
```

2. Replace the following list of IF-THEN instructions with a nested IF-THEN-ELSE instruction.

```
IF Num < 5
   THEN WRITELN ('Number is too small.') ;
IF (Num >= 5) AND ( Num <= 13 )
   THEN WRITELN ('Number is just right.') ;
IF Num > 13
   THEN WRITELN ('Number is too big.')
```

1. `(NumA >= NumB) AND (NumA >= NumC)` must have value `FALSE`. `NumB >= NumC` must have value `FALSE`.
2.
```
IF Num < 5
   THEN WRITELN ('Number is too small.')
   ELSE IF (Num >= 5 ) AND ( Num <= 13)
           THEN WRITELN ('Number is just right.')
           ELSE WRITELN ('Number is too big.')
```

Vocabulary   Page

Compound instruction   A collection of Pascal instructions bracketed by the words   91
  BEGIN and END.

Efficiency   One instruction is said to be more efficient than another instruction if it   98
  does the same job with less work. A nested IF-THEN-ELSE is more efficient
  than a series of IF-THEN instructions.

Nested control instruction   A control instruction that itself contains a control in-   94
  struction as one of its instructions. For example,

```
IF NumA > 10
  THEN IF NumA < 20
          THEN WRITE ('OK')
```

is a nested IF-THEN instruction.

Glad You Asked

Q In the IF-THEN-ELSE instruction, can I ever replace the THEN instruction with an
IF-THEN instruction?

A No. The general form of the IF-THEN-ELSE is

```
IF BOOLEAN expression
   THEN < InstructionA >
   ELSE < InstructionB >
```

Replacing InstructionA with an IF-THEN instruction would yield

```
IF BOOLEAN expression
   THEN IF BOOLEAN expression2
           THEN < Instruction >
   ELSE < InstructionB >
```

Now, as stated in the *Warning* earlier, the ELSE would be paired with the nearest
THEN. The results would be

```
IF BOOLEAN expression
   THEN IF BOOLEAN expression2
           THEN < Instruction >
           ELSE < InstructionB >
```

However, through the miracle of compound instructions, the desired instruction can be achieved. Consider the following:

```
IF BOOLEAN expression
  THEN
    BEGIN
      IF BOOLEAN expression2
        THEN < Instruction >
    END
  ELSE < InstructionB >
```

The use of BEGIN-END serves much like parentheses in an arithmetic computation. That is, the BEGIN-END brackets off the IF-THEN instruction. A good analogy is $7 + 3 * 5 = 22$, whereas $(7 + 3) * 5 = 50$.

Q Earlier, you said a list of IF-THEN instructions could usually be written as a nested IF-THEN-ELSE instruction. How could the following instructions be written as a nested IF-THEN-ELSE?

```
IF (NumA > 5) AND (NumA < 20)
  THEN WRITE (NumA , ' is okay.') ;
IF NumA <= 5
  THEN WRITE (NumA , ' is too small.') ;
IF NumA >= 20
  THEN WRITE (NumA , ' is too big.')
```

A A replacement for the series of IF-THEN instructions is

```
IF NumA >= 20
  THEN WRITE (NumA , ' is too big.')
  ELSE IF NumA <= 5
          THEN WRITE (NumA , ' is too small.')
          ELSE WRITE (NumA , ' is okay.')
```

Q How could I write the following nested instruction without nesting?

```
IF (A <= 3) OR (B >= 10)
  THEN D := A * B
  ELSE IF C > 8
          THEN D := A + B + C
          ELSE D := A + B
```

A To do so requires using more complicated BOOLEAN expressions. The instruction could be replaced by these instructions:

```
IF (A <= 3) OR (B >= 10)
  THEN D := A * B ;
IF (A > 3) AND (B < 10 ) AND (C > 8)
  THEN D := A + B + C ;
  ELSE D := A + B
```

Making replacements of this type is a good personal exercise to improve your skill with control instructions and BOOLEAN expressions. The best way of writing the information depends on the way you understand the instruction. A good guideline is "use the form that is easiest to read."

Section 2–3 Exercises

In problems 1 through 6, select the best description for each instruction from the following list:

    a. a nested IF-THEN-ELSE instruction
    b. an input instruction
    c. a compound IF-THEN instruction
    d. a decision control instruction
    e. an assignment instruction
    f. an output instruction

_____ **1.** READLN (NumA , NumB , NumC)
_____ **2.** WRITE ('The largest number is ' , Num : 1 : 2)
_____ **3.** IF NumA > 18
      THEN WRITELN ('Number is too large.')
_____ **4.** NumA := NumB – SQR (NumC)
_____ **5.** IF NumA > NumB
      THEN NumA := SQR (NumB)
      ELSE IF NumA > NumC
          THEN NumA := 5 * NumB
_____ **6.** IF NameA < NameB
      THEN
        BEGIN
          WRITE ('I''m sorry, please re-enter name: ') ;
          READLN (NameA)
        END .

  7. Give the output of the following (NumA contains the value 8) .

```
a. Ans := 5 ;                       b. Ans := 5 ;
   IF NumA < 10                        IF NumA > 10
     THEN                                THEN
       BEGIN                               BEGIN
         NumB := SQR (NumA) ;                NumB := SQR (NumA) ;
         Ans := NumB – NumA                  Ans := NumB – NumA
       END ;                               END
   WRITE (Ans)                           ELSE Ans := NumA ;
                                         WRITE (Ans)
```

  8. Give the output of the instructions in problem 7 if NumA contains the value 12.

  9. Given the following nested instruction,

```
IF (Ch1 = 'A') AND (Ch2 = 'T')
  THEN IF Ch3 = 'I'
          THEN WRITE ('Not possible')
          ELSE WRITE (Ch1 , 'C' , Ch2)
  ELSE IF (Ch1 = '0') AND (Ch2 = 'P')
          THEN WRITE ('M' , Ch1 , Ch2)
```

    a. If variables Ch1, Ch2, and Ch3 contain the values 'A', 'T', and 'C', respectively, give the output.
    b. If variables Ch1, Ch2, and Ch3 contain the values '0', 'P', and 'B', respectively, give the output.

10. Write a Pascal instruction that will output Number OK if the value in variable NumA is between 5 and 20 exclusively, and output Number too small if the value in variable NumA is less than or equal to 5.

11. Given the following boxed instruction,

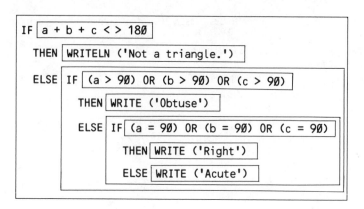

```
IF  a + b + c < > 180
   THEN  WRITELN ('Not a triangle.')
   ELSE  IF  (a > 90) OR (b > 90) OR (c > 90)
            THEN  WRITE ('Obtuse')
            ELSE  IF  (a = 90) OR (b = 90) OR (c = 90)
                     THEN  WRITE ('Right')
                     ELSE  WRITE ('Acute')
```

    a. Give values for a, b, and c that would cause the instruction WRITE ('Acute') to execute.

    b. Give values for a, b, and c that would cause the instruction WRITE ('Not a triangle.') to execute.

12. Given the instruction

```
IF NameA < NameB
   THEN WRITE (NameA)
   ELSE IF NameB < NameC
            THEN WRITE (NameB)
            ELSE WRITE (NameC)
```

    a. If NameA contains 'Robin', NameB contains 'Katie', and NameC contains 'Charlie', then the output will be _____ .

    b. If NameA contains 'Mick', NameB contains 'Mike', and NameC contains 'Mack', then the output will be _____ .

    c. If NameA contains '1234', NameB contains '1234', and NameC contains '1235', then the output will be _____ .

13. Given the instructions

```
WRITE ('Enter sales in dollars: ') ;
READLN (Sales) ;
IF Sales > 2000
   THEN IF Sales > 4000
            THEN Salary := 200 + 0.1 * Sales + 0.05 * (Sales - 4000)
            ELSE Salary := 200 + 0.1 * Sales
   ELSE Salary := 200 ;
WRITELN ( 'Your salary is: $' , Salary : 1 : 2 )
```

    a. For an input of 3500, the output is _____ .

    b. For an input of 5500, the output is _____ .

    c. For an input of 1500, the output is _____ .

14. Rewrite the following Pascal program using the style rules:

```
program style ; var numa , numb , numc : real ; count : integer ;
begin readln (numa , numb , numc) ; if numa < 10 then begin
count := round (numb + numc) ; write (count) end else
write (' no good!') ; writeln ; writeln ('thank you, that is all.') end .
```

15. The EZA Electric Company has embarked on an energy savings program. It has developed the following payment schedule:

> 7¢ per kilowatt hour (KWH).
> Add 2¢ for each KWH used over 1000 KWH.
> Add 4¢ for each KWH used over 3000 KWH.

For example, 1700 KWH used yields a cost of 0.07(1700) + 0.02(700). Complete the following Pascal program such that it will accept as input the number of KWH used. The output is the cost.

```
PROGRAM ElectPower ;

VAR NumHr ,
    Cost : REAL ;

BEGIN
  WRITE ('Enter number KWHs used this month: ') ;
  READLN (NumHr) ;
  IF NumHr < 1000
    THEN _____

    _____
    _____

END .
```

16. Box the following instruction:

```
IF NumA >= 100
  THEN WRITELN (NumA , ' is too large.')
  ELSE IF NumA > 20
          THEN
            BEGIN
              NumB := SQR (NumA) ;
              WRITELN (NumA , ' ' , NumB)
            END
          ELSE WRITELN (NumA , ' is too small.')
```

17. For the instruction in problem 16,
    a. Give the output if the variable NumA contains the value 17 and NumB contains the value 5.
    b. Give the output if the variable NumA contains the value 30 and NumB contains the value 5.
    c. Remove the words BEGIN and END. Will the resulting instruction be a valid Pascal instruction?

18. The price of an item equals cost plus profit (that is, Price = Cost + Profit). At Joan & Sons, the profit is 30% of cost. Thus, Price = Cost + 0.3(Cost), or Price = 1.3(Cost). Complete the following Pascal program. The program is to allow the user to input a C or a P. If C is input, the output is to be the Price of the item. If P is input, the output is to be the Cost.

```
PROGRAM Profit ;

VAR Cost , Price : REAL ;
    Ans : CHAR ;

BEGIN
  WRITE ('Please indicate type of entry Price or Cost (P/C): ') ;
  READLN (Ans) ;
  IF Ans = 'P'
    THEN _____

    _____

END .
```

19. Boot up Pascal; set the workfile to the file `CHANGEIT.PAS` from the `Source` diskette. Enter the Turbo Pascal editor. Replace the series of IF-THEN instructions with a nested IF-THEN-ELSE instruction. Quit the editor, and execute the program several times to test the alteration.

Programming Problems

For the following problems, follow the process presented in Section 1-1. Write a design for the solution, refine the design, test the design with hand simulations, convert the design to a Pascal program, enter the Pascal system, use the editor to create the text of the program, use the compiler to convert the text to code, execute the code, and debug the program. Turn in a copy of your design and its refinement. Turn in a hard copy of the text of the program and its output.

20. Write a Pascal program that allows an input of the number of hours worked. The output is the employee's pay based on the following: If number of hours is 40 or less, then pay is $8 per hour. If number of hours is more than 40 and less than or equal to 56, then pay is $8 for each of the first 40 hours plus $10.50 for each hour over 40 hours. If number of hours is more than 56, then pay is $8 for each of the first 40 hours plus $10.50 for each hour over 40 and less than or equal to 56 hours plus $13 for each hour over 56 hours. Remember, start with a design of the problem's solution.

Sample Execution

```
Please enter number of hours worked: 60
Your pay is: $540
```

21. A car rental company has three types of cars to rent. The charge per day for each car type is as follows

Car Type	Rent Per Day
1	$24.95
2	$32.95
3	$44.90

Sample Execution

```
Enter car type: 3
Enter number of days rented: 5
Enter miles driven: 1000

Cost of the rental is: $274.50
```

The daily rate includes an allowence of 150 miles per day. The extra mileage charge is 20¢ per mile. Write a Pascal program that allows the user to enter a car type, number of days rented, and the number of miles driven. The program is to output the cost of the rental.

22. Given an equation of the form $ax^2 + bx + c = 0$, the solution has the following form (Discriminant = $b^2 - 4ac$):

Discriminant > 0: solution is 2 numbers:
$(-b + \sqrt{\text{Discriminant}}) / (2*a)$ and
$(-b - \sqrt{\text{Discriminant}}) / (2*a)$
Discriminant $= 0$: solution is one number: $(-b) / (2*a)$
Discriminant < 0: solution is no real numbers.

Write a Pascal program to accept as input *a, b,* and *c.* The output is the solution to the equation (accurate to two decimal places). Remember, start with a design of the solution.

Sample Execution

```
Please enter a the x square coefficient: 1
Please enter b the x coefficient: -3
Please enter c the number term: -2

Solution is: 3.56 and -0.56
```

23. The MyTie Restaurant has a rather limited menu. A typical conversation with a waitress or waiter at the MyTie is as follows:

Sample Execution

```
Welcome to MyTie's
Would you care for a salad? (Y/N): Y
Would you care for the steak or fish? Fish
Would you care for anything to drink? (Y/N): Y
Tea or milk? Tea
```

The prices for the MyTie are as follows:

Salad:	$2.00
Steak:	$9.60
Fish:	$7.40
Tea:	$0.75
Milk:	$1.00

Write a Pascal program that plays the part of the waitress or waiter. After the order is taken, the program should write to the screen the order, the menu total price, 6% sales tax, and the total price. The output of the program should consist of a dialogue with a customer and a summary similar to the one shown.

Sample Execution (continued)

```
Your order is:
            Salad
            Fish dinner
            Tea
Price is: $ 10.15
Tax:      $  0.61
Total:    $ 10.76
Thank you for eating at MyTie's.
```

Section 2–4

CASE-OF-END

In this section, you will be introduced to another of the control instructions in the Pascal language. You have seen the decision control instruction IF-THEN-ELSE. In this section, you will study the decision control instruction CASE-OF-END. This decision control instruction can be used as an alternative to some nested IF-THEN-ELSE instructions.

2-4.1 Multiple Decision Making

The IF-THEN-ELSE instruction provides for selecting one of two instructions to execute. To make a selection from one of several instructions to execute, the **CASE-OF-END** decision control instruction can be used. An example of a CASE-OF-END instruction is

```
CASE Code OF
  1 : WRITELN ('Freshman') ;
  2 : WRITELN ('Sophomore') ;
  3 : WRITELN ('Junior') ;
  4 : WRITELN ('Senior')
  ELSE WRITELN ('Error in code.')
END
```

COMMENT
A common error is to forget the reserved word END in writing the CASE instruction.

The above CASE-OF-END instruction evaluates the BOOLEAN expression Code = 1. If Code = 1 has value TRUE, the string Freshman is output, and the execution of the CASE instruction is completed. If Code = 1 has value FALSE, the BOOLEAN expression Code = 2 is evaluated. If Code = 2 has value TRUE, the string Sophomore is output, and the execution of the CASE instruction is finished. This process continues until the reserved word ELSE is reached. If the ELSE is reached, the ELSE instruction is executed, and the execution of the CASE instruction is finished.

The CASE-OF-END instruction just presented is an alternative to the following nested IF-THEN-ELSE instruction:

```
IF Code = 1
  THEN WRITELN ('Freshman')
  ELSE IF Code = 2
          THEN WRITELN ('Sophomore')
          ELSE IF Code = 3
                  THEN WRITELN ('Junior')
                  ELSE IF Code = 4
                          THEN WRITELN ('Senior')
                          ELSE WRITELN ('Error in code.')
```

Figure 2–11

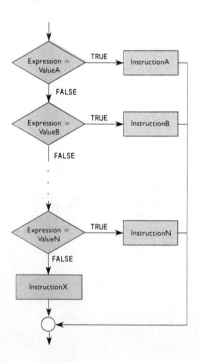

A picture of the CASE-OF-END instruction is shown in Figure 2–11. The general form is as follows.

```
CASE expression OF
  ValueA : <InstructionA>;
  ValueB : <InstructionB>;
    .
    .
  ValueN : <InstructionN>
  ELSE <InstructionX>
END .
```

The *expression* in Figure 2–11, is a variable or a valid combination of variables, operations, and values. The *expression* must yield a value of type INTEGER, CHAR, or BOOLEAN. Type REAL and type STRING *cannot* be used. The values listed after the word OF are used to select the instruction to be executed. **The values listed must be of the same type as the *expression.*** Only one instruction will be selected by the CASE-OF-END instruction. Also, the ELSE can be omitted. If so, the instruction after the CASE instruction is executed.

The *expression* is known as the **case selector.** The style for the instruction requires the selections to be indented under the CASE line. The END has the same indentation as the CASE.

The CASE-OF-END instruction is boxed as follows:

1. The word CASE starts the CASE-OF-END box.
2. Following the word CASE, an expression is sought and boxed.
3. The word OF is sought.
4. Following the word OF,
   a. A selection box is started.
   b. A value (or list of values), a colon, and an instruction are sought.
   c. The instruction is boxed.
   d. The selection box is closed.
   Steps 1 through 4 are repeated until the word ELSE (or END) is found. If ELSE is found, the ELSE instruction is boxed, and then the word END is sought.
5. The CASE-OF-END box is closed.

As you can see from the boxed instruction in Figure 2–12, only the selection boxes are adjacent boxes. Thus, the only semicolons needed are those used to separate the selections. (If semicolons are needed in the instructions of the selections, they are inserted.) Note that there is no semicolon between the last selection and the ELSE.

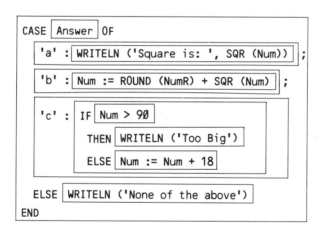

Figure 2–12

DO IT NOW

For the following CASE-OF-END instruction:

```
CASE Number OF
   1 : WRITELN ('The number is too small.') ;
   2 : IF Letter < 'Z'
          THEN Number := SQR (Number) ;
   3 : NumA := ROUND (RealNum) ;
   5 : WRITELN (Number , ' is too big.')
   ELSE WRITELN ('None of the above!')
END
```

1. If the variable `Number` contains the value 5, give the results of executing the instruction.
2. The case selector is _____.
3. Convert the instruction to a nested IF-THEN-ELSE instruction.

DO IT NOW ANSWERS

1. `5 is too big` would be written to the screen.
2. `Number`
3.
```
IF Number = 1
   THEN WRITELN ('The number is too small.')
   ELSE IF Number = 2
           THEN
             BEGIN
               IF Letter < 'Z'
                  THEN Number := SQR (Number)
             END
           ELSE IF Number = 3
                   THEN  NumA := ROUND (RealNum)
                   ELSE IF Number = 5
                           THEN WRITELN (Number , ' is too big.')
                           ELSE WRITELN ('None of the above.')
```

COMMENT

The selection for **Number** equal to 2 is an IF-THEN instruction. Without bracketing the IF-THEN instruction with BEGIN and END, the next ELSE would have been placed with the THEN in the instruction IF Letter < 'Z'

```
                THEN Number := SQR (Number)
```

2-4.2 Additional Features

In addition to the form just given, the CASE-OF-END also allows more than one value for a selection. The following CASE-OF-END instruction is a valid Pascal instruction:

```
CASE Grade OF
  'A' : WRITELN ('Very GOOD!') ;
  'B' : WRITELN ('Good') ;
  'C' : WRITELN ('You made it') ;
  'D' : WRITELN ('You should consider retaking the course.') ;
  'F' , 'W' , 'I' : WRITELN ('Better luck next time!')
END
```

The last selection choice means that if the BOOLEAN expression

```
(Grade = 'F') OR (Grade = 'W') OR (Grade = 'I')
```

is `TRUE`, then the instruction `WRITELN ('Better luck next time!')` is executed. (As usual, a comma is used to separate the items in the list: `'F', 'W', 'I'`.)

A sequence of values can be listed for a selection in which case the symbol .. is used. For example,

```
CASE Score OF
   90 .. 100 : LetGrade := 'A' ;
   80 .. 89 : LetGrade := 'B' ;
   70 .. 79 : LetGrade := 'C' ;
   60 .. 69 : LetGrade := 'D'
   ELSE LetGrade := 'F'
END
```

In this CASE-OF-END instruction, if `Score` has a value of 9∅, 91, 92, 93, 94, 95, 96, 97, 98, 99, or 1∅∅, then `LetGrade` is assigned the character `A`.

In addition to allowing multiple values for the case selector, the CASE-OF-END also allows a compound instruction for a selection instruction. Consider the following example:

```
CASE Class OF
   1 : BEGIN
          Over := NumGrade - 70 ;
          NumGrade : = 70 + Over DIV 3 ;
          WRITELN ('Your makeup grade is: ' , NumGrade)
       END ;
   2 : WRITELN ('Your makeup grade is: ' , NumGrade) ;
   3 : BEGIN
          WRITELN ('Your test score was ' , NumGrade) ;
          WRITELN ('You should take another makeup test.')
       END
END
```

DO IT NOW

1. For the previous CASE-OF-END instruction,
   a. Give the results if Class contains the value 1 and NumGrade is 92.
   b. Give the results if Class contains the value 5 and NumGrade is 13.
2. Write a nested IF-THEN-ELSE instruction that cannot be converted to a CASE-OF-END instruction.

DO IT NOW ANSWERS

1a. Over is assigned the value 22. NumGrade is assigned the value 77.
   Your makeup grade is: 77 is written to the screen.
 b. Since the value in Class does not match any of the values listed, the next instruction after the CASE-OF-END would be executed.
2. Any nested IF-THEN-ELSE instruction where the BOOLEAN expressions involve REAL or STRING variables would do. For example,

```
IF (NameA <= NameB) AND (NameA <= NameC)
   THEN WRITELN (NameA)
   ELSE IF NameB <= NameC
           THEN WRITELN (NameB)
           ELSE WRITELN (NameC)
```

where NameA, NameB, and NameC are of type STRING, cannot be converted directly to a CASE-OF-END instruction.

2-4.3 A Programming Example

As an example of the CASE-OF-END instruction, consider the following problem.

PROBLEM

The Ace Shipping Company's charges are based on the following table:

Weight	Cost
Less than 2 oz.	$0.75
2 to less than 4 oz.	$0.95
4 to less than 6 oz.	$1.25
6 to less than 8 oz.	$1.50
8 oz. and up	$2.00 + $0.25 per oz. over 8 oz.

Write a Pascal program that has as input a value for weight (of type REAL). The output is the cost of shipping.

Sample Execution

```
Please enter weight of package (in ounces): 6.5
Cost to ship package is $1.50
```

SOLUTION

First, think about the problem. Afterwards, construct a design for its solution.

Weight	Cost
Less than 2 oz.	$0.75
2 to less than 4 oz.	$0.95
4 to less than 6 oz.	$1.25
6 to less than 8 oz.	$1.50
8 oz. and up	$2.00 + $0.25 per oz. over 8 oz.

Design: Write ('Please enter weight . . .')
          Read (Weight)
          IntWeight := TRUNC (Weight)
          CASE IntWeight OF
              0, 1 : Cost := 0.75
              2, 3 : Cost := 0.95
              4, 5 : Cost := 1.25
              6, 7 : Cost := 1.50
              ELSE Cost := 2.0 + 0.25 * (IntWeight − 8)
          END
          WRITE ('Cost to ship package is: $')
          WRITELN (Cost : 1 : 2)

COMMENT

The value in `Weight` will be a REAL value and cannot be used for a case selector. Thus, `IntWeight` of type INTEGER is introduced. The field width in outputting `Cost` is set to `1`, since if the real value needs more space, it will be allotted. The decimal specification is set to `2`, since dollars and cents are involved.

Next, the design is tested by walking through it with various values for `Weight`. A value for `Weight` of **3.45** ounces is demonstrated as follows:

    Please enter weight . . . is written to the screen.
    The user enters 3.45.
    Weight is assigned the value 3.45.
    IntWeight is assigned the value 3.
    The second selection in the CASE-OF-END is made.
    Cost is assigned the value 0.95.
    Cost to ship package is: $0.95 is written to the screen.

Suppose the user enters a negative value for `Weight`. Although this situation should not occur, it is easy enough to handle (see the conversion of the design to a Pascal program in Figure 2–13).

Figure 2–13

```
PROGRAM CostToShip ;

VAR Weight, Cost : REAL ;
    IntWeight : INTEGER ;

BEGIN
  WRITE ('Please enter weight of package (in ounces): ') ;
  READLN (Weight) ;
  IntWeight := TRUNC (Weight) ;
  IF Weight <= 0
    THEN WRITELN ('Must enter a positive value for weight.')
    ELSE BEGIN
            CASE IntWeight OF
              0, 1 : Cost := 0.75 ;
              2, 3 : Cost := 0.95 ;
              4, 5 : Cost := 1.25 ;
              6, 7 : Cost := 1.50
              ELSE Cost := 2.0 + 0.25 * (IntWeight - 8)
            END ;
            WRITELN ('Cost to ship package is: $' , Cost : 1 : 2)
         END
END .
```

COMMENT
Notice that a semicolon is not used between the last selection and the ELSE.

2–4.4 Summary of CASE-OF-END

Use The CASE-OF-END instruction can be used as an alternative to some nested IF-THEN-ELSE instructions.

Form The form is

```
CASE expression OF
  ValueA : < InstructionA > ;
  ValueB : < InstructionB > ;
       .
       .
       .
  ValueN : < InstructionN >
  ELSE  < InstructionX >
END
```

The expression (case selector) is usually a variable (such as `Number` or `Letter`). However, it can be a combination of variables, operations, and values (such as `Number MOD 4 + 3`). The expression must evaluate to a value of type INTEGER, CHAR, or BOOLEAN. The values listed after OF must be of the same type as the expression. A list of values separated by commas can be used to make a selection. Also, a sequence of values can be used in a selection.

An instruction listed in a selection can be any valid Pascal instruction. This includes

1. A simple instruction (like READLN, etc.).
2. A control instruction (like IF-THEN-ELSE, etc.).
3. A compound instruction.
    The end of a CASE-OF-END instruction is marked by the word END.

Style and Punctuation The selections are indented under the CASE line. The word END has the same indentation as the word CASE. The selections (value, colon, instruction) are separated by a semicolon. If more than one value is listed for a selection, the values are separated by a comma or by .. (as in `'A' .. 'F'`).

Special Information The case selector or a value in the list of values *cannot* be of type REAL or STRING. The case selector and the values in the list of values must be of the same type (INTEGER, CHAR, or BOOLEAN for the present). A value can appear exactly once in the list of values. At most, one of the selections listed will be made (that is, only one of the instructions listed will be executed).

Vocabulary

Page		
106	**CASE-OF-END**	A decision control instruction in Pascal. The instruction is used to make a decision about which one of several instructions to execute.
107	**Case selector**	A term used as reference to the expression in the CASE-OF-END instruction.
106	**Multiple decision making**	The process of selecting one instruction for execution from a list of several instructions.

Glad You Asked

Q Is there such a thing as a nested CASE-OF-END instruction? If so, could you show an example of one?

A Yes. Consider the following:

```
CASE FirstCh OF
  'T' , 't' : CASE SecondCh OF
                'h' : ThCount := ThCount + 1 ;
                'r' : TrCount := TrCount + 1 ;
                'a', 'e', 'i', 'o', 'u' : TVowelCt := TVowelCt + 1
              END ;
  'C' , 'c' : CASE SecondCh OF
                'h' : ChCount := ChCount + 1 ;
                'r' : CrCount := CrCount + 1 ;
                'a', 'e', 'i', 'o', 'u' : CVowelCt := CVowelCt + 1
              END
END
```

Q I tried to use the following CASE-OF-END instruction:

```
CASE Height OF
  < 62 : WRITELN ('Short') ;
  62, 63, 64, 65 : WRITELN ('Medium Short') ;
  66, 67, 68, 69, 70 : WRITELN ('Average') ;
  > 70 : WRITELN ('Tall')
END
```

Of course, I got an error. I realize now that `< 62` and `> 70` cannot be used to list values. My question is, How would you write a Pascal instruction to do this?

A The following instructions will accomplish what you want:

```
CASE Height OF
   62, 63, 64, 65 : WRITELN ('Medium Short') ;
   66 .. 70 : WRITELN ('Average')
   ELSE IF Height < 62
           THEN WRITELN ('Short')
           ELSE WRITELN ('Tall')
END
```

Q You said the case selector could be of type INTEGER, CHAR, or BOOLEAN. What would be an example of the case selector's being of type BOOLEAN?

A Consider the following CASE-OF-END instruction:

```
CASE Num MOD 7 = 0 OF
   TRUE : WRITELN ('7 is a divisor of ' , Num) ;
   FALSE : WRITELN ('7 is not a divisor of ' , Num)
END
```

If the value in the variable Num is 49, then this instruction will write to the screen

```
7 is a divisor of 49
```

Of course, the instruction could be written as

```
IF Num MOD 7 = 0
   THEN WRITELN ('7 is a divisor of ' , Num)
   ELSE WRITELN ('7 is not a divisor of ' , Num)
```

Which form do you think is easiest to read?

Section 2–4 Exercises

1. The CASE-OF-END instruction is classified as
   a. an input instruction.
   b. a decision control instruction.
   c. an assignment instruction.
   d. a compound instruction.
   e. an output instruction.
2. The CASE-OF-END instruction is an alternative to a(n) _____ instruction.
3. Which of the following cannot be a selection in a CASE-OF-END instruction?
   a. `'13' : WRITELN ('This is the PBS station')`
   b. `37 : WRITELN ('The number is even.')`
   c. `'J' : WRITELN ('You have selected the president')`
   d. `9, 10, 11 : IF Number < 3.78`
      `                THEN Code := 3`
4. Which of the following cannot be a case selector (Number is of type INTEGER; Value is of type REAL)?
   a. `Number MOD 4 + 3`
   b. `SQR (Number)`
   c. `ROUND (Value) DIV 2`
   d. `Number`
   e. `ROUND (Value) / Number`

5. Given the following instructions (with `Number` of type INTEGER),

```
CASE Number MOD 4 OF
   0 : WRITE ('Hi Ho') ;
   1 : WRITE ('Hi ') ;
   2 : WRITE ('Ho ') ;
   3 : WRITELN ('It''s off to work we go')
END ;
```

a. The case selector is _____.

b. Give the BOOLEAN expression that must be satisfied for the instruction `WRITE ('Ho ')` to execute.

c. If the variable `Number` contains `10`, the results of executing the instruction will be _____.

d. If the variable `Number` contains `15`, the results of executing the instruction will be _____.

e. Write a nested IF-THEN-ELSE instruction to replace the instruction.

6. Box the following instruction:

```
CASE Ans OF
  'A' : WRITELN ('Very good!') ;
  'B' : WRITELN ('Sorry, check your addition.') ;
  'C' : WRITELN ('You used the wrong operation.') ;
  'D' : WRITELN ('Wrong. Don''t guess.')
END
```

7. For the following instruction (where `Height` is of type INTEGER),

```
IF Height < 62
  THEN WRITELN ('Short')
  ELSE IF Height > 70
          THEN WRITELN ('Tall')
          ELSE CASE Height OF
                  62, 63, 64, 65 : WRITELN ('Medium Short') ;
                  66 .. 70 : WRITELN ('Average')
               END
```

a. If `Height` contains the value `71`, the output is _____.

b. If `Height` contains the value `70`, the output is _____.

c. The BOOLEAN expressions that must be evaluated to get an output of `Average` are _____.

d. If the variable `Height` is changed to type REAL, discuss how the case selector should be altered so as to prevent an error in the CASE-OF-END instruction.

8. Given the following instruction,

```
Case Ch OF
  'a' : Ch := 'b' ;
  'b' : Ch := 'c' ;
  'c' : Ch := 'a'
END
```

if `Ch` contains the value `'a'`, the value in `Ch` after the instruction executes is _____.

9. Rewrite the following based on the style rules:

```
program style ; var number : integer ; ch : char ; begin
write ('please enter letter (a .. d): ') ; readln (ch) ;
      case ch of
'a' : number := 1 ; 'b' , 'c' : number := sqr (number) ;
'd' : number := number + 3 end ; writeln (number : 16) end .
```

10. Given the following Pascal program,

```
PROGRAM PayDay ;

VAR Code , Hours : INTEGER ;
Pay : REAL ;

BEGIN
  Pay := 0 ;
  WRITE ('Enter employee code (1, 2, 3): ') ;
  READLN (Code) ;
  IF (Code = 1) OR (Code = 2)
    THEN
      BEGIN
        WRITE ('Enter number of hours worked (0 .. 80): ') ;
        READLN (Hours)
      END ;
  CASE Code OF
    1 : Pay := 7.80 * Hours ;
    2 : Pay := 12.50 * (Hours MOD 41) + 18 * (Hours - 40) ;
    3 : Pay := 2000
  END ;
  WRITELN ('Your pay is $' , Pay : 1 : 2)
END .
```

   a. If 2 is entered for Code and 43 is entered for Hours, give the output of the program.
   b. If 3 is entered for Code and 10 is entered for Hours, give the output of the program.
   c. If 4 is entered for Code and 50 is entered for Hours, give the output of the program.
   d. Remove the assignment instruction Pay := 0. Now, repeat part c.

11. Find and comment on the errors in the following.

   a.
```
CASE Cost OF
   1.98 : WRITE ('Price too low.') ;
   2.0 : WRITE ('Great price.') ;
   3.0 : WRITE ('Price too high.')
END
```

   c.
```
CASE Number OF
   1 , 2 , 3 : Cost := SQR (Value) + 12 ;
   4 , 5 : Cost := 15 * Number - 5 ;
   3 , 6 : Cost := 129 - SQR (Number)
END
```

   b.
```
READLN (Name) ;
CASE Name OF
   'John' : WRITELN ('Bad choice.') ;
   'Susan' : WRITELN ('Good choice.') ;
   'Peggy' : WRITELN ('Don''t think so.')
END
```

12. Boot up Pascal; set the workfile to the file COSTSHIP.PAS from the Source diskette. Enter the Turbo Pascal editor. Rearrange the program commands to match the following design:

```
WRITE ('Please enter weight ...)
READLN (Weight)
IntWeight : = TRUNC (Weight)
CASE IntWeight OF
   .
   .
   .
IF Weight < = 0
   THEN WRITELN ('Must enter a positive value for weight.')
   ELSE WRITELN ('Cost to ship package is: $', Cost : 1 : 2)
```

Programming Problems

For the following problems, follow the process presented in Section 1–1. Write a design for the solution, refine the design, test the design with hand simulations, convert the design to a Pascal program, enter the Pascal system, use the editor to create the text of the program, use the compiler to convert the text to code, execute the code, and debug the program. Turn in a copy of your design and its refinement. Turn in a hard copy of the text of the program and its output.

13. A car rental company has four types of cars to rent. The charge per day for each car type and the charge for extra miles is as follows.

Sample Execution

```
Enter car type: 3
Enter number of days rented: 5
Enter miles driven: 1000

Cost of the rental is: $304.50
```

Car Type	Rent Per Day	Cost Per Extra Mile
1	$24.95	$0.20
2	$32.95	$0.27
3	$44.90	$0.32
4	$52.00	$0.40

The daily rate includes an allowance of 150 miles per day. The extra mileage charge is shown in the table. Write a Pascal program that allows the user to enter a car type, number of days rented, and the number of miles driven. The program is output the cost of the rental.

14. Write a program that has input a number between 0 and 15. The program is to write to the screen the number if the number is less than 10. It should write `'A'` if the number is 10; `'B'` if the number is 11; and so forth up to `'F'` for 15.

Sample Execution

```
Please enter whole number from 0 to 15: 12
The name is: C
```

A possible design:
```
WRITE ('Please enter value . . . )
READ (Number )
IF (Number < 0) OR (Number > 15)
  THEN WRITE (Number , ' out of range.')
  ELSE
    BEGIN
      WRITE ('The name is: ')
      IF Number < = 9
        THEN WRITELN (Number)
        ELSE CASE Number OF
               10 : WRITE ('A')
               11 : WRITE ('B')
                       .
                       .
               15 : WRITE ('F')
             END
    END
```

15. Susan is planning her 100th birthday party. She wants to know for which day of the week to plan. Her 100th birthday will be October 5, 2065. An algorithm to output the day of the week for a given date is as follows.

Let `MonthNum` be the month of year computed as follows:

March is `MonthNum` 1
April is `MonthNum` 2

.
.
.

January is `MonthNum` 11
February is `MonthNum` 12   (For Susan `MonthNum` is 8)
Let `DayNum` be the day of the month.   (For Susan `DayNum` is 5)
Let `YearNum` be the year of the century. (For Susan `YearNum` is 65)
Let `CenturyNum` be the previous century. (For Susan `CenturyNum` is 20)

```
A := (13*MonthNum - 1) DIV 5
B := YearNum DIV 4
C := CenturyNum DIV 4
D := A + B + C + DayNum + YearNum - 2 * CenturyNum
```

The day of the week is found as follows:
```
CASE D MOD 7 OF
    0 : Day := 'Sunday'
    1 : Day := 'Monday'
    2 : Day := 'Tuesday'
    3 : Day := 'Wednesday'
    4 : Day := 'Thursday'
    5 : Day := 'Friday'
    6 : Day := 'Saturday'
```

Convert this algorithm to a Pascal program. The program is to write to the screen the day of the week on which the date input falls.

Sample Execution

```
Please enter month number (1 = March ..): 8
Please enter day number (1 .. 31): 5
Please enter year number (0 .. 3000): 2065

Day of the week is: Monday
```

CHAPTER TEST

1. The IF-THEN-ELSE and CASE-OF-END instructions are classified as _____ control instructions.

2. Which of the following is a BOOLEAN value?
  a. FALSE   **b.** 13 MOD 7   **c.** 17 >= 3   **d.** 'A'   **e.** 2.13

3. Which of the following is a BOOLEAN expression (`Number` is a variable of type INTEGER)?
  a. Number MOD 5   **d.** Number := 16 MOD 3
  b. (Number <= 19) OR (Number >= 5)   **e.** Number > 9 AND Number < 15
  c. Number - 6

4. Which of the following can be used for multiple decision making?
   a. assignment instructions   **d.** READLN instructions
   b. compound instructions   **e.** the VAR section
   c. CASE-OF-END instructions

5. The three operations available for data of type BOOLEAN are _____, _____, and _____.

6. Rewrite the following using the style rules:

```
program class ; var number : integer ; value : boolean ; begin
write ('Please enter a number: ') ; readln (number) ;
case number mod 4 of 0 : writeln ('4 is a divisor') ;
1 , 3 : writeln ('four is not a divisor') ; 2 :
writeln ('2 is a divisor')
end end.
```

7. Which of the following could be used for a case selector (where Number is of type INTEGER and Value is of type REAL)?
   a. Number / Value   **d.** SQR (Value) − 0.6
   b. ROUND (Value) MOD 4   **e.** (Number − 6) / ROUND (Value)
   c. Number + SQR (Value)

8. Replace the following nested IF-THEN-ELSE instruction with a CASE-OF-END instruction (Ch is of type CHAR):

```
IF Ch = 'A'
  THEN WRITE ('Sears')
  ELSE IF Ch < 'D'
          THEN WRITE ('K mart')
          ELSE IF Ch = 'D'
                  THEN WRITE ('Safeway')
```

9. Complete the following Pascal program. The program is to allow the user to input the name of one of the four planets Jupiter, Saturn, Uranus, or Neptune. The output is to be the length of time it takes light from the sun to reach the planet (in minutes, accurate to hundredths). The following information will be helpful:

   Jupiter is 480 million miles from the sun.
   Saturn is 900 million miles from the sun.
   Uranus is 1800 million miles from the sun.
   Neptune is 2800 million miles from the sun.
   Light travels at 186,282 miles per second. Thus, time (in seconds) will be equal to the distance divided by 186,282.

Design: Read planet name.
          Look up distance from sun.
          Time is assigned (distance / 186282) / 60.
          Report Time.

Sample Execution

```
Please enter planet (Jupiter, Saturn, Uranus, Neptune): Uranus
It takes 161.05 minutes for the sun's light to reach Uranus.
```

The Turbo Editor

Search and Replace Commands

Earlier, the block commands of the Turbo Pascal editor were discussed. The Turbo Pascal editor has two other word-processing features known as the SEARCH command and the FIND/REPLACE command. These commands allow you to search through a TEXT file for a specified target and to find, then replace a target with a pre-selected string.

The SEARCH Command

The SEARCH command is selected by using the key sequence Ctrl-Q F. Once selected, the prompt Find: appears on the top line of the screen. A target (the string you wish to find) is entered. After the target is entered, the prompt Options: appears on the top line of the screen. Some of the options and their codes are as follows.

G (Global search)	The entire document is searched.
B (Backwards)	The search is conducted from cursor location back to start of the document.
U (Upper/lower)	Uppercase and lowercase letters are considered equal.
W (Whole words)	Matching patterns embedded in other words are ignored.

Once the desired options are entered, the search is started. Once an occurrence of the target is found, the cursor is positioned to the right of the target. You could now edit the target. To continue the search for other occurrences, the key sequence Ctrl-L is used.

As a hands-on experience with this command, bootup Turbo Pascal. Set the work file to the file BARGR from the Source diskette, then enter the editor. Do the following.

1. Hold down the Ctrl key then press the Q key (the symbols ^Q should appear at the top left of the screen). Press the F key.
2. Respond to the Find: prompt by entering the target Write
3. Respond to the Options: by entering U (ignore upper/lowercase).
4. After the first occurrence is found, use Ctrl-L to find the next occurrence of the target Write   Continue to use Ctrl-L until the prompt
       Search string not found. Press <ESC>
   appears at the top of the screen. Press the ESC key.

Play with the SEARCH command. When you are finished, use Ctrl-K D to quit the editor. If the save prompt appears, respond by pressing the N key for no.

The FIND/REPLACE Command

The FIND/REPLACE command is selected by using the key sequence Ctrl-Q A. The prompt Find: appears on the top line of the screen. Once a target is entered, the prompt Replace with: appears on the top line. Once the replacement string is entered, the prompt `Options:` appears on the top line. Some of the options available and their codes are as follows.

G (Global search)   The entire document is searched.

B (Backwards)   The search is conducted from cursor location back to start of the document.

U (Upper/lower)   Uppercase and lowercase letters are considered equal.

W (Whole words)   Matching patterns embedded in other words are ignored.

N (No ask)   Makes replacements without presenting the prompt `Replace (Y/N)?`

To escape the FIND/REPLACE command, the key sequence Ctrl-U is used.

As a hands-on experience with the FIND/REPLACE command, bootup Turbo Pascal. Set the workfile to the file `BARGR` from the diskette `Source` then enter the editor. Do the following.

1. Hold down the Ctrl key then press the Q key (the symbols `^Q` should appear at the top left of the screen). Press the A key.
2. Respond to the `Find:` prompt by entering the target `WRITE`
3. Respond to the `Replace with:` prompt by entering `Write`
4. Respond to the `Options:` by entering `UW` (ignore upper/lowercase and look for whole words).

COMMENT

If the option G is selected, the Ctrl-L sequence is not needed.

5. After the first occurrence is found, respond by pressing the N key for no. Use Ctrl-L to find the next occurrence of the target `WRITE` and press the Y key for yes. Continue to use Ctrl-L (respond to the replace prompt by pressing the Y key for yes) until the prompt

    `Search string not found. Press <ESC>`

appears at the top of the screen. Press the ESC key.

Play with the FIND/REPLACE command. When you are finished, use Ctrl-K D to quit the editor. Respond to the save prompt by pressing the N key for no.

Chapter Three

Repetition Control

Introduction

In this chapter, you will study another fundamental feature of any computer language: the ability to repeat the execution of an instruction. Repetition is often called **looping**. Like making decisions, it deals with controlling the flow of the execution of instructions by the program. To repeat the execution of an instruction, three different instructions are available in Pascal.

The chapter starts by looking at the repetition control instruction known as a WHILE-DO instruction. Next, a closely related repetition control instruction, the REPEAT-UNTIL instruction, is discussed. Finally, a very special repetition control instruction, known as a FOR-DO instruction, is covered. After finishing this chapter, you will be able to write a Pascal program that can repeat the execution of an instruction.

```
PROGRAM Chapter3 ;
{$U+}                                    {page 128}

VAR Count, Ct, LCV : INTEGER ;
    Ans : CHAR ;

BEGIN
  CLRSCR ;                               {page 144}
  REPEAT                                 {page 141}
    WRITE ('Enter times to loop (0 .. 8): ') ;
    READLN (Ct) ;
    Outer := 1 ;                         {page 123}
    WHILE Outer <= Ct DO                 {page 122}
      BEGIN                              {page 123}
        GOTOXY (5,Outer) ;               {page 159}
        CLREOL ;                         {page 159}
        WRITE (Outer) ;
        Outer := Outer + 1               {page 123}
      END ;
    WRITELN ;
    FOR LCV := 1 TO Ct DO                {page 154}
      WRITELN ('Loop ', LCV) ;
    WRITE ('Do another?(Y/N): ') ;
    READLN (Ans)
  UNTIL Ans = 'N'                        {page 141}
END .
```

WHILE-DO

In this section, you will be introduced to another control instruction, the WHILE-DO loop control instruction. This instruction provides for executing an instruction more than once. In fact, the WHILE-DO instruction will execute an instruction as long as (while) its BOOLEAN expression has the value `TRUE`.

3–1.1 Introduction to WHILE-DO

There are certain essentials in any computer language. The language must

1. Allow the input of data (this is accomplished in Pascal by the use of READ, READLN, and assignment `:=`).
2. Allow the output of data (this is accomplished in Pascal by the use of WRITE and WRITELN).
3. Allow for operations on data.
4. Allow for comparison of data.
5. Allow for decisions (the IF-THEN-ELSE instruction is one way of making a decision).
6. Allow for repetition.

Repetition means repeating an action over and over. Action, in a programming sense, means executing an instruction. That is, the language must allow for the repeated execution of an instruction. In the Pascal language, repetition can be accomplished by use of the **WHILE-DO instruction.**

The form of the WHILE-DO instruction is shown in Figure 3–1.

Figure 3–1

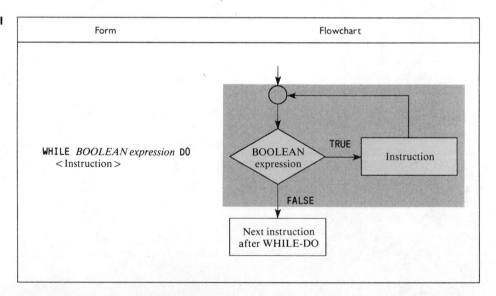

In Figure 3–1, the Instruction will be executed if the *BOOLEAN expression* has the value `TRUE`, and the execution will be repeated as long as the *BOOLEAN expression* has this value. Consider the following example:

```
Ch := ' ' ;
WHILE Ch < > 'Q' DO
  READLN (Ch)
```

Sample Execution

```
A
e
D
Q
>
```

First, the CHAR variable `Ch` is initialized to a blank. The assignment instruction `Ch := ' '` is called **initializing a variable** (`Ch`). Remember, until an assignment is made to a variable, the value that the variable contains is unknown. The WHILE-DO will execute its instruction, `READLN (Ch)`, since the expression `Ch < > 'Q'` has value `TRUE`. The instruction `READLN (Ch)` is executed "WHILE" the BOOLEAN expression has value `TRUE`. Once the user enters `Q`, the BOOLEAN expression has value `FALSE`. At this point, the execution of the WHILE-DO instruction is finished.

To execute more than one instruction in a WHILE-DO loop, a compound instruction is used. Consider the following example:

```
Count := 0 ;
WHILE Count < 10 DO
  BEGIN
    WRITE (Count : 3) ;
    Count := Count + 1
  END
```

The *BOOLEAN expression* in this WHILE-DO instruction is `Count < 10`. The instruction (to be repeated) is the compound instruction

```
BEGIN
  WRITE (Count : 3) ;
  Count := Count + 1
END
```

When the WHILE-DO instruction is executed,

```
WHILE Count < 10 DO
  BEGIN
    WRITE (Count : 3) ;
    Count := Count + 1
  END
```

Sample Execution

1. The BOOLEAN expression `Count < 10` has a value of `TRUE`.
2. Thus, the compound instruction is executed:
   a. The instruction `WRITE (Count : 3)` produces an output of ⬚⬚0
   b. The instruction `Count := Count + 1` assigns the variable `Count` the value in `Count` plus the number 1 (so `Count` now contains the number 1).
3. The BOOLEAN expression `Count < 10` is evaluated again and is found to have a value of `TRUE`.
4. Thus, the compound instruction is executed:
   a. The instruction `WRITE (Count : 3)` produces an output of ⬚⬚1 (so the output is continued: ⬚⬚0⬚⬚1).
   b. The instruction `Count := Count + 1` assigns the variable `Count` the value in `Count` plus the number 1 (so `Count` now contains the number 2).

COMMENT
`Count` was initialized to zero prior to the WHILE-DO.

This repetition continues. Finally, the variable `Count` is assigned the value `10` by the assignment instruction `Count := Count + 1`. The BOOLEAN expression `Count < 10` now yields a value of `FALSE`. The program then moves to the next instruction after the WHILE-DO instruction.

Punctuation   The WHILE-DO instruction is boxed as follows:

1. The word WHILE starts the WHILE-DO box.
2. A BOOLEAN expression is sought and enclosed in a box.
3. The word DO is sought.
4. Following the word DO, an instruction is sought and boxed.
5. The WHILE-DO box is closed.

As you can see in Figure 3–2, the only punctuation needed is inside the compound instruction, since only in the compound instruction box are there adjacent boxes. The BOOLEAN expression box is separated from the instruction box by the word DO. Of course, if there is an instruction after the WHILE-DO instruction, a semicolon will be needed to separate the two instructions.

Figure 3–2

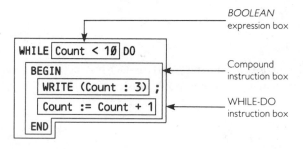

3-1.2 Accumulation and Sentinels

A common use of repetition is to accumulate (sum) a collection of numbers. The key instruction in an **accumulation loop** is an instruction like

        Sum := Sum + Value

This assignment instruction assigns to the memory location referenced by `Sum` the value currently in the memory location `Sum` plus the value in the variable `Value`. Suppose prior to executing the assignment instruction, the value in `Sum` was `56` and the value in `Value` was `20`. The assignment instruction would store in the memory location `Sum` the value `56 + 20`. That is, after the execution of the assignment instruction, the memory location referenced by `Sum` would contain the value `76`.

Consider the following instructions, where the user is to enter a collection of numbers. The numbers are to be accumulated (summed). The average of the collection of numbers is to be output to the screen.

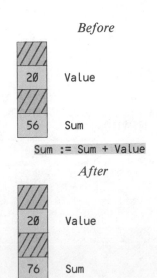

```
Count := Ø ;
Sum := Ø ;
WRITELN ('To sum a collection of numbers , press RETURN') ;
WRITE ('Otherwise, enter Q: ') ;
READLN (Ans) ;
WHILE Ans < > 'Q' DO
  BEGIN
    WRITE (Count + 1,'. Enter integer value: ') ;
    READLN (NumA) ;
    Count := Count + 1 ;
    Sum := Sum + NumA ;
    WRITE ('Enter Q to quit, press RETURN to continue ') ;
    READLN (Ans)
  END ;
IF Count < > Ø
  THEN BEGIN
         WRITE ('The average of the ' , Count , ' numbers ') ;
         WRITELN ('is ' , Sum / Count : 1 : 2)
       END
  ELSE WRITELN ('No values entered.')
```

In constructing an accumulation loop, a **sentinel** is often used. A sentinel is a guard. The value `Q` serves as a sentinel for the WHILE-DO loop. The first two instructions initialize the variables `Count` and `Sum`. The WRITE and WRITELN instructions ouput the message

Sample Execution

```
To sum a collection of numbers, press RETURN       .
Otherwise, enter Q:
```

If the user enters `Q` (the sentinel value), the BOOLEAN expression for the WHILE-DO instruction is `FALSE`. Thus, the instruction part of the WHILE-DO loop is skipped. The ELSE instruction of the IF-THEN-ELSE instruction after the WHILE-DO is executed. The screen would appear as

Sample Execution

```
To sum a collection of numbers, press RETURN
Otherwise, enter Q: Q
No values entered.
```

If the user presses the RETURN key, the sentinel allows the execution of the instruction part of the WHILE-DO loop. Thus, the compound instruction

```
BEGIN
  WRITE (Count + 1 , '. Enter integer value: ') ;
  READLN (NumA) ;
  Count := Count + 1 ;
  Sum := Sum + NumA ;
  WRITE ('Enter Q to quit , press RETURN to continue ') ;
  READLN (Ans)
END
```

```
READLN (NumA) ;
Count := Count + 1 ;
Sum := Sum + NumA ;
```

Before First Pass

NumA	Count	Sum
???	0	0

After First Pass

NumA	Count	Sum
17	1	17

After Second Pass

NumA	Count	Sum
31	2	48

is executed. A typical execution of the compound instruction would appear as

Sample Execution

```
1. Enter integer value: 17
Enter Q to quit, press RETURN to continue <ret>
```

where <ret> indicates pressing the RETURN key.

   After the compound instruction is executed, the BOOLEAN expression is evaluated again. Again, it yields a value of TRUE. Thus, the compound instruction is executed again. After the compound instruction is executed again, the screen might appear as follows:

Sample Execution

```
1. Enter integer value: 17
Enter Q to quit, press RETURN to continue <ret>
2. Enter integer value: 31
Enter Q to quit, press RETURN to continue
```

This repetition will continue until the user enters Q. After the user enters Q, the BOOLEAN expression is evaluated to have a value of FALSE. At this point, the compound instruction is skipped, and control is passed to the next instruction after the WHILE-DO. Since Count < > 0 has value TRUE, the instructions

```
WRITE ('The average of the ' , Count , ' numbers ') ;
WRITELN ('is ' , Sum / Count : 1 : 2)
```

will be executed. A possible output of the instruction might be

Sample Execution

```
1. Enter integer value: 17
Enter Q to quit, press RETURN to continue <ret>
2. Enter integer value: 31
Enter Q to quit, press RETURN to continue Q  <ret>
The average of the 2 numbers is 24.00
```

   The sentinel is used to control the number of times the loop's instruction is executed. Programmers often use the value read in, as a sentinel. That is, the previous accumulation loop could be written as follows (provided only non-negative values are to be accumulated).

```
Count := Ø ;
Sum := Ø ;
WRITE ('Enter first value (-1 to quit): ') ;
READLN (NumA) ;
WHILE NumA >= Ø DO
  BEGIN
    Sum := Sum + NumA ;
    Count := Count + 1 ;
    WRITE ('Enter value ' , Count + 1, ' (-1 to quit): ') ;
    READLN (NumA) ;
  END ;
IF Count > Ø
  THEN BEGIN
         WRITE ('The average of the ' , Count , ' numbers ') ;
         WRITELN ('is ' , Sum / Count : 1 : 2)
       END
  ELSE WRITELN ('No values entered. ')
```

Walk through

NumA	Count	Sum
???	Ø	Ø.Ø
13.2	1	13.2
12.8	2	26.Ø
1.3	3	27.3
-1		

Sample Execution

```
Enter first value (-1 to quit): 13.2
Enter value 2 (-1 to quit): 12.8
Enter value 3 (-1 to quit): 1.3
Enter value 4 (-1 to quit): -1
The average of the 3 numbers is 9.10
```

In these instructions, -1 serves as the sentinel. If the user enters -1, then the instruction of the WHILE-DO loop is not executed. Also, the IF-THEN-ELSE instruction is used to prevent a division-by-zero error in the event no numbers are entered by the user.

DO IT NOW

1. For the following instructions,

```
Count := Ø ;
WHILE Count < 5 DO
  Count := Count + 2
```

what is the value in Count after execution?

2. For these instructions,

```
NumberA := 1 ;
WHILE NumberA < > 27 DO
  BEGIN
    WRITE (NumberA + 2 : 3) ;
    NumberA := NumberA * 3
  END ;
WRITELN (NumberA : 3)
```

give the output.

3. For the WHILE-DO instruction in problem 2, what value serves as the sentinel?

DO IT NOW ANSWERS
1. 6
2. ☐☐3☐☐5☐11☐27
3. 27

3-1.3 Compiler Directives

Before discussing the topic of infinite loops, **compiler directives** must be discussed. A compiler directive is a comment to the compiler to compile the text of a Pascal program with selected optional features. Compiler directives are invoked by writing a line in the text of the Pascal program like the following:

```
{$U+}
```

There *cannot* be a space between the characters { and $.

The directive (indicated by $U+) is known as the **user interrupt directive**. It is used to allow the program user to stop the Pascal program at any time by using CONTROL-C. That is, the user holds down the CONTROL key while pressing the C key. The execution of the program halts, and the user is returned to the Pascal command line.

The easiest way to insert the directive is to start your Turbo Pascal program as follows:

```
{$U+}            or        PROGRAM ...
PROGRAM ...                 {$U+}
```

With the user interrupt directive in effect, your Turbo Pascal program will respond as stated in the next section.

3–1.4 Infinite (Endless) Loops

When a WHILE-DO instruction is executed, there must be some action in its Instruction to insure the BOOLEAN expression will eventually have a value of FALSE. Consider the following instructions:

```
Count := 0 ;
WHILE Count < 10 DO
   WRITE (Count)
```

The assignment instruction Count := 0 initializes the variable Count to 0. When the WHILE-DO instruction is executed, the BOOLEAN expression Count < 10 is evaluated to TRUE. The instruction WRITE (Count) is executed. The BOOLEAN expression Count < 10 is evaluated to TRUE. The instruction WRITE (Count) is executed. This process will continue forever. That is, the screen will fill up with zeroes, since the value of the variable Count never changes. The program has entered an **infinite loop**.

The instruction part of the WHILE-DO instruction WRITE (Count) did nothing to make the BOOLEAN expression take on a value of FALSE. Thus, once the WHILE-DO loop is entered, there is no exit.

PROGRAMMING POINT

To stop a program that has entered an infinite loop, CONTROL-C is used. This action will stop the execution of the program and return you to the Pascal system prompt. Press the space bar, and you are presented the main menu. You can also use CONTROL-BREAK to stop a program's execution.

Compare the instructions given previously with the following:

```
Count := 0 ;
WHILE Count < 10 DO
   BEGIN
     WRITE (Count) ;
     Count := Count + 1
   END
```

Here, the instruction for the WHILE-DO is a compound instruction. More importantly, the value in the variable `Count` is altered in such a way that the BOOLEAN expression `Count < 10` will eventually take on a value of `FALSE`.

3–1.5 Nested WHILE-DO Instructions

In the last chapter, nested IF-THEN-ELSE instructions were discussed. To create a **nested WHILE-DO instruction**, the instruction part of the WHILE-DO is replaced by a WHILE-DO instruction. Consider the instructions in Figure 3–3.

Figure 3–3

```
NumberA := 1 ;
NumberB := 0 ;
WHILE NumberA < 5 DO
  WHILE NumberB < 3 DO
    BEGIN
      WRITE (NumberA, ' ', NumberB) ;
      NumberB := NumberB + 1 ;
      NumberA := NumberA + 2
    END ;
WRITELN ;
WRITELN ('That is it!')
```

Sample Execution

```
1□03□15□2

That is it!
```

The first two instructions initialize the variables `NumberA` and `NumberB`. The next instruction is a nested WHILE-DO instruction. The BOOLEAN expression `NumberA < 5` is evaluated to have a value of `TRUE`, so the instruction is executed. The instruction is itself a WHILE-DO instruction called the inner loop. The BOOLEAN expression `NumberB < 3` is evaluated. It has a value of `TRUE`, so the compound instruction

```
BEGIN
  WRITE (NumberA, ' ', NumberB) ;
  NumberB := NumberB + 1 ;
  NumberA := NumberA + 2
END
```

is executed. This compound instruction is executed while the BOOLEAN expression `NumberB < 3` has a value of `TRUE`. After the value is `FALSE`, the BOOLEAN expression `NumberA < 5` is evaluated. If it has a value of `TRUE`, the inner loop is executed again. If it is `FALSE`, the nested WHILE-DO loop is exited.

To understand (analyze) a collection of instructions like the ones in Figure 3–3, a walk through of the instructions is performed. A walk through chart is shown in Table 3–1 for the instructions in Figure 3–3.

Table 3–1

NumA	NumB	Output (to this point)
1	0	1□0
3	1	1□03□1
5	2	1□03□15□2
7	3	Inner WHILE-DO loop exited (**NumberB < 3 FALSE**) Outer WHILE-DO loop exited (**NumberA < 5 FALSE**)

DO IT NOW

1. Which of the following will result in an infinite loop?

   a.
   ```
   Count := 3 ;
   WHILE Count < 10 DO
      Count := Count + 1
   ```

   b.
   ```
   Count := 3 ;
   WHILE Count < 10 DO
      BEGIN
        WRITE (Count) ;
        Count := Count - 1
      END
   ```

   c.
   ```
   NumberA := 3 ;
   NumberB := 2 ;
   WHILE NumberA < > 6 DO
      BEGIN
        NumberA := NumberA + NumberB ;
        WRITE (NumberA)
      END
   ```

2. Give the output of the following instructions:

   ```
   NumberA := 1 ;
   WHILE NumberA < 5 DO
     BEGIN
       NumberB := 1 ;
       WHILE NumberB < 3 DO
         BEGIN
           WRITE (NumberA : 3 , NumberB : 3) ;
           NumberB := NumberB + 1
         END ;
       NumberA := NumberA + 3
     END ;
   WRITELN ;
   WRITELN ('That is it!')
   ```

3. Complete the following instructions so as to allow a user to enter a comment about each section (a maximum of 5) of each of the ten chapters of a textbook:

   ```
   Chapter := 1 ;
   WHILE Chapter <= 10 DO
     BEGIN
       Section := 1 ;
       MoreSections := TRUE ;
       WRITELN ('Chapter ', Chapter) ;
       WHILE (Section <= 5) AND MoreSections DO
         BEGIN
           WRITE (' Section ', Section);
           WRITE (' Enter comment: ') ;
           READLN (Comment) ;
           WRITE ('Enter N for next chapter, ') ;
           WRITE ('press RETURN to continue- ') ;
           READLN (Ans);
           IF Ans = 'N'
             THEN _____

           _____
         END ;

       _____
     END ;
   ```

DO IT NOW ANSWERS

1a. Ends when `Count` contains the value **10**.
 b. Endless, since `Count` never contains a value larger than **10**.
 c. Endless, since `NumberA` never contains the value **6**.

2.

Sample Execution

```
□□1□□1□□1□□2□□4□□1□□4□□2

That is it!
```

3.
```
        IF Ans = 'N'
           THEN MoreSections := FALSE ;
           Section := Section + 1
      END ;
   Chapter := Chapter + 1
END
```

3-1.6 Programming Example

To increase your understanding of nested WHILE-DO instructions, study the following example.

EXAMPLE

Write a Pascal program to accumulate the payroll for the employees of MR Creations Company. The program should allow the user to enter the number of hours worked for each employee for each day of the week. The pay rate is the same for all employees and is given by the table shown here. The program should output the pay for each employee and the total payroll for all employees.

Day	Rate
1 through 5	$ 8.00 per hour
6 and 7	$12.50 per hour

Sample Execution

```
Press RETURN for new employee (enter -1 to quit): <ret>
Enter hours for day1 (-1 to quit): 8
Enter hours for day2 (-1 to quit): 12
Enter hours for day3 (-1 to quit): -1
Pay for employee1 is $160.00
Press RETURN for new employee (enter -1 to quit): <ret>
Enter hours for day1 (-1 to quit): 0
Enter hours for day2 (-1 to quit): 3
Enter hours for day3 (-1 to quit): -1
Pay for employee2 is $24.00
Press RETURN for new employee (enter -1 to quit): -1

Total payroll is $184.00
```

SOLUTION

A design to solve the problem is as follows.

Day	Rate
1 through 5	$ 8.00 per hour
6 and 7	$12.50 per hour

Design: Initialize EmployNum and AllSal
           WHILE MoreEmployees DO
               Initialize EmploySal and DayNum
               WHILE NumHours > = 0 DO
                   Accumulate Employee Salary
                   READ hours worked
               WRITE Employee Salary
               Accumulate payroll
           WRITE payroll

Inner loop / Outer loop

COMMENT

From the design, we know a nested loop will be used. The outer loop keeps up with the employee number and the total of all the salaries. The inner loop keeps up with the days worked and the salary for a given employee. When an exit is made from the inner loop,

1. The salary for the employee is written to the screen.
2. EmploySal and DayNum are initalized back to their start values.
3. Payroll is increased

When an exit is made from the outer loop, the payroll for all employees is written to the screen.

Sample Execution

```
Press RETURN for new employee (enter -1 to quit): <ret>
Enter hours for day1 (-1 to quit): 8
Enter hours for day2 (-1 to quit): 12
Enter hours for day3 (-1 to quit): -1
Pay for employee1 is $160.00
Press RETURN for new employee (enter -1 to quit): <ret>
Enter hours for day1 (-1 to quit): 0
Enter hours for day2 (-1 to quit): 3
Enter hours for day3 (-1 to quit): -1
Pay for employee2 is $24.00
Press RETURN for new employee (enter -1 to quit): -1

Total payroll is $184.00
```

Refinement of: *outer loop*
                  WRITE (Press RETURN for new employee (− 1 to quit): ')
                  READLN (Ans)
                  WHILE Ans > = 0 DO
                      EmployNum : = EmployNum + 1
                      DayNum : = 1
                      EmploySal : = 0
                      Initialize NumHours
                      WHILE NumHours > = 0 DO
                          Accumulate Employee Salary
                          READ hours worked
                      WRITE ('Pay for employee' , EmployNum, 'is: $ ')
                      WRITELN (EmploySal :1 : 2)
                      AllSal : = AllSal + EmploySal
                      WRITE ('Press RETURN for new employee (− 1 to quit): ')
                      READLN (Ans)

COMMENT

The WHILE-DO is controlled by the sentinel −1. That is, when the user is finished entering employees, the value stored in Ans will be less than 0. Thus, an exit will be made from the outer WHILE-DO loop. Also, the user could choose not to enter values for any employees by entering −1 at the start.

Refinement of: *inner loop*
                  WRITE ('Enter hours for day', DayNum, ' (− 1 to quit): ')
                  READLN (NumHours)
                  WHILE NumHours > = 0 DO

```
IF DayNum > 5
   THEN EmploySal := EmploySal + 12.5*NumHours
   ELSE EmploySal := EmploySal + 8.0*NumHours
DayNum := DayNum + 1
WRITE ( 'Enter hours for day', DayNum, ' ( −1 to quit): ' )
READLN ( NumHours )
```

COMMENT
Again, −1 serves as a sentinel for the WHILE-DO loop. The user can quit entering hours worked for an employee by entering −1. Also, the user can use 0 hours worked for an employee by entering −1 at the start.

PROGRAMMING POINT

A useful technique in converting a design to a Pascal program is

1. Write the program header section.
2. Write the program execution section.
3. From the execution section, construct the VAR and CONST sections.

Using this technique, less time is wasted on undeclared indentifier errors at compile time.

Converting the design to a Pascal program yields the program in Figure 3–4.

Figure 3–4

```
PROGRAM EmploySal ;

VAR EmployNum, Ans, DayNum : INTEGER ;
    AllSal, EmploySal, NumHours : REAL ;

BEGIN
  EnployNum := Ø ;
  AllSal := Ø ;
  WRITE ('Press RETURN for new employee (-1 to quit): ') ;
  READLN (Ans) ;
  WHILE Ans >= Ø DO                              {the payroll}
    BEGIN
      EmployNum := EmployNum + 1 ;
      DayNum := 1 ;
      EmploySal := Ø ;
      WRITE ('Enter hours for day', DayNum, ' (-1 to quit): ') ;
      READLN (NumHours) ;
      WHILE NumHours >= Ø DO                     {an employee}
        BEGIN
          IF DayNum > 5
            THEN EmploySal := EmploySal + 12.5 * NumHours
            ELSE EmploySal := EmploySal + 8.Ø * NumHours ;
          DayNum := DayNum + 1 ;
          WRITE ('Enter hours for day', DayNum,' (-1 to quit): ') ;
          READLN (NumHours)
        END ;
      WRITE ('Pay for employee', EmployNum,' is $') ;   {output employee pay}
      WRITELN (EmploySal : 1 : 2) ;
      AllSal := AllSal + EmploySal ;              :   {accumulate payroll}
      WRITE ('Press RETURN for new employee (-1 to quit): ') ;
      READLN (Ans)
    END ;
  WRITELN ;
  WRITELN ('Total payroll is $', AllSal : 1 : 2)        {output payroll}
END .
```

Vocabulary

Page

124   **Accumulation loop**   A loop used to sum a collection of numbers.

127   **Compiler directives**   A comment to the compiler to have the Pascal program compiled with selected options. To invoke such a directive, a line such as

        `{$U+}`

is inserted (usually at the start) in the text of the Pascal program.

128   **Infinite loop**   A repetition (loop) that continues to execute an instruction over and over without end. When used in the context of WHILE-DO instructions, it means a WHILE-DO instruction where the instruction never causes the BOOLEAN expression to assume a value of `FALSE`.

123   **Initializing a variable**   The act of assigning a value to a variable to insure that the variable contains the proper value. This is especially important for variables used in BOOLEAN expressions.

129   **Nested WHILE-DO instruction**   A WHILE-DO instruction where the instruction is, itself, a WHILE-DO instruction.

125   **Sentinel**   A value used to signal the end of the execution of a loop.

128   **User interrupt directive**   A compiler directive that allows the user to stop the execution of the program by using Ctrl-C.

121   **Looping**   executing an instruction repeatedly.

122   **WHILE-DO instruction**   A control instruction that allows for repetition of an instruction. The form is

        `WHILE `*BOOLEAN expression*` DO`
         `< Instruction >`

The *BOOLEAN expression* is evaluated. If the value is `FALSE`, the program skips the Instruction. If the value is `TRUE`, the Instruction is executed. After the Instruction is executed, the *BOOLEAN expression* is evaluated again. The repetition will continue while the *BOOLEAN expression* has a value of `TRUE`.

Glad You Asked

Q   I tried to execute a Pascal program that contained the following instructions (with Count of type INTEGER):

```
Count := 0 ;
WHILE Count > -1 DO
  BEGIN
    WRITE (Count ,' ') ;
    Count := Count + 2
  END
```

I expected to get an infinite loop; however, after printing a lot of numbers, the program ended. Please explain.

A   The BOOLEAN expression `Count > -1` is always `TRUE` and should have led to an infinite loop. However, the variable `Count` cannot handle integers larger than MAXINT (32767). Thus, the assignment instruction `Count := Count + 2` made an assignment to the variable `Count` of `-MAXINT - 1` (`Count` contained `-32768`). This is often referred to as *wrap around*. When this assignment occurred, the BOOLEAN expression `Count > -1` assumed a value of `FALSE`, and the execution of the WHILE-DO instruction was completed. To obtain an infinite loop, try the program again using the BOOLEAN expression `Count < MAXINT`.

Q Our instructor mentioned something about syntax errors and semantic errors. I always thought errors were errors! What's the difference?

A *Syntax* has to do with the order in which elements are arranged. A syntax error in Pascal is an error dealing with the arrangement of the elements (this includes spelling errors). For example, writing

```
X := (3 + 2 * (X + 1)
```

or

```
DO Count := Count + 1 WHILE Count < 10
```

would be syntax errors, since in the first example a parenthesis is missing, and in the second example the elements are out of order. Syntax errors are usually found when the program is being compiled. Thus, they are sometimes called compile time errors.

    Semantics has to do with the meaning of statements. A semantic error in Pascal is an error dealing with the meaning of an instruction. That is, the meaning given the instruction by the Pascal language is not the meaning intended by the programmer. An example of a semantics error would be

```
WHILE NOT (Ch = 'Q') OR (Ch = 'E') DO
   READ (Ch)
```

Suppose the programmer meant to write an instruction where a value for the CHAR variable Ch would be read as long as the user did not enter the value Q or the value E. However, the BOOLEAN expression NOT (Ch = 'Q') OR (Ch = 'E') means (Ch < > 'Q') OR (Ch = 'E'). Thus, an entry of an E will not stop the loop. The programmer meant to write the BOOLEAN expression

```
NOT ((Ch = 'Q') OR (Ch = 'E'))
```

Semantics errors are more difficult to deal with, since they are not discovered until the program is executed. Semantics errors are often called execution errors or logic errors.

Q I really understood the "river" picture you gave for the IF-THEN-ELSE instruction. Do you have one for the WHILE-DO instruction?

A Sure. However, it is a little more complicated. The flow of instruction execution is down the river (InstructionA is executed). When the WHILE-DO instruction is encountered, the BOOLEAN expression is like a gate. If the BOOLEAN expression has value FALSE, the flow of instruction execution moves to InstructionC. If the BOOLEAN expression has value TRUE, the flow is channeled into the loop.

Duck!

Where?

Semantics error

```
<InstructionA> ;
WHILE BOOLEAN Expression DO
   <InstructionB> ;
<InstructionC>
```

Once the loop is entered, InstructionB is executed. The flow of instruction execution encounters the gate (the BOOLEAN expression) again. If the BOOLEAN expression is TRUE, the flow of instruction execution remains in the loop. If the BOOLEAN expression is FALSE (as a result of InstructionB), the flow of instruction returns to the river (InstructionC is executed).

Section 3–1 Exercises

1. Insert TRUE for a true statement. Insert FALSE for a false statement.
   _____ **a.** A variable used in the BOOLEAN expression of a WHILE-DO instruction should be initialized.
   _____ **b.** An instruction like

   ```
   WHILE Ct < 10 DO
       WRITELN ('Hello')
   ```

   is known as an infinite loop.
   _____ **c.** A nested WHILE-DO instruction is a WHILE-DO instruction where the instruction part is an IF-THEN-ELSE instruction.
   _____ **d.** There is always a limit on the number of times a WHILE-DO instruction will execute its instruction.
   _____ **e.** When the execution of the instruction

   ```
   WHILE Ch < > 'q' DO
       READ (Ch)
   ```

   is completed, the value in the variable Ch is Q.

2. Which of the following is a repetition control instruction?
   a. `READ (Ch)`
   b. `IF Ch < > 'a'`
       `THEN WRITE ('Bye')`
   c. `Ch := 'p'`
   d. `WHILE Ch < > 'q' DO`
       `READ (Ch)`
   e. `CASE Ch OF`
       `'a' : WRITE ('Bye') ;`
       `'b' : WRITE ('Hi')`
       `END`

3. The WHILE-DO instruction is used to control the flow of instruction execution by causing the _____ of the execution of an instruction.

4. A nested WHILE-DO instruction is a WHILE-DO instruction where the instruction part of the WHILE-DO instruction is a(n) _____ instruction.

5. An infinite loop results when the instruction part of the WHILE-DO instruction fails to cause the BOOLEAN expression to assume a value of _____.

6. Classify the following instructions by inserting *A* for assignment, *D* for decision control, and *R* for repetition control.
   _____ **a.** `Ch := 'A'`
   _____ **b.** `IF NumA < 5`
              `THEN WRITE (NumA)`
   _____ **c.** `WHILE NumA < 5 DO`
              `READ (NumA)`
   _____ **d.** `CASE NumA OF`
              `1, 2, 3 : WRITE (NumA) ;`
              `4, 5 : WRITE (-NumA)`
              `END`

7. Give the output of the following instructions.
   a.
   ```
   FibN := 0 ;
   FibF := 1 ;
   FibS := 1 ;
   WHILE FibN < 50 DO
     BEGIN
       FibN := FibF + FibS ;
       WRITE (' ', FibN) ;
       FibF := FibS ;
       FibS := FibN
     END
   ```
   b.
   ```
   Exp := 1 ;
   Base := 3 ;
   Power := Base ;
   WHILE Exp < 5 DO
     BEGIN
       Power := Base * Power ;
       Exp := Exp + 1
     END ;
   WRITE (Power)
   ```

8. Which of the following are infinite loops?

a.
```
Count := 1 ;
WHILE Count < > 8 DO
    Count := Count + 1
```

b.
```
Count := -3 ;
WHILE Count < 5 DO
    BEGIN
        WRITE (Count) ;
        IF Count < 5
            THEN Flag := TRUE
            ELSE Flag := FALSE
    END
```

9. Complete the following program. It should allow the input of a collection of positive numbers and output the largest value entered.

```
PROGRAM Largest ;

VAR InNum, Hold, : REAL ;
    Ch : CHAR ;

BEGIN
  Ch := ' ' ;
  Hold := Ø ;
  WHILE Ch < > 'Q' DO
    BEGIN
      WRITE ('Please enter a positive number: ') ;
      READLN (InNum) ;
      IF InNum > Hold
        THEN Hold := InNum ;

      _____
      _____
      _____
```

10. Alter the Pascal program written in problem 9 to accept as input a collection of names. The output is the name that is alphabetically first in the collection. A typical execution of the program might produce a screen like this:

Sample Execution

```
Please enter a name: John
Press RETURN key for another entry/ Q to quit: <ret>
Please enter a name: Alice
Press RETURN key for another entry/ Q to quit: <ret>
Please enter a name: Jose
Press RETURN key for another entry/ Q to quit: Q <ret>

The alphabetically first is: Alice
```

11. Boot up Pascal; set the workfile to the file **AVERNUM.PAS** from the Source diskette. Enter the Turbo Pascal editor. First, alter the program such that the user can enter Q or q to quit. Second, initialize Count to 1 (rather than Ø). Alter the program to handle this alteration (output the same results as before).

12. Boot up Pascal; set the workfile to the file **MRCREATE.PAS** from the Source diskette. Enter the Turbo Pascal editor. Expand the program to output the average salary of the employees.

13. An important area of mathematics and computers is approximation. The square root of a number can be approximated by use of the formula

```
Root = (Root + A / Root) / 2
```

where A is the number whose square root is sought and Root is the approximation. To use this method, a value is assigned to Root at the start (generally 1). The value of Root is refined by the formula until the desired accuracy is obtained. Complete the program below to approximate the square root of a positive number.

```
PROGRAM SqRoot ;

VAR Root, A : REAL ;

BEGIN
  WRITE ('Please enter a positive number: ') ;
  READLN (A) ;
  IF A > 0
    THEN
      BEGIN
        Root := 1 ;
        WHILE ABS (SQR (Root) - A) > 0.01 DO
          .
          .
          .
      END
    ELSE WRITE (A : 1 : 2, ' is not a positive number.')
END .
```

14. Walk through the instructions below. In doing so, complete the chart for each value the variables NumA and NumB take on.

```
NumA := 1 ;
NumB := 0 ;
WHILE NumA < 6 DO
  BEGIN
    WHILE NumB < 4 DO
      BEGIN
        NumB := NumB + 2 ;
        WRITE (NumB)
      END ;
    NumA := NumA + 3 ;
    WRITE (NumA)
  END
```

NumA	NumB	Output (to this point)
1	0	None (just initialized variables)
———	———	

15. In problem 14 above, remove the reserved words BEGIN and END from the inside (second) WHILE-DO instruction. Rewrite the resulting instructions based on the style rules. Give the output.

16. Complete the following Pascal program. It should allow the user to enter the base and exponent (a positive integer). The output is to be the base to the exponent power.

```
PROGRAM Power ;

VAR Exp, Count : INTEGER ;
    Base, Pow : REAL ;

BEGIN
  WRITE ('Please enter base for power: ') ;
  READLN (Base) ;
  WRITE ('Please enter exponent for power: ') ;
  READLN (Exp) ;
  Pow := 1 ;
  Count := 0 ;
  WHILE Count < Exp DO
    BEGIN

      _____
      _____

  _____

END .
```

Sample Execution

```
Please enter base for power:3
Please enter exponent for power:4
The result is: 81.00
```

Programming Problems

17. The manager at Shoe World has data on shoe sales organized in the following table form.

Item	Number Sold	Price/Item
Tennis	143	$45.78
Golf	56	$65.34
Soccer	203	$38.90

Write a Pascal program that allows the manager to enter the item name, number sold, and price/item. The program is to compute and accumulate the gross (number sold times price/item). The manager should be allowed to enter data while the item XXX is not entered. Once the item XXX is entered, the program is to output the gross of all the sales.

Sample Execution

```
Enter item name (XXX to quit): Tennis
Enter number of items sold: 143
Enter price per item: $45.78
Enter item name (XXX to quit): Golf
Enter number of items sold: 56
Enter price per item: $65.34
Enter item name (XXX to quit): XXX

Gross for all sales is $10205.58
```

18. A student's GPA (grade point average) is computed by finding the total number of quality points, then dividing by the total number of credit hours. For example, suppose Jose takes the following courses with the indicated results:

Course	Credit Hours	Grade	Quality Points
Math	3	C	3*2 = 6
Chemistry	4	B	4*3 = 12
Speech	2	A	2*4 = 8
Total credit hours	9	Total quality points	26

Thus, Jose has a GPA of 26/9, or 2.89. Write a Pascal program that allows a student to input a course, credit hours for the course, and grade received. The program should allow such input while (as long as) the student wishes to enter data. The program should write to the screen the total number of hours taken, the total number of quality points earned, and the student's GPA for the courses (accurate to two decimal places).

Sample Execution

```
Please enter course name: Math
Enter credit hours for math: 3
Enter grade earned: C
Press RETURN to continue, enter Q to quit: <ret>
Please enter course name: Chemistry
```

19. The binary (base two) numbering system is a system with only two digits: 0 and 1. Each place value in this system is a power of 2. That is, the binary number **10010** yields **1*16 + 0*8 + 0*4 + 1*2 + 0*1**, or 18, in the decimal (base ten) numbering system. A problem that is often the bane of many students is converting a decimal number to a binary number. This problem can be solved with the following design:

```
Get positive integer value
WHILE Value > 0 DO
    WRITE ( Value MOD 2 )
    Value := Value DIV 2
```

However, the number written is the binary name reversed. Use this design to write a Pascal program that allows the user to input a positive integer. The program is to write to the screen the reversed binary number name for the input value.

Sample Execution

```
Please enter positive integer (1 ... 32000): 47
The binary name (reversed) is: 111101
```

COMMENT
The user would now have to interpret the results as follows:
The binary name for **47** is **101111**. Later in the course you will get the opportunity to complete this problem.

20. A mil is 0.001 of an inch. Suppose a piece of notebook paper is 6 mils thick. If the paper is folded, the new thickness is 12 mils. If it is folded again, the thickness is 24 mils. Write a Pascal program that allows the user to input the number of times to fold the paper. The output will be the resulting thickness in miles.
Hint: 1000 mils = 1 inch; 12 inches = 1 foot; 5280 feet = 1 mile.

Sample Execution

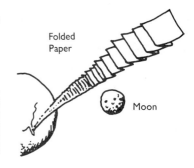

Folded Paper

Moon

```
Please enter number of times to fold paper: 50
Thickness would be 1.0661900000E+08 miles.
```

Section 3–2

REPEAT-UNTIL

In the last section, to repeat the execution of an instruction you used the Pascal control instruction WHILE-DO. In this section, you will study another instruction that allows repeated execution of an instruction. This instruction, REPEAT-UNTIL, is closely related to WHILE-DO.

3-2.1 REPEAT-UNTIL Loops

The WHILE-DO and the **REPEAT-UNTIL** instructions have the forms shown.

Figure 3–5

```
WHILE BOOLEAN expression DO
    < Instruction >
```

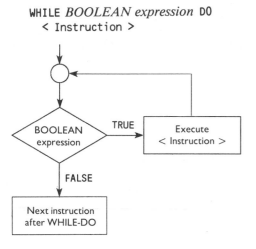

Figure 3–6

```
REPEAT
    < Instruction(s) >
UNTIL BOOLEAN expression
```

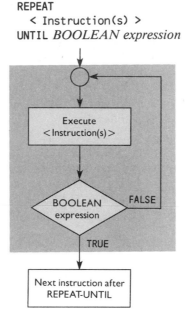

The list of instructions between the words REPEAT and UNTIL are executed. The BOOLEAN expression is evaluated. If it has the value **FALSE**, the list of instructions are executed again. If it has the value **TRUE**, the next instruction (if one exists) after the REPEAT-UNTIL instruction is executed.

The REPEAT-UNTIL instruction will execute the instruction(s) between the Pascal reserved words REPEAT and UNTIL until the *BOOLEAN expression* has the value `TRUE`. Since the words REPEAT and UNTIL bracket the instruction(s) to be repeated, there is no need to use BEGIN and END to bracket the instructions.

The following is an example of the use of the REPEAT-UNTIL instruction:

```
Count := 1 ;
Base := 3 ;
Power := 1 ;
REPEAT
  Power := Power * Base ;
  Count := Count + 1
UNTIL Count = 5 ;
WRITELN ( 'Three to the fifth power is: ', Power : 1 )
```

COMMENT
This is an example of exponentiation in Pascal.

Walking through this instruction yields the information shown in Table 3–2. The output of these instructions is `Three to the fifth power is 81`

Table 3–2

	Power	Count	Test (Count = 5)
At start	1	1	FALSE
First pass	3	2	FALSE
Second pass	9	3	FALSE
Third pass	27	4	TRUE
Fourth pass	81	5	Exit REPEAT-UNTIL

These instructions show an example of the *off-by-one* design error; indeed 3^5 is not 81 but 243. The problem here is that when `Count` contains 5 the instruction `Power := Power * Base` has been executed only four times. This is a common semantics error in programming, that can be overcome with experience and testing. To correct the error in this collection of instructions, the variable `Count` should be initialized to 0.

Comparing the WHILE-DO and REPEAT-UNTIL loop control instructions yields the following:

1. The WHILE-DO may or may not execute its instruction. The REPEAT-UNTIL always executes the instruction at least once.
2. The WHILE-DO will execute the instruction *while* the BOOLEAN expression has the value `TRUE`. The REPEAT-UNTIL will execute the instruction *until* the BOOLEAN expression has the value `TRUE` (that is, while the BOOLEAN expression is `FALSE`).

The major difference between the instructions is that the REPEAT-UNTIL executes the instruction, then runs the test (called a *post-test*); the WHILE-DO runs the test before executing the instruction. That is, the WHILE-DO runs a *pretest*.

EXAMPLE

Write the following WHILE-DO instruction as a REPEAT-UNTIL instruction.

```
Count := Ø ;
WHILE Count < 1Ø DO
  BEGIN
    WRITE ('Hello') ;
    Count := Count + 2
  END
```

Walk Through

Count	Output
Ø	Hello
2	HelloHello
4	HelloHelloHello
6	HelloHelloHelloHello
8	HelloHelloHelloHelloHello
1Ø	

SOLUTION

```
Count := Ø ;
REPEAT
  WRITE ('Hello') ;
  Count := Count + 2
UNTIL Count = 1Ø
```

Walk Through

Count	Output
Ø	Hello
2	HelloHello
4	HelloHelloHello
6	HelloHelloHelloHello
8	HelloHelloHelloHelloHello
1Ø	

Figure 3–7

The REPEAT-UNTIL instruction is boxed as follows:

1. The word REPEAT starts the REPEAT-UNTIL box.
2. Following the word REPEAT, an instruction is sought and boxed.
3. If another instruction is found, it is boxed.
4. Step 3 is repeated until the word UNTIL is found.
5. Following the word UNTIL, a BOOLEAN expression is sought.
6. The BOOLEAN expression is enclosed in a box.
7. The REPEAT-UNTIL box is closed.

```
REPEAT
  WRITE (Count : 3) ;
  Sum := Sum + Count ;
  WRITELN (' Sum is ' , Sum) ;
  Count := Count + 2
UNTIL Count = 1Ø
```

As you can see in Figure 3–7, the only adjacent boxes are the instruction boxes, so the only semicolons required are the ones to separate the instructions. Of course, if there is an instruction after the REPEAT-UNTIL instruction, a semicolon will be needed to separate the instructions.

DO IT NOW

1. Give the output of the following instructions if
   (a) −1234 is entered for InNum; (b) 14567 is entered for InNum.

```
BEGIN
  NumOfDigits := Ø ;
  READLN (InNum) ;
  REPEAT
    InNum := InNum DIV 1Ø ;
    NumOfDigits := NumOfDigits + 1
  UNTIL InNum = Ø ;
  WRITELN (NumOfDigits : 1)
END
```

2. Box the compound instruction in problem 1.

3. Write a compound instruction to find the sum of the even numbers less than 100. Use a REPEAT-UNTIL instruction. Assume that EvenNum and Sum have been declared as variables of type INTEGER.

DO IT NOW ANSWERS

1a. 4   b. 5

2.
```
BEGIN
   NumOfDigits := 0 ;
   READLN (InNum) ;
   REPEAT
      InNum := InNum DIV 10 ;
      NumOfDigits := NumOfDigits + 1
   UNTIL InNum = 0 ;
   WRITELN (NumOfDigits : 1)
END
```

3.
```
BEGIN
   Sum := 0 ;
   EvenNum := 0 ;
   REPEAT
      Sum := Sum + EvenNum ;
      EvenNum := EvenNum + 2
   UNTIL EvenNum > 98
END
```

3-2.2 *Interactive Programs*

The REPEAT-UNTIL repetition control instruction is usually used in situations where the programmer *knows* the instructions will be executed at least once. One such situation is with an **interactive program**—one that requires input from a user. Interactive programs use the keyboard to obtain data from the user. The screen is often used to output the results of the program. Most of the programs you have seen up to this point have been interactive programs. Since these programs deal with the screen, a method of clearing the screen is needed. The built-in procedure **CLRSCR** is used to clear the screen and place the cursor at the top of the screen.

As an illustration of this use of the REPEAT-UNTIL instruction, consider the following problem.

PROBLEM

Write a Pascal program that allows the user to select from the following menu:

A. Find square
B. Find square root
C. Find cube
D. Quit

After the selection is made, a number is entered by the user. The output is to be the result of the operation selected by the user. This process will continue until the user selects option D.

Sample Execution

```
A. Find square
B. Find square root
C. Find cube
D. Quit
Please select from above list (enter A,B,C,D): B
Please enter number: 15.68
The square root of 15.68 is 3.96
Press RETURN key to continue-
{screen clears and instructions are repeated until user wants to quit}
```

SOLUTION

After thinking about the problem, write a design for its solution.

Design: REPEAT
      Clear the screen
      Present the menu
      WRITE (Please select ....)
      READLN (Choice)
      WRITE (Please enter number)
      READLN (Number)
      CASE Choice OF
         'A' : WRITE (The square of , Number : 1 : 2)
            WRITELN (is, SQR(Number) : 1 : 2)
         'B' : WRITE (The square root of, Number : 1 : 2)
            WRITELN (is, SQRT (Number) : 1 : 2)
         'C' : Cube : = Number∗Number∗Number
            WRITE (The cube of, Number : 1 : 2)
            WRITELN (is, Cube : 1 : 2)
      END
      UNTIL Choice = 'D'

The next step in solving the problem is to test the design. That is, the programmer walks through the design with various inputs. Such a walk through follows:

- Execute program.
- Screen clears.
- Menu appears.
- Menu selection requested.
- User enters B.
- Number input requested.
- User enters −13.5.
- Second selection of the CASE instruction is executed.
- The square root of −13.5 is written to the screen.
- An attempt is made to find SQRT (− 13.5): <<<<ERROR>>>> .

The programmer, in testing the design, tries situations most likely to produce errors. The error here in the design is fixed, and the testing continues. Another design error found in walking through this design is that after the information is output, the screen clears before the user can see the information.

Once the design has been corrected and retested, the next step is to convert the design to a Pascal program. Such a conversion is presented in Figure 3–8.

COMMENT

Yet another design error is found upon testing the program MenuExample after it has been compiled. When the user selected 'D' to quit, the program still requested a number. Thus, the IF-THEN instruction is employed for the entry of the number. This error should have been found in the testing of the design (it simply was not found).

Figure 3–8

```
PROGRAM MenuExample ;

CONST Blank = ' ' ;

VAR Choice , Ans : CHAR ;
    Number , Cube : REAL ;

BEGIN
  REPEAT
    CLRSCR ;
    WRITELN ('A. Find Square') ;
    WRITELN ('B. Find Square root') ;
    WRITELN ('C. Find Cube') ;
    WRITELN ('D. Quit') ;
    WRITELN ;
    WRITE ('Please select from above list (enter A,B,C,D): ') ;
    READLN (Choice) ;
    IF Choice < > 'D'
      THEN
        BEGIN
          WRITELN ('Please enter number: ') ;
          READLN (Number) ;
          CASE Choice OF
           'A' : BEGIN
                   WRITE ('The square of ' , Number : 1 : 2) ;
                   WRITELN (' is ' , SQR (Number) : 1 : 2)
                 END ;
           'B' : IF Number < 0
                   THEN WRITELN ('Entry must be positive.')
                   ELSE BEGIN
                         WRITE ('The square root of ', Number : 1 : 2) ;
                         WRITE (' is ' , SQRT (Number) : 1 : 2)
                       END ;
           'C' : BEGIN
                   Cube := Number*Number*Number ;
                   WRITE ('The cube of ' , Number : 1 : 2) ;
                   WRITELN (' is ' , Cube : 1 : 2)
                 END
          END ;
          WRITE ('Press RETURN key to continue-') ;   {let user see screen}
          READLN (Ans)
        END
  UNTIL Choice = 'D'
END .
```

As a program gets longer, it gets harder to read when all the instructions are placed in the execution block. In the next chapter, a method of breaking up the program into more manageable pieces (called modules) will be presented. The use of modules is the essence of the Pascal language.

DO IT NOW

1. In the program MenuExample (Figure 3–6), there is only one instruction in the execution block, the REPEAT-UNTIL instruction. This instruction calls for the repetition of how many instructions?
2. If the user selects C from the menu and enters −4 for Number, what will be the output of the CASE-OF-END instruction?
3. If the user selects B from the menu and enters −9 for Number, what will be the output of the CASE-OF-END instruction?

3-2.3 User Input

Before finishing this section, the user rules discussed in Section 1–3 need to be expanded. The first two user rules dealt with prompts to the user. The next user rule deals with user anxiety.

USER RULE 3 Any time an instruction results in no output for an extended period of time, the user should be warned.

This user rule is designed to relieve user anxiety about whether the program has entered an error state. If it is known ahead of time that an instruction will take a long time to execute and that no output will be produced during this time, a message should appear to that effect on the screen. Suppose your program contains an instruction such as rolling a pair of dice until a sum of 12 is reached. An instruction to accomplish this is

```
REPEAT
  DieA := RANDOM (6) + 1 ;
  DieB := RANDOM (6) + 1 ;
  Sum := DieA + DieB
UNTIL Sum = 12
```

When this instruction executes, the CPU will process the assignment instructions until the value in Sum is 12. This could take some time. While the instruction is being executed, the user often thinks the program has an error. A simple way to avoid this user anxiety is to insert a line such as

```
WRITELN ('This will take some time-')
```

prior to entering the REPEAT-UNTIL instruction. Another way would be to insert an instruction in the REPEAT-UNTIL instruction such as

```
WRITE ('*')
```

Now, on each pass through the loop, the character '*' is written to the screen. Thus, the user knows the program is still working.

The other user rule we will discuss at this time deals with user input to the program.

USER RULE 4 Any time a program requests input from the user, the program must screen the input for errors.

Consider the following instructions:

```
WRITELN ('Please enter a positive number: ') ;
READLN (Num) ;
Results := SQRT (Num)
```

If the user enters the value −6 to the prompt, an error will occur and the execution of the program will stop. To avoid situations like this, the following instructions could be employed:

Sample Execution

```
Please enter a positive number: -6
Number must be positive.
Please enter a positive number:
```

```
REPEAT
  WRITELN ('Please enter a positive number: ') ;
  READLN (Num) ;
  IF Num <= 0
    THEN WRITELN ('Number must be positive.')
UNTIL Num > 0 ;
Results := SQRT (Num)
```

This type of instruction is often referred to as an error-trapping instruction. Not only does it check the user's input; it also presents the user with a message about the nature of the problem.

COMMENT

User Rules 3 and 4 were presented at this time, since they both involve loops. You are not yet ready to fully implement User Rule 4. For example, suppose the user enters the character 'a' to the prompt

```
Please enter a positive number:
```

Even with the error-trapping instruction, the program execution will halt with a type-conflict error. Later, you will be introduced to some techniques to use to avoid this situation.

Vocabulary

Page		
144	**CLRSCR**	The built-in procedure CLRSCR is used to clear the screen.
144	**Interactive program**	A program that requires input from a user. Usually, the input is from the keyboard.
141	**REPEAT-UNTIL instruction**	A repetition control instruction in Pascal. The form is

```
REPEAT
  < Instruction(s) >
UNTIL BOOLEAN expression
```

The instruction(s) bracketed by the words REPEAT and UNTIL will be repeated until the BOOLEAN expression has the value TRUE. The instruction(s) will be executed at least once.

Glad You Asked

Q What would the REPEAT-UNTIL instruction look like in terms of the "river" picture you gave for the IF-THEN-ELSE and WHILE-DO instructions?

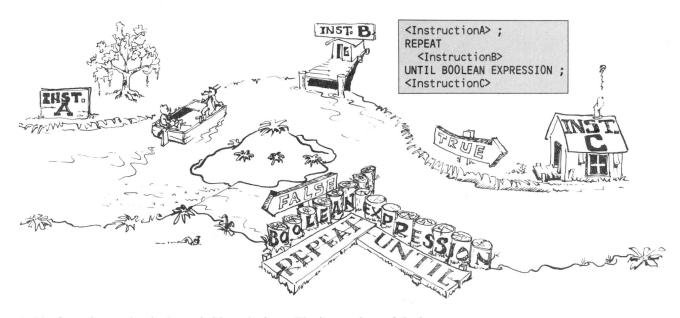

```
<InstructionA> ;
REPEAT
   <InstructionB>
UNTIL BOOLEAN EXPRESSION ;
<InstructionC>
```

A The flow of execution is channeled into the loop. The instructions of the loop are executed. The BOOLEAN expression acts as a gate. If it has the value **TRUE**, the flow of execution continues on down the river. If it has the value **FALSE**, the flow of execution goes around the island again.

Q IF-THEN-ELSE, CASE-OF-END, WHILE-DO, REPEAT-UNTIL . . . why have all of these? A friend who knows Pascal says she just uses IF-THEN-ELSE and WHILE-DO. Do I really need to know these other instructions?

A The most often used decision control instruction is IF-THEN-ELSE. The most often used repetition control instruction is WHILE-DO. These two are the important ones, and you must know them. However, the idea of the Pascal language is to provide the programmer with a set of tools. These tools are used to construct a program that mirrors the design of the problem's solution. The main idea is to use the right tool for the job. In an interactive program such as the one presented in this section, REPEAT-UNTIL was the right tool for repeating the instructions. This is because the instructions were to be executed at least once. Thus, the use of the REPEAT-UNTIL instruction allowed the program to match the problem solution design.

Section 3–2 Exercises

1. The WHILE-DO and REPEAT-UNTIL instructions are known as _____ control instructions.
2. For a REPEAT-UNTIL instruction, the instructions will be executed until the BOOLEAN expression has the value _____.
3. A program requiring input from the program's user is called a(n) _____ program.

4. Insert TRUE for a true statement, and FALSE for a false statement.
_____ **a.** The instruction of a WHILE-DO instruction will be executed at least once.
_____ **b.** The instructions to be repeated in a REPEAT-UNTIL instruction must be bracketed with BEGIN and END.
_____ **c.** `Number MOD 4`, where `Number` is of type INTEGER, could be used for a BOOLEAN expression in a REPEAT-UNTIL instruction.
_____ **d.** The REPEAT-UNTIL instruction is a post-test instruction.
_____ **e.** Any WHILE-DO instruction can be replaced by a REPEAT-UNTIL instruction.
_____ **f.** Any REPEAT-UNTIL instruction can be replaced by a WHILE-DO instruction.
_____ **g.** The terms *loop instruction* and *repetition instruction* refer to the same type of instruction.

5. Give the output of the following.

a.
```
Total := 0 ;
Count := 0 ;
REPEAT
  Count := Count + 2 ;
  Total := Total + Count
UNTIL Count > 10 ;
WRITELN (Total)
```

b.
```
Sum := 0 ;
Count:= 1 ;
REPEAT
  IF Count MOD 2 = 0
    THEN Sum := Sum + Count ;
  Count := Count + 1
UNTIL Count = 5 ;
WRITELN (Sum)
```

6. Find the error(s) in the following effort to find the sum of the numbers 1, 2, 3, . . . , 99, 100.

```
Count := 1 ;
REPEAT
  Count := Count + 1 ;
  Total := Total + Count
UNTIL Count = 100 ;
WRITELN (Total)
```

7. Box the following instruction:

```
REPEAT
  WRITE ('Please enter a positive number (-1 to quit): ') ;
  READLN (Number) ;
  IF Number >= 0
    THEN
      BEGIN
        WRITE ('The square root is: ') ;
        WRITELN (SQRT (Number) : 1 : 3)
      END
UNTIL Number < 0
```

8. Rewrite the following program using the style rules:

```
program power ; var base , exponent, count : integer ; results : real;
begin write ('Enter base for power: ') ; readln (base) ;
write ('Enter exponent for power: ') ; readln (exponent) ; Results := 1;
Count := 0;
repeat results := results * base ; count := count + 1 until
count >= exponent ; write ('Power is: '); writeln (results : 1 : 1) end.
```

9. Complete the following Pascal program. It should allow the user to enter a series of positive numbers separated by a blank space. The output is to be the largest value entered, the smallest value entered, and the average of the numbers entered.

Sample Execution

```
Enter a series of positive numbers (enter -1 to quit):
13 15 16 8 87 38.3 -1
The largest was 87
The smallest was 8
The average was 29.55
```

```pascal
PROGRAM MaxMinAv ;

CONST Big = 1E20 ;

VAR Number , Max , Min , Sum : REAL ;
    Count : INTEGER ;
BEGIN
  Max := 0 ;
  Min := Big ;
  WRITELN ('Enter a series of positive numbers (-1 to quit): ');
  Count := 0 ;
  Sum := 0 ;
  REPEAT
    READ (Number) ;
    IF Number >= 0
      THEN
        BEGIN
          IF Number > Max
            THEN Max := Number ;
          _____
  UNTIL Number < 0 ;
  WRITELN ('The largest value was: ', Max) ;
  _____
END .
```

WARNING
User must press the RETURN key to terminate the input of a number.

10. Boot up Pascal; set the workfile to the file **MENUEX.PAS** from the **Source** diskette. Enter the Turbo Pascal editor. Alter the program instructions to match the following design:

```
REPEAT
    ClearScreen
    PresentMenu
    GetSelection
    CASE Choice OF
        'A' : DoSquare
        'B' : DoSquareRoot
        'C' : DoCube
        'D' : QUIT
    END
UNTIL Choice = 'D'
```

Each of the selections **'A'**, **'B'**, and **'C'** should include a request for a number. For selection **'B'**, the request should be repeated until the user enters a non-negative value.

Programming Problems

11a. (Random numbers) Write a Pascal program that allows the user to input an integer from 1 to 6 inclusive. The program will then simulate the rolling of a die until the input value is obtained. The program should execute until the user is ready to quit. Remember, start with a design.

Sample Execution

```
Please enter number (1 . . . 6): 5
A die is being rolled . . .
It took 3 rolls to reach a 5.
Enter Q to QUIT. Press RETURN key for another trial.
```

b. Expand your program to allow the user to find the average number of rolls to reach the input value.

Sample Execution

```
Please enter number (1 . . 6): 3
Please enter number of trials to run (1 . . 1000): 100
Please wait ...
The average number of rolls to obtain a 3 was 2.456
```

12. Write a Pascal program that allows the user to select an option from the following menu.

A. Generate a new value
B. Report average to this point
C. Report highest value to this point.
Q. Quit

If option A is selected, the program is to generate and report a random number from 0 to 99.

If option B is selected, the program is to write to the screen the average of all the numbers generated.

If option C is selected, the program is to write to the screen the largest value of all the numbers generated.

If option Q is selected, the program is to write to the screen the number of values generated, the sum of the values generated, the average of the values generated, and the largest value generated. The program execution will then stop.

After each option, the program is to request that user press the RETURN key. After the RETURN key is pressed, the screen is to be cleared and the menu presented.

Sample Execution

```
A.  Generate a new value
B.  Report average to this point
C.  Report highest value to this point
Q.  Quit

Please enter A,B,C, or Q:  A
New value generated is 78
Press RETURN key to continue-
```

13. Write a Pascal program that allows the user to select a range of positive integers. A number is selected at random from the range. The user is to enter a "guess" as to the mystery number. The user is then given a report of "Too large," "Too small," or "You guessed it!" The guessing is to be repeated until the user guesses the number or enters 0 to quit. Remember, start with a design.

Sample Execution

```
Enter positive integer for maximum value: 100 <ret>
Enter positive integer for minimum value: 1 <ret>
Random number is being selected.
Enter guess for mystery number: 40 <ret>
Too large (press RETURN key or enter 0 to quit): <ret>
Enter guess for mystery number: 30 <ret>
Too large (press RETURN key or enter 0 to quit): <ret>
Enter guess for mystery number: 23 <ret>
Too small (press RETURN key or enter 0 to quit): 0 <ret>
The mystery number was 26.
```

Hint: RANDOM ((Maximum – Minimum + 1)) + Minimum will yield the mystery number.

14. On the planet Zephod, which orbits the star Betelgeuse, the sharks increase at a rate of 5% of the guppy population per day, provided there are 50 or more guppies per shark. Otherwise, the sharks die off at a rate of 50% per day. The guppies increase at a rate of 80% per day, provided the shark population is less than 20% of the guppy population. Otherwise there is no increase in the guppy population. Each shark eats five guppies a day. Write a Pascal program that allows the user to input the initial shark population, the initial guppy population, and the number of days the observation is to cover. The program is to output a day-by-day account of the populations until one species dies off or the end of the observation period is reached. All reproductions and deaths occur overnight. Any fractional fish are discarded. (These sharks only feed during the day.)

Sample Execution

```
Please enter number of sharks: 54
Please enter number of guppies: 1000
Number of days to observe: 15
End of day 1    sharks 54    guppies 730
Start of day 2  sharks 27    guppies 1314
_____        _____     _____
```

COMMENT
Use integer arithmetic. This is, to compute 80% of a value, use 80 * Value DIV 100 rather than 0.8 * Value .

FOR-DO

Up to this point, to repeat the execution of an instruction, you have used the Pascal control instruction WHILE-DO and the Pascal control instruction REPEAT-UNTIL. In this section, you will study the last of the control instructions that allow for repeated execution of instructions. This instruction is the FOR-DO instruction. It allows for specifying the number of times an instruction is to be repeated.

3–3.1 Introduction to FOR-DO

To introduce the **FOR-DO instruction,** consider the following:

```
FOR Count := 2 TO 5 DO
   WRITE (Count : 3)
```

Sample Execution

```
  2  3  4  5
```

The variable `Count` is known as the **loop control variable (lcv)** since its value determines when the repetition will end.

When this instruction executes, the loop control variable `Count` will be assigned the value 2. The instruction `WRITE (Count : 3)` will be executed. The value in the variable `Count` is increased to the next value (**incremented** to the value 3). The instruction `WRITE (Count : 3)` will be executed. This process continues until the value in `Count` is greater than 5. At that point, the execution of the instruction is completed, and the next instruction (if there is one) after the FOR-DO instruction is executed.

The general form of this repetition control instruction follows:

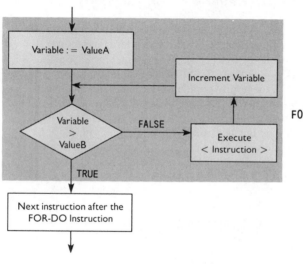

```
FOR Variable := ValueA TO ValueB DO
   < Instruction >
```

Variable, ValueA, and ValueB must be of type INTEGER, CHAR, or BOOLEAN. The data types REAL and STRING are not allowed.

To understand the FOR-DO instruction, consider the following list of instructions:

```
Total := 0 ;
FOR Count := 1 TO 5 DO
   BEGIN
      READLN (Score) ;
      Total := Total + Score
   END ;
WRITELN ('Average is: ', Total / 5 : 1 : 3)
```

Sample Execution

```
5
3
7
2
8
Average is: 5.000
```

The FOR-DO instruction does the following:

1. `Count` is assigned the value 1.
2. `Count` is then compared to the value 5. If `Count` is greater than 5, then the FOR-DO instruction is finished.
3. A value for `Score` is read, and `Total` is increased by the value in `Score`.
4. `Count` is incremented (increased to the next value).
5. Steps 2, 3, and 4 are repeated until `Count` takes on a value greater than 5. That is, the loop is exited at Step 2.

A walk through for a possible execution of this FOR-DO instruction is shown in Table 3–3.

Count	Count < 5	Score	Total
1	FALSE	5	5
2	FALSE	3	8
3	FALSE	7	15
4	FALSE	2	17
5	FALSE	8	25
6	TRUE	Instruction finished (loop exited)	

Table 3–3

The FOR-DO instruction is boxed as follows:

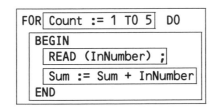

Figure 3–9

1. The word FOR starts the FOR-DO box.
2. Following the word FOR, an assignment instruction, the word TO, and a value are sought and enclosed in a box.
3. The word DO is sought.
4. Following the word DO, an instruction is sought and boxed.
5. The FOR-DO box is closed.

As you can see in Figure 3–9, the only adjacent boxes in the FOR-DO instruction are those that appear in the Instruction. Thus, the FOR-DO instruction itself requires no semicolons.

The FOR-DO repetition control instruction is used when the programmer knows exactly how many times the instruction is to be executed. The number of times the instruction is executed depends on the values listed in the following line:

`FOR Variable := ValueA TO ValueB`

1. If ValueA is greater than ValueB, then the instruction of the FOR-DO is *not* executed.
2. If ValueA is equal to ValueB, then the instruction of the FOR-DO is executed exactly once.
3. If ValueA is less than ValueB, then the instruction of the FOR-DO is executed ValueB − ValueA + 1 times (when the values are of type INTEGER).

DO IT NOW

1. For the following FOR-DO instruction,

```
FOR Value := 4 TO 8 DO
  WRITE (2 * Value : 3)
```

   a. The loop control variable is _____.
   b. The instruction `WRITE (2 * Value : 3)` will be executed _____ times.
   c. The output will be _____.
2. For the following FOR-DO instruction,

```
FOR Letter := 'a' TO 'e' DO
  WRITE (Letter : 3)
```

   a. The loop control variable is _____.
   b. The instruction `WRITE (Letter : 3)` will be executed _____ times.
   c. The output will be _____.
3. Write the following using a FOR-DO instruction:

```
Count := 0 ;
WHILE Count < 12 DO
  BEGIN
    WRITE ('The square of ', Count : 1) ;
    WRITELN (' is ', SQR (Count)) ;
    Count := Count + 1
  END
```

DO IT NOW ANSWERS

```
1a. Value    b. (8 − 1) + 1, or 5    c. □□8□10□12□14□16
2a. Letter    b. 5    c. □□a□□b□□c□□d□□e
3. FOR Count := 0 TO 11 DO
   BEGIN
     WRITE ('The square of ', Count : 1) ;
     WRITELN (' is ', SQR (Count))
   END
```

3–3.2 Extensions

It is now time to consider some extensions to the FOR-DO instruction. First, ValueA and ValueB can be any valid expression of the same data type as Variable. That is, the FOR-DO instruction could be used as in the following list of instructions:

```
WRITE ('Please enter base:') ;
READLN (Base) ;
WRITE ('Please enter exponent:') ;
READLN (Exponent);
Power := 1 ;
FOR Count := 1 TO Exponent DO
  Power := Power * Base ;
WRITELN ('The power is: ', Power)
```

Sample Execution

```
Please enter base: 3
Please enter exponent: 4
The power is: 81
```

Here, ValueB is the value in the variable Exponent. A walk through of the FOR-DO instruction where 3 has been entered for Base and 4 has been entered for Exponent is shown in Table 3–4.

Count	Base	Exponent	Power	Count > Exponent	Table 3–4
1	3	4	1 * 3 = 3	FALSE	
2	3	4	3 * 3 = 9	FALSE	
3	3	4	9 * 3 = 27	FALSE	
4	3	4	27 * 3 = 81	FALSE	
5	3	4	81	TRUE (loop exited)	

A second extension to the FOR-DO instruction is in the form that it can assume. Consider the following form:

```
FOR Variable := ValueA DOWNTO ValueB DO
    < Instruction >
```

In this form, rather than the loop control variable's being incremented (increased to the next value), it is **decremented** (decreased to the preceding value). An example of this form follows:

```
FOR Ch := 'Z' DOWNTO 'A' DO
    WRITE (Ch)
```

The output of this instruction will be ZYXWVUTSRQPONMLKJIHGFEDCBA

DO IT NOW

1. For each of the following instructions, state the number of times the Instruction will be repeated.
   a. `FOR Ch := 'a' TO 'e' DO`
      `< Instruction >`
   b. `FOR Num := 9 DOWNTO 5 DO`
      `< Instruction >`
   c. `FOR Ct := 3 TO 3 DO`
      `< Instruction >`
2. Write a Pascal program that has as input a whole number less than 10,000. The output of the program is to be the divisors of the number. A possible design follows:

```
REPEAT
   GetNumber
   IF SizeOk                                    {number less than 10,000}
   THEN
      BEGIN
         WRITELN ( 'The divisors are: 1 ' )
         FOR Count : = 2 TO ROUND (SQRT ( Number )) DO
            IF InNum MOD Count = 0
               THEN WRITE ( Count : 1, ' ' )
         WRITELN ( ' and ', Number )
      END
   WRITE ( 'Do you want to do another number? (Y/N): ' )
   READLN ( Ans )
UNTIL user wants to quit
```

DO IT NOW ANSWERS

1a. Five times.   b. Five times.   c. One time.

2.
```
PROGRAM Divisors ;

  VAR InNum, Count : INTEGER ;
      Ans : CHAR ;

  BEGIN
    REPEAT
      WRITE ('Enter whole number less than 10,000: ') ;
      READLN (InNum) ;
      IF InNum < 10000
        THEN BEGIN
               WRITE ('The divisors are: 1 ') ;
               FOR Count := 2 TO ROUND (SQRT ( InNum )) DO
                 IF InNum MOD Count = 0
                   THEN WRITE (Count : 1 ,' ') ;
               WRITELN (' and ', InNum)
             END ;
      WRITELN ;
      WRITE ('Enter Q to QUIT- ') ;
      WRITE ('Press RETURN key for another number') ;
      READLN (Ans)
    UNTIL Ans = 'Q'
  END .
```

3-3.3 Nested FOR-DO Loops

A nested FOR-DO instruction is one that contains a FOR-DO instruction in its instruction. An example of a nested FOR-DO loop follows:

```
FOR Outer := 1 TO 2 DO              Sample Execution
  FOR Inner := 'A' TO 'C' DO
    WRITE (Inner)                   ┌─────────────────────┐
                                    │  ABCABC             │
                                    └─────────────────────┘
```

A walk through this nested FOR-DO instruction is shown in Table 3-5.

Table 3-5	Outer	Outer > 2	Inner	Inner > 'C'	Output
	1	FALSE	'A'	FALSE	A
	1	FALSE	'B'	FALSE	AB
	1	FALSE	'C'	FALSE	ABC
	1	FALSE	'D'	TRUE	Inner loop exited
	2	FALSE	'A'	FALSE	ABCA
	2	FALSE	'B'	FALSE	ABCAB
	2	FALSE	'C'	FALSE	ABCABC
	2	FALSE	'D'	TRUE	Inner loop exited
	3	TRUE	Outer loop exited		

3-3.4 Screen Control

Before considering the next example of a nested FOR-DO instruction, we will discuss another built-in procedure dealing with the screen. In the last section, the built-in procedure CLRSCR was discussed. This instruction was used to clear the screen. It is now time to consider a built-in procedure for placing the cursor at a particular location on the screen. Such a procedure is **GOTOXY**.

The screen can be thought of as a table with 80 columns by 25 rows, as shown in Figure 3–10. The GOTOXY procedure allows the programmer to specify where the output to the screen will occur. Output starts at column 1, row 1; the top left corner of the screen is (1,1).

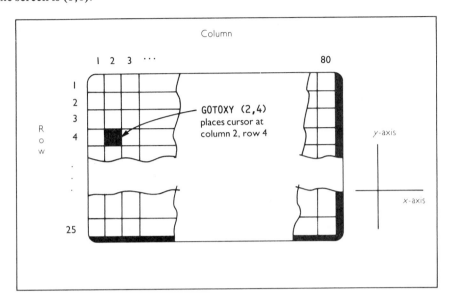

Figure 3–10

As an example of nested FOR-DO loops and of screen control, consider the instructions in Figure 3–11. These instructions produce a bar graph of the data entered. That is, the user enters the number of years for which the graph is to be drawn. Next, the sales for each year is entered. A bar of '*' is drawn using the inner FOR-DO loop.

Figure 3–11

```
WRITE ('For how many years is graph?(2 .. 9) ') ;
READLN (NumOfYears) ;
CLRSCR ;
WRITE ('Enter sales for year  : ') ;
FOR Year := 1 TO NumOfYears DO
  BEGIN
    GOTOXY (25 , 1) ;
    WRITE (Year) ;
    GOTOXY (29 , 1) ;
    CLREOL ;                          {Clear to end of line}
    READLN (AmtOfSales) ;
    GOTOXY (4*(Year - 1) + 1 , 23) ;
    WRITE (Year) ;
    FOR Sales := AmtOfSales DOWNTO 1 DO
      BEGIN
        GOTOXY (4*(Year - 1) + 1 , 23 - Sales) ;
        WRITE ('*')
      END
  END ;
GOTOXY (1 , 2) ;
WRITE ('Press RETURN key to quit- ') ;
READLN (Ch)
```

COMMENT
The build-in procedure **CLREOL** clears from cursor location to the end of the line. The cursor location is not changed.

Figure 3–12 shows a sample execution of the instructions in Figure 3–11 when 5 is entered for `NumOfYears` and sales data of 6, 2, 8, 4, and 5 are entered for `AmtOfSales`.

Figure 3–12

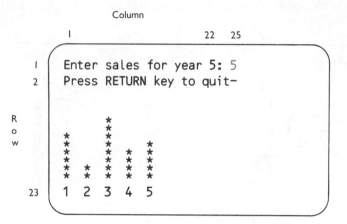

DO IT NOW

1. For the bar graph example in Figure 3–11, construct the VAR section to list the variables needed for the instructions listed.
2. A friend is trying to write a nested FOR-DO instruction to print out the following pattern:

```
*****
*****
*****
```

Discuss the problems with the following attempts.

```
a. FOR CtA := 1 TO 3 DO
      FOR CtB := 1 TO 5 DO
        WRITE ('*') ;
   WRITELN
b. FOR CtA := 1 TO 3 DO
      FOR CtB := 1 TO 5 DO
        BEGIN
          WRITE ('*') ;
          WRITELN
        END .
```

```
c. FOR CtA := 1 TO 3 DO
      BEGIN
        FOR CtB := 1 TO 5 DO
          WRITE ('*') ;
        WRITELN
      END .
d. FOR CtA := 1 TO 3 DO
      FOR CtB := 1 TO 5 DO
        BEGIN
          GOTOXY (CtB, CtA) ;
          WRITE ('*')
        END .
```

DO IT NOW ANSWERS

```
1. VAR NumOfYears, Year, AmtOfSales, Sales : INTEGER ;
       Ch : CHAR
```
2a. This attempt outputs

```
****************
```

The WRITELN instruction is not executed until the outer FOR-DO instruction is executed.

b. This attempt outputs

```
  *
  *
  *         that is, a column of 15 asterisks.
  .
  .
  .
  *
```

   The WRITELN instruction is executed for each pass through the inner FOR-DO loop.

c. There is no problem with this attempt. The output is the desired pattern.

d. This attempt also outputs the desired pattern.

3–3.4 Summary of FOR-DO

Some pointers about programming with the FOR-DO instruction follow:

1. The loop control variable must be of the same type as ValueA and ValueB (the beginning and ending values for the loop control variable). It should *not* be changed in the loop (that is, it is always incremented or decremented to the next value automatically). For example,

```
FOR Count := 1 TO 18 DO
  BEGIN
    WRITE (Count : 2, ' ') ;
    Count := Count + 2
  END
```

   is considered poor programming. If `Count` is to be incremented by a value other than 1, a WHILE-DO or REPEAT-UNTIL instruction should be used.

2. The value in the loop control variable should *not* be accessed after the FOR-DO has executed. On some implementations of Pascal (not Turbo), the value is undefined after the loop is executed. For example, in

```
FOR Count := 1 TO 120 DO ;
  WRITELN (Count)
```

   the FOR-DO instruction will do nothing other than delay long enough to count from 1 to 120. The second instruction will attempt to output the value in `Count`. This could yield an error on some implementations of the Pascal language (for Turbo Pascal, `Count` will contain 121). The variable `Count` should be reinitialized before further use.

   To summarize the three repetition control instructions:

1. The WHILE-DO control instruction is the workhorse of the Pascal language. The power of this instruction lies in its ability to test prior to entering the repetition. The value of the WHILE-DO becomes evident later when working with file-type data.

2. The REPEAT-UNTIL instruction is used when it is known that the instruction is to be repeated at least once. A typical use of this instruction is with interactive programs.

3. The FOR-DO instruction is the most specialized of this type of instruction. It is used when the programmer knows exactly how many times the instruction is to be executed.

Vocabulary

159   **CLREOL**   A built-in procedure that clears the screen from the cursor location to the end of the line. The cursor location is not altered.

157   **Decrement**   Decrease a value to the preceding value.

154   **FOR-DO instruction**   A repetition control instruction in Pascal. The form is

FOR Variable := ValueA TO ValueB DO
  < Instruction >
or
FOR Variable := ValueA DOWNTO ValueB DO
  < Instruction >

The loop control variable must be of type BOOLEAN, INTEGER or CHAR. If ValueA and ValueB are of type INTEGER, the instruction will be repeated (ValueB − ValueA + 1) times or (ValueA − ValueB + 1) times, depending on the use of TO or DOWNTO.

159   **GOTOXY (col, row)**   A built-in procedure for directing output to the screen to a given location. The screen is 80 columns wide and 25 rows long. The location (1,1) is the upper left corner, and the location of the lower right corner is (80, 25).

154   **Increment**   Increase a value to the next value.

154   **Loop control variable**   The variable used in a FOR-DO instruction to count the number of times an instruction is executed.

Glad You Asked

Q How do I get out of a FOR-DO loop, if I want to get out before the loop control variable is greater than the ending value? I tried

```
EndValue := 20 ;
FOR Count := 1 TO EndValue DO
  BEGIN
    READ (InNum);
    IF InNum < 0
      THEN EndValue := Count
      ELSE ...
  END
```

I didn't get an error, but I didn't get out of the loop, either.

A In your attempt, all you changed was the value in the variable EndValue. This is not an error; however, the values that control the loop are recorded upon entry into the loop and cannot be changed. If you do not want to execute the instructions a fixed number of times, use a WHILE-DO or REPEAT-UNTIL instruction.

Q Can you settle an argument? I claim the FOR-DO is like the REPEAT-UNTIL, since the instruction is executed until the loop control variable is larger than the second value listed. My friend says the FOR-DO is like the WHILE-DO, since the instruction is executed while the loop control variable is less than or equal to the last value. Am I right?

A In a way, you are both right. However, the FOR-DO instruction is simply a repetition control instruction. Although it can be replaced by the WHILE-DO instruction, it has its place in the tools that the programmer uses to construct a program that is easy to read, alter, and update.

Q I tried the following nested FOR-DO instruction:

```
FOR Count := 1 TO 5 DO
  FOR Count := 3 TO 7 DO
    WRITE (Count : 2)
```

Shouldn't I have gotten an error or some other bad thing?

A On some implementations of Pascal, this instruction would yield an error. The instruction is bad programming. The programmer should not alter the loop control variable (Count in this case). It leads the reader to think the second FOR-DO instruction will be executed five times. If the instruction does execute, it will not do what it implies it will do.

Q What is a holding loop?

A A *holding loop* (sometimes referred to as a *timing loop*) is a loop used to hold the program for a short period of time. Often the FOR-DO instruction is used to process such a loop. For example, the instruction

```
FOR Count := 1 TO 10000 DO ;
```

does nothing other than hold the program up long enough for the CPU to count to 10,000 (10,001, actually). Often this type of instruction is used to hold a title of a message on the screen for a short period of time or to slow down output to the screen.

Q Can you give a summary of all the different control instructions?

A Often a diagram is a helpful way to get an overall picture. Consider Figure 3–13. The left branch of the diagram shows the decision control instructions. These instructions are used to decide whether to execute or skip an instruction. The right branch of the diagram shows the repetition control instructions. These instructions are used to repeat the execution of an instruction (or group of instructions).

Figure 3–13

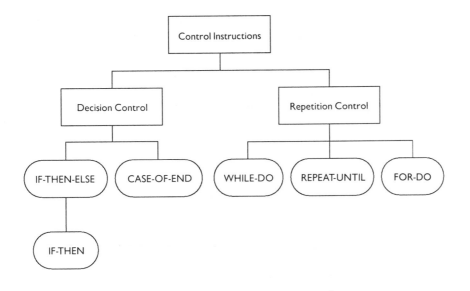

Section 3–3 Exercises

1. Which of the following is *not* a repetition control instruction?
    a. the REPEAT-UNTIL instruction
    b. the WHILE-DO instruction
    c. the FOR-DO instruction
    d. the CASE-OF-END instruction

Answer questions 2 through 5 based on the following FOR-DO instruction:

```
FOR Count := Start TO Finish DO
   WRITE (Count : 4)
```

2. The loop control variable is _____.
3. Which of the following could not be a value for Finish?
   a. 'z'   b. 9   c. 0.0   d. 0   e. −8
4. If Start contains −4 and Finish contains 0, the instruction WRITE (Count : 4) will be executed _____ times.
5. If Start contains 0 and Finish contains −4, the instruction WRITE (Count : 4) will be executed _____ times.
6. A FOR-DO instruction in which the instruction to be repeated contains a FOR-DO instruction is called a _____ FOR-DO instruction.
7. Which of the following applies to this FOR-DO instruction?

```
FOR Count := 1 TO Finish DO
   IF Finish > 4
      THEN Count := Finish
      ELSE WRITE (Count)
```

   a. The instruction to be repeated should never be an IF-THEN-ELSE instruction.
   b. The value in the loop control variable cannot be output while the loop is executing.
   c. It is a bad programming practice to assign the loop control variable a value while the loop is executing.
   d. Neither the beginning nor the ending value can be a variable.
8. Give the output of the following.
   a.
```
FOR Letter := 'a' TO 'f' DO
   WRITE (Letter : 2)
```
   b.
```
FOR Number := 6 DOWNTO 0 DO
   IF Number MOD 2 = 0
      THEN WRITE (Number)
```
   c.
```
FOR Count := 1 TO 6 DO
   CASE Count MOD 4 OF
      1 : WRITE ('Hi ');
      2 : WRITE ('Ho ');
      3 : WRITE ('It''s off to work we go. ')
   END
```
   d.
```
FOR CountA := 1 TO 6 DO
   BEGIN
      WRITE (CountA, ' ') ;
      FOR CountB := CountA TO 5 DO
         WRITE (CountB : 2) ;
      WRITELN
   END
```
   e.
```
FOR Outer := 1 TO 6 DO
   BEGIN
      FOR Inner := 1 TO 5 DO
         IF Inner < > Outer
            THEN WRITE (Inner) ;
      WRITELN
   END
```

9. Use a FOR-DO instruction to compose instructions to find the sum of the whole numbers from 1 to 100.

10. Find the errors in the following.
    a. FOR Index := 1 TO 45
        WRITE (Index : 3)
    b. FOR Number := 3.2 TO 3.9 DO
        WRITELN (SQRT (Number : 1 : 2))

11. Boot up Pascal; set the workfile to the file **BARGR.PAS** from the **Source** diskette. Enter the Turbo Pascal editor. Expand the program to output the sales for the year (value in **AmtOfSales**) at the top of each bar drawn in the bar graph.

12 **a.** The power of a number is (base)^{exponent} and is found as follows:
      If exponent is a positive integer the power is base*base* . . . *base.
      If exponent is a negative integer the power is 1/(base*base* . . . *base).
      If exponent is zero the power is 1.
      Write a Pascal program that lets the user input a value for base and an integer value for exponent. The output of the program is the resulting power.

Sample Execution

```
Please enter base: 4
Please enter exponent: -3
Power is 0.0156
```

   b. For your program in part a, what is the output when the user enters **0** for base and **-3** for exponent?

13. The factorial of a positive integer is the product of the number with each positive integer less than the number. That is,
        5 factorial is 5*4*3*2*1
        3 factorial is 3*2*1
    Write a Pascal program that has as input a positive integer from 1 to 17. The program is to output to the screen the factorial of the number. Use a FOR-DO loop. Remember, start with a design.

Sample Execution

```
Enter number (1..17): 4
4 factorial is 24
```

Programming Problems

14. Write a Pascal program to output the following multiplication table:

```
x| 1  2  3  4  5  6  7  8  9
--------------------------------
1| 1  2  3  4  5  6  7  8  9
2| 2  4  6  8 10 12 14 16 18
3| 3  6  . . .              .
4| 4  8  . . .              .
5| 5                        .
6| .
7| .
8| .
9| 9 18 27 36 45 54 63 72 81
```

The output should start at column 5, row 2. Use a nested FOR-DO loop and the built-in procedure GOTOXY.

15 **a.** Two BOOLEAN expressions are logically equivalent if they have the same truth value for every possible value of the statements that compose the BOOLEAN expressions. For example, the BOOLEAN expression **NOT (A and B)** is logically equivalent to **(NOT A) OR (NOT B)**, since no matter what the value of **A** and what the value of **B**, the two expressions yield the same truth value. To demonstrate this, a truth table is used.

A	B	NOT (A AND B)	(NOT A) OR (NOT B)
TRUE	TRUE	FALSE	FALSE
TRUE	FALSE	TRUE	TRUE
FALSE	TRUE	TRUE	TRUE
FALSE	FALSE	TRUE	TRUE

(continued)

Since the truth value of NOT (A and B) matches the truth value of (NOT A) OR (NOT B) for each possible value of A and each possible value of B, the two are logically equivalent.

Write a Pascal program to write to the screen a truth table such as the one just shown. The program should help you establish whether or not the BOOLEAN expression (NOT A) OR B is logically equivalent to A OR (NOT B). *Hint:*

```
FOR A := TRUE DOWNTO FALSE DO
  FOR B := TRUE DOWNTO FALSE DO
    WRITE ( A : 10 , B : 10 )
    Express1 := (NOT A) OR B
    Express2 := A OR (NOT B)
    WRITELN ( Express1 : 10, Express2 : 10 )
```

b. Alter your program in part a to help you determine if the BOOLEAN expression A AND (B OR C) is logically equivalent to (A AND B) OR (A AND C).

c. Expand your program in part a to output the results of the evaluation. That is, after writing the truth table to the screen, the program should write to the screen lines like these:

```
The expressions (NOT A) OR B and A OR (NOT B)
are not logically equivalent.
```

16. The tuition costs at a local university is computed using the following table.

Schedule of Charges

full-time		part-time	
in-state $545	out-of-state $1,184	in-state $44/hour	out-of-state $94/hour

Write a Pascal program that allows the user to enter a student's name and whether the student is an in-state or out-of-state student. The program is to randomly assign the student a number of hours between 3 and 18. The program is to compute, then output the student's tuition bill. A student is considered full-time if more than 12 hours are taken. The user should be allowed to enter exactly five student names. After the five tuition bills are computed, the program should output the total of the tuition bills and the average tuition bill.

Sample Execution

```
1.  Enter student name: Hardman, Linda
    Is student in-state?(Y/N): Y
    Number of hours taken is 12
    Tuition bill is $528
2.  Enter student name:
```

17. Write a Pascal program that allows the user to use the screen as a drawing pad for rectangles. The screen should be cleared and the cursor placed at row 21 column 1. The user should be allowed to enter the height (from 2 to 18 inclusive) and width (from 2 to 70 inclusive) of the rectangle. The program should print the character * to the screen to draw the rectangle. The top left vertex of the rectangle should be at screen location row 1 column 3.

Sample Execution

```
******
*    *
*    *
******

Enter height of rectangle (2..18): 4
Enter width of rectangle (2..70): 6
Press RETURN to continue, enter Q to quit:
```

CHAPTER TEST

1. Identify each of the following as a decision control instruction (write *Decision* in the blank) or a repetition control instruction (write *Repetition* in the blank).
   _____ **a.** an IF-THEN-ELSE instruction
   _____ **b.** a REPEAT-UNTIL instruction
   _____ **c.** a FOR-DO instruction
   _____ **d.** a CASE-OF-END instruction
   _____ **e.** a WHILE-DO instruction

2. Insert *True* to indicate a true statement or *False* to indicate a false statement.
   _____ **a.** A major use of the REPEAT-UNTIL instruction is with interactive programs.
   _____ **b.** The WHILE-DO instruction executes its instruction as long as its BOOLEAN expression is FALSE.
   _____ **c.** In a WHILE-DO instruction, the instruction executed must contain some action to alter the value of the BOOLEAN expression so as to avoid an infinite loop.
   _____ **d.** The FOR-DO instruction is used when the programmer is unsure of the number of times the instruction is to be executed.
   _____ **e.** A variable of type REAL can never be used for a loop control variable in a FOR-DO instruction.

3. Give the output of each of the following. Number and Sum are of type INTEGER.

```
a. Sum := 3 ;                        b. Number := 0 ;
   Number := 0 ;                        REPEAT
   WHILE Number < 5 DO                     Sum := 0 ;
     BEGIN                                 Number := Number + 2 ;
       Sum := Number - 2 ;                 Sum := Sum + Number
       Number := Number + 2             UNTIL Number > 5 ;
     END ;                              WRITELN ('Sum is: ', Sum)
   WRITELN ('Sum is '; Number)
```

4. Write a FOR-DO instruction to output KJIHGFED. Use Letter of type CHAR as the loop control variable.

5. Complete the following program. The program is to allow the user to enter positive integer data until ready to quit. The program is to output the **Range** of the data (range = high − low).

```
PROGRAM RANGE ;

VAR InNumber, High, Low, Range : INTEGER ;

BEGIN
  InNumber := Ø ;
  High := Ø ;
  Low := MAXINT ;
  WHILE InNumber >= Ø DO
    BEGIN
      WRITE ('Please enter positive integer value (-1 to quit): ') ;
      _____

END .
```

Sample Execution

```
Please enter positive integer value (-1 to quit): 8
Please enter positive integer value (-1 to quit): 2Ø
Please enter positive integer value (-1 to quit): 14
Please enter positive integer value (-1 to quit): 3
Please enter positive integer value (-1 to quit): -1

The range is 2Ø - 3 or 17
```

6. Write a Pascal program that allows the user to enter an upper value and a lower value, both of type INTEGER. The program is to write to the screen the sum of the even integers between (excluding the input values) the upper value and lower value.

Sample Execution

```
Please enter lower value: -12
Please enter upper value: 16
The sum of the even integers between -12 and 16 is 26
```

7. Dr. Ashad needs a program that allows him to enter five numeric scores. The program is to output the average of the four highest scores (drop the lowest score). Write a Pascal program to accomplish this task.

Sample Execution

```
Enter score 1: 9Ø
Enter score 2: 34
Enter score 3: 82
Enter score 4: 96
Enter score 5: 1ØØ
The average is 92.Ø
```

Debugging

As programs get longer and the structure becomes more complex, program errors appear. This is natural. The process of removing the program errors is known as debugging the program.

Avoid Random Changes

Once the text of a Pascal program is compiled (converted to object code), the program is executed. When the program does not perform its intended task, a program error is present. To remove the program error, you must locate the source of the error. Do not make random changes in the hope of correcting the error. In doing so, you often change a correctly functioning piece of code. This will induce even more errors.

To find the source of the error, your solution design is the place to start the search. Check to see that the design was coded properly. If the translation from the design to the program is accurate, walk through the design to make sure it solves the problem.

Tracing

When an execution section consists of a sequence of simple instructions, the programmer knows which instructions are executed. When an execution section contains decision control instructions and/or loop control instructions, the programmer is less sure of exactly which instructions will be executed and in which sequence. To trace through the execution of the program instructions, the WRITELN and READLN instructions can be used. For example, suppose the instructions below appeared in an execution section.

```
FOR Outer := 1 TO 10 DO
  BEGIN
    IF Outer MOD 3 = 1
      THEN FOR Inner := 1 TO 8 DO
             BEGIN
               Sum := Outer + Inner ;
               MyLimit := MyLimit + 2
             END ;
  Total := Total + Outer
END
```

To trace through the instructions, as they are being executed, insert WRITE and/or WRITELN instructions at strategic locations in the code.

```
FOR Outer := 1 TO 10 DO
  BEGIN
    WRITELN ('Entered outer loop, Outer is: ' , Outer) ;
    READLN (Ans) ;
    IF Outer MOD 3 = 1
      THEN FOR Inner := 1 TO 8 DO
             BEGIN
               WRITE ('Entered inner loop, Inner is: ');
               WRITELN (Inner) ;
               READLN (Ans);
               Sum := Outer + Inner ;
               MyLimit := MyLimit + 2
             END ;
    Total := Total + Outer
  END
```

Other tracing WRITELN's and READLN's could be inserted as needed. Through the use of the above technique, the programmer can visualize what is happening during the execution of the code. Once the program is debugged, the tracing WRITELN's and READLN's are deleted.

Chapter Four

Modules

Introduction

You now have at your disposal essentially all the tools needed to write a computer program (except for input/output to and from the disk drive). In this chapter, you will be introduced to a tool that allows you to write a *good* computer program: the **module.** Modules fall into two classes: procedures and functions. Modules allow the programmer to break a problem's solution into more manageable tasks. By using modules, the programmer can write a program that has a logical organization.

The chapter will start with a discussion of the design of a problem's solution and how the design can be reflected in the computer program by the use of procedures. Next, functions and their use in problem solving are discussed. Finally, program construction using modules is covered. When you finish this chapter, you will be able to write a Pascal program by using a modular approach.

```
PROGRAM Chapter4 ;

VAR Num : INTEGER ;
    Choice : CHAR ;

PROCEDURE PresentMenu ;                              {page 173}

  BEGIN                                              {page 173}
    CLRSCR ;
    WRITELN ('A. Option1') ;
    WRITELN ('B. Option2') ;
  END ;

PROCEDURE DoOption1 (TheCh : CHAR ;                  {page 190}
                     VAR TheNum : INTEGER) ;         {page 195}

  VAR Local : INTEGER ;                              {page 177}

  BEGIN
    {DoOption 1 instructions}
  END ;

PROCEDURE DoOption2 ;

  PROCEDURE NestedIn2 ;

    BEGIN
      {Instructions for NestedIn2}                   {page 226}
    END ;

  BEGIN
    {Instructions for DoOption2}
  END ;

FUNCTION Op2 (AChar : CHAR) : INTEGER ;              {page 212}

  BEGIN
    IF AChar < 'M'
      THEN Op2 := SQR (5)                            {page 213}
      ELSE Op2 := RANDOM (7)
  END ;

BEGIN
  PresentMenu ;                                      {page 179}
  READLN (Choice) ;
  CASE Choice OF
    'A', 'a' : DoOption1 ('Z', Num) ;                {page 195}
    'B', 'b' : DoOption2                             {page 179}
    ELSE WRITELN (Op2 ('P') : 5)                     {page 213}
  END
END .
```

Procedures

In this section, you will review the problem-solving technique discussed in Chapter 1. A major step in the approach was to design a solution to the problem. In this section, you will study how to convert that design to a Pascal program that mirrors the design. A major factor in this conversion is the use of procedures.

In Chapter 1, the approach given for solving problems on the computer consisted of the following steps:

1. Obtain a problem to be solved.
2. Outline the solution to the problem.
3. Fill in the outline with details (test the design; return to Step 2 if necessary).
4. Write a program; that is, convert the solution to a language the computer can understand.
5. Enter the program into the computer.
6. Have the computer compile and execute the program.
7. Verify that the program solves the original problem (test the program).

The major steps needed to solve the problem are listed *(outline the solution to the problem)*. Afterwards, the steps are refined *(fill in the outline with details)* until only simple tasks are left. This is called **stepwise refinement**. The problem solver starts (at the top) by thinking of the major steps that will solve the problem; the small details of how to do these steps are left until later. The design of the solution is a **top-down design**.

4–1.1 The Use of Modules

In solving problems up to this point, we have stressed the ideas just summarized. In this chapter, we will explore a method of physically separating the major steps and their refinements from the main execution section of the program. That is, the program will be constructed as a collection of modules with the main execution sections coordinating the execution of the modules. This approach to program development is called the **modular approach** and is illustrated in Figure 4–1.

Figure 4–1

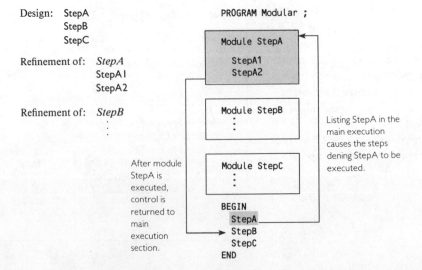

As you can see in Figure 4–1, the program mirrors the solution design through the use of modules (subprograms). A program becomes a list of modules and a main execution section that describes the sequence in which the modules are to be executed (called). The modules can be developed, tested, and debugged independently of one another, then assembled to form the program. This well-organized approach to program development leads to programs that are easier to read, test, debug, and maintain.

In Pascal, modules fall into two classes: procedures and functions. We will start by discussing procedures (the more general of the two). Later in the chapter, we will discuss functions. You will also learn how to develop and test modules independently and then assemble the modules to build a Pascal program. For now, it is important that you learn the fundamentals of procedures and their use in Pascal programs.

4-1.2 Procedures and Problem Solving

A procedure is like a small program. Just as a program tells the computer how to solve a problem, a procedure tells the computer how to do one of the major steps (subtasks) in the solution. The program layout becomes as follows: (1) list the major steps in the execution section, and (2) define how to do a complex step in a procedure block.

Declaring a Procedure A procedure block in a program looks very much like the program itself. The block begins with a **procedure header** section. This section begins with the reserved word **PROCEDURE,** which is followed by the procedure's identifier. The word PROCEDURE tells the compiler that the identifier will be defined as an instruction. Following the procedure header section, a CONST section and a VAR section can appear. Finally, the **procedure execution section** appears. The execution section is bracketed by the words BEGIN and END and contains the instructions that define the procedure.

The position of the procedure block is between the VAR section and the execution section of the program block (see Figure 4–2).

Figure 4–2

```
PROGRAM ProDemo ;                                    {program header section}

VAR VarA : REAL ;                                    {program VAR section}

PROCEDURE Demo ;                                     {procedure header section}

  VAR ProVar : CHAR ;                                {procedure VAR section}

  BEGIN                                              {procedure execution section}
      {instructions that define the procedure}
  END ;

BEGIN                                                {program execution section}
    {instructions of the program}
END .
```

Consider the following demonstration problem.

PROBLEM

Write a Pascal program that allows the user to select from a menu listing: triangle, rectangle, and trapezoid. After the selection is made, the user enters the information necessary to compute the area of the shape. The output of the program is the area measurement of the selected shape.

Sample Execution

```
Geometric shapes available are:
  A. Triangle
  B. Rectangle
  C. Trapezoid

Please select by entering A, B, C, Q=Quit: A
```

{screen clears}

```
Enter height of triangle: 12.3
Enter base of triangle: 5.2
Area measure of triangle is: 36.98

Press RETURN key for main menu-
```

SOLUTION

As usual, the starting place is the construction of a design.

Design: REPEAT
          Clear screen
          Present menu
          Read selection
          Clear screen
          CASE selection OF
              'A' : DoTriangle
              'B' : DoRectangle
              'C': DoTrapezoid
          END
          UNTIL user wants to quit

The next step is to refine the main steps in the solution that need explanation. The steps "Clear screen" and "Read selection" do not require further refinement.

Refinement of: *Present menu*
          WRITELN ('The geometric shapes available are:')
          WRITELN (' A. Triangle')
          WRITELN (' B. Rectangle')
          WRITELN (' C. Trapezoid')
          WRITELN
          WRITE ('To select shape enter A, B, C, Q = Quit: ')

Refinement of: *DoTriangle*
          WRITE ('Enter height of triangle: ')
          READLN (Height)
          WRITE ('Enter base of triangle: ')
          READLN (Base)
          WRITE ('The area measure is: ')
          WRITELN (Base*Height/2)
          WRITELN
          WRITE ('Press RETURN key for main menu-')
          READLN

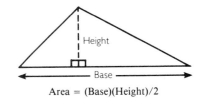

Area = (Base)(Height)/2

Refinement of: *DoRectangle*
          WRITE ('Enter length of rectangle: ')
          READLN (Length)
          WRITE ('Enter width of rectangle: ')
          READLN (Width)
          WRITE ('The area measure is: ')
          WRITELN (Length*Width)
          WRITELN
          WRITE ('Press RETURN key for main menu-')
          READLN

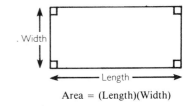

Area = (Length)(Width)

Refinement of: *DoTrapezoid*
          WRITE ('Enter length of major base of trapezoid: ')
          READLN (BigBase)
          WRITE ('Enter length of minor base of trapezoid: ')
          READLN (SmallBase)
          WRITE ('Enter height of trapezoid: ')
          READLN (Height)
          WRITE ('The area measure is: ')
          WRITELN (0.5*(BigBase + SmallBase)*Height)
          WRITELN
          WRITE ('Press RETURN key for main menu-')
          READLN

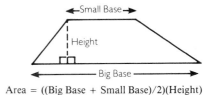

Area = ((Big Base + Small Base)/2)(Height)

After testing this design by walking through it with several examples, convert the design to a Pascal program. The program will have the form shown in Figure 4–3.

Figure 4–3

```
PROGRAM GeometricShapes ;

VAR Select : CHAR ;

PROCEDURE PresentMenu ;

  BEGIN
    {instructions for this main step go here}
  END ;

PROCEDURE DoTriangle ;

  VAR {variables this procedure needs go here} ;

  BEGIN
    {instructions for this main step go here}
  END ;

PROCEDURE DoRectangle ;

  VAR {variables this procedure needs go here} ;

  BEGIN
    {instructions for this main step go here}
  END ;

PROCEDURE DoTrapezoid ;

  VAR {variables this procedure needs go here} ;

  BEGIN
    {instructions for this main step go here}
  END ;

BEGIN
  REPEAT
    CLRSCR ;
    PresentMenu ;
    READLN (Select) ;
    CLRSCR ;
    CASE Select OF
      'A' : DoTriangle ;
      'B' : DoRectangle ;
      'C' : DoTrapezoid
    END
  UNTIL Select = 'Q'
END .
```

COMMENT

The word *stub* is used in the sense that a plumber stubs in all the pipes for a house under construction.

The form of the program GeometricShapes shown in Figure 4–3 is called a *stub*. That is, the program has been stubbed in. The stub can be compiled and executed (and often is, as a test).

It is now time to fill in the procedure blocks with their instructions. Again, the design and its refinements enter the process. The definition of each procedure is much like writing a small program. The refinement of the step (developed in the design of the solution) is used as a guide to write the procedure.

Refinement of: *Present menu*
```
WRITELN ('The geometric shapes available are:')
WRITELN (' A. Triangle')
WRITELN (' B. Rectangle')
WRITELN (' C. Trapezoid')
WRITELN
WRITE ('To select shape enter A, B, C, Q = Quit: ')
```

From this refinement, the procedure will be as follows:

```
PROCEDURE PresentMenu;

  BEGIN
    WRITELN ('The geometric shapes available are:') ;
    WRITELN ('  A. Triangle') ;
    WRITELN ('  B. Rectangle') ;
    WRITELN ('  C. Trapezoid') ;
    WRITELN ;
    WRITE ('To select shape enter A, B, C, Q=Quit: ')
  END
```

Refinement of: *DoTriangle*

```
                WRITE ('Enter height of triangle: ')
                READLN (Height)
                WRITE ('Enter base of triangle: ')
                READLN (Base)
                WRITE ('The area measure is: ')
                WRITELN (Base*Height/2)
                WRITELN
                WRITE ('Press ENTER key for main menu- ')
                READLN
```

COMMENT

Much as WRITELN by itself results in the output of a blank line to the screen, READLN by itself results in halting the program until the RETURN key is pressed. This allows the user to read the output of the procedure. Otherwise, the results would vanish from the screen almost as soon as they were printed (due to CLRSCR).

From the refinement of `DoTriangle`, the procedure will need variables `Height` and `Base`. Thus, the procedure produced from this refinement is

```
PROCEDURE DoTriangle ;

  VAR Height, Base : REAL ;

  BEGIN
    WRITE ('Enter height of triangle: ') ;
    READLN (Height) ;
    WRITE ('Enter base of triangle: ') ;
    READLN (Base) ;
    WRITE ('The area measure is: ') ;
    WRITELN (Base*Height/2) ;
    WRITELN ;
    WRITE ('Press RETURN key for main menu-') ;
    READLN
  END
```

A procedure is given everything it needs to do the task for which it is designed. The procedure `DoTriangle` needs variables `Height` and `Base`. Thus, they are declared in the VAR section for the procedure block. This procedure is said to be *self-contained* (or **modular**). Continuing the process, the program `GeometricShapes` is as shown in Figure 4–4.

Figure 4-4

Sample Execution

```
The geometric shapes available are:
   A. Triangle
   B. Rectangle
   C. Trapezoid

To select shape enter A,B,C,Q=Quit: A
```

{screen clears}

```
Enter height of triangle: 10
Enter base of triangle: 8
The area measure is:  4.0000000000E+01

Press RETURN key for main menu-
```

Sample Execution

```
The geometric shapes available are:
   A. Triangle
   B. Rectangle
   C. Trapezoid

To select shape enter A,B,C,Q=Quit: B
```

{screen clears}

```
Enter length of rectangle: 30
Enter width of rectangle: 10
The area measure is:    3.0000000000E+02

Press RETURN key for main menu-
```

Sample Execution

```
The geometric shapes available are:
   A. Triangle
   B. Rectangle
   C. Trapezoid

To select shape enter A,B,C,Q=Quit: C
```

```pascal
PROGRAM GeometricShapes ;

VAR Select : CHAR ;

PROCEDURE PresentMenu ;

  BEGIN
    WRITELN ('The geometric shapes available are:') ;
    WRITELN ('   A. Triangle') ;
    WRITELN ('   B. Rectangle') ;
    WRITELN ('   C. Trapezoid') ;
    WRITELN ;
    WRITE ('To select shape enter A, B, C, Q=Quit: ')
  END ;

PROCEDURE DoTriangle ;

  VAR Height, Base : REAL ;

  BEGIN
    WRITE ('Enter height of triangle: ') ;
    READLN (Height) ;
    WRITE ('Enter base of triangle: ') ;
    READLN (Base) ;
    WRITE ('The area measure is: ') ;
    WRITELN (Base*Height/2) ;
    WRITELN ;
    WRITE ('Press RETURN key for main menu-') ;
    READLN
  END ;

PROCEDURE DoRectangle ;

  VAR Length, Width : REAL ;

  BEGIN
    WRITE ('Enter length of rectangle: ') ;
    READLN (Length) ;
    WRITE ('Enter width of rectangle: ') ;
    READLN (Width) ;
    WRITE ('The area measure is: ') ;
    WRITELN (Length*Width) ;
    WRITELN ;
    WRITE ('Press RETURN key for main menu-') ;
    READLN
  END ;

PROCEDURE DoTrapezoid ;

  VAR BigBase, SmallBase, Height : REAL ;

  BEGIN
    WRITE ('Enter major base of trapezoid: ') ;
    READLN (BigBase) ;
    WRITE ('Enter minor base of trapezoid: ') ;
    READLN (SmallBase) ;
    WRITE ('Enter height of trapezoid: ') ;
    READLN (Height) ;
    WRITE ('The area measure is: ') ;
    WRITELN (0.5*(BigBase + SmallBase)*Height) ;
```

```
      WRITELN ;
      WRITE ('Press RETURN key for main menu-') ;
      READLN
   END ;

BEGIN
  REPEAT
    CLRSCR ;
    PresentMenu ;
    READLN (Select) ;
    CLRSCR ;
    CASE Select OF
      'A' : DoTriangle ;
      'B' : DoRectangle ;
      'C' : DoTrapezoid
    END
  UNTIL Select = 'Q'
END .
```

Figure 4-4
Continued

{screen clears}

```
Enter major base of trapezoid: 50
Enter minor base of trapezoid: 20
Enter height of trapezoid: 10
The area measure is:   3.5000000000E+02

Press RETURN key for main menu-
```

COMMENT

To read a Pascal program, always start reading at the program execution section. One reason for using procedures is to allow the reader to read the program in as much or as little detail as desired. The reader can read the main steps in the program execution section, and if he or she desires to see how a step is done, he or she can look up in the program to the desired step definition in the appropriate procedure block.

When the program is run, it starts executing the instructions in the main execution section. When a **procedure identifier** is encountered, like DoTriangle or PresentMenu, control is sent to the procedure's execution section, where the corresponding instructions are executed. Control is then returned to the main execution section. The procedure is said to be *called* (or executed). That is, the program *calls* (executes) the procedure PresentMenu.

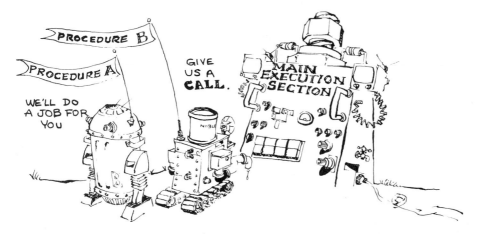

DO IT NOW

In the program `GeometricShapes` (see Figure 4–4),

1. If the user selects **B**, the procedure _____ will be called.
2. Which of the procedures listed must be called when the program executes?
3. Suppose the programmer wishes to expand the program to include circles. Describe the process, and write a procedure for circles.

DO IT NOW ANSWERS

1. DoRectangle   2. PresentMenu
3. In the procedure `PresentMenu`, a fourth selection, `D. Circle`, would be included in the menu. A procedure, `DoCircle`, would be written to define how to do this selection. The procedure would need a variable, `Radius`. In the program execution section, in the CASE-OF-END instruction, the selection `'D' : DoCircle` would be added.

Area = (Pi)(Radius)²

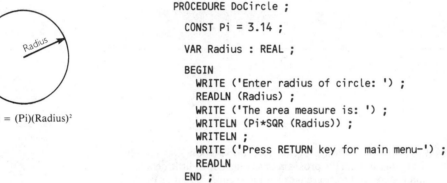

```
PROCEDURE DoCircle ;

   CONST Pi = 3.14 ;

   VAR Radius : REAL ;

   BEGIN
     WRITE ('Enter radius of circle: ') ;
     READLN (Radius) ;
     WRITE ('The area measure is: ') ;
     WRITELN (Pi*SQR (Radius)) ;
     WRITELN ;
     WRITE ('Press RETURN key for main menu-') ;
     READLN
   END ;
```

4-1.3 Style and Punctuation

A procedure (module) block *must* contain a procedure header and an execution section. It *may* contain a CONST section and a VAR section. The word PROCEDURE is a Pascal reserved word (thus, it is capitalized). The sections of a procedure are indented under the procedure. This indentation indicates that these sections belong to the procedure. A procedure is boxed much the same way as a program is boxed:

1. The word PROCEDURE starts the procedure box and the procedure header box.
2. An identifier is sought and boxed.
3. The procedure header box is closed.
4. If the word CONST is found, the CONST section is boxed.
5. If the word VAR is found, the VAR section is boxed.
6. The word BEGIN is sought and starts the execution section box.
7. The instructions in the execution section are boxed.
8. The word END is sought, and the execution section box is closed.
9. The procedure box is closed.

From the boxed procedure in Figure 4–5, you can see that a semicolon is needed to separate the procedure header section from the VAR section, and a semicolon is needed to separate the VAR section from the execution section. Also, semicolons are needed to separate the instructions within the procedure execution section.

Figure 4-5

```
PROCEDURE DoTriangle ;

  VAR Height, Base : REAL ;

  BEGIN
    WRITE ('Enter height of triangle: ') ;
    READLN (Height) ;
    WRITE ('Enter base of triangle: ') ;
    READLN (Base) ;
    WRITE ('The area measure is: ') ;
    WRITELN (Base*Height/2) ;
    WRITELN ;
    WRITE ('Press RETURN key for main menu-') ;
    READLN
  END
```

A semicolon will be needed to separate one procedure section from another. Also, a semicolon will be needed to separate the last procedure block from the program execution section. For this reason, every procedure block must be followed by a semicolon.

4-1.4 Documentation

Like a program, a procedure should have a comment section. In this comment section, the purpose of the procedure and a brief description of its input and its output should be recorded. As an example, see the procedure in Figure 4-6.

Figure 4-6

```
PROCEDURE DoRectangle ;

  {Purpose:   To compute the area of a rectangle.                          }
  {Input:     The Length and Width of the rectangle will be entered by the program user}
  {Output:    The area will be written to the screen.                      }

  VAR Length, Width : REAL ;

  BEGIN                                 {DoRectangle}
    WRITE ('Enter length of rectangle: ') ;
    READLN (Length) ;
    WRITE ('Enter width of rectangle: ') ;
    READLN (Width) ;
    WRITE ('The area measure is: ') ;
    WRITELN (Length*Width) ;           {output area}
    WRITELN ;                          {skip a line}
    WRITE ('Press RETURN key for main menu-') ;
    READLN                             {wait for RETURN key}
  END ;                                {DoRectangle}
```

When the program is compiled (converted to object code), the comments are ignored.

COMMENT

Just as a program should have a comment section, so should a procedure. Often a programmer waits until the program is tested and debugged before inserting comments. Before a program is finished, it must be documented properly. Due to space considerations, most comment sections will be omitted in the programs presented in the remainder of this book.

Vocabulary

Page

177   **Modular**   A description of a program that indicates it is developed as a collection of independent modules.

172   **Modular approach**   An approach to program construction that entails physically separating a major step (and its refinement) from the main execution section.

171   **Module**   An independent collection of instructions that describes how to do a particular task in the problem solution design. When implemented in the Pascal language, a module is written as a procedure or a function.

173   **Procedure**   A module (or small program) that lists the instructions needed to define how to do a particular task. The task is often one of the major steps in the problem solution design.

173   **PROCEDURE**   A reserved word in Pascal that is used to tell the compiler that an identifier is going to be defined as an instruction. The instructions that define the identifier are listed in the procedure's execution section.

173   **Procedure execution section**   The section of the procedure containing the instructions that define the procedure. These instructions will be executed when the procedure's identifier appears in an execution section.

173   **Procedure header**   The first line of the procedure block, which contains the reserved word PROCEDURE and the identifier of the procedure.

179   **Procedure identifier**   The word (identifier) used to name the procedure. When this word appears in an execution section, the instructions listed in the corresponding procedure's execution section are executed (provided the procedure has been defined prior to the identifier's appearance). The use of this identifier in an execution section is known as a *procedure call*.

172   **Stepwise refinement**   The idea of refining the steps needed to solve a problem. This refinement is continued until simple or primitive tasks are all that are left in the design.

172   **Top-down design**   The concept of designing a solution to a problem by first listing the major steps to be done. The details of writing the code for a major step are deferred until all major steps have been identified by the programmer.

Glad You Asked

Q What do I do if I can't come up with a design for the solution of a problem?

A Research the problem. That is, make sure you understand all its terms. Try walking through the problem with sample data. Pick up a pencil and try to sketch out a design, even if you know it will not work. Often, writing something can generate an idea. Just staring at the problem is seldom productive.

Q You said the problem should be solved and the Pascal program written before sitting down at the computer. I can just type in the solution without all that design junk. What is wrong with that?

A Your method might work for a while, especially with programs that are short. However, this approach will lead to trouble with larger programs; often, your approach generates programs that are hard to alter or update. In industry, programs often must be altered or expanded. This work on the program may or may not be done by the original programmer. The production of programs that cannot be read (except possibly by the original programmer) and that must thus be altered is one of the factors that led to the development of the Pascal approach to programming.

Remember, the work you are doing now is developmental work. You are to develop good programming habits. This work will help you develop good communication skills (these skills are valuable whether you enter programming or not). After all if you are smart enough to arrive at the solution your way, you are smart enough to deliver a well-written program for your solution. No matter how good you are at problem solving, you must communicate your solution to others.

Q Does it make any difference about the order in which the procedures are defined?

A Yes. A procedure must be defined before it is called in an execution section. Usually, it is best to write the procedure definitions in the order they appear in the program execution section.

Q What does the phrase *invoke a procedure* mean?

A To invoke (or call) a procedure means to use the procedure's identifier in an execution section. Invoking (calling) a procedure causes the program to execute the instructions in the procedure's execution section.

Section 4–1 Exercises

1. A procedure is used to
   a. assign a value to a constant.
   b. list instructions for doing a major step in the solution design.
   c. skip the execution of a collection of instructions.
   d. declare an identifier a variable and list its type.
   e. declare an identifier a constant and list its value.
2. To cause the execution of the instructions of a procedure
   a. use the procedure's identifier in an execution section.
   b. use the word GOTO, then the procedure's identifier.
   c. use a CASE instruction with the procedure's identifier as the case selector.
   d. simply write PROCEDURE, then the procedure's identifier.
3. Insert TRUE for a true statement, and FALSE for a false statement.
   _____ a. A program stub can be compiled and executed.
   _____ b. If a procedure is defined, it must be called.
   _____ c. A self-contained (modular) procedure is one that uses the variables listed in the program VAR section.
   _____ d. Every procedure must have a VAR section.
   _____ e. Every procedure must have an execution section.
   _____ f. If a Pascal program has a procedure, then the first instruction executed by the program is the first instruction in the procedure execution section.
   _____ g. The one section a procedure is not allowed is a CONST section.
   _____ h. To insert a comment in a program, commas are used.
   _____ i. One reason to use procedures is to make a program easier to alter.
   _____ j. When a procedure's identifier is found in the program execution section, the next instructions executed are the ones in the procedure's execution section.
   _____ k. The phrases *invoke a procedure, call a procedure,* and *execute a procedure* all have the same meaning.
   _____ l. Every procedure is followed by a semicolon.

4. Given the following Pascal program,

```
PROGRAM ProDemo ;

VAR Select : CHAR ;

PROCEDURE Add2AndSquare ;

  VAR Number : REAL ;

  BEGIN                              {Add2AndSquare}
    WRITE ('Please enter number: ') ;
    READLN (Number) ;
    WRITELN ('Result is ', SQR (Number + 2)) ;
    WRITE ('Press RETURN key to continue-') ;
    READLN                           {wait for RETURN key press}
  END ;                              {Add2AndSquare}

PROCEDURE SquareAndAdd2 ;

  VAR Number REAL ;

  BEGIN                              {SquareAndAdd2}
    WRITE ('Please enter number: ') ;
    READLN (Number) ;
    WRITELN ('Result is ', SQR (Number) + 2) ;
    WRITE ('Press RETURN key to continue-') ;
    READLN                           {wait for RETURN key press}
  END ;                              {SquareAndAdd2}

BEGIN                                {ProDemo}
  REPEAT
    CLRSCR ;
    WRITELN ('Please select:') ;
    WRITELN ('A. Function one') ;
    WRITELN ('B. Function two') ;
    WRITE ('Enter A, B, or Q=Quit: ') ;
    READLN (Select) ;
    IF Select = 'A'
      THEN Add2AndSquare
      ELSE SquareAndAdd2
  UNTIL Select = 'Q'
END .                                {ProDemo}
```

a. If the user enters **B**, then enters **3**, the output is _____
b. If the user enters **A**, then enters **−5**, the output is _____
c. If the user enters **B**, then enters **−6**, then presses the RETURN key, the next instruction executed is _____

5. Given the following Pascal program,

```
PROGRAM Grades ;

VAR Name : STRING [30] ;

PROCEDURE GiveGrade ;

  VAR StudentAver : REAL ;
      Aver : INTEGER ;

  BEGIN                              {GiveGrade}
    WRITE ('Please enter your test average: ') ;
    READLN (StudentAver) ;
    Aver := ROUND (StudentAver) ;
    WRITE (Aver : 1 , ' is ') ;
```

```
        IF Aver >= 90
          THEN WRITELN (' very good-an A.')
          ELSE IF Aver >= 80
                  THEN WRITELN ( ' good- a B.')
                  ELSE IF Aver >= 70
                          THEN WRITELN ( ' fair- a C.')
                          ELSE IF Aver >= 60
                                  THEN WRITELN (' poor work- a D.') ;
                                  ELSE WRITELN (' to low- an F.')
      END ;                             {GiveGrade}

    BEGIN                               {Grades}
      WRITE ('Please enter your name: ') ;
      READLN (Name) ;
      GiveGrade
    END .                               {Grades}
```

a. If Joanne is entered for Name and 73 is entered for StudentAver, give the output.
b. If Carl is entered for Name and 59.6 is entered for StudentAver, give the output.

6. Rewrite the following procedure following the style rules:

```
procedure doubleit; var count, times, amt : integer;
begin count := 0; write ('Enter number to double: ') ;
readln (amt); write ('Enter number of times to double: ') ;
readln (times); while count <= times do begin
double := 2 * amt; count := count + 1 end; write (amt) end;
```

7. Box the procedure DoubleIt in problem 6.
8. Boot up Pascal; set the workfile to the file GEOSHAPE.PAS from the Source diskette. Enter the Turbo Pascal editor. Alter the program to output the perimeter of the shape selected by the user.
9. Boot up Pascal; set the workfile to the file MENUEX.PAS from the Source diskette. Enter the Turbo Pascal editor. Alter the program so that the selections DoSquare, DoSquareRoot, and DoCube are written as procedures. The main execution section should appear as follows:

```
BEGIN                            {main execution section}
  REPEAT
    CLRSCR ;                     {clearscreen}
    PresentMenu ;
    WRITE ('Please select from above list (enter A,B,C,D) : ') ;
    READLN (Choice) ;
    CASE Choice OF
      'A' : DoSquare ;
      'B' : DoSquareRoot ;
      'C' : DoCube
    END ;
    IF Choice < > 'D'
      THEN BEGIN                 {hold screen}
              WRITE ('Press RETURN key to continue-') ;
              READLN (Ans)
           END
  UNTIL Choice = 'D'
END .                            {main execution section}
```

Delete the variable declarations for Number and Cube from the program VAR section.

10. Find the errors in the program below:

```
PROGRAM Errors ;

VAR Ans : CHAR ;

PROCEDURE FirstOne ;

  BEGIN                                        {FirstOne}
    WRITELN ('This is procedure one')
  END                                          {FirstOne}

PROCEDURE SecondOne

  BEGIN                                        {SecondOne}
    WRITELN ('This is procedure two')
  END ;                                        {SecondOne}

BEGIN                                          {Errors}
  WRITELN ('This program demonstrates procedure calls.') ;
  WRITE ('Which procedure do you want ') ;
  WRITE ('called? (enter 1 or 2): ') ;
  READLN (Ans) ;
  IF Ans = 1
    THEN FirstOne ;
  IF Ans = '2'
    THEN Procedure SecondOne
END .                                          {Errors}
```

11. Complete the following Pascal program. The program is to allow the user to select the type of temperature conversion desired, input a temperature, do the conversion, and output the results.

Sample Execution

```
Please select
  A. Fahrenheit to Centigrade
  B. Centigrade to Fahrenheit
Enter A, B, Q=Quit : A

Enter Fahrenheit temperature: 32
Centigrade temperature is: 0.0
Press RETURN key for main menu-
```

```
PROGRAM Conversions ;

VAR Select : CHAR ;

PROCEDURE ToCentigrade ;

  VAR InValue : REAL ;

  BEGIN
    .
    .
  END ;
    .
    .
    .

BEGIN                                          {Conversions}
  REPEAT
    CLRSCR
    WRITELN ('Please select') ;
    WRITELN ('  A. Fahrenheit to Centigrade') ;
    WRITELN ('  B. Centigrade to Fahrenheit') ;
    WRITE ('Enter A, B, Q=Quit : ') ;
    READLN (Select) ;
    .
    .
END .                                          {Conversions}
```

Programming Problems

12. Write a Pascal program that presents the prompt

        Select (A=Clear screen B=Place * C=Quit):

on line 21 of the screen. If the user enters B, then the user inputs a column location (1 .. 80) and a row location (1 .. 20). The character * is output to the screen at the screen location (column,row). Write a procedure to handle the selection *Place*. Use the Pascal program to create the design shown in the following sample execution.

Sample Execution

```
    *
    **
****  *
   *       *
   *         *
   *       *
****  *
    **
    *



Select (A=Clear screen  B=Place *  C=Quit): B
Column: 9   Row: 6
```

COMMENT
You must select option B 22 times to draw the design.

13. Write a Pascal program that allows the user to select from a menu listing the planets Mercury, Venus, Earth, and Mars. The program is to write to the screen information on the selection made. Refer to a science book for facts on planets.

Sample Execution

```
For information on the planets listed below,

A. Mercury  B. Venus  C. Earth  D. Mars

Please select (A, B, C, D, Q=Quit): B

The planet Venus:

Mean distance from Sun is 67.27 million miles.
Revolves around Sun every 224.701 days.
Diameter = 7,700 miles
Rotation on axis is 243.2 days.
Velocity in orbit is 22 miles per second.

Press RETURN for main menu-
```

14. Write a Pascal program that allows the user to select from the menu shown. For a given selection, the program should generate the selected type of problem, present the problem, allow the user to input an answer, write to the screen a response as to correctness of the answer, and allow the user the choice of another problem of the selected type or returning to the main menu.

Sample Execution

```
Main menu for Arithmetic Drill
A. Addition of whole numbers
B. Subtraction of whole numbers
C. Multiplication of whole numbers
D. Division of whole numbers
Q. Quit

To select, enter A, B, C, D, Q:
```

15. Write a Pascal program that allows the user to select from the following menu:

```
A. Find price given cost and percent profit
B. Find cost given price and percent profit
C. Find price given percent markup
D. Find price given percent markdown
Q. Quit
```

After the selection is made, the user is to enter data appropriate for the selection made. The output will be the price (or cost). The program is to execute until the user selects option **Q**.

Hint: (Percent Cost) (Price) = Cost, where Percent Cost = 1 − Percent Profit.

COMMENT
Markup means to add a percentage to the original cost. A markup of 10% does not yield a 10% profit.

Sample Execution

```
Please select-
    A. Find price given cost and percent profit
    B. Find cost given price and percent profit
    C. Find price given percent markup and original cost
    D. Find price given percent markdown and original cost
    Q. Quit
Enter A,B,C,D, or Q: A
Enter cost of item: 56.70
Enter percent profit: 40
Price should be set at $94.50 to obtain 40% profit.
Press RETURN key to continue-
```

Parameters

In the last section, you were introduced to procedures and their use in Pascal programs. In this section, we will extend the use of procedures to include the use of parameters. Parameters are used to allow the transfer of data to and from procedures. The parameters used with procedures fall into two classes: value and variable. Both classes will be discussed, as well as procedure calls involving parameters.

4-2.1 Value Parameters

A collection of parameters is used to define a particular instance of a process. For example, a linear function has the general form $y = mx + b$. Suppose m has the value 6 and b has the value 12. Then you have a particular instance of a linear function, $y = 6x + 12$. The symbols m and b are called **parameters** for a linear function. To introduce parameters and their use in programming, consider the following problem.

PROBLEM

Write a Pascal program that accepts as input a base and an exponent (both positive integers). The program is to output the resulting base to the exponent power.

SOLUTION

After thinking about the problem, develop the following design:

Design: ReadBase&Exponent
           DoPower

Refinement of: *ReadBase&Exponent*
                 WRITE('Please enter base: ')
                 READLN (Base)
                 WRITE ('Please enter exponent: ')
                 READLN (Exponent)

Refinement of: *DoPower*
                 Count : = 1
                 Power : = 1
                 WHILE Count < = ExpNum DO
                     Power : = Power*BaseNum
                     Count : = Count + 1
                 WRITELN ('The power is: ' , Power)

Sample Execution

```
Please enter base: 6
Please enter exponent: 5
The power is: 7776
```

To convert the step DoPower to a procedure, the procedure will require the transfer of values from the program, namely, a value for BaseNum and a value for ExpNum.

To perform this transfer, parameters are used. Consider the conversion of the step DoPower to a procedure presented in Figure 4–7.

Figure 4–7

```
PROCEDURE DoPower (BaseNum, ExpNum : INTEGER) ;

   VAR Count : INTEGER ;
       Power : REAL ;

   BEGIN                              {DoPower}
     Count := 1 ;
     Power := 1 ;
     WHILE Count <= ExpNum DO
         BEGIN                        {WHILE-DO instruction}
           Power := Power*BaseNum ;
           Count := Count + 1
         END ;                        {WHILE-DO instruction}
     WRITELN ('The power is: ' , Power)
   END ;                              {DoPower}
```

As you can see in Figure 4–7, the procedure header has been changed. Additional information has been added. The information enclosed in parentheses,

    BaseNum, ExpNum : INTEGER

is called a **parameter list** for the procedure. The list indicates that two values will be sent to the procedure DoPower when it is called. The first value will be placed in the variable BaseNum; the second value will be placed in the variable ExpNum. The values sent must be of type INTEGER, since the variables are declared to hold integer values. The parameters BaseNum and ExpNum are called **value parameters.**

With this change in the procedure header, there is a change in the call to the procedure DoPower. The following would be a valid call to the procedure DoPower:

    DoPower (Base, Exponent)

A valid call must include two values of type INTEGER. In the call to the procedure, DoPower (Base, Exponent), the value in the variable Base is passed to the procedure and is then placed in the variable BaseNum. The value in the variable Exponent is passed to the procedure and placed in the variable ExpNum.

When the procedure DoPower is called, memory locations are set aside for the variables BaseNum and ExpNum. The values passed are stored in these memory locations. When the execution of DoPower is finished, the variables BaseNum and ExpNum are forgotten (along with any variables or constants listed in the procedure's VAR and CONST sections); that is, the memory space allotted to store the values of these variables is taken back by the system.

Header: DoPower (BaseNum, ExpNum
                    ⇧   ⇧
Call: DoPower (Base, Exponent)

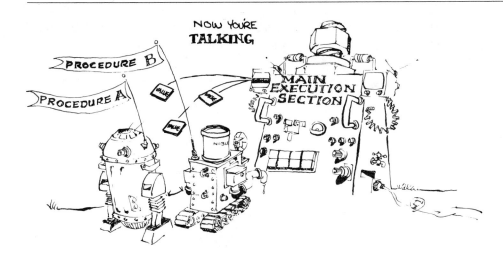

The conversion of the design to a Pascal program is shown in Figure 4–8.

Figure 4–8

```
PROGRAM Powers ;

VAR Base , Exponent : INTEGER ;

PROCEDURE DoPower (BaseNum , ExpNum : INTEGER) ;

  VAR Count : INTEGER ;
      Power : REAL ;

  BEGIN                                   {DoPower}
    Count := 1 ;
    Power := 1 ;
    WHILE Count <= ExpNum DO
      BEGIN                               {WHILE-DO instruction}
        Power := Power*BaseNum ;
        Count := Count + 1
      END ;                               {WHILE-DO instruction}
    WRITELN ('The power is: ' , Power)
  END ;                                   {DoPower}

BEGIN                                     {Powers}
  WRITE ('Please enter base: ') ;
  READLN (Base) ;
  WRITE ('Please enter exponent: ') ;
  READLN (Exponent) ;
  DoPower (Base , Exponent)
END .                                     {Powers}
```

Sample Execution

```
Please enter base: 7
Please enter exponent: 2
The power is:   4.9000000000E+01
```

COMMENT

The procedure call `DoPower (Base, Exponent)` in Figure 4–8 is an instruction that tells the program to execute the instructions listed in the execution section of the procedure `DoPower`. The execution of these instructions should be done using the values sent in the procedure call (namely, the values in the program variables `Base` and `Exponent`).

In the previous example, the procedure DoPower will process any two numbers of type INTEGER. When the call is made to DoPower, the two values are passed to request a particular instance of the procedure DoPower. In the call

    DoPower (Base, Exponent)

the values passed are the values stored in the program variables Base and Exponent. Actually, any two expressions could be passed. All the following calls are valid:

    DoPower (16, 7) $\{16^7$ is computed$\}$

    DoPower (5, Exponent*3) $\{5^{Exponent*3}$ is computed$\}$

    DoPower (Base*3, Exponent + 4) $\{(Base*3)^{Exponent+4}$ is computed$\}$

The following calls are invalid:

    DoPower (4)   (needs a value for ExpNum)

    DoPower (3.2, 5)   (the first value must be of type INTEGER)

4-2.2 The Procedure Header

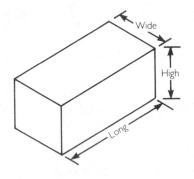

The general form of a procedure header contains the procedure identifier, then a set of parentheses containing the parameter list. For example, suppose a procedure is to find the volume of a box and output the result. This procedure would require parameters for the height, width, and length of the box, since these values determine the particular box. A header for this procedure might be

    PROCEDURE Volume (High, Long, Wide : REAL)

A call to this procedure would require values for each parameter. Thus, a call to this procedure might be

    Volume (18.2, 20.12, 5.2)

Notice that the items in the parameter list for the procedure header and in the procedure call are separated by a comma. The identifiers in the procedure header parameter list do not have to be previously declared in the program.

Consider the following procedure header:

    PROCEDURE Example (Num : INTEGER ; ChA, ChB : CHAR)

A call to this procedure must include values for the parameters Num, ChA, and ChB. For example,

    Example (19, 'A', 'G')

As you can see, a parameter list is stated much like declared variables in a VAR section. In fact, the procedure header just given could be presented as follows:

    PROCEDURE Example (Num : INTEGER ;
                       ChA, ChB : CHAR)

Also notice, in the call to the procedure, that the values sent to the procedure parameters are *ordered*. That is,

    Example ('A', 19, 'Q')

would yield an error, since an attempt would be made to assign to Num a value of type CHAR and to assign to ChA a value of type INTEGER.

DO IT NOW

1. Given the following procedure,

```
PROCEDURE SurfaceArea (High, Wide, Long : INTEGER) ;

   VAR Area, TopBottom, Sides, FrontBack : INTEGER ;

   BEGIN                              {SurfaceArea}
     FrontBack := 2*High*Wide ;
     Sides := 2*High*Long ;
     TopBottom := 2*Wide*Long ;
     Area := FrontBack + Sides + TopBottom ;
     WRITE ('The Surface Area is: ') ;
     WRITELN (Area)
   END .                             {SurfaceArea}
```

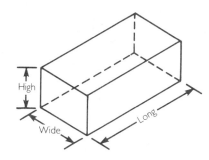

a. What would be the output for the following call? `SurfaceArea (3, 5, 2)`
b. What would be the output for the following call? `SurfaceArea (5, 2, 3)`

2. Match the following with the given errors.
   a. The procedure header: `PROCEDURE Inside (NumA, NumB : INTEGER)`
   and the call: `Inside (3)`
   b. The procedure header: `PROCEDURE Missing (Hold)`
   and the call: `Missing ('A')`
   c. The procedure header: `PROCEDURE Junk (Initial : CHAR; Age : INTEGER)`
   and the call: `Junk ('J', 26.3)`
   _____ Mismatch of parameter and value.
   _____ Incorrect number of values sent.
   _____ Missing type declaration for parameter.

3. Write a procedure that will take as input the height, length, and width of a box. The output is to be the message `The volume of the box is:` and the value of the volume of the box. Write a call to the procedure.

DO IT NOW ANSWERS

```
1a. The Surface Area is: 62
 b. The Surface Area is: 62
```

2.   __c__   Mismatch of parameter and value.
     __a__   Incorrect number of values sent.
     __b__   Missing type declaration for parameter.

```
3. PROCEDURE Volume (High, Long, Wide : REAL) ;

   VAR Vol : REAL ;

   BEGIN                              {Volume}
     Vol := High * Long * Wide ;
     WRITE ('The volume of the box is: ') ;
     WRITELN (Vol : 1 : 2)
   END                                {Volume}
```

Typical call: `Volume (3.2, 1.5, 3)`

4-2.3 *Variable Parameters*

Up to this point, the procedures presented can be classified as procedures without parameters, and procedures with value parameters. The first class of procedures simply defines a set of instructions to be executed. The second class defines a set of instructions to be executed based on a set of values (parameters) sent in the call to the procedure. It is now time to discuss the third and last class of procedures called procedures with **variable parameters.** Procedures in the third class do the following:

1. Define a set of instructions to be executed.
2. Allow for a set of values to be sent when the procedure is called.
3. Allow for a set of values to be returned after the instructions have been executed.

Consider the procedure DoPower discussed previously:

```
PROCEDURE DoPower (BaseNum, ExpNum : INTEGER) ;

   VAR Count : INTEGER ;
       Power : REAL ;

   BEGIN                                    {DoPower}
     Count := 1 ;
     Power := 1 ;
     WHILE Count <= ExpNum DO
        BEGIN                               {WHILE-DO instruction}
          Power := Power*BaseNum ;
          Count := Count + 1
        END ;                               {WHILE-DO instruction}
     WRITELN ('The power is: ' , Power)
   END ;                                    {DoPower}
```

COMMENT

A value parameter provides one-way communication similar to a radio. A variable parameter provides two-way communication, similar to a telephone.

The procedure's action can be limited to one thought. DoPower finds the power and writes the results to the screen. The instruction

```
    WRITELN ('The power is: ' , Power)
```

in the procedure DoPower can be moved to the main execution section. However, the variable Power would have to be declared a program variable. Additionally, a method of transferring the value for Power back to the calling execution section must be devised. This is due to the fact that the program variable Power and the procedure variable Power reference different memory locations. The transfer of the information back to the calling execution section can be accomplished by using a variable parameter.

A variable parameter is used to return a value to the calling execution section. The return of the value is accomplished by the procedure placing a value in a memory location referenced by a variable from the calling execution section. That is, the variable parameter shares a memory location with a variable from the calling execution section. Thus, a variable parameter *must* be given a variable identifier when the procedure is called. The instructions defined in the procedure execution section place a value in the location named by the variable identifier. Once the procedure execution is completed, the value in the variable parameter remains. (With value parameters, the values in memory are lost after the procedure execution.) The procedure DoPower using a variable parameter to return the results to the calling execution section is shown in Figure 4–9.

Figure 4-9

```
PROCEDURE DoPower (BaseNum, ExpNum : INTEGER ;
                   VAR Results : REAL) ;

  VAR Count : INTEGER ;

  BEGIN                                 {DoPower}
    Count := 1 ;
    Results := 1 ;
    WHILE Count <= ExpNum DO
       BEGIN                            {WHILE-DO instruction}
         Results := Results*BaseNum ;
         Count := Count + 1
       END                              {WHILE-DO instruction}
  END ;                                 {DoPower}
```

Figure 4–10 shows a valid call to the procedure DoPower in Figure 4–9.

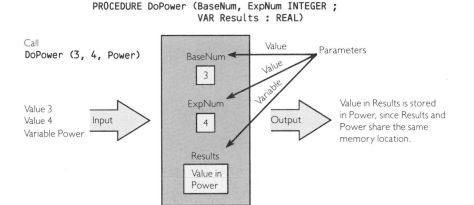

Figure 4-10

To indicate variable parameters, the word VAR must precede the variable parameter identifiers when they are listed in the procedure header. In a call to a procedure that has variable parameters, variable identifiers *must* be sent to the variable parameters. Consider Figure 4–10. The value in Results is returned to the calling execution execution section, since its value is stored in the memory location referenced by Power. That is, Results and Power share the same memory location. The entire program Powers is shown in Figure 4–11.

Figure 4-11

```
PROGRAM Powers ;

VAR Base , Exponent : INTEGER ;
    Power : REAL ;

PROCEDURE DoPower (BaseNum , ExpNum : INTEGER ;
                   VAR Results : REAL) ;

  VAR Count : INTEGER ;

  BEGIN                                    {DoPower}
    Count := 1 ;
    Results := 1 ;
    WHILE Count <= ExpNum DO
      BEGIN                                {WHILE-DO instruction}
        Results := Results*BaseNum ;
        Count := Count + 1
      END                                  {WHILE-DO instruction}
  END ;                                    {DoPower}

BEGIN                                      {Powers}
  WRITE ('Please enter base for power: ') ;
  READLN (Base) ;
  WRITE ('Please enter exponent: ') ;
  READLN (Exponent) ;
  DoPower (Base , Exponent , Power) ;
  WRITELN ('The power is: ' , Power)
END .                                      {Powers}
```

COMMENT

The program execution section of **Powers** in Figure 4-11 now needs the variable **Power** to be declared in the program VAR section. When **DoPower** is called, values are sent to the procedure. After execution of the procedure, the value in **Results** is returned to the main execution section since it shared a memory location with the program variable **Power**.

As another example of variable parameter use, consider the following problem.

PROBLEM

Write a Pascal program to take as input an investment amount (*P*), interest rate per month (*r*), and a number of months (*n*). The output is to be the value of the investment (*V*) after being compounded for the number of months input. The formula is $V = P(1 + r)^n$.

SOLUTION

Design: Get investment data
Compute compound interest factor $\{(1 + r)^n\}$
Compute investment value
Write investment value

Refinements: *Get investment data*
Get investment amount
Get interest rate
Get number of months

Compute compound interest factor
Compute: (1 + rate) to the *n*th power

Compute investment value
Value : = Amount*factor

Write investment value
WRITE ('Investment value is: $')
WRITE (Value)

Sample Execution

```
Please enter investment amount: $2000
Please enter interest rate per month: 0.01
Please enter number of months: 60
Investment value is: $3860.00
```

Further refinement of: *Compute: (1 + rate) to the* n*th power*
Count : = 0
Factor : = 1
WHILE Count < time DO
    Factor : = (1 + rate) * Factor
    Count : = Count + 1

A walk through of the design is as follows:

1. *Get investment data*
amount: $2000
rate: 0.01 per month
time: 60 months

2. *Compute compound interest factor*
Factor : = $(1 + 0.01)^{60}$ {results is 1.93}
    Compute: (1 + rate) to the 60th power
    Count : = 0
    Factor : = 1
    WHILE Count < 60 DO
        Factor : = (1 + 0.01)*Factor
        Count : = Count + 1

3. *Compute investment value*
Value : = 2000 * 1.93

4. *Write investment value*
    Investment value is: $3860.00

From the design, the program's main execution section is constructed:

```
BEGIN                                      {main program}
   GetInvestData (Amount , IntRate , Time) ;
   ComputeFactor (IntRate , Time , Factor) ;
   Value := Amount * Factor ;
   WRITELN ('Investment value is: $', Value : 1 : 2)
END .                                      {main program}
```

The procedures and their parameter needs are as follows:

■ GetInvestData

Three parameters, and all three must be variable parameters, since the values are needed in the calling section.

■ ComputeFactor

Three parameters, but only the parameter Factor needs to be a variable parameter, since only the value of Factor is needed in the calling section.

A Pascal program based on the design is shown in Figure 4–12.

Figure 4–12

```
PROGRAM Finance ;

VAR Amount , IntRate : REAL ;
    Time : INTEGER ;
    Factor , Value : REAL ;

PROCEDURE GetInvestData (VAR Amt , Rate : REAL ;
                         VAR Time : INTEGER) ;

   BEGIN                                   {GetInvestData}
     WRITE ('Please enter amount invested: $') ;
     READLN (Amt) ;
     WRITE ('Please enter interest rate per month: ') ;
     READLN (Rate) ;
     WRITE ('Please enter number of months: ') ;
     READLN (Time)
   END ;                                   {GetInvestData}

PROCEDURE ComputeFactor (TheRate : REAL ; Time : INTEGER ;
                         VAR Fact : REAL) ;

   VAR Count : INTEGER ;

   BEGIN                                   {ComputeFactor}
     Count := 0 ;
     Fact := 1 ;
     WHILE Count < Time DO
       BEGIN                               {WHILE-DO}
         Fact := (1 + TheRate) * Fact ;
         Count := Count + 1
       END                                 {WHILE-DO}
   END ;                                   {ComputeFactor}

BEGIN                                      {Finance}
   GetInvestData (Amount , IntRate , Time) ;
   ComputeFactor (IntRate , Time , Factor) ;
   Value := Amount * Factor ;
   WRITELN ('Investment value is: $' , Value : 1 : 2)
END .                                      {Finance}
```

Sample Execution

```
Please enter amount invested: $2000
Please enter interest rate per month: 0.01
Please enter number of months: 60
Investment value is: $3633.39
```

4-2.4 *Actual and Formal Parameters*

In defining a procedure, any valid identifier can be used in the parameter list. The identifier does not have to be declared before it is listed in the procedure header. This allows procedures to be written independently (perhaps by another programmer). The identifiers listed in the procedure header are called **formal parameters.** The word *formal,* in this context, means the outward form of something rather than its content.

Header:

DoPower (BaseNum, ExpNum

formal parameters

Call:

DoPower (Base, Exponent)

actual parameters

COMMENT

A variable parameter and the variable in the procedure call share the same memory location. That is, the *actual* memory location being used is the variable in the procedure call. The variable parameter is just a *formality*.

The identifiers used in the procedure call *must* be declared prior to this use. The list of parameters in the procedure call are known as **actual parameters.** The list of actual parameters must match the list of formal parameters (the ones in the procedure heading). That is,

1. The number of actual parameters in the call must be the same as the number of formal parameters in the procedure header.
2. The types of the parameters must match.
3. A variable parameter in the procedure header must be matched with a variable identifier in the procedure call.

Any reference to a (formal) parameter within the procedure execution section uses the identifier listed in the procedure header. When writing a procedure, think and write in a local sense. That is, act as if you know nothing of the program except what is required of the procedure you are writing.

To illustrate these points, consider the following procedure headers and the corresponding calls to the procedure:

Example 1

```
PROCEDURE ProcessPair (VAR Ans : BOOLEAN ;
                         FNum, SNum : INTEGER)     {formal}
```

Call:

```
ProcessPair (First, 13, -29)          {actual}
```

The actual parameter First must be a variable whose type is BOOLEAN.

Example 2

```
PROCEDURE CheckList (StudentID, CourseID : INTEGER ;
                     VAR Grade : CHAR ;
                     VAR NumHrs : INTEGER)
```

Call:

```
CheckList (StudentN, 1104, Grade, Hours)
```

StudentN must contain a value whose type is INTEGER, Grade must be a variable identifier whose type is CHAR, and Hours must be a variable identifier whose type is INTEGER.

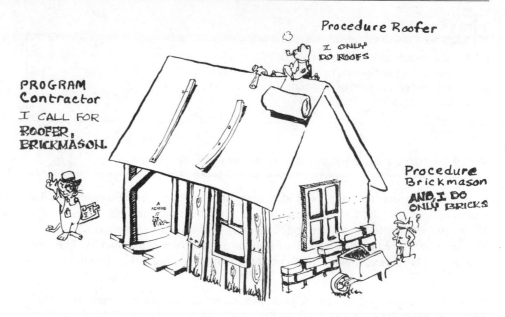

Consider the analogy in this illustration. When the PROGRAM Contractor calls for the Roofer, information needs to be passed. Roofer takes this information and does her job. Sometimes she returns information to the PROGRAM Contractor.

DO IT NOW

1. Given the following program VAR section,

```
VAR FirstN, SecondN : INTEGER ;
    Class : CHAR ;
    GPA : REAL
```

   a. Write a valid call to the procedure whose header is

```
PROCEDURE Fib (VAR FNumA, FNumB : INTEGER)
```

   b. Write a valid call to the procedure whose header is

```
PROCEDURE UpRec (StudentNumber : INTEGER ;
                 Grade : CHAR ;
                 VAR NumHrs : INTEGER ;
                 VAR Aver : REAL)
```

2. Update the program Finance (Figure 4–12) to allow the program user to find the value of several investments.
3. Update the procedure GetInvestData in the program Finance such that the user can enter the interest rate as a yearly percentage and enter the time as a number of years.
4. Given the following program VAR section and procedure heading,

```
VAR FlightN, DestNum : INTEGER ;
    Seats, NumPass : INTEGER ;
    Opening : BOOLEAN ;
    Cost : REAL

PROCEDURE CkFlight (FlightID, CityID : INTEGER ;
                    VAR SeatAvail : BOOLEAN ;
                    VAR Price : REAL)
```

which of the following are valid calls to CkFlight?

a. CkFlight (12345, New York, Opening, Cost)

b. CkFlight (9832, DestNum, Opening, Cost)

c. CkFlight (Ø23, 'Mobile', Opening, Cost)

d. CkFlight (FlightN, DestNum, Opening, 457.23)

DO IT NOW ANSWERS

1a. Fib (FirstN, SecondN)

b. UpRec (1234, 'B', FirstN, GPA)

2. Declare the variable **Ans** and state its type as CHAR in the program VAR section. Alter the program execution section to

```
BEGIN                                      {Finance}
  REPEAT
    GetInvestData (Amount , IntRate , Time) ;
    ComputeFactor (IntRate , Time , Factor) ;
    Value := Amount*Factor ;
    WRITELN ('The investment is worth $', Value:1:2) ;
    WRITELN ;
    WRITE ('Do you want another calculation?(Y/N): ') ;
    READLN (Ans)
  UNTIL Ans = 'N'
END .                                      {Finance}
```

3. The procedure GetInvestData could be written as follows:

```
PROCEDURE GetInvestData (VAR Amt, Rate : REAL ;
                         VAR Time : INTEGER) ;

  BEGIN                                    {GetInvestData}
    WRITE ('Please enter amount invested: $') ;
    READLN (Amt) ;
    WRITE ('Enter percent interest per year: ') ;
    READLN (Rate) ;
    Rate := Rate / 100 / 12 ;
    WRITE ('Enter number of years: ') ;
    READLN (Time);
    Time := Time * 12
  END ;                                    {GetInvestData}
```

4a. Invalid (second parameter not declared in VAR section)

b. Valid.

c. Invalid (second parameter must be of type INTEGER).

d. Invalid (fourth parameter must be a variable identifier).

4-2.5 *Modularization*

A module (procedure) should be self-contained. That is, if it needs values from the calling execution section, value parameters are used. If it needs to return information to the calling execution section, variable parameters are used. Any variables and/or constants needed locally in the procedure execution section are declared in the module's CONST and/or VAR section. To check a procedure for modularity, observe the execution section. Each identifier should be one of the following:

1. A built-in procedure, function, constant, or reserved word.

2. A parameter listed in the procedure header.

3. An identifier listed in the procedure's CONST section or VAR section.

Consider the procedure `ComputeFactor` from the program `Finance` in Figure 4–12.

```
PROCEDURE ComputeFactor (InRate : REAL ; Time : INTEGER ;
                                VAR Fact : REAL) ;

    VAR Count : INTEGER ;

    BEGIN                                    {ComputeFactor}
      Count := 0 ;
      Fact := 1 ;
      WHILE Count < Time DO
        BEGIN                                {WHILE-DO}
          Fact := (1 + InRate) * Fact ;
          Count := Count + 1
        END                                  {WHILE-DO}
    END ;                                    {ComputeFactor}
```

Checking the procedure for modularity involves observing the execution section. This observation reveals that each identifier is a reserved word, is a built-in instruction, or appears in the procedure header section or the procedure VAR section.

Vocabulary

Page

199   **Actual parameters**   The parameters listed in the call to the procedure.

199   **Formal parameters**   The parameters listed in the procedure header.

190   **Parameter list**   A list indicating which values and which variables will be sent to a procedure by the calling execution section.

189   **Parameters**   A method of discussing a particular instance of a general process or concept. In Pascal, a parameter is used to select a particular execution of a procedure. In effect, parameters enable values and variables to be passed to a procedure.

190   **Value parameters**   In a procedure header, when an identifier is listed and its type is stated, a value parameter is defined. When the procedure is invoked (called), a value is passed to the identifier. This value is used when the instructions of the procedure are executed. After execution, the identifier and its contents are lost.

194   **Variable parameters**   In a procedure header, when an identifier and its type are preceded by the reserved word VAR, a variable parameter is created. When the procedure is invoked (called), a variable identifier is passed to the parameter. The contents of the memory location can be altered by the instructions of the procedure. That is, after execution, the value of the parameter is returned to the calling execution section.

Glad You Asked

Q I want to write a procedure that needs two input values. Which of the following should I use?

```
PROCEDURE FindCDem (A, B : INTEGER)
```
or
```
PROCEDURE FindCDem (VAR A, B : INTEGER)
```

A It depends on whether the calling execution section needs the results of any operations done on the identifiers sent. If the procedure simply needs the values sent, use the first form (value parameters). If the procedure is to return information to the calling execution section, use the second form (variable parameters). There are other alternatives.

Suppose the procedure needs to return only one value to the calling execution section. One of the following might be the procedure header:

```
PROCEDURE FindCDem (A : INTEGER ; VAR B : INTEGER)
```
or
```
PROCEDURE FindCDem (VAR A : INTEGER ; B : INTEGER)
```

Q When a program like `Finance` (page 198) has several procedures, I have trouble seeing where one procedure stops and another starts. Is there a way to visually separate procedure blocks?

A Some programmers visually separate the blocks of a program by inserting a comment like

```
{**************************}
```

between the procedure blocks.

Q Why use different identifiers for the procedure header? A friend told me a procedure can use the program's variables. The different identifiers just confuse me.

A One of the ideas behind procedure use was to allow separate parts of the program design to be developed independently. That is, one programmer might write the first procedure while another programmer writes the second procedure, and so forth. The program could then be assembled by putting together the parts. For this to be accomplished, the programmers should not worry about which identifiers to use. They should only worry about what the procedure *needs* and what the procedure should *accomplish*. Also, by using this approach to procedures, a procedure written for one program could be used in another program (that is, the procedure becomes a tool).

Q Why use parameters at all? Why not just use the program variables?

A The use of parameters allows the reader to see quickly the needs of a procedure and the information returned by the procedure. As a programmer and problem solution designer, you should develop the concept of breaking the solution into modules. Also, you should develop the ability to state the inputs to, and the outputs from, the modules. Finally, always using program variables can result in an error called side-effect. This error occurs when a procedure alters a variable without the programmer's being aware of the alteration.

Q What would happen if I declared an identifier in a procedure VAR section that was already declared in the program VAR section?

A The memory locations for the variables in the program VAR section are set aside at the start of the program. When a procedure is called, temporary memory locations are created for any variables (or constants) declared for the procedure. Thus, even if the two variables have the same identifier, they reference two different memory locations. After the execution of the procedure is completed, the memory locations created for the procedure are taken back by the system (that is, any values in the locations are lost). The same reasoning applies to value parameters.

Q I saw the following in another book on Pascal. The procedure heading

```
PROCEDURE NextNum (Last : INTEGER ; VAR Next : INTEGER)
```

was given. Then this statement was made: "Obviously, the call

```
NextNum (15, InNum + LastNum)
```

would yield an error." Why is this obvious?

A The parameter `Next` is a variable parameter. It must be sent a variable identifier. That is, `Next` is given the memory address of some variable. This allows `Next` to contain the value of the variable sent at the start of the execution of the procedure and to return a value to the calling execution section. Any alteration to the value in `Next` is recorded in the memory location referenced by the variable identifier sent. By sending `InNum + LastNum`, there is no way the procedure would know which memory location to use since `InNum + LastNum` is an expression and does not reference a memory location.

Q Is WRITELN a procedure with a value parameter?

A Close, but you could not write a procedure to do what WRITELN does. That is, for the header

```
PROCEDURE WRITELN (InValue : ?????)
```

how would you know the type to give `Invalue`? Remember, you can have calls to WRITELN like `WRITELN ('Hello')` and `WRITELN (3.456)`.

Q Variable parameters, value parameters, formal parameter list, actual parameter list, passing values, passing variables, returning values—are you kidding? This is just too much! I am totally confused. Is there another way to explain all this (maybe a picture)?

A Consider this example and Figure 4–13.

```
PROCEDURE Illust (NumA, NumB : INTEGER ;
                  VAR NameID : INTEGER ;
                  VAR Cost : REAL)
    Call:  Illust (Weight, Height, Student, Price)
```

When `Illust` is invoked, temporary memory locations are created for the value parameters `NumA` and `NumB`. `Weight` and `Height` place their values in the temporary memory locations created for `NumA` and `NumB`. When the instructions in the execution section for `Illust` are executed, the temporary memory locations `NumA` and `NumB` are used. After the instructions in the execution section for `Illust` are executed, the temporary memory locations `NumA` and `NumB` are destroyed.

When `Illust` is invoked, the variable parameters `NameID` and `Cost` are given the same memory locations as `Student` and `Price`. `NameID` and `Cost` are formal identifiers used when the instructions for `Illust` are executed. The actual memory locations

Figure 4–13

Call
Illust (Weight, Height, Student, Price)

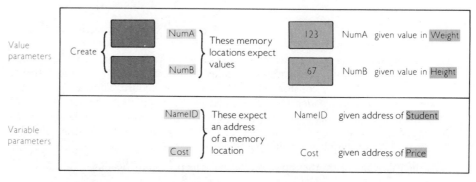

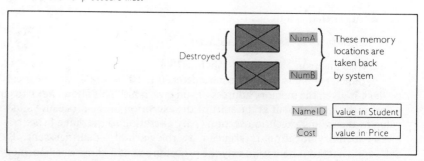

being used are `Student` and `Price`. Thus, after the instructions in the execution section of `Illust` are executed, the values in `NameID` and `Cost` are passed back to the calling execution section (these values were placed in the memory locations identified by `Student` and `Price`).

Section 4–2 Exercises

1. For the procedure header `PROCEDURE Demo (NumA, NumB : INTEGER)`
   a. The parameters are _____ and _____.
   b. These parameters are _____ parameters.
   c. A possible call to the procedure is _____.
2. For the procedure header `PROCEDURE Demo (VAR Letter : CHAR)`
   a. The parameter is _____.
   b. The parameter is a(n) _____ parameter.
   c. In a call to the procedure `Demo`, the parameter `Letter` must be sent a(n) _____ identifier.
3. Insert TRUE for a true statement. Insert FALSE for a false statement.
   _____ a. The identifiers for parameters in the procedure header must be declared in the program VAR section.
   _____ b. Value parameters are used to send values to a procedure.
   _____ c. After a procedure executes, to access a value in a value parameter, simply use its identifier.
   _____ d. For `PROCEDURE Demo (VAR Letter : CHAR)`, a valid call would be `Demo ('A')`.
   _____ e. A variable parameter must be sent an identifier of a variable.
   _____ f. A value parameter must be sent a value. To send an identifier of a variable would yield an error.
   _____ g. In a procedure call, any identifiers listed must be declared.
   _____ h. In a procedure header, the identifiers in the parameter list are known as formal parameters.
   _____ i. In a procedure header, the identifiers in the parameter list cannot be identifiers declared in the program VAR section.
4. Given: `PROCEDURE DoubleAdd3 (Num : INTEGER) ;`

   ```
   BEGIN
     Num := 2 * Num + 3 ;
     WRITELN (Num)
   END;
   ```

   Give the results of the following calls to `DoubleAdd3`.
   a. `DoubleAdd3 (5)`
   b. `DoubleAdd3 (-1)`
   c. `DoubleAdd3`
   d. `DoubleAdd3 (5.3)`
   e. `DoubleAdd3 (InNum * 3)`, where `InNum` is a variable of type INTEGER and contains the value `9`.

5. Given these program variables and their data types,

```
NameID        INTEGER
Position      CHAR
Age           INTEGER
Salary        REAL
```

match the following calls with these procedure headers.

a. Over21 (NameID, Age)
b. Over21 (Age)
c. Over21 (Age, NameID, Position)
d. InName (Salary, NameID)
e. InName (35000, 'S', 35)
f. InName (NameID, Salary)

_____ 1. PROCEDURE InName (Employee : INTEGER ; Cost : REAL)
_____ 2. PROCEDURE InName (Value : REAL ; PosType : CHAR ;
                              Num : INTEGER)
_____ 3. PROCEDURE Over21 (Num : INTEGER)
_____ 4. PROCEDURE Over21 (Employee : INTEGER ; Old : INTEGER)
_____ 5. PROCEDURE Over21 (Years : INTEGER ;
                              Person : INTEGER ; JobType : CHAR)
_____ 6. PROCEDURE InName (Cost : REAL ; Employee : INTEGER)

6. Given this program VAR section and the following procedure heading,

```
VAR Age,
    Weight : INTEGER ;
    Rating : REAL ;
    Status : CHAR

PROCEDURE CheckPat (Years, Pounds : INTEGER ; Rating : REAL ;
                      VAR Results : CHAR)
```

mark the following calls as *Valid* or *Invalid*. If invalid, state why.

_____ a. CheckPat (38, 123, Rating, 'G')
_____ b. CheckPat (Weight, Age, 0.05, Status)
_____ c. CheckPat (18, 129, Rating, Status)
_____ d. CheckPat
_____ e. CheckPat (Status)
_____ f. CheckPat (Weight, Age, Rating, Status)

7. Give the output of the following Pascal program:

```
Program Illust ;

VAR NumA,
    NumB : INTEGER ;

PROCEDURE CallIt (FNum : INTEGER ; VAR SNum : INTEGER) ;

  BEGIN                              {CallIt}
    FNum := FNum + SNum ;
    SNum := FNum * 3 ;
    WRITELN (FNum)
  END ;                              {CallIt}

BEGIN                                {Illust}
  NumA := 5 ;
  NumB := 4 ;
  CallIt (NumA, NumB) ;
  WRITELN (NumA : 5, NumB: 5)
END .                                {Illust}
```

8. Given the following procedure,

```
PROCEDURE Volume (Object : CHAR ; Height, Radius : REAL) ;

  CONST Pi = 3.14 ;

  VAR Vol : REAL ;

  BEGIN
    IF Object = 'C'
      THEN Vol := 1/3 * Pi * SQR(Radius) * Height
      ELSE IF Object = 'T'
              THEN Vol := Pi * SQR(Radius) * Height
              ELSE IF Object = 'S'
                      THEN Vol := 4/3 * Pi * SQR(Radius) * Radius ;
    WRITELN ('Volume is: ', Vol : 1 : 3)
  END
```

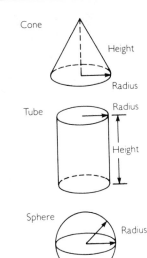

Cone
Height
Radius

Tube
Radius
Height

Sphere
Radius

give the output of the procedure for the following calls.
a. Volume ('C', 10, 3.0)
b. Volume ('S', 7, 10)

9. Write a Pascal program that allows the user to input one of three solids (Cone, Tube, Sphere) and the radius and height of the solid. The program is to output the volume of the shape. *Hint:* Use the procedure in problem 8.

Sample Execution

```
Please select solid (C=Cone, T=Tube, S=Sphere): C
Please enter height of cone: 21
Please enter radius of base: 10
Volume is 2198.000
```

10. Is the following procedure modular? If not, specify the offending identifier(s).

```
PROCEDURE ReverseDigits (InNum : INTEGER) ;

  BEGIN                   {ReverseDigits}
    Ct := InNum DIV 10 ;
    InNum := InNum - 10*Ct ;
    WRITE ('The number reversed is: ') ;
    WRITELN (10*InNum + Ct)
  END ;                   {ReverseDigits}
```

11. A procedure AverTwoLargest has the following execution section. The procedure has input three integers. It is to return to the calling execution section the average of the two largest integers. Write a procedure header and a VAR section for the procedure AverTwoLargest that insures modularity.

```
  BEGIN                   {AverTwoLargest}
    Sum := 0 ;
    IF NumA <= NumB
      THEN IF NumA <= NumC
              THEN Sum := NumB + NumC
              ELSE Sum := NumB + NumA
      ELSE IF NumB <= NumC
              THEN Sum := NumA + NumC
              ELSE Sum := NumA + NumB ;
    Aver := Sum/2
  END ;                   {AverTwoLargest}
```

12. Boot up Pascal; set the workfile to the file POWERS.PAS from the Source diskette. Enter the Turbo Pascal editor. Alter the procedure DoPower to use a variable parameter to return the results of the computation to the calling execution section. Alter the main execution section to work with the new version of DoPower.

13. Boot up Pascal; set the workfile to the file BARGR.PAS from the Source diskette. Enter the Turbo Pascal editor. Alter the program by replacing the instruction of the outer FOR-DO instruction with a call to the procedure DoABar. The procedure DoABar should be sent the value in the variable Year. Use TheYear as the identifier for the procedure's value parameter.

14. Boot up Pascal; set the workfile to the file FINANCE.PAS from the Source diskette. Enter the Turbo Pascal editor. Expand the program to also output the value of the investment at the end of each year.

Sample Execution

```
Please enter investment amount: $2000
Please enter interest per month: 0.01
Please enter number of months: 26

Value at end of year 1: $2253.65
Value at end of year 2: $2539.47
Value of the investment is $2590.51
```

Programming Problems

15. Write a Pascal program that allows the user to input three integers. The output of the program is the three integers ordered from smallest to largest. Use a procedure OrderThem that takes as input the three values of the three integers and writes to the screen the three integers in their proper order.

Sample Execution

```
Please enter first integer: 13
Please enter second integer: -12
Please enter third integer: 5
The integers in order are: -12  5  13
```

16. An annuity is the money resulting from investing a fixed amount of money (P) each month into an account. The money is compounded at an interest rate (r) per month. This investment process is done for a number of months (n). The value of the investment is given by:

$$V = P(1 + r)((1 + r)^n - 1)/r$$

Alter the Pascal program Finance (Figure 4–12) to compute the value of an annuity. The user is allowed to enter the amount invested each month, the interest rate (as a percent per year) and the length of time (in years).

Sample Execution

```
Please enter investment per month: $100
Please enter yearly interest rate in percent: 12
Please enter length of time in years (1...60): 35
The value of the annuity would be: $636300.00
```

17a. The experimental probability of an event is the ratio of the number of successes to the total number of trials. Suppose a die is rolled eight times and results in the following: 1, 3, 5, 3, 4, 6, 6, 2. The experimental probability of a 6 would be 2/8 (or 0.25). Write a Pascal program to find the experimental probability of obtaining a sum of 9 when a pair of dice is rolled 100 times. A possible design for the solution to this problem is:

Design: Count : = 0   {Initialize Count}
          WHILE Count < 100 DO
              Roll Dice
              GetSum
              CheckFor9
          Report Experimental Probability

b. Alter the Pascal program in part a to find the experimental probability of rolling a pair of dice and obtaining a double (both dice have same number). Use 1000 rolls.

18a. Write a procedure that takes as input the value parameters `NumerA`, `DenomA`, `NumerB`, `DenomB`, and the variable parameters `SumN` and `SumD`. The procedure is to return to the calling execution block the numerator and denominator of the sum of the two fractions. *Hint:* $a/b + c/d = (ad + bc)/bd$.

b. Use the procedure developed in part a to write a Pascal program that has input two fractions. The program is to output the sum of the two fractions (in fraction notation).

Sample Execution

```
For first fraction—
Enter numerator: 2
Enter denominator: 3

For second fraction—
Enter numerator: 1
Enter denominator: 5

Sum of the fractions is 13/15
```

19. Write a Pascal program that allows the user to input the coordinates of two points, then outputs the equation of the line through the two points. A possible design for the problem solution follows:

Design: Get coordinates of points
          Compute slope of line
          Compute *y* intercept
          Write equation of line

Get coordinates: Will need to return $X1$, $Y1$, $X2$, $Y2$

Compute slope: Will need input of $X1$, $Y1$, $X2$, $Y2$
                   and will return slope
                   Slope $= (Y2 - Y1)/(X2 - X1)$

Compute Y intercept: Will need input of $X1$, $Y1$, slope
                         Will return *y*int ($y$int $= Y1 -$ slope $* X1$)

Write equation of line: Will need input slope and *y*int
                            WRITELN ('The equation of the line is: ')
                            WRITELN ('y = ', slope:1:2, 'x + ', yint:1:2)

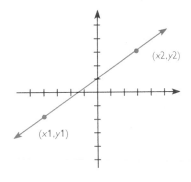

Sample Execution

```
For first point—
Enter x coordinate: 5
Enter y coordinate: 2
For second point—
Enter x coordinate: 10
Enter y coordinate: 22
The equation of the line is:
y = 4.00x + -18.00
```

20a. A car rental company has two types of cars to rent. The charge per day for each car type and the charge for extra miles is as follows

Car Type	Rent Per Day	Cost Per Extra Mile
1	$24.95	$0.20
2	$32.95	$0.27

The daily rate includes an allowance of 150 miles per day. The extra mileage charge is shown in the table. Write a Pascal program that randomly generates a car type, number of days rented (from 1 to 14 inclusive), and the number of miles driven per day (from 0 to 600 inclusive). The program is to output the car type, days rented, total miles driven, and the cost of the rental.

b. Expand your program to allow the user to input the number of car rental records to be generated. The program should output each record, then a summary. The summary should show the averages of days rented, miles driven, and cost for each car type. Also, the average cost of all car rentals should be output.

Sample Execution

```
Car type: 2
Number of days rented: 5
Total miles driven: 1000

Cost of the rental is: $232.25
```

Sample Execution

```
                        Averages
Car Type      Days Rented      Miles Driven        Cost
   1              7.75            1846.75        $535.41
   2              7.67            2500.33        $888.47

All rentals: $613.14
```

21. The z score of a data value (score) is given by: (Score − mean)/standard deviation. Write a Pascal program that allows the user to input a collection of data. The program then allows the user to request the z score of one of the data values. A possible design for this program follows:

Count	Score	Squares
1	10	100
2	13	169
3	17	289
:	:	:
n	14	196
	Sum	SumSq

Design: GetData
              ComputeMean&Standard Deviation
              GetScore
              Compute z score
              Report z score

GetData: Needs to return n (the number of scores input);
               Sum (the sum of the scores); and
               SumSqr (the sum of the squares of the scores)

ComputeMean&Standard Deviation: Needs n, Sum, and SumSqr
                                      Returns Mean and Std Dev

     Remember:
        Mean = Sum / n
        Standard dev = SQRT $((n*\text{SumSq} - \text{SQR(Sum)}) / ((n)*(n-1)))$

GetScore: WRITE ('Please enter score: ')
              READ (Score)

Compute z score: Needs Score, Mean, Std Dev
                       Will return z score

Report z score: WRITELN ('The z score of ', Score : 1, ' is ', z score)

22. (Simulation) A tank of capacity V gallons has input from pipe A at a gallons per hour and pipe B at b gallons per hour. The tank has a drain that outputs D gallons per hour. The input pipes and the drain are equipped with timers that allow them to open and close in cycles (open 3, closed 2, open 3, closed 2, etc.).

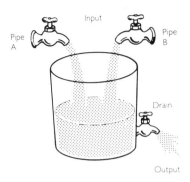

   Write a Pascal program that allows the user to (a) set the capacity of the tank; (b) set the initial level of the tank; (c) set the rate of input of pipe A and pipe B, and the rate of output of the drain; and (d) set timer A, timer B, and timer drain, to cycle. The program is to output a chart of the progression of the water level in the tank until it is full or the user wishes to quit.

Sample Execution

```
Tank simulation
Enter capacity of tank (gal): 40000
Enter initial level of tank (gal): 10000
Enter rate of pipe A (gal/hr): 800
Enter rate of pipe B (gal/hr): 500
Enter rate of drain (gal/hr): 1000
For timer on pipe A,
open cycle (hrs): 4
closed cycle (hrs): 2
For timer on pipe B,
open cycle (hrs): 2
closed cycle (hrs): 3
For timer on drain,
open cycle (hrs): 1
closed cycle (hrs): 1
```

{Screen Clears}

```
The following is a simulation of the tank's level.
Press RETURN key for next hour. Enter Q to quit.

Hour   Pipe A   Pipe B   Drain    Level
  0                               10000    <ret>
  1      800      500     1000    10300    <ret>
  2      800      500        0    11600    <ret>
  3      800        0     1000    11400    <ret>
  4      800        0        0    12200    <ret>
  5        0        0     1000    11200    <ret>
  6        0      500        0    11700    <ret>
...

Tank is full!! Hours = 124
Press RETURN key for another simulation, enter Q to quit-
```

Hint: Pipe A makes a complete cycle in `OnA + OffA` hours.
```
      IF Time MOD (OnA + OffA) <= (OnA - 1)
          THEN Pipe A is on.
```

Functions

So far in this chapter, you have studied procedures. Essentially, procedures are used to define new instructions in Pascal. In this section, you will study functions. A **function** is used to define a new operation. Functions and procedures are both viewed as subprograms in Pascal. Thus, you already know much of the information on functions from your work with procedures.

4–3.1 User-Defined Functions

Consider the predefined (built-in) function SQR. This function has a number as input. The function SQR takes the number and multiplies it times itself. The result (output) of the function is stored in the function identifier SQR. We now want to discuss functions defined by the programmer. In general, a function defined by the programmer

1. Has input values (value parameters).
2. Has an execution section to operate on the input values.
3. Produces an output value and assigns this value to the function identifier to be returned to the calling execution section.

When a programmer defines a function, the process follows the general path of defining a procedure. For example, suppose the programmer wanted a function that would cube a number. The definition would appear as follows:

```
FUNCTION Cube (Num : INTEGER) : INTEGER ;

  BEGIN
    Cube := Num * Num * Num
  END ;
```

A typical call to the function `Cube` would be `Volume := Cube (6)`

The function definition starts with the **function header.** This section of the function starts with the reserved word **FUNCTION**. The word FUNCTION indicates that the function identifier will be defined as an operation. Following the reserved word FUNCTION is the function identifier. Next in the function header is a parameter list in parentheses. The last item in the function header is a data type for the function identifier.

```
      reserved word      parameter list
            ⇓                  ⇓
      FUNCTION Cube (Num : INTEGER) : INTEGER ;
                ⇑                      ⇑
         function identifier      data type for function identifier
```

A function can have a CONST section and a VAR section. It must have an execution section. The **function execution section** is bracketed by the reserved words BEGIN and END. In the execution section, the instructions that define the function are listed. One of these instructions (usually the last one) *must* assign a value to the function identifier of the type declared in the function header.

You should note two major differences between FUNCTION blocks and PROCEDURE blocks:

1. A function identifier has a data type declared for it in the header. A procedure identifier does not.

```
FUNCTION Cube (Num : INTEGER) : INTEGER
```

2. In the execution section of a function, the function identifier *must* be assigned a value. A procedure identifier *cannot* be assigned a value. The reason for this is that a function is designed to perform a list of instructions, then return exactly one value. A procedure is designed to perform a list of instructions and possibly return several values (using variable parameters).

```
Cube := Num*Num*Num
```

Another major difference between procedures and functions occurs in the **function call.** A function executes a set of instructions, then assigns a value to the function identifier. Thus, a function identifier in the calling execution section represents a value. The function identifier must be used like a value in the calling execution section. A procedure identifier must be used as an instruction in the calling execution section.
Consider the following example.

```
Volume := Cube (6)
```

EXAMPLE

Write a function to find the average (mean) of a collection of five numbers. The input to the function will be the five numbers. The output of the function is the average of the collection of numbers. Also, give a typical call to this function.

SOLUTION

```
FUNCTION MeanOf5 (Num1, Num2, Num3, Num4, Num5 : REAL) : REAL ;

  VAR Sum : REAL ;

  BEGIN
    Sum := Num1 + Num2 + Num3 + Num4 + Num5 ;
    MeanOf5 := Sum / 5
  END
```

A typical call to this function would be

```
WRITE (MeanOf5 (12.3 , 14 , 19 , 23.8 , 3) : 7 : 3)
```

Consider the following function `NewPrice`. The input to this function consists of a character indicating whether price is to be marked up or marked down, the original price, and the percent of change. The function is to return the new price.

```
FUNCTION NewPrice (Which : CHAR ; OrigPrice, PerCent : REAL) : REAL ;

  VAR Amt : REAL ;

  BEGIN
    Amt := PerCent*OrigPrice ;
    IF (Which = 'U') OR (Which = 'u')
      THEN NewPrice := OrigPrice + Amt
      ELSE NewPrice := OrigPrice - Amt
  END
```

A possible call to `NewPrice` is: `ThePrice := NewPrice ('D', 9.87, 0.30)`

A function is boxed much as a procedure is boxed. In the header box, there *must* be an identifier for the function and a data type for the identifier. In the parentheses in the header box, the parameters for the function and their types are listed. The rest of the function is boxed in the usual way (see Figure 4–14).

Figure 4–14

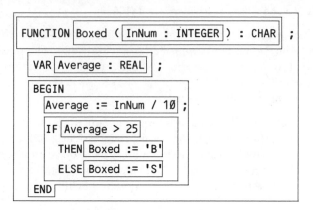

DO IT NOW

1. Write a function to compute the standard deviation of a collection of numbers. The function is to have the value parameters n (the number of numbers in the collection), Sum (the sum of the numbers), and SumSq (the sum of the squares of the numbers). The output of the function is to be the standard deviation. The formula for the standard deviation follows:

$$\text{SQRT } ((n * \text{SumSq} - \text{SQR}(\text{Sum})) / (n * (n{-}1)))$$

2. Write a function to compute a number to a whole number exponent. The function is to have the value parameters Base (the number) and Exponent (the number of times the number is to be multiplied by itself).

DO IT NOW ANSWERS

```
1. FUNCTION StdDev (n : INTEGER ; Sum ,
                    SumSq : REAL) : REAL ;

     BEGIN
       StDev := SQRT ((n*SumSq - SQR(Sum)) / (n * (n - 1)))
     END
2. FUNCTION Power (Base : REAL ; Exponent : INTEGER) : REAL ;

     VAR Count : INTEGER ;
         Hold : REAL ;

     BEGIN
       Count := 0 ;
       Hold := 1 ;
       WHILE Count < Exponent DO
         BEGIN
           Hold := Hold * Base ;
           Count := Count + 1
         END ;
       Power := Hold
     END
```

4–3.2 *Using Functions*

Here are some guidelines for using functions in Pascal programs:

1. If the subprogram is to return more than one value to the calling execution section, do not use a function. Use a procedure.
2. Use only value parameters in the function header. (To use a variable parameter would return more than one value and would confuse the readers of the program.)
3. Remember to list a data type for the function identifier in the function header.
4. Remember to assign a value to the function identifier in the function execution section. This assignment often is the last instruction in the function execution section.
5. A function call must list actual parameters that match the formal parameters in the function header both in number of parameters and in data type.
6. A function call (such as `Cube (31)`) is a call to have the instructions in the execution section of the function executed using the value(s) listed. The call also represents a value (of the type listed for the function in its header) and must appear in the calling execution section in an assignment instruction, BOOLEAN expression, etc. For example, `NumA := Cube (31)` or `WRITELN (Cube (31))`

4–3.3 *Programming Example*

To further your understanding of functions and to see functions used in a Pascal program, consider the following example.

EXAMPLE

Write a Pascal program to process a checking account. The program is to allow the user to enter a name and the starting balance for the account. The program will then process a collection of withdrawals and deposits for the account. The output of the program will be the account name and the starting and ending balances of the account.

SOLUTION

Design: GetName
　　　　 WHILE Transaction < > Q DO
　　　　　　 Get Starting Balance
　　　　　　 Get Transaction
　　　　　　 Update Balance
　　　　 Report Results

Refinement of: *Update Balance*
　　　　　 If Withdrawal
　　　　　　 Then Balance = Balance − Amount
　　　　　 If Deposit
　　　　　　 Then Balance = Balance + Amount

Sample Execution

```
Please enter account name: Thelma M. Dobbs
Please enter starting balance: $123.45
Please enter transaction (W/D/Q): W
Please enter amount: $23
Please enter transaction (W/D/Q): Q

Thelma M. Dobbs
Starting Balance $123.45
Ending Balance $100.45
```

COMMENT

A function will be used for this module. The input will be type of transaction and `Amount`. The function will return the `Balance`.

Refinement of: *Report Results*
                   Give Account Name
                   Give Starting Balance
                   Give Ending Balance

This design yields the Pascal program in Figure 4–15.

Figure 4–15

```
PROGRAM CheckAccount ;

VAR Name : STRING [30] ;
    StartBal ,
    Amount ,
    Balance : REAL ;
    Transaction : CHAR ;

FUNCTION UpDate (OldBal : REAL ;
                   Trans : CHAR ; Amt : REAL) : REAL ;

  BEGIN                              {UpDate}
    IF Trans = 'D'
      THEN UpDate := OldBal + Amt ;
    IF Trans = 'W'
      THEN UpDate := OldBal - Amt
  END ;                             {UpDate}

PROCEDURE Report (FirstBal , LastBal : REAL) ;

  BEGIN                              {Report}
    WRITELN ('Starting Balance $', FirstBal : 1 : 2) ;
    WRITELN ('Ending Balance $' , LastBal : 1 : 2)
  END ;                             {Report}

BEGIN                                {CheckAccount}
  WRITE ('Please enter account name: ') ;
  READLN (Name) ;
  WRITE ('Please enter starting balance: $') ;
  READLN (StartBal) ;
  Balance := StartBal ;
  Transaction := ' ' ;             {initialize Transaction to blank}
  WHILE Transaction < > 'Q' DO
    BEGIN                            {WHILE-DO}
      WRITE ('Please enter transaction (W/D/Q): ') ;
      READLN (Transaction) ;
      IF (Transaction = 'W') OR (Transaction = 'D')
        THEN
          BEGIN                      {IF-THEN instruction}
            WRITE ('Please enter amount: $') ;
            READLN (Amount) ;
            Balance := UpDate (Balance , Transaction , Amount)
          END                        {IF-THEN instruction}
    END ;                            {WHILE-DO}
  WRITELN ;
  WRITELN (Name) ;
  Report (StartBal , Balance)
END .                                {CheckAccount}
```

Sample Execution

```
Please enter account name: Thelma M.
Please enter starting balance: $123.4
Please enter transaction (W/D/Q): W
Please enter amount: $23
Please enter transaction (W/D/Q): Q

Thelma M. Dobbs
Starting Balance $123.45
Ending Balance $100.45
```

Consider the conditional instruction and the program in Figure 4–15.

```
IF (Transaction = 'W') OR (Transaction = 'D')
   THEN ...
```

What problems might arise if the BOOLEAN expression were replaced by
Transaction < > 'Q'? Suppose the user entered an S for the variable Transaction.
The function UpDate would be called. The value S would be passed to the actual parameter Trans. The instructions in the execution block of UpDate would be executed,
but no value would be assigned to the function identifier UpDate. An error would be
produced, since the function identifier *must* be assigned a value.

DO IT NOW

1. Suppose you were given the program CheckAccount (see Figure 4–15) and were in-
   structed by your boss to alter the program so as to have a program execution section of

```
BEGIN
  WRITE ('Please enter account name: ') ;
  READLN (Name) ;
  WRITE ('Please enter starting balance: $') ;
  READLN (StartBal) ;
  Balance := UpDate (StartBal) ;
  Report (StartBal , Balance)
END .
```

The updated version of the program is to have the following VAR section:

```
VAR Name : STRING [30] ;
    StartBal , Balance : REAL
```

Write the function UpDate. (*Hint:* Use local variables for Transaction, Amount,
and NewBal).

2. As mentioned earlier, a procedure should not be allowed to alter a program variable unless it is a variable parameter. A function simply should not alter a program
   variable. If it does, a semantics error called a **side effect** can occur. To see such an
   error, consider the following program:

```
PROGRAM SideExample ;

VAR NumA , NumB , NumC : INTEGER ;

FUNCTION SideEffect (Number : INTEGER) : INTEGER ;

  BEGIN                          {SideEffect}
  NumA := NumA + 1 ;
    SideEffect := NumA * Number
  END ;                          {SideEffect}

BEGIN                            {SideExample}
  NumA := 10 ;
  NumB := 3 ;
  NumC := 2 * SideEffect (NumB) ;
  WRITE ('NumA is: ' , NumA , ' NumB is: ' , NumB) ;
  WRITELN (' NumC is: ' , NumC)
END .                            {SideExample}
```

Give the output of the program SideExample.

DO IT NOW ANSWERS

```
1. FUNCTION UpDate (InNum : REAL) : REAL ;

   VAR Transaction : CHAR ;
       NewBal , Amount : REAL ;

   BEGIN
     NewBal := InNum ;
     Transaction := ' ' ;
     WHILE Transaction < > 'Q' DO
       BEGIN
         WRITE ('Please enter transaction (W/D/Q): ') ;
         READLN (Transaction) ;
         WRITE ('Please enter amount: $') ;
         READLN (Amount) ;
         IF Transaction = 'D'
           THEN NewBal := NewBal + Amount ;
         IF Transaction = 'W'
           THEN NewBal := NewBal - Amount
       END ;
     Update := NewBal
   END
```

2. NumA is: 11 NumB is: 3 NumC is: 66

The semantics error occurs in reading the execution section of SideExample. Since NumA was assigned the value 10 and none of the instructions that follow the assignment instruction involve NumA, the program reader should expect the output

NumA is: 10 NumB is: 3 NumC is: 66

Vocabulary

Page		
212	**Function**	A subprogram used to define a new operation.
212	**FUNCTION**	A reserved word in the Pascal language that indicates that the next word is an identifier of a function. A function definition (declaration) block must have a function header and a function execution section (it can contain a VAR section, and a CONST section). One of the instructions in the function execution section must assign a value to the function identifier.
213	**Function call**	A listing of a function identifier in an execution section. The function's identifier is listed; then, in parentheses, values for the function's parameters (if any exist) are stated. Since a value will be returned by the function, the function's identifier must appear in an assignment instruction, BOOLEAN expression, etc.
212	**Function execution section**	A list of instructions bracketed by the Pascal reserved words BEGIN and END. One of the instructions in this section *must* assign a value to the function identifier.
212	**Function header**	The first line in the definition of a function. It starts with the Pascal reserved word FUNCTION. Next comes the function identifier. The identifier can be followed by a parameter list in parentheses. Finally, a data type for the value that the function will return to the calling execution section *must* be stated.
217	**Side effect**	A semantics error that can occur if a function or procedure is allowed to alter the value of a program variable by means other than a variable parameter.

Glad You Asked

Q I wrote a program with a function `HowMany`. The function had a value parameter of type CHAR, and the output was of type INTEGER. I used the instruction `HowMany := 6` in the program execution section. I got an error when the program was being compiled. Isn't `HowMany` a memory location? And if so, why can't I assign a value to it?

A Any reference to the identifier `HowMany` outside the function's execution section is a call to have the function execute. The memory location that the function `HowMany` uses to store its output in can only be altered in the execution section of the function `HowMany`. Thus, in the sense you are using it, `HowMany` is not a memory location.

Q I had a function `CountEm` of type INTEGER that had as input a value of type INTEGER. I put the instruction

    CountEm := CountEm (5) + 3

in the execution section of the function. When I executed the program, I got the error message `STACK OVERFLOW`. What happened?

A You made a common error in the use of functions. A function identifier can be used in its own execution section. When you placed the instruction

    CountEm := CountEm (5) + 3

in the `CountEm` execution section, no error occurred while the program was compiling. When an attempt was made to execute the instruction
`CountEm := CountEm (5) + 3`, the following occurred:

1. The memory location set aside for the output was to get the value `CountEm (5) + 3`.
2. To find the value `CountEm (5)`, the function `CountEm` was called.
3. When the instructions of `CountEm` were executed, the instruction
   `CountEm := CountEm (5) + 3` appeared. To execute this instruction, the function `CountEm` was called to get the value of `CountEm (5)`.
4. When the instructions of `CountEm` were executed, the instruction
   `CountEm := CountEm (5) + 3` appeared. To execute this instruction, the function `CountEm` was called to get the value of `CountEm (5)`.

And so forth. Each time the function `CountEm` is called, a memory location is created to store the value for `CountEm`. This area of memory is called a *stack*. Eventually this area of memory becomes full (overflows). Thus, the error message `STACK OVERFLOW` appears.

This action (a function or procedure calling itself) is known as *recursion*. When used properly, it is a valuable problem-solving technique. You will see recursion used in a later chapter of this book.

Q I tried the program `CheckAccount` (page 216). I replaced the BOOLEAN expression `(Transaction = 'W') OR (Transaction = 'D')` with the BOOLEAN expression `Transaction < > 'Q'`. I ran the program and entered `A` for `Transaction`. No error occurred. I thought you said an error would occur. What happened?

A Although your compiler did not give a run-time error, you did get a logic error. Check the value in `Balance`. It will not be correct.

Section 4–3 Exercises

1. Given the function header,

        FUNCTION Discriminant (a, b, c : INTEGER) : REAL

   a. The function identifier is _____.
   b. The type of the function is _____.
   c. The parameters of the function are _____ parameters.
   d. A possible call to this function would be

        Radicand := _____

   e. For the call in part d, the variable Radicand must be of type _____.
2. Given the function header,

        FUNCTION Slope (x1 , y1 , x2 , y2 : INTEGER) : REAL

   a. The function type is _____.
   b. The function is to be sent the coordinates of two points, $(x1, y1)$ and $(x2, y2)$, and return the slope of the line through the points. Complete the execution section of the function:

        BEGIN   {Slope}
          .
          .
        END   {Slope}

3. Insert TRUE for a true statement. Insert FALSE for a false statement.
   _____ **a.** In the execution section of a function, the function identifier must be assigned a value.
   _____ **b.** A major difference between functions and procedures is that functions are not allowed a VAR section or a CONST section.
   _____ **c.** For a function of type INTEGER with identifier CheckName, the following would be a valid instruction in the program execution section:
        READLN (CheckName)
   _____ **d.** A function should not have variable parameters.
   _____ **e.** Any procedure can be replaced by a function.
   _____ **f.** A function should be used when a module is to return exactly one value to the calling execution section.
   _____ **g.** In the execution section of a procedure, the procedure identifier must be assigned a value.
   _____ **h.** A function must have a type declared for its identifier in the function header.
   _____ **i.** Every function block must be followed by a semicolon.
   _____ **j.** A function can be of type REAL or INTEGER, but not BOOLEAN.
4. Given the following function,

        FUNCTION Quad (x : INTEGER) : INTEGER ;
          BEGIN
            Quad := 3 * SQR (x) - 2 * x - 5
          END

   give the value in NumA after each of the following instructions.
   a. NumA := Quad (4)
   b. NumA := Quad (-3)
   c. NumA := Quad (10) + 10
   d. NumA := Quad (Quad (2))

5. Given the function header

```
FUNCTION Hypot (LegA , LegB : INTEGER) : REAL
```

insert *Valid* for a valid instruction and *Invalid* for an invalid instruction (assume LongSide is of type REAL).

_____ **a.** Hypot (13 , 20)
_____ **b.** WHILE Hypot < 300 DO
         WRITE ('Too small')
_____ **c.** LongSide := Hypot (2.6 , 5.0)
_____ **d.** LongSide := Hypot (5 , −3)

6. Find at least three errors in the following Pascal program:

```
Program Sleuthing ;

VAR FNum , SNum : INTEGER ;

FUNCTION FindIt (OneN , OtherN : INTEGER) ;

  VAR Count : INTEGER ;

  BEGIN                              {FindIt}
    Count := 0 ;
    WHILE Count < OtherN DO
      BEGIN
        OneN := OtherN + Count ;
        Count := Count + 1
      END
  END ;                              {FindIt}

BEGIN                                {Sleuthing}
  FNum := 6 ;
  FindIt (FNum , SNum)
END .                                {Sleuthing}
```

7. Given the following program,

```
PROGRAM FunExp ;

VAR NumA , NumB : INTEGER ;

FUNCTION BlackBox (FNum , SNum : INTEGER) : INTEGER ;

  BEGIN                              {BlackBox}
    IF FNum > SNum
      THEN BlackBox := SQR (SNum)
      ELSE BlackBox := 3 * FNum − SNum
  END ;                              {BlackBox}

BEGIN                                {FunExp}
  WRITE ('Please enter first number: ') ;
  READLN (NumA) ;
  WRITE ('Please enter second number: ') ;
  READLN (NumB) ;
  NumA := BlackBox (NumA , NumB) ;
  WRITELN (NumA , BlackBox (NumB,NumA) : 5)
END .                                {FunExp}
```

if 8 is input for NumA and 10 is input for NumB, what is the output of the program?

8. Suppose you turned in a program with the following conditional instruction:

```
IF ((First = 'S') OR (First = 'P')
     OR (First = 'R')) AND ((Second = 'S')
     OR (Second = 'P') OR (Second = 'R'))
  THEN GiveWinner (First , Second)
```

Your boss says the instruction should read as follows:

```
IF PlayOk (First , Second)
  THEN GiveWinner (First , Second)
```

Write the BOOLEAN function PlayOk.

9. Discuss the differences between functions and procedures in the following areas:
   a. the header   **b.** the execution section   **c.** the call

10. Label the following built-in modules as a *procedure* or as a *function*.
   _____ **a.** CLRSCR
   _____ **b.** SQRT
   _____ **c.** ABS
   _____ **d.** READLN

11. Determine from the way identifier ModuleA is used in the program execution section whether it is a procedure or function.
   _____ **a.** ModuleA ('B')
   _____ **b.** Ch := ModuleA ('C')
   _____ **c.** WRITELN (ModuleA ('Z'))
   _____ **d.** IF Ch = 'Z'
                   THEN ModuleA ('D')

12. Boot up Pascal; set the workfile to the file CKACC.PAS from the Source diskette. Enter the Turbo Pascal editor. Expand the function UpDate to output

    ```
    Sorry, account overdrawn.
    ```

    If the value sent for Trans is the character W and the value sent for OldBal minus the value sent for Amt is less than zero.

13. For the following procedure headers write a function header if it is possible to write the procedure as a function. If the procedure cannot be written as a function, explain why.
   a. PROCEDURE ProFun (NumA : INTEGER ;
                            VAR Ch : CHAR) ;
   b. PROCEDURE ProFun (NumA : INTEGER) ;
   c. PROCEDURE ProFun ;
   d. PROCEDURE ProFun (VAR TheNum : REAL) ;
   e. PROCEDURE ProFun (VAR Ach : CHAR ;
                            VAR FNum, SNum : INTEGER) ;

Programming Problems

14. Write a Pascal program that allows the user to input an amount invested (A), an interest rate per compound period (r), and a number of compound periods (n). The program is to output the value of the investment. The program should have two functions. The function DoPower should have input the interest rate per compound period and the number of compound periods. It should return the results $(1 + r)^n$. The function Compound should have input the amount invested (A), the interest rate per compound period (r), and the number of compound periods (n). It should return the results $A*(1 + r)^n$.

Sample Execution

```
Enter amount invested: $10000
Enter interest rate per compound period: 0.01
Enter number of compound periods: 240

Value of investment is: $108925.54
```

15. Write a Pascal program that allows the user to input the lengths of the sides of a triangle. The program should call a function `AreaTri` that is sent the lengths of the sides and returns the area measure of the triangle. The program should output the area measure of the triangle.
Hint: Area = $SQRT(s*(s - A)*(s - B)*(s - C))$
     where $s = (A + B + C)/2$

Sample Execution

```
Enter length of side A: 12
Enter length of side B: 16
Enter length of side C: 20

Area measure of triangle is: 96.00
```

16a. Write a function `Convert` that has as input an amount (a number from 1 to 1000) and a magnitude (million, billion, trillion). The function is to convert the input amount and magnitude in seconds to years. (Assume 365.25 days per year.)
   Example: Input: `15.3 million (seconds)`
           Output: `0.48 (years)`

   b. Use the function `Convert` to write a Pascal program that allows the user to input a number (from 1 to 1000), then select a magnitude (million, billion, trillion). The output of the program is to be how many years ago that input amount of seconds represents.

Sample Execution

```
Please enter an amount (1 .. 1000) : 15.3
Please select a magnitude:
A. Million
B. Billion
C. Trillion
(enter A , B , or C) : A

15.3 million seconds ago was 0.48 years ago.
```

   c. Expand the Pascal program in part b to allow the user to also select a unit of time (seconds, minutes, hours, days). The program is to output how many years ago the input amount of time represents.

Program Construction

In the first section of this chapter, you were introduced to the general concept of procedures. In the second section, you studied the finer points of procedures (parameters). In the third section, you studied functions. In this section, you will learn about program construction. First, the topics of nested procedures, structured diagrams, and scope will be discussed. Next, an approach to program construction using modules will be presented.

Modules (procedures and functions) are the essence of the Pascal language. The use of modules makes a program easier to read, test, debug, alter, and/or maintain. Additionally, using modules allows the program to mirror the problem solution design. The programmer does nearly all the work in the design stage, when the major steps are listed. These steps are then refined and tested for correctness. When the design is converted to a Pascal program, the major steps of the design are written as modules.

4–4.1 Nested Modules

Since a module is like a small program, it can itself have modules. In Section 4–1, the program GeometricShapes was presented. The program allowed the user to select from a menu one of three shapes (triangle, rectangle, or trapezoid). The program then output the area measurement of the shape. Suppose the programmer wanted to expand the program GeometricShapes (Figure 4–4) to allow the user also to find the perimeter of the shape selected. The program structure might now appear as shown in Figure 4–16.

After making the alterations shown in Figure 4–16, the structure of the program GeometricShapes is more complex. To show the structure of a program like GeometricShapes, programmers often use a **structured diagram.** Such a diagram shows the network of the program's modules. Figure 4–16 shows a structured diagram for the program GeometricShapes. The network consists of levels. The main execution section is at level 0, and the program procedures are at level 1. The nested procedures are at level 2.

Figure 4–16

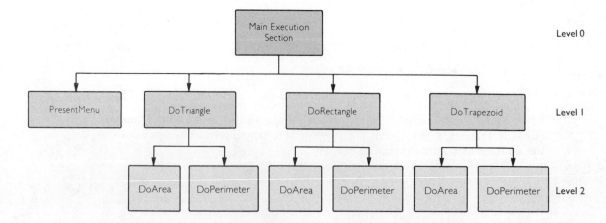

Figure 4-17

```
PROCEDURE DoTriangle ;

  VAR Ans : CHAR ;

  PROCEDURE DoArea ;

    VAR Height, Base : REAL ;

      BEGIN                              {DoArea of triangle}
        WRITE ('Enter height of triangle: ') ;
        READLN (Height) ;
        WRITE ('Enter base of triangle: ') ;
        READLN (Base) ;
        WRITE ('The area measure is: ') ;
        WRITELN (Base*Height/2) ;
        WRITELN ('Press ENTER key for main menu-') ;
        READLN                           {wait for RETURN key}
      END ;                              {DoArea of triangle}

  PROCEDURE DoPerimeter ;

    VAR Side, Sum : REAL ;
        Count : INTEGER ;

      BEGIN                              {DoPerimeter for triangle}
        Sum := 0 ;                       {initialize Sum}
        FOR Count := 1 TO 3 DO
          BEGIN                          {FOR-DO instruction}
            WRITE ('Enter length of side', Count:1, ' : ') ;
            READLN (Side) ;
            Sum := Sum + Side
          END ;                          {FOR-DO instruction}
        WRITELN ('Perimeter is ' , Sum) ;
        WRITELN ('Press ENTER key for main menu-') ;
        READLN                           {wait for RETURN key}
      END ;                              {DoPerimeter for triangle}

  BEGIN                                  {DoTriangle}
    CLRSCR ;
    WRITELN ('Triangles: ') ;
    WRITELN ('  1. Area measurement') ;
    WRITELN ('  2. Perimeter') ;
    WRITELN ;
    WRITE ('Enter 1, 2, Q=Quit: ') ;
    READLN (Ans) ;
    IF Ans = '1'
      THEN DoArea
      ELSE IF Ans = '2'
              THEN DoPerimeter
  END ;                                  {DoTriangle}
```

Sample Execution

```
Triangles:
  1. Area measurement
  2. Perimeter
Enter 1, 2, Q=Quit : 1
Enter height of triangle: 10
Enter base of triangle: 40
The area measure is: 2.0000000000E+02
Press ENTER key for main menu-
```

Sample Execution

```
Triangles:
  1. Area measurement
  2. Perimeter
Enter 1, 2, Q=Quit: 2
Enter length of side1: 20
Enter length of side2: 10
Enter length of side3: 15
Perimeter is 4.5000000000E+01
Press ENTER key for main menu-
```

Structured Diagram

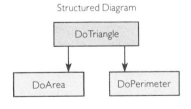

The box at the top (in Figure 4–16) coordinates the boxes at level 1. That is, the main execution section calls the program procedures. The procedures at level 1 call the procedures at level 2 that are subordinate to them. It is often recommended that the design of the solution to a problem start with a structured diagram. For solutions that are long and have many steps, a structured diagram is a valuable tool.

Altering the procedure DoTriangle to find the perimeter as well, produces the procedure shown in Figure 4–17. Here, the procedures DoArea and DoPerimeter are said to be **nested procedures** in the procedure DoTriangle. A similar alteration would be made to procedures DoRectangle and DoTrapezoid to produce the desired change to GeometricShapes.

DO IT NOW

1. Given that the alterations just discussed are made to the program GeometricShapes,
   a. If the user enters A and then enters 2, trace the action through the program.
   b. If the user next enters the values 5, 2.7, and 8, give the output.
2. Alter the procedure DoTrapezoid in a manner similar to the alteration made for DoTriangle.

DO IT NOW ANSWERS

1a. When the user enters A to select from the main menu, the procedure DoTriangle is called. When the user enters 2 to select from the menu for DoTriangle, the procedure DoPerimeter is called.

  b. The output will be The perimeter is 1.5700000000E+01
                       Press RETURN key for main menu–

2. PROCEDURE DoTrapezoid ;

     VAR Ans : CHAR ;

     PROCEDURE DoArea ;

       VAR BigBase , SmallBase , Height : REAL ;

       BEGIN   {DoArea of trapezoid}
         WRITE ('Enter height of trapezoid: ') ;
         READLN (Height) ;
         WRITE ('Enter major base of trapezoid: ') ;
         READLN (BigBase) ;
         WRITE ('Enter minor base of trapezoid: ') ;
         READLN (SmallBase) ;
         WRITE ('The area measure is: ') ;
         WRITELN (0.5*(BigBase + SmallBase)*Height) ;
         WRITELN ('Press RETURN key for main menu–') ;
         READLN   {wait for RETURN key}
       END ;   {DoArea of triangle}

     PROCEDURE DoPerimeter ;

       VAR Side, Sum : REAL ;
           Count : INTEGER ;

       BEGIN   {DoPerimeter for trapezoid}
         Sum := 0 ;   {initialize Sum}
         FOR Count := 1 TO 4 DO
           BEGIN   {FOR-DO instruction}
             WRITE ('Enter length of side', Count:1 , ' : ') ;
             READLN (Side) ;
             Sum := Sum + Side
           END ;   {FOR-DO instruction}
         WRITELN ('Perimeter is ' , Sum) ;
         WRITELN ('Press ENTER key for main menu–') ;
         READLN   {wait for RETURN key}
       END ;   {DoPerimeter for triangle}
```
```

```
BEGIN                              {DoTrapezoid}
  CLRSCR ;
  WRITELN ('Trapezoids: ') ;
  WRITELN ('  1. Area measurement') ;
  WRITELN ('  2. Perimeter') ;
  WRITELN ;
  WRITE ('Enter 1, 2, Q=Quit: ') ;
  READLN (Ans) ;
  IF Ans = '1'
    THEN DoArea
    ELSE IF Ans = '2'
           THEN DoPerimeter
END ;                              {DoTrapezoid}
```

4-4.2 *Global and Local Identifiers*

The alterations made to the procedures `DoTriangle`, `DoRectangle`, and `DoTrapezoid` were made independently of the program `GeometricShapes`. That is, the programmer was told what the procedure should do and then a local alteration in that procedure was made to accomplish this objective. The programmer did not need to concern himself with the rest of the program, since it stayed the same. This is part of the power of module use. Modules allow the programmer to concentrate on the task at hand without worrying about the other parts of the program. To understand how this is accomplished, we will discuss the terms global identifiers and local identifiers.

Figure 4-18

Consider the demonstration Pascal program in Figure 4–18. When the program `Demo` is compiled, memory locations are set aside for the program variables `NumA`, `Name`, and `Results`. These variables are called **global variables** or **global identifiers**. That is, they are known (can be used) throughout the program. This means that one of instructions in the procedure `Trial` could use one or more of the variables identifiers `NumA`, `Name`, or `Results`.

When the procedure `Trial` is called, memory locations are set aside for the procedure variables (`FNum` and `SNum`). After the instructions of the procedure have been executed, these memory locations are taken back by the system (their contents are lost). They are known (can be used) only when the procedure `Trial` is executing, and cannot be used in the execution section of the program `Demo`. For this reason, the variables `FNum` and `SNum` are said to be **local variables** or **local identifiers**.

Local variables are destroyed (the memory locations are taken back by the Pascal system and used for other purposes) after the instructions of the module are executed. Thus, any local variables should be initialized each time the module is called (since the old values are lost). For example, suppose you made a call to the procedure `Trial` and at the end of `Trial`'s execution, `FNum` contained the value 5. Do not assume that `FNum` will contain the value 5 when `Trial` is called again!

Earlier, we said that a module can be written independently of the rest of the program. The writer of the module does not have to worry about which identifiers to use. What happens if a variable identifier is declared in a module that has the same name as a global identifier? When the module is called (executed), the system reserves a different memory location than the one used for the global identifier. For example

```
Program Demo ;

VAR NumA : INTEGER ;
    Name : STRING [30] ;
    Results : REAL ;

PROCEDURE Trial ;

  VAR FNum ,
      SNum : INTEGER ;

  BEGIN
    {Procedure Instructions}
  END ;

BEGIN
  {Program Instructions}
END .
```

```
PROGRAM Example ;

VAR NumB : INTEGER ;

PROCEDURE One ;

  VAR NumB : INTEGER ;

  BEGIN
    NumB := 3 ;
    WRITELN ('NumB is ', NumB : 3)
  END ;

BEGIN
  NumB := 12 ;
  One ;
  WRITELN ('NumB is ', NumB : 3)
END .
```

Sample Execution

```
NumB is   3
NumB is  12
```

When procedure One was called, NumB was assigned the value 3 during the execution of the procedure. After the execution of procedure One, the memory cell NumB is taken back by the system. To the rest of the program, NumB references a different memory location whose contents is 12.

4-4.3 Scope

A procedure (or function) defined at the program level is known (can be used) by any procedure/function that follows it. Also, the procedure (or function) is known in the program execution section. Consider a procedure nested in another procedure. Where is the nested procedure known? That is, in which execution sections can the identifier of the nested procedure be used? Questions of this nature deal with the **scope** of an identifier.

Before presenting a rule for scope, we will first explore a graphic technique known as **blocking.** To block a program, start the box at the program header, and conclude the box at the END of the program execution section. To block a module, draw a box starting at the header section and ending at the END of the module's execution section. See Figure 4–19.

Figure 4–19

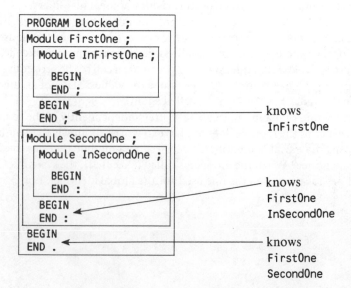

The scope rule for module identifiers is as follows:

> A module identifier is known by (can be used in the execution section of) any module that is in the same block and follows it.

Using this rule, consider the program form in Figure 4–19. The following observations are made.

1. The main execution section knows modules `FirstOne` and `SecondOne`. The main execution section does not know `InFirstOne` and `InSecondOne`. That is, if the identifier `InFirstOne` (or `InSecondOne`) appears in the program execution section, the compiler will stop and issue the error message `undeclared identifier`.
2. The module `FirstOne` knows the module `InFirstOne`.
3. The module `SecondOne` knows modules `FirstOne` and `InSecondOne`.

Something to keep in mind when thinking about scope is that *nothing happens with a procedure/function until it is called*. That is, until module `FirstOne` is called, the module `InFirstOne` does not exist. Thus, `InFirstOne` could not possibly be known outside the `FirstOne` block.

DO IT NOW

1. Construct a structured diagram for the program form in Figure 4–19.
2. Construct a program form where program `President` knows modules `VicePresA` and `VicePresB`, module `VicePresA` knows `VicePresB` and `DepartHead1`, and module `VicePresB` knows `DepartHead2`.
3. Construct a structured diagram for the program form in problem 2.

DO IT NOW ANSWERS

1.

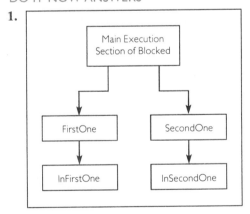

2.

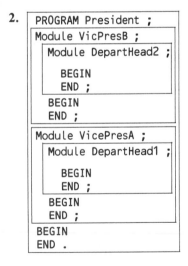

3.

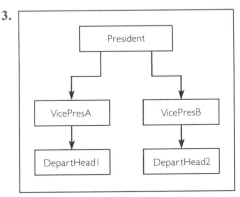

4-4.4 *Building a Pascal Program*

A Pascal program can be constructed by putting together modules (modularization). That is, the programmer can concentrate on one part (module) of the program at a time. Thus, rather than approach a program as a long sequence of instructions, the programmer breaks the program into smaller and smaller pieces. The programmer develops the code for one small piece of the program. This piece is tested and debugged, then inserted into the program.

In Pascal, this approach can be implemented as follows:

1. A design of the solution for the problem is developed, refined, and tested.
2. A shell (stub) of the Pascal program is entered. The shell is saved, then tested and debugged.
3. Each module in the design is written as a Pascal program. The program corresponding to the module is saved, tested, and debugged. Next, the program for the module is converted to a procedure or function and saved. The module is then plugged into the main program shell.

COMMENT

This last part is accomplished using the Copy application of the editor. That is, in the program shell, the cursor is moved to the point where the module is to be inserted. Ctrl-K R is used to read a file from the diskette. The name of the file containing the module is entered. The text of the file containing a module is inserted at the cursor location.

Once the module is plugged in, the partial program is tested again.

4. Step 3 is repeated until the program construction is complete.

By using this approach, the program is tested as it is constructed. That is, the programmer knows that each module works by itself and that it works with the main execution section. Additionally, some of the modules developed can be used in other Pascal programs. That is, a collection of utilities are developed.

PROGRAMMING POINT

With longer programs, when the program is developed straight from the design and its refinements, errors naturally occur. It is difficult to locate the source of an error when working with the entire program. Often modules that are correct are altered in an attempt to fix an error in the program.

As an example of the modular approach to program construction, consider the following example.

EXAMPLE

An item is to be depreciated by the straight line depreciation method. Write a Pascal program to output a chart of year versus value of the item. The program is to have as input the original value of the item, the salvage value of the item, and the number of years to depreciate the item.

Sample Execution

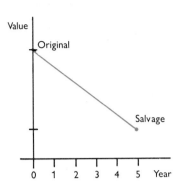

```
Please enter original value of item: $10000
Please enter salvage value of item: $2000
Enter life of item in years: 5

Year    Value
 1      $8400.00
 2      $6800.00
 3      $5200.00
 4      $3600.00
 5      $2000.00
```

SOLUTION

Depreciating an item means reducing its value year by year by a selected amount. For example, if an item orginally has a value of $10,000 and after five years the salvage value is $2000, then the depreciation is $8000. To depreciate the item by the straight line method, the amount of depreciation is divided by the life of the item, then the value is reduced by this amount each year.

   Using this information, a design is constructed.

Design: GetData
         Compute AmtOfDep
         WriteChart

Refinement of: *GetData*
         ClearScreen
         WRITE ('Please enter original value of item: $')
         READLN (OrigValue)
         WRITE ('Please enter salvage value of item: $')
         READLN (SalValue)
         WRITE ('Enter life of item in years: ')
         READLN (Years)

Refinement of: *Compute AmtofDep*
         AmtOfDep : = OrigVal − SalValue

Refinement of: *WriteChart*
         GOTOXY (1,5)
         WRITE ('Year', 'Value' : 20)
         FOR Ct : = 1 TO NumYears DO
              Value : = Value − AmtOfDep/NumYears
              WRITELN (Ct : 3, '$':15, Value : 1 : 2)

After testing the design, the editor is entered and a program shell is created (see Figure 4–20).

Figure 4–20

```
PROGRAM StLine ;                    {the shell}

VAR OrigValue, SalValue : REAL ;
    Years : INTEGER ;

PROCEDURE GetData (VAR TheValue, TheSal : REAL ;
                   VAR Time : INTEGER) ;

  BEGIN
    WRITELN ('GetData called')
  END ;

PROCEDURE WriteChart (Value, AmtOfDep : REAL ;
                      NumYears : INTEGER) ;

  BEGIN
    WRITELN ('WriteChart called')
  END ;

BEGIN                   {Main execution section}
  GetData (OrigValue, SalValue, Years) ;
  AmtOfDep := OrigVal - SalValue ;
  WriteChart (OrigValue, AmtOfDep, Years)
END .                        {Main execution section}
```

The file is saved. Next, the shell is executed to test and debug it.

Since the steps `GetData` and `ComputeAmtOfDep` are fairly simple, the step `WriteChart` will be used to demonstrate the modular program construction approach.

The step `WriteChart` is first developed as a Pascal program. See Figure 4–21.

Figure 4–21

```
PROGRAM WriteChart ;

VAR Value, AmtOfDep : REAL ;
    Ct, NumYears : INTEGER ;

BEGIN
  Value := 10000 ;                          {an input value later}
  AmtOfDep := 1600 ;                        {an input value later}
  NumYears := 5 ;                           {an input value later}
  CLRSCR ;                                  {just for testing}
  GOTOXY (1,5) ;
  WRITELN ('Year', 'Value' : 20) ;          {do header for chart}
  FOR Ct := 1 TO NumYears DO
    BEGIN                                   {output line of chart}
      Value := Value - AmtOfDep/NumYears ;  {depreciate Value for year}
      WRITELN (Ct : 3, '$' : 15, Value : 1 : 2)
    END                                     {output line of chart}
END .
```

After entering the text, the file is saved. Next, the program is run, tested, and debugged. After the programmer is sure the program works properly, the program is converted to a procedure. See Figure 4–22.

Figure 4–22

```
PROCEDURE WriteChart (Value, AmtOfDep : REAL ;
                      NumYears : INTEGER) ;

VAR Ct : INTEGER ;

BEGIN
  GOTOXY (1,5) ;
  WRITE ('Year', 'Value' : 20) ;              {do header for chart}
  FOR Ct := 1 TO NumYears DO
    BEGIN                                      {output line of chart}
      Value := Value - AmtOfDep/NumYears ;     {depreciate value for year}
      WRITELN (Ct : 3, '$' : 15, Value : 1 : 2)
    END                                        {output line of chart}
END ;
```

After the conversion, the file is saved. The program shell is loaded into the editor. The procedure WriteChart is inserted in the program shell at the desired location. The program is tested again to insure that the procedure interfaces correctly with the program.

By using this approach to program development, each piece of the program is developed and tested separately. Next, the parts are pieced together to form a program. If there are difficulties, they are localized to a module of the program. Also, some of the modules developed will become utilities that can be used in other programs.

Vocabulary

		Page
Blocking	A graphic technique used to show a module's scope.	228
Global identifier	An identifier known throughout the program block.	227
Local identifier	An identifier known only in a module block.	227
Module block	The area of the program that starts with the module's header and ends with the END of the module's execution section.	228
Nested procedures	Procedures that are defined (declared) in a procedure block.	226
Scope	A description of where an identifier is known (can be used). The scope of a program constant is the entire program. The scope of a variable declared in a module is the module block. The scope of a program module is the program execution section and any program module block that physically follows it.	228
Structured diagram	A diagram that shows the network of a program's modules.	224

Glad You Asked

Q When should I use nested procedures?

A A general guideline to use in making a decision to nest a procedure is as follows: If the procedure is not needed by the rest of the program, then it can be nested.

The stepwise refinement of a procedure will reveal the need for a nested procedure, just as the program design revealed the need for the original procedure. For beginners, it is sometimes recommended that all procedures be written at the program level (that is, without nesting). Doing this makes it much easier to deal with the scope of a procedure. However, not using nested procedures destroys the idea of writing a program that mirrors the solution design.

Figure 4–23

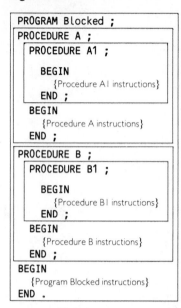

```
PROGRAM Blocked ;
  PROCEDURE A ;
    PROCEDURE A1 ;

      BEGIN
          {Procedure A1 instructions}
      END ;
    BEGIN
        {Procedure A instructions}
    END ;
  PROCEDURE B ;
    PROCEDURE B1 ;

      BEGIN
          {Procedure B1 instructions}
      END ;
    BEGIN
        {Procedure B instructions}
    END ;
  BEGIN
      {Program Blocked instructions}
  END .
```

Q What is meant by *level?* I heard someone say, "A procedure is known by any procedure that follows it and that is at the same *level*."

A *Level* is usually used to refer to modules. It can be described by example better than it can be defined. Consider program Blocked in Figure 4–23. The procedures A and B are said to be at the program level. Procedure A1 is said to be at Procedure A level; Procedure B1 is said to be at Procedure B level. Using the term *level* makes it much easier to give the scope of a procedure. The statement you mentioned means that Procedure B does not know Procedure A1. Procedure B follows Procedure A1, but they are not at the same level. Procedure B is at the program level, and Procedure A1 is at the Procedure A level. The scope of a procedure could be stated as follows:

1. A procedure is known in any procedure that follows it and that is at the same level.
2. A procedure is known by the procedure (if any) that defines its level. For example, Procedure A1 is known by Procedure A but not by the program Blocked (Procedure A1's level is defined by Procedure A).

Q Can a procedure call itself?

A Yes. A procedure can make a call to itself (its identifier can be used in its own execution section). This area will be covered in a later chapter under the topic of recursion.

Section 4–4 Exercises

1a. Construct a structured diagram for the following Pascal program:

```
PROGRAM Scope ;

VAR Num : INTEGER ;
    Ans : CHAR ;

PROCEDURE FirstOne ;

  VAR FNum : INTEGER ;

  BEGIN
      {instructions for FirstOne}
  END ;

PROCEDURE SecondOne ;

  VAR SecNum : INTEGER ;

  PROCEDURE SubSecond ;

    VAR SNuBA : INTEGER ;

    BEGIN
        {instructions for SubSecond}
    END ;

  BEGIN
      {instructions for SecondOne}
  END ;

BEGIN
    {instructions for Program Scope}
END .
```

b. Block the Pascal program in Part a.

c. Mark the following instructions and the given execution sections as *Valid* or *Invalid*.

_____ **1.** FirstOne in SecondOne execution section
_____ **2.** SecondOne in Scope execution section
_____ **3.** SecondOne in FirstOne execution section
_____ **4.** FirstOne in SubSecond execution section
_____ **5.** SubSecond in Scope execution section

2. Write the following Pascal program as a procedure. The procedure is to have an input of Investment, Goal, and IntRate (as a decimal per month). The procedure is to return the Time to the calling execution block.

(*Hint:* Remove the procedure GetData. It will be replaced by parameters in the new procedure header. Also, the two WRITELN instructions in the program execution section can be removed.)

```
PROGRAM HowLong ;

VAR Investment , Goal , IntRate : REAL ;
    Time : INTEGER ;

PROCEDURE GetData (VAR MoneyIn , MoneyOut : REAL ;
                   VAR Rate : REAL) ;

  BEGIN                                         {GetData}
    WRITE ('Please enter amount invested: $') ;
    READLN (MoneyIn) ;
    WRITE ('Please enter goal: $') ;
    READLN (MoneyOut) ;
    WRITE ('Interest rate as percent per year is: ') ;
    READLN (Rate) ;
    Rate := Rate / 100 / 12
  END ;                                         {GetData}

PROCEDURE DoNextMonth (IntRate : REAL ; VAR NextMonth : REAL ;
                       VAR Months : INTEGER) ;

  BEGIN                                         {DoNextMonth}
    NextMonth := NextMonth  * (1 + IntRate) ;
    Months := Months + 1
  END ;                                         {DoNextMonth}

  BEGIN                                         {HowLong}
    GetData (Investment , Goal , IntRate) ;
    Time := 0 ;
    WHILE Investment <= Goal DO
       DoNextMonth (IntRate , Investment , Time) ;
    WRITELN ('It will take ', Time:1 , ' months') ;
    WRITELN ('for your money to grow to $' , Goal : 1 : 2)
  END .                                         {HowLong}
```

3. Sketch a program layout (give blocks) to satisfy the following.

a. Variable NumA is known by procedure Zap but not by procedure Zip or program ZipZap.

b. Procedure Duke is known by procedure Queen but is not known by procedure King or program Domain.

c. Variable Serf is known by procedure LandLord and by procedure OverLord but not by program Kingdom.

4. Circle the errors in the following program:

```
PROGRAM ErrScope ;

VAR ProgA , ProgB : INTEGER ;

PROCEDURE Para (VAR A , B , C : INTEGER) ;
   BEGIN
     ScopeIt (A,B)
   END ;

PROCEDURE ScopeIt (Var A: INTEGER ; B : INTEGER) ;
   PROCEDURE SubScope ;
     VAR InnerValue : BOOLEAN ;
     BEGIN
       InnerValue := TRUE
     END ;
   BEGIN
     IF A < B
       THEN Para (A,B,A)
   END ;
PROCEDURE LevelErr ;
   BEGIN
     SubScope ;
     ScopeIt (5 , 3)
   END ;
BEGIN
   WRITELN ('No errors here!')
END .
```

5. Boot up Pascal; set the workfile to the file `STLINE.PAS` from the `Source` diskette. Enter the Turbo Pascal editor. Use the Copy application to read in the contents of the TEXT file `WRCHART.PAS` from the `Source` diskette. Alter the material read in by the Copy application to a procedure. Execute the altered program several times to test the alterations.

Programming Problems

6. Write a Pascal program that allows the user to input one of the outcomes from rolling a pair of dice (2,3, . . . , 12). The program should then request from the user the number of trials (rolls) on which the experimental probability should be based. The output of the program is to be the experimental probability of obtaining the outcome input by the user.

Sample Execution

```
Please enter one of the outcomes
from rolling a pair of dice (2..12): 5
On how many rolls should the
experimental probability be based? 200
The experimental probability of a 5 is 0.178
```

7. The monthly payments (*MP*) on a loan are based on the amount of the loan (*L*), the interest rate per month (*r*), and the number of months (*n*). The formula for the computation is

$$MP = (r * L * (1 + r)^n)/((1 + r)^n + 1)$$

Write a Pascal program that allows the user to input the amount of the loan, the interest rate as a percent per year, and the number of years. The output is to be the monthly payments on the loan.

Sample Execution

```
Please enter amount of loan: $8000
Please enter percent interest rate per year: 18
Please enter number of years: 5
Your monthly payments will be: $203.15
```

8. Joe Smart, marketing director for Go Get Em Software, Inc., has come up with a sales program to boost sales. The plan is to price each piece of software based on the number of pieces ordered by a customer. The price of an order of one piece is $40. The price of an order of two pieces is $40 for the first piece and $36 for the second piece; that is, each additional piece ordered is reduced in price by 10% of the price of the previous piece. Write a Pascal program that allows the user to input the size of an order. The output of the program should be the price of the order.

   Hint: Joe's plan is just like compound interest, except rather than gaining value, there is a loss in value. The price of nth piece is $40 (1 - 0.10)^n$. How many pieces of software must be ordered so as to get any additional pieces free (*Free* meaning the cost is less than 1 cent)?

Sample Execution

```
Please enter number of pieces ordered: 30
Price of order is: $383.04
Price of piece 30 was $1.88

Press RETURN to do another order, enter Q to quit
```

9. Write a Pascal program that requests two fractions from the user. The program will then present the following menu:

```
A. Find sum of fractions
B. Find difference of fractions
C. Find product of fractions
D. Find quotient of fractions
Q. Quit
Please select option by entering letter (A .. D, Q):
```

The output of the program is to be the results (as a fraction) of the operation selected.

10. Write a Pascal program that allows the user to select from the following menu:

```
A. Value of an investment
B. Value of an annuity
C. Monthly payments on a loan
Please select A, B, C, or Q=Quit:
```
                                                (continued)

Hint: Convert to procedures the program `Finance` (page 198) and the programs written for an annuity (page 208) and monthly payments (page 237). The procedure to compute the compound interest factor $(1 + r)^n$ should appear as the first procedure at the program level, since it will be used by each of the procedures.

11a. Write a Pascal program that randomly generates 5 grades for a student. The grades generated should be based on the following algorithm.

1. Select a random number from 1 to 10 (inclusive).
2. If number is less than 3,

    `Grade := RANDOM (50)`

    If number is between 3 and 6 inclusive,

    `Grade := RANDOM (30) + 50`

    If number is greater than 6,

    `Grade := RANDOM (21) + 80`

The program should output the grades generated, and the student's numeric average (rounded to nearest whole number) based on the following plan.

1. Drop the lowest grade (that is, average four highest grades).
2. If score on Test3 is greater than 85, add 5 points to average.

Sample Execution

```
Student's grades are:
78  91  86  36  68
Student's average is: 86
```

b. Convert your program in part a to a procedure. Use the procedure to write a program that generates grades for 30 students. The program is to output the percentage of students passing (any average greater than 59 is passing), the highest average generated, and the percentage of A's (an A is given for averages over 92).

Sample Execution

```
Percent passing is 68%
Highest average was 101
Percent A's is 9%
```

12. An amortization table is a listing of the progress made in paying off an installment loan. Part of an amortization table is presented here (the loan is for $12,000 at 12% interest for 4 years).

Payment#	Amount	Interest	Principal	Remaining Balance
1	316.01	120.00	196.01	11803.99
2	316.01	118.04	197.97	11606.02
. . .	. . .	. . .	. . .	. . .
48	315.99	3.13	312.86	0.00

Write a Pascal program that allows the user to input the loan amount, interest rate per year, and number of years. The output is to be an amortization table for the loan. The program should pause at the end of each 12 lines of output and wait for the user to press the RETURN key to continue the output of the table.

Design: Get loan data
          Compute monthly payment   {see problem 7 page 237}
          RemainingBalance : = LoanAmount
          Write table header
          Month : = 1
          REPEAT
              Compute InterestPaid, Principal, RemainingBalance
              Write Table Line
              IF Month MOD 12 = 0
                THEN READLN
                ELSE WRITELN
              Month : = Month + 1
          UNTIL MONTH = LengthOfLoanInMonths

Refinement of: *Compute InterestPaid, Principal, RemainingBalance*
                 InterestPaid : = IntRate * RemainingBalance
                 Principal : = MonthlyPayment − Interest
                 RemainingBalance : = RemainingBalance − Principal

CHAPTER TEST

Select the best choice for problems 1 through 9 from the list on the left.

a. procedure
b. top down
c. variable parameter
d. function
e. scope
f. value parameter
g. procedure call
h. structured diagram
i. formal parameters
j. actual parameters

_____ **1.** a module that always returns exactly one value to the calling execution section
_____ **2.** the parameters listed in the procedure header
_____ **3.** the areas of the program where an identifier has meaning
_____ **4.** a parameter that must be sent a variable identifier
_____ **5.** a method of showing the levels of a Pascal program
_____ **6.** the parameters listed in the procedure call
_____ **7.** the listing of a procedure's identifier in an execution section
_____ **8.** a design approach in which major steps in the solution are listed and tested first
_____ **9.** a feature of the Pascal language that allows the programmer to define a complex step in the solution's design as a module

10. Insert TRUE for a true statement. Insert FALSE for a false statement.
_____ **a.** The identifiers used as formal parameters must be declared in the program VAR section.
_____ **b.** To declare a variable parameter in a procedure header, the reserved word VAR is used.
_____ **c.** A function's identifier must be assigned a value in the function's execution section.
_____ **d.** A module identifier declared in the VAR section of a function can be used in the program execution section.
_____ **e.** A function should not have variable parameters.

11. Given the following procedure header,

```
PROCEDURE CountAs (Letter : CHAR ; VAR Number : INTEGER) ;
```

if `Count` and `Alpha` are program variables of type INTEGER and CHAR, respectively, insert *Valid* for a valid call, and *Invalid* for an invalid call to `CountAs`.
_____ **a.** CountAs ('T' , 22)
_____ **b.** Count := CountAs (Alpha , Count)
_____ **c.** CountAs ('A' , Number)
_____ **d.** CountAs (Count, Alpha)
_____ **e.** WRITE (CountAs ('A', Count))
_____ **f.** CountAs (Alpha, Count)

12. Given the following Pascal program stub,

```
PROGRAM ComputeSinX ;

VAR X , SinX , XRadians : REAL ;
    NumTerms , Count : INTEGER ;

FUNCTION Factorial (n : INTEGER) : REAL ;

  BEGIN
    {function will return factorial of input number}
  END ;

FUNCTION Power (Base , Exponent) : REAL ;

  BEGIN
    {function will return base to exponent power}
  END ;

BEGIN                          {main program}
  WRITE ('Enter value of x in degrees (0 .. 90 ): ') ;
  READLN (X) ;
  WRITE ('Use how many terms in estimation (3 .. 15 ): ') ;
  READLN (NumTerms) ;
  XRadians := 2*3.14*X/360 ;
  Count := 1 ;
  WHILE _____

  _____

END .                          {main program}
```

COMMENT
The notation 3! means 3 factorial.
That is, $3! = 3*2*1$ or 6.

complete the execution section of `ComputeSinX`. Use the following formula:

$$Sin(x) = x^1/1! - x^3/3! + x^5/5! - x^7/7! + \ldots$$

Sample Execution

```
Enter value of x in degrees (0 .. 90): 60
Use how many terms in estimation (3 .. 15): 12
The sin of 60 degrees is approximately: 0.866
```

13. Write a Pascal procedure that has as input a three-digit number. The procedure is to write to the screen the hundreds digit and return to the calling execution section the number represented by the tens and ones digit.
Input: **759**
Output: **7** written to the screen and the value **59** returned.

14. Write a Pascal function `SumDigits` that has as input a two-digit number. The value returned is the numerological value of the number. That is, the digits are summed; if the value is greater than 9, the digits are summed again.
Input: **75**
Output: **3**　(*Note:* 7 + 5 = 12, and 1 + 2 = 3.)

15. Use the function `SumDigits` in problem 14 to write a Pascal program that allows the user to enter a birthday as a month number, day number, and year number. The program is to output the numerological value of the birthday.

Sample Execution

```
Please enter birth month number (1 .. 12): 3
Please enter birth day number (1 .. 31): 25
Please enter birth year number: 1953

Your birth number is: 1
```

```
Design:   For Ct := 1 To 3 DO
             CASE Ct OF
                1 : WRITE ( 'Please enter birth month number (1..12): ' )
                2 : WRITE ( 'Please enter birth day number (1..31): ' )
                3 : WRITE ( 'Please enter birth year number: ' )
             END
             READLN ( Value )
             BirthNum := BirthNum + SumDigits ( Value )
             WHILE BirthNum > 9 DO
                BirthNum := SumDigits ( BirthNum )
           WRITELN ( 'Your birth number is: ' , BirthNum )
```

Programming Projects

Project 4–1.
You may have received a form letter such as the following one. The parts filled in by the program user are underlined for demonstration. In the actual letter, there would be no underlining.

The Liscombe's
6578 South A Street   December 15, 1990
Yonkers
New York

Dear Mr. and Ms. Liscombe:

Only you have been selected from the Yonkers area to apply for our once-a-year special discount on our nuclear food processor. The Liscombe family will glow when they show off this processor to their neighbors on A Street. Apply before October 31, 1998, and receive at no cost an attachment that can be used for light landscaping jobs.

Sincerely,

Write a Pascal program that does the following.

   a. Allows the user to enter in the underlined parts.
   b. Presents the completed letter and allows the user to verify the letter.
   c. Writes the completed form letter to the printer.

Turn in the following for this project:
   a. A program design and its refinements.
   b. A hard copy of your Pascal program.
   c. Two form letters produced by the program.

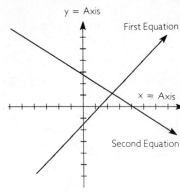

y = Axis

First Equation

x = Axis

Second Equation

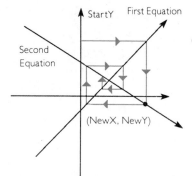

StartY   First Equation

Second
Equation

(NewX, NewY)

Project 4-2.

A system of equations like

$$3x + 5y = 10$$
$$2x - 3y = 3$$

In general,
$Ax + By = C$
$Dx + Ey = F$

has as a solution an ordered pair of numbers, that is, a value for x and a value for y. Such a system can be solved by a method known as *iteration*. An algorithm for solving this system by the iterative method is as follows:

1. Rewrite the first equation: $3x + 5y = 10$ for x.
   Thus, $x = (10 - 5y)/3$.
   Rewrite the second equation: $2x - 3y = 3$ for y.
   Thus, $y = (3 - 2x)/(-3)$.
2. Enter an initial approximation for y. For example, $y = 4$. Next, compute the new value for x by using the equation in part 1.
3. Enter a closeness factor (a small positive number): 0.01.
4. Define `CloseEnough` as
   $(ABS(3x + 5y - 10) < 0.01)$ AND $(ABS(2x - 3y - 3) < 0.01)$
5. WHILE NOT CloseEnough DO
      NewApproximation
   where NewApproximation is
      NewX := (10 - 5 * Old Y)/3
      NewY := (3 - 2 * OldX)/(- 3)
6. Report solution: NewX, NewY

NewX := (C - B•OldY)/A
NewY := (F - D•OldX)/E

Write a Pascal program to solve systems of equations by iteration.

Sample Execution

```
This program solves a system of equations by iteration.
For first equation-  enter x coefficient: 3
                     enter y coefficient: 5
                     enter number term: 10
For second equation- enter x coefficient: 2
                     enter y coefficient: -3
                     enter number term: 3
                     enter start value for y: 7
Enter closeness factor (a small positive number): 0.005

Now, solving system ....................

Solution is: x = 2.368
             y = 0.579

Enter Q to quit, press RETURN to do another problem:
```

Hint:
```
IF A/B = D/E
  THEN WRITE ('No solution')
IF ABS (A/B) < ABS (D/E)
  THEN Swap (A,D)
       Swap (B,E)
       Swap (C,F)
```

Turn in the following:
a. A design and a structured diagram.
b. A hard copy of your Pascal program.
c. A hard copy of at least three test executions.

Chapter Five

Data

Introduction

The Pascal language requires the programmer to state a type for the data a variable will hold. Thus, knowledge of data is essential to solving problems on the computer. In the first section of this chapter, the simple data types will be reviewed. Two new classes of data types will be introduced. These classes are subrange data types and enumerated data types. The second section introduces the idea of structuring simple data into more complex data structures. As examples of data structures, we will consider the data types STRING and SET. In the third section, a data structure known as a TEXT file will be introduced. TEXT files provide for storing information generated by a computer program on a diskette. Such storage allows information to be retained after the computer is turned off. In the last section of this chapter, problems and examples dealing with characters and numbers in TEXT files will be presented.

```
PROGRAM Chapter5 ;
{$R+}                                      {page 249}

TYPE WholeNum = 0 .. MAXINT ;              {page 248}
    DayType = (Mon, Tue, Wed, Thr) ;       {page 250}
    String40 = STRING [40] ;               {page 262}

VAR Num : WholeNum ;                        {page 249}
    Choices : SET OF 'A' .. 'E' ;          {page 268}
    TheDay : DayType ;                     {page 249}
    TheName : String40 ;
    TheFile : TEXT ;                       {page 281}

PROCEDURE OpenFile (VAR AFile : TEXT) ;    {page 288}

  VAR Name : STRING [8] ;

  BEGIN
    WRITE ('Enter file name: ') ;
    READLN (Name) ;
    ASSIGN (AFile, Name) ;                 {page 282}
    RESET (AFile)                          {page 283}
  END ;

BEGIN
  OpenFile (TheFile) ;                     {page 288}
  WHILE NOT EOF (TheFile) DO               {page 284}
    READLN (TheFile,TheName) ;             {page 283}
  CLOSE (TheFile) ;                        {page 284}
  Choices := ['A' .. 'E'] ;               {page 268}
  ASSIGN (TheFile, 'NewName.TXT') ;        {page 282}
  REWRITE (TheFile) ;                      {page 285}
  FOR The Day := Mon TO Wed DO             {page 251}
    BEGIN
      Ch := CHR (ORD (TheDay) + 65) ;      {page 245}
      IF Ch IN Choices                     {page 269}
        THEN WRITE (TheFile,Ch)            {page 300}
    END ;
  CLOSE (TheFile)
END .
```

Data Types

In this section, the data types that are predefined (intrinsic to the Turbo Pascal language) will be reviewed and summarized, and additional predefined functions for the different data types will be covered. Included are the functions PRED, SUCC, CHR, and ORD. Two methods of constructing new data types will be studied. The first method yields subrange data types. The second method yields enumerated data types. You will also learn about a new program section called a TYPE declaration section.

5-1.1 Standard Types

Up to this point, each variable declared has been given one of the following types: BOOLEAN, CHAR, STRING, INTEGER, or REAL. These five types are the predefined types for most implementations of Pascal on personal computers. The types BOOLEAN, CHAR, INTEGER, and REAL are called the **standard data types,** since they are the predefined types for Standard Pascal. As you will soon see, an unlimited number of types is available to the Pascal programmer. In fact, much of the rest of the Pascal language deals with data types. To understand data types, you must have a good knowledge of the standard types just listed.

COMMENT
See Appendix C for differences between Turbo Pascal and ISO Standard Pascal.

In discussing data types, two classifications of data are used: scalar and ordinal. **Scalar data** is a collection of data that can use the relational operators: $<$, $<=$, $>$, $>=$, $<>$, and $=$. For two members (a and b) of a collection of scalar data, one of the following must be true: $a < b$, $a > b$, or $a = b$ (you might recall from mathematics that this is called the law of trichotomy). As the word *scalar* implies, the data can be used to indicate a scale. **Ordinal data** is a collection of scalar data with the additional property that each member (except the first) has a unique predecessor, and each member (except the last) has a unique successor. As the word *ordinal* implies, the data can be used to indicate order such as first, second, third, and so forth.

COMMENT
The data type STRING is considered a data structure and will be discussed in the next section.

All the standard types (BOOLEAN, CHAR, INTEGER, and REAL) are examples of scalar data. However, data of type REAL is not ordinal data (see Figure 5-1). Given a value of type REAL, the value that precedes (or succeeds) it depends on the accuracy allowed. In mathematics, the real numbers are said to be *dense;* that is, given any two real numbers, there is a real number between them. Thus, a real value has no predecessor or successor.

Figure 5-1

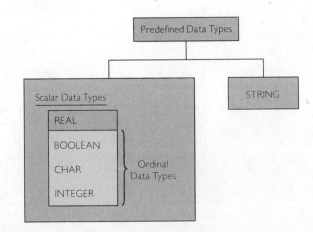

5-1.2 Ordinal Types

For ordinal data types BOOLEAN, CHAR, and INTEGER, there are three predefined functions: PRED, SUCC, and ORD. These functions are defined as follows:

PRED (value)

This function has as input a value of ordinal data. It returns the piece of ordinal data that precedes the value sent. Examples:

PRED ('B') returns A.

PRED (-3) returns -4.

PRED (TRUE) returns FALSE.

PRED (FALSE) is undefined, since FALSE is the first value of the data type BOOLEAN.

SUCC (value)

This function has as input a value of ordinal data. It returns the piece of ordinal data that succeeds the value sent. Examples:

SUCC ('s') returns t.

SUCC (FALSE) returns TRUE.

SUCC (982) returns 983.

SUCC (MAXINT) is undefined, since MAXINT is the last value of the data type INTEGER.

ORD (value)

This function has as input a value of ordinal data. It returns the position of the value in the collection. Although this function is designed for all the ordinal data types, it is used mainly with the data type CHAR. Examples:

ORD ('A') returns 65 (the ASCII code for A).

ORD ('0') returns 48 (the ASCII code for 0).

ORD ('a') returns 97 (the ASCII code for a).

ORD (5) returns 5 (the value sent).

ORD (FALSE) returns 0.

To increase your understanding of these built-in functions, consider the following example.

EXAMPLE

Compose a collection of instructions that write to the screen every other lowercase letter of the alphabet, starting with a. Assume the variable Letter has been declared to be of type CHAR.

SOLUTION

```
Letter := 'a' ;
WHILE Letter <= 'z' DO
  BEGIN
    IF ORD (Letter) MOD 2 = 1
      THEN WRITE (Letter : 3) ;
    Letter := SUCC (Letter)
  END
```

These instructions write to the screen every other letter of the alphabet (that is, ⎵⎵a⎵⎵c⎵⎵e and so forth). Looking up 'a' in the ASCII table (Appendix E) yields a value of 97. Thus, ORD (Letter) MOD 2 yields 1, and the BOOLEAN expression

ORD (Letter) MOD 2 = 1 yields TRUE. Thus, a is written to the screen. The ASCII value for 'b' is 98. Thus, the expression ORD (Letter) MOD 2 yields Ø when Letter contains 'b'. The BOOLEAN expression of the IF-THEN instruction yields FALSE and b is not written to the screen.

DO IT NOW

Give the value in the variable after the following assignments.

1. Num := ORD ('A') - ORD ('a')
2. Ans := PRED ('Ø')
3. Test := SUCC (5)
4. Ans := SUCC (PRED (ORD ('A')))

5-1.3 *Analysis of a Type*

In studying data types, it is helpful to view them by observing the following areas:

1. The elements of the data type.
2. The operations available for the data type.
3. The predefined functions and procedures available for the data type.

To illustrate this approach and to review the standard data types (BOOLEAN, CHAR, INTEGER, and REAL), consider the following:

BOOLEAN
Values: FALSE, TRUE
Operations: NOT, AND, OR, assignment
Predefined functions: PRED, SUCC, ORD
Predefined procedures: WRITE, WRITELN

CHAR
Values: ... '!', ..., 'Ø', '1', ..., 'A', 'B', ..., 'a', 'b', ...
Operations: assignment, relationals (>, <, =,...)
Predefined functions: PRED, SUCC, ORD
Predefined procedures: READ, READLN, WRITE, WRITELN

REAL
Values: Ratios of integers (list of values is very long)
Operations: +, -, *, /, assignment, relationals
Predefined functions: ABS, SQR, SQRT, ROUND, TRUNC
Predefined procedures: READ, READLN, WRITE, WRITELN

INTEGER
Values: -MAXINT - 1, .., -3, -2, -1, Ø, 1, 2, 3, .., MAXINT
Operations: +, -, *, DIV, MOD, assignment, relationals
Predefined functions: PRED, SUCC, ORD, ABS, SQR, SQRT, ODD, CHR
Predefined procedures: READ, READLN, WRITE, WRITELN

The predefined function **ODD** has as input a value of type INTEGER. The function ODD returns the value TRUE if the input number has a remainder of 1 after division by 2 (that is, the integer sent is an odd number). The function ODD returns FALSE if the input number has a remainder of 0 after division by 2 (that is, the integer sent is an even number).

Example Results := ODD (3) assigns the value TRUE to the BOOLEAN variable Results.

DO IT NOW ANSWERS
1. -32
2. /
3. 6
4. 65

The predefined function **CHR** has as input a value of type INTEGER in the range 0 to 255. The function returns the character whose ASCII number is the value sent.

Example `WRITE (CHR (65))`   writes the character A on the screen.
           `Answer := CHR (49)` assigns the character 1 to the CHAR variable
                 `Answer`.

COMMENT
For `Ch` of type CHAR,
`Ch := CHR (256)` yields an error, since the last CHAR value has ORD 255.

An additional collection of functions defined for data of types INTEGER and REAL is available. The following is a list of these functions:

Function	Explanation
SIN (number)	This function has as input an integer or real value. The value returned is the real number that is the trigonometric sine of the input value. The input value is the radian measure of an angle.
COS (number)	This function has as input an integer or real value. The value returned is the real number that is the trigonometric cosine of the input value. The input value is the radian measure of an angle.
ARCTAN (number)	This function has as input an integer or real value. The value returned is the real number that is the trigonometric arc tangent of the input value.
LN (number)	This function has as input a positive integer value or a positive real value. The function takes the input value and writes it as a power of e (e is Euler's constant, which is approximately 2.72). The value returned by the function is the real number that is the exponent of the resulting power of e. This exponent is called the natural logarithm of the number.
EXP (number)	This function has as input an integer or real value. The function takes the input value and computes Euler's constant, e, to the input value power. The value returned is the result of this computation as a real number.

The functions LN and EXP are very useful in solving problems involving powers and radicals. Consider the following example:

EXAMPLE

Write a Pascal instruction to compute the cube root of 15.

SOLUTION

In general, $a^n = \text{EXP} (n * \text{LN} (a))$.
The cube root of a number is the number to the one-third power. That is, cube root 15 is $15^{(1/3)}$.
Thus, `CubeRoot15 := EXP ((1/3) * LN (15))` would compute the cube root of 15 and assign the value to the REAL variable `CubeRoot15`.

COMMENT
To find the power of a number in Pascal, the programmer can use a loop, provided the exponent is an integer. However, for noninteger exponents (like 1.3 or ⅓), the programmer *must* use.

$$a^n = \text{EXP} (n * \text{LN} (a))$$

5-1.4 Subrange Types

It is good programming practice to identify the range of values required by a variable for a particular application. Suppose you have a variable `Count` that is used to count the passes through a WHILE-DO loop. Suppose you plan to have at most 12 passes through the loop. To declare the variable `Count` and give it type INTEGER is overstating the needs of the variable. To list a data type for a variable that fits its needs, **subrange types** are often used.

Requiring that a variable have a data type is a form of error checking in Pascal. The programmer must be aware of the type of values that are stored in a variable location. The use of subrange data types extends this idea. Using subranges (and the resulting value range errors), the program is easier to test and debug.

A subrange type can be created for the ordinal data types CHAR and INTEGER. For example, the declaration of variable `Count` could be

```
VAR Count : 1 .. 13 ; rather than VAR Count : INTEGER ;
```

Suppose a variable `Ans` is to take on only the character values A, B, C, D, and E. `Ans` could be declared as

```
VAR Ans: 'A' .. 'E' ; rather than VAR Ans : CHAR ;
```

The general form of a subrange type of declaration is

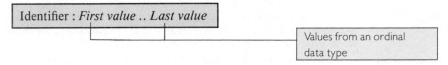

Identifier : *First value .. Last value*

Values from an ordinal data type

The first value and/or last value can be a constant. The following is a valid declaration of a subrange type:

```
CONST Tops = 18 ;

VAR NumA : 3 .. Tops ;
```

The operations and predefined functions available for a subrange type are the same operations and predefined functions available for the parent type. For the variables `NumA` and `NumB` declared as follows,

```
VAR NumA : 1 .. 20 ;
    NumB : 0 .. 20 ;
```

all of the following would be valid instructions:

```
NumA := 13 ;
READ (NumB) ;
NumB := SQR (5) - 12 ;
```

Consider the instructions:

```
NumA := 1 ;
WHILE NumA <= 20 DO
  NumA := SUCC (NumA) ;
```

If `NumA` is of type 1 .. 20, a **value range error** will occur when the loop instruction is executed. A value range error occurs when an attempt is made to store a value in a variable location that is not in the range declared for the variable (in the VAR block). In the loop just given, an attempt would be made to store the number 21 in the variable location `NumA`. However, since `NumA` is declared to hold numbers from 1 to 20, a value range error occurs.

COMMENT

To obtain value range checking in Turbo Pascal, the compiler directive **$R+** must be inserted in the program (usually on a line prior to the program header). This directive instructs the compiler to compile the program text so that value range errors are detected. That is, when a value is assigned to a variable outside the range stated in the variable declaration, the program execution stops and issues a `value range error` message. The checking occurs only on assignment instructions using `:=` (READ and READLN assignments are not checked). Typically, this directive is inserted during program development. Once the program is tested and debugged, the directive is removed.

Example: `{$R+}`

```
PROGRAM OrdinalCheck ;
        ⋮
        ⋮
```

DO IT NOW

1. Give the value in the variable after the following assignment.

   a. `NumA := TRUNC (-2.35)`   **c.** `Ans := CHR (68)`
   b. `Which := ODD (132)`   **d.** `Value := EXP (3 * LN (2))`

2. Declare the following variables, and give a subrange type to fit the stated needs.

   a. `NumA` needs a whole number from 1 to 19.
   b. `Ans` needs the lower-case letters.
   c. `xAxis` needs the integers from −14 to 14.
   d. `InNum` needs the characters 0 to 9.

5-1.5 User-Defined Types

Just as the Pascal programmer can declare an identifier to be a variable (using the VAR section) or a constant (using the CONST section), the programmer can define an identifier to be a data type. That is, the programmer can define new data types. These data types are known as **user-defined types.** To define a user-defined type, you must use a **TYPE declaration section. TYPE** is a reserved word that indicates that the declared identifiers are of a data type. The TYPE section follows the CONST section in the program structure.

There are two ways to create a user-defined type. The first (and easiest) involves a subrange. Consider the example in Figure 5–2.

```
CONST Tops = 45 ;

TYPE GoodNum = 0 .. Tops ;

VAR NumA : GoodNum ;
    Count : 1 .. 40 ;

BEGIN
  FOR Count := 1 TO 40 DO
    BEGIN
      NumA := Count MOD 16 ;
      WRITE (NumA : 3)
    END
END
```

DO IT NOW ANSWERS

```
1a. -2
 b. FALSE
 c. D
 d. 8.0
2a. VAR NumA : 1 .. 19 ;
 b. VAR Ans : 'a' .. 'z' ;
 c. VAR xAxis : -14 .. 14 ;
 d. VAR InNum : '0' .. '9' ;
```

Figure 5–2

As you can see in Figure 5–2 (and in Figure 5–3), the TYPE section is placed after the CONST section (if it exists). In the TYPE section, the instruction GoodNum = Ø .. Tops creates a type identified as GoodNum. The values in this type are the values from the subrange of integers 0 to 45 inclusive. In the VAR section, NumA is declared, and its type is stated as GoodNum.

The second way to create a user-defined type is to list the values that make up the data type. This approach is called enumerating (listing) the values. A data type created in this way is called an **enumerated type**. For example,

```
TYPE Days = (Monday, Tuesday, Wednesday,
             Thursday, Friday, Saturday, Sunday)
```

creates an enumerated data type identified as Days. The values in this data type are listed in the parentheses, separated by commas. The values listed for an enumerated type must be identifiers; values from a predefined or a previously defined type cannot appear in the list.

COMMENT

The declaration

```
TYPE Numbers = (1, 2)
```

yields an error since the values 1 and 2 are from the predefined type INTEGER.

COMMENT

An identifier in Pascal is a combination of alphanumerics (letters of the alphabet plus the digits) and the underscore symbol. There are program identifiers, procedures and function identifiers, variable identifiers, constant identifiers, data type identifiers, and identifiers of the elements of an enumerated data type.

Figure 5–3

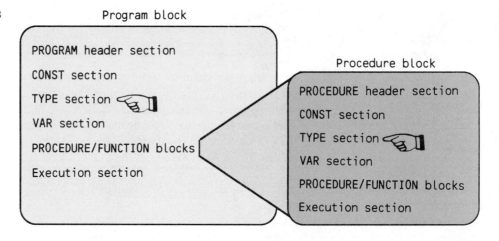

Program block

PROGRAM header section

CONST section

TYPE section

VAR section

PROCEDURE/FUNCTION blocks

Execution section

Procedure block

PROCEDURE header section

CONST section

TYPE section

VAR section

PROCEDURE/FUNCTION blocks

Execution section

5-1.6 Using Enumerated Data Types

Enumerated data types are ordinal data types (see Figure 5–4). Thus, they can use the relationals and the predefined functions ORD, SUCC, and PRED. For the data type Days,

```
TYPE Days = (Monday, Tuesday, Wednesday,
             Thursday, Friday, Saturday, Sunday)
```

if Number and Day were of type Days, then

```
Number := ORD (Monday) assigns the value Ø to the variable Number;
Day := SUCC (Tuesday) assigns the value Wednesday to the variable Day.
```

COMMENT

ORD returns Ø for the first element of an enumerated data type.

Figure 5–4

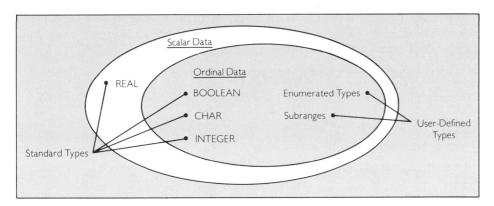

The programmer would declare a variable `Day` to be of type `Days` as follows:

```
VAR Day : Days
```

A possible use of this variable might be

```
Day := Monday ;
WHILE Day < > Sunday DO
  BEGIN
    IF Day = Saturday
      THEN Wage := 2.5 * Rate * Hours
      ELSE Wage := Rate * Hours ;
    Total := Total + Wage ;
    Day := SUCC (Day)
  END
```

The variable `Day` is declared, and its type is listed as `Days`. The values stored in the variable `Day` must be the values listed in the type declaration for `Days`.

Once an enumerated type is defined in the TYPE section, another type can be created as a subrange type. Consider the following example:

```
TYPE Days = (Monday, Tuesday, Wednesday,
             Thursday, Friday, Saturday, Sunday) ;
     HardDays = Monday .. Thursday
```

A new data type, `HardDays`, has been created by giving a subrange of a previously declared type `Days`.

Enumerated types are used to increase the readability of a Pascal program. The values of such a data type cannot be used with READ, READLN, WRITE, or WRITELN. For example, an instruction like the following (where `Day` is of type `Days`)

```
FOR Day := Monday TO Wednesday DO
  WRITE (Day)
```

is invalid (an error message is issued at compile time). To input/output the values of an enumerated data type, some form of coding must be employed. For example,

```
FOR Day := Monday TO Friday DO
  CASE Day OF
    Monday : WRITE ('Monday') ;
    Tuesday : WRITE ('Tuesday') ;
    Wednesday : WRITE ('Wednesday')
  END
```

COMMENT
Defining `HardDays` as `HardDays = (Monday, Thursday)` would yield an error since it uses previously defined identifiers.

A major reason for the use of a TYPE section involves procedure headers and function headers. A subrange listing or an enumeration of values cannot be used in a procedure or function header. Therefore, the following is invalid:

```
PROCEDURE FindIt (Num : 1 .. 20)
```

However, suppose the following TYPE section were in the program:

```
TYPE Range = 1 .. 20
```

The procedure header could be written as

```
PROCEDURE FindIt (Num : Range)
```

DO IT NOW

1. Construct a TYPE section that defines LargeLetters as a data type and gives as its values the characters 'A' through 'Z', and defines Evens as a type and gives as its values the words that represent the even numbers from two through ten inclusive.
2. For the TYPE section

```
TYPE Days = (Monday, Tuesday, Wednesday,
                  Thursday, Friday, Saturday, Sunday)
```

and the instructions

```
Day := Monday ;
WHILE Day < > Sunday DO
  BEGIN
    IF Day = Saturday
       THEN Wage := 2.5 * Rate * Hours
       ELSE Wage := Rate * Hours ;
    Total := Total + Wage ;
    Day := SUCC (Day)
  END
```

where Day is of type Days, if Rate contains the value 8.50, Hours contains the value 2, and Total contains the value 0.0, then the value in Total after execution of the instructions is _____.

3. Suppose that after hand simulating the instructions in problem 2, you disagreed with the answer listed (it is correct). How would you use the computer to verify the correctness of the answer?

DO IT NOW ANSWERS

1. ```
   TYPE LargeLetters = 'A' .. 'Z' ;
        Evens = (two , four , six , eight , ten)
   ```
2. 127.5
3. Write a debugging version of a Pascal program involving the instructions. Execute the code of the program, and observe the output. A debugging version might appear as follows:

```
PROGRAM CheckResults ;

TYPE Days = (Monday, Tuesday, Wednesday, Thursday,
                  Friday, Saturday, Sunday) ;
```
```

```
VAR Day : Days ;
    Rate, Hours, Wage, Total : REAL ;

  BEGIN                                              {set up for debugging instructions}
    Rate := 8.5 ;                                    {initialize values as stated}
    Hours := 2.0 ;                                   {initialize values as stated}
    Total := 0.0 ;                                   {initialize values as stated}
    Day := Monday ;
    WHILE Day < > Sunday DO
      BEGIN
        IF Day = Saturday
          THEN Wage := 2.5 * Rate * Hours
          ELSE Wage := Rate * Hours ;
        Total := Total + Wage ;
        WRITE ('Day# ', ORD (Day)) ;                 {for debugging}
        WRITE (' Wage ', Wage : 1 : 2) ;             {debugging}
        WRITELN (' Total ', Total : 1 : 2) ;         {debugging}
        Day := SUCC (Day)
      END ;
    WRITELN ('Value in Total is: ', Total : 1 : 2)   {debugging}
  END .                                              {set up for debugging instructions}
```

Sample Execution

```
Day# 0 Wage 17.00 Total 17.00
Day# 1 Wage 17.00 Total 34.00
Day# 2 Wage 17.00 Total 51.00
Day# 3 Wage 17.00 Total 68.00
Day# 4 Wage 17.00 Total 85.00
Day# 5 Wage 42.50 Total 127.50
Value in Total is: 127.50
```

COMMENT

A more involved version would write to the screen the name of each day rather than just the day number. To accomplish this, a CASE-OF-END instruction would be used to output a string value representing the value in the variable Day.

Vocabulary

	Page
Enumerated type A user-defined type created by listing (enumerating) the values of the type. Example: TYPE Colors = (Red, Blue, Green, Yellow)	250
ORD (value) A predefined Pascal function that has as input a value from an ordinal data type. The value returned by the function is the order of the input value. Example: CharValue := ORD ('H') assigns the number 72 to the variable CharValue.	245
Ordinal data A collection of scalar data that has the property that each element except the first has a unique predecessor, and each element except the last has a unique successor. The types BOOLEAN, CHAR, and INTEGER represent ordinal data.	244
PRED (value) A predefined Pascal function that has as input a value from an ordinal data type. The value returned by the function is the predecessor of the input value. Example: NewChar := PRED ('H') assigns the character G to the variable NewChar.	245
Scalar data A collection of data values that has an ordering. The types BOOLEAN, CHAR, INTEGER, and REAL all represent scalar data.	244
Standard data types BOOLEAN, CHAR, INTEGER, and REAL.	244
Subrange type A type that contains a continuous range of values from any ordinal data type. By using a subrange type, the entire range of values of the type need not be listed. Example: VAR Num : −5 .. 5 ; Letter : 'A' .. 'Z' declares Num a variable and states that Num can be assigned the integer values from −5 to 5 inclusive. Letter is declared a variable to reference the character values A through Z.	248
SUCC (value) A predefined Pascal function that has as input a value from an ordinal data type. The value returned by the function is the successor of the input value.	245

Example: `NextNum := SUCC (-6)`

assigns the integer −5 to the variable `NextNum`.

249   **TYPE**   A Pascal reserved word that indicates that the identifiers listed are identifiers of a data type.

249   **TYPE declaration section**   A section of a Pascal program in which a data type is defined. Its position is after the CONST section (if one exists).

249   **User-defined types**   Data types defined by the programmer in a TYPE section.

248   **Value range error**   An error that occurs when a value is assigned to a variable that is not in the range declared for the variable.

Glad You Asked

Q What is a transfer function?

A A *transfer function* is a predefined function that has as input a value from one data type and has as output a value from a different data type. ROUND and TRUNC are referred to as transfer functions. These functions transfer REAL values to INTEGER values. Another example of a transfer function is ORD. The function ORD transfers a CHAR value to an INTEGER value. Similarly, CHR is a transfer function from INTEGER to CHAR.

Q Can I declare a variable to take on the values that are positive even integers: 2, 4, 6, . . . , MAXINT − 1?

A No. The subrange of values must be continuous.

Q I tried to use the function SUCC in the following instructions and got an error message while the program was executing. What happened?

```
VAR Count : 0 .. 12 ;

BEGIN
  Count := 0 ;
  WHILE Count <= 12 DO
    BEGIN
      WRITE (CHR (Count + 65) : 3) ;
      Count := SUCC (Count)
    END
END
```

COMMENT
The FOR-DO instruction
`FOR Count := 0 TO 12 DO`
`WRITE (Count)`
does not yield a value range error. This is due to the way the compiler handles a FOR-DO loop.

A The error was a value range error. On the last pass through the compound instruction for the WHILE-DO, `Count` contained the value `12`. When the instruction `Count := SUCC (Count)` was executed, an attempt was made to place the value `13` (the successor of `12`) in the variable `Count`. However, `Count` was declared to hold values from `0` to `12` inclusive, thus the value range error.

Q What is meant by the phrase *type compatible*?

A Two variables are said to be type compatible if the values they represent are from the same parent (base) type. For example, `NumA : 0 .. 13` and `NumB : 3 .. 10` would be type compatible. An instruction like `NumB := NumA` would pass through the compiler but may result in an error at execution. If `NumA` referenced a value outside the range stated for `NumB`, a value range error would result.

Section 5–1 Exercises

1. Which of the following is *not* an ordinal data type?
   a. REAL   **b.** CHAR   **c.** INTEGER   **d.** BOOLEAN

2. Which of the following is *not* a standard data type?

    a. REAL   **b.** CHAR   **c.** STRING   **d.** BOOLEAN   **e.** INTEGER

3. Which of the following is an *invalid* listing of values for a subrange data type?

    a. 1 .. 7   **b.** 'a' .. 'v'   **c.** -9 .. 28   **d.** 3.0 .. 3.9

4. Which of the following is an *invalid* enumerated type declaration?

    a. `Color = (Red, Blue, Green, Yellow)`

    b. `Order = (President, VicePres, Secretary, Treasurer, Sergeant)`

    c. `Smalls = (one, two, three, four, five, six, seven)`

    d. `Letters = ('A', 'B', 'C')`

5. The statement `TYPE Evens = (2, 4, 6, 8, 10)` is *invalid,* since

    a. the list of values must be continuous.

    b. values from a previously defined type cannot be listed.

    c. the values should be separated by semicolons.

    d. the identifier `Evens` is a reserved word in Pascal.

6. The procedure header

```
PROCEDURE CheckColor (InColor : (Red, Blue, Green, Brown))
```

is *invalid,* since

    a. a nonstandard type cannot be used as a parameter data type.

    b. an enumerated type cannot be used as a parameter data type.

    c. enumerated type declarations are not allowed in the formal parameter list for a procedure.

    d. the enumerated type should be listed as a subrange.

7. Insert *True* for a true statement. Insert *False* for a false statement.

    _____ **a.** To increment a variable of type CHAR, use the PRED function.

    _____ **b.** The ORD function returns a value of type CHAR.

    _____ **c.** The values returned by ROUND and TRUNC are the same when a value of type REAL is sent.

    _____ **d.** A subrange data type can be declared for any standard type.

    _____ **e.** The TYPE section position in the program's structure is after the VAR section (if a VAR section exists).

    _____ **f.** In the TYPE section, user-defined data types are defined.

8. Give the value in the variable after the assignment.

    a. `NumA := SUCC (-12)`

    b. `Save := ORD (CHR (69))`

    c. `Ans := SUCC (SUCC ('C'))`

    d. `Num := TRUNC (-0.23)`

    e. `Value := EXP (2 * LN (3))`

9. State one of the standard types (BOOLEAN, CHAR, INTEGER, or REAL) for the value stored in the variable by the assignment.

    a. `Sample := ORD ('Y')`

    b. `Sample := SUCC (CHR (45))`

    c. `Sample := SQRT (ROUND (13.2))`

    d. `Sample := ODD (9)`

10. Write an assignment instruction to assign the following expressions to the variable `RealNum`.

    a. 3^8 **b.** $500(1.03)^{36}$ **c.** cube root of 135   **d.** $123^{(2/3)}$

11. Construct a `TYPE` section to declare the following data types:

    `Years` consisting of the values 1965 through 1990

    `CarTypes` consisting of USA, German, Japanese, French, Swedish

    `RunWays` consisting of 100, 200, . . . , 800

    `Letters` consisting of 'A' . . . 'Z'.

12. Construct a TYPE section to declare the following data types:

    `Colors` consisting of `Red, Blue, Green, Yellow, Brown, Black`

    `MyColors` consisting of `Blue, Green, Yellow`

13. Find and circle the errors in the following:

```
TYPE Opinion = ('Against', 'Neutral', 'Favor') ;
     Taste = (Sour, Bitter, Sweet, Salty) ;
     CarYear : 1965 .. 1995 ;

VAR SubTaste : (Sour, Sweet) ;
    MyCar : CarYear ;
    Odds : 1, 3, 5, .., 19 ;
```

14. For `VAR ChessPieces : (Queen, Rook, Bishop, Knight, Pawn)`, give the value in the variable after the assignment.

_____ **a.** `Try := ORD (Rook)`
_____ **b.** `Try := SUCC (Bishop)`
_____ **c.** `Try := ORD (Queen)`
_____ **d.** `Try := PRED (Pawn)`

15. Write a Pascal program to output a chart with the headings `Number`, `CHR`, `Letter`, and `ORD`. The values listed under these headers are shown here (`Number` is to range from 65 to 85; `Letter` is to range from a to u; the values under `CHR` and `ORD` are to be the values returned by the functions CHR and ORD).

16. Complete the following procedure to total up monthly sales:

```
PROCEDURE GetSalesData (VAR Total : REAL) ;

   TYPE Months = (Jan, Feb, Mar, Apr, May, Jun, Jul,
                  Aug, Sep, Oct, Nov, Dec) ;

   VAR Month : Months ;
       Value : REAL ;

   BEGIN
     Month := Jan ;
     WHILE _____ DO
       BEGIN
         WRITE ('Enter sales data for month') ;
         WRITE (ORD (Month) : 3, ': ') ;
         READLN (Value) ;
         Month := _____
         Total := Total + Value
       END
   END
```

17. Boot up Pascal; set the workfile to the file **TYPEDEMO.PAS** from the `Source` diskette. Enter the Turbo Pascal editor. Alter the program by inserting a procedure **WritePay** that outputs the day name (use the procedure **PrDay**) and the amount of pay for the day. The screen design for the program's output should present the request for data starting at line 15 and output the day and pay for the day starting at line 1 (see the sample execution).

18. Write a Pascal function **Step** to replace the predefined function ROUND. (*Hint:* Use the predefined function TRUNC).

19. Write a Pascal function **IntOfNum** to replace the predefined function TRUNC. (*Hint:* Use the predefined function ROUND.)

20. Write a Pascal function **OddParity** that replaces the predefined function ODD.

21. Find and circle at least five errors in the following program:

```
PROGRAM TypeErr ;

CONST Max = 25 ;

VAR NumA : 0 .. Max ;
    RNum : 2.3 .. 6.3 ;
    Ans : 'A' to 'Z' ;
```

```
BEGIN
  RNum := CHR (66) ;
  NumA := ORD ('A') - 66 ;
  Ans := 'A' ;
  WRITE (PRED (Ans))
END .
```

22. Given the following function,

```
FUNCTION Mystery (Which : BOOLEAN ; Symbol : CHAR) : CHAR ;

  BEGIN
    IF Which
      THEN Mystery := CHR (ORD (Symbol) + 1)
      ELSE Mystery := CHR (ORD (Symbol) - 1)
  END
```

   a. for the call `Ans := Mystery (TRUE, 'A')`, give the output of `WRITE (Ans)`.
   b. for the call `Ans := Mystery (FALSE, 'K')`, give the output of `WRITE (Ans)`.

23. You are given the following procedure to incorporate in a program you are composing. Write a program TYPE section to handle the parameter `Status`, and insert a procedure TYPE section to handle the local variables of the procedure.

```
PROCEDURE CkSeats (VAR Status : Which) ;

CONST LowEnd = 101 ;
      HighEnd = 599 ;
      MaxCap = 120 ;

VAR Flight : FltNumber ;
    NumSeats : Capacity ;

BEGIN
  WRITE ('Please enter flight # (') ;
  WRITE (LowEnd : 4, '-', HighEnd : 4,') : ') ;
  READLN (Flight) ;
  NumSeats := GetPresentSeats (Flight) ;
  IF NumSeats < MaxCap
    THEN Status := SeatOpen
    ELSE Status := FlightFull
END
```

24. Write a Pascal program that allows the user to enter a flight number from 101 to 599. The output is to be whether or not the flight has an open seat. Use the procedure `CkSeats` developed in problem 23 and the function `GetPresentSeats` listed here.

```
FUNCTION GetPresentSeats (FlightNumber : FltNumber) : Capacity ;

VAR Number : 0 .. 140 ;

BEGIN
  IF FlightNumber <= 300
    THEN Number := RANDOM (50) + 90
    ELSE Number := RANDOM (90) + 40 ;
  IF Number > 120
    THEN Number := 120 ;
  GetPresentSeats := Number
END
```

Sample Execution

```
Please enter flight# (101 - 599): 236
Sorry that flight is full.
Press RETURN key to continue.
Enter Q to Quit.
```

Start at column 39, row 11
Select random direction
Select random number of steps (1..5)

Programming Problems

25. Write a Pascal program that writes the character ∗ to the screen location column 39, row 11. The character is then to perform a *random walk;* that is, a random direction (up, down, right, left) is selected, and a random amount (1 . . . 5) is selected. The character ∗ is then written to the screen to simulate the random walk. The walk should end if the character is outside the range
$5 \leq$ column ≤ 75 and $2 \leq$ row ≤ 22.

Use the following TYPE section:

```
TYPE ColNum = 5 .. 75 ;
     RowNum = 2 .. 22 ;
     Direction = (Up, Right, Down, Left)
```

26. Character graphics deals with the text screen. A common screen layout for interactive programs employs windows. A window is a small area of the screen that acts as if it were the entire screen. That is, all CLRSCR, GOTOXY's, etc. respond relative to the smaller screen (window). To create windows, Turbo Pascal provides the built-in procedure WINDOW which has the following form.

```
WINDOW (X1, Y1, X2, Y2)
```

where X1, Y1 is the column/row location of the top left corner of the window and X2, Y2 is the column/row location of the bottom right corner. After a window is created, it is framed. That is, a box is drawn around the window. Write a procedure to create and frame a window on the screen. To frame the window, use the following design.

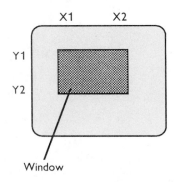

Screen

Character	ASCII
┌	218
─	196
┐	191
│	179
└	192
┘	217

Design   GOTOXY (X1-1,Y1-1)
           WRITE (CHR (218))   {do left top corner}
           FOR Ct := X1 TO X2 DO   {top and bottom}
              GOTOXY (Ct,Y1-1)
              WRITE (CHR (196))
              GOTOXY (Ct, Y2 + 1)
              WRITE (CHR (196))   {a dash}
           GOTOXY (X2 + 1, Y1-1)
           WRITE (CHR (191))   {do right top corner}
           FOR Ct := Y1 TO Y2 DO   {sides}
              GOTOXY (X1-1,Ct)
              WRITE (CHR (179))
              GOTOXY (X2 + 1,Ct)
              WRITE (CHR (179))
           GOTOXY (X1-1,Y2 + 1)
           WRITE (CHR (192))   {do left lower corner}
           GOTOXY (X2 + 1,Y2 + 1)
           WRITE (CHR (217))   {do right lower corner}

COMMENT
This design will create a frame for a window from column X1, row Y1 to column X2, row Y2. The window will have Y2 − Y1 + 1 rows with each row being X2 − X1 + 1 columns wide.

27. Write a Pascal program that presents the following prompt:

```
M(ove T(urn E(rase Q(uit
```

on line 22 of the screen. In the center of the screen the character ∗ appears. The program is to allow the user to enter one of the characters M, T, E, or Q. The action taken for each input is as follows:

COMMENT

Turbo Pascal provides a special form of the READ instruction that is helpful in this type of problem. Rather than using READ (Ch) to input a character, use READ (KBD, Ch).

   M: Writes the character ∗ to the screen either above, below, or to the right or left of the last ∗ written to the screen. The direction depends on the value in the variable Dir (Dir is initialized to Up at the start of the program).

   T: Alters the value in the variable Dir in the following order: Up, Right, Down, Left. That is, if the value in Dir is Up, then if the user presses the T key, the value in Dir is altered to Right. If the T key is pressed again, the value in Dir becomes Down, and so forth.

   E: Erases the screen and resets the ∗ to the center of the screen. Also, the value in Dir is set to Up.

   Q: Quits the program.

28. Expand your program in problem 27 to write to the screen on line 23 a status report like the following (X represents the column, Y represents the row):

```
X = 40  Y = 10  Direction = Left
```

On each input by the user of M or T, the status is updated.

Structured Data

In the last section, you learned about simple data types. These types included the predefined types (BOOLEAN, CHAR, INTEGER, and REAL), the enumerated (user-defined) types, and subranges of ordinal types (CHAR, INTEGER, and enumerated types). These types are called **simple data types,** since the values of the types cannot be decomposed. In this section, you will be introduced to **structured data types.** A structured data type consists of values that are composed from a simple data type. The structured types you will learn about in this section are STRING and SET. Later, you will study other structured data types such as TEXT files, arrays, and records.

5-2.1 A List of Characters: STRINGS

As discussed earlier, STRING is a predefined data type in most implementations of Pascal on personal computers. STRING is not a simple data type, since the values (lists of characters) can be decomposed (to characters, in this case). The data type STRING is an example of a structured data type. A **data structure** is a data type that provides a particular structuring of values from simpler data types. The structuring provided by the data type **STRING** is that of a list. The simpler data type for which the structuring is provided is CHAR. That is, the values of the data type STRING are lists of characters. Some of the values of data type STRING are 'A'; 'John Q. Public'; 'The old blue dog?'; and '1984 wasn''t that bad.'.

To study and analyze the data type STRING, consider the following:

COMMENT

Simple data types are BOOLEAN, CHAR, INTEGER, REAL, subranges of ordinal types, and enumerated types.

1. The *values* of the data type.
2. The *operations* available for the data type.
3. The *predefined procedures* and *functions* for the data type.

The *values* of data type STRING are lists of characters. The length of a list must be less than 256 (or the length stated in the VAR block). The operations available for this data type are assignment and relationals. Examples of these operations are as follows:

Assignment: `Sentence := 'The price is $2.98.'`
               `InName := ''`
Relationals: `'Joan' < 'Joanne'` has BOOLEAN value `TRUE`.
               `'123' = '125 - 2'` has BOOLEAN value `FALSE`.

COMMENT

`InName := ''` (the null string) is valid. However, for `Ch` of type CHAR, `Ch := ''` (the null character) is invalid.

As stated earlier, comparisons of STRING values are made character by character based on the ASCII code for the characters (see Appendix E). Assignment of STRING-type data can also be accomplished by the instruction READLN.

5-2.2 Predefined STRING Procedures and Functions

There are several predefined procedures and functions available for working with STRING-type data. The most commonly used are the following:

READLN (value)

A predefined procedure for reading in a value of type STRING from the keyboard.

WRITELN (value)

A predefined procedure for writing to the screen a value of type STRING.

CONCAT (valueA, valueB, . . , valueN)

The predefined function **CONCAT** has as input two or more STRING values. The value returned is the STRING value made up of joining (concatenating) the STRING values together.

Example: `Full := CONCAT ('John', 'Smith')` assigns the STRING value
            `'JohnSmith'` to the STRING variable `Full`.

LENGTH (value)

The predefined function **LENGTH** has as input a STRING value. The function returns the length of the string—that is, the number of characters in the STRING value.

Example: `HowLong := LENGTH ('Today')` assigns the value 5 to the
          INTEGER variable `HowLong`.

A particular character in the list of characters that make up a string can be accessed. Consider the following example:

```
VAR Name : STRING [20] ;
    FirstInit : CHAR ;

BEGIN
  Name := 'Carol Mendalsohn' ;
  FirstInit := Name [1] ;
  WRITE (FirstInit)
END
```

index
`1234567890123456`
`Carol Mendalsohn`

The instruction `FirstInit := Name [1]` assigns to the CHAR variable `FirstInit` the character that is in position 1 in the value in the STRING variable `Name`. In these instructions, `FirstInit` is assigned the value `'C'`. In general, variable [number] (where variable is of type STRING) is the character found at position number in the STRING variable. The value in number must be from 1 to the length of the STRING value. The number position is called the **index.** Another example is

```
Count := 1 ;
WHILE Count < 6 DO
  BEGIN
    WRITE (Name [Count]) ;
    Count := Count + 1
  END
```

If the value stored in the STRING variable `Name` has length greater than 5, the first five characters are written to the screen. If the value has less than five characters, meaningless trailing characters will be written to the screen.

DO IT NOW

1. Give the output of the following:
   a.
   ```
   Number := LENGTH ('Good-bye.') ;
   WRITELN (Number : 2)
   ```
   b.
   ```
   LastName := ' Murphy' ;
   Name := CONCAT ('Eddie ', LastName) ;
   WRITELN (Name)
   ```
   c.
   ```
   Index := 1 ;
   Name := 'Robert Frost' ;
   WHILE Index <= LENGTH (Name) DO
     BEGIN
       WRITE (Name [Index]) ;
       Index := Index + 2
     END
   ```

2. Discuss the errors in the following:
   a.
   ```
   Title := 'Fire and Ice' ;
   Letter := Title [13]
   ```
   b.
   ```
   Author := 'Sinclair Lewis' ;
   Title := 'Main Street' ;
   CONCAT (Author, '-', Title)
   ```

3. For `StringA := 'If March comes in like a '` and

   `StringB := ' then March goes out like a '`,

   give the output in the following:
   a. `WRITELN (CONCAT (StringA, 'lion', StringB, 'lamb.'))`
   b. `WRITELN (CONCAT (StringA, 'gnu', StringB, 'gnat.'))`

DO IT NOW ANSWERS

1a. `□9`   b. `Eddie□□Murphy`   c. `Rbr□rs`   (where □ represents a blank)
2a. The length of `Title` is 12; `Title [13]` is undefined.
  b. CONCAT is a function; it returns a value. Thus, it must appear in a place appropriate to values (such as in an assignment instruction, etc.).
3a. `If March comes in like a lion then March goes out like a lamb.`
  b. `If March comes in like a gnu then March goes out like a gnat.`

5-2.3 Strings as Parameters

When using variables of type STRING as parameters for procedures or functions, you cannot specify a length of the string in the parameter listing. That is, a procedure header like

```
PROCEDURE BumpUp (InString : STRING [30])
```

yields an error message when compiled. Thus, a data type is declared in the program TYPE section. A possible declaration follows:

```
TYPE String30 = STRING [30]
```

With this type declaration, the procedure header would be

```
PROCEDURE BumpUp (InString : String30)
```

To increase your understanding of STRING-type data, consider the following example.

EXAMPLE

```
PEA RIDGE
```

Construct a Pascal procedure, BumpUp, that has as input a STRING value. The procedure is to alter the STRING value to all uppercase characters.
Sample use:

```
CityName := 'Pea Ridge' ;
BumpUp (CityName) ;
WRITELN (CityName)
```

SOLUTION

Design: Index := 1
     WHILE Index < = LENGTH (InString) DO
        Letter := InString [Index]
        IF (Letter > = 'a') AND (Letter < = 'z')
          THEN InString [Index] := CapitalOf (Letter)
        Index := SUCC (Index)

Letter	Place	OffSetInCaps	CapitalOf
'a'	97	0	'A'
'y'	121	24	'Y'

Refinement of: *CapitalOf (Letter)*
     Place := ORD (Letter)
     OffSetInCaps := Place − ORD ('a')
     CapitalOf := CHR (ORD('A') + OffSetInCaps)

The procedure will have the variable parameter InString. The WHILE-DO instruction will search through the STRING value character by character. The IF-THEN instruction will check for a lowercase letter. If such a character is found, the function CapitalOf is called and is sent the lowercase letter. The function operates on the letter and returns the uppercase letter. The Index position in InString is then assigned the character returned by the function CapitalOf. The search continues while the value in Index is less than or equal to the length of the value sent. The value in InString is returned to the calling execution section.

This design yields the Pascal procedure in Figure 5–5. The data type String80 is declared in the program TYPE section.

COMMENT

The Turbo Pascal language provides a built-in function called **UPCASE** that simplifies the procedure BumpUp in Figure 5–5. This function is passed a value of type CHAR and returns the uppercase equivalent of the character sent. If the value passed has no uppercase equivalent or is an uppercase letter, the value is unchanged. Using UPCASE, the procedure BumpUp could be written as follows:

```
PROCEDURE BumpUp (VAR InString : String80) ;

  VAR Index : 1 .. 80 ;

  BEGIN
    FOR Index := 1 TO LENGTH (InString) DO
      InString [Index] := UPCASE (InString [Index])
  END ;
```

```
PROCEDURE BumpUp (VAR InString : String80) ;

  VAR Index : 1 .. 81 ;
      Letter : CHAR ;

  FUNCTION CapitalOf (Letter : CHAR) : CHAR ;

    VAR Place : 1 .. 256 ;
        OffSetInCaps : 0 .. 26 ;

      BEGIN                                        {CapitalOf}
        Place := ORD (Letter) ;
        OffSetInCaps := Place - ORD ('a') ;
        CapitalOf := CHR (ORD ('A') + OffSetInCaps)
      END ;                                        {CapitalOf}
  BEGIN                                            {BumpUp}
    Index := 1 ;
    WHILE Index <= LENGTH (Instring) DO
      BEGIN                                        {WHILE-DO}
        Letter := InString [Index] ;
        IF (Letter >= 'a') AND (Letter <= 'z')
          THEN InString [Index] := CapitalOf (Letter) ;
        Index := SUCC (Index)
      END                                          {WHILE-DO}
  END ;                                            {BumpUp}
```

Figure 5–5

Letter	Place	OffSetInCaps	CapitalOf
'a'	97	0	'A'
'y'	121	24	'Y'

5-2.4 Error Checking

Chapter 3 stated that the programmer must screen values entered by the program user for possible errors. For example, if a request is made for a numeric input and the user enters a character or a string of characters that cannot be converted to a numeric value, the program execution stops, and a type conflict error message is issued. To avoid situations such as this, many programmers input all values as strings then convert the numeric inputs to numbers. To aid in this process, Turbo Pascal provides the procedure **VAL**. This procedure has as input a value parameter of type STRING. The STRING value is converted to a numeric value. The numeric value and an error status on the conversion is returned to the calling execution section.

The general form of the VAL procedure is

VAL   (*STRING value, numeric variable, INTEGER variable*)

The string to be
converted to a
number

Storage for
resulting
number

This records
position of
error

If the *numeric variable* is of type INTEGER, an attempt is made to convert the STRING value to an integer. If the *numeric variable* is of type REAL, an attempt is made to convert the STRING value to a REAL value. The INTEGER variable is used to record the results of the attempted conversion. A zero is returned if the conversion was successful. The index of the first offending character in the string is returned if the conversion was not successful.

COMMENT

Even with **$R+** (the range checking compiler option) no error checking is performed on values input by the user.

A typical use of the procedure VAL is as follows:

```
PROGRAM ErrorTrap ;

VAR NumString : STRING [80] ;
    TheNum : REAL ;
    ErrCode : INTEGER ;

BEGIN
  REPEAT
    WRITE ('Please enter real number: ') ;
    READLN (NumString) ;
    VAL (NumString, TheNum, ErrCode) ;
    IF ErrCode > 0
      THEN WRITELN ('Error at character ', ErrCode)
  UNTIL ErrCode = 0 ;
  WRITELN ('Square of number entered is: ', SQR (TheNum):1:2)
END .
```

Sample Execution

```
Please enter real number: 3.24A
Error at character 5
Please enter real number: 3e1
Square of number entered is: 9.00
```

COMMENT
If ErrCode contains 0 then the conversion to a number was successful.

WARNING
If the conversion to a number is unsuccessful, then the value returned for the numeric variable by VAL is undefined. Additionally, only type INTEGER and type REAL are allowed for the numeric variable. That is, subranges are not allowed.

DO IT NOW

1. What is the error in the following procedure header?

   ```
   PROCEDURE LowCase (InString : STRING [80]) ;
   ```

2. If TheString contains the value

   ```
   1234 W. Elm Street
   ```

   give the output of the following instructions:

   ```
   FOR Ct := 1 TO LENGTH (TheString) DO
     TheString [Ct] := UPCASE (TheString) ;
   WRITE (TheString)
   ```

3. In the program ErrorTrap, if the data type of TheNum is changed to INTEGER,
   a. What other changes would have to be made?
   b. How would the program be affected?

DO IT NOW ANSWERS

1. The data type for InString must be previously declared in the TYPE section of the calling execution section.
2. 1234 W. ELM STREET
3a. No other changes need be made. However, the field width and decimal specification for outputting SQR (TheNum) could be removed and the prompt for the number should be altered.
 b. The VAL procedure would return TheNum as a value of type INTEGER.

5-2.5 Additional STRING Routines

Following are additional predefined procedures and functions dealing with STRING-type data.

COPY (Value, StartNum, LengthNum) The predefined function COPY has as input a string value, a number indicating where to start in the string (the index), and a number indicating the number of characters to copy. The output of the function is the string starting at the index of the input string and ending at index plus the length minus 1.

Example: `MidName := COPY ('John Smith', 3, 5)`

assigns the STRING value hn Sm to the variable `MidName`.

```
index
1234567890
John Smith
```

`POS (Pattern, Value)` The predefined function POS has as input two STRING values. The function searches through the second STRING value for the pattern string. If the pattern string is *not* found, the output of the function is Ø. If the pattern is found, the output of the function is the position in (the index of) the value string where it was found.

Examples: `Location := POS ('York', 'New York')`

assigns the number 5 to the variable `Location`.

`Location := POS ('Yorks', 'New York City')`

assigns the number Ø to the variable `Location`.

```
index
12345678
New York
```

`INSERT (Source, Destination, Index)` The predefined procedure INSERT has value parameter `Source`, variable parameter `Destination`, and value parameter `Index`. The value in `Destination` is altered by inserting the string in `Source` in `Destination` starting at the position in `Index`.

Example: `Name := 'John Public' ;`

`INSERT ('Q. ', Name, 6)`

alters the value in `Name` to John Q. Public.

```
index
12345678901
John Public
```

`DELETE (Destination, Index, Length)` The predefined procedure DELETE has variable parameter `Destination` and value parameters `Index` and `Length`. The STRING value in `Destination` is altered by deleting the length of characters starting at the position in `Index`.

Example: `City := 'New York City' ;`

`DELETE (City, 6, 3)`

alters the value in `City` to the value New Y City.

```
index
1234567890123
New York City
```

`STR (Num, Result)` The predefined procedure STR is passed a value of type INTEGER and a variable parameter of type STRING. The procedure converts the number to a string and returns the results to the STRING variable `Results`.

Example: `STR (123, NumString)`

converts the numeric value `123` to the string `'123'` and assigns the string to STRING variable `NumString`.

The following example illustrates the use of strings and some of the additional predefined procedures and functions just listed.

EXAMPLE

Suppose a STRING value contains a list of characters like the following:

`Butler, Jack   93`

(that is, a last name, comma, space, first name, spaces, and a score). Write a Pascal procedure, `ReOrder`, to create a new STRING value of the form
Score␣␣␣first name␣last name (where ␣ represents a blank space). Thus, the procedure `ReOrder` will return the value

`93   Jack Butler`

SOLUTION

Design: GetScore
  New String := CONCAT (Score, '   ')
  Get FName
  New String := CONCAT (New String, FName, ' ')
  Get LName
  New String := CONCAT (New String, LName)

A picture is often helpful:

```
12345678901234567      Index
Butler, Jack    93     TheString
```

Refinement of: *GetScore*
  Blank := ' '   {one blank space}
  Blanks := ' '   {two blank spaces}
  Index := POS (Blanks, TheString)
  Score := COPY (TheString, Index, LENGTH (TheString) − Index + 1)
  WHILE Score [1] = Blank DO
    DELETE (Score, 1,1)

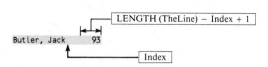

Refinement of *GetFName*
  Comma := ','
  Blanks := ' '   {two blank spaces}
  Index := POS (Comma, TheString) + 2
  Long := POS (Blanks, TheString) − Index
  FName := COPY (TheString, Index, Long)

Refinement of: *Get LName*
  Comma := ','
  Index := POS (Comma, TheString)
  LName := COPY (TheString, 1, Index − 1)

  This design leads to the Pascal procedure in Figure 5–6. The data type String80 is defined in the program TYPE section.

DO IT NOW

1. For the STRING variable DataLine with value

     MidNight□Cowboy□□□$39.95□□□□4

   (each □ represents a blank space), give the output of the following:
   a. WRITELN (LENGTH (DataLine))
   b. WRITELN (POS ('Cow', DataLine))
   c. WRITELN (COPY (DataLine, 4, 5))
   d. DELETE (DataLine, 1, 9) ;
      WRITELN (DataLine)
   e. INSERT ('2', DataLine, 29) ;
      WRITELN (DataLine)

2. If the procedure ReOrder (see Figure 5–6) is sent the STRING value 'Boillot, Michel 100', then the value returned in TheString is _____.

3. If the procedure ReOrder (see Figure 5–6) were rewritten as a function, discuss the alterations required.

```
PROCEDURE ReOrder (VAR TheString : String80) ;

  TYPE String25 = STRING [25] ;

  VAR NewString ,
      Score , FName , LName : STRING [25] ;

  PROCEDURE GetScore (TheLine : String80 ;
                      VAR Numeral : String25) ;

    CONST Blanks = '  ' ;                      {two blanks}

    VAR Index : 1 .. 81 ;

    BEGIN
      Index := POS (Blanks , TheLine) ;
      Numeral := COPY (TheLine , Index , LENGTH (TheLine) - Index + 1) ;
      WHILE Numeral [1] = ' ' DO              {remove blanks}
        DELETE (Numeral, 1, 1)
    END ;

  PROCEDURE GetFName (TheLine : String80 ;
                      VAR Name : String25) ;

    CONST Blanks = '  ' ;                      {two blanks}
          Comma = ',' ;

    VAR Index, Long : 1 .. 81 ;

    BEGIN
      Index := POS (Comma , TheLine) + 2 ;
      Long := POS (Blanks , TheLine) - Index ;
      Name := COPY (TheLine , Index , Long)
    END ;

  PROCEDURE GetLName (TheString : String80 ;
                      VAR Name : String25) ;

    CONST Comma = ',' ;

    VAR Index : 1 .. 81 ;

    BEGIN
      Index := POS (Comma , TheString) ;
      Name := COPY (TheString , 1 , Index - 1)
    END ;

BEGIN
  GetScore (TheString , Score) ;             {ReOrder}
  NewString := CONCAT (Score , '    ') ;     {four blanks}
  GetFName (TheString , FName) ;
  NewString := CONCAT (NewString , FName , ' ') ;
  GetLName (TheString , LName) ;
  NewString := CONCAT (NewString , LName) ;
  TheString := NewString                     {send NewString back}
END                                          {ReOrder}
```

Figure 5–6

LENGTH (TheLine) − Index + 1

Butler, Jack   93

Index

Long

Butler, Jack   93

Index

Index − 1

Butler, Jack   93

Index

DO IT NOW ANSWERS

DO IT NOW ANSWERS

1a. `30`   b. `10`   c. `Night`   d. `Cowboy░░░░$39.95░░░░4`
  e. `MidNight░Cowboy░░░░$39.95░░░2░4`
2. `100░░░░Michel Boillot`
3.   The header would be altered to

```
FUNCTION ReOrder (TheString : String80) : String80 ;
```

In the execution section, the assignment instruction, `TheString := NewString`
would be altered to `ReOrder := NewString`

5-2.6 *SET OF*

As another example of structured data, consider the data structure called **SET.** In mathematics, a set is a collection of objects. The objects might be numbers, colors, etc. In Pascal, a set is a collection of objects all of the same data type. The objects must be from an ordinal data type (CHAR, INTEGER, etc.). The data structure SET provides a structuring of a mathematical set on a simple data type, such as characters.

To create a data type whose values are sets, the TYPE section can be used:

```
TYPE BaseValue = SET OF 2 .. 16
```

COMMENT

If the base type is numerical, the values must be non-negative.

The data type following the Pascal reserved words **SET OF** is called the set's **base type.** The base type must be an ordinal data type. In this example, it is a subrange of INTEGER type data. Also, the number of values in the base type (its cardinality) is limited to 256 in Turbo Pascal.

Once the data type `BaseValue` is declared, it can be used in a variable declaration. For example,

```
VAR GoodNum : BaseValue
```

WARNING

A common error is to forget to assign a value to a variable of type SET.

creates a variable whose values will be sets. The sets will contain as elements the integers from 2 through 16 inclusive. As with any variable, `GoodNum` has no value until it is initialized. An example of an assignment instruction involving `GoodNum` is

```
GoodNum := [2, 4, 8, 16]
```

This assignment instruction stores in the memory locations referenced by `GoodNum` the set whose elements are the numbers `2`, `4`, `8`, and `16`. In mathematics, the symbols { and } are used to denote a set. However, in Pascal, these symbols are used for comments, so the symbols [and] are used to bracket the elements in a set. The elements listed for the set are each separated by a comma. Also, elements can be indicated by using subrange notation. For example, `GoodNum := [5 .. 8, 12]` assigns to `GoodNum` the set whose elements are 5, 6, 7, 8, and 12.

The Pascal language offers the programmer a wide range of data types. The variations are almost limitless. Consider the following:

```
TYPE People = (John, Sue, Bill, Jose, Amy) ;
     Committee = SET OF People ;

VAR Possible : Committee ;
```

COMMENT

Defining `Committee` as `SET OF (John, Sue, Bill, Jose, Amy)` is valid provided the definition of `People` is deleted. Otherwise, a *duplicate identifier* error message is issued.

The first instruction in the TYPE section,

```
People = (John, Sue, Bill, Jose, Amy)
```

creates an enumerated data type whose values are identifiers. The second instruction in the TYPE section,

```
Committee = SET OF People
```

uses the enumerated data type `People` to create a **SET data type** whose values are sets. The sets will contain as elements the identifiers `John`, `Sue`, `Bill`, `Jose`, and `Amy`. The identifier `Possible` is declared a variable, and its type is listed as `Committee`; that is, the variable `Possible` will hold values that are sets. An assignment to `Possible` could be

```
Possible := [Sue, Bill, John]
```

Analysis of SET Data   Just as with a standard data type, SET data can be analyzed by observing its values, operations, and predefined procedures and functions. It is helpful in this discussion to have an example:

```
TYPE People = (John, Sue, Bill, Jose, Amy) ;
     Committee = SET OF People ;
```

Values: Subsets of the set declared. In this case, some of the values of the data type
Committee are
[ ]; [John]; [Sue, Amy]; [Bill, Jose, John]; etc.

Operations:
Assignment (`:=`): A value of type `Committee` can be assigned to a variable of type `Committee`.
Example: `CashGroup := PartyGroup`. The variable `CashGroup` is assigned the value in the variable `PartyGroup`. Both variables must be of type `Committee`.

SET relationals: <, <=, >, >=, =, < >
Examples: `[John] < [Sue, Bill, John]` has BOOLEAN value `TRUE`.
         `[Sue, Amy] = [Amy, Sue]` has BOOLEAN value `TRUE`.
One value of `Committee` is less than another value if it is a subset. Two values of `Committee` are equal if they have elements that are the same (the order of listing of the elements in a set is ignored).

SET arithmetic: union (`+`), intersection (`*`), difference (`-`)
Examples: `[John, Bill] + [Sue, Bill]` yields `[John, Sue, Bill]`.
         `[Jose, Amy] * [Sue, Amy]` yields `[Amy]`.
         `[Sue, Bill, John] - [John]` yields `[Sue, Bill]`.
The union (`+`) of two sets produces the set that contains all the elements in the two sets. No element is ever listed more than once. The intersection (`*`) of two sets produces the set that contains the elements common to both sets. If the sets have no elements in common, the intersection produces [ ] (the empty set). The difference (`-`) of two sets (`A - B`) produces the set that contains the elements in the first set (`A`) that are not in the second set (`B`).

SET Relational IN   A relational not mentioned in the previous list of SET relationals is the relational **IN**. This relational tests for set membership. A BOOLEAN expression using this relational is

```
'A' IN ['a' .. 'z']
```

The value of this BOOLEAN expression is `FALSE`, since the character `'A'` is not a member of the set `['a' .. 'z']`.

A common use of the relational IN is to replace BOOLEAN expressions like

```
(Letter >= 'a') AND (Letter <= 'z')
```

with a BOOLEAN expression like

```
Letter IN LowerCase
```

Of course, `LowerCase` would have to be declared a SET variable and assigned the SET value `['a' .. 'z']`.

Consider the procedure `GetSelection` in Figure 5–7, which is to return a valid selection (a character from A to E inclusive).

Figure 5–7

```
PROCEDURE GetSelection (Column, Row : INTEGER ;
                        VAR Select : CHAR) ;

  VAR ValidCh : SET OF CHAR ;

  BEGIN                                    {GetSelection}
    ValidCh := ['A' .. 'E','a' .. 'e'] ;
    REPEAT
      GOTOXY (Column,Row) ;                {screen location}
      CLREOL ;                             {clear to end of line}
      READLN (Select)
    UNTIL Select IN ValidCh ;
    Select := UPCASE (Select)             {make sure capital letter}
  END ;                                    {GetSelection}
```

The major uses of the data type SET involve the relational IN. To make sets easier to use, a SET value can be listed (created) in an execution section, provided its base type is a predefined ordinal type or an ordinal type declared in the TYPE section. That is, the procedure `GetSelection` could be written as shown in Figure 5–8.

Figure 5–8

```
PROCEDURE GetSelection (Column, Row : INTEGER ;
                        VAR Select : CHAR) ;

  BEGIN                                    {GetSelection}
    REPEAT
      GOTOXY (Column,Row) ;                {screen location}
      CLREOL ;                             {clear to end of line}
      READLN (Select)
    UNTIL Select IN ['A' .. 'E','a' .. 'e'] ;
    Select := UPCASE (Select)             {make sure capital letter}
  END ;                                    {GetSelection}
```

There are situations where the programmer wishes to test for an element *not* in a set. Suppose an instruction is to be executed while the value in the CHAR variable `Ch` is not in the set `['A' .. 'E']`. To write the BOOLEAN expression for this WHILE-DO instruction requires caution:

```
WHILE NOT (Ch IN ['A' .. 'E']) DO
     <Instruction>
```

`Ch IN ['A' .. 'E']` is a BOOLEAN expression. Thus, `NOT (Ch IN ['A' .. 'E'])` is a BOOLEAN expression. A common error involving this BOOLEAN expression is to write

```
Ch NOT IN ['A' .. 'E']     <<<<error>>>>
```

Summary The SET data structure is used to improve the readability of a program. A variable of type SET cannot be used with READ, READLN, WRITE, or WRITELN. That is, for `LowerCase`, a variable of type SET OF CHAR, instructions like `WRITELN (LowerCase)` and `READLN (LowerCase)` are invalid. An additional weakness of the data structure is that the elements of a SET value cannot be accessed directly (unlike the elements of a STRING value). Finally, the base type of SET is quite limited. For example, `SET OF REAL`, `SET OF INTEGER`, and `SET OF STRING` are all *invalid*. However, the use of sets and the relational IN can be used to improve the readability of some complex BOOLEAN expressions.

DO IT NOW

1. Complete the following TYPE section to declare a data type consisting of sets of characters from `'A'` through `'Z'` and to declare a data type consisting of sets of `Colors`.

```
TYPE Colors = (red, yellow, blue, green, black);
     BigCharSet = _____ ;
     ColorSet = _____
```

2. Use the TYPE section in problem 1 to declare variable

   `Answers` to be a variable of type `BigCharSet`
   `Primary` to be a variable of type `ColorSet`
   `ColorNum` to be a variable of a SET data type whose values are the numbers 1, 2, 3, and 4

3. Using the TYPE and VAR sections of problems 1 and 2, write an assignment instruction to accomplish the following:
   a. Store a set in variable location `Answers` with elements `'A'`, `'C'`, `'P'`, and `'Z'`.
   b. Store a set in variable location `ColorNum` with elements 1 and 4.
   c. Store a set in variable location `Primary` that contains no elements.

4. Replace the following BOOLEAN expressions with a BOOLEAN expression using IN.
   a. ```
      IF (Number >= 18) AND (Number <= 56)
         THEN WRITELN (Number, ' is good.')
      ```
   b. ```
      IF (Value = 2) OR (Value = 4) OR (Value = 8)
         THEN WRITELN (Value)
      ```
   c. ```
      IF ODD (Value) AND (Value <= 10) AND (Value > 0)
         THEN Value := 2 * Value + 1
      ```
      ```

DO IT NOW ANSWERS

1. BigCharSet = SET OF 'A' .. 'Z' ;
   ColorSet = SET OF Colors;
2. VAR Answers : BigCharSet ;
       Primary : ColorSet ;
       ColorNum : SET of 1 .. 4 ;
3a. Answers := ['A', 'C', 'P', 'Z']
 b. ColorNum := [1, 4]
 c. Primary := [ ]

4a. IF Number IN [18 .. 56]
       THEN WRITELN (Number, ' is good.')
 b. IF Value IN [2, 4, 8]
       THEN WRITELN (Value)
 c. IF Value IN [1, 3, 5, 7, 9]
       THEN Value := 2 * Value + 1

Vocabulary

Page

268   **Base type**   A phrase used to refer to the data type from which the values in a set originate. The base type must be ordinal, and the number of values in the base type must be less than 256 in Turbo Pascal. If the base type is made up of numbers, the numbers must be non-negative integers that are no larger than 255 (that is, 0 .. 255).

260   **CONCAT**   A predefined function that has as input two or more strings. The function returns a string composed from concatenating (joining) the STRING values together.

Example: FullName := CONCAT (FName, LName) assigns to the STRING value FullName the value in FName and the value in LName.

259   **Data structure**   A data type that provides a structuring for simpler data types. STRING and SET data types are examples of data structures.

269   **Empty set**   The set which contains no elements. Indicated by [ ].

269   **IN**   A Pascal reserved word that represents a test for set membership. IN is a relational for values from the data type SET. Examples:

```
        WHILE NOT (Ans IN ['Y', 'N', 'y', 'n']) DO
          READ (Ans) ;
        IF Num IN Primes
          THEN WRITE (Num : 4)
```

260   **Index**   A number used to reference a particular character in a STRING value. Example: WRITE (Person [3]) writes the character in position 3 of the STRING value referenced by the STRING variable Person.

260   **LENGTH**   A predefined function that has as input a STRING value. The function returns the number of characters in the STRING value. Example:

```
        WHILE Count < LENGTH (DataLine) DO
          <instruction>
```

268   **SET**   A structured data type. The simpler type in this data structure is an ordinal type called the base type. The structuring provided is that of a mathematical set.

269   **SET data type**   A data type defined in a TYPE section. The values of the data type are sets.

268   **SET OF**   A Pascal reserved word used to create a SET data type. What follows can be a previously defined ordinal type or a subrange type; however, the number of values in the type must be no more than 256 in Turbo Pascal. Example:

```
        TYPE NumSet = SET OF 10 .. 99 ;
             CharSet = SET OF CHAR ;
             Colors = (Red, Blue, Green, Yellow) ;
             ColorSet = SET OF Colors
```

This reserved word can also be used in a VAR section to list a variable's type as SET data. That is, the variable will take on a value that is a set. Example:

```
VAR Primes : SET OF 2 .. 100 ;
    Smalls : SET OF 'a' .. 'z' ;
    Color : ColorSet
```

Simple data types Data types whose values cannot be decomposed.	259
STRING A data structure in which the simpler type is CHAR and the structuring is that of a list. Example: `'All good persons.'` is a value of type STRING.	259
Structured data type A data type that can be decomposed to a simpler data type. Examples: `STRING [50]` and `SET OF CHAR`.	259
UPCASE A predefined function that has as input a value of type CHAR. The value returned is the capital of the character sent (if it exists).	262
VAL A predefined procedure used to convert a string value to a number.	263
[...] Symbols used to reference a particular character in a string of characters. Example: `Letter := Name [3]`. Also, the symbols used in reference to a value of SET data. Example: `Primes := [2, 3, 5, 7]`	268

Glad You Asked

Q Can a procedure or function have a TYPE section?

A Yes. Remember, a main idea in writing a procedure or function is that it can be written independently of the program; that is, it can be *self-contained* or *modular*. Often, a procedure is first written as a program, then converted to a procedure by providing an interface (the parameter list) to the main program.

Q In trying out the TYPE section, I inserted the following instructions:

```
TYPE Days = (Mon, Tue, Wed, Thu, Fri, Sat, Sun) ;
     WeekEnd = (Sat, Sun) ;
```

At compile time, I got an error. Next, I tried

```
TYPE Days = SET OF (Mon, Tue, Wed, Thu, Fri, Sat, Sun) ;
     WeekEnd = SET OF (Sat, Sun) ;
```

I still got an error. Would you please explain?

A In your first try, you were defining enumerated data types. Once you listed the identifiers for `Days`, the instruction `WeekEnd = (Sat, Sun)` was invalid. The reason is that its identifiers are previously defined values (values from the data type `Days`). One way to understand why this restriction exists is to consider the predefined function ORD. What would `ORD (Sat)` yield: 5 or 0? You could have used `WeekEnd = Sat .. Sun`. Here, `Sat .. Sun` is a subrange of the previously declared type `Days`.

   In your second attempt, you defined two different SET types. However, in defining the set type `Days`, you listed identifiers for the base type (thus, defining an enumerated data type). In defining the set type `WeekEnd`, you used one of the previously listed identifiers (in effect, you declared the same identifier twice). You could have used `WeekEnd = SET OF Sat .. Sun`. In this situation, you are using a subrange of a previously declared type created in the definition of `Days`.

Q I saw a statement in another book that said to define a SET type, you write `SET OF`, then a simple type. What is meant by the term *simple type*?

A *Simple type* is used to refer to a data type whose values cannot be decomposed. Simple type takes in the predefined types, BOOLEAN, CHAR, INTEGER, and REAL. Also, it includes user-defined ordinal types. The statement is an error. `SET OF INTEGER` is invalid. Likewise, `SET OF 3.2 .. 7.8` is invalid.

Q Can SET variables be type compatible?

A Yes. When two variables are of different types, yet the underlying type is the same for both types, the variables are said to be *type compatible*. Example:

```
VAR SetA : SET OF 1 .. 12 ;
    SetB : SET OF 3 .. 8 ;
```

SetA and SetB do not have identical types. However, the underlying type of both variables is INTEGER. Thus, they are type compatible. This means that for the example given, SetA := SetB is always valid. However, SetB := SetA may be invalid (for instance, suppose SetA contains the value 9).

Q Is SET-type data scalar data? Is it ordinal data?

A No. With structured data types such as STRING and SET data types, the terms *scalar* and *ordinal* are not used.

Q Can I have a function of type SET?

A No. Functions are limited to the scalar data types. Turbo Pascal does allow functions to be of type STRING.

Q Can I build a STRING value by reading a series of characters from the keyboard? I tried the following instructions:

```
Ch := ' ' ;                {a blank}
Ct := 1  ;
WHILE ORD (Ch) < > 13 DO    {13 is ASCII for RETURN}
  BEGIN
    READ (Ch) ;
    Line [Ct] := Ch ;
    Ct := Ct + 1
  END ;
WRITELN ('String is ', Line)
```

When I executed the program, I could enter characters but I could not exit the WHILE-DO loop. I had to use Ctrl-C to exit the program. Can you help?

A Yes, but not using your instructions. The variable Line was not initialized. Thus, Line [Ct] := Ch may not assign the value in Ch to a position in Line. One approach would be to initialize Line to a collection of blanks. However, this fixes the length of the STRING value. Also the READ (Ch) instruction does not end until you press RETURN. Thus, if you ran the instructions and typed The old then pressed RETURN, Ch will contain the character T. If you now pressed the RETURN key again, Ch still would not contain the code for the RETURN key. To build a STRING value from characters read from the keyboard, start by inserting the compiler option $B-. This compiler option allows the READ instruction involving a character to end without the user pressing the RETURN key. Now, use the following instructions.

```
Ch := ' ' ;                {a blank}
Line := '' ;               {the null string}
WHILE ORD (Ch) < > 13 DO    {13 is ASCII for RETURN}
  BEGIN
    READ (Ch) ;
    IF ORD (Ch) < > 13
      THEN Line := CONCAT (Line, Ch)
  END ;
WRITELN ('String is ', Line)
```

Section 5–2 Exercises

1. If STRING variable `Line` contains the value `'J.R.R. Tolkien The Hobbit'`, then
   a. `WRITE (Line [5])` has output _____.
   b. `WRITELN (LENGTH (Line))` has output _____.
2. Which of the following is a data structure?
   a. REAL **b.** STRING **c.** CHAR **d.** INTEGER **e.** BOOLEAN
3. The base type of `SET OF 5 .. 16` is
   a. undefined.
   b. a subrange of INTEGER.
   c. 16
   d. REAL.
   e. 11
4. For `Line := 'The Age of Innocence'` the instruction `Letter := Line [21]`
   a. assigns the character `T` to `Letter`.
   b. deletes the first character of the value stored in `Line`.
   c. yields an error if `Line` is of type `STRING [2Ø]`.
   d. is a valid instruction, but does nothing.
5. The type declaration `Numbers = SET OF 1 .. MAXINT` is invalid, since _____.
6. Insert *True* for a true statement. Insert *False* for a false statement.
   _____ a. `Numbers := 1 .. 5Ø` assigns to the variable `Numbers` the set whose elements are the numbers from 1 to 50.
   _____ b. The length of a string must be less than 256.
   _____ c. CONCAT is a predefined procedure that has two value parameters of type STRING.
   _____ d. Data of type SET is ordinal-type data.
   _____ e. For a variable `Example` whose data type is a data structure, the instruction `WRITE (Example)` is always invalid.
   _____ f. For the procedure call `VAL (TheStr, TheNum, TheErr)`, if the value in `TheStr` is `'1A3'` then the value returned in `TheErr` is 2.
   _____ g. The base type of a set can be any subrange type.
   _____ h. The data type SET is used mainly to improve the readability of a Pascal program.
7. The STRING variable `MessageA` contains the string `'The solution to a problem'`. STRING variable `MessageB` contains the string `'changes the problem.'` Give the output of the following instructions.
   a. `WRITELN (CONCAT (MessageA, ', ', MessageB))`
   b. `WRITELN (LENGTH (MessageA))`
8. For `Letter`, a variable of type CHAR, write an IF-THEN instruction that calls the procedure `UpVowels` if `Letter` is in the set whose elements are `'A'`, `'E'`, `'I'`, `'O'`, `'U'`.
9. Write a function `CkVowel` that has input `Letter`, a parameter of type CHAR. The function should return `TRUE` if `Letter` is in the set of vowels and `FALSE` if `Letter` is not in the set of vowels.
10. Mark the following as *Valid* or *Invalid* Pascal instructions:
    a. `TYPE Attitude = SET OF ('Good', 'Bad', 'Ugly')`
    b. `VAR GPASet : SET OF 1.Ø .. 4.Ø`
    c. `CharSet := SET OF 'A' .. 'z'`
    d. `IF NumA NOT IN [ 1, 2, 3, 5 ]`
       `    THEN WRITE ('NumA is not small')`
    e. `TYPE Numbers = Ø .. 2Ø ;`
       `        MiddleNums = SET OF Numbers`
11. Discuss the error in the following:

    `TYPE Num = SET OF 1 .. 1ØØ ;`

    `VAR Bum : SET OF Num ;`

12. Given the following procedure,

```
PROCEDURE Mystery ;

  VAR InString : STRING [30] ;
      OutString : STRING [30] ;
      Num, Index : 0 .. 30 ;

  BEGIN
    Num := 1 ;
    WRITELN ('Enter string up to 30 characters long: ') ;
    READLN (InString) ;
    OutString := InString ;
    Index := LENGTH (InString) ;
    WHILE Index > 0 DO
      BEGIN
        OutString [Num] := InString [Index] ;
        Num := SUCC (Num) ;
        Index := PRED (Index)
      END ;
    WRITELN ('Mystery is: ', OutString)
  END
```

   a. If the string `noon day sun` is entered for `InString`, give the output of the procedure.

   b. If the string `able was I ere I saw elba` is entered for `Instring`, give the output of the procedure.

   c. The input string in part b is called a *palindrome*. A palindrome is a string that has the same value when its characters are reversed. Expand the procedure to output the following message if the input string is a palindrome:

   ```
   _____ is a palindrome
   ```

   where _____ represents the input string. To test the expanded procedure, input values like `'noon'`, `'1991'`, `'tenet'`, and `'a man a plan a canal panama'`.

   d. Expand the procedure in part c to ignore blanks in the string input when testing for a palindrome.

13. Write a Pascal function `Convert` that has the following header:

```
FUNCTION Convert (Numeral : String80) : WholeNum ;
```

   where `WholeNum` is declared type `0 .. MAXINT` and `String80` is declared type `STRING [80]`. The function is to convert the STRING value sent (`Numeral`) to a number. Example of use:

```
WRITE ('Enter number of parts to order: ') ;
READLN (NumString) ;
NumParts := Convert (NumString) ;
Total := Present + NumParts ;
```

14. Boot up Pascal; set the workfile to the file `BUMPUP.PAS` from the `Source` diskette. Enter the Turbo Pascal editor. Alter the procedure `BUMPUP` to use the built-in UPCASE function as described in the comment in section 5–2.3. Test the alteration.

15. Boot up Pascal; set the workfile to the file `TYPEDEMO.PAS` from the `Source` diskette. Enter the Turbo Pascal editor. Use the copy application to read in the contents of the file `ERRTRAP.UTL` from the `Source` diskette. Use the procedure `NumErrCk` to check the user's input for errors. Test the alterations by executing the program with user inputs such as `A3`, `12.6`, and `34r`.

16. Boot up Pascal; set the workfile to the file `STRDEMO.PAS` from the `Source` diskette. Execute the program. Select option `A`. Enter the following STRING value:

`The ostrich has no wings. This is due to the fact that it doesn't fly.`

Use the options `B` and `C` to alter the STRING value to

`The ostrich has no wings. This is fine since it doesn't fly.`

Use option `D` to search the string for the substring `as`.

17. Boot up Pascal; set the workfile to the file `OPSTRING.PAS` from the `Source` diskette. Alter the program to allow the user to enter the date in the form `12-6-89`. The program is to output the date in the form `Dec. 6, 1989`.

18. Boot up Pascal; set the workfile to the file `MENUEX.PAS` from the `Source` diskette. Use the copy application to read in the file `GETSEL.UTL` from the `Source` diskette. Use the procedure `GetSelection` to read the user's menu selection.

Programming Problems

19. The following problem was presented in Chapter 3 (Section 3–1, programming problem 19):

> The binary (base two) numbering system is a system with only two digits: 0 and 1. Each place value in this system is a power of 2. That is, the binary number `10010` yields `1*16 + 0*8 + 0*4 + 1*2 + 0*1`, or 18, in the decimal (base 10) numbering system. A problem that is often the bane of many students is converting a decimal number to a binary number. This problem can be solved with the following design.
>
> ```
> Get positive integer value
> WHILE Value > 0 DO
>       WRITE (Value MOD 2)
>       Value := Value DIV 2
> ```
>
> However, the number written is the binary name reversed.
>
> Use this design to write a Pascal program that allows the user to input a positive integer. The program is to write to the screen the reversed binary number name for the input value.
>
> **Sample Execution**
>
> ```
> Please enter positive integer (1 ... 32000): 47
> The reversed binary name is: 111101
> ```

Using your work with the data type STRING, the program can now be altered to write the conversion to a binary number in normal form. Do this alteration.

Sample Execution

```
Please enter positive integer (1 ... 32000): 47
The binary name is: 101111
```

20. Alter your program in problem 19 to allow the user to input the desired base (from 2 to 9 inclusive) for the conversion. The program is to write to the screen the input value in the numbering system selected by the user.

Sample Execution

```
Please enter positive integer (1 ... 32000): 47
Please select base (2 .. 9): 8
The base 8 name is: 57
```

21. Expand your Pascal program in problem 20 to handle bases up to 32. A common such base is base 16 (known in computer science as hexadecimal). The hexadecimal numbering system has 16 digits: 0, 1, 2, 3, 4, 5, 6, 7, 8, 9, A, B, C, D, E, and F. Thus, when the result of the MOD operation is larger than 9, a character is employed.

Sample Execution

```
Please enter positive integer (1 ... 32000): 47
Please select base (2 .. 32): 16
The base 16 name is: 2F
```

22. Write a Pascal program to count the number of words in a string. The program is to allow the user to input a string of up to 120 characters. A word is defined to be one or more characters followed by a space or one of the characters in `['.', ',', ';', '?', '!', ':']`. The program will output the number of words in the string.

Sample Execution

```
Please enter text (up to 120 characters):
Supercomputers such as the Cray-2 have about reached their limit.
Danny Hillis has a fresh idea.  <ret>
Your text contains 16 words.
```

23a. Write a Pascal procedure that has as input a positive number of type REAL less than 100 and with accuracy less than four decimal places. The procedure is to return the string value form of the number. The procedure header is:

```
PROCEDURE NumToString (Num : REAL; VAR NString : String80) ;
```

b. Use the procedure `NumToString` to write a Pascal program that allows the user to input a positive number of type REAL less than 100, with accuracy less than four decimal places. The output of the program is the number of times the digit 3 appears in the number.

Sample Execution

```
Please enter a real number: 35.334
The digit 3 appears 3 times.
```

24. A deck of 52 letter cards in the word game SCOWL! can be thought of as the following STRING value:

Deck: AAAAABCDDEEEEEEFGGHIIIIJKLMNNNOOOOPQRRRSSSTTTUUVWXYZ

a. Write a Pascal procedure to shuffle the deck. A possible design follows:

```
Design:   Index : = 1
          WHILE Index < 52 DO
              Pick random number from Index + 1 to 52
              Swap Deck [ RandomNum ] and Deck [ Index ]
              Increment Index
```

b. Write a Pascal procedure to deal a five-card hand to player 1 and a five-card hand to player 2.

c. In the game of SCOWL!, a player can either lay the cards down to form a five-letter word or discard a letter and be dealt a new card. The game continues until a player lays down a five-letter word. Write a Pascal program to simulate the game SCOWL!

A possible design follows:

```
Get Player Names
Shuffle cards
Deal hands
WHILE No Winner DO
    GetPlay
ReportWinner
```

Refinement of:
GetPlay
```
Write Name and hand
Write prompt: Have word?(Y/N):
IF yes
    THEN GetWord
             CheckAgainstHand
             If CheckGood
                 Then SetWinner
    ELSE GetExchangeCard
             DealNewCard
SwitchPlayers
```

Sample Execution

```
Mona your hand is PWAVE
Have word? (Y/N) : N
Discard which card? W
Your new hand is PQAVE
Harvey your hand is PAONC
Have word? (Y/N) : Y
Enter word: CAPON
Harvey you win!
```

25. Write a Pascal program using sets that has as input a number less than 256. The program has as output the numbers that are less than or equal to the input value and prime (divisible only by itself and 1). Name the program `FindPrimes`.

```
Design:   Get UpperLimit
          Primes : = [ ]                          {the empty set}
          WHILE Num < = UpperLimit DO
              Num : = 2
              CkForPrime ( Num, Print )
              IF Prime
                THEN Add to Primes
              Num : = Num + 1
          Write Set to Screen
```

Refinement of: *CkForPrime (Input Target; Return Prime)*
```
                 Count : = 2
                 Prime : = TRUE
                 WHILE (Count < Target) AND Prime DO
                     IF Target MOD Count = 0
                         THEN Prime : = FALSE
                         ELSE Count : = Count + 1
```

Refinement of: *AddToPrimes*
```
                 Primes : = Primes + [ Num ]        {union of sets}
```

Refinement of: *WriteSetToScreen*
```
                 FOR Count : = 1 TO UpperLimit DO
                     IF Count IN Primes
                         THEN Write (Count : 4)
```

26. Convert the program `FindPrimes`, developed in problem 25, to a procedure, `FindPrimes`. Write a Pascal program, `PrimeFactor`, which uses the procedure `FindPrimes` to prime factor a number input by the program's user.

Sample Execution

```
Please enter whole number (2 .. 255): 221
The prime factors are: 13 and 17
```

27. More than 2000 years ago, a Greek mathematician named Eratosthenes used the following method of finding the prime numbers that are less than or equal to a given positive integer:
a. Form the set of numbers from 2 to the input number.
b. Starting with 2, remove all set members that are multiples of 2.
c. Take the next number in the remaining set (3, at this point), and remove all multiples of this number.
d. Repeat step c until the next number is larger than the square root of the input number.
e. The remaining set contains all the primes less than or equal to the input number.
Write a Pascal program that allows the user to input a positive integer less than 256. The output should be all primes less than or equal to the input value. The program should be based on Eratosthenes' algorithm.

Sample Execution

```
Please enter number (2 .. 255): 22
Finding primes ........
Primes less than 22 are: 2 3 5 7 11 13 17 19
```

28. A common use of sets is with surveys. Suppose you desire to have a class of 30 students complete the following survey:

Sample Execution

```
Enter your assigned student number (1 .. 30): 17
Do you take a course in math?(Y/N): Y
Do you take a chemistry course?(Y/N): N
Do you take a physics course?(Y/N): Y
```

Write a Pascal program that will conduct the survey. The program should build the sets `MathSet`, `ChemSet`, and `PhySet`. The program should then output the student numbers of the students in the following sets:
a. The students taking math but not chemistry.
b. The students taking math, chemistry, and physics.
c. The students taking only physics.

Hint: To output the values of the set `MathSet`, the following instructions could be used:

```
WRITELN ('The students taking only math are: ') ;
FOR Num := 1 TO 30 DO
  IF Num IN MathSet
    THEN WRITE (Num) ;
WRITELN
```

Section 5–3

TEXT Data Type

In the first section of this chapter, you considered the standard data types BOOLEAN, CHAR, INTEGER, and REAL. In the second section, you were introduced to data structures. In this section, you will study another data structure known as TEXT, which provides a way of storing and using data outside the main memory of the computer. To work with data of type TEXT, you need to know how to use the predefined procedures RESET, REWRITE, and CLOSE. Also, the predefined BOOLEAN function EOF will be studied.

5–3.1 File of Lines

A **file** is a collection of data in which each member of the collection has the same data type. This data is usually stored on a diskette, outside the main memory of the computer. The data in a file is a sequence of components. These components could be values from BOOLEAN-type data, CHAR-type data, INTEGER-type data, and so forth. In this section, you will only be concerned with files consisting of lines of characters. Such files have a reserved word, **TEXT,** to identify them and are called TEXT files.

A TEXT file is not new to you. Every time you have composed a Pascal program in the editor, you have created a TEXT file. In fact, the only kind of file that can be created in the editor is a TEXT file. Just like STRING and SET data types, the data type TEXT is a data structure. The values in this data type are files (usually stored on a diskette) that contain lines of characters. The structure provided by a TEXT file is as follows:

```
_____ < end-of-line marker >
_____ < end-of-line marker >
< end-of-line marker >
_____ < end-of-line marker >
< end-of-file marker >
```

A TEXT file is a collection of lines, and the lines are made up of characters (see Figure 5–9). Suppose you used the editor to insert the following text:

```
A bird in the hand
is worth
two
in the bush.
```

Figure 5–9

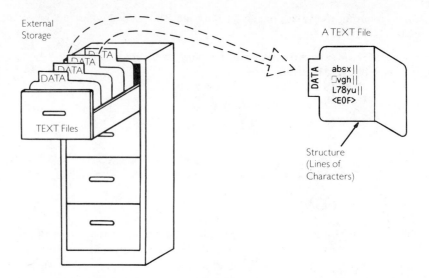

If you then quit the editor and saved the contents, a TEXT file would be created. The data is stored on a diskette in a form similar to the following (where || represents the end-of-line marker):

A bird in the hand||is worth||two||in the bush.|| <end-of-file marker>

While you were in the editor, each time the RETURN key was pressed, the keystroke was recorded as an end-of-line marker in the TEXT file. When you quit the editor, the end-of-file marker was inserted to mark the end of the TEXT file.

5–3.2 Reading a TEXT File

Suppose you wish to write a Pascal program to write to the screen the contents of a TEXT file. That is, you want to output the components of the data structure. A design to accomplish this would be as follows:

Design: Prepare the file for processing
           WHILE More lines in the Text file DO
                READ a line from the file
                WRITE the line to the screen
           Close the file

Opening the File   To prepare the file for processing, first a name must be associated with a variable of type TEXT. To declare a variable and state its type as TEXT, the VAR section is used. For example,

VAR InFile : TEXT

declares the variable InFile and states its data type as TEXT. To associate a filename with the variable InFile, the built-in procedure **ASSIGN** is used. For example,

ASSIGN (InFile, 'MyFile.PAS')

associates the file named MyFile.PAS with the TEXT file variable InFile.

COMMENT

The period followed by **PAS** is known as a file extension. The use of file extensions enables easier identification of the files' contents in a directory listing of the files on a diskette. Some commonly used extensions are **.PAS** (for TEXT of Pascal programs), **.COM** (for the object code of a program), and **.TXT** (for a TEXT file). The extension is composed by the programmer and can be up to three alphanumeric characters in length.

The general form of the ASSIGN instruction is

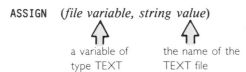

ASSIGN   (*file variable, string value*)

           a variable of   the name of the
           type TEXT   TEXT file

Next, the TEXT file must be opened. To open a file means the Pascal system prepares the file for processing. To open an existing file, the procedure **RESET** is used. For example,

    RESET (InFile)

will open the file whose name has been assigned to the variable InFile.

WARNING

If the file assigned to InFile does not exist, the program execution stops and an error message is issued. If no file has been assigned to InFile, the compiler will stop compilation and issue an error message.

Reading a Line   So far, we have seen how to assign a filename to a variable of type TEXT and how to open the file for processing. To access the components of the TEXT file data structure, the READLN instruction is used. For example,

    READLN (InFile, TheLine)

will assign a line of the TEXT file to the STRING variable TheLine. The general form of the READLN procedure is

READLN   (*file variable, variable*)

        a variable of   a variable of data type CHAR
        type TEXT   or STRING, or a numeric type

COMMENT
We will cover the situation where *variable* is a numeric type or of type CHAR in the next section.

If the *file variable* parameter is omitted, the value for the *variable* is read from the keyboard by default.

The File Pointer   When a TEXT file is opened for processing with RESET, the Pascal system uses a file pointer to keep up with the current position in the file. After RESET is executed, the pointer is positioned at the start of the file. For each READLN instruction executed, the file pointer is moved to the start of the next line in the file. For example, suppose the TEXT file assigned to InFile appears as follows (where || represents an end-of-line marker):

    A bird in the hand||is worth||two in the bush.|| < end-of-file marker >

After the instruction `RESET (InFile)` is executed, the file pointer is positioned as

A bird||in the hand||is worth||two in the bush.|| <end-of-file marker>
⇑

After the instruction `READLN (InFile, TheLine)` is executed, the file pointer is positioned as

A bird||in the hand||is worth||two in the bush.|| <end-of-file marker>
         ⇑

If the file pointer is positioned at the end-of-file marker:

A bird||in the hand||is worth||two in the bush.|| <end-of-file marker>
                                                ⇑

and the instruction `READLN (InFile, TheLine)` is executed, the program execution stops, and the error message

    Tried to read past end-of-file marker.

is issued. To prevent this error, the Pascal language provides the BOOLEAN function **EOF.**

COMMENT
If RESET is performed on a TEXT file that is already open, the file pointer is moved to the start of the first line of the file.

End-of-File Function   A typical use of the end-of-file (EOF) function is as follows:

    WHILE NOT EOF (InFile) DO
        READLN (InFile, TheLine)

The BOOLEAN expression `NOT EOF (InFile)` protects the program from executing the READLN instruction when the file pointer is at the end-of-file marker. If the file pointer is at the end-of-file marker, then `EOF (InFile)` returns the value `TRUE`. Thus, the expression `NOT EOF (InFile)` has value `FALSE`, and the execution of the WHILE-DO instruction is completed.

Closing a File   After processing a TEXT file, the file must be closed. To accomplish this, the built-in procedure **CLOSE** is used. For example,

    CLOSE (InFile)

closes the TEXT file assigned to the variable `InFile`.

To write the contents of a TEXT file to the screen we could use the Pascal program in Figure 5–10.

Figure 5–10

```
PROGRAM SeeTxtFile ;

VAR TheLine : STRING [80] ;
    InFile : TEXT ;                        {declare InFile a variable}
                                           {and state its data type as TEXT}
BEGIN
  ASSIGN (InFile, 'MyFile.PAS') ;
  RESET (InFile) ;                         {open the file}
  WHILE NOT EOF (InFile) DO
    BEGIN
      READLN (InFile, TheLine) ;           {get a line from the file}
      WRITELN (TheLine)                    {write the line to the screen}
    END ;
  CLOSE (InFile)                           {close the file}
END .
```

DO IT NOW

1. Suppose the WHILE-DO instruction in the program `SeeTxtFile` (see Figure 5–10) is replaced by a REPEAT-UNTIL instruction:

```
REPEAT
  READLN (InFile, TheLine) ;
  WRITELN (TheLine)
UNTIL EOF (InFile)
```

What difficulties could arise from this replacement?

2. The instruction `READLN (TheFile)` can be used to skip a line of the TEXT file assigned to `TheFile`. Suppose the file `Silly.TXT` is assigned to `TheFile` and is as follows:

```
A carelessly planned project||takes three times as||
long to complete||whereas a carefully planned project||
only takes twice as long to complete.||   <end-of-file marker>
```

Give the output of the following instructions (`TheFile` is of type TEXT, and `ALine` is of type `STRING [40]`):

```
ASSIGN (TheFile, 'Silly.TXT') ;
RESET (TheFile) ;
READLN (TheFile) ;
READLN (TheFile, ALine) ;
WRITELN (ALine) ;
CLOSE (TheFile)
```

DO IT NOW ANSWERS

1. If the TEXT file is empty (that is, contains no lines), the execution of the instruction `READLN (TheFile, TheLine)` will stop the program and issue the error message
`Tried to read past end-of-file marker.`
2. `takes three times as`

5-3.3 Creating a TEXT File

Up to this point, the editor has been the only way to create a TEXT file. It is possible to write a Pascal program to create a TEXT file. A design to accomplish this would be as follows:

Design: Assign a name to the file variable
        Open the file to receive data
        REPEAT
           GetALine
           WriteLineToTheFile
           Check with user about quitting
        UNTIL user wants to quit
        CLOSE the file

To assign a name to a variable of type TEXT, the ASSIGN procedure is used. To open a file to receive information, the built-in procedure **REWRITE** is used. For example the following two instructions (where `OutFile` is a variable of type TEXT)

```
ASSIGN (OutFile, 'NewFile.TXT') ;    {assign name to variable}
REWRITE (OutFile) ;                  {open the file to receive data}
```

opens the file to receive information and names the file `NewFile.TXT`.

WARNING
If a file exists on diskette named `NewFile.TXT`, the instruction `REWRITE (OutFile)` will destroy the contents of that file.

To write information to a TEXT file, the built-in procedure **WRITELN** is used. For example,

```
WRITELN (OutFile, TheLine)
```

where `TheLine` is of type STRING, writes to the TEXT file the string of characters stored in `TheLine`.

COMMENT

If the file variable parameter (`OutFile`) is omitted, the material is written to the screen. When writing to a TEXT file, unlike writing to the screen, the parameter of type STRING (`TheLine` in the WRITELN procedure given here) must be a variable parameter. That is, `WRITELN (OutFile, 'Hello Rick')` will stop the program's execution and issue an error message.

A Pascal program to create a TEXT file is shown in Figure 5–11.

Figure 5–11

```
PROGRAM CreateAFile ;

VAR TheFile : TEXT ;
    ALine, FileName : STRING [80] ;
    Ans : CHAR ;
BEGIN
  WRITE ('Enter name of new TEXT file: ') ;
  READLN (FileName) ;
  ASSIGN (TheFile, FileName) ;
  REWRITE (TheFile) ;                  {create and open file to receive data}
  REPEAT
    WRITELN ('Enter line to add to the TEXT file: ') ;
    READLN (ALine) ;
    WRITELN (TheFile, ALine) ;    {send line to file}
    WRITE ('Enter another line?(Y/N): ') ;
    READLN (Ans)
  UNTIL Ans IN ['N', 'n'] ;
  CLOSE (TheFile)                      {close the file}
END .
```

DO IT NOW

1. Suppose you executed the program `CreateAFile` and created a TEXT file whose contents represented a valid Pascal program. How would you compile and execute the program?
2. Describe how you would expand the program `CreateAFile` to allow the user to see the contents of the TEXT file created.

DO IT NOW ANSWERS

1. Set the workfile to the name of the TEXT file created. From the Turbo Pascal main menu, press the R key for Run and the contents of the TEXT file created will be compiled then executed.
2. Set the workfile to `CreateAFile`. Enter the editor and move the cursor to the blank line prior to the execution section. Use `Ctrl-K R` to read in the contents of the TEXT file `SeeTxt.PAS` (which contains the source code for the program `SeeTxtFile`). Convert the program `SeeTxtFile` to a procedure. The procedure header would be

```
        PROCEDURE SeeTxtFile (FileName : String8Ø) ;
```

Alter the line `ASSIGN (InFile, 'MyFile.PAS')`
to the line `ASSIGN (InFile, FileName)`

In the main execution section of `CreateAFile`, insert a call to the procedure `SeeTxtFile`.

5–3.4 *Processing a TEXT File*

So far, we have looked at how to read a TEXT file and how to create one from a Pascal program. Next, we will look at how to process the data contained in a TEXT file. A summary of the instructions introduced so far follows:

- `ASSIGN (FileVariable, StringValue)`
  A procedure used to assign a name to a variable of type TEXT
  Example: `Assign (OutFile, 'MyFile.PAS')`

- `RESET (FileVariable)`
  A procedure used to open an existing file. Prior to executing this instruction, `FileVariable` must be assigned a STRING value that is the name of an existing file on the diskette. If no such file exists, the program stops and issues an error message. The instruction moves the file pointer to the start of the file. Executing RESET on an open file moves the file pointer to the first line of the file (the file's contents are not altered).

- `REWRITE (FileVariable)`
  A procedure used to open a new file. Prior to executing this instruction, `FileVariable` must be assigned a STRING value that is the desired name of the file. The instruction moves the file pointer to the start of the file. If the file is an existing file, its contents are erased. Executing REWRITE on an open file moves the file pointer to the start of the file, erasing the contents of the file.

- `READLN (FileVariable, TheLine)`
  A procedure used to read a line from an existing TEXT file (a file opened with RESET). If the file pointer is at the end-of-file marker, the program stops and issues an error message. The line read from the file is stored in the STRING variable `TheLine`.

- `WRITELN (FileVariable, ALine)`
  A procedure used to write a line to a TEXT file (a file opened with REWRITE). The STRING value stored in `ALine` is written to the current end of the file.

- `EOF (TheFile)`
  A BOOLEAN-valued function that returns the value `TRUE` if the file pointer is at the end-of-file marker.

- `CLOSE (TheFile)`
  A procedure used to close a file.

To increase your understanding of TEXT files, study the following example of processing a TEXT file:

EXAMPLE

On the diskette, there is a TEXT file named `History.TXT`. Write a Pascal program to count the number of vowels in the file.

SOLUTION

Design: Open the file named History.TXT
           WHILE NOT EOF (TheFile) DO
                ProcessALine
           Close the file
           Report number of vowels

Refinement of: *Open the file named History.TXT*
                  ASSIGN (InFile, 'History.TXT')
                  RESET (InFile)

Refinement of: *ProcessALine*
                  READLN (InFile, TheLine)
                  FOR Ct   := 1 TO LENGTH (TheLine) DO
                       IF TheLine [Ct] is a vowel
                            THEN increment vowel count

Refinement of: *Close the file*
                  CLOSE (InFile)

Refinement of: *Report number of vowels*
                  WRITE (The number of vowels in the file is:')
                  WRITELN (NumVowels)

Note that RESET is used to open the file, since the file already exists on the diskette. This design yields the Pascal program in Figure 5–12.

Figure 5–12

```
PROGRAM ProcessText ;

TYPE WholeNum = 0 .. MAXINT ;

VAR NumVowels : WholeNum ;
    InFile : TEXT ;

PROCEDURE ProcessALine (VAR VowelCt : WholeNum ;
                        VAR TheFile : TEXT) ;

  VAR ALine : STRING [255] ;
      Vowels : SET OF CHAR ;
      Ct : 0 .. 255 ;

  BEGIN
    Vowels := ['A','E','I','O','U','a','e','i','o','u'] ;
    READLN (TheFile, ALine) ;
    FOR Ct := 1 TO LENGTH (ALine) DO
      IF ALine [Ct] IN Vowels
        THEN VowelCt := VowelCt + 1
  END ;

BEGIN
  NumVowels := 0 ;
  ASSIGN (InFile, 'History.TXT') ;
  RESET (InFile) ;
  WHILE NOT EOF (InFile) DO
    ProcessALine (NumVowels, InFile) ;
  CLOSE (InFile) ;
  WRITE ('Number of vowels in the file is ') ;
  WRITELN (NumVowels)
END .
```

WARNING
A variable of type TEXT must be passed to a module as a variable parameter.

For the program `ProcessText` in Figure 5–12, the data type for `NumVowels` is `WholeNum`. This data type was defined in the TYPE section, since `NumVowels` was passed as a parameter to the procedure `ProcessALine`. Also, note that `InFile` was passed as a variable parameter to `ProcessALine`. This is a requirement. A variable of type TEXT must always be a variable parameter in a procedure header. Finally, `NumVowels` is initialized to `Ø`. When the procedure `ProcessALine` is executed, `VowelCt` is initialized to the value passed (the value in `NumVowels`). After the execution of `ProcessALine`, `NumVowels` contains the value sent to `ProcessALine` plus the number of vowels in the line read in from the TEXT file. Thus, a running total of the number of vowels is stored in the program variable `NumVowels`.

DO IT NOW

1. Suppose the file `History.TXT` contains the following lines:

```
Niklaus Wirth designed the language Pascal in 197Ø.||
In 1983, Philippe Kahn and Borland International||
developed Turbo Pascal.||   <end-of-file marker>
```

Do a walk through for the program `ProcessText` in Figure 5–12. Give the output.

2. Expand the program `ProcessText` (in Figure 5–12) to ouput a line number and the number of vowels in the line.

Sample Execution

```
Line 1: Number vowels- 15
Line 2: Number vowels- 14
Line 3: Number vowels- 8
Number of vowels in the file is: 37
```

3. What would be the output of `ProcessText` (see Figure 5–12) if
   a. `History.TXT` were empty?
   b. `History.TXT` did not exist?

DO IT NOW ANSWERS

1. `Number of vowels in the file is: 37`

2.
```
PROGRAM ProcessText ;

TYPE WholeNum = Ø .. MAXINT ;

VAR TotalVowels, NumVowels, LineNum : WholeNum ;
    InFile : TEXT ;

PROCEDURE ProcessALine (VAR VowelCt : WholeNum ;
                        VAR TheFile : TEXT) ;

  VAR ALine : STRING [255] ;
      Vowels : SET OF CHAR ;
      Ct : Ø .. 255 ;
  BEGIN
    Vowels := ['A','E','I','O','U','a','e','i','o','u'] ;
    READLN (TheFile, ALine) ;
    FOR Ct := 1 TO LENGTH (ALine) DO
      IF ALine [Ct] IN Vowels
        THEN VowelCt := VowelCt + 1
  END ;
```

```
BEGIN
  TotalVowels := 0 ;
  LineNum := 0 ;
  ASSIGN (InFile, 'History.TXT') ;
  RESET (InFile)
  WHILE NOT EOF (InFile) DO
    BEGIN
      NumVowels := 0 ;
      LineNum := LineNum + 1 ;
      ProcessALine (NumVowels, InFile) ;
      WRITELN ('Line ', Number, ': Number vowels- ', NumVowels) ;
      TotalVowels := TotalVowels + NumVowels
    END ;
  CLOSE (InFile) ;
  WRITE ('Number of vowels in the file is: ') ;
  WRITELN (TotalVowels)
END .
```

3a. If History.TXT is empty, the output is

Number of vowels in the file is: 0

Since the file is empty, the BOOLEAN expression NOT EOF (InFile) has value FALSE; thus, the procedure ProcessALine is not called.

b. If History.TXT does not exist, there is no output. When an attempt is made to execute the instruction RESET (InFile), the program stops and issues an error message.

5-3.5 *Special Procedures*

Three special procedures are available in Turbo Pascal for working with TEXT files. These procedures are ERASE, RENAME, and APPEND.

ERASE:

The procedure ERASE is used to remove a file from a diskette.

Example: ERASE (TheFile) removes from the diskette the file assigned to the file variable TheFile.

COMMENT
The TEXT file should be closed prior to using the procedures ERASE, RENAME, and APPEND.

RENAME:

The procedure RENAME is used to change the name of a file.

Example: RENAME (TheFile, 'MyFile.TXT') changes the name of the file assigned to the file variable TheFile to the name MyFile.TXT.

APPEND:

The procedure APPEND opens an existing file and moves the file pointer to the end-of-file marker. After APPEND has been executed, the WRITELN procedure can be used to add lines to the end of the file.

Example: APPEND (TheFile) opens the TEXT file assigned to file variable TheFile and moves the file pointer to the end of the file.

Vocabulary

Page		
	290	**APPEND** A predefined procedure used to add material to the end of a TEXT file.
	282	**ASSIGN** A Turbo Pascal predefined procedure for assigning a name to a file variable. The procedure has as input a file variable and a value. The procedure assigns to the file variable the value input.

Example:

ASSIGN (OutFile , 'B:MyFile.TXT')

CLOSE   A Pascal predefined procedure for closing a file. The procedure has as input a file variable. 284
Example:

```
CLOSE (OutFile)
```

EOF   A predefined BOOLEAN function that is used to avoid trying to read past the end-of-file marker. The function has a file variable as input. The value returned by the function is TRUE if the file pointer is on the end-of-file marker. 284
Example:

```
WHILE NOT EOF (InFile) DO
  ProcessALine
```

ERASE   A predefined procedure used to remove a file from a diskette. 290
File   A sequence of values, all of the same data type. The data is usually stored outside the main memory of the computer on a diskette. 281
READLN   When used with TEXT files, an instruction that provides for getting one of the components (a line) of the file. The file pointer is advanced to the start of the next line. 283
Example:

```
READLN (InFile , TheLine)
```

RENAME   A predefined procedure used to rename a file on a diskette. 290
RESET   A Pascal predefined procedure for opening an existing file. This procedure opens the file and sets the file pointer to the start of the file. 283
Example:

```
RESET (InFile)
```

REWRITE   A Pascal predefined procedure for creating a new file. The file is opened (prepared for processing) to receive data. 285
Example:

```
REWRITE (OutFile)
```

TEXT   A Pascal reserved word for a file made up of lines of text with each line made up of characters. TEXT is a data type (just as CHAR or INTEGER is a data type) where the values are files. 281
WRITELN   When used with TEXT files, an instruction that provides for placing a component (a line) in the file. The next output to the file will start at the beginning of the next line. 286
Example:

```
WRITELN (OutFile ,TheLine)
```

Glad You Asked

Q How do I create a TEXT file on a diskette in the second disk drive?

A The second disk drive is named B:. Thus, you would use the following:

```
ASSIGN (OutFile, 'B:Names.TXT') ;
REWRITE (Outfile) ;
```

Q How can I write the contents of a TEXT file to the printer?

A One approach would be to alter the program SeeTxtFile (see Figure 5–10) to write the line to the printer rather than to the screen, that is, WRITELN (LST, TheLine). You should use a line counter to keep from printing across pages. A page contains 66 lines.

Q Why use CLOSE? I read in another book that when the program ends, all open files are closed by the Pascal system.

A All open files are closed at the end of the program. However, it is good programming to close any files that have been opened. When a file is opened, a memory location is used to hold the file identifier. When the file is closed, the memory location is taken back by the system. If files are not closed, this area of memory could fill and result in an error. Additionally, failing to close a file can result in "trash" being written to the file when the system closes the file.

Q I tried to write a procedure named `LowerCase`. The procedure header was

```
PROCEDURE LowerCase (PassFile : TEXT) ;
```

In the program execution block, the call to the procedure was to be `LowerCase ('MyFile')`. The program stopped compiling with a `File value parameter not allowed` error message. Would you please explain this?

A The error message means that to pass a file to a procedure or function, a variable identifier for the file must be used. If you opened the file with a statement like `RESET (InFile)`, then a valid call to the procedure would be `LowerCase (InFile)`. Remember, as mentioned earlier in this section, for a TEXT file, a variable parameter must be used. That is, a correct procedure header would be `PROCEDURE LowerCase (VAR PassFile : TEXT)`, and a correct call would be of the form `LowerCase (a variable identifier)`.

Q What is a buffer?

A Buffer, in normal usage, means to soften the shock of something, as in buffered aspirin or a buffer state. In computers, a *buffer* is a storage area of memory. In this buffer, data coming from or going to an external source (a diskette file, the keyboard, etc.) is temporarily held. The buffer serves as an adjustment to the difference in speed of the CPU and the IO device. That is, it softens the shock of the slow input/output of data to the fast processing of data performed by the CPU.

Q If a TEXT file is opened with REWRITE, can it be read from? If a TEXT file is opened with RESET, can it be written to?

A If a TEXT file is opened with REWRITE, the file pointer is moved to the start of the file, and the contents of the file are destroyed. Thus, there is nothing to read. If you write material to the file, you still cannot read the material (without closing and starting over), since the file pointer cannot be moved backward. Thus, a TEXT file opened with REWRITE is by default for writing only.

　　If a TEXT file is opened with RESET, the file pointer is moved to the start of the file, and the contents are not altered. The only IO operation allowed is READ (or READLN).

Q I keep getting an `IO error` (input/output error) message when I try to open an existing file. I either forget the file's name or I misspell it. Is there a way to see the directory from a Pascal program?

A No. There is no easy way to produce a directory listing from a Pascal program. However, there is a compiler directive that can help. Consider the following instructions. (`FileName` is of type `STRING [40]`, and `ErrCode` is of type INTEGER.)

```
{$I-}                    {turn off IO error checking}
REPEAT
  WRITELN ('Enter name of file to open: ') ;
  READLN (FileName) ;
  RESET (TheFile) ;
  ErrCode := IORESULT ;
  IF ErrCode < > 0
    THEN WRITELN ('Sorry, ', FileName, ' does not exist!')
UNTIL ErrCode = 0 ;
{$I+}                    {turn IO error checking back on}
```

The compile directive {$I-} is used to turn off IO error checking.

IORESULT is a built-in INTEGER-valued function that returns Ø when no error has been made during an IO operation. When using the function IORESULT, be aware of the following logic error:

```
{$I-}                         {turn off IO error checking}
REPEAT
  WRITELN ('Enter name of file to open: ') ;
  READLN (FileName) ;
  RESET (TheFile) ;
  IF IORESULT < > Ø
    THEN WRITELN ('Sorry, ', FileName, ' does not exist!')
UNTIL IORESULT = Ø ;
{$I+}                         {turn IO error checking back on}
```

The REPEAT-UNTIL has no effect in this situation. That is, even if an error is made in opening the file in `FileName`, the instructions will not be repeated. When the WRITELN instruction (in the IF-THEN instruction) was executed, the value Ø was stored in IORESULT, since no error was recorded. Thus, the BOOLEAN expression for the REPEAT-UNTIL has value `TRUE`. The error's source is in using the identifier IORESULT after another IO operation (the WRITELN) has occurred.

Section 5–3 Exercises

Match these instructions with the descriptions that follow (assume `OutFile` and `InFile` are of type TEXT and `TheLine` is of type STRING).

a. WRITELN (OutFile , TheLine)
b. READLN (InFile , TheLine)
c. EOF (InFile)
d. REWRITE
e. RESET
f. WRITELN (OutFile)
g. CLOSE (OutFile)
h. VAR InFile : TEXT

_____ 1. declares the identifier `InFile` as a variable of type TEXT.

_____ 2. checks for an end-of-file marker in the TEXT file.

_____ 3. is a predefined procedure to open an existing file.

_____ 4. places a line of text in a TEXT file.

_____ 5. closes the TEXT file listed.

_____ 6. gets a line from a TEXT file and advances the file pointer to the start of the next line.

_____ 7. inserts a blank line in a TEXT file.

_____ 8. is a predefined procedure that creates a new file.

9. Insert *True* for a true statement. Insert *False* for a false statement.

_____ a. A TEXT file is a data structure.

_____ b. The only way a programmer can create a TEXT file is to use the editor.

_____ c. The predefined procedures REWRITE and RESET are used to open a TEXT file.

_____ d. If a TEXT file exists on a diskette, using RESET to open the file destroys the contents of the file.

_____ e. RESET is used to open an existing TEXT file.

_____ f. The predefined procedure READLN is used to insert data in a TEXT file.

_____ g. If the file pointer is moved past the end-of-file marker in a TEXT file, a runtime error is issued.

_____ h. A TEXT file must be opened before values can be read from, or written to, the file.

_____ i. The predefined procedure SHUT is used to close a TEXT file.

10. List the steps required to create a new TEXT file from a Pascal program.

11. List the steps required to see the contents of an existing TEXT file from a Pascal program.

12. a. Alter the Pascal program `SeeTxtFile` (Page 000) to allow the user to input the name of the file to be processed.

    b. Further alter the program `SeeTxtFile` to output the contents of the TEXT file double spaced. That is, every other line of output is a blank line.

For problems 13 through 16, assume the TEXT file `Grades.TXT` exists and contains the following lines (|| represents an end-of-line marker):

```
Adams, John||96||Bell, Alex||67||Cather, Willa||85||
Davy, Hump||76||Earp, Wyatt||46||Kilmer, Joyce||88||
North, Ollie||23||Stern, Bertha||72||   <end-of-file marker>
```

Also, assume the following TYPE and VAR sections:

```
TYPE WholeNum = 0.. 100 ;
     String20 = STRING [20] ;

VAR InFile, OutFile : TEXT ;
    TheLine, SecLine : String20 ;
    ANumber : WholeNum ;
    ErrCode : INTEGER ;
```

13. Give the output of

```
ASSIGN (InFile, 'Grades.TXT') ;
RESET (InFile) ;
WHILE NOT EOF (InFile) DO
  BEGIN
    READLN (InFile, TheLine) ;
    WRITELN (TheLine) ;
    READLN (InFile)
  END
```

14. Give the output of

```
ASSIGN (InFile, 'Grades.TXT') ;
RESET (InFile) ;
WHILE NOT EOF (InFile) DO
  BEGIN
    READLN (InFile) ;
    READLN (InFile, TheLine) ;
    WRITELN (TheLine)
  END
```

15. Give the contents of `Altered.TXT` after the following instructions are executed:

```
ASSIGN (InFile, 'Grades.TXT') ;
RESET (InFile) ;
ASSIGN (OutFile, 'Altered.TXT') ;
REWRITE (OutFile) ;
WHILE NOT EOF (InFile) DO
  BEGIN
    READLN (InFile, TheLine) ;
    READLN (InFile, SecLine) ;
    TheLine := CONCAT (TheLine, '*', SecLine) ;
    WRITELN (OutFile, TheLine)
  END ;
CLOSE (InFile) ;
CLOSE (OutFile)
```

16. Give the output of

```
ASSIGN (InFile, 'Grades.TXT') ;
RESET (InFile) ;
WHILE NOT EOF (InFile) DO
   BEGIN
     READLN (InFile , TheLine) ;
     VAL (TheLine, TheNum, ErrCode) ;
     IF ErrCode = 0
        THEN WRITE (TheNum : 3)
   END
```

17. Boot up Pascal; set the workfile to the file **PROTEXT.PAS** from the Source diskette. Enter the editor. Alter the program to allow the user to input the name of the TEXT file to be processed.

18. Boot up Pascal; set the workfile to the file **TEXTEX.PAS** from the Source diskette. Use the copy application to read the contents of the files **SEETXTFI.PAS**, **CREATEFI.PAS**, and **PROTEXT.PAS** from the Source diskette. Alter the material read in to procedures that interface with the main execution section of the program **AllOfIt**. Test the program **AllOfIt** by executing the program and creating several TEXT files (including one containing no text).

Programming Problems

19. Write a Pascal program to create a TEXT file named **RandomGr.TXT**. Each line of the TEXT file is to have the form

       LastName, FirstName* LetterGrade

   where **LetterGrade** is a character from **'A'** to **'F'**. The program should allow the user to enter the name and the letter grade.

20. Write a Pascal program that will process a TEXT file whose contents consist of the text of a Pascal program. The program is to output to the screen each line of the TEXT file that starts with the letter *P*. The user is to enter the name of the file to be processed.

Sample Execution

```
Enter name-
First: Ron
Last: Deep
Enter letter grade: A
Enter another record?(Y/N):
```

Sample Execution

```
Enter name of TEXT file: ProTEXT.PAS
The lines starting with letter P are:
PROGRAM ProcessText;
PROCEDURE ProcessALine (VAR VowelCt : WholeNum) ;
```

21. Alter the program **ProcessText** (Page 288) to count the number of nonblank characters in a TEXT file. The name of the TEXT file to be processed is to be input by the user.

Sample Execution

```
Enter name of TEXT file: MyFile.TXT
The file contains 8512 nonblank characters.
```

22. Write a Pascal program that allows the user to enter the name of a TEXT file. The program is to output the number of words in the TEXT file. A word is a string of characters that is succeeded by a blank space or end-of-line marker.

Sample Execution

```
Enter name of TEXT file: YourFile.TXT
The file contains 142 words.
```

23. Joan's teacher has requested that each TEXT file containing a Pascal program contain a comment after the program header section. The comment is to have the following form:

```
{*************************************************************}
{ Name:                                                       }
{ Program's purpose:                                          }
{ Date:                                                       }
{*************************************************************}
```

Joan has decided to write a Pascal program to open a TEXT file containing a Pascal program and to insert the comment section just shown in the text of the program. She has sketched out the following design:

```
Create TempFile
Open program TEXT file
Write header section to TempFile
Fill in comment section
Write comment section to TempFile
Write rest of program TEXT file to TempFile
Check TempFile for accuracy
Close files
```

Write a Pascal program to accomplish this task. You might start by refining Joan's design. How would you destroy the old TEXT file containing the program and rename the new TEXT file containing the comment section and the program text?

Character Reference for TEXT Files

In Section 5–1, you studied simple data types. In Section 5–2, you were introduced to data structures (STRING and SET). In Section 5–3, you studied the data structure TEXT. In this section, the work with TEXT files will continue. You will learn how to work with the characters of a TEXT file. Additionally, you will learn to work with numbers and TEXT files.

5-4.1 Characters in TEXT Files

Up to this point, you have considered a TEXT file as a collection of lines. That is, you have accessed the components of the data structure TEXT by accessing the lines of the data structure. The Pascal language also provides for accessing the characters that make up the lines of the TEXT file. This access is accomplished by using the READ and WRITE procedures.

Reading a Character The **READ** procedure can be used with a TEXT file. For example,

        READ (TheFile, Ch)

where TheFile is a variable of type TEXT and Ch is a variable of type CHAR, will access the TEXT data structure to obtain a character to be stored in Ch. The general form of the READ instruction is

    READ (*file variable, variable*)

          a variable of   a variable of type CHAR
          type TEXT   or a numeric type

Suppose a TEXT file named 'History.TXT' exists on the diskette and contains the lines

        Niklaus Wirth designed the language Pascal in 1970.||
        In 1983, Philippe Kahn and Borland International||
        developed Turbo Pascal.|| <end-of-file marker>

When the instructions

        ASSIGN (TheFile, 'History.TXT') ;
        RESET (TheFile) ;

are executed, the file pointer is positioned at the start of the file:

        Niklaus Wirth designed the language . . .
        ⇑
when the instruction

        READ (TheFile, Ch)

is executed, the character N is assigned to Ch, and the file pointer is advanced to i (the next character):

        Niklaus Wirth designed the language . . .
         ⇑

EOLN Just as Pascal provides a BOOLEAN-valued function, EOF, for testing for the end-of-file marker, there is a BOOLEAN-valued function for testing for the end-of-line marker. The function has identifier **EOLN.** Consider the instruction

        WHILE NOT EOLN (TheFile) DO
          READ (TheFile, Ch)

The function EOLN is called. Next, the BOOLEAN expression NOT EOLN (TheFile) is evaluated. If the file pointer is at the end-of-line marker, EOLN (TheFile) returns the value TRUE. Thus, the BOOLEAN expression NOT EOLN (TheFile) has value FALSE, and the execution WHILE-DO instruction is completed. The WHILE-DO instruction will read a character from the TEXT file while the file pointer is not at the end-of-line marker.

Suppose the file pointer is at the start of a nonempty TEXT file. Compare

```
        READLN (TheFile, ALine)
```

with the following instructions using the READ procedure:

```
        ALine := '' ;                    {the null string}
        WHILE NOT EOLN (TheFile) DO
          BEGIN
            READ (TheFile, Ch) ;
            CONCAT (ALine, Ch)
          END ;
```

After executing these instructions, the STRING variable `ALine` would contain the first line of the TEXT file. However, the file pointer would be positioned at the end-of-line marker. To move the file pointer to the start of the next line, the instruction `READLN (TheFile)` would need to be used.

To increase your understanding of using the READ procedure to process a TEXT file, study the following example.

EXAMPLE

A TEXT file named `Company.TXT` exists on a diskette and is made of lines like the following:

```
    General Mills*       Battle Creek, Michigan||
```

That is, each line is a company name followed by an asterisk, some blanks, a city name, a comma, a blank, and a state name. Write a Pascal program that has as input the TEXT file `Company.TXT` and writes to the screen the names of the companies headquartered in Florida.

SOLUTION

One approach to solving this problem would be to read a line of the TEXT file, then use the STRING procedures and function to separate from the line the company name and the state name. To demonstrate processing a TEXT file character by character, the following design is used.

Design: Open the file
        WHILE NOT EOF (TheFile) DO
            ProcessALine
        Close (TheFile)

Refinement of: *ProcessALine*
            GetCompanyName
            GetStateName
            IF StateName = 'Florida'
               THEN WRITELN (CompanyName)

Refinement of: *GetCompanyName*
            CoName := ''   {the null string}
            Ch := ' '   {a blank}
            WHILE Ch < > '*' DO
               READ (TheFile,Ch)   {end of company name marked with *}
               CONCAT (CoName,Ch)

Refinement of: *GetStateName*

```
                  Ch := ''                          {a blank}
                  WHILE Ch < > ',' DO               {city name followed by comma}
                        READ (TheFile,Ch)
                  READ (TheFile,Ch)                 {skip blank after the comma}
                  READLN (TheFile, StateName)       {get state name and move pointer}
                                                    {to start of next line}
```

After this design is tested (by walking through it with a typical line from the TEXT file), the design is converted to a Pascal program. The program resulting from this design is shown in Figure 5–13.

Figure 5–13

```
PROGRAM Company ;

VAR TheFile : TEXT ;

PROCEDURE ProcessALine (VAR AFile : TEXT) ;

  VAR CoName, StateName : STRING [40] ;
      Ch : CHAR ;

  BEGIN                                  {ProcessALine}
    CoName := '' ;                       {the null string}
    Ch := ' ' ;                          {a blank}
    WHILE Ch < > '*' DO                  {get company name}
      BEGIN
        READ (AFile, Ch) ;
        CoName := CONCAT (CoName, Ch)
      END ;
    WHILE Ch < > ',' DO                  {skip to end of city name}
      READ (AFile, Ch) ;
    READ (AFile, Ch) ;                   {skip blank after comma}
    READLN (AFile, StateName) ;          {get state name}
    IF StateName = 'Florida'
      THEN WRITELN (CoName)
  END ;                                  {ProcessALine}

BEGIN                                    {Company}
  ASSIGN (TheFile, 'B:Company.TXT') ;
  RESET (TheFile) ;
  WHILE NOT EOF (TheFile) DO
    ProcessALine (TheFile) ;
  CLOSE (TheFile)
END .                                    {Company}
```

General Mills* Battle Creek, Michigan||
file pointer

General Mills* Battle Creek, Michigan||
file pointer

COMMENT

The state name could have been obtained by using the following instructions:

```
        StateName := '' ;               {the null string}
        WHILE NOT EOLN (TheFile) DO
          BEGIN
            READ (TheFile, Ch) ;
            StateName := CONCAT (StateName, Ch)
          END
```

Writing a Character   The **WRITE** procedure can be used to write a character to a TEXT file. For example,

    WRITE (ToTheFile, Ch)

where `ToTheFile` is a variable of type TEXT and `Ch` is a variable of type CHAR, will write the character stored in `Ch` to the TEXT file. The general form of the WRITE procedure follows:

    WRITE   (*file variable, variable*)

          a variable of   a variable of type CHAR
          type TEXT   or a numeric type

Consider the instruction `WRITELN (ToThefile, ALine)` and the following instruction using the WRITE procedure (where `ALine` is of type STRING, `Ct` is of type 1 .. 255, and `ToTheFile` is of type TEXT):

    FOR Ct := 1 TO LENGTH (ALine) DO
      WRITE (ToTheFile, ALine [Ct])

The FOR-DO instruction would write to the TEXT file the characters of the string stored in `ALine`. However, the instruction would not write the end-of-line marker to the TEXT file. Suppose the following instructions are executed (where `ToTheFile` is of type TEXT, `TheString` is of type STRING[80], and `Ct` is of type 1 .. 255):

    ASSIGN (ToTheFile, 'NewFile.TXT') ;
    REWRITE (ToTheFile) ;   {create file}
    WRITE ('Enter a string of characters: ') ;
    READLN (TheString) ;
    FOR Ct := 1 TO LENGTH (TheString) DO
      WRITE (ToTheFile , TheString [Ct]) ;   {send first line}
    WRITE ('Enter a string of characters: ') ;
    READLN (TheString) ;
    FOR Ct := 1 TO LENGTH (TheString) DO
      WRITE (ToTheFile , TheString [Ct]) ;   {send second line}

If the user enters `I am 20` for the first string and `YEARS OLD` for the second string, the TEXT file would appear as `I am 20YEARS OLD`. If we had used

    WRITELN (ToTheFile, TheString)

instead of the FOR-DO instructions, the results would have been
`I am 20||YEARS OLD||`

DO IT NOW

The TEXT file `MyStuff.TXT` contains the lines

    First, I bought some stuff. Next, I had to buy a house||
    in which to keep the stuff. Of course, I had to buy some||
    more stuff with which to fill the house.|| <end-of-file marker>

1. What is wrong with the following attempt to write the contents of the file to the screen (`TheFile` is of type TEXT, and `Ch` is of type CHAR)?

```
        ASSIGN (TheFile, 'MyStuff.TXT') ;
        RESET (TheFile) ;
        REPEAT
          WHILE NOT EOLN (TheFile) DO
            BEGIN
              READ (TheFile, Ch) ;
              WRITE (Ch)
            END
        UNTIL EOF (TheFile) ;
        CLOSE (TheFile)
```

2. Write a Pascal program that will create a new TEXT file containing the nonblank characters of the file `MyStuff.TXT`. Name the new TEXT file `YourStuff.TXT`.

DO IT NOW ANSWERS

1. The program will enter an endless (infinite) loop after writing to the screen the line

```
    First, I bought some stuff. Next, I had to buy a house
```

At this point, the function EOLN returns the value `TRUE`. Thus, the BOOLEAN expression `NOT EOLN (TheFile)` has value `FALSE`, and the instruction of the WHILE-DO will not execute. However, EOF still returns the value `FALSE`, so the REPEAT-UNTIL will execute the WHILE-DO instruction endlessly. If you insert the instruction `READLN (TheFile)` after the WHILE-DO instruction, the program will output the contents of `MYStuff.TXT`.

COMMENT
To recover from this type of infinite loop, you must reboot the computer (use `Ctrl-Alt-Del` keys).

2.
```
PROGRAM NoBlanks ;

VAR OldFile, NewFile : TEXT ;

PROCEDURE MoveALine (VAR SourceFile, DestFile : TEXT) ;

  CONST ABlank = ' ' ;

  VAR Ch : CHAR ;

  BEGIN
    READLN (SourceFile, TheLine) ;
    FOR Ct := 1 TO LENGTH (TheLine) DO
      IF TheLine [Ct] < > ABlank
        THEN WRITE (Destfile, TheLine [Ct]) ;     {send nonblank characters}
    WRITELN (DestFile)                            {insert end-of-line marker}
  END ;

BEGIN
  ASSIGN (OldFile, 'MyStuff.TXT') ;
  RESET (OldFile) ;
  ASSIGN (Newfile, 'YourStuff.TXT') ;
  REWRITE (Newfile) ;
  WHILE NOT EOF (OldFile) DO
    MoveALine (OldFile, NewFile) ;
  CLOSE (OldFile) ;
  CLOSE (NewFile)
END .
```

5-4.2 *Numbers in TEXT Files*

A TEXT file is made up of lines of text, and each line is made up of characters. Suppose the TEXT file `TestScor.TXT` is the following:

```
Apes, Harry*      98     <end-of-line marker>
Blue, Sky*        72     <end-of-line marker>
Care, Ido*        65     <end-of-line marker>
Care, Wedo*       88     <end-of-line marker>
Ideal, High*      82     <end-of-line marker>
<end-of-file marker>
```

Although the file is made up of characters, special provision is made to work with numbers in TEXT files. Consider the following instructions, where `Number` is a variable of type INTEGER and `InFile` is a variable of type TEXT.

```
Apes, Harry*  98||
Apes, Harry*  98||
Blue, Sky*    72||
```

```
ASSIGN (InFile , 'TestScor.TXT') ;
RESET (InFile) ;
Ch := ' ' ;                        {initialize Ch to blank character}
WHILE Ch < > '*' DO                {skip over name}
  READ (InFile , Ch) ;
READLN (InFile , Number)
```

RESET moves the file pointer to the top of the file. The WHILE-DO instruction moves the file pointer to the first blank after the first name (`Apes, Harry*`). The instruction `READLN (InFile , Number)` assigns the number 98 to the variable `Number` and moves the file pointer to the start of the next line.

In working with numbers in TEXT files, the instruction `READ (InFile , Number)`, where `Number` is of type INTEGER or REAL, will:

1. Skip over blanks and end-of-line markers until a nonblank character is found.
2. Take the string of characters that follows, up to the next blank space or nonnumeric character (end-of-file marker, etc.).
3. Attempt to convert the characters to a number.

WARNING

If no such conversion is possible, an `IO error` message is issued. Trying to read past end-of-line and end-of-file markers is a common error in working with numbers in TEXT files (see next DO IT NOW exercise).

Consider these instructions:

```
ASSIGN (InFile , 'TestScor.TXT') ;
RESET (InFile) ;
READLN (InFile , Number)
```

where `Number` is a variable of type INTEGER. The execution of these instructions would lead to an error, since `READLN (InFile , Number)` would attempt to convert the character `A` (from the line `Apes, Harry* 98`) to a number (see Figure 5–14).

Figure 5–14

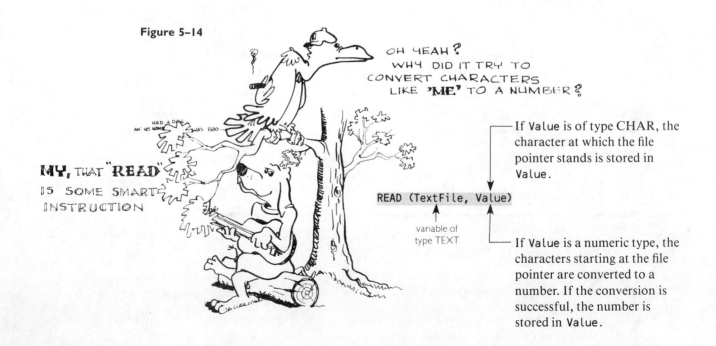

OH YEAH? WHY DID IT TRY TO CONVERT CHARACTERS LIKE 'ME' TO A NUMBER?

MY, THAT "READ" IS SOME SMART INSTRUCTION

If `Value` is of type CHAR, the character at which the file pointer stands is stored in `Value`.

`READ (TextFile, Value)`

variable of type TEXT

If `Value` is a numeric type, the characters starting at the file pointer are converted to a number. If the conversion is successful, the number is stored in `Value`.

Suppose you had a TEXT file composed of numbers separated by end-of-line markers:

23||34||78||98||45|| <end-of-file marker>

An instruction like (assume `Count` and `Sum` have been initialized to `0`):

```
WHILE NOT EOF (InFile) DO
  BEGIN
    READLN (InFile , Number) ;
    Sum := Sum + Number ;
    Count := Count + 1
  END
```

Walk Through

Number	Sum	Count
23	23	1
34	57	2
78	135	3
98	233	4
45	278	5

could be used to find the sum of the numbers. The instruction would return 278 for `Sum` and 5 for `Count`. Each time READLN is called, a value is assigned to `Number`, and the file pointer is moved to the start of the next line.

If the instruction `READLN (Number)` is replaced by `READ (Number)`, the value returned for `Sum` would be 278. However, the value returned for `Count` would be 6.

```
WHILE NOT EOF (InFile) DO
  BEGIN
    READ (InFile , Number) ;
    Sum := Sum + Number ;
    Count := Count + 1
  END
```

The first time READ is called, the value 23 is assigned to `Number`. The file pointer is left at the end of the line. The next call to READ skips over the end-of-line marker and assigns the variable `Number` the next value. After the value 45 has been assigned, the file pointer is at the end-of-line marker. Since `NOT EOF (InFile)` is `TRUE`, another call is made to `READ (InFile,Number)`. This is the extra call recorded in `Count`. The end-of-line marker after the value 45 is skipped, but the next object found is the end-of-file marker. Thus, `Number` is assigned `0`, and the value assigned `Sum` is still 278.

23||34||78||98||45|| <end-of-file>

23||34||78||98||45|| <end-of-file>

Suppose the TEXT file values were

23A||34B||78C||98D||45E|| <end-of-file marker>

The original instructions, with `READLN (InFile,Number)`, would process the file without difficulty. On each call to READLN, the string of characters up to the letter would be converted to a number value and assigned to the variable `Number`. Also, on each call, the file pointer would be moved to the start of the next line.

If READLN were replaced by READ, an IO error would result after the first call. After the first call, the value 23 would be assigned to `Number`. However, the file marker would be at the letter `A`. On the next call, an attempt would be made to convert the value `A` to a number value. Since such a conversion is impossible, the error results.

As an example of processing a TEXT file involving numbers, consider the program `Average` in Figure 5–15 which reads the TEXT file `TestScor.TXT` and computes, then prints, the averages of the scores. The program processes each line using the procedure `ReadScores`. The procedure skips over the characters in the name, then reads the score into the variable `Num`.

Figure 5–15

WARNING
File variables must be passed as variable parameters.

```
PROGRAM Average ;

TYPE WholeNum : 0 .. MAXINT ;

VAR InFile : TEXT ;
    NumSc , Total : WholeNum ;
    Aver : REAL ;

PROCEDURE ReadScores (VAR SumOfScores , N : WholeNum ;
                           VAR WorkFile : TEXT) ;

  VAR Ch : CHAR ;
      Num : WholeNum ;

  BEGIN                                    {ReadScores}
    Ch := ' ' ;
    WHILE Ch < > '*' DO                    {skip over name}
      READ (WorkFile , Ch) ;
    READ (WorkFile , Num) ;                {read the test score}
    READLN (WorkFile) ;                    {move pointer to next line}
    N := SUCC (N) ;                        {keep up with number of scores}
    SumOfScores := SumOfScores + Num
  END ;                                    {ReadScores}
BEGIN                                      {main program}
  Total := 0 ;
  NumSc := 0 ;
  ASSIGN (InFile , 'TestScor.TXT') ;
  RESET (InFile) ;
  WHILE NOT EOF (InFile) DO
    ReadScores (Total , NumSc , InFile) ;
  Aver := Total / NumSc ;
  WRITE ('The average of the test scores is: ' , Aver : 1 : 3) ;
  CLOSE (InFile)
END .                                      {main program}
```

TestScor.TXT
```
Apes, Harry*  98||
Blue, Sky*    72||
Care, Ido*    65||
Care, Wedo*   88||
Ideal, High*  82||
<end-of-file  marker>
```

DO IT NOW

1. What would happen if the instruction READLN (WorkFile) were left out of the procedure ReadScores (see Figure 5–15)?

2. What would happen if, in the procedure ReadScores (see Figure 5–15), the WHILE-DO instruction were replaced by

```
    WHILE Ch < > ' ' DO        {skip over name}
      READ (WorkFile, Ch)
```

3. Rename the program Average (see Figure 5–15) to Maximum, and alter it so as to output the highest test score.

DO IT NOW ANSWERS

1. The file would be processed. However, after the call to ReadScores (where the line Ideal, High* 82 is processed), the file pointer is on the end-of-line marker after the score 82. In the program execution section, NOT EOF (InFile) is TRUE. Thus, ReadScores is called. When ReadScores executes, Ch < > '*' is TRUE. Thus, an error message is issued, since an attempt is made to read past the end-of-file marker (on some systems, the WHILE-DO would become an infinite loop).

2. An exit from the WHILE-DO loop would occur after the comma in the name `Apes, Harry`. This would leave the file pointer on the `H` in `Harry`. When `READ (WorkFile, Num)` executes, an attempt would be made to convert `'H'` to a number of type `WholeNum`. An `IO error` message would be issued.

3. `Program Maximum:`

```
Type WholeNum = Ø .. MAXINT ;

VAR InFile : TEXT ;
    Max : WholeNum ;

PROCEDURE ReadScores (VAR Largest : WholeNum ;
                      VAR InFile : TEXT) ;

  VAR Ch : CHAR ;
      Num : WholeNum ;

  BEGIN                              {ReadScores}
    Ch := ' ' ;
    WHILE CH < > '*' DO              {skip over name}
      READ (InFile , Ch) ;
    READ (InFile , Num) ;           {read the test score}
    READLN (InFile) ;               {move pointer to next line}
    IF Num > Largest
      THEN Largest := Num
  END ;                             {ReadScores}
BEGIN                                {main program}
  Max := Ø ;                        {initialize Max to zero}
  ASSIGN (InFile , 'TestScor.TXT') ;
  RESET (InFile) ;
  WHILE NOT EOF (InFile) DO
    ReadScores (Max , InFile) ;
  WRITELN ('The maximum of the test scores is: ', Max) ;
  CLOSE (InFile)
END .                                {main program}
```

```
TestScor.TXT
Apes, Harry*  98||
Blue, Sky*    72||
Care, Ido*    65||
Care, Wedo*   88||
Ideal, High*  82||
<end-of-file  marker>
```

5-4.3 *Control Breaks*

As a last example of working with numbers in TEXT files, we will consider a problem known as a **control breaks** problem. Suppose a TEXT file named `GMSales.TXT` exists on diskette and has the following form:

Salesperson Number	Date of Sales	Item Number	Amount of Sales
111	02/07/92	J12	125.60
111	02/09/92	J28	52.00
111	02/23/92	A15	23.00
215	02/01/92	M19	256.00
215	02/05/92	A23	334.56
215	02/20/92	Z45	101.02
215	02/25/92	T56	9.17

The file `GMSales.TXT` is to be processed to obtain the total sales. Additionally, subtotals for each salesperson are to be obtained. The screen output is to have the following form:

Sample Execution

```
Salesperson          Sales        Totals
111                 125.60
111                  52.00
111                  23.00
                                  200.60
215                 256.00
215                 334.56
215                 101.02
215                   9.17
                                  700.75
Total Sales                       901.35
```

The TEXT file GMSales.TXT is organized by groups. The groups in this situation are groups of sales for a particular salesperson. When this file is processed, the output must be broken down into groups of sales by salesperson. Controlling the breaks requires recognizing the breaks between groups of data. In the GMSales.TXT file, the breaks will be controlled by the salesperson number.

A design to solve the problem is as follows:

Design: WriteHeader
          OpenFile
          Total : = 0
          ProcessfirstLine
          WHILE NOT EOF (TheFile) DO
              ProcessALine
          WRITELN (SubTotal : 38 : 2)
          Total : = Total + SubTotal
          WRITELN ('Total sales:', Total : 25 : 2)

```
GMSales.TXT
111   02/07/92   J12   125.60
111   02/09/92   J28    52.00
111   02/23/92   A15    23.00
215   02/01/92   M19   256.00
215   02/20/92   Z45   101.02
215   02/25/92   T56     9.17
```
└— Control Break

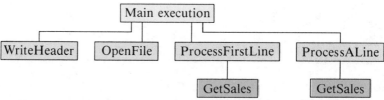

Refinement of: *WriteHeader*
                 WRITE ('Salesperson', 'Sales' : 9, 'Totals': 16)

Refinement of: *OpenFile*
                 ASSIGN (TheFile, 'GMSales.TXT')
                 RESET (TheFile)

Refinement of: *ProcessFirstLine*
                 IF NOT EOF (TheFile)
                   THEN Get SPNumber
                       Get SalesAmt
                       PrevNum : = SPNumber
                       WRITE (SPNumber)
                       WRITELN (SalesAmt : 17 : 2)
                       SubTotal : = SalesAmt

Refinement of: *ProcessALine*
          Get SPNumber
          Get SalesAmt
          IF SPNumber = PrevNum
            THEN SubTotal : = SubTotal + SalesAmt
                WRITE (SPNumber)
                WRITELN (SalesAmt :17 : 2)
            ELSE WRITELN (SubTotal : 30 : 2)
                Total : = Total + SubTotal
                SubTotal : = SalesAmt
                PrevNum : = SPNumber
                WRITE (SPNumber)
                WRITELN (SalesAmt : 17 : 2)

Refinement of: *Set SalesAmt*
          Skip over blanks
          Skip over Date
          Skip over blanks
          Skip over Item code
          READLN (TheFile, SalesAmt)

COMMENT
`GetSPNumber` can be accomplished by using `READ (TheFile, SPNumber)`.

When the first line of the TEXT file is processed, the instruction

`READ (TheFile, SPNumber)`

is used to assign the variable `SPNumber` (salesperson number) a value. Next, the sales amount for this person is obtained by moving the file pointer past the item code, using READLN. The value obtained for sales amount is used to initialize the variable `SubTotal`. The value obtained for `SPNumber` is used to initialize the variable `PrevNum`.

After the first line is processed, the remaining lines are processed. For each line, values for `SPNumber` and `SalesAmt` are obtained. If the value in `SPNumber` is equal to the value in `PrevNum`, the values are output to the screen, and `SubTotal` is updated. If the value in `SPNumber` is not equal to `PrevNum`, a control break is executed. That is, the value in `SubTotal` (the sales for a given salesperson) is written to the screen. Also, `Total` is increased by the amount in `SubTotal`, `SubTotal` is assigned the value in `SalesAmt`, and `PrevNum` is assigned the value in `SPNumber`.

The design is tested by walking through it with data from the file `GMSales.TXT`; then it is converted to a Pascal program. See Figure 5–16.

Walk Through

SPNumber	SalesAmt	PrevNum	Subtotal	Total
111	125.60	111	125.60	0
111	52.00		177.60	
111	23.00		200.60	
215	256.00			
		215	256.00	200.60
215	334.56		590.56	
215	101.02		691.58	
215	9.17		700.75	
WRITELN (SubTotal:38:2)				
Total := Total + SubTotal				901.35
WRITELN ('TotalSales:', Total:25:2)				

Output

Salesperson	Sales	Totals	
111	125.60		ProcessFirstLine
111	52.00		ProcessALine
111	23.00		ProcessALine
		200.60	ProcessALine
215	256.00		
215	334.56		ProcessALine
215	101.02		ProcessALine
215	9.17		ProcessALine
		700.75	
Total Sales:		901.35	

Figure 5–16

```
PROGRAM ControlBreaks ;

TYPE CodeNum = 100 .. 999 ;

VAR TxtFile : TEXT ;
    PrevNum : CodeNum ;
    SubTotal, Total : REAL ;

PROCEDURE WriteHeader ;

  BEGIN
    WRITELN ('Saleperson', 'Sales':9, 'Totals':16)
  END ;

PROCEDURE GetSales (VAR TheFile : TEXT ;
                    VAR SalesAmt : REAL) ;

  VAR Ch : CHAR ;

  BEGIN
    Ch : = ' ' ;                          {initialize Ch to a blank}
    WHILE Ch = ' ' DO                     {skip over blanks}
      READ (TheFile, Ch) ;
    WHILE Ch < > ' ' DO                   {skip over date}
      READ (TheFile, Ch) ;
    WHILE Ch = ' ' DO                     {skip over blanks}
      READ (TheFile, Ch) ;
    WHILE Ch < > ' ' DO                   {skip over item code}
      READ (TheFile, Ch) ;
    READLN (TheFile, SalesAmt)
  END ;

PROCEDURE ProcessFirstLine (VAR TheFile : TEXT ;
                            VAR PrevNum : CodeNum ;
                            VAR SubTotal : REAL) ;

  VAR SPNumber : CodeNum ;
      SalesAmt : REAL ;

  BEGIN                                   {ProcessFirstLine}
    IF NOT EOF (TheFile)
      THEN BEGIN
            READ (TheFile, SPNumber) ;
            GetSales (TheFile, SalesAmt) ;
            PrevNum := SPNumber ;         {initialize PrevNum}
            SubTotal := SalesAmt ;        {initialize SubTotal}
            WRITE (SPNumber) ;
            WRITELN (SalesAmt : 17 : 2)
          END
  END ;                                   {ProcessFirstLine}

PROCEDURE ProcessALine (VAR TheFile : TEXT ;
                        VAR PrevNum : CodeNum ;
                        VAR SubTotal, Total : REAL) ;

  VAR SPNumber : CodeNum ;
      SalesAmt : REAL ;

  BEGIN                                   {ProcessALine}
    READ (TheFile, SPNumber) ;
```

GMSales.TXT

111	02/07/92	J12	125.60
111	02/09/92	J28	52.00
111	02/23/92	A15	23.00
215	02/01/92	M19	256.00
215	02/05/92	A23	334.56
215	02/20/92	Z45	101.02
215	02/25/92	T56	9.17

Figure 5–16
Continued

```
         GetSales (TheFile, SalesAmt) ;
         IF SPNumber = PrevNum
           THEN BEGIN                          {continue subtotal}
                   SubTotal := SubTotal + SalesAmt ;
                   WRITE (SPNumber) ;
                   WRITELN (SalesAmt : 17 : 2)
                END
           ELSE BEGIN
                   WRITELN (SubTotal : 30 : 2) ;  {control break}
                   Total := Total + SubTotal ;    {update Total}
                   SubTotal := SalesAmt ;         {restart SubTotal}
                   PrevNum := SPNumber ;          {set new PrevNum}
                   WRITE (SPNumber) ;
                   WRITELN (SalesAmt : 17 : 2)
                END
      END ;                                    {ProcessALine}

BEGIN                                          {main execution}
  WriteHeader ;
  ASSIGN (TxtFile, 'GMSales.TXT') ;
  RESET (TxtFile) ;                            {open file}
  Total := 0 ;
  ProcessFirstLine (TxtFile, PrevNum, SubTotal) ;
  WHILE NOT EOF (TxtFile) DO
    ProcessALine (TxtFile, PrevNum, SubTotal, Total) ;
  WRITELN (SubTotal : 38 : 2) ;
  Total := Total + SubTotal ;
  WRITELN ('Total sales: ', Total : 25 : 2)
END .                                          {main execution}
```

COMMENT

In the program `ControlBreaks`, the procedure `ProcessFirstLine` protects against reading from an empty file. Also, the procedure is used to initialize the variables `PrevNum` and `SubTotal`. For this reason, it is often called a priming read (as in priming a pump).

Vocabulary   Page

EOLN A predefined BOOLEAN-valued function used to detect when the end of a   297
line in a TEXT file has been reached.

READ A predefined procedure that obtains a value from a TEXT file. The proce-   297
dure has two variable parameters, the first of type TEXT and the second of type
CHAR (or a numeric type). The procedure obtains a value from a TEXT file
and then advances the file pointer.

WRITE A predefined procedure that places a value in a TEXT file. The procedure   300
has two variable parameters, the first of type TEXT and the second of type
CHAR (or a numeric type). The procedure places the value in the second parameter in the TEXT file and then advances the file pointer.

Glad You Asked

Q I have a TEXT file in which the lines appear as follows:

```
Name            Company          Total Compensation
Iacocca, L.     Chrysler         $11,500,000
Pickens, T.     Mesa Petroleum   $ 9,900,000
Spiegel, T.     Columbia S&L     $ 9,000,000
  .
  .
  .
Lazarus, C.     Toys "R" Us      $ 3,000,000
```

How can I process the TEXT file to obtain the average compensation of all of the executives?

A First, you must skip the first line (the headers). Next, you process each line to obtain the amount of compensation. To accomplish this, you move the file pointer to the first numeric character right of the dollar ($) character. Once the pointer is positioned, the commas must be filtered (deleted) from the amount. This could be accomplished by using the following instructions:

```
Num := 0 ;
WHILE NOT EOLN (Thefile) DO
  BEGIN
    READ (TheFile, Ch) ;
    IF Ch IN ['0' .. '9']                    {digits}
      THEN Num := 10*Num + ORD (Ch) - ORD ('0')
END
```

Once the number is obtained it could be accumulated in a variable (say Sum), after which the next line would be processed.

Q I have a TEXT file with the lines appearing as follows:

```
Name           Birthday
Gosett, L.     5/27/36
Guthrie, A.    7/10/47
Penn, S.       8/17/60
Ciccone, M.    8/16/58
  .
  .
  .
Zappa, F.      12/21/40
```

How can I process the TEXT file to write to the screen the names of the people born prior to the 15th of the month?

A Skip over the first line (the titles). Process each line by doing the following:
1. Obtain the name by using instructions similar to the following:

```
Name := '' ;                {the null string}
Ch := ' ' ;                 {a blank}
WHILE Ch < > '.' DO         {a period}
  BEGIN
    READ (TheFile, Ch) ;
    Name := CONCAT (Name, Ch)
  END
```

2. Move the file pointer to the right of the slash (/) character.
3. Use an instruction like

```
READLN (TheFile, BDay)
```

where BDay is a numeric type. The characters from the file pointer's location to the next non-numeric character (the second slash character) will be converted to a number and then stored in the variable BDay. The file pointer will move to the start of the next line.

4. Compare the value in the variable BDay to the value 15. If it is less, then write the value in Name to the screen.

Section 5–4 Exercises

For problems 1 through 5 assume the following:

```
TYPE WholeNumber : Ø .. MAXINT ;

VAR InFile : TEXT ;
    Number, Sum, Count,
    Maximum , Minimum,
    Range , TempHold : WholeNumber ;
```

The TEXT file SampleDa.TXT contains only whole numbers separated by a space and/or an end-of-line marker. From the editor, the file appears as follows (where || represents an end-of-line marker):

17 23 56 78 89 92 23||34 78 78 89 65 23||12 15 99 34|| < end-of-file marker >

1. Complete the following list of instructions to output the number of values in the file, the sum of the values in the file, and the average of the values in the file:

```
ASSIGN (InFile , 'SampleDa.TXT') ;
RESET (InFile) ;
Sum := Ø ;
Count := Ø ;
WHILE NOT EOF (InFile) DO
  BEGIN
    WHILE NOT EOLN (InFile) DO
      BEGIN
        READ (InFile , Number) ;
        Count := Count + 1 ;
        Sum := Sum + Number
      END ;
      _____
  END
  _____
```

2. Complete the following instructions to output the *range* of the values in the file:

```
ASSIGN (InFile , 'SampleDa.TXT') ;
RESET (InFile) ;
Minimum := MAXINT ;
Maximum := -MAXINT - 1 ;
WHILE NOT EOF (InFile) DO
  BEGIN
    WHILE NOT EOLN (InFile) DO
      BEGIN
        READ (InFile , Number) ;
        IF Number >= Maximum
          THEN _____ ;
          _____
      END
  END ;
Range := Maximum - Minimum ;
_____
```

```
Enter low value for search: 45
The values greater than
or equal to 45 are:
56 78 89 92 78 78 89 65 99
Press RETURN key to continue.
Enter Q to Quit.
```

```
Enter low value for search: 45
Enter high value for search: 78
The values between 45 and 78 are:
56 65
Press RETURN key to continue.
Enter Q to Quit.
```

3. Write a Pascal program to list to the screen all the values in `SampleDa.TXT` greater than or equal to a value input by the user. Use the following design:

```
REPEAT
   RESET InFile
   Get Value from user
   WHILE NOT EOF (InFile) DO
       READ (Number)
       IF Number > = Value
          THEN WRITE ( Number : 1 , ' ')
UNTIL user wants to quit
Close InFile
```

4. Expand the program in problem 3 to allow the user to input two values (low value, high value). The program is to output all the values between the input values (exclusive).

5. Write a Pascal program to allow the user to add values to the end of the `TEXT` file `SampleDa.TXT`.

6. Boot up Pascal; set the workfile to the file `PROCOMP.PAS` from the `Source` diskette. Enter the editor. Alter the program to output the names of the companies with headquarters in the state of New York.

7. Boot up Pascal; set the workfile to the file `AVERAGE.PAS` from the `Source` diskette. Enter the editor. Expand the program to output each line of the TEXT file and whether the score is above or below average.

Sample Execution

```
The average of the test scores is: 81.00
Apes, Harry*     98   Above
Blue, Sky*       72   Below
```

8. Boot up Pascal; set the workfile to the file `CtrlBrk.PAS` from the `Source` diskette. Enter the editor. Expand the program to output the item number in a column to the right of the sales column. Alter the program to write its output to the printer.

Programming Problems

9. Each line of text in the TEXT file `Donors.TXT` has the following form:

   LName,⬚FName*⬚⬚Address*⬚County

   A typical text line is

   Butler, Candy* 132 West Garden Quincy Fl 32571* Gasden

   a. Write a Pascal procedure that has a county as input. The output is to be a list of names (presented on the screen) of donors from the input county.
   b. Write a Pascal program to delete a text line specified by the program user from the TEXT.

For problems 10 through 13 assume the TEXT file `Grades2.TXT`. The file consists of lines with the following form:

   LName,⬚FName*⬚⬚⬚Score

A typical line is `Cika, Rab*    93`. All scores are from `0` to `100`; all `LName` and `FName` values are limited to 15 characters.

10. Write a Pascal program to find the minimum score and output the name of the person and the score. Use the following design:

Design: Open InFile
Min : = 101
LineNum : = 1
WHILE NOT EOF (InFile) DO
    CheckForMin (Min , LineNum , TargetLine)
RESET (InFile)
Count : = 1
WHILE Count < TargetLine DO
    READLN (InFile, TextLine)
    Count : = Count + 1
WRITE ('Lowest grade was made by: ')
WRITELN (TextLine)

Sample Execution

```
Processing file ...
Lowest grade was made by: Clown, Joe*    50
```

11. Write a Pascal program that allows the user to input two scores (low value, high value). The program will output each name and score in the given range, exclusive of end values.

12. Write a Pascal program that allows the user to input a name (FirstName LastName). The program will search the TEXT file. The output will be the name and score, if name is found. If name is not found, the output will be Sorry, can't find that name.

13. Write a Pascal program that will write the contents of Grades2.TXT to the screen with the addition of a letter grade for each name. Use this grade scale:

Above 94	A
86 to 94	B
73 to 85	C
66 to 72	D
65 or below	F

Sample Execution

```
Cika, Rab*       93   B
Boles, Sharon*   67   D
Stalle, Ron*     95   A
  :
```

14. Write a Pascal program to search the text of a Pascal program for the word WHILE. The output should be the number of times the word appears in the TEXT file.

15. Expand the program in problem 14 to allow the user to enter the word for which the search will be conducted.

16. Write a Pascal procedure to scan the text of a Pascal program and list to the screen each procedure header.

17. Write a Pascal program that has as input the TEXT file of a Pascal program. The program will write the contents of the file to the screen. However, each character between the character { and the character } will be replaced by the character *. (This type of program is a tool for checking a Pascal program's text for errors with comments.)

18. The TEXT file KPark.TXT has the following form:

Department	Item No.	Quantity	Cost/Item
03	1137	7	3.20
03	1082	2	7.80
03	1792	5	17.90
09	2317	1	247.00
12	1005	10	52.00
12	8791	2	7.47

Sample Execution

Department	Sales	Totals
03	22.40	
03	15.60	
03	89.50	
		127.50
09	247.00	
		247.00
12	520.00	
12	14.94	
		534.94
Total for all departments		909.44

That is, each line of the TEXT file is made up of a department number, an item number, the quantity sold, and the cost per item. Write a Pascal program that processes the TEXT file to output to the screen the department number and value of the sales for each line of the TEXT file. A control break should occur for each department to output the total sales for the department. After processing the TEXT file, the total sales value for all the departments should be output to the screen.

CHAPTER TEST

Match these items with the following descriptions:

a. scalar data type   f. TEXT file
b. IN   g. index
c. PRED   h. EOF
d. ordinal data type   i. RESET
e. enumerated type   j. REWRITE

_____ 1. a predefined function used to check for the end of a TEXT file
_____ 2. a relational used to check for set membership
_____ 3. a number used to refer to a particular character in a string
_____ 4. a predefined function used to find the preceding value of an ordinal value
_____ 5. a user-defined data type created by listing its values
_____ 6. a data structure
_____ 7. a predefined procedure for opening an existing TEXT file
_____ 8. the data type REAL
_____ 9. the data type CHAR
_____ 10. a predefined procedure for creating a new TEXT file

11. List three ordinal data types.

12. List three data structures.

13. Complete the following TYPE and VAR sections to
    a. declare `Colors` a data type with values `red, yellow, blue, green`.
    b. declare `MoneyValues` a data type with values from `10` to `200`.
    c. declare `MyColor` a set variable with base type `yellow, blue, green`.
    d. declare `GoodMoney` a set variable with base type `50` to `100`.

    ```
    TYPE COLORS _____ ;
         MoneyValues _____ ;

    VAR MyColor_____ ;
        GoodMoney_____
    ```

14. Write a Pascal procedure that has as input a string of length 80. The procedure is to remove all blank spaces from the string and return the altered string. Assume that `String80 = STRING [80]` has been defined in the program TYPE section.

    Sample Execution

    ```
    Enter string value (up to 80 characters):
    Marvin Cohen, where are you?
    Value returned is:
    MarvinCohen,whereareyou?
    ```

15. Complete the following Pascal program. It is to count the total number of periods, semicolons, colons, question marks, and exclamation marks in the TEXT file `MyLetter.TXT`.

```
PROGRAM PunctCount ;

VAR InFile : Text ;
    Count : 0 .. MAXINT ;
    Ch : CHAR ;

BEGIN
  Count := 0 ;
  _____

END .
```

```
The TEXT file contains 30 of the punctuation marks.
```

16. The TEXT file **'Sample.TXT'** contains a collection of numbers from 0 to 300. The values are separated by blank spaces and end-of-line markers. Write a Pascal program to output the values between **70** and **150** inclusive. The program should also output the average of these values.

```
Now reading Sample .....
Values between 70 and 150 inclusive are:
73 78 93 95 102 147 149
The average of these values is: 105.29
```

Programming Projects

Project 5-1. Write a Pascal program that generates a TEXT file named Weather.TXT. The lines of the TEXT file should appear as follows:

```
01/01/89 54 28 0.20  <end-of-line marker>
01/02/89 57 32 0.00  <end-of-line marker>
    :
03/31/89 91 78 1.34  <end-of-line marker>
<end-of-file marker>
```

The values in each line represent the date and the high temperature, low temperature, and rainfall for the date. The temperatures and rainfall amounts can be assigned randomly.

Write a Pascal program that allows the user to select from the following menu:

```
A. See weather conditions for a given day
B. See last entry
C. Append next entry
D. See statistics for year so far
Q. Quit
```

If the user selects option **A**, the user is given the following prompts:

Sample Execution

```
Last entry was made ......     {date of last entry}
Please enter month: February
Please enter day: 23
```

The output will have the following form:

Sample Execution

```
February 23, 1989, had: a high temperature of 45 F
                        a low temperature of 13 F
                        rainfall was 0.53 inches
```

If the user selects option **B**, the output has the following form:

Sample Execution

```
Last entry was made ........     {date of last entry}
The high temperature was 65 F
The low temperature was 45 F
The rainfall was 0.00 inches
```

If the user selects option **C**, the user is presented the following prompts:

Sample Execution

```
Next entry is for ...........     {date of new entry}
Enter high temperature for day (in Fahrenheit): 89
Enter low temperature for day (in Fahrenheit): 78
Enter rainfall for day (in inches): 0
```

If the user selects option **D**, the user is presented the following statistics:

Sample Execution

```
Last entry was made ........     {date of last entry}
Average temperature to date: 76.4 F
Maximum temperature to date: 87 F on May 7
Minimum temperature to date: 13 F on February 17
Total rainfall to date: 34.46 inches
Maximum rainfall to date: 4.56 inches on April 16
Average rainfall to date: 0.31 inches per day

Press RETURN key for main menu-
```

Turn in a design, a hard copy of your program, a hard copy of the TEXT file
Weather.TXT, and a hard copy of a test run for each option.

Project 5–2. A popular game is based on a contestant's spinning a large wheel that randomly selects a money value. The contestant then guesses in order to uncover a letter in a mystery phrase. If successful, the contestant is credited with the money value times the number of letters uncovered for that spin. At this point, the contestant can guess the mystery phrase, spin again, or pass to the next contestant. If the mystery phrase is correctly identified, the contestant then wins the money that has been placed on credit for the round. Otherwise, play passes to the next contestant. If the first contestant is unsuccessful at uncovering a letter, the next contestant gets a turn. A contestant cannot guess a vowel. A contestant, however, can buy a vowel for $250 prior to spinning the wheel. All the letters in the mystery phrase that match the vowel are uncovered.

Write a Pascal program named `SpinForDollars` that simulates this game. A possible screen design is as follows:

Sample Execution

```
 __M_I_ D_M_I_
 (fictional character)

          WHEEL SPIN: $250
 Mickey $1500        Robin $2350
 Enter letter: C     Enter Letter: ▯

 Sorry. No C .

 Totals: Phase 2 of 3 in game

         Mickey $0        Robin $4350
```

COMMENT
This program uses only one screen and the GOTOXY procedure.

From the above screen, the following observations are made:

The mystery phrase is from the category fictional characters.

The letters *D, M,* and *T* have been uncovered.

The contestant Mickey has $1500 on credit.

The contestant Robin has $2350 on credit.

On Mickey's last turn, a *C* was guessed. The mystery phrase does not contain a *C*.

It is now Robin's turn. The wheel has been spun, yielding a value of $250. Robin is now to enter a letter as a guess. If the letter appears in the phrase, Robin will be credited another $250 times the number of times the guessed letter appears in the mystery phrase. Also, Robin will be given the opportunity to solve the mystery phrase or to spin again.

The totals at the bottom indicate that the contestants have selected a game consisting of three puzzles. Robin solved the first puzzle and won $4350.

Your program should start with a screen that allows the contestants to enter the following required information for the game:
a. The number of contestants (2 or 3).
b. The contestants' names (up to eight characters).
c. The number of puzzles in the game (1 to 5).
The values on the wheel and their frequencies follow:

Value	Frequency	Value	Frequency
$ 50	3	$ 250	5
$100	4	$ 300	4
$150	5	$ 500	2
$200	6	$1000	1

Enter the editor, and build a TEXT file containing the phrase and the category. The TEXT file should appear as follows:

```
OAKLAND CALIFORNIA*(a place)  <end-of-line marker>
STEVEN SPIELBERG*(a person)  <end-of-line marker>
MONEY FOR NOTHING*(a title)  <end-of-line marker>
PETER RABBIT*(fictional character)  <end-of-line marker>
MICROWAVE OVEN*(an object)  <end-of-line marker>
    .
    .
    .
<end-of-file marker>
```

Your program should read in the number of mystery phrases selected at the start of the game from the TEXT file. The mystery phrases should be selected randomly from the TEXT file. At the end of the game, the winner should be announced and the winnings for each contestant stated.

For extra credit, insert any of the following additional features:

d. Add these selections to the wheel: skip turn; lose turn; bankrupt.

e. Add the option of one contestant with a timer. The contestant should be allowed to select a level of play. The level of play yields the amount of time allowed for the guess and the decision to solve the puzzle and/or guess again. In this game, only one vowel can be bought.

f. Add the extra feature of the game's winner playing a victory round for $10,000. A puzzle for this victory round should be selected when the other puzzles are selected. To play the round, the contestant selects five consonants and one vowel. Any of the selected letters appearing in the puzzle are revealed. The contestant has three minutes to enter the puzzle.

Turn in a hard copy of your TEXT file for the mystery phrases, a design, a structured diagram, and a hard copy of your program.

Chapter Six

Lists

Introduction

A computer program is a well-defined set of instructions that acts on a well-defined data structure. Up to this point, you have studied the instruction part of a computer program. From this point on, you will mainly study the data part. You have already seen some of the data structures available in Pascal (SET OF, STRING, and TEXT files). In this chapter, you will study lists, one of the most basic of the data structures.

Another name for a list is a one-dimensional array. The list data structure in the Pascal language is referenced by ARRAY OF. You will learn how to declare a variable and state its type as ARRAY OF. You will also learn how to access a component of a list, search a list, and sort a list. Finally, you will study an application of the list data structure known as parallel arrays. When you finish this chapter, you will be able to write a Pascal program that uses the data structure ARRAY OF.

```
PROGRAM Chapter6 ;

CONST Max = 6 ;

TYPE WholeNum = 0 .. 100 ;
     ListType = ARRAY [1 .. Max] OF CHAR ;        {page 327}

VAR Value : CHAR ;
    NDex, Found : WholeNum ;
    TheList : ListType ;                          {page 328}

PROCEDURE SelectSort (TheLen : WholeNum ;
                             VAR List : ListType) ;  {page 327}

  BEGIN
    {instructions for Selection sort}            {page 361}
  END ;

PROCEDURE InsertSort (TheLen : WholeNum ;
                            VAR TheList : ListType) ;

  BEGIN
    {instructions for Insertion sort}            {page 358}
  END ;

PROCEDURE BinarySearch (TheLen : WholeNum ; List : ListType ;
                              Target : CHAR ;
                              VAR Found : WholeNum) ;

  BEGIN
    {instructions for binary search}             {page 347}
  END ;
BEGIN
  FOR Ndex := 1 TO Max DO
    TheList [NDex] := CHR (RANDOM (26) + 65) ;   {page 323}
  WRITELN ('Select sort routine (S/I): ') ;
  READLN (Which) ;
  IF Which IN ['S','s']
    THEN SelectSort (Max, TheList)
    ELSE InsertSort (Max, TheList) ;
  WRITE ('Enter value to search for (A .. Z): ') ;
  READLN (Value) ;
  BinarySearch (Max, TheList, Value, Found) ;
  IF Found > 0
    THEN WRITELN ('Found in cell ', Found)
    ELSE WRITELN (Value, ' not found.')
END .
```

Arrays

In this section, you will be introduced to the **one-dimensional array.** This data structure is much like a simple list of items. You will learn how to declare a variable of type ARRAY and how to access a component of an array.

6-1.1 Review

Before starting with arrays, a general review is in order. First, a computer program involves both instructions and data. Up to this point, you have studied simple instructions such as assignments, READ, and WRITE; the control instructions (WHILE-DO, IF-THEN–ELSE, etc.); and procedures and functions. All of these involve the instruction part of a computer program. You have also studied simple data types such as BOOLEAN, CHAR, INTEGER, REAL, subranges, and enumerated types, as well as the data structures STRING, SET OF, and TEXT files (see Table 6–1). These deal with the data on which the instructions of a computer program operate. The remainder of this book is mainly concerned with the data part of a computer program.

Table 6–1

Instructions		
Simple Instructions	Procedures/Functions	Control Instructions
READ	SQR	IF-THEN-ELSE
WRITE	CHR	CASE-OF-END
Assignment	MyRoutine	WHILE-DO
⋮	⋮	REPEAT-UNTIL
		FOR-DO

Data		
Simple Data Types		Data Structures
BOOLEAN	subrange	STRING
CHAR	enumerated	SET OF
INTEGER		TEXT
REAL		ARRAY OF

6-1.2 The Need for Arrays

Some problems are difficult (practically impossible) to solve without the use of the array data structure. Consider the following problem.

PROBLEM

Write a Pascal program that has input (from the keyboard) of six grades. The program is to compute then output their average. Additionally, the program is to output (write to the screen) each grade that is above the average.

Sample Execution

```
Enter grade 1: 89
Enter grade 2: 78
Enter grade 3: 56
Enter grade 4: 97
Enter grade 5: 46
Enter grade 6: 88

Average is: 75.67
Grades above average are 89 78 97 88
```

SOLUTION

To compose a Pascal program to solve this problem with the tools we have on hand would require a VAR section such as:

```
VAR Gr1, Gr2, Gr3, Gr4, Gr5, Gr6 : 0 .. 100 ;
    Average : REAL ;
```

To read in the scores from the keyboard would require a sequence of six different pairs of instructions (one for each grade entered) like:

```
WRITE ('Enter grade 1: ') ;
READLN (Gr1)
```

To compute the average of the grades, the following assignment instruction could be used:

```
Average := (Gr1 + Gr2 + Gr3 + Gr4 + Gr5 + Gr6)/6
```

Finally, to write to the screen each grade that is above average would require a sequence of six different IF-THEN instructions such as:

```
IF Gr1 > Average
   THEN WRITE (Gr1)
```

Even with the use of modules, such a program would be difficult to read and alter. Imagine altering the program to handle 100 or 1000 grades.

Obviously, a data structure is needed that can store the grades as they are read in and then provide easy access to them later. Such a data structure is called an **ARRAY**. A variable whose data type is ARRAY references a list of memory locations where the memory locations are indexed (labeled or numbered in some sense). Some everyday examples of indexed lists (arrays) follow:

A Shopping List	A Football Roster	A Final Grade Sheet
1. Bread	18 Killum, Harry	112 36 8971 A
2. Milk	19 Squats, Phil	234 87 1123 D
3. Wheat germ	20 Backs, Fast	239 12 3456 B
4. Toothpaste	⋮	⋮
	⋮	⋮

6-1.3 Declaring an ARRAY Variable

To declare a variable and state its data type as an ARRAY data structure, the reserved words **ARRAY** and **OF** are used. For example,

```
VAR Grades = ARRAY [1 .. 6] OF 0 .. 100
```

declares the variable `Grades` and states that its data type will be an ARRAY. Unlike the variables `Gr1`, `Gr2`, `Gr3`, `Gr4`, `Gr5`, and `Gr6`, the memory locations for `Grades` form a continuous block of memory locations (see Figure 6–1).

Figure 6–1

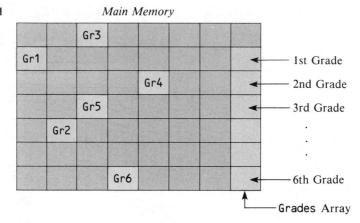

This memory arrangement allows the individual memory locations (called cells) to be accessed. Often an array is visualized as follows:

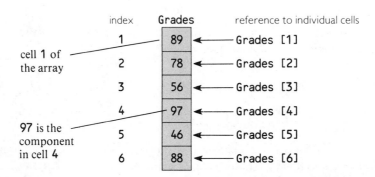

`Grades [1]` references the value **(component)** stored in the first memory location (cell) of the ARRAY variable `Grades`. Likewise, `Grades [4]` references the component stored in the fourth cell of the ARRAY variable `Grades`.

Taking a closer look at the declaration of a variable to be of type ARRAY reveals the following:

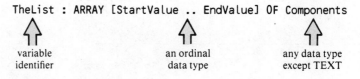

Following the reserved word ARRAY, a data type known as the **index type** appears. This data type is enclosed in brackets and usually listed as a subrange. The number of values in the index type determines the number of memory locations (cells) the ARRAY variable will reference. Following the reserved word OF, another data type known as the **component type** appears. This data type determines the data type of the values stored in the cells of the array. The component type can be any data type except TEXT.

Suppose the variable `Grades` had been declared as

```
                                        component type
Grades : ARRAY ['a' .. 'f'] OF 0 .. 100
                                        index type
```

The array would be visualized as follows:

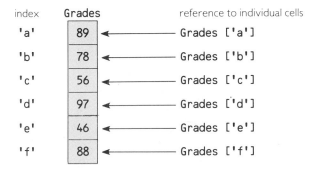

6-1.4 Subscripts

The ARRAY data structure provides the structure of an indexed list for any data type (except TEXT). To access a component of this data structure, a **subscript** (or an **index**) is used. For the variable `Grades`, where

```
Grades : ARRAY [1 .. 6] OF 0 .. 100
```

`Grades [1]` (read "Grades sub one") references (accesses) the component of the data structure `Grades` that is in cell 1. Consider the instruction for reading a list of scores from the keyboard into the data structure `Grades`:

```
FOR Ct := 1 TO 6 DO
   BEGIN
      WRITE ('Enter grade ', Ct, ': ') ;
      READLN (Grades [Ct])
   END
```

```
Enter grade 1:  89
Enter grade 2:  78
Enter grade 3:  56
Enter grade 4:  97
Enter grade 5:  46
Enter grade 6:  88
```

Grades   reference to individual cells

Grades [1]
Grades [2]
Grades [3]
Grades [4]
Grades [5]
Grades [6]

WARNING
READLN (Grades) yields an
IO not allowed error
message.

COMMENT
An important difference between working with the variables `Gr1`, `Gr2`, `Gr3`, `Gr4`, `Gr5`, and `Gr6` and the components of the ARRAY variable `Grades` is the ability to work with the components of `Grades` using a loop. Often the loop structure used to manipulate the subscript is a FOR-DO loop, since the programmer knows how many times the loop's instruction is to be executed.

Not only does the ARRAY data structure `Grades` provide storage for the six values entered, it also provides easy access to the values at some later point in the program. Consider finding the average of the six grades. One way to accomplish this would be to sum the components (the values stored in the cells) of the array. After the sum is found, the average would be the sum divided by 6. The following instructions could be used to find the sum of the components and assign a value to `Average`:

```
Sum := 0 ;
FOR Ct := 1 TO 6 DO
  Sum := Sum + Grades [Ct] ;
Average := Sum/6
```

| | **Walk Through** | |
Ct	Grades [Ct]	Sum
1	89	89
2	78	167
3	56	223
4	97	320
5	46	366
6	88	454

DO IT NOW

1. Declare a variable with identifier `TheList`, and state its type as an array with ten cells. The array is to store INTEGER-type data, and the cells are to be indexed from 11 to 20.

2. Suppose `TheList` (from problem 1) contains the value:

index	11	12	13	14	15	16	17	18	19	20
TheList	-4	5	8	-2	9	3	-1	2	-10	12

Give the output of the following instructions:

a. `WRITE (TheList [12])`

b. `WRITE (TheList [19] - 4)`

c. `FOR Ct := 11 TO 20 DO`
  `IF TheList [Ct] >= 0`
    `THEN WRITE (TheList [Ct] : 4)`

d. `WRITE (TheList [19 - 4])`

DO IT NOW ANSWERS

```
1. VAR TheList : ARRAY [11 .. 20] OF INTEGER
2a. 5  b. -14  c.    5   8   9   3   2  12  d. 9
```

6-1.5 Manipulation of ARRAY Components

The key to understanding arrays and thus using the ARRAY data structure is developing the ability to manipulate the components of an array. To develop this ability, study the following series of short examples of component manipulation.

EXAMPLE

For the VAR section

```
VAR Ct : 1 .. 4 ;
    TheList : ARRAY [1 .. 4] OF CHAR ;
```

write a FOR-DO loop to assign the characters from `A` to `D` to the cells of `TheList`.

SOLUTION

Because each component is indexed by a number from 1 to 4, the identifiers
TheList [1], TheList [2], . . . TheList [4] are a collection of variables of type
CHAR. Thus, they can be assigned a value of type CHAR using an assignment in-
struction. The following instruction solves the problem:

```
FOR Ct := 1 TO 4 DO
   TheList [Ct] := CHR (64 + Ct)
```

index	TheList
1	A
2	B
3	C
4	D

EXAMPLE

For the VAR section

```
VAR Ct : 1 .. 5 ;
    ListA, ListB : ARRAY [1 .. 5] OF REAL ;
```

write a FOR-DO instruction to assign to each cell of ListB the square of the corresponding component of ListA.

SOLUTION

```
FOR Ct := 1 TO 5 DO
   ListB [Ct] := SQR (ListA [Ct])
```

index	1	2	3	4	5
ListA	3.1	2.0	5.2	1.2	-2.0
ListB	9.61	4.0	7.04	1.44	4.0
index	1	2	3	4	5

EXAMPLE

For the VAR section

```
VAR Index : 1 .. 7 ;
    ArrayA : ARRAY [1 .. 7] OF 1 .. 100 ;
```

write instructions that write to the screen the components of ArrayA while the components are greater than 50.

SOLUTION

```
Index := 1 ;
WHILE ArrayA [Index] > 50 DO
   BEGIN
      WRITE (ArrayA [Index] : 4) ;
      Index := Index + 1
   END
```

Sample Execution

```
72  68
```

WARNING
The instruction WRITE (ArrayA)
yields an IO not allowed error
message.

index	ArrayA
1	72
2	68
3	13
4	98
5	12
6	100
7	86

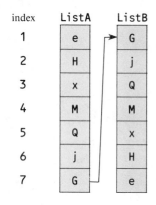

index	ListA	ListB
1	e	G
2	H	j
3	x	Q
4	M	M
5	Q	x
6	j	H
7	G	e

EXAMPLE

For the VAR section

```
VAR Ct : 1 .. 7 ;
    ListA, ListB : ARRAY [1 .. 7] OF CHAR ;
```

write a FOR-DO loop that will fill ListB with the components from ListA in reverse order. That is, ListB [1] will contain the component stored in ListA [7], ListB [2] will contain the component stored in ListA [6], and so forth.

SOLUTION

```
FOR Ct := 1 TO 7 DO
  ListB [Ct] := ListA [8 - Ct]
```

EXAMPLE

For the VAR section

```
VAR Subscript, TheSpot : 1 .. 100 ;
    Max : 0 .. MAXINT ;
    TheList : ARRAY [1 .. 100] OF 1 .. MAXINT ;
```

write instructions to fill TheList with random numbers from 1 to 1000, and then output to the screen the maximum (largest) component in the list and the index of the cell in which it is stored.

SOLUTION

```
WRITELN ('Filling list with random numbers ..') ;
FOR Subscript := 1 TO 100 DO                        {fill TheList}
  TheList [Subscript] := RANDOM (1000) + 1 ;
Max := 0 ;                                          {initialize Max}
FOR Subscript := 1 TO 100 DO                        {search for Max}
  IF TheList [Subscript] > Max
    THEN BEGIN
            Max := TheList [Subscript] ;            {update Max}
            TheSpot := Subscript                    {record the index}
         END ;
WRITE ('The maximum is ' , Max) ;
WRITELN (' and it is stored in cell ', TheSpot)
```

Sample Execution

```
Filling list with random numbers ..
The maximum is 965 and it is stored in cell 67
```

DO IT NOW

1. For the VAR section

```
VAR ChList : ARRAY [1 .. 100] OF CHAR ;
    Ct, TCt : 1 .. 100
```

write instructions to fill the array with randomly selected characters from a to z then write to the screen the number of t's in the list.

2. For the VAR section

```
VAR NumList : ARRAY [1 .. 10] OF INTEGER ;
    Temp : INTEGER ;
    Index : 1 .. 10
```

write instructions to swap the components in each pair of cells. That is, the values in NumList [1] and NumList [2] are swapped, the values in NumList [3] and NumList [4] are swapped, and so forth.

Sample Execution

```
Filling list with random characters ..
The list contains 15 t's.
```

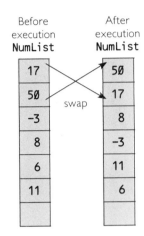

DO IT NOW ANSWERS

```
1. WRITELN ('Filling list with random characters .. ') ;
   FOR Ct := 1 TO 100 DO
     ChList [Ct] := CHR (ORD ('a') + RANDOM (26)) ;
   TCt := 0 ;
   FOR Ct := 1 TO 100 DO                          {Count the t's}
     IF ChList [Ct] = 't'
       THEN TCt := TCt + 1 ;
   WRITELN ('The list contains ', TCt, ' t''s.')
2. FOR Index := 1 TO 5 DO
     BEGIN
       Temp := NumList [2*Index - 1] ;            {components 1, 3, 5, 7, 9}
       NumList [2*Index - 1] := NumList [2*Index] ;
       NumList [2*Index] := Temp
     END
```

6-1.6 Using Arrays in Programs

To use a variable of type ARRAY in a Pascal program, the variable will often be passed as a parameter to a module (a procedure or function). To do so, the variable type must be previously defined. That is, a header such as

```
PROCEDURE SearchList (TheList : ARRAY [1 .. 100] OF CHAR) ;
```

yields an error at compile time. The data type for the array has to be defined in a TYPE section. Thus, if the type section defines ListType as

```
TYPE ListType = ARRAY [1 .. 100] OF CHAR
```

then the header could be written as

```
PROCEDURE SearchList (TheList : ListType) ;
```

In addition to defining an array type in the TYPE section, it is a good programming practice to define the beginning and ending index values in the CONST section. This allows the length of the array to be easily altered. For example,

COMMENT

The data type for a function cannot be a data structure. The only exception to this (in Turbo Pascal) is the data structure STRING.

```
CONST MaxIndex = 100 ;

TYPE IndexType = 1 .. MaxIndex ;
     ListType = ARRAY [1 .. MaxIndex] OF CHAR ;

VAR TheList : ListType ;
```

allows the programmer to alter the length of the list by altering the value in MaxIndex. Consider the following:

```
PROCEDURE SearchList (ListLen : IndexType ; TheList : ListType) ;

  VAR Ct : IndexType ;

  BEGIN
    FOR Ct := 1 TO ListLen DO
         .
         .
         .
```

By using the CONST, TYPE, and VAR sections just given, the procedure header allows alterations at some later date. That is, if the length of the list is to be altered, the change is made in the CONST section only.

For our first example of a Pascal program that uses arrays, we return to the problem presented at the beginning of Section 6–1.2.

EXAMPLE

Write a Pascal program that has input (from the keyboard) of six grades. The program is to process the grades to obtain their average. It is to output (write to the screen) the average and each grade that is above the average.

SOLUTION

Sample Execution

```
Enter grade 1: 89
Enter grade 2: 78
Enter grade 3: 56
Enter grade 4: 97
Enter grade 5: 46
Enter grade 6: 88

Average is: 75.67
Grades above average are 89 78 97 88
```

Design: GetScores
           FindAverage
           ReportResults   {average and scores above average}

Refinement of: *GetScores*
                  FOR Ct := 1 TO ListLen DO
                      WRITE ('Enter score', Ct, ':')
                      READLN (List [Ct])

Refinement of: *FindAverage*
                  Sum := 0
                  FOR Ct := 1 TO ListLen DO
                      Sum := Sum + List [Ct]
                  Average := Sum / ListLen

Refinement of: *ReportResults*
                  WRITELN ('The average is:', Average)
                  WRITE ('Scores above average are:')
                  FOR Ct := 1 TO ListLen DO
                      IF List [Ct] > Average
                         THEN WRITE (List [Ct])

Converting the design and its refinements to a Pascal program yields the program in Figure 6–2.

Figure 6-2

```
PROGRAM AboveAverage ;

CONST MaxIndex = 6 ;

TYPE IndexType = 1 .. MaxIndex ;
     ComponentType = 0 .. 100 ;
     ListType = ARRAY [1 .. MaxIndex] OF ComponentType ;

VAR TheList : ListType ;
    ListLen : IndexType ;
    Average : REAL ;

PROCEDURE GetScores (TheLen : IndexType ;
                     VAR TheList : ListType) ;

  VAR Ct : IndexType ;

  BEGIN                                        {GetScores}
    FOR Ct := 1 TO TheLen DO
      BEGIN
        WRITE ('Enter grade', Ct, ' : ') ;
        READLN (TheList [Ct])
      END                                      {GetScores}
  END ;

PROCEDURE FindAverage (ListLen : IndexType ; List : ListType ;
                       VAR TheAverage : REAL) ;

  VAR Ct : IndexType ;
      Sum : REAL ;

  BEGIN                                        {FindAverage}
    Sum := 0 ;
    FOR Ct := 1 TO ListLen DO                  {Sum List components}
      Sum := Sum + List [Ct] ;
    TheAverage := Sum / ListLen
  END ;                                        {FindAverage}

PROCEDURE ReportResults (ListLen : IndexType ; List : ListType ;
                         Aver : REAL) ;

  VAR Index : IndexType ;

  BEGIN                                        {Report Results}
    WRITELN ;
    WRITELN ('The average is: ' , Aver : 1 : 2) ;  {Write average}
    WRITE ('Grades above average are: ') ;
    FOR Index := 1 TO ListLen DO               {Output values above average}
      IF List [Index] > Aver
        THEN WRITE (List [Index] : 4)
  END ;                                        {ReportResults}

BEGIN
  GetScores (MaxIndex , TheList) ;
  FindAverage (MaxIndex , TheList , Average) ;
  ReportResults (MaxIndex, TheList, Average)
END .
```

In the program AboveAverage (in Figure 6–2), the ARRAY data structure provides storage for the grades. If only the average of the grades were needed, storage for all the values would not have been needed. Thus, an ARRAY data structure would not have been used.

DO IT NOW

1. Alter the program AboveAverage (in Figure 6–2) to process 50 grades.
2. Alter the program AboveAverage (in Figure 6–2) to process at most 50 grades. That is, the user is allowed the option to enter fewer than 50 grades.

DO IT NOW ANSWERS

1. Change the value of MaxIndex in the CONST section from 6 to 50.
2. Change the value of MaxIndex in the CONST section from 6 to 50. Add the program variable TheLen of type IndexType to the VAR section. In the main execution section, replace each reference to MaxIndex with TheLen, and insert the instruction TheLen := 0 as the first instruction. Alter the procedure GetScores to

```
PROCEDURE GetScores (VAR TheLen : IndexType ;
                     VAR TheList : ListType) ;

   VAR Grade : INTEGER ;

   BEGIN
     WRITE ('Enter grade ', TheLen + 1, ' (-1 to quit): ') ;
     READLN (Grade) ;                              {do a priming read}
     WHILE Grade < > -1 DO
       BEGIN
         TheLen := TheLen + 1 ;
         TheList [TheLen] := Grade ;
         WRITE ('Enter grade ', TheLen + 1, ' (-1 to quit): ') ;
         READLN (Grade)
       END
   END ;
```

This procedure allows the user to partially fill the array. With this possibility, the actual number of cells filled is made a variable parameter for GetScores and is passed to the other procedures. This is essential for the procedure FindAverage, since using MaxIndex (the value 50) would produce erroneous results if fewer than 50 grades were entered.

6-1.7 Random Access

The next example of array use in a program demonstrates the ability of the ARRAY data structure to store values and to provide random access to them. Access to the components of the data structure TEXT is sequential. That is, only the next component can be accessed. With the ARRAY data structure and the use of subscripts, any component can be accessed. This is known as **random access** and is a major feature of the ARRAY data structure. Additionally, the example demonstrates the use of an array where the index is of type CHAR. The index can be any ordinal data type. The following example uses an array whose components are indexed from A to Z.

EXAMPLE

Write a Pascal program that allows the user to input the name of a TEXT file. The program is to process the TEXT file to produce a list of the number of times each letter appears in the file. An uppercase letter and its lowercase equivalent are to be considered the same letter. The user is allowed to enter a letter. The program is to output the number of times the letter appeared in the file.

Sample Execution

```
Enter TEXT file name: B:NumberFun.TXT
Processing file .....
Enter character to check (A .. Z): d
The letter D appeared 7 times.
Press RETURN to continue, enter Q to quit: q
Do you want to process another file? (Y/N): n
```

SOLUTION

Design: REPEAT
           Get FileName
           Open file
           Initialize Array components
           ProcessFile
           ReportResults
           Close file
     UNTIL user wants to quit

Refinement of: *ProcessFile*
           WHILE NOT EOF (InFile) DO
              ProcessALine
              READLN (InFile)   {move file marker to start of next line}

Refinement of: *ProcessALine*
           WHILE NOT EOLN (InFile) DO
              READ (Ch)
              IF Ch IN ['a' .. 'z']
                THEN Ch : = UPCASE (Ch)
              IF Ch IN ['A' .. 'Z']
                THEN Increment LetterCt [Ch]

COMMENT

A one-dimensional array `LetterCt`, with 26 components (indexed from `A` to `Z`) of type `Ø` to `Max` (where `Max` is declared in the CONST section), is used to hold the count of the number of times each letter appears in the file.

The design just given yields the Pascal program in Figure 6–3.

Figure 6–3

```
PROGRAM LetterCount ;

CONST Max = 3ØØØ ;

TYPE LetterList = ARRAY ['A' .. 'Z'] OF Ø .. Max ;
     String2Ø = STRING [2Ø] ;

VAR InFile : TEXT ;
    FName : String2Ø ;
    LetterCt : LetterList ;
    Ans , Ch : CHAR ;
```

Figure 6-3
Continued

```
PROCEDURE ProcessFile (VAR LetCt : LetterList ;
                       VAR InFile : TEXT) ;

  VAR Ch : CHAR ;

  BEGIN                                    {ProcessFile}
    WRITE ('Processing file ') '
    WHILE NOT EOF (InFile) DO              {nested WHILE-DO instruction}
      BEGIN                                {outer WHILE-DO loop}
        WHILE NOT EOLN (InFile) DO         {ProcessALine}
          BEGIN                            {inner WHILE-DO loop}
            READ (InFile , Ch) ;           {get a character from file}
            IF Ch IN ['a' .. 'z']          {set lowercase to uppercase}
              THEN Ch := UPCASE (Ch) ;
            IF Ch IN ['A' .. 'Z']          {increment letter count}
              THEN LetCt [Ch] := SUCC (LetCt [Ch])
          END ;                            {inner WHILE-DO loop}
        READLN (InFile) ;                  {move file marker to next line}
        WRITE ('.')                        {avoid user anxiety}
      END ;                                {outer WHILE-DO loop}
    WRITELN                                {start fresh line}
  END ;                                    {ProcessFile}

PROCEDURE ReportResults (LetterCt : LetterList) ;

  VAR Ch : Ans: CHAR ;

  BEGIN                                    {ReportResults}
    REPEAT
      WRITE ('Enter letter to check (A .. Z): ') ;
      READLN (Ch) ;
      Ch := UPCASE (Ch) ;                  {allow entry of lowercase}
      IF Ch IN ['A' .. 'Z']
        THEN BEGIN                         {output number of occurrences}
               WRITE ('The letter ', Ch, ' appeared ') ;
               WRITELN (LetterCt [Ch], ' times.')
             END                           {output number of occurrences}
        ELSE WRITE ('Entry must be from A to Z') ;
      WRITE ('Press RETURN to continue, enter Q to quit- ') ;
      READLN (Ans)
    UNTIL Ans IN ['Q', 'q']
  END ;                                    {ReportResults}

BEGIN                                      {main program}
  REPEAT
    WRITE ('Enter TEXT file name: ') ;
    READLN (FName) ;
    ASSIGN (InFile , FName) ;
    RESET (InFile) ;                       {open the file}
    FOR Ch := 'A' TO 'Z' DO                {initialize components of LetterCt}
      LetterCt [Ch] := Ø ;
    ProcessFile (LetterCt) ;
    ReportResults (LetterCt) ;
    CLOSE (InFile) ;
    WRITE ('Do you want to process another file?(Y/N): ') ;
    READLN (Ans)
  UNTIL Ans IN ['N' , 'n']
END .                                      {main program}
```

COMMENT

For the program `LetterCount` in Figure 6–3, `LetterCt` was passed as a variable parameter to the procedure `ProcessFile`, since the procedure was to alter the values of `LetterCt`. `LetterCt` was passed as a value parameter to the procedure `ReportResults`, since the procedure only used the values of `LetterCt`.

DO IT NOW

1. For the program `LetterCount` in Figure 6–3, alter the procedure `ReportResults` to output a chart of the letters and the frequency of each letter (number of times the letter appears).

2. Further alter the procedure `ReportResults` (of program `LetterCount`) to output a line similar to

   ```
   The most often occurring letter was R.
   ```

   The line should appear after the chart is output.

3. In the program `LetterCount`, the array `LetterCt` was initialized by assigning each component the value **0**. Why was this necessary?

Sample Execution

```
Enter TEXT file name: NumberFun.TXT

Letter              Frequency
  A                    13
  B                     7
  C                     0
  .                     .
  .                     .
  .                     .
  Z                     1
```

DO IT NOW ANSWERS

1.
```
PROCEDURE ReportResults (LetterCt : LetterList) ;

  VAR Ch : CHAR ;

  BEGIN                                    {ReportResults}
    WRITELN ;                              {skip a line}
    WRITELN ('Letter', 'Frequency' : 20)   {do header for chart}
    FOR Ch := 'A' TO 'Z' DO                {dump array values}
      BEGIN
        WRITELN (Ch : 3, LetterCt [Ch] : 20) ;
        IF Ch = 'T'
          THEN READLN                      {pause for user to see screen}
      END
  END ;                                    {ReportResults}
```

2. In the procedure `ReportResults`, add the following instructions:

```
Target := ' ' ;           {a blank}
Mark := 0 ;
FOR Ch := 'A' TO 'Z' DO
  IF LetterCt [Ch] > Mark
    THEN BEGIN
            Mark := LetterCt [Ch] ;
            Target := Ch
         END ;
WRITE ('The most often occurring letter was ');
WRITELN (Target, '.')
```

   `Target` and `Mark` need to be declared in the VAR section of `ReportResults`.

3. In the procedure `ProcessFile`, a component of the array `LetterCt` is to be assigned the successor of the value in that component. If the component is undefined, the SUCC function will probably yield an error (it most likely will not yield the desired results). Also, if a letter does not appear in the TEXT file, the scan of `LetterCt` for `ReportResults` will produce erroneous results.

6-1.8 Merging Lists

The power of arrays lies in the ability to access any component of the array (that is, random access). In the example LetterCount, the use of an array saved the programmer from having to declare a variable for each letter in the alphabet. The array provided storage space for the number of times each letter occurred, as well as random access to this data.

A weakness of arrays is their fixed length. Once the length of the array is set (when the type is defined or the variable is declared), the length cannot be altered by a program instruction. Arrays are referred to as static data structures. Dynamic data structures (lists with variable lengths) will be discussed in Chapter 10.

As a final example of using the ARRAY data structure in a Pascal program, the following processes two array values by merging them into a third array. To merge two arrays means to form a third array whose components are the components from the two arrays. Usually, the values in the first two arrays are ordered and it is desired that the resulting array also be ordered. For example,

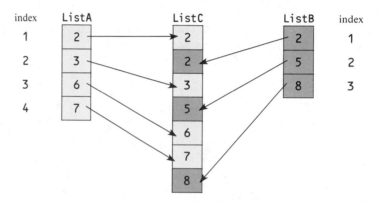

An algorithm for merging two arrays follows:

1. Start by comparing the value in cell 1 of ListA with the value in cell 1 of ListB.
2. The smallest of the two values is stored in cell 1 of ListC.
3. The next value of the array from which the smallest value came is obtained.
4. This new value is compared with the other value (the one not stored in ListC).
5. The smallest of these two values is stored in the next cell of ListC.

Steps 3, 4, and 5 are repeated until one of the lists is exhausted. The values from the remaining list are then stored in ListC.

EXAMPLE

Write a Pascal program to fill ListA (of length 10) and ListB (of length 7) with random numbers from 1 to 100 inclusive. The values stored in ListA and ListB should be ordered from smallest to largest. The list should then be merged into ListC (of length 17). The value stored in ListC should be ordered (from smallest to largest). The values stored in ListA, ListB, and ListC should be written to the screen.

SOLUTION

First, a plan to fill a list with random numbers that are ordered from smallest to largest must be devised. Consider the following loop:

```
Ct := 1 ;
FOR Index := 1 TO ListLen DO
  BEGIN
    WHILE (RANDOM (4) <= 2) AND (Ct < 100) DO
      Ct := Ct + 1 ;
    List [Index] := Ct
  END
```

	Walk Through	
index	Ct	List [index]
1	1	
	2	
	3	3
2	4	
	5	5
3	6	
	7	
	8	
	.	
	.	
	.	

The outer loop (the FOR-DO) loops through the indices of the array List. The inner loop (the WHILE-DO) loops through Ct, the value that will be stored in a cell of List. The function RANDOM returns a value from 0 to 3 inclusive. While the value is less than 3, Ct is increased by 1. At some point, a 3 is returned, and List [Index] is assigned the value in Ct. The FOR-DO moves to the next cell of List. The WHILE-DO continues to increment Ct. Thus, the values in List are ordered.

A design to solve the problem of merging two lists is as follows:

Design: FillListA
          FillListB
          MergeLists
          ShowLists

Refinement of: *FillList*
                 Ct := 1
                 FOR Index := 1 TO ListLen DO
                     WHILE (RANDOM (4) < = 2) AND (Ct < 100) DO
                         Ct := Ct + 1
                     List [Index] := Ct

COMMENT
The procedure FillList will be sent an array and its length.

Refinement of: *MergeLists*
                 CtA := 1
                 CtB := 1
                 WHILE (CtA < = LenA) AND (CtB < = LenB) DO
                     IF ListA [CtA] < = ListB [CtB]
                         THEN ListC [CtA + CtB − 1] := ListA [CtA]   {value from ListA stored}
                             CtA := CtA + 1
                         ELSE ListC [CtA + CtB − 1] := ListB [CtB]   {value from ListB stored}
                             CtB := CtB + 1
                 IF CtA < = LenA
                   THEN FOR Ct := CtA TO LenA DO
                           ListC [Ct + CtB − 1] := ListA [Ct]   {finish out ListA}
                   ELSE FOR Ct := CtB TO LenB DO
                           ListC [CtA + Ct − 1] := ListB [Ct]   {finish out ListB}

Refinement of: *ShowLists*
                 FOR Ct := 1 TO ListLen DO
                     WRITE (TheList [Ct] :4)
                 WRITELN

COMMENT
The procedure ShowList will be sent an array and its length. A set-up for the call to this procedure will be

```
WRITELN ('ListA is: ') ;
ShowList (LenA, ListA)
```

Converting this design to a Pascal program produces the program MergeList in Figure 6–4.

Figure 6–4

```
PROGRAM MergeList ;

CONST MaxLen = 17 ;

TYPE CompType = 1 .. 100 ;
     Index = 1 .. MaxLen ;
     ListType = ARRAY [1 .. MaxLen] OF CompType ;

VAR ListA, ListB, ListC : ListType ;
    LenA, LenB, LenC : Index ;

PROCEDURE FillList (TheLen : Index ; VAR TheList : ListType) ;

  VAR Ct, Subscript : Index ;

  BEGIN                                                {FillList}
    Ct := 1
    FOR Subscript := 1 TO TheLen DO                    {loop through indices}
      BEGIN
        WHILE (RANDOM (4) <= 2) AND (Ct < 100) DO      {select ever increasing}
          Ct := Ct + 1 ;                               {random value}
        TheList [Subscript] := Ct                      {fill cell of array}
      END
  END ;                                                {FillList}

PROCEDURE MergeTheList (Len1 : Index ; List1 : ListType ;
                        Len2 : Index ; List2 : ListType ;
                        VAR MergeList : ListType) ;

  VAR Ct1, Ct2 , Ct : Index ;

  BEGIN                                                {MergeTheList}
    Ct1 := 1 ;
    Ct2 := 1 ;
    WHILE (Ct1 <= Len1) AND (Ct2 <= Len2) DO
      IF List1 [Ct1] <= List2 [Ct2]
        THEN BEGIN
               MergeList [Ct1 + Ct2 - 1] := List1 [Ct1] ;  {value from List1}
               Ct1 := Ct1 + 1                              {stored}
             END
        ELSE BEGIN
               MergeList [Ct1 + Ct2 - 1] := List2 [Ct2] ;  {value from List2}
               Ct2 := Ct2 + 1                              {stored}
             END ;
    IF Ct1 <= Len1
      THEN FOR Ct := Ct1 TO Len1 DO                    {finish out List1}
             MergeList [Ct + Ct2 - 1] := List1 [Ct]
      ELSE FOR Ct := Ct2 TO Len2 DO                    {finish out List2}
             MergeList [Ct1 + Ct - 1] := List2 [Ct]
  END ;

PROCEDURE ShowList (TheLen : Index ; TheList : ListType) ;

  VAR Ct : Index ;

  BEGIN                                                {ShowList}
    FOR Ct := 1 TO TheLen DO
      WRITE (TheList [Ct] : 4) ;
    WRITELN
  END ;                                                {ShowList}
```

Figure 6–4

Continued

```
BEGIN                                              {Main execution}
  LenA := 10 ;
  LenB := 7 ;
  LenC := LenA + LenB ;
  FillList (LenA, ListA) ;
  FillList (LenB, ListB) ;
  MergeTheList (LenA, ListA, LenB, ListB, ListC) ;
  WRITELN ('ListA is: ') ;
  ShowList (LenA, ListA) ;
  WRITELN ('ListB is: ') ;
  ShowList (LenB, ListB) ;
  WRITELN ('The merged list is: ') ;
  ShowList (LenC, ListC)
END .                                              {Main execution}
```

DO IT NOW

1. Expand the program MergeList (Figure 6–4) to handle two arrays of lengths 100 and 150.
2. Alter the program MergeList to work with arrays whose components are of type CHAR.

DO IT NOW ANSWERS

1. In the CONST section, change MaxLen = 17 to MaxLen = 250. In the program execution section, change LenA := 10 to LenA := 100 and LenB := 7 to LenB := 150.
2. In the program TYPE section, change CompType = 1 .. 100 to CompType = CHAR. In the procedure FillList, replace Ct with Ch of type CHAR, and change the WHILE-DO instruction to

```
        WHILE (RANDOM (4) <= 2) AND (Ch < 'z') DO
          Ch := SUCC (Ch)
```

6-1.9 Summary

In concluding this introductory section on the ARRAY data structure, the following points and warnings need to be made:

1. The ARRAY data structure provides storage for a collection of values from any data type (except TEXT). The structure provided by the data type is that of an indexed (subscripted) list. The index provides for random access to the components of the list. The index is a subrange of an ordinal data type. Thus, a declaration such as

```
        VAR RealList : ARRAY [1.0 .. 3.2] OF INTEGER
```

   would be invalid, since the index type is not a subrange of ordinal data.
2. An ARRAY value cannot be input or output directly. That is, for TheList of type ARRAY, instructions like READLN (TheList) and WRITELN (TheList) will result in the error message IO not allowed being written to the screen. To input the value to be stored in a variable of type ARRAY, a loop is used. To output the value stored in an ARRAY variable, a loop is used.

3. An error the programmer must guard against is a subscript range error. This error occurs when the subscript (index) is out of the range listed in the declaration of the array. For example, if `TheList` is declared as

```
VAR TheList : ARRAY [1 .. 10] OF INTEGER
```

then `TheList [21] := 13` and `WRITELN (TheList [0])` yield subscript range errors. For these errors to be detected in Turbo Pascal, the compiler directive `{$R+}` must be inserted (usually as the first line) in the program.

4. Variables of type ARRAY can be used in assignment instructions. For `ListA` and `ListB`, both of the same ARRAY type, the instruction `ListA := ListB` is valid. It assigns to the cells of `ListA` the values stored in the cells of `ListB`. The relationals cannot be used with ARRAY values.

5. In a procedure header, the data type of a parameter must be a built-in or a previously defined type. Thus, if a parameter is of type ARRAY, the ARRAY data type must be defined in a TYPE section. For example,

```
PROCEDURE SwapEm (TheList : ARRAY [1 .. 100] OF INTEGER)
```

is invalid. The data type for `TheList` must be defined in a TYPE section.

6. Once the number of components to be stored in an ARRAY variable is set (when the variable is declared), it cannot be altered while the program is executing.

Vocabulary

Page

Glad You Asked

Q How many components (cells) can an array have?

A The number of components is limited by the amount of memory available. Each cell takes up memory locations in the main memory of the computer. Since the number of locations is finite, this limits the size of (number of components in) the array.

Q In playing with the program `LetterCount` (see Figure 6–3), I defined `LetterList` as follows:

```
LetterList = ARRAY ['A' .. 'Z', 'a' .. 'z'] OF 0 .. MAX
```

In compiling the program, I got the following error message:

```
Base type must be scalar.
```

Can you explain why?

A The index declaration must be one subrange. That is, it must be a continuous collection of values (for a one-dimensional array). Actually, you have defined `LetterList` to be a two-dimensional array. That is why you did not get an error on the line you gave here. When an attempt was made to assign the variable `LetterCt` (in the execution section of `LetterCount`) a value for a component, the compiler expected a reference to a component using two index values. In a two-dimensional array, you must reference a component by using two index values—thus, the error. The subject of two-dimensional arrays will be covered in Chapter 7.

Q Is type STRING the same thing as an array of CHAR?

A Yes and no. Type STRING is an intrinsic (built-in) data type. It has some features the programmer could not replicate (much as READ has features that the programmer could not develop from just writing a procedure). One such feature is variable length.

   Consider `Line` of type `STRING [8]` and `ListA` of type `ARRAY [1..8] OF CHAR`. In Turbo Pascal, `Line` and `ListA` are compatible. That is, `ListA` can be used as if it were a string. However, `ListA := Line` yields an error at compile time.

Q Could the problem at the start of this section that produced the program `AboveAverage` be solved using a TEXT file? That is, could the scores be stored in a TEXT file, then the TEXT file be processed?

A Yes. However, processing a TEXT file is slow compared with processing an array. The reason for this time difference is that the TEXT file stores its components on a diskette, and the array stores its components in main memory.

Q I saw the following TYPE definition in another book:

```
TYPE Days = (Mon, Tue, Wed, Thu, Fri, Sat, Sun) ;
     HourList = ARRAY [Days] OF 0 .. 24 ;
```

Is this valid?

A Yes. The definition of `HourList` is equivalent to

```
HourList = ARRAY [Mon .. Sun] OF 0 .. 24
```

The subscript type must be one of the following:
1. The built-in type BOOLEAN or CHAR.
2. An enumerated type.
3. A subrange of an ordinal type.

Section 6–1 Exercises

1. For `Letters` of type `ARRAY ['a' .. 'd'] OF 1 .. 12`, the number of components in a value stored in `Letters` is
   a. 12. **b.** 4. **c.** 11. **d.** 'a'. **e.** undefined.

2. Which of the following cannot be a component type of an array?
   a. REAL   **b.** CHAR   **c.** TEXT   **d.** INTEGER   **e.** BOOLEAN

3. For NumList of type ARRAY [1 .. 15] OF REAL, which of the following is *valid*?
   a. NumList [5] := 3.45   **c.** WRITE (NumList)
   b. Numlist [0] := -4.67   **d.** READLN (NumList)

4. Insert *True* for a true statement. Insert *False* for a false statement.
   _____ **a.** To access the components of an array, the index is used.
   _____ **b.** The index of an array can be of type REAL.
   _____ **c.** The components of an array can be of type REAL.
   _____ **d.** An array must be accessed sequentially.
   _____ **e.** The number of cells an array has can be altered while the program is executing.
   _____ **f.** A value parameter cannot be of type ARRAY.
   _____ **g.** The terms *index* and *subscript* have the same meaning.
   _____ **h.** An ARRAY variable can be assigned the value in another ARRAY variable of the same type.
   _____ **i.** An array variable should be initialized.
   _____ **j.** To write a value in the ARRAY variable NumList to the screen, the programmer can use WRITELN (NumList).

5. For Temp of type ARRAY [1 .. 10] OF INTEGER with the following value,

13	3	11	-2	5	6	-8	0	7	10

   index   1   2   3   4   5   6   7   8   9   10

   give the output of the following (What is of type INTEGER).
   a. WRITE (Temp [4])
   b. WRITE (Temp [9])
   c. Temp [2] := Temp [5] - Temp [1] ;
       WRITE (Temp [2])
   d. FOR Ct := 3 TO 9 DO
           What := Temp [Ct] + Temp [Ct + 1] ;
       WRITE (What)
   e. What := 0 ;
       Ct := 1 ;
       WHILE Ct < 11 DO
         BEGIN
           What := Temp [Ct] + What ;
           Ct := SUCC (Ct)
         END ;
       WRITE (What)

6. For NameList, an ARRAY ['a' .. 'g'] OF STRING [20] with this value,

Robin	Joshua	Gary	Emory	Jose	Ida	Marsha

   index   'a'   'b'   'c'   'd'   'e'   'f'   'g'

   give the output of the following.
   a. WRITE (NameList ['c'])
   b. WRITE (NameList ['b'])
   c. NameList ['f'] := CONCAT (NameList ['a'] , NameList ['f']) ;
       WRITE (NameList ['f'])
   d. FOR Ch := 'g' DOWNTO 'c' DO
           WRITE (NameList [Ch] , ' ')
   e. Ch := 'b' ;
       WHILE NameList [Ch] < 'Judy' DO
         Ch := SUCC (Ch) ;
       WRITELN (NameList [Ch])

7. **a.** Alter `NumList : ARRAY [Ø .. 5] OF REAL` such that the array will have ten components.

   b. Declare `PartList` to be an array indexed from `1Ø1` to `12Ø` with components of type `Ø .. 8Ø`.

   c. Given `TYPE Days = (Mon, Tue, Wed, Thu, Fri, Sat, Sun)`, define `WorkDays` (in a TYPE section) to be an array indexed from `Mon` to `Fri` with components of type `Ø .. 24`.

   d. For

```
TYPE Color = (Red, Blue, Green, Black, White);
     ColorList = ARRAY [Red .. White] OF 'A' .. 'Z';

VAR Mix : ColorList
```

give a value for the variable `Mix`:

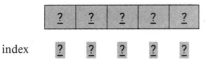

index

8. **a.** Given `NumList = ARRAY [1 .. 5] OF Ø .. 1ØØ` and `Grades` of type `NumList`, complete the following procedure to return the minimum of the values in the cells of `Grades`.

```
PROCEDURE Minimum (GradeList : NumList ; VAR Min : INTEGER) ;

VAR Index : 1 .. 5 ;

BEGIN
    .
    .
    .
END ;
```

   b. If the value in `Grades` is

62	70	78	91	82

index   1   2   3   4   5

and `Mark` is of type INTEGER and contains `Ø`, give the output of

```
Minimum (Grades , Mark) ;
WRITE (Mark : 3)
```

9. Given `ListType = ARRAY [1 .. 1ØØ] OF WholeNum`, where `WholeNum = Ø .. 1Ø1`; `TheList` is of type `ListType`; and `ListLen, Ct, Hi`, and `Lo` are of type `WholeNum`, what is the output of the following instructions?

```
FOR Ct := 1 TO 1ØØ DO
  TheList [Ct] := Ct ;
ListLen := 1ØØ ;
Hi := ListLen + 1 ;
Lo := Ø ;
WHILE (Hi - Lo) > 1 DO
  BEGIN
    WRITELN (List [(Hi + Lo) DIV 2]) ;
    IF RANDOM (2) > Ø
      THEN Hi := (Hi + Lo) DIV 2
      ELSE Lo := (Hi + Lo) DIV 2
  END
```

10. Write a Pascal program that will fill, then output to the screen the value of, an array like the following:

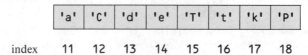

index   11   12   13   14   15   16   17   18

11. Write a Pascal program that will fill the array `NumList` (of type `ARRAY [1 .. 40] OF 0 .. MAXINT`) with the first 40 odd integers. Do *not* use the keyboard to input values.

12. Consider the following Pascal procedure. Assume that `NumList` of type `ARRAY [1 .. 10] OF INTEGER` has been defined.

```
PROCEDURE SearchArray (MyList : NumList ; Target : INTEGER) ;

  VAR Index : 1 .. 11 ;

  BEGIN
    Index := 1 ;
    WHILE (Index <= 10) AND (MyList [Index] < > Target) DO
      Index := SUCC (Index);
    WRITELN ('Target = ' , Target : 1, ' found at index ', Index : 1)
  END ;
```

Assuming that the following ARRAY value is passed for `MyList`,

MyList | −3 | 4 | 6 | 5 | 7 | −12 | 0 | 6 | 8 | −13 |

index   1   2   3   4   5   6   7   8   9   10

determine the output of `SearchArray` under the following conditions.
   a. 5 is passed for `Target`. **b.** −3 is passed for `Target`. **c.** 2 is passed for `Target`.

13. Alter the procedure in problem 12 to handle the case where the value in `Target` is not found by printing a message like

```
Target of 2 not found in array.
```

14. Find and comment on the errors in the following.
   a.
```
TYPE NumList = ARRAY [1 .. 20] OF REAL ;

VAR MyList : NumList ;
    Ct : 1 .. 21 ;

BEGIN
  FOR Ct := 1 TO 21 DO
    MyList [Ct] := 0
END
```
   b.
```
TYPE NumList = ARRAY [1 .. 20] OF REAL ;

VAR MyList : NumList ;
    Ct : 0 .. MAXINT ;

BEGIN
  NumList [5] := 3
END
```
   c.
```
TYPE Parts = (Gasket, Plugs, Points, Rings) ;

VAR PartList : ARRAY [103 .. 120] OF Parts ;

BEGIN
  WRITE (PartList [105])
END
```

15. Alter the program `LetterCount` (presented in Figure 6–3) to also output the *relative frequency* of the letters. For example, if the letter *A* appeared 20 times and there were 100 characters in the TEXT file, then the relative frequency of *A* is 20%.

16. Boot up Pascal; set the workfile to the file **AboveAvg.PAS** from the **Source** diskette. Enter the editor. Alter the program to allow the user to enter the number of numeric grades to be processed (up to a maximum of 100 grades).

17. Boot up Pascal; set the workfile to the file **LetterCt.PAS** from the **Source** diskette. Enter the editor. Expand the program to output a horizontal bar graph of the frequency of the letters *b,c,d,f,g,j,* and *k*.

18. Boot up Pascal; set the workfile to the file **MergeLst.PAS** from the **Source** diskette. Enter the editor. Alter the program to allow the user to enter a collection of names in alphabetical order to fill the two lists to be merged.

Sample Execution (Problem 17)

```
b  **************************
c  **********
d  ***********
f  ****************************
g  *******
j  **
k  *

Press RETURN key to continue—
```

Programming Problems

19. One of the earliest methods of encoding a secret message was simply to shift the alphabet. For example, the shift

        Original: A B C D E F G H I J K . . X Y Z
        Shifted: M N O P Q R S T U V W . . J K L

    would translate the message

        Adding manpower to a late software
        project makes it later

    to

        Mppuzs ymzbaiqd fa m xmfq earfimdq
        bdavqof ymwqe uf xmfqd

    Write a Pascal procedure that generates a code such as the one just given by assigning a value to a variable of type **ARRAY ['A' .. 'Z'] OF CHAR**. Use a random number from 1 to 25 to select the start point for **'A'**. A lowercase letter should be translated to its uppercase equivalent for conversion to the code. Use the procedure to write a Pascal program that allows the user to enter up to a 60-character message. The output is to be the encoded message. The program should encode messages until the user is ready to quit.

20. The TEXT file **Names.TXT** contains 20 names in alphabetical order, one name per line, similar to the following lines:

        Albertson, Mary||
        Apples, John||
        Bedelia, Bob||
              :
        Zhmed, Alice|| < end-of-file marker >

    Write a Pascal program that reads the names from the TEXT file into an array. The program will allow the user to enter a number from 1 to 20. The program will write to the screen the name in the list whose index is the number entered.

21. Expand your program in problem 20 to spin the list. That is, name 1 (**Albertson, Mary**) becomes name 20, name 2 (**Apples, John**) becomes name 1, and so forth. The program should start by presenting the menu shown. The user should be able to select from the menu.

Sample Execution (Problem 21)

```
A. Fill list from names file
B. See name on list
C. Spin list
Q. Quit
Please select (enter A,B,C,Q):
```

22. Write a Pascal program that allows the user to survey a list of up to 100 students. The survey questions are as follows:

Sample Execution

```
1. Name: Igor Gorin
2. Are you taking physics?(Y/N): N
3. Are you taking math?(Y/N): Y
4. Are you taking chemistry?(Y/N): Y

Press RETURN for next survey subject (enter Q to quit):
```

The program should build the sets PhyClass, MathClass, and ChemClass. Also, the program should write the following to the screen.
a. The names of the students taking all three courses.
b. The names of the students taking chemistry but not math.
c. The names of the students taking math and chemistry but not physics.
d. The names of the students not taking any of the three courses.
Hint: Store the names entered in an array. Use the index of the array to build the sets.

Section 6–2

Searching

In the last section, you were introduced to the ARRAY data structure. In this section, the topic of searching an array will be covered. The search techniques discussed are the linear search and the binary search. Also, you will see more applications of the ARRAY data structure.

6-2.1 Linear Search

Suppose you have the following variable declaration:

```
Numbers : NumList
```

where NumList = ARRAY [1 .. 100] OF 0 .. MAXINT

Also, suppose Numbers contains a value (that is, a list of 100 numbers from 0 to MAXINT). If you wanted to search this array for a given value, the following instructions could be used. (Assume the searched-for value is referenced by the variable Target.)

```
BEGIN
  Ct := 1 ;
  WHILE (Target < > NumList [Ct]) AND (Ct <= 100) DO    {Search the List}
    Ct := SUCC (Ct) ;
  IF NumList [Ct] = Target
    THEN WRITELN (Target : 1, ' found at position ', Ct)
    ELSE WRITELN (Target : 1, ' not found in array.')
END
```

This type of search is called a **linear search.** It starts at index 1 and searches through the array component by component. Often, this is the only type of search possible on an array. Notice that the worst case (with regard to execution time) occurs when the value in `Target` is not found; the instruction for the WHILE-DO is executed 100 times.

As an example of a linear search, consider the following problem.

PROBLEM

Write a Pascal program that allows the user to select from the menu shown. The list is limited to 50 names, and each name is limited to 30 characters.

```
A. Enter list of names
B. Search for a name
Q. Quit

Please select (enter A, B, Q):
```

SOLUTION

After thinking about the problem, propose the following design:

```
Design:   REPEAT
              PresentMenu
              Get user's selection
              CASE Select OF
                  'A' : Fill list with names
                  'B' : Search List
              END
          UNTIL Select = 'Q'
```

Next, after walking through this design, refine the steps. (The refinement of the steps *PresentMenu* and *Get user's selection* will not be shown.)

Refinement of: *FillList*
```
              ListLen := 0
              REPEAT
                ListLen := ListLen + 1
                WRITE ('Enter name', ListLen, ': ')
                READLN (NameList [ListLen])
                WRITE ('Enter Q to quit, ')
                WRITE ('press RETURN to continue- ')
                READLN (Ans)
              UNTIL (Ans IN ['Q','q']) OR (ListLen > 50)
```

COMMENT
`FillList` will need variable parameters `NameList` and `ListLen`.

Refinement of: *SearchList*
```
              WRITE ('Enter name to search for: ')
              READLN (Name)
              Count := 1
              WHILE (Name < > List [Count]) AND (Count < = ListLen) DO
                  Count := Count + 1
              IF Count > Count + 1
                THEN WRITE ('Name not found.')
                ELSE WRITE ('Found at position ', Count)
```

COMMENT
`SearchList` will need value parameters `NameList` and `ListLen`.

Conversion of this design produces the Pascal program in Figure 6–5.

Figure 6–5

```pascal
PROGRAM LinearSearch ;

TYPE String30 = STRING [30] ;
     Names = ARRAY [1 .. 50] OF String30 ;
     Index = 0 .. 51 ;                          {51 to handle WHILE-DO}

VAR NameList : Names ;
    ListLen : Index ;
    Select : CHAR ;

PROCEDURE PresentMenu ;

  BEGIN                                          {PresentMenu}
    WRITELN ;
    WRITELN ('A. Fill list');
    WRITELN ('B. Search list');
    WRITELN ('Q. Quit');
    WRITE ('Please select (enter A, B, or Q): ')
  END ;                                          {PresentMenu}

PROCEDURE FillList (VAR NameList : Names ; VAR ListLen : Index) ;

  VAR Count : Index ;
      Ans : CHAR ;

  BEGIN                                          {FillList}
    ListLen := 0 ;
    REPEAT
      ListLen := ListLen + 1 ;
      WRITE ('Enter name', ListLen, ': ') ;
      READLN (NameList [ListLen]) ;
      WRITE ('Enter Q to quit, press RETURN to continue- ') ;
      READLN (Ans)
    UNTIL (Ans IN ['Q', 'q']) OR (ListLen > 50)
  END ;                                          {FillList}

PROCEDURE SearchList (TheList : Names ; TheLen : Index) ;

  VAR Count : Index ;
      Name : STRING [30] ;

  BEGIN                                          {SearchList}
    WRITE ('Enter name to search for: ') ;
    READLN (Name) ;
    Count := 1 ;
    WHILE (Name < > NameList [Count]) AND (Count <= TheLen) DO
      Count := Count + 1 ;
    IF Count > TheLen
      THEN WRITELN ('Name not found.')
      ELSE WRITELN ('Found at position ', Count)
  END ;                                          {SearchList}

BEGIN                                            {LinearSearch}
  REPEAT
    PresentMenu ;
    READLN (Select) ;
    CASE Select OF
     'A', 'a' : FillList (NameList , ListLen) ;
     'B', 'b' : SearchList (NameList , ListLen)
    END
  UNTIL (Select = 'Q') OR (Select = 'q')
END .                                            {LinearSearch}
```

6-2.2 Binary Search

Suppose you have a situation similar to the search just described, except this time the values in the array are *ordered*. A much better search routine, called a **binary search,** can be used to search the list for a value. A binary search can be used only if the data is ordered in some fashion. The basic idea of a binary search is to start looking for the target in the middle of the list of values. If it is found, then quit. If the target is less than the middle value, then look in the half of the list containing the smaller values. If the target is greater than the middle value, then look in the half of the list containing the larger values. To see how a binary search works, observe the similar but smaller ordered array in Figure 6–6 involving numbers.

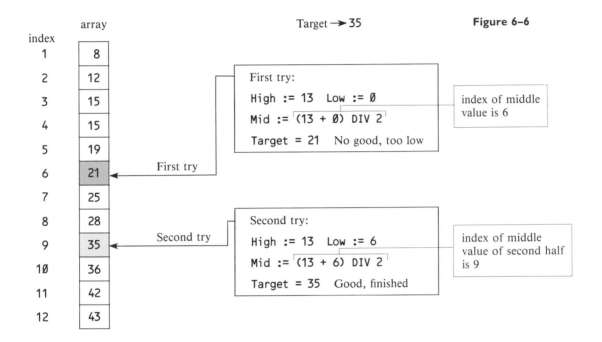

Figure 6–6

In Figure 6–6, the target (the value searched for) is **35**. To find the middle value, the high position is set to the highest index value plus 1. The low position is set to the lowest index value minus 1. The middle value is set to (High + Low) DIV 2. Now, (13 + 0) DIV 2 yields **6**, so the target value is tested against the sixth value in the array (21 in this case). There is no matchup. Since the target (35) is greater than the middle value, the second half of the list is searched next.

For the next try, the high position is not changed. The low position is set to the middle value (6 in this case). A new middle value is computed. The middle value for the second half of the list is (6 + 13) DIV 2 or **9**. So the target value (35) is tested against the ninth value in the array. This is a match and the search is finished.

The worst case with a search is when the value is not found. Suppose the target value in this case were **5**. Walking through the process yields the following:

```
Initial try:   High := 13        {highest index plus 1}
               Low := 0          {lowest index minus 1}
               Mid := (13 + 0) DIV 2   {thus Mid is assigned 6}
```

Look up sixth value. Is it equal to the target (5)? No, 5 is less than 21.

index	array
1	8
2	12
3	15
4	15
5	19
6	21
7	25
8	28
9	35
10	36
11	42
12	43

Second try: High := 6   {High assigned Mid}
               Low := 0   {Low unchanged}
               Mid := (6 + 0) DIV 2   {thus Mid is assigned 3}

Look up third value. Is it equal to the target (5)? No, 5 is less than 15.

Third try: High := 3   {High assigned Mid}
               Low := 0   {Low unchanged}
               Mid := (3 + 0) DIV 2   {thus Mid is assigned 1}

Look up first value. Is it equal to the targe (5)? No, 5 is less than 8.

Fourth try: High := 1   {High assigned Mid}
               Low := 0   {Low unchanged}
               Mid := (1 + 0) DIV 2   {thus Mid is assigned 0}

There is no zeroth value. Thus, search must end.

If High is assigned Mid, High is assigned the value 0 (the same value as Low). A test is needed as a stopping condition. Is High = Low? If yes, then stop.

From this work, the following design is developed for the binary search:

Design: High := Upper index + 1
           Low := Lower index − 1
           Found := 0
           WHILE (High < > Low) AND (Found = 0) DO
               Mid := (High + Low) Div 2   {get index}
               IF Target = Array [Mid]
                 THEN Found := Mid   {finished}
                 ELSE IF Target > Array [Mid]
                     THEN Low := Mid   {move to larger values}
                     ELSE High := Mid   {move to smaller values}

COMMENT
The variable Found stores the index of the component matching Target. If Target is not found then Found will contain 0.

DO IT NOW

Given the following one-dimensional array,

5	8	11	13	17	18	25	30	32

index   1   2   3   4   5   6   7   8   9

Target   13

Try#	High	Low	Mid	Value	Result
1	10	0	5	17	high
2	5	0	2	8	low
3	5	2	...	...	...
4					
5					

fill in a chart like the one here to do the following.
1. Walk through the binary search design for a target of 13.
2. Walk through the binary search design for a target of 26.
3. Walk through the binary search design for a target of 98.

DO IT NOW ANSWERS

1. Target 13

Try #	High	Low	Mid	Value	Result	
1	10	0	5	17	high	
2	5	0	2	8	low	
3	5	2	3	11	low	
4	5	3	4	13	Hit!	Found := 4

2. Target 26

Try #	High	Low	Mid	Value	Result	
1	10	0	5	17	low	
2	10	5	7	25	low	
3	10	7	8	30	high	
4	8	7	7	25	low	
5	7	7	High = Low		Quit	Found := 0

3. Target 98

Try #	High	Low	Mid	Value	Result	
1	10	0	5	17	low	
2	10	5	7	25	low	
3	10	7	8	30	low	
4	10	9	9	32	low	
5	10	9	9	32	low	Stuck!

*************DESIGN ERROR!!*************

Note the design error in problem 3 of the last DO IT NOW section. The BOOL-EAN expression for the WHILE-DO should be

((High - Low) > 1) AND (Found = 0)

With this correction and the design just given, a Pascal procedure for the binary search is as shown in Figure 6–7.

Figure 6–7

```
PROCEDURE BinarySearch (ListLen : INTEGER ; Target : ComponentType ;
                        List : ArrayType ; VAR Found : INTEGER);

  VAR High , Low , Mid : INTEGER ;

  BEGIN                                    {BinarySearch}
    Found := 0 ;
    High := ListLen + 1 ;
    Low := 0 ;
    WHILE ((High - Low) > 1) AND (Found = 0) DO
      BEGIN                                {WHILE-DO}
        Mid := (High + Low) DIV 2 ;
        IF List [Mid] = Target
          THEN Found := Mid
          ELSE IF Target > List [Mid]
                  THEN Low := Mid
                  ELSE High := Mid
      END                                  {WHILE-DO}
  END                                      {BinarySearch}
```

COMMENT

The procedure in Figure 6–7 assumes that the parameter List has type ArrayType and is ordered from smallest to largest; the index type range is 1 .. ListLen; and the components of the array have type ComponentType. The procedure returns the value in Found. If 0 is returned, then Target was not found. If Target was found, the value returned in Found is the index of the component. A typical call to the procedure would be

BinarySearch (100 , 19 , NumList , Found)

This call would result in a search of an array NumList indexed from 1 to 100. The search would be for the value 19.

6-2.3 Efficiency

The **efficiency** of a technique such as searching refers to the time it takes to complete the task. This can be estimated by the number of times a set of instructions must be executed. Technique A is more efficient than technique B if technique A does the same task as technique B in less time (fewer executions). To obtain a feel for efficiency, consider the Pascal program `Compare` in Figure 6–8. The program outputs lines like the following:

Sample Execution

```
Input Target (0 .. 2000): 18
Linear search: Found at position 18. Accessed List 18 times.
Binary search: Found at position 18. Accessed List 10 times.

Do another comparison? (Y/N) : Y
Input Target (0 .. 2000): 250
Linear search: Found at position 18. Accessed List 250 times.
Binary search: Found at position 18. Accessed List 2 times.

Do another comparison? (Y/N) : N
```

`Accessed List` represents how many times the array was accessed. The array components are simply the numbers from 1 to 1000.

Figure 6–8

```
PROGRAM Compare ;

TYPE WholeNum = 0 .. 2000 ;
     ArrayType = ARRAY [1 .. 1000] OF WholeNum ;

VAR List : ArrayType ;
    Ct, Time , Target , Found : WholeNum ;
    Ans : CHAR ;

PROCEDURE LinearSearch (ListLen, Target : WholeNum ;
                        List : ArrayType ;
                        VAR Found , Time : WholeNum) ;

  VAR Ct : WholeNum ;

  BEGIN                                            {LinearSearch}
    Ct := 1 ;
    Time := 1 ;
    WHILE (Target < > List [Ct]) AND (Ct < ListLen) DO
      BEGIN                                        {WHILE-DO}
        Ct := SUCC (Ct) ;
        Time := SUCC (Time)
      END ;                                        {WHILE-DO}
    IF List [Ct] = Target
      THEN Found := Ct
      ELSE Found := 0
  END ;                                            {LinearSearch}
```

Figure 6–8

Continued

```
PROCEDURE BinarySearch (ListLen , Target : WholeNum ;
                        List : ArrayType ;
                        VAR Found , Time : WholeNum) ;

  VAR High , Low , Mid : Ø .. MAXINT ;

  BEGIN                                              {BinarySearch}
    Found := Ø ;
    Time := Ø ;
    High := ListLen + 1 ;
    Low := Ø ;
    WHILE ((High - Low) > 1) AND (Found = Ø) DO
      BEGIN                                          {WHILE-DO}
        Time := SUCC (Time) ;
        Mid := (High + Low) DIV 2 ;
        IF List [Mid] = Target
          THEN Found := Mid
          ELSE IF Target > List [Mid]
                  THEN Low := Mid
                  ELSE High := Mid
      END                                            {WHILE-DO}
  END ;                                              {BinarySearch}
BEGIN                                                {main program}
  FOR Ct := 1 TO 1000 DO                             {initialize array}
    List [Ct] := Ct ;
  REPEAT
    Found := Ø ;
    Time := Ø ;
    WRITE ('Input Target (Ø .. 2000): ') ;
    READLN (Target) ;
    WRITELN ('Searching... Position Ø means value not found!') ;
    LinearSearch (1000 , Target , List , Found , Time) ;
    WRITE ('Linear search: ', Target , ' Found at position ', Found) ;
    WRITELN ('. Accessed List ', Time, ' times.') ;
    BinarySearch (1000 , Target , List , Found , Time) ;
    WRITE ('Binary search: ', Target , ' Found at position ', Found) ;
    WRITELN ('. Accessed List ', Time, ' times.') ;
    WRITELN ;
    WRITE (Do another comparison?(Y/N): ') ;
    READLN (Ans)
  UNTIL Ans = 'N'
END .                                                {main program}
```

COMMENT

The number of times the binary search accesses the array is an example of *logarithmic growth*. This type of growth is the opposite of exponential growth. The maximum number of times the array is accessed is $\log_2(\texttt{ListLen}) + 1$. A logarithmic growth pattern is a very slow growth pattern. $T = \log_2(\texttt{ListLen}) + 1$ means that if $\texttt{ListLen}$ is written as a power of 2, the exponent will be T. That is, $T = \log_2(\texttt{ListLen}) + 1$ yields the equation

$$\texttt{ListLen} = 2^{T-1}$$

Thus, for an array of length 1000, the equation becomes

$$1000 = 2^{T-1}$$

2^{10} is 1024. Therefore, the array will be accessed at most 11 times to find a component. Does this agree with the results of the program $\texttt{Compare}$?

WARNING
The components of an array must be ordered to use a binary search.

From the execution of the program Compare, you can see that a binary search is more efficient than a linear search.

DO IT NOW

1. Alter the procedure BinarySearch to search the array LetterList whose type is ArrayType where

    ArrayType = ARRAY [1 .. 100] OF CHAR

    Assume the value in LetterList has its components ordered based on ASCII values (smallest to largest). Also, give a typical call to the procedure.

2. Alter the procedure BinarySearch to search the array PartList whose type is ArrayType where

    ArrayType = ARRAY [101 .. 999] OF WholeNum

    Assume WholeNum = 0 .. MAXINT and that the value in PartList has its components ordered from smallest to largest. Also, give a typical call to the procedure.

3. For a one-dimensional array of length 70, what is the greatest number of accesses a binary search would make to find a value in the array?

DO IT NOW ANSWERS

1. Change the procedure header to

```
PROCEDURE BinarySearch (ListLen : INTEGER ;
                        Target : CHAR ;
                        List : ArrayType ;
                        VAR Found : INTEGER) ;
```

   Call: BinarySearch (100, '!', LetterList, Found)

2. Change the instruction Low := 0 to the instruction Low := 100
   Call: BinarySearch (999, 378, PartList, Found)

3. Find the smallest integer value for T such that $2^{T-1} >= 70$; $2^6 = 64$; $2^7 = 128$. So 8 times is the greatest number of times the array would be accessed.

Vocabulary

Page		
347	**Binary search**	The process of searching an ordered list. The search starts at the middle item in the list, then repeatedly moves to the middle item of a shorter and shorter list. The process is continued until the item is found or the length of the shortened list is zero.
350	**Efficiency**	A relative measure of a process's use of time and memory space. Process A is more efficient than process B if process A takes less time and/or memory space to accomplish the same task as process B. For example, for an array with a large number of components, the binary search is more efficient than the linear search.
345	**Linear search**	The process of searching through a list by starting at the first item and going item by item through the list. This is the only search possible if the items in the list are not ordered.

Glad You Asked

Q Will a binary search work on a list of names?

A Yes, if the list of names is ordered (say, alphabetically). Of course, the target would be of type STRING.

Q How would I search a list to find all occurrences of a value in the list?

A If the list is not ordered, repeatedly doing a linear search is your only choice. If the list is ordered, you can improve the efficiency by using a binary search. The binary search will give you the location of an occurrence of the value. The problem is that the occurrence found might be the first occurrence, the last occurrence, or an occurrence somewhere in between. The design would be as follows:

Design: Get Target
        BinarySearch (ListLen, Target, List, Found)
        IF Found = StartIndex   {Target first item in List}
          THEN CountOccur
                ReportResults
        IF Found > StartIndex   {Target found in List}
          THEN MoveToHead   {find first occurrence}
                CountOccur
                ReportResults
        IF Found = 0
          THEN Report Target not found

Refinement of: *MoveToHead (Found , List , Target , Head)*
                Ct : = Found − 1
                WHILE Ct > 0 AND List [Ct] = Target DO   {find index of first occurrence}
                    Ct : = PRED (Ct)
                Head : = Ct + 1   {return Head to main program}

Refinement of: *CountOccur (Head, Target, List, NumOcc)*
                Ct: = 0
                WHILE List [Head] = Target DO   {Count number times Target appears}
                    Head : = SUCC (Head)
                    Ct : = SUCC (Ct)
                NumOcc : = Ct   {return NumOcc to main program}

Refinement of: *ReportResults (Target, Head, NumOcc)*
                WRITE (Target, ' found at ', Head)
                WRITE ('It occurred ', NumOcc, ' times.')

The conversion of this design to a Pascal program is left as an exercise.

Section 6–2 Exercises

1. Insert either *Linear* or *Binary* in the following blanks.
    _____ **a.** the search used to search for a value when the list is not ordered in some fashion
    _____ **b.** for an ordered list, the most efficient of the two searches
    _____ **c.** the search that moves component by component through the list being searched
    _____ **d.** the search that starts with the middle value in the list

2. Insert *True* for a true statement and *False* for a false statement.
  _____ **a.** The linear search can be used on any array.
  _____ **b.** If an array is ordered, the linear search is the most efficient search.
  _____ **c.** A search cannot be done on a list whose components are of type REAL.
  _____ **d.** The number of times an array will be accessed in the binary search when the target value is not found is the length of the array.
  _____ **e.** The binary search can only be used when the list is ordered in some fashion.

3. For the following one-dimensional array (list) value (where the component values are of type CHAR),

A	B	D	F	G	H	J	L	M	M	N	P	R	V	W	Z

index   1   2   3   4   5   6   7   8   9   10 11 12 13 14 15 16

if a binary search is used on the array, complete this chart:

```
Try#   High   Low   Mid   Value   Result
1      ...    ...   ...   ...     ...
2      ...    ...   ...   ...     ...
....   ...    ...   ...   ...     ...
```

for a target value of
a. J   **b.** A   **c.** W   **d.** a

4. For the one-dimensional array (list) value in the margin (where the component values are of type STRING [10]), if a binary search is used on the array, then complete the following chart:

```
Try#   High   Low   Mid   Value   Result
1      ...    ...   ...   ...     ...
2      ...    ...   ...   ...     ...
```

for a target value of
a. Portland   **b.** Falmouth   **c.** Richmond   **d.** Atlanta

index	
1	Baltimore
2	Bono
3	Falmouth
4	Loma
5	Naples
6	Omaha
7	Portland
8	Seward
9	Warsaw
10	Yuma

5. Alter the procedure BinarySearch to search the list in problem 4. Write a Pascal program that allows the user to input a STRING value (the name of a city). The program is to search a list of cities. The output is to be the position found or the statement . . . not in list. where the ellipsis represents the target city.

6. RealList is a one-dimensional array of type

```
ARRAY [1 .. 100] OF REAL
```

where the value in RealList has its component values ordered from lowest to highest. Each component value is accurate to two decimal places (hundredths). Alter the procedure BinarySearch to search the array RealList.

7. For List of type ArrayType, where

```
ArrayType = ARRAY [1 .. 100] OF WholeNum
```

rewrite the procedure BinarySearch as a Pascal function. The function header should be

```
FUNCTION BinarySearch (ListLen , Target : WholeNum ;
                       List : ArrayType) : WholeNum ;
```

where WholeNum = 0 .. MAXINT

8. Boot up Pascal; set the workfile to the file Linear.PAS from the Source diskette. Enter the editor. Alter the program to fill the list with random numbers from 1 to 500 (inclusive).

9. Boot up Pascal; set the workfile to the file `BinaryEx.PAS` from the `Source` diskette. Enter the editor. Alter the program to fill the list with the alphabet letters *A* to *Z* (inclusive).

10. Boot up Pascal; set the workfile to the file `Compare.PAS` from the `Source` diskette. Enter the editor. Alter the FOR-DO instruction in the program execution section as follows:

```
FOR Ct := 1 TO 1000 DO
  List [Ct] := 10001 - Ct
```

Alter the remainder of the program to work with this array.

Programming Problems

11. Write a Pascal program to do the following.
    a. Fill a list with 100 cells with random numbers from 12 to 22 inclusive.
    b. Allow the user to input a value from 12 to 22 inclusive, then output the frequency (number of occurrences) of the value in the list.
    (*Hint:* Use a linear search for the input value, since the list is not ordered.)

12. Expand your program in problem 11 to output a frequency distribution for each value in the list. That is, the output should be similar to the sample execution shown.

13. Suppose `NumList` is of type `ARRAY [1 .. 200] OF INTEGER`. Write a Pascal program to do the following:
    a. Fill the list with random numbers between 10 to 40 inclusive where the values are ordered from lowest to highest.
    b. Allow the user to enter a value from 10 to 40 inclusive.
    c. Search the list for the value entered in part b.
    d. Report where the value was found in the list and the number of occurrences of the value. (See Glad You Asked of Section 6–2 for a design.)
    To accomplish part a, use this design:

Sample Execution

Value	Frequency
12	8
13	17
.	.
.	.
.	.

```
Total := 1
Ct := RANDOM (10) + 1
WHILE Total < = 200 DO
    Frequency : = RANDOM (20)
    Total : = Total + Frequency
IF Total > 200
  THEN Frequency : = Frequency - (Total - 200)
        Total : = 200
FOR Index : = (Total - Frequency) TO (Total - 1) DO
  NumList [Index] : = Ct + 9
IF Ct < 31
  THEN Ct : = Ct + 1
NumList [200] : = Ct + 9
```

Sample Execution

```
Enter value to search for (10..40): 13
13 found at 16
It occurred 12 times.

Press RETURN to continue, enter Q to quit:
```

14. The *median* of an ordered list of numbers is the middle value. To find the median of a collection of numbers in an array `List`, two different situations are considered.

Situation A: The length of the list is an *odd* number. The index of the median is given by the following formula:

```
index = (ListLen + 1) DIV 2
The median is List [index].
```

Situation B: The length of the list is an *even* number. The median is the average of the list values: `List [ListLen DIV 2]` and `List [ListLen DIV 2 + 1]`

That is, the median is

```
(List [ListLen DIV 2] + List [ListLen DIV 2 + 1]) / 2
```

Given: `List`, a one-dimensional array of type `NumList`, where

```
NumList = ARRAY [1 .. Max] OF INTEGER
```

and `List` contains a value whose components are ordered.

Write a Pascal procedure, `FindMedian`, that has as input the ARRAY value `List`. The procedure should return the median to the calling execution block. The procedure header should be

```
PROCEDURE FindMedian (List : NumList ; ListLen : INTEGER ;
                      VAR Median : INTEGER)
```

15. Given a score from an ordered list indexed from `1` to `Max` (a constant defined in the program CONST section), the score's *percentile* value is given by

$$Percentile = ROUND ((Index / (ListLen + 1)) * 100)$$

Index is the score's position in the list and *ListLen* is the number of components in the list.

COMMENT
If a score has a percentile of 42 then it is greater than 42% of the scores in the list (provided the list is ordered from smallest to largest).

Write a Pascal function `Percentile` that will return the percentile of a value. The function has as input a value from a component of `List` an array of type `ArrayType` (where `ArrayType = ARRAY [1 .. Max] OF WholeNum` and `WholeNum = 0 .. MAXINT`). The function header is

```
FUNCTION Percentile (Target, ListLen : WholeNum ;
                     List : ArrayType) : WholeNum
```

Section 6-3

Sorting

In the previous section, you studied searching a list. If the list was ordered in some fashion, the efficiency of the search could be greatly improved. In this section, you will study how to order a list of values. The process of ordering a list of values is called **sorting** the list. In this section, you will study two sort techniques, the insertion sort and the selection sort. In later chapters, you will study the Shell sort and the quicksort.

6-3.1 Building an Ordered List

Suppose you have a list of numbers to enter. You would like to have the numbers ordered by the computer from smallest to largest. For example, you enter 12, 13, 8, and 9. The numbers are processed by placing them in order. The output is

```
The numbers in order are: 8 9 12 13
```

One method of accomplishing this task is a technique called an **insertion sort.** Essentially, the idea is to use an array and the following steps:

1. Get the first entry. Place it in cell 1.
2. Get the next entry. Search for the proper insertion point; move the remaining cells to the right; and insert the entry at the proper insertion point.

Do Step 2 as long as there is more data to be entered and the array is not full.

Using these values and List (an `ARRAY [1 .. 4] OF INTEGER`), the technique appears as follows:

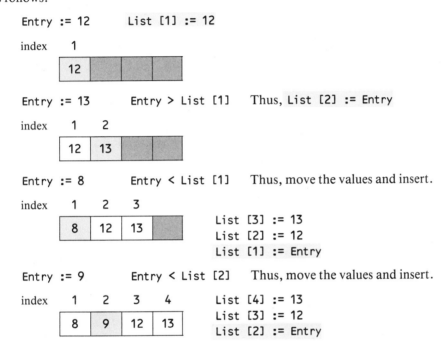

A design for the insertion sort follows:

Design: Get first Entry
Insert in cell 1
Pt := 1
WHILE MoreEntries AND Pt < LengthofArray DO
    GetNextEntry
    Ct := 1
    WHILE Ct < = Pt AND Entry > List [Ct] DO
        Ct := SUCC (Ct)   {find insertion point}
    IF Ct < = Pt
        THEN MoveValuesDown
    List [Ct] : = Entry
    Pt : = SUCC (Pt)

Refinement of: *MoveValuesDown*
                FOR I : = Pt + 1 DOWNTO Ct + 1 DO
                    List [I] : = List [I − 1]

DO IT NOW

1. Walk through the design just given for an entry of 15. Assume that the previous entries were 18, 9, 12, and 23. Thus, the array List now appears as follows (with Pt having a value of 4):

```
Entry := 15

index    1    2    3    4

        9   12   18   23
```

2. Walk through the design just given for an entry of 18. Assume that the previous entries were 18, 9, 12, and 23. Thus, the array List now appears as follows (with Pt having a value of 4). In which cell is the new entry placed?

```
Entry := 18

index    1    2    3    4

        9   12   18   23
```

3. Complete the conversion of the insertion sort design to a Pascal program:

```
PROGRAM InsertionSort ;

TYPE NumList = ARRAY [1 .. 100] OF INTEGER ;
     Index = 1 .. 101 ;

VAR List : NumList ;
    Pt, Ct : Index ;
    Entry : INTEGER ;
    MoreEntries : BOOLEAN ;
    Ans : CHAR ;

PROCEDURE MoveValuesDown (Start , Top : Index ;
                             VAR List : NumList) ;

    VAR NDex : Index ;

    BEGIN                             {MoveValuesDown}
      :
      :
    END ;                             {MoveValuesDown}

PROCEDURE PrintResults (Pt : Index ; List : NumList) ;

  VAR Ct : Index ;

  BEGIN                               {PrintResults}
    WRITELN ('Your entries in order are: ') ;
    FOR Ct := 1 TO Pt DO
      BEGIN                           {FOR-DO instruction}
        WRITELN (Ct, ' : ', List [Ct]) ;
        IF Ct MOD 20 = 0              {page full}
          THEN BEGIN
                 WRITE ('Press RETURN key') ;
                 READLN
               END
      END                             {FOR-DO instruction}
  END ;                               {PrintResults}
```

```
      BEGIN                                 {main program}
        Pt := 1 ;
        WRITE ('Enter first value (an integer): ') ;
        READLN (List [1]) ;
        MoreEntries := TRUE ;
        WHILE MoreEntries AND (Pt < 100) DO    {Get entries}
          BEGIN                              {outer WHILE-DO loop}
            WRITE ('Enter value ', Pt + 1 , '. ') ;
            READLN (Entry) ;
            Ct := 1 ;
            WHILE ....
              ⋮
              ⋮
          END ;                              {outer WHILE-DO loop}
        IF Pt = 100
          THEN WRITELN ('Array Full') ;
        PrintResults (Pt , List)
      END .                                  {main program}
```

DO IT NOW ANSWERS

1. Since the entries **9**, **12**, **18**, and **23** have already been made, the WHILE-DO loop is still executing, and **Pt** has the value **4**. If the array has length less than 5, nothing happens. Otherwise, the value **15** is entered. **Ct** is assigned the value **1**. The WHILE-DO instruction increases the value in **Ct** to **3**. Since 3 <= 4, the **MoveValuesDown** procedure is executed. The FOR-DO loop is from **5** DOWNTO **4**. It moves **23** to cell 5 and **18** to cell 4, then instruction **List [Ct] := Entry** places **15** in cell 3. **Pt** is assigned the value **5**.

2. The value **18** is entered. **Ct** is assigned the value **1**. The WHILE-DO instruction increases the value in **Ct** to **3**. Since 3 <= 4, the **MoveValuesDown** procedure is executed. The FOR-DO loop is from **5** DOWNTO **4**. It moves **23** to cell 5 and **18** to cell 4. Then instruction **List [Ct] := Entry** places **18** in cell 3. **Pt** is assigned the value **5**. Thus, the new entry (**18**) is placed in cell 3.

3.
```
   PROCEDURE MoveValuesDown (Start , Top : Index ;
                             VAR List : NumList) ;

   VAR NDex : Index ;

   BEGIN                                  {MoveValuesDown}
     FOR NDex := Top + 1 DOWNTO Start + 1 DO
       List [NDex] := List [NDex - 1]
   END ;                                  {MoveValuesDown}
```

```
        WHILE (Ct <= Pt) AND (Entry > List [Ct]) DO
          Ct := SUCC (Ct) ;
        IF Ct <= Pt
          THEN MoveValuesDown (Ct , Pt, List) ;
        List [Ct] := Entry ;
        Write ('Enter Q to quit, press RETURN to continue- ') ;
        READLN (Ans) ;
        IF (Ans = 'Q') OR (Ans = 'q')
          THEN MoreEntries := FALSE ;
        Pt := SUCC (Pt)
```

6-3.2 *Ordering an Existing List*

The insertion sort just developed was used to order a list as the data was entered. To use the insertion sort to sort an existing list would require only a few alterations. These would be as follows (where **ListLen** is the length of the array):

1. Since the values are not being read in, the outer WHILE-DO test becomes
Pt < ListLen

2. Rather than read `Entry,` `Entry` is assigned the next value in the list:
`Entry := List [Pt + 1]`

Further exploration of this situation is left for you to do as an exercise.

Rather than completely develop the insertion sort for an existing list, we will explore a different type of sort. This sort technique is called a **selection sort.** It approaches sorting an existing list much as you or I would. That is, if you had a list of values and wanted to order them from smallest to largest, you would form a new list. Get the lowest value and place it in the new list. Cross out the value. Get the lowest value remaining in the original list. Place it in the new list. Cross out the value in the original list. Continue this process until there are no values left in the original list. This sort process requires two arrays. After developing this algorithm, we will then discuss a related method that will use only one array.

Developing this idea as a design yields the following. Assume that the existing list is of type `ARRAY [1 .. Max] OF INTEGER`.

original list   new list

13   5
X̶   6
X̶
23

Design: *SelectionSort*
            Pt := 1
            WHILE Pt < = Length of List DO
                 Search List for smallest value (ListLen , Min , Index , List)
                 Place Min in NewList [Pt]
                 Replace List [Index] with very large value
                 Pt := SUCC (Pt)

Refinement of: *Search List for smallest value (ListLen , Min , Index , List)*
                  Min : = List [1]   {assume smallest in cell 1}
                  FOR Ct : = 2 TO ListLen DO   {check remaining cells}
                      IF List [Ct] < Min
                          THEN Min : = List [Ct]   {found smaller value}
                               Index : = Ct   {location of the cell}
                  {return Min and Index to main program}

Walking through this design for a smaller but similar array yields the picture shown in Figure 6–9.

Figure 6–9

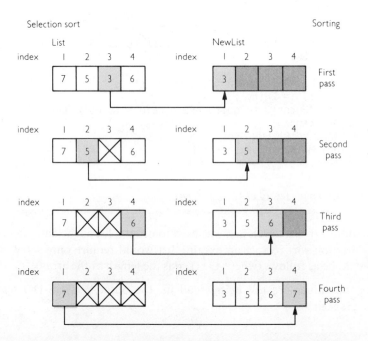

Selection sort   Sorting

First pass; Second pass; Third pass; Fourth pass

Converting the design of SelectionSort to a Pascal program yields the program in Figure 6–10.

Figure 6–10

```
PROGRAM SelectionSort ;

CONST Len = 100 ;
      LenPlus1 = 101 ;

TYPE NumList = ARRAY [1 .. Len] OF INTEGER ;
     Subscript = 1 .. LenPlus1 ;

VAR List , NewList : NumList ;
    Min : INTEGER ;
    Index, Pt : Subscript ;

PROCEDURE FindMin (TheLen : Subscript ; VAR Min : INTEGER ;
                   VAR Index : Subscript ; VAR List : NumList) ;

  VAR Ct : Subscript ;

  BEGIN                                 {FindMin}
    Min := List [1] ;
    Index := 1 ;
    FOR Ct := 2 TO TheLen DO
      BEGIN                             {FOR-DO instruction}
        IF List [Ct] < Min
          THEN BEGIN                    {THEN instruction}
                 Min := List [Ct] ;
                 Index := Ct
               END                      {THEN instruction}
      END ;                             {FOR-DO instruction}
    WRITE ('*')                         {relieve user's anxiety}
  END ;                                 {FindMin}

BEGIN                                   {main program}
  FOR Index := 1 TO Len DO             {fill array for test}
    BEGIN                               {FOR-DO instruction}
      List [Index] := Index * 32 MOD 99 ;
      WRITE (List [Index] : 4) ;        {show user old list}
      NewList [Index] := 0              {initialize NewList}
    END ;                               {FOR-DO instruction}
  WRITELN ;
  WRITELN ('Now sorting list- ') ;
  Pt := 1 ;
  Min := 0 ;
  Index := 1 ;
  WHILE Pt <= Len DO
    BEGIN                               {WHILE-DO instruction}
      FindMin (Len , Min , Index , List) ;
      NewList [Pt] := Min ;
      List [Index] := MAXINT ;
      Pt := SUCC (Pt)
    END ;                               {WHILE-DO instruction}
  WRITELN ;                             {start new line on screen}
  FOR Index := 1 TO Len DO             {show user new list}
    WRITE (NewList [Index] : 4)
END .                                   {main program}
```

COMMENT
The instruction
List [Index] := Index * 32 MOD 99
is used to fill the array List with some test values.

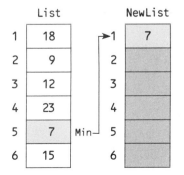

This design of `SelectionSort` can be improved with regard to its efficiency. That is, the procedure can be designed such that the array `NewList` is not needed. For large data structures, often there is not enough memory space to handle both `List` and `NewList`. The following design accomplishes the same task as `SelectionSort`, but it uses only the original array `List`.

Design: Pt : = 1
           WHILE Pt > Length of List DO
               FindMin (ListLen, Pt, List, Min, Index)
               TempHold : = List [Pt]   {swap values of List [Pt] and}
               List [Pt] : = Min   {List [Index]}
               List [Index] : = TempHold
               Pt : = SUCC (Pt)

The procedure `FindMin` needs to find the smallest value from the value in `Pt` to the end of the list. Thus, the procedure needs an input of the value in `Pt`.

Refinement of: *FindMin (ListLen, Pt, List, Min, Index)*
                  Min : = List [Pt]
                  FOR Ct : = Pt + 1 TO ListLen DO
                      IF List [Ct] < Min
                          THEN Min : = List [Ct]
                              Index : = Ct

Figure 6–11

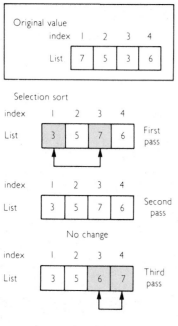

Walking through the design for the array `List` with length 4 and component values 7, 5, 3, and 6 yields the picture shown in Figure 6–11.

When the last cell is reached, the value in that cell must be the largest value. In the second pass (when `Pt` has value 2), the value returned for `Min` is 5, and the value returned for `Index` is 2. Thus,

    TempHold is assigned the value in List [Pt]   {5 in this case}
    List [Pt] is assigned the value in Min   {5 in this case}
    List [Index] is assigned the value in TempHold   {5 in this case}

There is no change when a value is in its proper position, yet the interchange is still carried out (see the following Do It Now Exercise 2).

DO IT NOW

1. For `List` of length 5 with component values of 17, 8, 9, 5, and 16, show the value in `List` at each of the four passes for `SelectionSort` (using only `List`).
2. Adjust the design in exercise 1 to skip the swap if the ARRAY value is in its proper position.
3. Convert the new design for `SelectionSort` to a Pascal program.

DO IT NOW ANSWERS

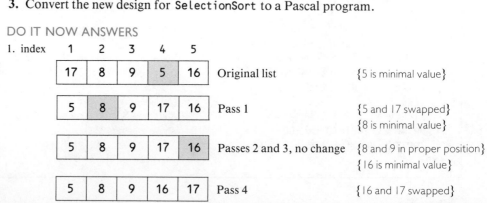

1.
index	1	2	3	4	5		
	17	8	9	5	16	Original list	{5 is minimal value}
	5	8	9	17	16	Pass 1	{5 and 17 swapped} {8 is minimal value}
	5	8	9	17	16	Passes 2 and 3, no change	{8 and 9 in proper position} {16 is minimal value}
	5	8	9	16	17	Pass 4	{16 and 17 swapped}

2. IF List [Pt] < > Min
       THEN
           TempHold : = List [Pt]   {swap values of List [Pt]}
           List [Pt] : = Min   {and List [Index]}
           List [Index] : = TempHold

3. PROGRAM SelectionSort ;

   CONST ListLen = 100 ;
         LenPlus1 = 101 ;

   TYPE NumList = ARRAY [1 .. ListLen] OF INTEGER ;
        Subscript = 1 .. LenPlus1 ;

   VAR List : NumList ;
       Min , TempHold : INTEGER ;
       Ct , Index , Pt : Subscript ;

   PROCEDURE FindMin (TheLen, Start : Subscript; List : NumList ;
                      VAR Min : INTEGER ;
                      VAR Index : Subscript) ;

      VAR Ct : Subscript ;

      BEGIN   {FindMin}
        Min := List [Start] ;
        Index := Start ;
        FOR Ct := Start TO TheLen DO
           BEGIN   {FOR-DO instruction}
             IF List [Ct] < Min
                THEN BEGIN   {THEN instruction}
                       Min := List [Ct] ;
                       Index := Ct
                     END   {THEN instruction}
           END ;   {FOR-DO instruction}
        WRITE ('*')   {relieve user's anxiety}
      END;   {FindMin}

   BEGIN   {main program}
     FOR Index := 1 TO ListLen DO   {fill array for test}
       List [Index] := Index * 32 MOD 99 ;
     FOR Index := 1 TO ListLen DO   {show user old list}
       WRITE (List [Index] : 4) ;
     WRITELN ;   {start new screen line}
     WRITELN ('Now sorting list-') ;
     Pt := 1 ;
     Min := 0 ;
     Index := 1 ;
     WHILE Pt < ListLen DO
       BEGIN   {WHILE-DO instruction}
         FindMin (ListLen, Pt, List, Min, Index) ;
         IF List [Pt] < > List [Index]   {swap only values not in proper position}
            THEN BEGIN   {swap values}
                   TempHold := List [Pt] ;
                   List [Pt] := Min ;
                   List [Index] := TempHold
                 END ;   {swap values}
         Pt := SUCC (Pt)
       END ;   {WHILE-DO instruction}
     WRITELN ;   {start new line on screen}
     FOR Index := 1 TO ListLen DO   {show user sorted list}
       WRITE (List [Index] : 4)
   END .   {main program}

Vocabulary

Glad You Asked

Q   Which sort technique is best?

A   That question is difficult to answer when considered from the context of the ideas behind the Pascal language. The selection sort is more efficient than the insertion sort. However, there is another sort called the quicksort (see Chapter 10) that is faster than either of these. Now, one purpose of Pascal is to write programs that are easy to read and maintain. For most people, the simpler the idea, the easier the idea is to read and comprehend. So which is best, the quicksort (which is fast but hard to understand) or a slower but easier-to-understand sort such as the selection sort?

     The insertion sort makes sense when building an ordered list, and the selection sort makes sense when ordering an existing list. Also, remember that you are in a learning situation at this point. Working with the different sort techniques also provides practice in working with arrays and the instructions of the Pascal language.

Q   In the procedure MoveValuesDown (in the answer to DO IT NOW exercise 3, section 6–3.1), I just do not see how to come up with the limits for the FOR-DO loop. Can you help?

A   First, the DOWNTO is used to avoid destroying the components to be moved down. To find the limits on the FOR-DO, the key is trial and error. However, this does not mean guessing. You try what you think will work. Walk through the design. If it does not work, you learn more about the situation for the next try. In the procedure you referred to, the FOR-DO instruction was as follows:

```
FOR NDex := Top + 1 DOWNTO Start + 1 DO
    List [NDex] := List [NDex - 1]
```

and the picture was

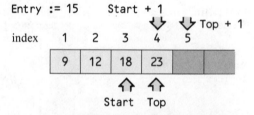

You wanted to put 23 in cell 5 and 18 in cell 4 to get the following:

Q What is a bubble sort? I was reading another textbook, and the author mentioned this sort. It has such a strange name.

A The bubble sort is just another of many sorts available. In fact, entire books are written just on search and sort techniques. The bubble sort works on the idea of taking the first two component values and ordering them. Next, the second and third are ordered, and so forth through the list. If the list is ordered, then quit. Otherwise, the process is repeated until the list is ordered. A picture of this follows:

First pass of bubble sort / Array after first pass

Is list sorted? No. Do second pass. Continue to do a pass until the list is sorted.

In the first pass, $n - 1$ (3, in this case) comparisons are made (n is the length of the list). Notice that the largest value is moved to the end of the list. Thus, the second pass must perform only $n - 2$ comparisons (2, in this case). The bubble sort is often classified as an *exchange sort* (that is, elements of the list are exchanged in some fashion). (For more on the bubble sort, see problem 12 in the exercises for Section 6–3.)

The bubble sort is *too slow* for long lists (as are the selection and insertion sorts). In Chapter 8, an alteration of the bubble sort will yield a much faster sort, known as the Shell sort. In Chapter 10, through the use of a technique known as recursion, an even faster sort, known as the quicksort, will be developed. For now, it is only important that you develop the idea of sorting and learn how to work with arrays.

Section 6–3 Exercises

1. Given the following array value, give the results of sorting the list from smallest to largest.

	1	2	3	4	5	6	7	8
original list	12	7	19	18	23	17	8	1Ø

	1	2	3	4	5	6	7	8
sorted list								

2. If the selection sort is used to sort the array value in problem 1, the first pass would exchange component _____ with component _____.

3. If a list of values is to be sorted as they are being read into the computer, the _____ sort would be used.

4. Insert *True* for a true statement. Insert *False* for a false statement.
   _____ **a.** The major reason for sorting a list is to improve the efficiency of a search of the list.
   _____ **b.** Once a list is sorted, the best search to use is the linear search.
   _____ **c.** To sort a list from smallest to largest by the selection sort, the algorithm starts by finding the largest element in the list.
   _____ **d.** The basic idea of the insertion sort is to keep the list ordered as the values are being entered.

5. For the insertion sort, suppose the array value so far appears as follows:

1	2	3	4	5	6	7
B	D	H	M	W	Z	

If the value K is entered, the K is inserted at position _____ , and the values _____ are moved down.

6. Do a walk through for the selection sort to produce a chart (like the one given as an answer for Do It Now exercise 1, section 6–3.2) for the following list. The list is to be sorted from smallest to largest.

1	2	3	4	5	6
P	U	L	S	E	S

7. Joan has a list of numbers to be ordered from largest to smallest. To accomplish this, she wants to use an insertion sort. She has altered the design presented in the text material to the following:

```
Design:  Get first Entry
         Insert in cell 1
         Pt := 1
         WHILE MoreEntries AND Pt < LengthOfArray DO
             GetNextEntry
             Ct := 1
             WHILE Ct <= Pt AND Entry < List [Pt] DO
                 Ct := SUCC ( Ct )
             IF Ct <= Pt
               THEN MoveValuesDown
             List [Ct] := Entry
             Pt := SUCC ( Pt )
```

Refinement of: *MoveValuesDown*
```
                 FOR I := Pt + 1 DOWNTO Ct + 1 DO
                     List [I] := List [I − 1]
```

Walk through this design for an entry of 15. Assume that the previous entries were 9 and 18. The array List now appears as follows (with Pt having a value of 2):

```
Entry := 15
index  1    2    3
```

18	9		

What is the value in Ct? _____. The FOR-DO instruction in MoveValuesDown is from _____ DOWNTO _____. The value in Pt is _____.

8. Boot up Pascal; set the workfile to the file Insert.PAS from the Source diskette. Enter the editor. Move the cursor to the main execution section. Do the following.
   a. Delete the first WRITE instruction.
   b. Alter the instruction READLN (List [1]) to List [1] := RANDOM (50)
   c. In the WHILE-DO instruction,
      i. Delete the WRITE instruction.
      ii. Alter the READLN instruction to Entry := RANDOM (100) − 30
      iii. Delete the next WRITE, READLN, and IF-THEN instructions.
   Execute the altered program. What is the smallest value in the list? What is the largest value in the list?

9. Boot up Pascal; set the workfile to the file BinaryEx.PAS from the Source diskette. Enter the editor. Move the cursor to the blank line prior to the procedure

BinarySearch. Use the F7 function key to insert a beginning marker. Move the cursor to the end of the procedure BinarySearch. Use the F8 function key to insert an ending marker. Use Ctrl-K W to select the Write block to a file option. Respond to the file name prompt by entering Binary.UTL. Quit the editor and set the workfile to the file Select.PAS from the Source diskette. Enter the editor. Move the cursor to the blank line prior to the program execution section. Use Ctrl-K R to select the Read file option. Respond to the file prompt by entering Binary.UTL. Expand the program to allow the user to enter a value (from 0 to 99) then have the list searched (using the binary search) for the value.

10. Boot up Pascal; set workfile to the file EffSelec.PAS from the Source diskette. Enter the editor. Alter the program to fill the list with 100 randomly selected characters. Write a procedure to replace the instructions that swap two components of the array.

Programming Problems

11. Write a Pascal program that will allow the members of a class of 40 students to sign in for a test by entering their last names (assume all students have different last names). The program is to yield an ordered list of names upon entry of the key word, roster. Use an insertion sort.

12. In the text material, it was mentioned that the insertion sort could be designed to order (sort) an existing list. The design is as follows:

Refinement of: *InsertionSort* (for existing list)
$$Pt := 1$$
WHILE Pt < LengthOfArray DO
    Entry := List [Pt + 1]
    Ct := 1
WHILE Ct <= Pt AND Entry > List [Ct] DO
    Ct := SUCC (Ct)
IF Ct <= Pt
  THEN MoveValuesDown
List [Ct] := Entry
Pt := SUCC (Pt)

a. Convert this design to a Pascal program.

b. Use the program to sort List, an array of type ARRAY [1 .. 100] OF CHAR. To test the program, you can use the following instruction to fill List:

```
FOR Ct := 1 TO 100 DO
   List [Ct] := CHR (Ct MOD 26 + 65)
```

13. A design for the bubble sort (see the Glad You Asked section) is as follows:

Design: Pt := 1
    WHILE ListNotSorted DO
      FOR Ct := 1 TO ListLen − Pt DO
        CheckPairs

Refinement of: *CheckPairs*
    IF List [Ct] > List [Ct + 1]
      THEN Temp := List [Ct + 1]   {swap}
          List [Ct + 1] := List [Ct]
          List [Ct] := Temp

a. Write a Pascal function ListNotSorted. The function should return value TRUE if the list is not in order.

b. Convert the design just given to a Pascal program, and test it by sorting the following list: 17, 3, 5, 6, 2, 12, 19, 5, 8, 23, 12

Altered file

NameList.TXT

Allred,␣Betty*␣␣␣458-9135
Boles,␣Sharon*␣␣␣255-0069
⋮

Altered file

States.TXT

Alaska*␣␣␣479
Wyoming*␣␣␣514
Vermont*␣␣␣525
⋮

Sample Execution

The students, by grade averages,

 1. Calley, Karen 98
 2. Zeal, Lotta 97
 3. Lively, Hank 92
    ⋮
120. Worm, Lowly 23

14. A TEXT file, NameList.TXT, is made up of 50 lines. On each line is a name and a phone number, for example, Killam,␣Jon*␣␣␣678-9345. (The ␣ represents a blank space.) Write a Pascal program that will alter the TEXT file NameList.TXT such that the names are ordered alphabetically. (*Hint:* Read the lines into an array of type ARRAY [1..50] OF STRING[40].)

15. A TEXT file, States.TXT, is made up of 50 lines. On each line is a state name and the state's population in thousands. For example,

Florida*␣␣␣6789
New York*␣␣␣18191
⋮

Write a Pascal program that will alter the TEXT file States.TXT such that the first line is the state with the lowest population and so forth by population size.

16. A TEXT file named Students.TXT is made up of 120 lines. On each line is a student's name and the student's average in MAT 1138. Write a Pascal program that will output the lines of the TEXT file ordered by grade average from highest to lowest.

Students.TXT
Denison,␣Marie*␣␣␣78
Zeal,␣Lotta*␣␣␣97
⋮

Parallel Arrays

In this section, you will study an application of the ARRAY data structure, that of parallel arrays. This application deals with arrays that are related in some sense. You will study how to search and how to sort parallel arrays. The purpose of this section is to provide more experience in working with one-dimensional arrays.

6–4.1 Matched Arrays

Parallel arrays are arrays that are related or matched in some way. As an introduction, consider the following lists:

	NameList		OccupationList
index 1	Chou En-lai	index 1	Politician
2	Forster, E. M.	2	Writer
3	Fourier, Jean	3	Mathematician
4	Goddard, Robert	4	Physicist
5	Kellogg, Frank	5	Politician
6	MacArthur, Douglas	6	Military Leader
7	Riemann, Bernhard	7	Mathematician
8	Tolstoy, Lev	8	Writer

Each component of NameList is the name of a noted personality of the past. The list is in alphabetical order. Each component of OccupationList is an occupation. The two lists are matched in the sense that component 1 of OccupationList matches the occupation of the person named in cell 1 of NameList. A typical use of these parallel arrays would be as follows:

1. The user enters a name.
2. The name is looked up in `NameList` and the index recorded.
3. The occupation in `OccupationList` at this index is obtained.
4. The occupation is written to the screen as the occupation of the name entered.

Arrays `NameList` and `OccupationList` are called parallel arrays.

6-4.2 *Searching and Parallel Arrays*

As an application of parallel arrays and searching, consider the following example. One array is a list of part numbers carried by the store; the other is a list of the current prices for the parts.

EXAMPLE

The Service Center has stored in an array the part numbers for the parts it has in stock. The values in the cells are four-digit part numbers from 1001 to 9999. The list is ordered from lowest part number to highest part number. The price of each part is stored in a second array. Write a Pascal program that allows the user to input a part number. The output of the program is whether or not the part is carried and, if so, the price.

Sample Execution

```
Please enter part number (Ø to quit): 9315
Price is $12.18
Please enter part number (Ø to quit): Ø
```

SOLUTION

The two parallel arrays, `PartList` and `PriceList`, appear as follows:

PartList

1138	1256	1290		9315	9887

index   1   2   3   ..   99   100

PriceList

1.98	3.79	2.05		12.18	5.20

index   1   2   3   ..   99   100

Suppose the user enters 1256 for the part number. The Service Center carries this part, and its price is $3.79. Suppose the user enters 1287 for the part number. The service center does not carry this part.

After thinking about and playing with the problem, compose the following design. Since the part numbers are ordered, the binary search can be used to search for the part number input by the user.

Index	PartList	PriceList
1	1138	1.98
2	1256	3.79
3	1290	2.05
.	.	.
.	.	.
99	9315	12.18
100	9887	5.20

Design: REPEAT
        WRITE ('Please enter part number (0 to quit): ')
        READLN (PartNum)
        BinarySearch (100, PartNum, PartList, Found)
        IF Found = 0
          THEN WRITE ('Part not carried. Must order.')
         ELSE Price : = PriceList [Found]
            WRITELN ('Price is $', Price : 4: 2)
      UNTIL PartNum = 0

Walking through the design for an input of `1003` yields the following:

    `BinarySearch (100, PartNum, PartList, Found)` is called.
    `Found` is assigned `0`.

Output is `Part not carried. Must order.`

Walking through the design for an input of `1290` yields the following:

    `BinarySearch (100, PartNum, PartList, Found)` is called.
    `Found` is assigned `3`. `PriceList [3]` is obtained.

Output is `Price is $2.05`

Walking through the design for an input of `0` yields the following:

    `BinarySearch (100, PartNum, PartList, Found)` is called.
    `Found` is assigned `0`.

Output is `Part not carried. Must order.`   {the program execution stops}

This last output is a minor design error. The design (adjusted for the error) yields the program in Figure 6–12.

Figure 6–12

```
PROGRAM PartSearch ;

TYPE WholeNum = 0 .. 10000 ;
     PartsArray = ARRAY [1 .. 100] OF WholeNum ;
     PriceArray = ARRAY [1 .. 100] OF REAL ;

VAR PartList : PartsArray ;
    PriceList : PriceArray ;
    Found , ListLen, PartNum : WholeNum ;
    Price : REAL ;

PROCEDURE LoadArrays (VAR PartList : PartsArray ;
                      VAR PriceList : PriceArray) ;

  VAR Ct : 1 .. 100 ;

  BEGIN                              {LoadArrays}
    FOR Ct := 1 TO 100 DO
      BEGIN                          {fill arrays with dummy values}
        PartList [Ct] := 1000 + 80 * Ct ;
        PriceList [Ct] := (Ct MOD 10) + 0.98
      END
  END ;                              {LoadArrays}
```

COMMENT
The procedure `LoadArrays` simply fills the arrays with some values to test the program. The array `PartList` will contain values from `1080` to `9000`.

```
PROCEDURE BinarySearch (ListLen , Target : WholeNum ;
                        List : PartsArray ;
                        VAR Found : WholeNum) ;

  VAR High , Low , Mid : INTEGER ;
  BEGIN                                    {BinarySearch}
    Found := 0 ;
    High := ListLen + 1 ;
    Low := 0 ;
    WHILE ((High - Low) > 1) AND (Found = 0) DO
      BEGIN                                {WHILE-DO instruction}
        Mid := (High + Low) DIV 2 ;
        IF List [Mid] = Target
          THEN Found := Mid
          ELSE IF Target > List [Mid]
                  THEN Low := Mid
                  ELSE High := Mid
      END                                  {WHILE-DO instruction}
  END ;                                    {BinarySearch}
BEGIN                                      {main program}
  ListLen := 100 ;
  LoadArrays (PartsList , PriceList) ;
  REPEAT
    WRITE ('Please enter part number (0 to quit): ') ;
    READLN (PartNum) ;
    IF PartNum < > 0
      THEN BEGIN                           {THEN instruction}
             BinarySearch (ListLen , PartNum, PartList, Found) ;
             IF Found = 0
               THEN WRITELN ('Part not carried. Must order.')
               ELSE BEGIN                  {inner ELSE instruction}
                      Price := PriceList [Found] ;
                      WRITELN ('Price is $', Price : 1 : 2)
                    END                    {inner ELSE instruction}
           END                             {THEN instruction}
  UNTIL PartNum = 0
END .                                      {main program}
```

Figure 6-12
Continued

DO IT NOW

Suppose the array PartList was of type

    ARRAY [1001 .. 9999] OF InvLevel

where InvLevel = -2 .. MAXINT. The values in the cells of PartList represent the present inventory level for a given part (-2 = no such part; -1 = not carried; 0 = carried, but out; a positive number = number in inventory). The array PriceList is of type

    ARRAY [1001 .. 9999] OF REAL

Design a Pascal program that allows the user to input a part number (`PartNum`) from `1001` to `9999`. The output of the program follows:

Please check part number and re-enter.	(if PartList [PartNum] = −2)
Part not carried. Please order.	(if PartList [PartNum] = −1)
Sorry. Out of part at this time.	(if PartList [PartNum] = 0)
22 items in inventory. Price: $2.56	(if PartList [PartNum] > 0)

DO IT NOW ANSWER

This program does not require a search, since `PartNum` is the index of the array. A design follows:

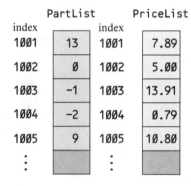

```
Design:   ShutDown : = FALSE
          REPEAT
            Get PartNum
            IF PartNum = 10000
              THEN BEGIN
                      WRITE ('Shutdown? (Y/N): ')
                      READLN (Ans)
                      IF Ans = 'Y'
                        THEN ShutDown : = TRUE
                   END
              ELSE BEGIN
                      Found : = PartList [PartNum]
                      CASE Found OF
                         -2 : WRITELN ('Please check part number and re-enter')
                         -1 : WRITELN ('Part not carried. Please order.')
                          0 : WRITELN ('Sorry. Out of part at this time.')
                      END
                      IF Found > 0
                        THEN Price : = PriceList [PartNum]
                             WRITE (PartList [PartNum] : 1)
                             WRITE (' items in inventory.')
                             WRITELN ('Price: $', PriceList [PartNum])
                   END
          UNTIL ShutDown
```

6-4.3 Sorting Parallel Arrays

The next application to consider is that of sorting parallel arrays. A typical situation involving this application is as follows.

EXAMPLE

A TEXT file named `Artist.TXT` is made of lines similar to the following (|| represents an end-of-line marker):

```
Alda, Alan||
New York, New York||
Arkin, Alan||
New York, New York||
Ashley, Elizabeth||
Ocala, Florida||
     .
     .
     .
Williams, Robin||
Chicago, Illinois||
<end-of-file marker>
```

One line contains a name and the next line, a birthplace. The names are in alphabetical order. Write a Pascal program that reads the names into an array `NameList` and the birthplaces into a parallel array `StateList`. The program should allow the user to input a state (such as Illinois), then write to the screen a list of people born in that state.

Sample Execution

```
Please enter state name: Texas
Born in Texas:
Baker, Joe Don
Busey, Gary
Duvall, Shelley
Fawcett, Farrah
Hagman, Larry
Martin, Steve
Nelson, Willie
Spacek, Sissy
Turner, Tina

Enter Q to quit, press RETURN to continue-
```

SOLUTION

After thinking about the problem, compose the following design:

Design:　Open file
　　　　　Fill NameList and StateList
　　　　　REPEAT
　　　　　　　WRITE ('Enter state: ')
　　　　　　　READLN (State)
　　　　　　　Search for state in StateList
　　　　　　　Write to screen names from NameList
　　　　　　　Offer user chance to quit
　　　　　UNTIL user is ready to quit

	NameList		StateList
index		index	
1	Cater, Nell	1	Alabama
2	Harris, Emmylou	2	Alabama
3	Elam, Jack	3	Arizona
4	Green, Al	4	Arkansas
.		.	
.		.	
.		.	

At this point, there are still major questions as to how to finalize the program. Many of these questions involve which of several ways to proceed. Most of these questions deal with searching and sorting the parallel arrays.

After considering how to search and how to sort the list of states, make the following refinements for the steps in the design:

Refinement of:　*FillLists*
　　　　　　　ListLen := 0
　　　　　　　WHILE NOT EOF (InFile) AND ListLen < Max DO
　　　　　　　　　READLN (InFile, Name)　　　　　　　{get Name}
　　　　　　　　　Ch := ' '　　　　　　　　　　　　　　{a blank}
　　　　　　　　　WHILE Ch < > ',' DO　　　　　　　　{skip over city}
　　　　　　　　　　　READ (InFile, Ch)
　　　　　　　　　READ (InFile, Ch)　　　　　　　　　{skip blank}
　　　　　　　　　READLN (InFile, State)　　　　　　{get State}
　　　　　　　　　ListLen := ListLen + 1
　　　　　　　　　InsertState
　　　　　　　　　InsertName

Refinement of: *InsertState*
                      InsertSort (State, StateList, ListLen, Pos)

COMMENT
`State` will be inserted in `StateList` in its alphabetical position with the insertion sort.
`StateList` has the length `ListLen`. Insertion occurred at position `Pos`. Thus, the procedure
`InsertSort` will need variable parameters `StateList` and `Pos` and value parameters `State`
and `ListLen`. Also, `Name` must be inserted in `NameList` at the same position that `State` is inserted in `StateList`. Thus, `NameList` and `Name` are needed as parameters.

Refinement of: *Search*
                      BinarySearch (State, StateList, ListLen, Start)
                      IF Start > 1
                        THEN WHILE StateList [Start − 1] = State DO   {move to head of entries}
                              Start : = Start − 1

COMMENT
`Search` will need variable parameters `StateList` and `Start` and value parameter `ListLen`.
`Search` will use `BinarySearch` to find an occurrence of the value `State` in `StateList`. Since
there can be several values for `State`, the WHILE-DO instruction is used to move to the first
occurrence of `State` in `StateList` (provided `State` is not in position 1 of `StateList`).

Refinement of: *WriteNames*
                      WRITELN ('Born in ', State , ' : ')
                      IF Start = 0
                        THEN WRITE ('Sorry no names in list for ')
                                WRITELN (State)
                        ELSE WHILE StateList [Start] = State DO   {output all names for the state}
                                WRITELN (NameList [Count])
                                Start : = Start + 1

After walking through this design with several test values (including the case where
the TEXT file `Artist.TXT` is empty), convert the design to the Pascal program in Figure 6–13.

Figure 6–13

```
PROGRAM ParLSort ;

CONST MaxIndex = 7Ø ;

TYPE String4Ø = STRING [4Ø] ;
     Names = ARRAY [1 .. MaxIndex] OF String4Ø ;
     States = ARRAY [1 .. MaxIndex] OF String4Ø ;
     Index = Ø .. MaxIndex ;

VAR InFile : TEXT ;
    NameList : Names ;
    StateList : States ;
    ListLen, Start : Index ;
    State : String4Ø ;
    Ans : CHAR ;
```

Figure 6–13
Continued

```
PROCEDURE FillList (VAR InFile : TEXT; VAR NameList : Names ;
                    VAR StateList : States ; VAR ListLen : Index) ;

  VAR Name, State : String40 ;
      Pos : Index ;
      Ch : CHAR ;

  PROCEDURE InsertState (State : String40 ; VAR StateList : States ;
                         Name : String40 ; VAR NameList : Names ;
                         ListLen : Index ; VAR Pos : Index) ;

    PROCEDURE MoveValuesDown (Pos, ListLen : Index ;
                             VAR StateList : States ;
                             VAR NameList : Names) ;

    VAR NDex : Index ;

    BEGIN                                 {MoveValuesDown}
      FOR NDex := ListLen DOWNTO (Pos + 1) DO
        BEGIN
          StateList [NDex] := StateList [NDex - 1] ;
          NameList [NDex] := NameList [NDex - 1]
        END
    END ;                                 {MoveValuesDown}

  BEGIN                                   {InsertState}
    Pos := 1 ;
    IF ListLen = 1
      THEN BEGIN
             StateList [1] := State ;     {fill first slot in StateList}
             NameList [1] := Name         {fill first slot in NameList}
           END
      ELSE
        BEGIN                             {insertion sort}
          WHILE (Pos < ListLen) AND (State >= StateList [Pos]) DO
            Pos := Pos + 1 ;
          IF Pos < ListLen
            THEN MoveValuesDown (Pos, ListLen, StateList, NameList) ;
          StateList [Pos] := State ;
          NameList [Pos] := Name
        END                               {insertion sort}
  END ;                                   {InsertState}

BEGIN                                     {FillList}
  ListLen := 0 ;
  WHILE NOT EOF (InFile) AND (ListLen < MaxIndex) DO
    BEGIN                                 {process a line of the TEXT file}
      READLN (InFile, Name) ;            {get Name}
      Ch := ' ' ;                         {initialize Ch}
      WHILE Ch < > ',' DO                 {skip over city name}
        READ (InFile, Ch) ;
      READ (InFile, Ch) ;                 {skip blank prior to state name}
      READLN (InFile, State) ;            {get State}
      ListLen := ListLen + 1 ;
      InsertState (State, StateList, Name, NameList, ListLen, Pos) ;
    END                                   {process a line of the TEXT file}
END ;                                     {FillList}
```

```
StateList   NameList
1. New York  Alda, Alan
2.
3.
```

```
StateList   NameList
1. Florida   Ashley, Elizabeth
2.                              ◄─┐
3. New York  Alda, Alan          │
4. New York  Arkin, Alan         │
5.                               │
   Illinois  Williams, Robin ────┘
```

```
Artist.TXT
Alda, Alan||
New York, New York||
  ⋮
```

```
Name
Williams, Robin

State
Illinois
```

Figure 6-13

Continued

```
PROCEDURE Search (VAR StateList : States ; VAR Start : Index ;
                   ListLen : Index ; State : String40) ;

  PROCEDURE BinarySearch (Target : String40 ; VAR StateList : States ;
                           ListLen : Index ; VAR Found : Index) ;

    VAR High, Low, Mid : Index ;

    BEGIN                                    {BinarySearch}
      {Include BinarySearch instructions}
    END ;                                    {BinarySearch}

  BEGIN                              {search StateList for first occurrence of State}
    BinarySearch (State, StateList, ListLen, Start) ;
    IF Start > 1
      THEN WHILE (StateList [Start - 1] = State) AND (Start > 1) DO
             Start := Start - 1 ;            {move to first occurrence}
    IF StateList [Start] < > State
      THEN Start := Start + 1
  END ;                                      {search StateList}

PROCEDURE WriteNames (Start : Index ; State : String40 ;
                       VAR NameList : Name ;
                       VAR StateList : States) ;

  BEGIN
    {see Do It Now exercise 3}
  END ;

BEGIN                                        {main program ParLSort}
  ASSIGN (InFile, 'Artist.TXT') ;
  RESET (InFile) ;
  FillList (InFile, NameList, StateList, ListLen) ;
  CLOSE (InFile) ;
  REPEAT
    WRITE ('Please enter state name: ') ;
    READLN (State) ;
    Search (StateList, Start, ListLen, State) ;
    WriteNames (Start, State, NameList, StateList) ;
    WRITELN ;
    WRITE ('Enter Q to quit, press RETURN to continue-') ;
    READLN (Ans) ;
  UNTIL (Ans = 'Q') or (Ans = 'q')
END .                                        {main program ParLSort}
```

Sample Execution

```
Please enter name of state: Texas
Born in Texas:
Baker, Joe Don
Busey, Gary
Duvall, Shelley
   :
```

COMMENT

For program **ParLSort** in Figure 6-13, **NameList** and **StateList** are passed as variable parameters, although in some procedures the arrays are not altered. This is because of memory concerns and is a common practice with data structures. The lengths of the list can be altered easily by using the declaration of **MaxIndex** in the program CONST section.

DO IT NOW

1. What would happen if you entered the program text in Figure 6-13 as is? Would it compile? Would the CPU execute the code?
2. Construct a structured diagram for the design.
3. Complete the procedure **WriteNames**.

DO IT NOW ANSWERS

1. If you entered the program text in Figure 6–13 as is to the Pascal compiler, the text would be compiled to code. However, in a call to the procedure Search, BinarySearch would be called. The value returned for Start would be "trash" (since there are no instructions listed in BinarySearch to give Found a value). At this point, an out-of-range error message would most likely be issued.

2. A structured diagram for the design would be as follows:

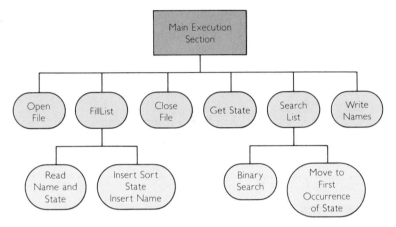

3.
```
   PROCEDURE WriteNames (Start : Index ; State : String40 ;
                         VAR NameList : Names ;
                         VAR StateList : States) ;
     BEGIN                             {WriteNames}
       WRITELN ('Born in ', State, ':') ;
       IF Start = Ø
         THEN WRITELN ('Sorry no names in list for ', State)
         ELSE WHILE StateList [Start] = State DO
                 BEGIN                 {write a name}
                   WRITELN (NameList [Start]) ;
                   Start := Start + 1
                 END                   {write a name}
     END ;                             {WriteNames}
```

Vocabulary

Page

Parallel arrays   Two arrays that are related in some regard, such as a list of names and a list of phone numbers.

368

Glad You Asked

Q I tried to alter the program ParLSort to work with the TEXT file Artist.TXT, where each line of the TEXT file has the following form:

> McNair, Barbara* Wisconsin, Racine ‹end-of-line marker›

That is, each line is made up of a name followed by a birthplace. The character * is used to mark the end of the name. To fill the two lists, I had to use the following for FillList:

```
                          BEGIN                                    {FillList}
                            ListLen := 0 ;
                            WHILE NOT EOF (InFile) AND (ListLen < MaxIndex) DO
                              BEGIN                          {process a line of the TEXT file}
                                Name := '            ' ;    {initialize Name to 20 spaces}
                                State := '            ' ;   {initialize State to 20 spaces}
                                Ch := ' ' ;                 {initialize Ch}
                                Ct := 1 ;                   {initialize Ct}
                                READ (InFile, Ch)
                                WHILE Ch < > '*' DO          {get Name}
                                  BEGIN
                                    Name [Ct] := Ch ;
                                    READ (InFile, Ch) ;
                                    Ct := Ct + 1
                                  END ;
                                READ (InFile, Ch) ;          {move pointer beyond *}
                                WHILE Ch = ' ' DO
                                  READ (InFile, Ch) ;        {skip over blanks}
                                Ct := 1 ;                    {initialize Ct}
                                WHILE Ch < > ',' DO          {get State}
                                  BEGIN
                                    READ (InFile, Ch) ;
                                    State [Ct] := Ch ;
                                    Ct := Ct + 1
                                  END;
                                READLN (InFile) ;            {move to next line}
                                ListLen := ListLen + 1 ;
                                InsertState (State, StateList, Name, NameList, ListLen, Pos) ;
                              END                       {process a line of the TEXT file}
                          END ;                         {FillList}
```

Artist.TXT
McNair, Barbara* Wisconsin, Racine
Nimoy, Leonard* Massachusetts, Boston
Plato, Dana* California, Maywood

When I enter the name of a state, such as Wisconsin, I always get the following:

    Sorry, no names in list for Wisconsin.

Can you help?

A Your problem is the comparison of the STRING values StateList [NDex] and State in the procedure Search. For two strings to be equal, they must have the same length and the same characters. If you entered Wisconsin for State, the length of State is 9. The length of StateList [NDex] is 20 (since you initialized it to 20 blanks). Thus, the Search procedure does not obtain a match (even though the first nine characters matched).

There are a couple of ways around this problem. One way is to "pad" the value input for State with blanks. That is, you add blanks to the value entered for State until the length is 20. The other approach is to remove the blanks from the value read in from TEXT file for StateList [NDex]. The removal could be accomplished by using the DELETE procedure:

    DELETE (StateList [NDex], Ct, 21 - Ct)

where Ct := POS (' ', StateList [NDex])

Section 6–4 Exercises

1. Given the following parallel arrays, complete the procedure FindHigh that follows. The program has the TYPE section shown.

index	CityList	HiList	LoList
1	Amsterdam	57	52
2	Athens	90	66
3	Bangkok	90	81
4	Barcelona	86	76
5	Beirut	79	61
6	Berlin	54	48
7	Bordeaux	80	69
8	Brussels	61	43
9	Buenos Aires	57	46
10	Cairo	106	84

```
TYPE String30 = STRING [30] ;
     Cities = ARRAY [1 .. 10] OF String30 ;
     Number = -65 .. 165 ;
     NumList = ARRAY [1 .. 10] OF Number ;
```

The procedure is to write to the screen the name of the city with the highest temperature and the city's temperature.

```
PROCEDURE FindHigh (VAR CityList : Cities ;
                    VAR HiList : NumList) ;

  VAR Index, Mark : 1..11 ;
      High : -65..165 ;
  BEGIN
    High := -MAXINT - 1 ;
    Index := 1 ;
    WHILE Index <= 10 DO            {linear search on HiList}
      BEGIN                        {search}
        IF HiList [Index] >= High
          THEN BEGIN               {record current high}
                 High := HiList [Index] ;
                 Mark := Index
               END                 {record current high}
        Index := Index + 1
      END ;                        {linear search on HiList}

  END
```

2. Write a procedure FindLo (similar to the procedure FindHigh in problem 1) to write to the screen the city with the lowest temperature of the day.

3. Write a procedure ReportTemp that has the same parameters as in problem 1 with the added value parameter LoList. The procedure is to write to the screen the difference of the high and low temperatures for each city in CityList.

4. Boot up Pascal; set the workfile to the file Parallel.PAS from the Source diskette. Enter the editor. Alter the program to allow the user to fill the array PartList with values from 1000 to 9999 (inclusive) and to fill the array PriceList with values from 10.00 to 99.99 (inclusive). Allow the user to quit entering values when desired (but before the end of the list). Expand the program by inserting the selection sort procedure to sort the array PartList.

5. Boot up Pascal; set the workfile to the file ParLSort.PAS from the Source diskette. Enter the editor. Alter the program to allow the user to add values to the list from the keyboard. That is, after the values in the parallel arrays are listed to the screen, the user should be allowed to enter a name and state. The newly entered values should then be inserted in the parallel arrays and saved to the TEXT file Artist.TXT.

6. Given the following,

```
TYPE WholeNum = 0 .. MAXINT ;
     Census = ARRAY [1 .. 50] OF WholeNum ;
     City = ARRAY [1 .. 50] OF STRING [40] ;

VAR CityList : City ;
    YearOne, YearTwo : Census ;
    Count : WholeNum ;
    CityFile : TEXT ;
    YearFile : TEXT ;
```

The file named `Alaska.TXT` is of type TEXT and contains the following lines:

Anchorage||Eielson AFB||Fairbanks||Juneau||Kenai Pen||
Ketchikan||Sitka|| < end-of-file marker >

The file named `AlasPop.TXT` is of type TEXT and contains the following lines:

1730 480 || 52 61 || 226 148 || 195 60 || 253 166 ||
72 70 || 78 34 || < end-of-file marker >

where || represents an end-of-line marker.

If the following instructions are executed,

```
ASSIGN (CityFile, 'Alaska.TXT') ;
RESET (CityFile) ;
ASSIGN (YearFile, 'AlasPop.TXT') ;
RESET (YearFile) ;
Count := 1;
WHILE (NOT EOF (CityFile)) AND (NOT EOF (YearFile)) DO
  BEGIN
    READLN (CityFile, CityList [Count]) ;
    READ (YearFile, YearOne [Count]) ;
    READLN (YearFile, YearTwo [Count]) ;
    Count := Count + 1
  END ;
```

give the output of the following.
a. `WRITE (CityList [2])`
b. `WRITE (YearOne [2] : 1)`
c. `WRITE (YearTwo [3] - YearOne [3])`
d. `WRITE (CityList [4])`
e. `WRITE (CityList [1], YearOne [1] : 5)`

Sample Execution

City	Change in population
Anchorage	260.42%
⋮	⋮

7. The two values in each line of the file `AlasPop.TXT` in problem 6 represent the 1980 and 1970 populations (in hundreds) of the cities in the file `Alaska.TXT`. Write a Pascal procedure that will output to the screen each city and the change in population as a percentage.
Hint: Percent change in population = ((1980 population − 1970 population) / 1970 population) ∗ 100.

Programming Problems

8. For the parallel arrays `NameList` and `PhoneNum` , both of type `StrList` (where `StrList = ARRAY [1 .. 100] OF STRING [40]`), write a Pascal procedure that has as value parameters the two arrays and a name. The output of the procedure is the phone number if the name is found. If the name is not found, the output should be `...not listed` (where ... represents the input name). Assume `NameList` is in alphabetical order.

index	NameList
1	Able, Sue
2	Baker, Tom
3	Calis, Marie
4	Elliot, Bill
5	Ellis, E.J.
:	:
100	Thompson, Dee

index	PhoneNum
1	623-9089
2	567-1234
3	994-3345
4	289-0089
5	994-3124
:	:
100	567-9812

9. Given the following parallel arrays,

index	TeamList	NickList	Conference
1	Air Force	Falcons	Western Athletic
2	Akron	Zips	Ohio Valley
3	Boston Univ	Terriers	Yankee
4	Duke	Blue Devils	Atlantic Coast
5	Kentucky	Wildcats	Southeastern
6	New Mexico	Lobos	Western Athletic
7	UCLA	Bruins	Pacific Ten
8	Wichita State	Shockers	Missouri Valley

complete the following procedure, which has parameters `TeamList`, `NickList`, `Conference`, and `Team`. The procedure is to write to the screen the values from `NickList` and `Conference` that match the values in `Team` where `StringList = ARRAY [1 .. MaxIndex] OF String30`.

```
PROCEDURE FindMatch (ListLen : Index ;
                     VAR TeamList, NickList,
                         Conference : StringList ;
                     Team : String30) ;

  VAR Ndex : Index ;

  BEGIN
    NDex := 1 ;
    WHILE (TeamList [NDex] < > Team) AND (NDex <= ListLen) DO
      NDex := NDex + 1 ;
    IF TeamList [NDex] < > Team
      THEN WRITELN ('Sorry, ' Team ' not found in list.')
      ELSE __________
  END ;
```

10a. Write a procedure `InsertTeam` with the same parameters as `FindMatch` in problem 9 and with the added parameters `Nick` and `Confer` of type `String30`. The procedure is to insert the value in `Team` in its alphabetically correct position in `TeamList`. Also, `Nick` and `Confer` are to be added to the lists `NickList` and `Conference` in their corresponding positions. The call

```
InsertTeam (ListLen, TeamList, NickList, Conference, Team, Nick, Confer)
```

where `Team` contains `Missouri`, `Nick` contains `Tigers`, and `Confer` contains `Big Eight` should insert these values at position 6 in the lists presented in problem 9. The other values in the lists should be moved down the list.

b. Write a procedure to write to the screen all the teams in `TeamList` that have the value in `Confer` in `Conference`. That is, if the value in `Confer` is `Western Athletic` and the lists are the ones in problem 9, then the output should be as shown.

Sample Execution

```
Teams from Western Athletic are:
Air Force, New Mexico
```

11. The TEXT file named `StateDr.TXT` contains 50 lines. Each line is similar to the following:

    `Alabama*⬜⬜⬜2330`

```
The states ordered by number
of licensed drivers:
 1. Alaska        343000
 2. Vermont       356000
              ⋮
50. California  16656000
```

The states are in alphabetical order. The number represents the number of licensed drivers (in thousands), and the ⬜ represents a blank space. Write a Pascal program to
   a. fill an array with the states.
   b. fill an array with the numbers.
   c. alter the lists such that the number list is ordered from smallest to largest (use the selection sort).
   d. output the data to the screen ordered from smallest to largest by number of drivers.

12. A researcher has a list of the colleges and universities in the United States. Additionally, there are lists of number of students, number of instructors, and year founded. Write a Pascal program that would allow the researcher to enter the data from the keyboard to fill the lists. The data is to be saved in a TEXT file. (Only the colleges with more than 15,000 students are listed, with the largest being Ohio State University, Columbus, 53,757. Allow for 120 entries.) Each line of the TEXT file should be as follows:

    ⋮

    ```
    Ohio State University Columbus*    53757*03262*1870
    Oklahoma State University*         22823*01921*1890
    ```

    ⋮

13. Write a Pascal program that will allow the researcher in problem 12 to see the school names from
   a. smallest to largest with respect to number of students.
   b. smallest to largest with respect to number of instructors.
   c. oldest to newest.

14. `FileA` and `FileB` are TEXT files on a diskette. Each contains a list of 20 names in alphabetical order. Write a Pascal program to *merge* the two files into a TEXT file, `FileC`. `FileC` should consist of the names in `FileA` and `FileB` in alphabetical order. Use the following design:

    Design: Read names in FileA into ListA
             Read names in FileB into ListB
             CtA := 1
             CtB := 1
             CtC := 1
             WHILE CtA <= 20 AND CtB <= 20 DO
                 IF ListA [CtA] <= ListB [CtB]
                    THEN ListC [CtC] := ListA [CtA]
                             CtA := CtA + 1
                    ELSE ListC [CtC] := ListB [CtB]
                             CtB := CtB + 1
                 CtC := CtC + 1
             Write names in ListC to FileC
             Close Files

```
Argentina, Buenos Aires*  23||
Argentina, Mendoza*       14||
Canada, Edmonton*         35||
    ⋅                      ⋅
    ⋅                      ⋅
    ⋅                      ⋅
Israel, Haifa*            15||
    ⋅                      ⋅
    ⋅                      ⋅
    ⋅                      ⋅
Venezuela, Caracas*       38||
  < end-of-file marker >
```

15. The company SpanGlobe has outlets in several different countries. The company has a TEXT file named `SpanGlob.TXT` with lines similar to the one shown in the margin. Each line is made up of a country, city, and number of employees (followed by an end-of-line marker ||). Write a Pascal program to fill the arrays `CountryList` and `Employees`. A component of `CountryList` is a country (like Argentina). The corre-

sponding component for `Employees` is the total number of employees in the country (37 for Argentina). The program is to write to the screen the lists ordered by number of employees per country from largest to smallest.

CHAPTER TEST

1. Which of the following is *not* a data structure?
   a. `ARRAY [1 .. 30] OF INTEGER`   **c.** `REAL`
   b. `SET OF CHAR`   **d.** `STRING [40]`

2. For `LetterList = ARRAY ['a' .. 'e'] OF INTEGER,`
   a. the component type is _____.
   b. the index type is a subrange of the type _____.

3. Which of the following cannot be a component type for an array?
   a. `REAL`   **b.** `0 .. 100`   **c.** `TEXT`   **d.** `CHAR`   **e.** `STRING [5]`

4. The binary search
   a. is used to order the values in a list.
   b. can only be used to find a value in an ordered list.
   c. cannot be used on an array where the component type is STRING.
   d. can be used to find a value in any list of REAL values.

5. A major feature of arrays is that
   a. the values in an array must be accessed sequentially.
   b. the values in an array can be accessed randomly.
   c. the values in an array can be TEXT files.
   d. the values in an array must be of type INTEGER.

6. One method of ordering a list of values is to use the _____ sort.

7. Parallel arrays
   a. are arrays that have the same component type.
   b. are arrays used in geometry.
   c. are arrays that are related in some sense.
   d. must have component type REAL.

Problem 8 refers to the following program sections:

```
TYPE String6 = STRING [6] ;
     LetterList = ARRAY ['A' .. 'F'] OF 1 .. 12 ;

VAR Title : LetterList ;
    Place : ARRAY [1 .. 6] OF String6 ;
```

8. Insert *Valid* for a valid Pascal instruction and *Invalid* for an invalid Pascal instruction.
   _____ **a.** `Title [2] := 'S'`   _____ **d.** `Place [1] := Title`
   _____ **b.** `Title ['B'] := 5`   _____ **e.** `Place [1] := 'Utah'`
   _____ **c.** `WRITE (Title ['C'] : 3)`   _____ **f.** `Place [5] := 'El Paso'`

9. For `NumList` (a variable of type `ARRAY [1 .. 6] OF 5 .. 12`) and `Count` (a variable of type INTEGER), write a FOR-DO instruction to assign a value to `NumList`.

10. Write a Pascal function `Location`. The function has value parameter `List` of type `Numbers` where `Numbers = ARRAY [1 .. 80] OF INTEGER`. The function is to return the numbers of values in `List` less than zero.

11. Write a Pascal procedure `Reverse`. The procedure has value parameters `InList` of type `CharList` and `Last` of type `Index`, where `Index` is declared in the program TYPE section as `1 .. 50` and `CharList` has the declared type `ARRAY [ 1 .. 50 ] OF CHAR`. `Last` contains the index of the last nonblank character in the ARRAY value in `InList`. The procedure `Reverse` has the variable parameter `OutList` of type `CharList`. The procedure `Reverse` is to return to the calling execution block the values sent in `InList` with its nonblank components reversed. For example, if the value sent is as follows,

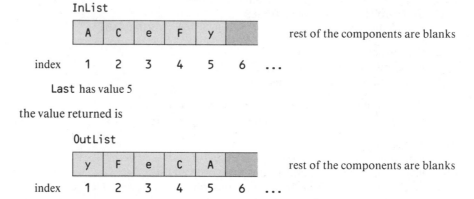

`Last` has value 5

the value returned is

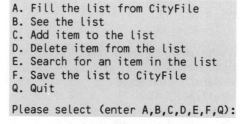

Programming Projects

Project 6-1. Write a Pascal program that allows the user to select from the following menu.

```
A. Fill the list from CityFile
B. See the list
C. Add item to the list
D. Delete item from the list
E. Search for an item in the list
F. Save the list to CityFile
Q. Quit

Please select (enter A,B,C,D,E,F,Q):
```

```
CityFile.TXT
New Iberia||
Davenport||
     .
     .
     .
San Diego||
< end-of-file marker >
```

The TEXT file `CityFile.TXT` has lines similar to the ones shown.

The city names are not ordered. Your program should sort the names as they are read into the list. The program should use the binary search to search for an item in the list. You are to turn in a copy of your design and its refinements and a copy of your program. Also turn in a hard copy of the following.

a. The initial list read in from `CityFile.TXT`.
b. The initial list after four values are inserted.
c. The list after two values are deleted.

Project 6-2. Write a Pascal program to simulate a bank with three tellers. Customers arrive at the bank in groups of zero, one, two, three, or four every tick (a tick is one cycle through the main loop). As the group of customers arrive, they distribute themselves to the shortest lines (no teller is favored). A teller waits on a customer in either one or two ticks. Once a customer enters a line, the customer remains (no switching lines). The program should start by allowing the user to enter the probability of each type of group arriving. That is, the program should start with the following:

Sample Execution

```
This is a simulation of a bank with three tellers.
Customers can arrive in groups of 0, 1, 2, 3, or 4.
Enter probability (as a percent) of a group of 4: 5
Enter probability (as a percent) of a group of 3: 20
Enter probability (as a percent) of a group of 2: 20
Enter probability (as a percent) of a group of 1: 30
Probability of a group of 0 is 25%.

Press RETURN key to see simulation-
```

After the user enters this information, the screen clears to present the simulation. A possible screen display follows:

Sample Execution

```
Teller A  Teller B  Teller C
   X         X         X
   X         X
             X

Door       XXXX
Group of 4 arrives.
Press RETURN key for next tick. Enter Q to quit.
```

When the user presses the RETURN key, the customers being served are removed (if service is finished). The customers at the door enter the lines. A new group appears. The program is to execute until the user enters **Q** to quit or a line is longer than ten customers.

Sample Execution

```
Teller A   Teller B   Teller C
   x          x          x
   x          x          x
   x          x

Door         x
Group of 1 arrives.
Press RETURN for next tick. Enter Q to quit.
```

Turn in a copy of your design and its refinement. Turn in a structured diagram for the design. Turn in a copy of your program.

For extra credit, expand (alter) your program to allow the following.
a. The user can select continuous or step execution (as illustrated here).
b. The user can enter the range of ticks for each teller.
c. The customers can switch lines.

Chapter Seven

Tables

Introduction

In this chapter, we will continue to work with the ARRAY data structure. The data structure will be expanded to two-dimensional arrays. A model for this type of array is a table. Additionally, some applications that use processing of table values will be presented. Included in these applications is the idea of a spreadsheet. At the end of this chapter, you will be able to write a Pascal program that uses the table data structure.

```
PROGRAM Chapter7 ;

CONST MaxRow = 6 ;
      MaxCol = 4 ;

TYPE WholeNum = 0 .. 100 ;
     RowIndex = 1 .. MaxRow ;
     ColIndex = 1 .. MaxCol ;
     TableType = ARRAY [1 .. MaxRow,1 .. MaxCol] OF
                                    WholeNum ;   {page 388}

VAR Sum, TheNum : INTEGER ;
    ATable : TableType ;                         {page 388}
    Row : RowIndex ;
    Col : ColIndex ;

PROCEDURE SumRow (TheTable : TableType ;         {page 393}
                  NumCol : ColIndex ; WhichRow : RowIndex ;
                  VAR TheSum : INTEGER) ;

  BEGIN
    {Instructions to sum row of table}          {page 404}
  END ;

PROCEDURE SumCol (TheTable : TableType ;
                  NumRow : RowIndex ; WhichCol : ColIndex ;
                  VAR TheSum : INTEGER) ;

  BEGIN
    {Instructions to sum column of table}       {page 404}
  END ;

BEGIN             {main program}
  FOR Row := 1 TO MaxRow DO                      {page 391}
    FOR Col := 1 TO MaxCol DO
      ATable [Row,Col] := RANDOM (99) + 1        {page 391}
  WRITE ('Sum Row or Column? (R/C): ') ;
  READLN (Ans) ;
  WRITE ('Which one? ') ;
  READLN (TheNum) ;
  IF Ans IN ['R','r']
    THEN SumRow (ATable, MaxCol, TheNum, Sum)
    ELSE SumCol (ATable, MaxRow, TheNum, Sum) ;
  WRITELN ('The sum is: ', Sum)
END .             {main program}
```

Two-Dimensional Arrays

In this section, the data structure ARRAY OF will be expanded to include **two-dimensional arrays.** This data structure is often referred to as a table. You will learn how to access the values in the cells of a two-dimensional array (table). Also, you will see more examples of the use of the top-down approach to problem solving.

7–1.1 Review of Lists

In the last chapter, you were introduced to the data structure ARRAY OF. The examples you saw of this data structure were lists (one-dimensional arrays). That is, each value of the data type was a list of components and each component was indexed. For example,

```
TYPE NumList = ARRAY [1 .. 9] OF INTEGER ;

VAR TempChange : NumList
```

declares `TempChange` a variable and states its type as `NumList`, a one-dimensional array. A value that the variable `TempChange` will hold is a list of integers. Each integer in the list will be indexed from 1 to 9. Such a value might be

index	1	2	3	4	5	6	7	8	9
TempChange	15	-2	5	-7	8	0	3	13	4

To access one of the components of a value in the variable `TempChange`, the index (subscript) is used. For example,

```
ThisHour := TempChange [3]
```

assigns to the variable `ThisHour` the value in the list that is indexed by **3** (the value **5**, in the example just given). Of course, the variable `ThisHour` must be of a compatible type (REAL, INTEGER or an appropriate subrange).

7–1.2 Introduction to Tables

Suppose the programmer desired to store several lists like `TempChange`; for example, a week (Monday to Friday) of temperature changes. The data structure ARRAY OF can be expanded to two-dimensional arrays. Consider the following TYPE and VAR sections:

```
                                                    rows
TYPE NumTable = ARRAY [1 .. 5, 1 .. 9] OF INTEGER ;

VAR WeekTable : NumTable                              columns
```

The data type `NumTable` has been defined as a two-dimensional array (table). The table will have five rows and nine columns. In each cell of the table, a value of type INTEGER will be stored. The variable `WeekTable` has been declared a variable and its type stated as `NumTable`. A typical value in `WeekTable` might be as shown in Figure

7–1. A list of values running vertically down the table is called a **column of the table**. A list of values running horizontally across the table is called a **row of the table**. To access a component of this value, a *pair of indices* are used. For example, if the value in WeekTable is as shown in Figure 7–1,

    Tuesday6 := WeekTable [2,6]

assigns to the variable Tuesday6 (of type INTEGER) the value 9. This value was found by going to row 2 then across to column 6.

Column

	1	2	3	4	5	6	7	8	9
1	15	−2	5	−7	8	0	3	13	4
2	6	2	−9	1	3	9	13	0	7
3	12	6	7	5	−2	11	3	1	3
4	9	5	−1	8	12	5	1	0	12
5	8	7	2	1	−1	11	8	3	1

Row

Figure 7–1

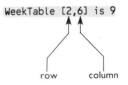

WeekTable [2,6] is 9

The general form used to define a type or to declare a variable to hold values that are tables (two-dimensional arrays) is

    ARRAY [_____ , _____] OF _____
              ↑   ↑   ↑
          row index   column   component type
            type   index type

The component type can be any standard data type (INTEGER, CHAR, REAL, BOOLEAN) or user-defined type. The data type TEXT *cannot* be used for the component type. The indices (subscripts) are subranges of built-in ordinal types (BOOLEAN, CHAR, INTEGER) or user-defined ordinal types.

From a readability standpoint, the definition of the data type NumTable could be improved by using an enumerated data type for the day index. Consider the following TYPE and VAR sections:

    TYPE Days = (Mon, Tue, Wed, Thu, Fri) ;
         NumTable = ARRAY [Mon .. Fri, 1 .. 9] OF INTEGER ;

    VAR WeekTable : NumTable

Now, a cell of WeekTable would be accessed as follows:

    WRITE (WeekTable [Tue,3])

This instruction would output to the screen the value stored in the second row and the third column of WeekTable, as shown in Figure 7–2.

Figure 7-2

WeekTable [Tue,3] is -9

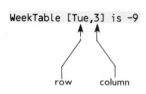

row   column

	Column								
	1	2	3	4	5	6	7	8	9
Mon	15	-2	5	-7	8	0	3	13	4
Tue	6	2	-9	1	3	9	13	0	7
Row Wed	12	6	7	5	-2	11	3	1	3
Thr	9	5	-1	8	12	5	1	0	12
Fri	8	7	2	1	-1	11	8	3	1

Often information encountered in everyday life is arranged as a table of values. Some examples follow.

1. A teacher's gradebook.

Student	Test1	Test2	Test3	Test4
1	78	82	87	94
2	89	96	82	88
⋮	⋮	⋮	⋮	⋮

3. Seats in an auditorium.

Seat [C,7]

Columns   Row

2. Seats on an airplane.

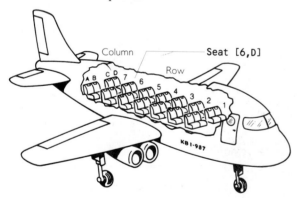

Column   Seat [6,D]
Row

KB1-987

4. Income tax tables.

		Classification		
	Single	Married Filing Jointly	Married Filing Separately	Head of a Household
22,000	3,574	2,744	4,386	3,307
22,050	3,587	2,755	4,402	3,319
Income 22,100	3,600	2,766	4,419	3,331
⋮	⋮	⋮	⋮	⋮

7-1.3 Filling a Table

To assign values to the cells of a two-dimensional table, a nested loop is commonly used. Consider the following TYPE and VAR sections.

```
TYPE Days = (Mon, Tue, Wed, Thu, Fri) ;
     NumTable = ARRAY [Mon .. Fri, 1 .. 9] OF INTEGER ;

VAR WeekTable : NumTable ;
    Row : Days ;
    Column : 1 .. 9 ;
```

The FOR-DO instruction

```
FOR Column := 1 TO 9 DO
  BEGIN
    WRITE ('Enter temperature change for hour ', Column, ' : ') ;
    READLN (WeekTable [Mon,Column])
  END
```

will allow the user to assign values to the first row of `WeekTable`. To assign values to each cell of the table `WeekTable`, a nested FOR-DO instruction can be used. Consider the following nested FOR-DO instruction to assign a random value to each cell of `WeekTable`.

```
FOR Row := Mon TO Fri DO
  FOR Column := 1 TO 9 DO
    WeekTable [Row, Column] := RANDOM (20) - 5
```

The outer loop starts with the first row. The inner loop assigns a value to each cell in this row. Next, the outer loop moves to the second row. The inner loop assigns a value to each cell in this row. This process is continued until the cells of the last row are assigned a value.

COMMENT

Since tables can be loaded in row fashion or column fashion, the FOR-DO instructions could be altered to:

```
FOR Column := 1 TO 9 DO
  FOR Row := Mon TO Fri DO
```

7-1.4 *Accessing the Cells of a Table*

To **access a cell of the table** data structure, two indices must be used. As an example of accessing the cells of a table, consider the program `MaxValue` in Figure 7–3. This sample program starts by filling the cells of the table. Next, the cells are searched for the largest value. The variable `Largest` is initialized to the value `Table [1,1]`. The search is conducted by starting at the first row. The value in each cell of this row is compared with the value stored in the variable `Largest`. If the value in the cell is greater than the value in `Largest`, the value is assigned to `Largest`. Next, the search moves to the second row. This process continues until each cell of the table is accessed.

Figure 7–3

```
PROGRAM MaxValue ;

TYPE NumTable = ARRAY [1 .. 5 , 1 .. 9] OF INTEGER ;

VAR Largest : INTEGER ;
    Row : 1 .. 5 ;
    Col : 1 .. 9 ;
    Table : NumTable ;

BEGIN                                    {MaxValue}
  FOR Row := 1 TO 5 DO                    {Init rows of table}
    FOR Col := 1 TO 9 DO                  {Init columns for testing}
      Table [Row, Col] := Row * Col MOD 12 - 8 ;
  Largest := Table [1,1] ;               {Initialize Largest}
  FOR Row := 1 To 5 DO                    {Search for max value}
    FOR Col := 1 TO 9 DO
      IF Table [Row, Col] > Largest
        THEN Largest := Table [Row, Col] ;
  WRITELN ('Largest value is: ', Largest)
END .                                     {MaxValue}
```

Sample Execution

```
Largest value is: 3
```

PROGRAMMING POINT

When working with two-dimensional arrays (tables), typically a nested FOR-DO loop is used to access the cells of the table.

DO IT NOW

Suppose `TempByDay` is of type `NumTable` where

NumTable = ARRAY [1 .. 5, 1 .. 9] OF INTEGER

and contains the value in Figure 7–4. Give the output of the following:

Figure 7–4

Column

Row	1	2	3	4	5	6	7	8	9
1	15	-2	5	-7	8	0	3	13	4
2	6	2	-9	1	3	9	13	0	7
3	12	6	7	5	-2	11	3	1	3
4	9	5	-1	8	12	5	1	0	12
5	8	7	2	1	-1	11	8	3	1

1. WRITE (TempByDay [4, 6])

2. WRITE (TempByDay [5, 3])

3. Count := 0 ;
    FOR Ct := 1 TO 9 DO
      IF Table [4, Ct] <= 0
        THEN Count := Count + 1 ;
    WRITELN (Count)

4. Min := MAXINT ;
    FOR Ct := 1 TO 5 DO
      IF Table [Ct, 3] <= Min
        THEN Min := Table [Ct, 3] ;
    WRITELN (Min)

7-1.5 Use of Tables

DO IT NOW ANSWERS

1. 5   2. 2   3. 2   4. –9

Your earliest encounter with numerical tables was probably with a multiplication table. Since that time, you have encountered (or soon will encounter) other numerical tables. Some of these tables are as follows: trigonometric tables for the sine, cosine, and tangent of a list of angle measurements; logarithmic tables for finding the logarithm of a number; binomial tables for finding the probability of an event; and the normal probability table in statistics. In chemistry, there is the periodic table of chemical elements. In finance, there are tables for compound interest, annuities, and installment loans.

As an example of the use of tables and to become familiar with programs that involve tables, consider the following example.

EXAMPLE

A table named *Square* is established as follows. The column indices represent the ones digit in a number. The row indices represent the tens digit in a number. Thus, to find the square of 32, the tens digit is 3 so you move to row 3; the ones digit is 2 so you move to column 2. The value there is 1024. Thus, the square of 32 is 1024.

Square Table

Column

Row	0	1	2	...	9
0	0000	0001	0004	. . .	0081
1	0100	0121	0144	. . .	0361
2	0400	0441	0484	. . .	0841
3	0900	0961	1024	. . .	1521
4	1600	1681	1764	. . .	2401
5	2500	2601	2704	. . .	3481
6	3600	3721	3844	. . .	4761
7	4900	5041	5184	. . .	6241
8	6400	6561	6724	. . .	7921
9	8100	8281	8464	. . .	9801

Write a Pascal program that allows the user to enter a value from 0 to 99. The value is looked up in the table and its square is reported.

Sample Execution

```
Enter whole number (0 .. 99): 71
The square of 71 is: 5041
Press RETURN key to continue, enter Q to quit-
```

SOLUTION

Design: REPEAT
        Get InValue
        Look-up table value
        ReportResults
        WRITE ('Press RETURN to continue, enter Q to quit ')
        READLN (Ans)
    UNTIL Ans = 'Q'

Refinement of: *Look-up Table value*
        Row : = InValue DIV 10
        Col : = InValue MOD 10
        Results : = Table [Row, Col]

COMMENT

The built-in function SQR could perform the example's task with ease. However, this example of *table use* is designed to give you an idea of how to use a table. Also, the use of look-up tables, rather than the use of a formula, is a common practice in computing.

This design yields the Pascal program in Figure 7–5.

```
PROGRAM SquareTable ;

TYPE WholeNum = 0 .. 10000 ;
     Index = 0 .. 10 ;
     TableType = ARRAY [0 .. 9, 0 .. 9] OF WholeNum ;

VAR Table : TableType ;
    Row, Column : Index ;
    Ans : CHAR ;
    InValue : WholeNum ;

PROCEDURE FindSquare (Row, Col : Index ; VAR Table : TableType ;
                      Value : WholeNum) ;

  BEGIN                                          {FindSquare}
    Row := Value DIV 10 ;
    Col := Value MOD 10 ;
    WRITELN ('The square of ', Value, ' is: ', Table [Row, Col])
  END ;                                          {FindSquare}

BEGIN                                            {main program}
  FOR Row := 0 TO 9 DO                           {Fill Square Table}
    FOR Column := 0 TO 9 DO
      Table [Row, Column] := SQR (10 * Row + Column) ;
  REPEAT
    WRITE ('Enter whole number (0 .. 99): ') ;
    READLN (InValue) ;
    FindSquare (Row, Column, Table, InValue) ;
    WRITE ('Press RETURN to continue, enter Q to quit- ') ;
    READLN (Ans)
  UNTIL Ans IN ['Q', 'q']
END .                                            {main program}
```

Figure 7–5

COMMENT

The index type can be any ordinal data type. Thus, rows and columns can be indexed with negative integer values.

DO IT NOW

1. For the program `SquareTable` in Figure 7–5, if the user enters 89 for the value, give the output.
2. For the program `SquareTable`, why would the programmer make `Table` a variable parameter?

7-1.6 Games

Another use for tables involves games. Not only are games a part of life's experiences, they often provide a model for real-world situations. Consider the game described by the table in Figure 7–6.

Figure 7–6

Row Player	Column Player: A	B	C	D
A	2	−1	4	−3
B	1	3	−1	5
C	−3	1	−2	6
D	−5	6	1	−1
E	3	−8	2	−2

The Row Player selects a letter, A, B, C, D, or E. The Column Player selects a letter, A, B, C, or D. The table gives the winnings for the Row Player. A negative value indicates that the Row Player loses (Column Player wins). For example, suppose the Row Player selects D and the Column Player selects A. The Row Player loses \$5; the Column Player wins \$5.

EXAMPLE

Write a Pascal program that simulates the game just presented with the computer as the Column Player.

SOLUTION

Design:

```
PresentPayOffTable
Get User's Name
REPEAT
   Get Player's Play
   Get Computer's Play
   PayOff := Table [ Row,Column ]
   GiveResults
   WRITE ('Press RETURN to continue, enter Q to quit- ') ;
   READLN (Ans)
UNTIL Ans = 'Q'
```

DO IT NOW ANSWERS

1. `The square is: 7921.`
2. Although `Table` should be a value parameter, using a variable parameter allows the procedure to use the memory area used by the main execution section. This approach conserves memory.

The design just given yields the Pascal program in Figure 7–7.

Figure 7–7

```
PROGRAM GameTable ;

TYPE TableType = ARRAY ['A' .. 'E', 'A' .. 'D'] OF INTEGER ;
     String20 = STRING [20] ;

VAR Table : TableType ;
    Ans : CHAR ;
    Name : String20 ;
    Row , Column : 'A' .. 'E' ;
    PayOff , Total : INTEGER ;

PROCEDURE WriteTable (Table : TableType) ;

  VAR Row , Col : 'A' .. 'E' ;
```

```
    BEGIN                                            {WriteTable}
      WRITELN ('Column Player' : 19) ;
      WRITE (' ') ;                                  {a blank}
      FOR Col := 'A' TO 'D' DO
        WRITE (Col : 6) ;
      WRITELN ;
      FOR Row := 'A' TO 'E' DO
        BEGIN                                        {Outer loop}
          WRITE (Row) ;
          FOR Col := 'A' TO 'D' DO                   {Inner loop}
            WRITE (Table [Row , Column] : 6) ;
          WRITELN
        END                                          {Outer loop}
    END ;                                            {WriteTable}

FUNCTION DoPlayer (Name : String20) : CHAR ;

  VAR Ans : CHAR ;

  BEGIN                                              {DoPlayer}
    GOTOXY (1, 14) ;
    CLREOL ;                                         {Clear line}
    WRITE (Name , ' enter choice: ') ;
    READLN (Ans);
    DoPlayer := Ans
  END ;                                              {DoPlayer}

FUNCTION DoComputer : CHAR ;

  BEGIN                                              {DoComputer}
    GOTOXY (1, 15) ;
    WRITE ('I selected: ') ;
    DoComputer := CHR (RANDOM (4) + ORD ('A')) {computer picks column number}
  END ;                                              {DoComputer}

PROCEDURE GiveResults (Name : String20 ; PayOff , Total : INTEGER) ;

  BEGIN                                              {GiveResults}
    GOTOXY (1, 17) ;
    CLREOL ;                                         {Clear line}
    IF PayOff > 0
      THEN WRITELN (Name , ' you win $' , PayOff)
      ELSE WRITELN ('I win $', - PayOff) ;
    GOTOXY (1, 19) ;
    CLREOL ;                                         {Clear line}
    IF Total > 0
      THEN WRITELN ('You have won $' , Total)
      ELSE WRITELN ('You have lost $' , Total)
  END ;                                              {GiveResults}

BEGIN                                                {main program}
  FOR Row := 'A' TO 'E' DO
    FOR Column := 'A' TO 'D' DO
      BEGIN                                          {Fill game table}
        WRITE ('Enter row ' , Row, ' column ' , Column,' : ') ;
        READLN (Table [Row,Column])
      END ;                                          {Fill game table}
```

Figure 7–7

Continued

Sample Execution

```
     Column Player
        A    B    C    D
  A     2   -1    4   -3
  B     1    3   -1    5
  C    -3    1   -2    6
  D    -5    6    1   -1
  E     3   -8    2   -2
```

Sample Execution

```
     Column Player
        A    B    C    D
  A     2   -1    4   -3
  B     1    3   -1    5
  C    -3    1   -2    6
  D    -5    6    1   -1
  E     3   -8    2   -2

Shirley enter choice: B
I selected: D

I win $1
You have won $7
```

Figure 7–7

Continued

```
Total := Ø ;
WRITE ('Row player please enter name: ') ;
READLN (Name) ;
CLRSCR ;                                        {clear screen}
WriteTable (Table) ;
REPEAT
  Row := DoPlayer (Name) ;
  Column := DoComputer ;
  WRITELN (Column) ;
  PayOff := Table [Row,Column] ;
  Total := Total + PayOff ;
  GiveResults (Name , PayOff , Total) ;
  GOTOXY (1, 23) ;
  WRITE ('Press RETURN to continue, enter Q to quit: ') ;
  READLN (Ans)
UNTIL Ans = 'Q'
END .                                           {main program}
```

Figure 7–8

Action	Weather		
	Heavy Rain	Average Rain	Light Rain
Corn	50	20	− 10
Wheat	− 30	60	10
Cotton	− 20	30	40
Peanuts	60	− 20	− 30

The idea of the row-column game just demonstrated appears in some real-life problems. Consider the table in Figure 7–8.

Here, the rows represent the actions a farmer can take. The columns represent the different amounts of rainfall that can occur. The components of the table represent the farmer's winnings (or losses). Suppose the farmer plants corn and the weather is heavy rain; then the farmer will win $50. However, if the weather is light rain, the farmer will lose $10. Could a computer program be written to solve the problem of finding the farmer's optional action given the probabilities of the different weather conditions?

COMMENT

If the farmer had 100 acres, the best plan would be to plant some combination of the four crops (perhaps 30 acres of corn, 20 acres of wheat, 40 acres of cotton, and 10 acres of peanuts). The proper combination to maximize the farmer's winnings would depend on the probability of each of the rainfall amounts. The actual solution to this problem is covered in an area of mathematics known as decision theory. In the future you may study decision theory.

7-1.7 Parallel Arrays and Tables

Up to this point, you have seen how to access the cells of a two-dimensional array (a table). Now it is time to look at the relationship between parallel arrays (discussed in Chapter 6) and tables. Parallel arrays are lists that are related in some sense. Consider the following parallel arrays, representing three different stores. The index of the arrays represents a part number and the cells of each array provide the current inventory level of a given part.

Bartow store		Dublin store		Paoli store	
index	inventory	index	inventory	index	inventory
1001	34	1001	12	1001	38
1002	Ø	1002	Ø	1002	Ø
⋮	⋮	⋮	⋮	⋮	⋮

These arrays can be replaced with a table data structure. That is, rather than using the following (where MaxRow represents the number of different parts):

```
TYPE ListType = ARRAY OF [1 .. MaxRow] OF 0 .. MAXINT ;

VAR Store1 , Store2 , Store3 : ListType
```

the following could be used (where MaxCol represents the number of stores):

```
TYPE TableType = ARRAY OF [1 .. MaxRow, 1 .. MaxCol] OF 0 .. MAXINT ;

VAR Table : TableType
```

Here, the row index represents the part numbers and the column index represents the stores. The advantage of the table data type in this situation is in processing the values in the data structures. Consider the problem of finding the total number of a given part for all the stores. In the parallel arrays situation, the design to solve this problem would be as follows:

```
Find proper row index                 {for the part number}
Total : = Store1 [Index] + Store2 [Index] + Store3 [Index]
```

This approach is not too bad as long as the number of stores is low. However, suppose that rather than three stores there were ten stores. In the TABLE data structure situation, the design to solve the problem would be as follows:

```
Find proper row index                 {for the part number}
Total : = 0
FOR Col : = 1 TO MaxCol DO             {sum across the stores}
    Total : = Total + Table [Row, Col]
```

The table data structure provides an advantage over parallel arrays for situations in which the values across the parallel arrays must be processed. In the next section, you will study processing tables in detail. For now, it is only important to know that the different data structures have different properties and purposes. The data structure chosen by the programmer depends on the problem to be solved. The choice of data structure affects the design of the solution to the problem.

Vocabulary

	Page

Accessing a cell of a table   The act of identifying a cell in a table. This is accomplished by specifying the row and column of the cell.   [391]

Example:

```
Value := Table [4, 5]
```

accesses the cell located at row 4 and column 5.

Column of a table   A list of values that runs vertically down a table. The second subrange given in the definition of a table is for the number of columns in the table.   [389]

Row of a table   A list of values that runs horizontally across a table. The first subrange given in the definition of a table is for the number of rows in the table.   [389]

Two-dimensional arrays   A data structure that consists of values in the form of a table. Each value of the table is referenced by a row index and a column index. A typical example is as follows: [388]

```
VAR NumTable : ARRAY [1 .. 5 , 1 .. 7] OF CHAR
```

In this example, the components of the table are of type CHAR. The rows of the table are indexed from 1 to 5. The columns of the table are indexed from 1 to 7.

Glad You Asked

Q Can any two parallel lists be replaced by a table?

A No. Suppose you had the data structures

```
ListA = ARRAY [1 .. 7] OF INTEGER
```

and

```
ListB = ARRAY [1 .. 7] OF INTEGER
```

An alternate data structure that could be employed is

```
Table = ARRAY [1 .. 7, 1 .. 2] OF INTEGER
```

However, suppose you had the data structures

```
ListA = ARRAY [1 .. 7] OF INTEGER
```

and

```
ListB = ARRAY [1 .. 7] OF CHAR
```

A table cannot be used to store the information that is in the two lists. This is because the components of a table must be of the same data type. In Chapter 8, you will study a data structure (known as a list of records) that is an alternative to the last two lists.

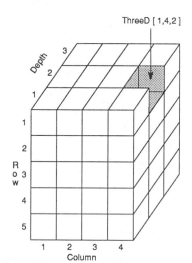

ThreeD [1,4,2]

Q Can a data type be a three-dimensional array? If so, how would it be defined?

A Yes. In fact, the number of dimensions is limited only by memory requirements. To define such a data type (structure), the form developed for lists and tables is continued:

```
VAR ThreeD : ARRAY [1 .. 5, 1 .. 4, 1 .. 3] OF INTEGER
```

To access a component of this structure, you would use an index for each dimension. For example, `WRITE (ThreeD [1, 4, 2])` would write to the screen a component of the value in the variable `ThreeD`. The component output would be the component in the first row, fourth column, with a depth of 2.

Q Can a table data structure be searched using a binary search?

A To use the binary search routine, the data must be ordered in some sense. Seldom is a table value ordered. To search a table value, usually a sequential search is used either by row or by column. That is, row 1 is searched, row 2 is searched, and so forth. However, if the values of a table are ordered, as was the case in the program `SquareTable`, a binary search could be conducted on a column of the table or a row of the table.

Q Is a table value ever sorted?

A In constructing a table, the rows and columns often provide the ordering for the table value. Usually, searching and sorting is limited to one-dimensional arrays. However, there are situations in which the value in a table is sorted.

Q What is an electronic spreadsheet? Is it just a table?

A An electronic spreadsheet is essentially a table. However, the operations available to the user are often quite sophisticated. The user can label the column headers of the table and can define the values to be placed in the columns by entering a formula for the values. The table is updated when the user alters values in the table. In section 7–2.3, you will see a simplified example of this type of program.

Q Do the subranges used to index a table have to start at 1?

A No. The subranges are from any ordinal type. Thus, if you had

```
TYPE Colors = (Red , Blue , Orange , Yellow , Green , Purple) ;
     Days = (rainy , cloudy , snowy , sunny , windy)
```

you could declare `Table` as follows:

```
VAR Table : ARRAY [Red .. Yellow , rainy .. windy] OF CHAR
```

You could then make an assignment to a cell of `Table` like this:

```
Table [Orange, snowy] := 'E'.
```

Q What does the notation `Table [2][3]` mean?

A An alternative way to define a table is

```
Table : ARRAY [1 .. 5] OF ARRAY [1 .. 7] OF INTEGER.
```

This is the same as

```
Table : ARRAY [1 .. 5, 1 .. 7] OF INTEGER.
```

Likewise, the notation `Table [2][3]` is an alternative to `Table [2,3]`.

Section 7–1 Exercises

Given the following:

```
TYPE WholeNum = 0 .. 300 ;
     NumTable = ARRAY [0 .. 9, 0 .. 7] OF WholeNum ;

VAR NumA, NumB : 0 .. 10 ;
    NumC, Count : WholeNum ;
    TimesTable : NumTable ;
```

1. The number of columns in a value in the variable `TimesTable` is _____.
2. The component type of a value in the variable `TimesTable` is _____.
3. The number of cells in a value in the variable `TimesTable` is _____.
4. Given the execution of the instruction:

```
FOR NumA := 0 TO 9 DO
   FOR NumB := 0 TO 7 DO
      TimesTable [NumA, NumB] := NumA * NumB
```

what would be the output of the following?
   a. `WRITE (TimesTable [3, 5])`
   b. `WRITE (TimesTable [5, 3])`
   c. `NumC := 0 ;`
```
   FOR NumA := 0 TO 7 DO
     NumC := TimesTable [3, NumA] ;
   WRITE (NumC)
```
   d. `NumC := 43 ;`
```
   Count := 0 ;
   NumA := 0 ;
   WHILE NumA <= 9 DO
     BEGIN
       IF NumC >= TimesTable [NumA, 7]
         THEN Count := Count + 1 ;
       NumA := SUCC (NumA)
     END ;
   WRITE (Count)
```

5a. Define `CharTable` to be a two-dimensional array with 6 rows, 8 columns, and component type CHAR.
   b. Write a nested FOR-DO instruction to fill `CharTable` with randomly selected characters.
   c. Write a nested FOR-DO instruction to write to the screen the values stored in the cells of `CharTable`.

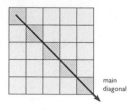

main
diagonal

Salespersons
  1 2 3 4

1				
2				
Items 3				
4				
5				

6. Given the variable `NumTable` of type

> `ARRAY [1 .. 5, 1 .. 5] OF WholeNum`   (where `WholeNum = 0 .. 300`)

write a nested FOR-DO instruction to find the maximum value of the main diagonal components. The main diagonal components are in the cells where the row index equals the column index.

7. Boot up Pascal; set the workfile to the file `SqTable.PAS` from the `Source` diskette. Enter the editor. Expand the program to output the row and column location of where the square of the value entered was found.

8. Boot up Pascal; set the workfile to the file `GameTabl.PAS` from the `Source` diskette. Enter the editor. Alter the program to fill the cells of the table with random values from − 6 to 5 (inclusive). Also, after each play, the table should filled with a new collection of random values.

9. A company has five products (numbered 1 to 5) and four salespersons (numbered 1 to 4). Write a Pascal program to allow the user to enter the number of each product sold by each salesperson. The program should store the number entered in a 5 by 4 table.

10. A common use of a table is a mileage chart like the one following. Suppose the table value is on a diskette in a TEXT file. Each line of the TEXT file contains the values (separated by a space) for a row of the table. The name of the file is `DistData.TXT`. Write a Pascal program that

a. reads the values of the TEXT file `DistData.TXT` into a table.

b. allows the user to enter one of the six cities in response to the prompt `From:` and one of the five remaining cities in response to the prompt `To:`.

The output of the program will be the table entry for the distance.

Sample Execution

```
Please select from the following cities
(Atlanta, Boston, Chicago, Dallas, New York, Tulsa)
From: New York
To: Tulsa
Distance is 1344 miles.
```

From	To Atlanta	Boston	Chicago	Dallas	New York	Tulsa
Atlanta	---	1037	674	795	841	772
Boston	1037	---	963	1748	206	1537
Chicago	674	963	---	917	802	683
Dallas	795	1748	917	---	1552	257
New York	841	206	802	1552	---	1344
Tulsa	772	1537	683	257	1344	---

11. Using the distance chart in problem 10, write a Pascal program that allows for a sample execution like the following.

Sample Execution

```
Entry cities are Atlanta, Boston, Chicago, Dallas, New York, Tulsa.

Please enter start city: Tulsa
Enter next city on trip (Q to Quit): Atlanta
Enter next city on trip (Q to Quit): Dallas
Enter next city on trip (Q to Quit): Boston
Enter next city on trip (Q to Quit): Q
Total round trip distance is 4852 miles.
```

12. Suppose a diskette contains a TEXT file named `Periodic.TXT`. In the TEXT file there are 103 lines. On each line is a listing for a symbolic name of a chemical element and its name. For example (where || represents the end-of-line marker),

    `H Hydrogen||He Helium||Li Lithium||Be Beryllium||B Boron||...`

    would be lines 1 through 5 of the TEXT file. Write a Pascal program to read the values of the TEXT file into a table. Also, the program should allow the user to select from the menu:

    A. Find symbolic name
    B. Find element name
    Q. Quit

    Sample Execution

    ```
    Please select (enter A, B, or Q): A
    Enter element's name: Silver
    Symbolic name is: Ag
    Press RETURN to continue (enter Q to quit):
    ```

13. Write a Pascal program to simulate the two-player game described here. The computer should play the part of player two.

    Player one has three cards: a 3 of clubs, a 5 of clubs, and a 9 of hearts.
    Player two has three cards: a 2 of hearts, a 7 of hearts, and an 8 of clubs.
    Each player displays one of the three cards. If the cards are the same color, player one wins the sum of values in dollars. If they are not of the same color, player two wins the sum of the values in dollars.

    The program should keep up with total winnings and display the total after each play. The game should continue until a player has won $40.
    Note: Hearts are red and clubs are black.

14. Write a Pascal program to allow two users to play the game of tic-tac-toe. The program should follow a design similar to the following.

    Design: Get player's names
              Draw board
              PlayerX := PlayerO
              Repeat
                  Get player move from 1 .. 9
                  record move in 3 by 3 array
                  Display move on board
                  Switch players
              Until Winner or Draw

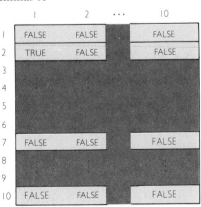

15. The XYZ Company wants a Pascal program that will (a) build `ExecList`, a list that contains the names of the ten executives of the company in alphabetical order; and (b) build `SubTable`, a 10 by 10 table showing which executive is subordinate to which executive. The value in this table is similar to

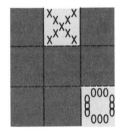

index	ExecList		1	2	...	10
1	Chou	1	FALSE	FALSE		FALSE
2	Gill	2	TRUE	FALSE		FALSE
3	Johns	3				
4	Kalin	4				
5	Lee	5				
6	McKee	6				
7	Rassbone	7	FALSE	FALSE		FALSE
8	Sanchez	8				
9	Wills	9				
10	Ying	10	FALSE	FALSE		FALSE

(continued)

The component at row 7, column 2 is the value TRUE. This indicates that executive 7 is subordinate to executive 2. Write a Pascal program to build the list and the table based on the organization shown.

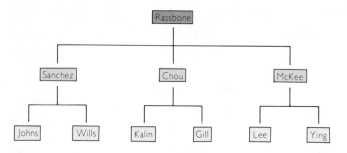

Must be a secret code

16. Expand your program in problem 15 to allow the user to enter the name of an executive. The program should then output a list of executives that are subordinate and a list of executives that are superiors.

17. The MR Ducks Company has five warehouses that are used to store four different items carried by the outlet stores of the company. Suppose the company has the inventory levels of the items in the warehouses in a 5 by 4 table similar to the following one. The numbers in the cells of the table represent the inventory level for the item. A zero indicates that the warehouse is out of the given item.

		Item		
Warehouse	1	2	3	4
Arcadia	23	67	12	64
Bartow	0	45	98	0
Bonifay	78	0	56	23
Naples	79	23	0	98
Ocala	13	45	32	7

Sample Execution

```
Enter item to check (1 .. 4) : 2
Warehouse(s) out of item: Bonifay
```

The value in CityList is a list of the warehouses. Write a Pascal procedure that has as value parameters a value of Table and a value of CityList. The procedure is to read a value for item number, then write to the screen the warehouses that are out of the item. Assume

```
CONST RowMax = 5 ;
      ColMax = 4 ;

TYPE TableType = ARRAY [1 .. RowMax,1 .. ColMax] OF 0 .. MAXINT ;
     ListType = ARRAY [1 .. RowMax] OF STRING [40] ;
```

18. The hexadecimal (base 16) numbering system uses 16 digits (0, 1, 2, 3, 4, 5, 6, 7, 8, 9, A, B, C, D, E, F). A table for converting a hexadecimal number to a decimal (base 10) number can be built using the data type

```
Hex = ARRAY [0 .. 15 , 0 .. 15] OF 0 .. 255
```

the variable HexTable : Hex

and the instruction

```
FOR Row := 0 TO 15 DO
  FOR Col := 0 TO 15 DO
    HexTable [Row, Col] := (16 * Row) + Col
```

Write a Pascal program that allows the user to enter a hexadecimal number from 0 to FF. (FF means (15*16) + 15.) The program is to write to the screen the decimal value for the input value.

Sample Execution

```
Please enter hexadecimal value (Ø .. FF): AB
The decimal name for AB is 171

Enter Q to quit, Press RETURN to continue-
```

19. Expand your program in problem 18 to allow the user to select the option of entering a decimal number. If this option is selected, the program should write to the screen the hexadecimal name for the number. Your program should use only the one table described in problem 18.

    Hint: Search the first column for the correct row. Search this row for the correct column.

20. Write a Pascal program that uses a table to aid in taking a survey. The survey is to classify each subject by age group (16–20, 21–25, 26–30, over 30). The subjects are to respond to the following yes/no questions:

    a. Do you invest in stocks?
    b. Do you have a savings account?
    c. Do you invest in bonds?
    d. Do you have a loan?

    The program should initialize the cells of the table to zero then increment the appropriate cell for each *yes* answer. The output should be the values stored in cells of the table.

Sample Execution

```
A. Hex to Decimal
B. Decimal to Hex
Q. Quit
Please select (A,B,Q) : B
Enter decimal name : 38
The hexadecimal name is 26.
```

Sample Execution

```
Please enter age: 19
Do you invest in stocks? (Y/N): Y
   .
   .
   .
{screen clears}
Age      Stocks    Savings    Bonds    Loan
16-2Ø      3         27         1       42
21-25     15         2Ø         5       68
   .        .          .         .       .
   .        .          .         .       .
```

Section 7-2

Processing Tables

In the last section, you were introduced to the data structure of tables (two-dimensional arrays). In this section, you will learn about processing a table value. You will learn how to manipulate the values in the rows and columns of a table.

7-2.1 Row and Column Processing

The major types of operations employed in processing a table value are

1. Accessing a value in a cell of the table.
2. Finding the sum of a column of the table.
3. Finding the sum of a row of the table.

Section 7-1 was mainly concerned with operation 1. To access a value in a cell of a table, the value is referenced by its row and its column. The other two operations will now be discussed. Operation 2, **column processing**, or finding the sum of a column, is illustrated in Figure 7-9.

Figure 7-9

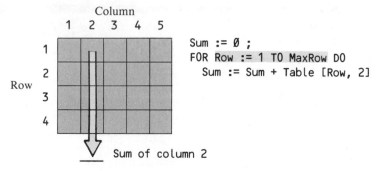

```
Sum := 0 ;
FOR Row := 1 TO MaxRow DO
   Sum := Sum + Table [Row, 2]
```

Operation 3, **row processing**, or finding the sum of a row, is illustrated in Figure 7-10.

Figure 7-10

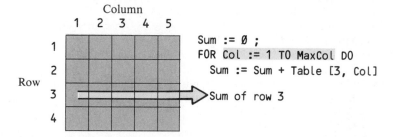

```
Sum := 0 ;
FOR Col := 1 TO MaxCol DO
   Sum := Sum + Table [3, Col]
```

As an example of processing a table value, consider the Pascal program in Figure 7-11 that computes and prints the average of each row in a table.

Figure 7-11

Sample Execution

```
Average of row 1 is -5.40
Average of row 2 is -6.00
Average of row 3 is -6.60
Average of row 4 is -7.20
Average of row 5 is -3.00
```

```
PROGRAM RowAverages ;

CONST RowMax = 5 ;
      ColMax = 9 ;

TYPE NumTable = ARRAY [1 .. RowMax , 1 .. ColMax] OF INTEGER ;

VAR Average : REAL ;
    Sum : INTEGER ;
    Row : 1 .. RowMax ;
    Col : 1 .. ColMax ;
    Table : NumTable ;

BEGIN                                       {RowAverages}
  FOR Row := 1 TO RowMax DO                 {Init cells of table}
    FOR Col := 1 TO ColMax DO               {for testing}
      Table [Row, Col] := Row * Col MOD 12 - 8 ;
  FOR Row := 1 To RowMax DO                 {find average of rows}
    BEGIN                                   {Outer FOR-DO loop}
      Sum := 0 ;
      FOR Col := 1 TO ColMax DO             {find sum of row}
        Sum := Sum + Table [Row, Col] ;
      Average := Sum / RowMax ;
      WRITELN ('Average of row ', row:1, ' is ' , Average:1:2)
    END                                     {Outer FOR-DO loop}
END .                                       {RowAverages}
```

DO IT NOW

Suppose `TempByDay` is of type `NumTable` where

    NumTable = ARRAY [1 .. 5, 1 .. 9] OF INTEGER

and contains the values in Figure 7–12.

Give the output of the following:

1. `WRITE (TempByDay [4, 6])`

2. `WRITE (TempByDay [5])`

3. `Total := Ø;`
`FOR Ct := 1 TO 9 DO`
`  Total := Total + TempByDay [4, Ct] ;`
`WRITE (Total)`

4. `Total := Ø ;`
`FOR Ct := 1 TO 5 DO`
`  Total := Total + TempByDay [Ct, 7] ;`
`WRITE (Total)`

Figure 7–12

Row	Column 1	2	3	4	5	6	7	8	9
1	15	-2	5	-7	8	Ø	3	13	4
2	6	2	-9	1	3	9	13	Ø	7
3	12	6	7	5	-2	11	3	1	3
4	9	5	-1	8	12	5	1	Ø	12
5	8	7	2	1	-1	11	8	3	1

7-2.2 *A Programming Example*

As a more sophisticated illustration of a Pascal program that processes a table, consider the following example.

EXAMPLE

The MR Ducks Company has five warehouses that are used to store four different items needed by their stores (see the following table).

Warehouse	Item 1	2	3	4
Arcadia	23	67	12	64
Bartow	Ø	45	98	Ø
Bonifay	78	Ø	56	23
Naples	79	23	Ø	98
Ocala	13	45	32	7

DO IT NOW ANSWERS

1. 5
2. Error. `TempByDay [5]` is a list of values and cannot be used with READ or WRITE.
3. 51
4. 28

The value in a cell of the table represents the inventory that the warehouse has in stock. A zero means the warehouse is out of the item. Write a Pascal program that allows the user to select from the menu shown.

    A. Find total inventory for an item
    B. Find warehouses out of an item
    C. Update inventory of a warehouse
    Q. Quit

Sample Execution

```
{after user enters values for the table}
A. Find total inventory for an item
B. Find warehouses out of an item
C. Update inventory of a warehouse
Q. Quit
Enter choice (A,B,C,Q) : A
Find total inventory for item (1..4) : 2
Inventory level is 180
{main menu reappears}
```

Sample Execution

```
{after user enters values for the table}
A. Find total inventory for an item
B. Find warehouses out of an item
C. Update inventory of a warehouse
Q. Quit
Enter choice (A,B,C,Q): B
Enter item to check (1..4): 2
Naples is out of item
Ocala is out of item
{main menu reappears}
```

SOLUTION

Design:
```
Fill CityList
Fill Table
REPEAT
    PresentMenu
    GetSelection
    CASE Select OF
        'A' : FindColumnSum
        'B' : SearchColumn
        'C' : UpdateTable
    END
UNTIL Select = 'Q'
```

Sample Execution

```
Enter warehouse #1 name: Arcadia
Enter warehouse #2 name: Barlow
Enter warehouse #3 name: Bonifay
Enter warehouse #4 name: ∎
```

Refinement of: *FillCityList*
```
FOR ROW := 1 TO RowMax DO
    WRITE ('Enter warehouse #',Row,' name: ')
    READLN (CityList [Row])
```

Refinement of: *FillTable*
```
FOR Row := 1 TO RowMax DO
    FOR Col := 1 TO ColMax DO
        WRITE ('For ' , CityList [Row])
        WRITE (' enter inventory level for item ')
        WRITE (Col , ' : ')
        READLN (Table [Row,Col])
```

Sample Execution

```
For Arcadia enter inventory for item 1: 23
For Arcadia enter inventory for item 2: 69
For Arcadia enter inventory for item 3: 13
For Arcadia enter inventory for item 4: 64
For Bartow enter inventory for item 1: 0
```

Refinement of: *FindColumnSum*
```
WRITE ('Find total inventory for item')
WRITE ('(1 ..' , ColMax, '): ')
READLN (Column)
Sum := 0
FOR Row := 1 TO RowMax DO
    Sum := Sum + Table [Row, Column]
WRITELN ('Inventory level is ' , Sum)
```

Sample Execution

```
Find total inventory for item (1..4): 5
Inventory level is 123
```

Refinement of: *SearchColumn*
```
WRITE ('Enter item to check')
WRITE (' (1 ..' , MaxCol, '): ')
```

```
            READLN (Column)
            FOR Row : = 1 TO RowMax DO
              IF Table [Row,Column] = 0
                 THEN WRITE (CityList [Row])
                      WRITELN (' is out of item.')
```

Refinement of: *UpdateTable*

```
            WRITELN ('Select warehouse to update- ')
            Ch : = 'A'
            FOR Row : = 1 TO RowMax DO
               WRITELN (Ch, '.' , CityList [Row])
               Ch : = SUCC (Ch)
            Ch : = PRED (Ch)
            WRITE ('Enter choice (A ..', Ch,'): ')
            READLN (Ans)
            Row : = ORD (Ans) − ORD ('A') + 1
            FOR Col : = 1 TO ColMax DO
               WRITE ('Enter change for item # ' , Col, ' : ')
               READLN (Change)
               Table [Row,Col] : = Change + Table[Row,Col]
```

This design leads to the Pascal program in Figure 7–13.

Figure 7–13

```
PROGRAM Warehouse ;

CONST RowMax = 5 ;
      ColMax = 4 ;

TYPE Inventory = 0 .. MAXINT ;
     Index = 1 .. 5 ;
     ListType = ARRAY [1 .. RowMax] OF STRING [40] ;
     TableType = ARRAY [1 .. RowMax, 1 .. ColMax] OF Inventory ;

VAR CityList : ListType ;
    Table : TableType ;
    Select : CHAR ;

PROCEDURE FillCityList (RowLen : Index ; VAR CityList : ListType) ;

  VAR Row : Index ;

  BEGIN                              {FillCityList}
    FOR Row := 1 TO RowLen DO
       BEGIN                         {FOR-DO instruction}
         WRITE ('Enter warehouse #',Row ,' name: ') ;
         READLN (CityList [Row])
       END                           {FOR-DO instruction}
  END ;                              {FillCityList}

PROCEDURE FillTable  (RowLen, ColLen : Index ;
                      VAR Table : TableType ; CityList : ListType) ;

  VAR Row , Col : Index ;

  BEGIN                              {FillTable}
    FOR Row := 1 TO RowLen DO
      FOR Col := 1 TO ColLen DO
```

Figure 7–13

Continued

Sample Execution

```
For Arcadia enter inventory for item 1: 23
For Arcadia enter inventory for item 2: 69
For Arcadia enter inventory for item 3: 13
For Arcadia enter inventory for item 4: 64
For Bartow enter inventory for item 1: 0
```

```
      BEGIN                               {nested FOR-DO instruction}
        WRITE ('For ' , CityList [Row]) ;
        WRITE (' enter inventory level for item ') ;
        WRITE (Col , ': ') ;
        READLN (Table [Row,Col])
      END                                 {nested FOR-DO instruction}
  END ;                                   {FillTable}

PROCEDURE PresentMenu (VAR Select : CHAR) ;

  BEGIN                                   {PresentMenu}
    WRITELN ;
    WRITELN ('A. Find total inventory for an item') ;
    WRITELN ('B. Find warehouses out of an item') ;
    WRITELN ('C. Update inventory of a warehouse') ;
    WRITELN ('Q. Quit') ;
    WRITELN ;
    WRITE ('Enter choice (A,B,C,Q): ') ;
    READLN (Select)
  END ;                                   {PresentMenu}

PROCEDURE FindColumnSum (RowLen, ColLen : Index ; Table : TableType) ;

  VAR Row , Column : Index ;
      Sum : 0 .. MAXINT ;
```

Sample Execution

```
Find total inventory for item (1..4): 5
Inventory level is 123
```

```
  BEGIN                                   {FindColumnSum}
    WRITE ('Find total inventory for item') ;
    WRITE (' (1 .. ' , ColLen,'): ') ;
    READLN (Column) ;
    Sum := 0 ;
    FOR Row := 1 TO RowLen DO
      Sum := Sum + Table [Row, Column] ;
    WRITELN ('Inventory level is ' , Sum)
  END ;                                   {FindColumnSum}

PROCEDURE SearchColumn (RowLen, ColLen : Index ;
                        Table : TableType ; CityList : ListType);

  VAR Row , Column : Index ;
```

Sample Execution

```
Enter item to check (1..4): 2
Naples is out of item.
Ocala is out of item.
```

```
  BEGIN                                   {SearchColumn}
    WRITE ('Enter item to check') ;
    WRITE (' (1 .. ' , ColLen, '): ') ;
    READLN (Column) ;
    FOR Row := 1 TO RowLen DO
      IF Table [Row,Column] = 0
        THEN WRITELN (CityList [Row] , ' is out of item.')
  END ;                                   {SearchColumn}

PROCEDURE UpdateTable (RowLen, ColLen : Index ;
                       VAR Table : TableType ; CityList : ListType) ;

  VAR Ch , Ans : CHAR ;
      Row , Col : Index ;
      Change : INTEGER ;
```

```
  BEGIN                                 {UpdateTable}
    WRITELN ('Select warehouse to update- ') ;
    Ch := 'A' ;
    FOR Row := 1 TO RowLen DO           {Menu}
      BEGIN                             {FOR-DO instruction}
        WRITELN (Ch, '. ' , CityList [Row]) ;
          Ch := SUCC (Ch)              {Next letter}
      END ;
    Ch := PRED (Ch) ;                   {Adjust letter}
    WRITE ('Enter choice (A .. ', Ch, '): ') ;
    READLN (Ans) ;                      {which warehouse}
    Row := ORD (Ans) - ORD ('A') + 1 ; {Find row number}
    FOR Col := 1 TO ColLen DO
      BEGIN                             {DoChange}
        WRITE ('Enter change for item #' , Col , ': ') ;
        READLN (Change) ;
        Table [Row,Col] := Change + Table [Row,Col]
      END                               {DoChange}
  END ;                                 {UpdateTable}
BEGIN                                   {Main program}
  FillCityList (RowMax, CityList) ;
  FillTable (RowMax, ColMax, Table, CityList) ;
  REPEAT
    PresentMenu (Select) ;
    CASE Select OF
      'A' : FindColumnSum (RowMax, ColMax, Table) ;
      'B' : SearchColumn (RowMax, ColMax, Table, CityList) ;
      'C' : UpdateTable (RowMax, ColMax, Table, CityList)
    END
  UNTIL Select = 'Q'
END .                                   {Main program}
```

Figure 7-13

Continued

Sample Execution

```
Select warehouse to update-
A. Arcadia
B. Bartow
C. Bonifay
D. Naples
E. Ocala
Enter choice (A .. E): D
Enter change for item #1: -3
Enter change for item #2: 5
```

DO IT NOW

1. Suppose the MR Ducks Company has added a new warehouse at Chipley and has added three more items to their inventory. How would you alter the program Warehouse to handle this alteration?

2. Describe how the MR Ducks Company would use the program Warehouse to find which warehouses are out of item 3.

3. Expand the program Warehouse to allow the user to check a warehouse. That is, the user should be able to select a warehouse, then obtain a listing of the out-of-stock items.

4. Could the list CityList be integrated into the data structure Table? If it can, do so. If it cannot, explain why.

DO IT NOW ANSWERS

1. The only changes needed are that the constants RowMax and ColMax would be altered to 6 and 7, and Index would be defined as 1 .. 7.

2. The user would select option B (Find the warehouses out of an item) from the main menu. In response to the prompt Enter item to check (1 .. 5): , the user would enter 3.

The program would then write to the screen the warehouses that are out of item **3**. For the table value given in section 7–2.2, `Naples` would be written to the screen. The user would then be returned to the main menu.

3. The main menu would be expanded by adding the option`D. Check stock level of a warehouse`. In the CASE–OF–END instruction in the main execution block, the selection `'D' : CheckWarehouse (RowLen, ColLen, Table, CityList)` would be added. The procedure `CheckWarehouse` would appear as shown:

```
PROCEDURE CheckWarehouse (RowLen, ColLen : Index ;
                          Table : TableType ;
                          CityList : ListType) ;

VAR Ch , Ans : CHAR ;
    Row , Col : Index ;

BEGIN                                          {CheckWarehouse}
  WRITELN ('Select warehouse to check- ') ;
  Ch := 'A' ;
  FOR Row := 1 TO RowLen DO                     {Menu}
    BEGIN                                       {FOR-DO instruction}
      WRITELN (Ch, '. ' , CityList [Row]) ;
      Ch := SUCC (Ch)                           {Next letter}
    END ;
  Ch := PRED (Ch) ;                             {Adjust letter}
  WRITE ('Enter choice (A .. ', Ch, '): ') ;
  READLN (Ans) ;                                {Which warehouse}
  Row := ORD (Ans) - ORD ('A') + 1 ;            {Find row number}
  FOR Col := 1 TO ColLen DO
    IF Table [Row,Col] = 0
      THEN WRITELN ('Out of item ', Col)
END                                             {CheckWarehouse}
```

4. `CityList` cannot be integrated into `Table`. In a table, each component must be of the same data type. The components of `CityList` are of type `STRING [40]`. The components of `Table` are of type `0 .. MAXINT` (a subrange of the data type INTEGER). In the next chapter, a data structure called RECORD OF will be introduced to handle this type of integration.

7–2.3 *Amortization Spreadsheet*

A major use of tables is that of an electronic spreadsheet. A spreadsheet allows the user to create a table of values. Next, the user is allowed to alter the makeup of the table to answer *"what-if"* questions. The example presented here is a simplified version of a spreadsheet to demonstrate processing the values in a table data structure. As always, the example provides a demonstration of the top-down approach to problem solving.

EXAMPLE

Write a Pascal program to create an amortization table for a loan. The program should allow the user to select from the following menu:

```
A. Enter loan information
B. See table
C. See sum of a column
D. Change a column value
Q. Quit
```

If option A is selected, the program allows the user to enter amount of the loan, interest rate, and length of the loan.

If option **B** is selected, the program writes the table to the screen one year at a time. For example:

```
Payment#  Amount  Interest  Principal  Remaining
   1      269.92   225.00     42.92    29955.08
   2      269.92   224.66     45.25    29909.03
   3      269.92   224.32     45.59    29864.23
   .        .        .          .         .
   .        .        .          .         .
   .        .        .          .         .
  12      269.92   221.15     48.77    29438.19
Press RETURN to see next year, enter Q to quit:
```

If option **C** is selected, the user is allowed to see the sum of one of the columns of the table (over a range of months). If option **D** is selected, the user is allowed to change one of the following: monthly payment, loan amount, interest rate, or length of the loan.

SOLUTION

Design: REPEAT
        Present main menu
        Get selection
        CASE Select OF
            'A' : GetLoanData
                UpDateTable
            'B' : PresentTable
            'C' : FindSum
            'D' : AlterValue
                UpDateTable
        END
        UNTIL Select = 'Q'

COMMENT
After selections **A** and **D**, the table of values needs to be updated. The table of values will be of type **ARRAY [1 .. MaxRow, 1 .. 4] OF REAL** where **MaxRow** is a program constant.

For a program of this size, a structured diagram showing the modules is helpful (see Figure 7–14).

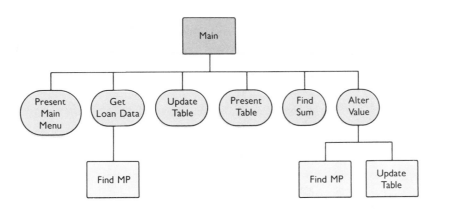

Figure 7–14

Sample Execution

```
A. Enter loan data
B. See table
C. Find sum of a column
D. Change header value
E. Quit

Enter selection (A,B,C,D,Q):
```

Refinement of: *PresentMainMenu*
WRITELN
WRITELN ('A. Enter loan data')
WRITELN ('B. See table')
WRITELN ('C. Find sum of a column')
WRITELN ('D. Alter a value')
WRITELN ('Q. Quit')
WRITELN
WRITE ('Enter selection (A, B, C, D, Q): ')
READLN (Select)

Refinement of: *GetLoanData*
WRITE ('Enter amount of loan: $')
READLN (Loan)
WRITE ('Enter interest rate per year as a percent: ')
READLN (Rate)
Rate : = Rate / 12 / 100
WRITE ('Enter length of loan in years: ')
READLN (Time)
Time : = Time * 12
FindMP

Sample Execution

```
Enter amount of loan: $3000
Enter yearly interest rate as a percent: 12
Enter length of loan in years: 30
```

COMMENT
The use of the built-in functions
EXP and LN allows for the future
expansion of entering a fractional
value for Time. That is, at some
future revision of the program,
the user could enter 12.5 years
for the length of the loan. The
mathematical formula for
Factor is $(1 + Rate)^{Time}$

Refinement of: *FindMP*
Factor : = EXP (Time * LN (1 + Rate))
MP : = Loan * Rate * Factor/(Factor − 1)

Refinement of: *UpdateTable*

Table [1,1] : = MP	{Monthly payment}
Table [1,2] : = Rate * Loan	{Interest owed}
Table [1,3] : = MP − Table [1,2]	{Principal}
Table [1,4] : = Loan − Table [1,3]	{Remaining balance}

Row : = 2
WHILE Table [Row 4] > = MP DO
    Table [Row,1] : = MP
    Table [Row,2] : = Rate * Table[Row − 1,4]
    Table [Row,3] : = Table[Row,1] − Table [Row,2]
    Table [Row,4] : = Table [Row − 1,4] − Table [Row,3]
    Row : = Row + 1
IF Table [Row − 1,4] < > 0   {Do last payment}
  THEN Table [Row,1] : = Table [Row − 1,4] + Rate * Table [Row − 1 ,4]
        Table [Row,2] : = Rate * Table[Row − 1,4]
        Table [Row,3] : = Table [Row − 1,4]
        Table [Row,4] : = 0
        Row : = Row + 1
FOR Ct : = Row TO MaxRow DO   {Zero rest of Table}
  FOR Col : = 1 TO 4 DO
    Table [Row,Col] : = 0

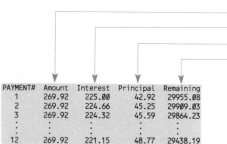

PAYMENT#	Amount	Interest	Principal	Remaining
1	269.92	225.00	42.92	29955.08
2	269.92	224.66	45.25	29909.03
3	269.92	224.32	45.59	29864.23
:	:	:	:	:
12	269.92	221.15	48.77	29438.19

COMMENT
The first row of the table is initialized based on the loan data.
Working off the previous row, the
rest of the row formulas in the
table are calculated in the
WHILE-DO instruction. The
IF-THEN instruction takes care of
the last payment. Finally, the rest
of the table cells are assigned a
zero.

Refinement of: *PresentTable*

```
Ct := 1
REPEAT
   WRITE ('Payment# ....')
   FOR Row := Ct TO Ct + 11 DO
      WRITE ( Row : 4 )
      WRITE (Table [Row,1] : 14 : 2)
      WRITE (Table [Row,2] : 14 : 2)
      WRITE (Table [Row,3] : 14 : 2)
      WRITE (Table [Row,4] : 14 : 2)
   Ct := Ct + 12
   WRITE ('Press RETURN for next year. Enter Q to quit: ')
   READLN (Ans)
UNTIL (Ans = 'Q') OR (Table [Ct,4] = 0)
```

Sample Execution

```
Payment# Amount Interest Principal
   1     500.00 225.00     42.92
   2     500.00 222.44     45.25
   3     500.00 220.86     45.59
```

Refinement of: *FindSum*

```
WRITE ('Enter column to sum (1 .. 5): ')
READLN (Column) ;
Count = 1
IF Column = 1
   THEN WHILE Table [Count,4] > 0 DO
               Count := Count + 1
         WRITE ('Length of loan in months is ')
         WRITELN (Count:1)
   ELSE WRITE ('Enter start month: ')
         READLN (Start)
         WRITE ('Enter end month: ')
         READLN (Finish)
         Sum := 0
         FOR Count := Start TO Finish DO
             Sum := Sum + Table [Count,Column]
         WRITE ('Sum of column ', Column)
         WRITELN (' is: ' , Sum : 1 : 2)
```

Sample Execution

```
Find Sum of column (1..5): 1
Number of payments = 240
```

Sample Execution

```
Find sum column (1..5): 2
Enter start month: 13
Enter end month: 24
The sum is $3963.91
```

Refinement of: *AlterValue*

```
WRITELN ('Please select value to change')
WRITELN ('A. Amount of loan')
WRITELN ('B. Rate of interest')
WRITELN ('C. Length of loan ')
WRITELN ('D. Monthly payment')
WRITELN
WRITE ('Please select: ')
READLN (Ans)
CASE Ans OF
   'A' : WRITE ('Enter loan amount: ')
         READLN (Loan)
         FindMP
   'B' : WRITE ('Enter yearly interest rate as percent: ')
         READLN (Rate)
         Rate := Rate / 12 / 100
         FindMP
```

Sample Execution

```
Change value of:
A. Interest rate
B. Length of loan
C. Payment amount
D. Loan amount
Please select: C
Enter new payment amount: 400
```

COMMENT

Because this procedure needs the procedure FindMP (as does GetLoanData), the procedure FindMP will be placed at the program level.

```
                        'C' : WRITE ('Enter length of loan in years: ')
                                READLN (Time)
                                Time : = Time * 12
                                FindMP
                        'D' : WRITE ('Enter payment amount: ')
                                READLN (MP)
```

The design just presented yields the Pascal program in Figure 7–15.

Figure 7–15

```
PROGRAM AmortTable ;

CONST MaxRow = 482 ;                              {handle loans up to 40 years}

TYPE TableType = ARRAY [1 .. MaxRow, 1 .. 4] OF REAL ;
     Number = 1 .. MaxRow ;

VAR Table : TableType ;
    Month : Number ;
    Loan, Rate, MP : REAL ;
    Select : CHAR ;

PROCEDURE PresentMenu (VAR Select : CHAR) ;

  BEGIN                                           {PresentMenu}
    WRITELN ;                                     {Skip a line}
    WRITELN ('A. Enter loan data') ;
    WRITELN ('B. See table') ;
    WRITELN ('C. Find sum of a column') ;
    WRITELN ('D. Change header value') ;
    WRITELN ('Q. Quit) ;
    WRITELN ;                                     {Skip a line}
    WRITE ('Enter selection ( A, B, C, D, Q): ') ;
    READLN (Select)
  END ;                                           {PresentMenu}

PROCEDURE FindMP (LoanAmt, IntRate : REAL ;LoanLen : Number ;
                    VAR Payment : REAL) ;

  VAR Factor : REAL ;

  BEGIN                                           {FindMP}
    Factor := EXP (LoanLen * LN (1 + IntRate)) ;
    Payment := LoanAmt * IntRate * Factor/(Factor - 1)
  END ;                                           {FindMP}

PROCEDURE GetLoanData (VAR Amount , Interest , MP : REAL ;
                         VAR Time : Number) ;

  VAR Factor : REAL ;

  BEGIN                                           {GetLoanData}
    WRITE ('Enter amount of loan: $') ;
    READLN (Amount) ;
    WRITE ('Enter yearly interest rate as a percent: ') ;
    READLN (Interest) ;
    Interest := Interest / 12 / 100 ;
    WRITE ('Enter length of loan in years: ') ;
    READLN (Time) ;
    Time := Time * 12 ;                           {Convert to months}
    FindMP (Amount, Interest, Time, MP)
  END ;                                           {GetLoanData}
```

Sample Execution

```
Enter amount of loan: $30000
Enter yearly interest rate as a percent
Enter length of loan in years: 30
```

Figure 7-15
Continued

```
PROCEDURE UpdateTable (RowLen : Number ; VAR Table : TableType ;
                       MP , Rate , Amount : REAL ;
                       LoanLen : Number) ;

  VAR Row, Col : Number ;
    BEGIN                                         {UpdateTable}
      WRITELN ('Please wait. Updating table. ') ;
      Table [1,1] := MP ;                         {Monthly payment}
      Table [1,2] := Amount * Rate ;              {Interest owed}
      Table [1,3] := Table [1,1] - Table [1,2] ;  {Principal}
      Table [1,4] := Amount - Table [1,3] ;       {Remaining balance}
      Row := 2 ;
      WHILE (Row <= LoanLen) AND (Table [Row - 1,4] > 0) DO
        BEGIN                                     {WHILE-DO}
          IF Table [Row - 1, 4] >= MP
            THEN
              BEGIN                               {THEN instruction}
                Table [Row,1] := MP ;
                Table [Row,2] := Rate * Table [Row - 1,4] ;
                Table [Row,3] := MP - Table [Row,2] ;
                Table [Row,4] := Table [Row - 1,4] - Table [Row,3] ;
                Row := Row + 1
              END                                 {THEN instruction}
            ELSE
              BEGIN                               {ELSE instruction}
                Table [Row,1] := Table [Row - 1,4] + Rate * Table [Row - 1,4] ;
                Table [Row,2] := Rate * Table [Row - 1, 4] ;
                Table [Row,3] := MP - Table [Row,2] ;
                Table [Row,4] := 0 ;
                Row := Row + 1
              END                                 {ELSE instruction}
        END ;                                     {WHILE-DO}
      LoanLen := Row ;
      FOR Row := LoanLen TO RowLen DO             {Zero rest of Table}
        FOR Col := 1 TO 4 DO
          Table [Row,Col] := 0
    END ;                                         {UpdateTable}
PROCEDURE PresentTable (RowLen : Number ;
                        VAR Table : TableType ; LoanLen : INTEGER);

  VAR Ct : Number ;
      Ans : CHAR ;

  PROCEDURE NextPage (VAR Ct : Number ; VAR Table : TableType) ;

    VAR Row : Number ;

    BEGIN                                         {Next Page}
      WRITE ('Payment# ', 'Amount ': 10, 'Interest':12) ;
      WRITELN ('Principal':13, 'Remaining':13) ;
      FOR Row := Ct TO Ct + 11 DO
```

COMMENT
Assign first row of Table a set of values.

COMMENT
Compute values for remaining rows of Table from row 2 until loan is paid off. Each set of values is based on values from previous row.

COMMENT
Do last payment.

COMMENT
Assign the remaining rows of Table a value of zero.

Figure 7-15

Continued

```
Payment#  Amount  Interest  Principal
   1      500.00   225.00     42.92
   2      500.00   222.44     45.25
   3      500.00   220.86     45.59
```

```
          BEGIN                                          {FOR-DO instruction}
            WRITE (Row : 4) ;
            WRITE (Table [Row, 1] : 14 : 2) ;
            WRITE (Table [Row, 2] : 12 : 2) ;
            WRITE (Table [Row, 3] : 13 : 2) ;
            WRITELN (Table [Row, 4] : 13 : 2)
          END                                            {FOR-DO instruction}
      END ;                                              {NextPage}

    BEGIN                                                {PresentTable}
      Ct := 1 ;
      REPEAT
        WRITE ('Press RETURN for next year. Enter Q to quit: ') ;
        READLN (Ans) ;
        IF (Ans < > 'Q') AND (Ct < LoanLen)
          THEN BEGIN
                  NextPage (Ct , Table) ;
                  Ct := Ct + 12
                END
      UNTIL (Ans = 'Q') OR (Ct > LoanLen) OR (Table [Ct,4] <= 0)
    END ;                                                {PresentTable}

PROCEDURE DoColumn (RowLen : Number ; VAR Table : TableType) ;

  VAR Sum : REAL ;
      Col , Start, Finish, Ct : Number ;

    BEGIN                                                {DoColumn}
      WRITE ('Find sum of column (1 .. 5): ') ;
      READLN (Col) ;
      IF Col = 1
        THEN BEGIN                                       {Find length of loan}
                Ct := 1 ;
                WHILE Table [Count,4] > 0 DO
                  Ct := Ct + 1 ;
                WRITELN ('Number of payments = ', Ct)
             END                                         {Find length of loan}
        ELSE BEGIN                                       {Find sum of column}
                WRITE ('Enter start month#: ') ;
                READLN (Start) ;
                WRITE ('Enter end month#: ') ;
                READLN (Finish) ;
                Sum := 0 ;
                FOR Ct := Start TO Finish DO
                  IF Table [Ct,4] >= 0
                    THEN Sum := Sum + Table [Ct,Col - 1] ;
                WRITELN ('The sum is $', Sum : 1 : 2)
             END                                         {Find sum of column}
    END ;                                                {DoColumn}

PROCEDURE AlterValue (VAR Loan, Interest, MP : REAL;
                          VAR Time : Number) ;

  VAR Ans , Ch : CHAR ;
```

```
Find Sum of column (1..5): 1
Number of payments = 240
```

```
Find sum column (1..5): 2
Enter start month: 13
Enter end month: 24
The sum is $3963.91
```

```
    BEGIN                                        {AlterValue}
      WRITELN ('Change value of: ') ;
      WRITELN ('A. Interest rate') ;
      WRITELN ('B. Length of loan') ;
      WRITELN ('C. Payment amount') ;
      WRITELN ('D. Loan amount') ;
      WRITELN ;
      WRITE ('Please select: ') ;
      READLN (Ans) ;
      CASE Ans OF
       'A': BEGIN                                {Change interest rate}
              WRITE ('Enter new interest rate (as percent): ') ;
              READLN (Interest) ;
              Interest := Interest / 12 / 100 ;
              FindMP (Loan, Interest, Time, MP)
            END ;                                {Change interest rate}
       'B': BEGIN                                {Change length of loan}
              WRITE ('Enter new length of loan: ') ;
              READLN (Time) ;
              WRITE ('Is this months or years?(M/Y): ') ;
              READLN (Ch) ;
              IF Ch < > 'M'
                THEN Time := Time * 12 ;
              FindMP (Loan, Interest, Time, MP)
            END ;                                {Change length of loan}
       'C': BEGIN                                {Change monthly payment}
              WRITE ('Enter new payment amount: ') ;
              READLN (MP)
            END ;                                {Change monthly payment}
       'D': BEGIN                                {Change amount of loan}
              WRITE ('Enter new loan amount: ') ;
              READLN (Loan) ;
              FindMP (Loan, Interest, Time, MP)
            END                                  {Change amount of loan}
      END                                        {CASE}
    END ;                                        {AlterValue}
BEGIN                                            {AmortTable}
  REPEAT
    PresentMenu (Select) ;
    CASE Select OF
     'A' : BEGIN
             GetLoanData (Loan, Rate, MP , Month) ;
             UpDateTable (MaxRow, Table, MP, Rate, Loan, Month)
           END ;
     'B' : PresentTable (MaxRow, Table, Month) ;
     'C' : DoColumn (MaxRow, Table) ;
     'D' : BEGIN
             AlterValue (Loan, Rate, MP, Month) ;
             UpdateTable (MaxRow, Table, MP, Rate, Loan, Month)
           END
    END                                          {CASE}
  UNTIL Select = 'Q'
END .                                            {AmortTable}
```

Figure 7–15

Continued

Sample Execution

```
Change value of:
A. Interest rate
B. Length of loan
C. Payment amount
D. Loan amount
Please select: C
Enter new payment amount: 400
```

Sample Execution

```
A. Enter loan data
B. See table
C. Find sum of a column
D. Change header value
E. Quit

Enter selection (A,B,C,D,Q):
```

DO IT NOW

1. Julia wants to buy a car for $12,000. A local bank will finance 90% of the price at 12% interest for four years. Suppose Julia wants to make payments for a year, then pay the loan off at the end of the first year. Describe how Julia would use the program `AmortTable` in Figure 7–15 to find the amount of the payoff.

2. Peter has an $80,000 house loan at 15% interest for 20 years. He has used the program `AmortTable` to find the monthly payments to be $1053.43. Peter now wants to ask, "What if I make double payments on the loan?" Describe how Peter would use the program to find how long it would take to pay off the loan at this new monthly payment.

3. Susan has heard that making a payment plus interest each month will greatly reduce the cost of the loan. That is, Susan will pay the regular monthly payment plus the interest owed for the month. As is, the program `AmortTable` cannot handle this type of alteration. Suggest how to alter the program to handle this type of *what-if* question.

DO IT NOW ANSWERS

1. From the main menu, Julia would select choice **A** and enter the loan data. After the table has been updated, she is returned to the main menu. She now selects choice **B** to see the table. At the bottom of the first page, in the `Remaining` column, she will see the payoff for the loan at the end of the first year. Julia could now enter **Q** to quit and return to the main menu.

2. Since Peter already has the table filled for the original loan data, he would now select **D** from the main menu to change a column value. At this point, Peter will see another menu for different values he can change. He will enter choice **C** (payment amount) and enter **2106.86** (double the monthly payment). After a short wait (to update the table), Peter is returned to the main menu. To find the length of time to pay off the loan at this new monthly payment, Peter selects choice **C** (find sum of column). Next, he enters the value **1** to select column 1. The result is: **The number of payments = 52**. That is, it will take Peter four years, four months (rather than 20 years) to pay off the loan if he makes double payments each month.

3. One approach to this alteration would be as follows:

   Step 1: Add the program variable `Interest` of type REAL.

   Step 2: Add the choice: **E. See MP plus Interest** to the menu in the procedure `PresentMenu`.

   Step 3: In the procedure `UpdateTable`, add the value parameter `Interest`. Change the procedure as follows:

```
        PROCEDURE UpdateTable (RowLen : Number ;
                               VAR Table : Table Type ;
                               MP, Rate, Amount : REAL ;
                               LoanLen : Number ;
                               Interest : REAL) ;

     VAR Row : Number ;
         Col : 0 .. 4 ;

     BEGIN                                          {UpdateTable}
       Table [1,1] := MP + (Interest * Amount) ;    {Monthly payment plus interest}
       Table [1,2] := Rate * Amount ;               {Interest owed}
       Table [1,3] := Table [1,1] − Table [1,2] ;   {Principal}
       Table [1,4] := Amount − Table [1,3] ;        {Remaining balance}
       Row := 2;
       WHILE Table [Row 4] >= MP DO
         BEGIN                                       {WHILE-DO}
           Table [Row,1] := MP + Interest * Table [Row−1, 4] ;
           Table [Row,2] := Rate * Table [Row−1,4] ;
           Table [Row,3] := Table [Row,1] − Table [Row,2] ;
           Table [Row,4] := Table [Row − 1,4] − Table [Row,3] ;
           Row := Row + 1
         END ;                                       {WHILE-DO}
```

```
IF Table [Row - 1,4] < > 0
   THEN BEGIN                                    {Do last table entry}
           Table [Row,1] := Table [Row - 1,4] + Rate * Table [Row - 1,4] ;
           Table [Row,2] := Rate * Table [Row - 1,4] ;
           Table [Row,3] := Table [Row - 1,4] ;
           Table [Row,4] := 0 ;
           Row := Row + 1
        END ;                                    {Last table entry}
   FOR Ct := Row TO MaxRow DO                    {Zero rest of Table}
     FOR Col := 1 TO 4 DO
       Table [Row,Col] := 0
END ;                                            {UpdateTable}
```

Step 4: In the CASE-OF-END of the main execution block, add the selection:

```
'E' : BEGIN
        Interest := Rate ;
        UpdateTable (MaxRow, Table, MP, Rate, Loan, Month, Interest)
      END
```

Also, adjust the other calls to `UpdateTable`. Other calls to `UpdateTable` will pass the value 0 for the parameter `Interest`.

Vocabulary

	Page
Column processing The act of operating on a column of a table to find the sum or product of the values in the column.	404
Row processing The act of operating on a row of a table to find the sum or the product of the values in the row.	404

Glad You Asked

Q In the program `Warehouse`, in the procedure `UpdateTable`, could the changes in inventory be read into a list, then could the list components be added to the appropriate row of `Table`?

A Yes. To do the addition part, the following loop could be used. The loop assumes that the changes have been read into `ChangeList`, a local variable of type `ARRAY [1 .. ColLen] OF INTEGER`.

```
FOR Col := 1 TO ColLen DO
  Table [Row,Col] := ChangeList [Col] + Table [Row, Col]
```

However, since the storage of these values is not needed, it would be best to use a variable of a simple type, as done in the program `Warehouse`. You should always try to use the appropriate data type. Often there is a temptation to *overuse* the list data structure. The decision as to which data type to use depends on whether or not the data must be stored before processing. If it must be stored first and then processed, a list data structure or a table data structure is appropriate.

Q How can the value in a table be stored on a diskette? Surely the user doesn't have to enter the table value, as was done in the program `Warehouse`.

A For now, the value in a table could be stored in a TEXT file, provided the components of the table are of an appropriate data type, such as CHAR, STRING, or one of the number types. For example, the value in the variable `Table` of the program `Warehouse` could be stored in a TEXT file using the following design:

COMMENT
In Chapter 9, we will study a file type that allows components of type ARRAY OF.

```
Open the file                            {use the variable InFile of type TEXT}
FOR Row : = 1 TO RowMax DO
   WRITE (InFile , CityList [Row])
   WRITE ('*')                           {a sentinel to mark the end of the city name}
   FOR Col : = 1 TO ColMax DO
      WRITE (InFile , Table [Row,Col])
      WRITE (InFile , ' ')               {two spaces to separate the numbers}
   WRITELN (InFile)                      {Move file marker to start of next line}
Close file
```

This design would create a TEXT file which each line contained (a) the name of the warehouse followed by an *; and (b) the inventory level of each item in the warehouse separated by two blank spaces. A typical line would appear as follows:

```
Bonifay* 23  45  67  Ø  12
```

Q How can I find the sum of the *diagonal* of a table?

A For a table to have a diagonal, the number of rows must equal the number of columns. There are two major diagonals. One runs from the top left to the bottom right of the table; the other runs from the top right to the bottom left of the table.

To find the sum of the top left to bottom right diagonal, the following design could be used:

```
Sum : = 0
FOR Row : = 1 TO RowMax DO
   FOR Col : = 1 TO ColMax DO
      IF Row = Col
         THEN Sum : = Sum + Table [Row,Col]
```

A more efficient alternative to this design is

```
Sum : = 0
FOR Row : = 1 TO RowMax DO
   Sum : = Sum + Table [Row, Row]
```

How would you find the sum of the components in the top right to bottom left diagonal?

Q In the program `AmortTable`, you said the program could be expanded to allow the user to enter a fractional number of years like 12.8. How could this be done? Wouldn't the program variable `Month` have to be of type REAL? If so, wouldn't that mess up the other uses of `Month`?

A In the procedure `GetLoanData`, a local variable `Year` of type REAL could be declared. All references to `Time` in the execution section of `GetLoanData` would be replaced by `Year`. An extra instruction,

```
IF Year < > TRUNC (Year)              {Year not a whole number}
   THEN Time := TRUNC (Year + 1)
   ELSE Time := Year
```

would be added as the last instruction in the execution section of `GetLoanData`. This way, the program variable `Month` (which is passed the value in `Time`) is still of type `Number`.

Section 7.2 Exercises

For problems 1 through 7 assume the following CONST, TYPE, and VAR sections:

```
CONST RowMax = 4 ;
      ColMax = 3 ;
```

```
TYPE TableType = ARRAY [1 .. RowMax, 1 .. ColMax] OF INTEGER ;

VAR Table : TableType ;
    Row , Col : 1 .. MAXINT ;
    Average , Sum , Mystery , Temp : INTEGER ;
```

1. The instructions:

```
Sum := Ø ;
Col := 2 ;
FOR Row := 1 TO RowMax DO
  Sum := Sum + Table [Row,Col]
```

will store in the variable Sum the sum of the values in column _____.

2. The instructions:

```
Mystery := 1 ;
FOR Row := 1 TO RowMax DO
  FOR Col := 1 TO ColMax DO
    IF Row = Col
      THEN Mystery := Mystery * Table [Row,Col]
```

will
   a. find the product of all the components of the table.
   b. find the sum of the components in row 1.
   c. find the product of all the components where the row and column indices are equal.
   d. find the product of all the components in column 3.

3. The instructions:

```
Row := 3 ;
FOR Col := 1 TO ColMax DO
  Table [Row,Col] := 1.1 * Table [Row,Col]
```

will
   a. assign each component in row 3 the value 1.1.
   b. increase each component in row 3 by 10%.
   c. find the sum of the components in column 3.
   d. increase each component in column 3 by 10%.

4. Write a collection of instructions that will write to the screen all the components of the value stored in Table that are greater than 12.

5. Write a collection of instructions that will *interchange* the components in row 2 with the components in row 3.

6. Write a collection of instructions that will write to the screen the *average* of the components in row 2.

7. Describe the alterations to the CONST, TYPE, and VAR sections required to allow the storage of a table with six rows and eight columns in the variable Table.

8. The Bayside Car Company has a table of the number of cars it sells. The rows of the table are indexed from 1 to 4 and represent the four different car types sold. The columns are indexed from 1 to 6 and represent the six different salespersons. Write a Pascal function SumCol that has as input a column of the table value. The function is to return the sum of the column. Use the following function header:.

	Salesperson					
	1	2	3	4	5	6
Car Type 1	5	2	Ø	Ø	1	Ø
2	7	Ø	1	Ø	2	2
3	Ø	1	3	Ø	1	1
4	3	2	1	1	4	Ø

```
FUNCTION SumCol (NumRows : Index ; TableColumn : ColumnList) : Sales ;
```

Assume
```
    Const RowMax = 4 ;
          ColMax = 6 ;

    Type Index = 1 .. 6 ;
         Sales = Ø .. MAXINT ;
         ColumnList = ARRAY [1 .. RowMax] OF Sales ;
```

9. Write a Pascal procedure `DoColumns` that uses the function `SumCol` in problem 8. The procedure has input `Table` of type `TableType` and `NameList` of type `ListType`. The procedure is to output the name of each salesperson followed by the total number of cars the person has sold. The value in `Table` is similar to the following table. The value in `NameList` is the names of the salespersons.

Salesperson

		1	2	3	4	5	6
	1	5	2	0	0	1	0
	2	7	0	1	0	2	2
Car Type	3	0	1	3	0	1	1
	4	3	2	1	1	4	0

Sample Execution

```
Salesperson     Cars sold
Morez , Tina       15
Killum, Bill        5
Holden, Susan       5
Lilly, Lil          1
Black , Jack        8
Star, Ira           3
```

10. Boot up Pascal; set the workfile to the file `WareH.PAS` from the `Source` diskette. Enter the editor. Alter the program to fill the inventory level for the warehouses by randomly assigning a value from 0 to 5 (inclusive).

11. Boot up Pascal; set the workfile to the file `Amort.PAS` from the `Source` diskette. Enter the editor. Expand the `See Table` option of the program to output the totals (for the 12 months shown on the screen) of the columns `Amount`, `Interest`, and `Principal`.

12. A *4 by 4 magic square* is a 4 by 4 array in which the components are 16 consecutive numbers (like 12 through 27). Also, each row, each column, and each diagonal must sum to the same value. Write a Pascal program that allows the user to fill a 4 by 4 array with 16 consecutive numbers. The output of the program is whether or not the result is a magic square.

Sample Execution

Magic Square

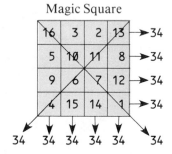

```
Enter value for row 1 column 1: 16
Enter value for row 1 column 2: 3
       .
       .
Enter value for row 4 column 4: 1

Your square is:
    16    3    2   13     Sum row1 is 34
     5   10   11    8     Sum row2 is 34
     9    6    7   12     Sum row3 is 34
     4   15   14    1     Sum row4 is 34
   Column sums are
   34   34   34   34
Diagonal sums are 34 and 34
It is a magic square with value 34
```

13. Expand the program `Warehouse` presented in this section (page 407) to allow the values in `CityList` and `Table` to be saved to a TEXT file. In the main menu there should be an option: `Save data to disk`. Each line of the TEXT file should appear similar to this one:

   `Bonifay* 45  78  13  56`

That is, each line should contain a city from the city list followed by the inventory levels for each of the four items.

14. Suppose the MR Ducks Company in the warehouse example presented in this section has a TEXT file named `Mileage.TXT`. Each line in this TEXT file contains the name of an outlet store followed by the miles to the five warehouse locations of the company. The outlet stores are named Orlando, Miami, Tampa, Pensacola, and Quincy. A line of the TEXT file appears as follows:

```
Orlando* 93 53 350 198 57
```

Thus, the distance from the warehouse in `Bonifay` to the outlet store in `Orlando` is `350` miles. Expand the program `Warehouse` to allow the user to enter an order for one of the four items carried by the MR Ducks Company. The user should enter the level of the order, then select the outlet store that is the destination of the order from the list of outlet stores. The program should then search the value in `DistTable` for the nearest warehouse (or warehouses) to fill the order.

	Arcadia	Bartow	Bonifay	Naples	Ocala
Orlando	93	53	350	198	57
Miami	180	210	562	130	163
Tampa	75	45	340	150	75
Pensacola	495	480	100	590	380
Quincy	315	300	60	410	200

Sample Execution

```
{after selecting the option: Fill order}
Enter item to order: 2
Enter number of item 2 to order: 56
Select store for the order to be sent to
A. Orlando
B. Miami
C. Tampa
D. Pensacola
E. Quincy
Enter selection (A,B,C,D,E): C
Order was filled as follows:
12 from Bartow
30 from Bonifay
14 from Ocala
```

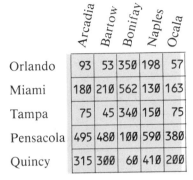

15. The Gill River Community College faculty is currently planning a new salary proposal. A faculty member's salary is computed as follows:

$$(\text{Base pay}) + (\text{Year factor}) * (\text{years of experience}) + (\text{Rank factor}) * \text{Rank} + (\text{Level factor}) * \text{Level}$$

Four different ranks and four different levels are available. The GRCC faculty has the information on the 130 faculty members in a TEXT file named `Salary.TXT`. Each line of the TEXT file appears similar to the following:

```
Reese, Richard* 18 3 4
```

The lines consist of a faculty member's name followed by values for years of experience, rank, and level. Write a Pascal program to allow the user to select from the menu:

```
A. Enter salary values
B. See table
C. Change a salary value by a percent
D. See percent increase (decrease) in budget
Q. Quit
```

Option `A` should allow the user to enter values for base, year factor, rank factor, and level factor. Option `B` should write to the screen the values in the table for 20 faculty members at a time.

Sample Execution

```
Enter base: $8000
Enter year factor: $00
Enter rank factor: $500
Enter level factor: $000
```

(Continued)

```
Member           Base      YrsExp    Rank      Level     Total
Gilly, Susan     15000     4000      2000      3000      24000
Homer, Sid       15000     300       1000      1000      17300
      .
      .
      .
Press RETURN to continue. Enter Q to quit-
```

Option `C` should allow the user to increase or decrease the value of `Base`, `YrsExp`, `Rank`, or `Level` by a percent. Option `D` should allow the user to see the total increase (decrease) in budget for each table value produced. The change should be based on the total salary of all faculty members when the table is first filled.

```
A. Change base
B. Change year factor
C. Change rank factor
D. Change level factor
Q. Quit
Please select (A..D,Q): A
Enter percent change: 8
Increase or Decrease (I/D): I
```

CHAPTER TEST

1. Which of the following defines a two-dimensional ARRAY data type?
   a. `ThisOne = ARRAY [1 .. 3] OF INTEGER`
   b. `ThisOne = SET OF ARRAY [1 .. 3, 1 .. 6] OF 1 .. 6`
   c. `ThisOne = Table [1 .. 8 , 1 .. 6] OF CHAR`
   d. `ThisOne = ARRAY [Ø .. 5 , Ø .. 3] OF REAL`
   e. `ThisOne = List [1 .. 4 , 1 .. 3]`

2. Which of the following cannot be the data type of `Component`, where
   `TableType = Array [1 .. MaxRow, 1 .. MaxCol] OF Component`?
   a. INTEGER   b. REAL   c. ARRAY [1 .. 4] OF INTEGER   d. TEXT

3. Which of the following could not be the data type of a function?
   a. `Inventory where Inventory = Ø .. MAXINT`
   b. `Which where Which = (Red , Blue , Green , Yellow)`
   c. `Block where Block = Array [1 .. 3 , 1 .. 5] OF REAL`
   d. `Total where Total = -89 .. 98`

4. Insert *True* for a true statement. Insert *False* for a false statement.
   _____ a. `ARRAY [1 .. 9] OF INTEGER` and
              `ARRAY [1 .. 6 , 1 .. 3] OF INTEGER`
              are equivalent data types.
   _____ b. A variable parameter cannot be of type two-dimensional array.
   _____ c. A function cannot be of type two-dimensional array.
   _____ d. The parallel arrays `NameList` of type
              `ARRAY [1 .. 9Ø] OF STRING [4Ø]` and `GradeList` of type
              `ARRAY [1 .. 9Ø] OF Ø .. 1ØØ` could be replaced by a two-dimensional
              array.
   _____ e. The components of a TEXT file could be of type
              `ARRAY [1 .. 9 , 1 .. 18] OF CHAR`.

5. For `Table` of type `ARRAY [1 .. 12 , 1 .. 12] OF INTEGER` the instructions:

   ```
   Sum := Ø ;
   FOR Row := 1 TO 12 DO
     FOR Col := 1 TO 12 DO
       Sum := Sum + Table [Row, Row]
   WRITELN (Sum)
   ```

   would
   a. write to the screen the sum of all the components in `Table`.
   b. write to the screen the sum of row 5 of `Table`.
   c. write to the screen the sum of a diagonal of `Table`.
   d. write to the screen the sum of column 12 of `Table`.

6. For `Table` of type `TableType` where

      `TableType = ARRAY [1 .. RowMax , 1 .. ColMax] OF INTEGER`

and `RowMax` and `ColMax` are program constants, write a Pascal procedure that has the value parameter `Table`. The procedure should write to the screen the number of the row with the largest sum.

Sample Execution

```
The row with the largest sum is 3
```

Programming Projects

Project 7–1. A regular multiplication table is a 10 by 10 table with the rows indexed from 0 to 9 and the columns indexed from 0 to 9. The product of 5 and 8 can be found by going to row 5, then reading across to column 8 to find the value 40. Suppose you had a multiplication table with rows indexed from 2 to 7 and columns indexed from 2 to 7. Any counting number less than 49 and not in this table is a prime number. For example, 17 is not in the table and 17 is a prime number.

x	2	3	4	5	6	7
2	4	6	8	10	12	14
3	6	9	12	15	18	21
4	8	12	16	20	24	28
5	10	15	20	25	30	35
6	12	18	24	30	36	42
7	14	21	28	35	42	49

Write a Pascal program to build a multiplication table with rows indexed from 2 to 30 and columns indexed from 2 to 30. The program should allow the user to enter a counting number less than 900. The program should then search the table for the input value. If the value is found, the factors (the row and column indices) should be written to the screen. If the value is not found, the program should report that the input value is prime.

Sample Execution

```
Please enter counting number (1 .. 900): 567
567 has factors 21 and 27

Enter Q to quit, anything else to continue-
```

Attempt to obtain the most efficient method of searching the multiplication table. Turn in a copy of your design and its refinements, a structured diagram, a copy of the program, and a hard copy of three test executions. For extra credit, expand the program to give the prime factors of the input value by searching the table for each factor found.

Project 7–2. A four-way traffic intersection can be modeled as shown.

The * character marks the roadway, the - and | characters mark the center lines of the lanes, and the C characters each represent a car.

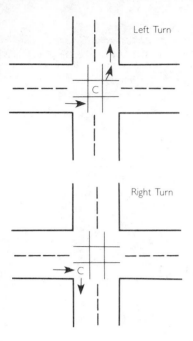

Left Turn

Right Turn

Write a Pascal program to simulate a four-way stop intersection. Each lane (north, east, south, and west) will hold up to ten cars. The program should start by allowing the user to enter the probability of a car entering one of the lanes. For example,

Sample Execution

```
Welcome to the four-way stop intersection.
Enter probability (as a percent) for North lane: 30
Enter probability (as a percent) for East lane: 10
Enter probability (as a percent) for South lane: 35
Enter probability (as a percent) for West lane: 5

Press RETURN to start simulation-
```

A possible design for the main loop for the simulation is as follows:

```
WHILE MoreTicks AND NOT GridLock DO
    IF intersection occupied
        THEN update intersection
        ELSE next car enters intersection
    Update lanes
    Ticks := Ticks + 1
    Check GridLock
```

Each car at the intersection randomly selects a direction to go (turn right, straight, turn left). After a car clears the intersection, it vanishes (is no longer of interest). The rules for the intersection are as follows (a *tick* is one cycle through the loop in the design presented):

a. First car at intersection gets to go first.

b. A right turn takes one tick.

c. A straight takes two ticks.

d. A left turn takes three ticks.

The simulation should run for a number of ticks input by the user or until a *gridlock* occurs. A gridlock occurs when one lane is full (contains ten cars).

The simulation should show a car moving through the intersection. A car arriving in one of the lanes fills the next empty slot.

Upon exit from the main loop, the following should be reported:

a. The condition of the intersection (gridlock, success).

b. The number of ticks.

c. The probabilities entered for each lane.

d. The number of cars in each lane.

Turn in a design and its refinements, a structured diagram, a copy of your program, and a copy of the report just described for three sample executions.

Chapter Eight

Records

Introduction

In this chapter, you will study the data structure called RECORD. This data structure solves one of the basic problems of arrays. In an array, all components must be of the same data type (BOOLEAN, INTEGER, etc.). With records, each record is made up of fields and each field can be of a different data type. You will study how to combine the data structure RECORD with the data structure ARRAY OF to produce a new data structure called a list of records, one of the most useful data structures in the Pascal language. You will study how to search and sort a list of records. When you finish this chapter, you will be able to write a Pascal program that uses the data structure RECORD.

```
PROGRAM Chapter8 ;

CONST ListLen = 6 ;

TYPE String20 = STRING [20] ;
     NameType = RECORD                              {page 428}
                     First : CHAR ;
                     Last : String20
                END ;
     Person = RECORD
                     Who : NameType ;              {page 442}
                     Age : INTEGER ;
                     Sex : BOOLEAN
                END ;
     ListType = ARRAY [1 .. ListLen] OF Person ;   {page 431}

VAR APerson : Person ;                             {page 443}
    AList :    ListType ;                          {page 431}
    TheFile : TEXT ;
    Index : 1 .. ListLen ;

PROCEDURE ShellSort (VAR TheList : ListType ;
                     TheLen : INTEGER) ;           {page 450}

  BEGIN
    {Instructions to do Shell sort}               {page 451}
  END ;

BEGIN               {main program}
  ASSIGN (TheFile, 'People.TXT') ;
  RESET (TheFile) ;
  FOR Index := 1 TO ListLen DO
    WITH AList [Index] DO                          {page 446}
      BEGIN
        READLN (TheFile, Who.First) ;             {page 429}
        READLN (TheFile, Who.Last) ;
        READLN (TheFile, Age)
      END ;
  CLOSE (TheFile) ;
  ShellSort (AList, ListLen) ;                     {page 451}
  WRITELN ('Records by age are:') ;
  FOR Index := 1 TO ListLen DO
    BEGIN
      WRITE (AList [Index].Who.Last:20) ;         {page 443}
      WRITELN (AList [Index].Age)                 {page 429}
    END
END .            {main program}
```

RECORDS and Arrays

In this section, you will be introduced to the data structure RECORD. You will see how fields are used to define record-type data and you will see how to access a field of a variable of type RECORD. Finally, you will study how the data structure RECORD is combined with the data structure ARRAY OF to yield the data structure array of records (list of records).

In Chapter 6, parallel arrays were introduced as lists that are related in some sense. In Chapter 7, it was stated that if parallel arrays had the *same* component type (CHAR, INTEGER, etc) they could be combined into a table. When the component types of parallel arrays are *different*, an array of records can be used to combine the data into one data structure. Consider the parallel arrays in Figure 8–1.

Figure 8–1

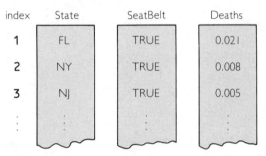

The array `State` has component type STRING. The array `SeatBelt` has component type BOOLEAN. The array `Deaths` has component type REAL. These parallel arrays *cannot* be combined into a two-dimensional array. However, by defining a record with fields of type STRING, BOOLEAN, and REAL, then using an array of records, the lists in Figure 8–1 can be combined into a single data structure (an array of records). To do this, you must first learn about records.

8-1.1 Defining a RECORD Type

As with any data structure, the **RECORD** data structure provides a structuring on simpler data types. The structuring provided is that of a record. The simpler data types can be any valid Pascal data type (except TEXT).

A good analogy of the Pascal data type RECORD is a record like your student record that is in the personnel department. On this record is your name, your parents' names, courses you are taking, scores you have made on standardized tests, comments made by some of your earlier teachers, and so forth. This collection of data is organized into a form. The pieces of data are of different types. Some of the information is string-type data, some is numerical data. Other everyday examples of records are credit records, military records, and social security records.

To define a RECORD type in a TYPE section, the following form is used:

```
TYPE identifier = RECORD
                    field1 identifier : type ;
                    field2 identifier : type ;
                        .
                        .
                    fieldn identifier : type
                 END
```

An example of a definition of a RECORD type is as follows:

```
TYPE Person = RECORD
              Name : STRING [40] ;
              Address : STRING [40] ;
              Age : INTEGER ;
              Income : REAL
          END
```

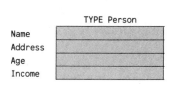

The identifiers `Name`, `Address`, `Age`, and `Income` are called **fields** of the record. With the type, `Person`, defined, a variable could now be declared and its type stated as `Person`. For example,

```
VAR Customer : Person
```

declares the identifier `Customer` to be a variable and states that the values it will hold are of type `Person` (a record). The following instructions would assign a value to the variable `Customer`:

```
Customer.Name := 'John Small' ;
Customer.Address := '123 Boxwood Av Helena, Montana' ;
Customer.Age := 26 ;
Customer.Income := 32000
```

A variable of type RECORD is assigned a value by assigning a value to each field of the record. A *period* is used to specify which field of the record is being *accessed*. The identifiers separated by a period (such as `Customer.Age`) are called **field selectors** (see Figure 8–2).

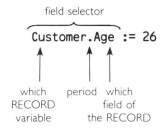

Figure 8–2

COMMENT

All variables of type `Person` have the field identifiers `Name`, `Address`, `Age`, and `Income`. That is, if `Supplier` is also of type `Person` then `Supplier.Name := 'Raoul Bliss'` is a valid assignment to the `Name` field of `Supplier`.

As an illustration of defining a record and accessing the fields of the record, consider this example.

EXAMPLE

Define a type `PartRec`, to be a record with fields `PartName`, `PartNum`, `Quantity`, and `Ordered`. Declare `Parts` to be a variable of type `PartRec`. Write instructions to assign a value to each field of the variable `Parts`. Allow the user to verify the assignment. That is, the code should echo the field assignments, then allow the user to re-enter the values if assignments are incorrect.

Sample Execution

```
Enter part name: spark plug
Enter part number (1000 .. 9999):
Enter quantity on hand: 58
Is part ordered?(Y/N): N

The record entered is:
Name: spark plug
ID Number: 1205
Quantity: 58
On order: No
Is record correct?(Y/N):
```

SOLUTION

See Figure 8–3.

Figure 8–3

```
TYPE Digits = 1000 .. 9999 ;
     WholeNum = 0 .. MAXINT ;
     PartRec = RECORD
                    PartName : STRING [40] ;
                    PartNum : Digits ;
                    Quantity : WholeNum ;
                    Ordered : BOOLEAN
                END ;

VAR Ans, OK : CHAR ;
    Parts : PartRec ;

BEGIN
  REPEAT
    WRITE ('Enter part name: ') ;            {Fill Record}
    READLN (Parts.PartName) ;
    WRITE ('Enter part number (1000 .. 9999): ') ;
    READLN (Parts.PartNum) ;
    WRITE ('Enter quantity on hand: ') ;
    READLN (Parts.Quantity) ;
    WRITE ('Is part ordered? (Y/N): ') ;
    READLN (Ans) ;
    IF (Ans = 'Y') OR (Ans = 'y')
      THEN Parts.Ordered := TRUE
      ELSE Parts.Ordered := FALSE ;
    WRITELN ;
    WRITELN ('The record entered is: ') ;    {Show record}
    WRITELN ('Name: ' , Parts.PartName) ;
    WRITELN ('ID Number: ' , Parts.PartNum) ;
    WRITELN ('Quantity: ' , Parts.Quantity) ;
    WRITE ('On order: ') ;
    IF Parts.Ordered
      THEN WRITELN ('Yes')
      ELSE WRITELN ('No')
    WRITELN ;
    WRITE ('Is record correct?(Y/N): ') ;    {verify record}
    READLN (OK)
  UNTIL (OK = 'Y') OR (OK = 'y')
END
```

Sample Execution

```
Enter part name: spark plug
Enter part number (1000 .. 9999):
Enter quantity on hand: 58
Is part ordered?(Y/N): N

The record entered is:
Name: spark plug
ID Number: 1205
Quantity: 58
On order: No
Is record correct?(Y/N):
```

Parts	TYPE PartRec
PartName	spark plug
PartNum	1205
Quantity	58
Ordered	FALSE

DO IT NOW

1. Given

```
TYPE StateRec = RECORD
                    Name : STRING [40] ;
                    Population : REAL ;
                    Area : REAL
                END ;

VAR State : StateRec ;
```

a. Write assignment instructions to assign to the variable `State` the record value: Utah; 1,461,037; 82,073.

b. Write instructions to output to the screen a record value stored in `State`.

2. Declare a record type called `AdRec` with the following fields: `Company`, a string of length 40; `Rank`, a number from 1 to 50; `Costs`, a number (in millions) from 129 to 726; `PerCent`, a REAL number representing percent of sales spent on advertising.

DO IT NOW ANSWERS

```
1a. State.Name := 'Utah' ;
    State.Population := 1461037 ;
    State.Area := 82073 ;
 b. WRITELN ('State: ' , State.Name) ;
    WRITELN ('Population: ', State.Population:1:0) ;
    WRITELN ('Area: ' , State.Area:1:0 , ' sq. miles') ;
 2. TYPE Number = 1 .. 50 ;
         Millions = 129 .. 726 ;
         AdRec = RECORD
                     Company : STRING [40] ;
                     Rank : Number ;
                     Costs : Millions ;
                     PerCent : REAL
                 END ;
```

8-1.2 *Array of RECORDS*

As mentioned at the start of this chapter, parallel arrays with different component types can be combined into a single data structure. This is accomplished by using the user-defined data structure **array of records**. Consider the parallel arrays presented at the start of this section (See Figure 8–4.)

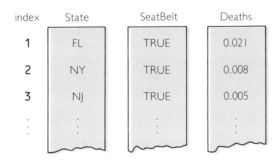

Figure 8–4

These three lists can be combined into an array of records as follows:

```
TYPE StateRec = RECORD
                    State : STRING [2] ;
                    SeatBelt : BOOLEAN ;
                    Deaths : REAL
                END ;
     RecList = ARRAY [1 .. 50] OF StateRec ;

VAR StateList : RecList
```

The identifier `StateList` has been declared a variable and its type stated as `RecList`. Thus, the values `StateList` will hold are one-dimensional arrays in which the components are of type `StateRec`. Each component of the array will be a record. An assignment to component 3 of `StateList` would be as follows:

```
StateList [3].State := 'NJ' ;
StateList [3].SeatBelt := TRUE ;
StateList [3].Deaths := 0.005
```

A picture of this data structure is presented in Figure 8–5.

Figure 8–5

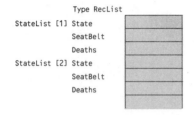

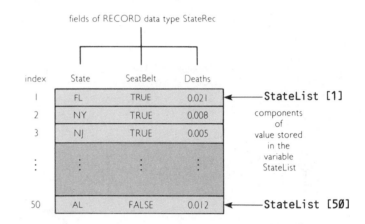

The following instruction could be used to assign a record value to each of the fifty cells of the variable `StateList`:

```
FOR Index := 1 TO 50 DO
  BEGIN
    WRITE ('Enter state name ', Index, ': ') ;
    READLN (StateList [Index].State) ;
    WRITE ('Does state have seat belt law?(Y/N): ') ;
    READLN (Ans) ;
    IF Ans = 'Y' OR Ans = 'y'
      THEN StateList [Index].SeatBt := TRUE
      ELSE StateList [Index].SeatBt := FALSE ;
    WRITE ('Enter highway death rate: ') ;
    READLN (StateList [Index].Deaths)
  END
```

Sample Execution

```
Enter state name 1: OH
Does state have seat belt law?(Y/N): Y
Enter highway death rate: 0.03
Enter state name 2: UT
Does state have seat belt law?(Y/N): N
```

DO IT NOW

1. Given

```
TYPE StateRec = RECORD
                  State : STRING [2] ;
                  SeatBelt : BOOLEAN ;
                  Deaths : REAL
                END ;
     RecList = ARRAY [1 .. 50] OF StateRec ;
VAR StateList : RecList
```

Write a Pascal procedure that has as input `StateList`. The procedure is to allow the user to alter the value in the variable parameter `StateList`. That is, the user is allowed enter new values for each of the fields of a record stored in the cells of `StateList`.

2. Write a Pascal procedure that has as input `StateList`. The procedure is to search the list of records for each state with a death rate higher than 0.01. The output is to be a listing of such states and the existence of a seatbelt law within those states.

3. Given

```
TYPE String2Ø = STRING [2Ø] ;
     Employees = ARRAY [1 .. 3] OF String2Ø ;
     Store = RECORD
                  Name : String2Ø ;
                  Location : String2Ø ;
                  Workers : Employees
             END ;
     Stores = ARRAY [1 .. 2Ø] OF Store ;
VAR StoreList : Stores
```

write an assignment instruction to assign Dot Dobbs to the second component of the `Workers` field for the fifth store in `StoreList`.

DO IT NOW ANSWERS

```
1. PROCEDURE AlterList (VAR StateList : RecList) ;

   VAR Index : 1 .. 5Ø ;
       Ans, OK : CHAR ;

   BEGIN                                              {AlterList}
     REPEAT
       WRITE ('Enter number of the record to alter (1..5Ø): ') ;
       READLN (Index) ;
       WRITELN ('Record number ', Index, ' is: ') ;
       WRITELN (StateList [Index].State) ;
       IF StateList [Index].SeatBelt
         THEN WRITELN (' has seatbelt law. ')
         ELSE WRITELN (' has no seatbelt law. ') ;
       WRITE ('Highway death rate is: ') ;
       WRITELN (StateList [Index].Deaths : 1 : 3) ;
       WRITE ('Re-enter state name?(Y/N): ') ;
       READLN (Ans) ;
       IF Ans = 'Y'
         THEN BEGIN                                   {alter State field}
               WRITE ('Enter state name: ') ;
               READLN (StateList [Index].State)
             END ;                                    {alter State field}
       WRITE ('Change law field? (Y/N): ') ;
       READLN (Ans) ;
       IF Ans = 'Y'                                   {alter SeatBelt field}
         THEN StateList [Index].SeatBelt := NOT (StateList [Index].SeatBelt) ;
       WRITE ('Change death rate? (Y/N): ') ;
       READLN (Ans) ;
       IF Ans = 'Y'
         THEN BEGIN                                   {alter Deaths field}
               WRITE ('Enter highway death rate: ') ;
               READLN (StateList [Index].Deaths)
             END ;                                    {alter Deaths field}
       WRITELN ('Press RETURN to alter another record.') ;
       WRITE ('Enter Q to quit. ') ;
       READLN (OK)
     UNTIL OK = 'Q'
   END                                                {AlterList}
```

```
2. PROCEDURE SearchRate (StateList : RecList) ;

     VAR Index : 1 .. 50 ;

     BEGIN                                          {SearchRate}
       WRITELN ('States with death rates over 1%: ') ;
       FOR Index := 1 TO 50 DO
         IF StateList [Index].Deaths > 0.01
           THEN BEGIN                               {THEN instruction}
                   WRITE (StateList [Index].State) ;
                   IF StateList [Index].SeatBelt
                     THEN WRITELN (' --Seatbelt law')
                     ELSE WRITELN (' --No seatbelt law')
                END                                  {THEN instruction}
     END                                            {SearchRate}
3. StoreList [5].Workers [2] := 'Dot Dobbs'
```

8-1.3 A Programming Example

Next, consider this problem involving an array of records and a TEXT file.

PROBLEM

A local bank has a summary of its customer records in a TEXT file. The lines of the TEXT file are similar to the following:

```
Polset, Thomas M.  <end-of-line marker>
546-0145  <end-of-line marker>
-23.56  <end-of-line marker>
Pursey, Lucy J.  <end-of-line marker>
567-1234  <end-of-line marker>
378.65  <end-of-line marker>
```

```
Menu

A. See a customer record
B. See list of overdrawn accounts
C. See total of all checking accounts
Q. Quit
```

Each set of three lines contains a name, an account number, and a balance. The bank needs a Pascal program that allows the user to select from the menu shown.

SOLUTION

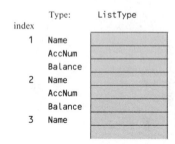

First, a data structure is selected. For this problem, a list of records is chosen:

```
Customer = RECORD
                Name : STRING [40] ;
                AccNum : STRING [8] ;
                Balance : REAL
             END ;

ListType = ARRAY [1 .. IndexMax] OF Customer
```

Design: REPEAT
              Present menu
              Get selection
              CASE Select OF
                  'A' : FindName
                  'B' : ScanBalance
                  'C' : SumBalance
              END
          UNTIL Select = 'Q'

Refinement of: *FillList*
        Open file
        Index : = 0
        WHILE NOT EOF (InFile) DO
            Index : = Index + 1
            READLN (InFile , List [Index].Name)
            READLN (InFile , List [Index].AccNum)
            READLN (InFile , List [Index].Balance)
        Close file

COMMENT
This procedure reads three lines of TEXT file to fill one cell of **List**.

Refinement of: *FindName*
        WRITE ('Enter name of customer')
        WRITE (' (last, first, middle initial): ')
        READLN (Name)
        BinarySearch (List, Length, Name, Found)
        IF Found = 0
          THEN WRITELN ('Name not found')
          ELSE WRITELN ('Name: ' , List [Found].Name)
              WRITE ('Account number:')
              WRITELN (List [Found].AccNum)
              WRITE ('Balance: $')
              WRITELN (List [Found].Balance:1:2)

COMMENT
The procedure **BinarySearch** must be altered to deal with a list of records.

Refinement of: *ScanBalance*
        Index : = 1
        WHILE (Index < = ListLen) DO
           IF List [Index].Balance < 0
             THEN WRITELN ('Name. ' , List [Index].Name)
                WRITE ('Account Number: ')
                WRITELN (List [Index].AccNum)
                 WRITE ('Balance: $')
                WRITELN (List [Index].Balance:1:2)
           Index : = Index + 1

COMMENT
Because this procedure and the procedure **FindRecord** must write the record to the screen, a procedure will be used to write the record to the screen.

Refinement of: *SumBalance*
        Sum : = 0
        FOR Index : = 1 TO ListLen DO
           Sum : = Sum + List [Index].Balance
        WRITE ('Sum of all accounts is: $' , Sum:1:2)

A structured diagram of this design is shown in Figure 8–6. The design yields the Pascal program in Figure 8–7.

Figure 8–6

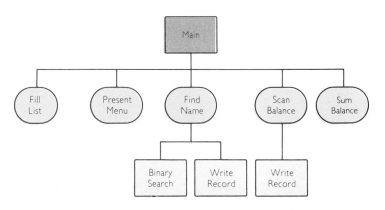

Figure 8-7

```pascal
PROGRAM CheckAccount ;

CONST IndexMax = 200 ;

TYPE Customer = RECORD
                     Name : STRING [40] ;
                     AccNum : STRING [8] ;
                     Balance : REAL
                 END ;
     ListType = ARRAY [1 .. IndexMax] OF Customer ;
     WholeNum = 0 .. MAXINT ;
     String40 : STRING [40] ;

VAR List : ListType ;
    Select : CHAR ;
    InFile : TEXT ;
    ListLen : WholeNum ;

PROCEDURE FillList (VAR InFile : TEXT ; VAR List : ListType ;
                    VAR Index : WholeNum) ;

  BEGIN                                    {FillList}
    ASSIGN (InFile, 'Accounts.TXT') ;
    RESET (InFile) ;
    Index := 0 ;
    WHILE NOT EOF (InFile) DO
      BEGIN
        Index := Index + 1 ;              {keep up with length of list}
        READLN (InFile , List [Index].Name) ;
        READLN (InFile , List [Index].AccNum) ;
        READLN (InFile , List [Index].Balance)
      END ;
    CLOSE (InFile)                         {Close file}
  END ;                                    {FillList}

PROCEDURE PresentMenu ;

  BEGIN                                    {PresentMenu}
    WRITELN ;
    WRITELN ('A. Find name') ;
    WRITELN ('B. Find overdrawn accounts') ;
    WRITELN ('C. Find sum of all accounts') ;
    WRITELN ('Q. Quit') ;
    WRITELN
  END;                                     {Present Menu}

PROCEDURE WriteRecord (TheRecord : Customer) ;

  BEGIN                                    {WriteRecord}
    WRITELN ('Name: ', TheRecord.Name) ;
    WRITELN ('Account number: ', TheRecord.AccNum) ;
    WRITELN ('Balance: $', TheRecord.Balance:1:2)
  END;                                     {WriteRecord}

PROCEDURE FindName (VAR List : ListType ; ListLen : WholeNum) ;

  VAR Name : STRING [40] ;
      Found : WholeNum ;

  PROCEDURE BinarySearch (ListLen : WholeNum ; Target : String40 ;
                          List : ListType ;
                          VAR Found : WholeNum) ;

    VAR High , Low , Mid : INTEGER ;
```

COMMENT

Read three lines of `InFile` to fill the fields of `List [Index]`

Sample Execution

```
Name: Polset, Thomas M.
Account number: 546-0145
Balance: $-23.56
```

```
      BEGIN                                       {BinarySearch}
        Found := 0 ;
        High := ListLen + 1 ;
        Low := 0 ;
        WHILE ((High - Low) > 1) AND (Found = 0) DO
          BEGIN                                   {WHILE-DO}
            Mid := (High + Low) DIV 2 ;
            IF List [Mid].Name = Target
              THEN Found := Mid
              ELSE IF Target > List [Mid].Name
                      THEN Low := Mid
                      ELSE High := Mid
          END                                     {WHILE-DO}
      END ;                                       {BinarySearch}

  BEGIN                                           {FindName}
    WRITE ('Enter name of customer') ;
    WRITE (' (last, first, middle initial): ') ;
    READLN (Name) ;
    BinarySearch (ListLen, Name, List, Found) ;
    IF Found = 0
      THEN WRITELN ('Name not found')
      ELSE WriteRecord (List [Found])
  END ;                                           {FindName}

PROCEDURE ScanBalance (VAR List : ListType ; ListLen : WholeNum) ;

  VAR Index : WholeNum ;

  BEGIN                                           {ScanBalance}
    Index := 1 ;
    WHILE (Index <= ListLen) DO
      BEGIN
        IF List [Index].Balance < 0
          THEN WriteRecord (List [Index]) ;
        Index := Index + 1
      END
  END ;                                           {ScanBalance}

PROCEDURE SumBalance (VAR List : ListType ; ListLen : WholeNum) ;

  VAR Sum : REAL ;
      Index : WholeNum ;

  BEGIN                                           {SumBalance}
    Sum := 0 ;
    FOR Index := 1 TO ListLen DO
      Sum := Sum + List[Index].Balance ;
    WRITELN ('Sum of all accounts is: $', Sum:1:2)
  END ;                                           {SumBalance}
BEGIN                                             {main program}
  FillList (InFile, List, ListLen) ;
  REPEAT
    PresentMenu ;
    WRITE ('Enter A,B,C,Q:') ;
    READLN (Select) ;
    CASE Select OF
      'A' : FindName (List, ListLen) ;
      'B' : ScanBalance (List, ListLen) ;
      'C' : SumBalance (List, ListLen)
    END
  UNTIL Select = 'Q'
END .                                             {main program}
```

Figure 8–7

Continued

Sample Execution

```
Enter name of customer (last, fir
Name: Pursey, Lucy J.
Account number: 576-1234
Balance: $378.65
```

Sample Execution

```
Name: Davis, L.S.
Account number: 437-5812
Balance: $-13.13
Name: Boles, Sam K.
Account number: 322-5117
Balance: $-52.28
```

Sample Execution

```
Sum of all accounts is: $17000.00
```

DO IT NOW

1. In program `CheckAccount` in Figure 8–7, what would happen if the user selected `A` from the main menu and entered the name `Thomas M. Polset` for the prompt `Enter name of customer (last, first, middle initial):`?
2. Could the `BinarySearch` procedure be used to search the account number fields of the list of records?
3. Alter the procedure `SumBalance` to sum only the accounts with a positive balance.

DO IT NOW ANSWERS

1. The message `Record not found` would be written to the screen since the `Name` field has the format `Last, First Middle initial`.
2. No. The list of account numbers is not ordered.
3. Change the instruction of the FOR-DO instruction to read as follows:

```
IF List[Index].Balance > Ø
   THEN Sum := Sum + List[Index].Balance
```

Vocabulary

Page		
431	**Array of records**	A user-defined data structure composed by using the data structures ARRAY OF and RECORD. The data structure is a list and the components of the list are records.
429	**Field selector**	A path for selecting a particular field of a record. The path is composed of the record variable identifier, a period, and the field identifier. Example: For `Customer` of type `Person` (where `Person` is a record type with fields `Name`, `Age`, and `Sex`), `Customer.Name` is a field selector.
428	**RECORD**	A structured data type. A value of type RECORD is a collection of a fixed number of fields. The fields can be of any standard type (except TEXT) or any user-defined type. Example:

```
Person = RECORD
           Name : STRING [15] ;
           Age : INTEGER ;
           Sex : (Male , Female)
         END
```

429	**Record field**	One of the components of a value of type RECORD. The field is made up of an identifier and a data type. Example: `Name` is a field of the following record type:

```
Person = RECORD
           Name : STRING [4Ø] ;
           Age : INTEGER
         END
```

Glad You Asked

Q How many fields can a record have?

A The only limit is the available memory. It is not uncommon for a record to have ten or more fields.

Q Can a list of records be sorted? If so, which field would be used for the sort?

A Yes. This is one of the attractions of an array of records. Suppose the records have fields `Name` and `Age`. The list can be sorted and output ordered alphabetically by name.

The list can be sorted again and output ordered by age. More on sorting lists of records will appear in the next section.

Q Can I use the same field identifier in the definition of different records?

A Yes. But it is not recommended! It is best to eliminate any source of possible confusion.

Q You said an array of records can be constructed. Can a field of a record be an array?

A Yes. When a field is of type STRING, the field is a list of characters. However, the idea can be expanded. You could have a record like this one:

```
State : RECORD
          Name : STRING [20] ;
          Population : REAL ;
          Size : REAL ;
          Cities : ARRAY [1 ..10] OF STRING [20]
        END
```

Here, the field `Cities` is an array. An assignment to this field might be as follows:

```
State.Cities [2] := 'Dubuque'
```

Suppose you wanted to select all cities whose name starts with N, the following instruction would select the cities.

```
FOR Ct := 1 TO 10 DO
  IF State.Cities [Ct][1] = 'N'
    THEN ...
```

Q Can a field of a record be a record?

A Yes. This type of data structure is called a *nested record* (like a nested FOR-DO). Nested records will be discussed in the next section.

Q Can a record value be written to a TEXT file?

A No. The components of a TEXT file are characters. That is, the data structure TEXT provides a structuring for the simpler data type CHAR. Although numbers can be written to a TEXT file, they are first converted to character data. In the next chapter, you will be introduced to a file whose components can be of type RECORD.

Section 8–1 Exercises

For problems 1 through 7, use the TYPE and VAR sections given here.

```
TYPE College = RECORD
                 Name : STRING [40] ;
                 Students : REAL ;
                 Teachers : 1 .. 3000 ;
                 City : STRING [20] ;
                 State : STRING [20] ;
                 ZIP : STRING [12]
               END ;

  VAR CollRec : College ;
```

1. Which of the following assigns to the `City` field of `CollRec` the value `Detroit`?
   a. `College.City := 'Detroit'`   c. `CollRec.City := 'Detroit'`
   b. `City := 'Detroit'`   d. `CollRec := 'Detroit'`
2. Which of the following assigns to the `Teachers` field of `CollRec` the value 1294?
   a. `Teachers := 1294`   c. `CollRec.Teachers := 1294`
   b. `Teachers.Field := 1294`   d. `College.Teachers := 1294`

```
TYPE College =
  RECORD
    Name : STRING [40] ;
    Students : REAL ;
    Teachers : 1 .. 3000 ;
    City : STRING [20] ;
    State : STRING [20] ;
    ZIP : STRING [12]
  END ;

VAR CollRec : College ;
```

3. Which of the following will write the value in the student field to the screen?
   a. WRITE (CollRec.Students)   **c.** WRITE (College.Students)
   b. WRITELN (Students)   **d.** WRITE (College)

4. Which of the following is a field?
   a. College   **b.** REAL   **c.** CollRec   **d.** ZIP

5. Which of the following is a field selector?
   a. College.ZIP   **b.** CollRec   **c.** College   **d.** CollRec.City

6. Write instructions to assign to CollRec the value:

   Butler University 4058 340 Indianapolis Indiana 46208

7. Write instructions to output to the screen a value in CollRec.

8. Which of the following is a user-composed data structure?
   a. STRING   **b.** REAL   **c.** CHAR   **d.** list of records   **e.** TEXT

9. Define a record data type called Scientists that has fields Name, BirthYear, Nationality, Occupation, and NotedFor. A typical value stored in the record is as follows:

   Bohr, Niels 1882 Danish physicist
   leading figure in development of quantum theory.

10. Define a record type called TVShows that has fields Program, Date, Network, Households. A typical value to be stored in the record is

    M*A*S*H Special 2/28/83 CBS 50150000

11. Design a record type ActressAward that will hold the data on one of the following lines. Also, define AwardList an array with component type ActressAward.

Year	Actress	Movie
1979	Sally Field	Norma Rae
1980	Sissy Spacek	Coal Miner's Daughter
1981	Katharine Hepburn	On Golden Pond
.	.	.
.	.	.
.	.	.

12. Boot up Pascal; set the workfile to the file CheckAcc.PAS from the Source diskette. Enter the editor. Alter the data type Customer by replacing the Name field with fields FName and LName of type STRING [20] and MidInit of type STRING [2]. Alter the remainder of the program to work with this data type.

Programming Problems

Problems 13 through 18 refer to the following CONST, TYPE, and VAR sections:

```
CONST MaxIndex = 50 ;

TYPE RecordType = RECORD
                    Park : STRING [20] ;
                    Location : STRING [20] ;
                    Year : 1850 .. 2000 ;
                    Acreage : REAL ;
                    Comment : STRING [255]
                  END ;
     ListType = ARRAY [1 .. MaxIndex] OF RecordType ;

VAR NatPark : RecordType ;
    ParkList : ListType ;
```

13. Write a Pascal procedure to write to the screen the contents of a value stored in the variable `NatPark`.

14. Write a Pascal procedure to allow the user to fill the list `ParkList` with records like the following:

Acadia	Maine	1919	38632	Rugged seashore on Mt. Desert Island.
Arches	Utah	1971	39056	Stone arches, pedestals caused by wind erosion.
Badlands	South Dakota	1978	243302	Arid land of fossils, prairie, bison, bighorn sheep, antelope.
:				

The user is to fill the list with the `Park` field in alphabetical order.

15. Write a Pascal procedure that allows the user to save the list of records `ParkList` to a TEXT file. The lines of the TEXT file should appear as follows:

```
Acadia  <end-of-line marker>
Maine  <end-of-line marker>
1919  <end-of-line marker>
38632  <end-of-line marker>
Rugged seashore on Mt. Desert Island.  <end-of-line marker>
Arches  <end-of-line marker>
Utah  <end-of-line marker>
1971  <end-of-line marker>
39056  <end-of-line marker>
Stone arches, pedestals caused by wind erosion.  <end-of-line marker>
:
:
```

16. Write a Pascal procedure that will read the TEXT file in problem 15 to fill the list of records `ParkList`.

17. Write a Pascal procedure that allows the user to enter a state's name. The procedure is to write to the screen all national parks located in the state.

Sample Execution

```
Please enter state name: Florida
Biscayne- Aquatic, coral reef park south of Miami.
Everglades- Subtropical swamp with abundant bird life.
```

18. Write a Pascal procedure that will write to the screen the total number of acres in all the national parks.

19. Ernie has a TEXT file (named `ErnieMov.TXT`) that contains lines like these:

Star Wars	1977	185138000	<end-of-line marker>
The Empire Strikes Back	1980	134209000	<end-of-line marker>
Jaws	1975	133435000	<end-of-line marker>
Grease	1978	96300000	<end-of-line marker>
:	:	:	

Sample Execution

```
Please enter year: 1973
The highest revenue movie
through 1973 was:
The Exorcist $88500000
```

Each line contains the name of a movie, year released, and sales. Write a Pascal program that will read the information into a list of records.

20. Expand the program written in problem 19 to allow the user to enter a year. The program is to write to the screen the movie that produced the highest revenue through the year input.

Sample Execution

```
Enter occupation: Traveler
Polo, Marco
Venice
Italy
1254 - 1324
```

21. Suppose a list of records exists that contains information about famous people. The fields of the record are `Name`, `Occupation`, `City`, `Country`, `Lived`. Typical entries in the list are

Jagger, Mick	Nostradamus, Michel	Renoir, Pierre
Singer	Astrologer	Painter
Dartford	St. Remy	Limoges
England	France	France
1944 -	1503 - 1566	1841 - 1919

Write a Pascal procedure that has variable parameter `Famous` (the list of records) and value parameter `ListLen` (the length of the list). The procedure is to allow the user to input an occupation. The procedure is to then write to the screen the records from the list that have the input occupation.

22. The MyT Quick stores in the Flat Hills area need a Pascal program to read a TEXT file named `MyTQ.TXT`. The lines of the TEXT file are similar to the following:

```
MyTQUICK #1    <end-of-line marker>
Blount Street    <end-of-line marker>
Kim Kline    <end-of-line marker>
Bill Downs    <end-of-line marker>
Sabina Salts    <end-of-line marker>
```

That is, each group of five lines yields a store name, location, and employees list. Each store has three employees. The TEXT file is to be read into a list of records with fields `Name`, `Location`, and `Workers`. There should be fifteen stores in the list of records.

Section 8–2

Working with Records

In the last section, you were introduced to the data structure RECORD. In this section, you will learn about some additional features of this data structure. These features are hierarchical (nested) records and the instruction WITH. You will learn a new sorting method called the Shell sort.

8-2.1 Hierarchical Records

As with most data structures in Pascal, the data structure RECORD can be built upon. That is, the fields of the record can be declared types like ARRAY or RECORD. Just as the instructions of a program can be refined by using procedures and functions, the fields of a record can be refined. Records which contain a field of type RECORD are called **hierarchical records**, **nested records**, or **tree structures**. Consider the record type given in the last section:

```
TYPE Person = RECORD
                 Name : STRING [40] ;
                 Address : STRING [80] ;
                 Age : INTEGER ;
                 Income : REAL
              END
```

The field `Name` could be refined as

```
NameRec = RECORD
            First : STRING [18] ;
            MidInit : STRING [2] ;
            Last : STRING [20]
          END
```

Likewise, the field `Address` could be refined as

```
AddRec = RECORD
            Street : STRING [40] ;
            City : STRING [20] ;
            State : STRING [20]
          END
```

Now the TYPE section would appear as shown in Figure 8–8.

Figure 8–8

```
TYPE NameRec = RECORD
                  First : STRING [18] ;
                  MidInit : STRING [2] ;
                  Last : STRING [20]
                END ;
     AddRec = RECORD
                  Street : STRING [40] ;
                  City : STRING [20] ;
                  State : STRING [20]
                END ;
     Person = RECORD
                  Name : NameRec ;
                  Address : AddRec ;
                  Age : INTEGER ;
                  Income : REAL
                END
```

Declaring variable `Customer` to be of type `Person`, a value would now be assigned to `Customer` as follows:

```
Customer.Name.First := 'John' ;
Customer.Name.MidInit := 'G' ;
Customer.Name.Last := 'Small' ;
Customer.Address.Street := '125 Boxwood Av.' ;
Customer.Address.City := 'Helena' ;
Customer.Address.State := 'Montana' ;
Customer.Age := 26 ;
Customer.Income := 31000 ;
```

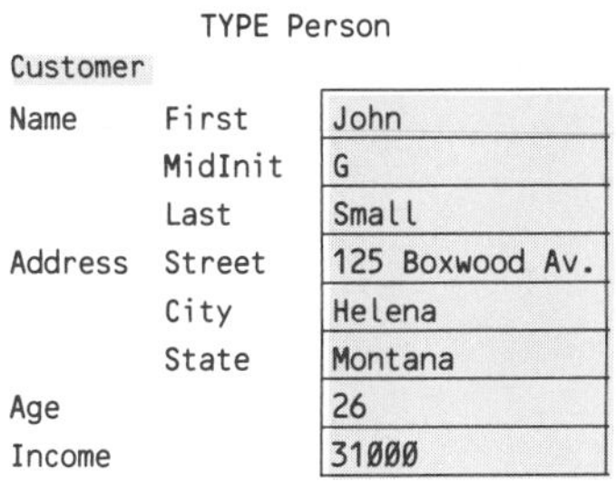

	TYPE Person	
Customer		
Name	First	John
	MidInit	G
	Last	Small
Address	Street	125 Boxwood Av.
	City	Helena
	State	Montana
Age		26
Income		31000

As you can see, to access the inner fields a **path** is followed. The field selector, `Customer.Name.Last`, accesses the record `Customer`, then the field `Name`, then the field `Last`. A diagram of the record type `Person` would be as shown in Figure 8–9.

Figure 8–9

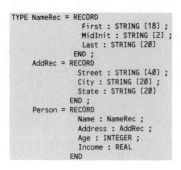

```
TYPE NameRec = RECORD
                First : STRING [18] ;
                MidInit : STRING [2] ;
                Last : STRING [20]
              END ;
     AddRec = RECORD
                Street : STRING [40] ;
                City : STRING [20] ;
                State : STRING [20]
              END ;
     Person = RECORD
                Name : NameRec ;
                Address : AddRec ;
                Age : INTEGER ;
                Income : REAL
              END
```

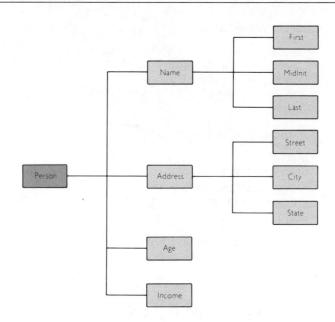

This diagram is called a *tree diagram* of the data structure. Often a data structure such as `Person` is called a *tree structure*. The box labeled `Person` is called the *root* of the tree. Each field that is not subdivided (`Last, Age`, etc.) is called a *leaf* of the tree.

Assignments (with the assignment operator : = , `READ`, etc.) with RECORD-type data are done by fields. Thus, for variables `Debtor` and `Customer` of type `Person`, the following instructions are valid assignments:

```
Debtor := Customer ;
Debtor.Name := Customer.Name ;
Debtor.Name.First := Customer.Name.First
```

COMMENT
RECORD variables cannot be used with the relationals in Turbo Pascal. That is,
`Debtor <= Customer` yields the error message
`structured variables are not allowed.`

That is, two records of the same type and/or two fields of the same type can be used with the assignment operation. Also, for `Debtor` of type `Person` and `Owner` of type `Name`, the following are valid assignments:

```
Debtor.Name := Owner ;
Debtor.Name.Last := Owner.Last
```

DO IT NOW

Given the TYPE and VAR sections in Figure 8–10,

1. Draw a diagram of the record type `Day`.
2. Write an instruction to make an assignment to the `Clouds` field of the variable `Today`.
3. On February 10 the clouds were of type stratus, the low temperature was − 6, the high temperature was 35, and the average temperature was 28.6. Record this information in the appropriate record in the variable `Month`.

Figure 8-10

```
    TYPE CloudType = (cirrus, cumulus, nimbus, stratus);
         Temp = RECORD
                     HiTemp : INTEGER ;
                     LoTemp : INTEGER ;
                     AvTemp : REAL
                  END ;
           DateType = RECORD
                          DayNum : 1 .. 31 ;
                          MonthNum : 1 .. 12
                       END ;
           Condition = RECORD
                           Clouds : CloudType ;
                           Thermo : Temp
                        END ;
           Day = RECORD
                     Date : DateType ;
                     Weather : Condition
                  END ;
    VAR Today : Day ;
        Month : ARRAY [1 .. 31] OF Day ;
```

DO IT NOW ANSWERS

1. A diagram of **Day** would be as follows:

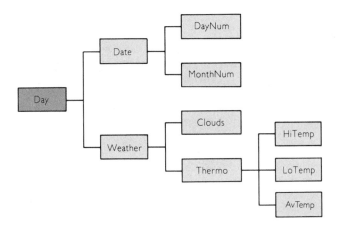

2. One possible assignment is

        Today.Weather.Clouds := cirrus

3. Month [10].Date.DayNum := 10 ;
   Month [10].Date.MonthNum := 2 ;
   Month [10].Weather.Clouds := stratus ;
   Month [10].Weather.Thermo.HiTemp := 35 ;
   Month [10].Weather.Thermo.LoTemp := -6 ;
   Month [10].Weather.Thermo.AvTemp := 28.6

8-2.2 WITH

As you can see from the last Do It Now exercise, nested records often require quite a lot of information to be written to access a field of the record. The Pascal instruction **WITH** can be used to reduce the amount written to access a field of a record. For example, suppose you wanted to write to the screen the high and low temperature for the record value in the variable Today (see Figure 8–10 or Figure 8–11). Using the WITH instruction, this could be accomplished as follows:

```
WITH Today.Weather.Thermo DO
  BEGIN
    WRITELN ('High temperature was: ', HiTemp) ;
    WRITELN ('Low temperature was: ' , LoTemp)
  END
```

The record path (Today.Weather.Thermo) is stated once in the WITH instruction. Throughout the block bracketed by the BEGIN-END, only the field selector is used. This WITH instruction replaces the instructions

```
WRITELN ('High temperature was: ', Today.Weather.Thermo.HiTemp) ;
WRITELN ('Low temperature was: ', Today.Weather.Thermo.LoTemp)
```

The general form of the WITH instruction is

```
WITH record identifier DO
     < instruction >
```

The *record identifier* can be the root of the record or part of the path up to the leaf of the record. In the example just given, Today.Weather.Thermo was a path of the record. For a nested record such as

```
TYPE NameRec = RECORD
                   First : STRING [18] ;
                   MidInit : STRING [2] ;
                   Last : STRING [20]
                 END ;
     AddRec = RECORD
                   Street : STRING [40] ;
                   City : STRING [20] ;
                   State : STRING [20]
                 END ;
     Person = RECORD
                   Name : NameRec ;
                   Address : AddRec ;
                   Age : INTEGER ;
                   Income : REAL
                 END ;

VAR Customer : Person ;
```

two possible forms of the WITH instruction are as follows:

```
WITH Customer DO              and         WITH Customer.Address DO
     < instruction >                           < instruction >
```

The instruction part of the WITH instruction can be a simple or compound instruction.

For a compound instruction, BEGIN-END is used to mark the scope of the WITH instruction. Any reference to an identifier in the BEGIN-END block of the

WITH instruction that matches a field of the record is a reference to the field selector. That is, suppose `First` is a program variable which is also used as a field selector for the RECORD-type variable `Customer` (this is not a recommended practice). In the instructions

```
First := 'Mary' ;
WITH Customer.Name DO
  BEGIN
     .
     .
    First := 'John' ;          {Assignment to Customer.Name.First}
     .
     .
  END ;
WRITE (First) ;                {outputs Mary}
  .
  .
```

the field selector `Customer.Name.First` is assigned the value `'John'`. However, the instruction `WRITE (First)` will output `Mary`. Outside the BEGIN-END block of the WITH instruction, the instruction

```
WRITE (Customer.Name.First)
```

must be used to output `John`. Inside the BEGIN-END block of the WITH instruction, the instruction `WRITE (First)` is all that is needed to output the value in the `First` field of `Customer.Name`.

DO IT NOW

Given the TYPE and VAR sections in Figure 8–11,

1. Write an instruction using `WITH` to assign a value to the variable `Today`. (Add any variables needed to the VAR section.)
2. Write a FOR-DO instruction to write to the screen the `Temp` field of the records in `Month`. (Add any variables needed to the VAR section.)

Figure 8–11

```
TYPE CloudType = (cirrus, cumulus, nimbus, stratus);
     Temp = RECORD
               HiTemp : INTEGER ;
               LoTemp : INTEGER ;
               AvTemp : REAL
            END ;
     DateType = RECORD
                   DayNum : 1 .. 31 ;
                   MonthNum : 1 .. 12
                END ;
     Condition = RECORD
                    Clouds : CloudType ;
                    Thermo : Temp
                 END ;
     Day = RECORD
              Date : DateType ;
              Weather : Condition
           END ;

VAR Today : Day ;
    Month : ARRAY [1 .. 31] OF Day ;
    Index : 1 .. 31 ;
```

Add Ans : CHAR and Finished : BOOLEAN to the VAR section.

```
Enter day of month (1..31): 5
Enter month of the year (1..12): 1
Select cloud type for day:
A=Cirrus B=Stratus C=Cumulus D=Nimbus
Enter A,B,C,D: A
Enter high temperature: 52
Enter low temperature: 35
Enter average temperature: 43.5
```

```
1. BEGIN
    WITH Today.Date DO
      BEGIN
        WRITE ('Enter day of month (1 .. 31): ') ;
        READLN (DayNum) ;
        WRITE ('Enter month of the year (1 .. 12): ') ;
        READLN (MonthNum)
      END ;
    WRITELN ('Select cloud type for day.') ;
    WRITELN ('A=Cirrus B=Stratus C=Cumulus D=Nimbus') ;
    WRITE ('Enter A,B,C,D: ') ;
    READLN (Ans) ;
    WITH Today.Weather DO
      BEGIN
        Clouds := Cirrus ;
        Finished := FALSE ;
        WHILE NOT Finished DO
          IF ORD (Clouds) < > (ORD (Ans) - ORD ('A'))
            THEN Clouds := SUCC (Clouds)
            ELSE Finished := TRUE
      END ;
    WITH Today.Weather.Thermo DO
      BEGIN
        WRITE ('Enter high temperature: ') ;
        READLN (HiTemp) ;
        WRITE ('Enter low temperature: ') ;
        READLN (LoTemp) ;
        WRITE ('Enter average temperature: ') ;
        READLN (AvTemp)
      END
  END
2. FOR Index := 1 TO 31 DO
    WITH Month [Index].Weather.Thermo DO
      BEGIN
        WRITE (Index , '. High temperature: ' , HiTemp) ;
        WRITE (' Low temperature: ' , LoTemp) ;
        WRITELN (' Average temperature: ' , AvTemp : 1 : 2)
      END
```

8-2.3 Shell Sort

Before considering sorting records, we will look at a new sort technique. This technique is known as the **Shell sort** (named for its inventor, Donald Shell). The Shell sort is similar to the bubble sort (see Glad You Asked in Section 6–3). The Shell sort is often employed for its simplicity of design and speed advantage over the selection, insertion, and bubble sorts. A design for the Shell sort is as follows.

Design: *ShellSort (List , ListLen)*

```
Gap : = (ListLen + 1) DIV 2
WHILE Gap > = 1 DO
    REPEAT
        NoSwaps : = TRUE
        FOR Ct : = 1 TO ListLen − Gap
            IF List [Ct] > List [Ct + Gap]
                THEN Swap ( List[Ct], List[Ct + Gap] )
                    NoSwaps : = FALSE
    UNTIL NoSwaps
Gap : = Gap DIV 2
```

The Shell sort starts by comparing the first component with the middle component of the array (rather than the next component as is done in the bubble sort). On each pass through the WHILE-DO loop, the gap between the components being compared is divided in half. A walk through of the Shell sort is presented in Figure 8–12.

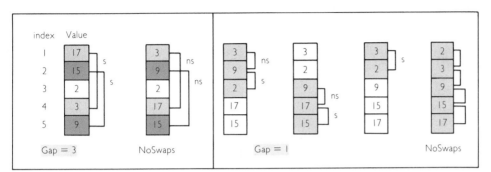

Figure 8–12

After the first pass through the WHILE-DO loop (in Figure 8–12), Gap is assigned the value **1**. After the second pass through the WHILE-DO loop, Gap is assigned the value **0**. Thus, the WHILE-DO loop is exited and the list is sorted.

The conversion of this design to a Pascal procedure yields the procedure shown in Figure 8–13.

COMMENT
When Gap is 1, the Shell sort degenerates to the bubble sort.

Figure 8–13

```
PROCEDURE ShellSort (VAR List : ListType ; ListLen : Index) ;

  VAR Gap , Ct : Index ;
      NoSwaps : BOOLEAN ;

  PROCEDURE Swap (VAR First , Second : Component) ;

    VAR Temp : Component ;

    BEGIN                                    {Swap}
      Temp := First ;
      First := Second ;
      Second : = Temp
    END ;                                    {Swap}

  BEGIN                                      {ShellSort}
    Gap := (ListLen + 1) DIV 2 ;
    WHILE Gap >= 1 DO
      BEGIN                                  {WHILE-DO loop}
        REPEAT
          NoSwaps := TRUE ;
          FOR Ct := 1 TO ListLen - Gap DO    {a pass through list}
            IF List [Ct] > List [Ct + Gap]
              THEN BEGIN                      {Swap elements}
                Swap (List [Ct], List [Ct + Gap]) ;
                NoSwaps := FALSE
              END                            {Swap elements}
        UNTIL NoSwaps ;
        Gap := Gap DIV 2
      END                                    {WHILE-DO loop}
  END                                        {ShellSort}
```

COMMENT
This procedure assumes `ListType` is an array with `ListLen` components and the components are of type `Component`.

8-2.4 Sorting Records

In Section 8-1, you learned how to use the binary search to search through a list of records. For this search to work, the records had to be ordered in some sense. Sorting a list of records means to order the records based on one of the fields of the record. The following example illustrates sorting a list of records.

EXAMPLE

Suppose List is of type ARRAY [1 .. MaxIndex] OF Person where Person is the record type defined as in Figure 8-8. Also, suppose the value in List is ordered based on the Name field; that is, the records in the list are ordered alphabetically. Write a Pascal procedure to write to the screen the Name field of the record and the Income field of the record from highest income to lowest income. The screen should appear as follows:

Sample Execution

```
Pruitt, Lois A.   $89000.00
Paulo, Frank K.   $78000.00
Gordon, David S.  $45000.00
         .
         .
         .
```

TYPE Person

Customer		
Name	First	John
	MidInit	G
	Last	Small
Address	Street	125 Boxwood Av.
	City	Helena
	State	Montana
Age		26
Income		31000

SOLUTION

A "brute force" approach to this problem would be to search through the Income field of the list for the highest income, write the results to the screen, find the next highest income, write the results to the screen, and so forth. A more elegant approach to this problem would be to alter the Shell sort just discussed to handle a list of records. Such an alteration is presented in Figure 8-14.

The alterations made to the Shell sort are as follows:

1. The list of records is passed as a value parameter.
2. The list is sorted from largest to smallest.
3. The objects being moved about in the list are now records. That is, the procedure Swap now exchanges data of type Person.
4. Material is now written to the screen. This material is only part of the component in the list; that is, only the Name field and Income field are written to the screen.

There are some problems with this approach:

1. The objects being moved around are records. Thus, more time is consumed in doing the sort.
2. The list of records is passed as a *value* parameter to the procedure RecShellSort. If the list has several components, there may not be enough memory available to store the list.
3. If the list of records is passed as a *variable* parameter, the memory problem is solved. However, the list itself is altered. That is, sorting the list based on the Income field destroys the alphabetical ordering based on the Name field.

Figure 8–14

```
PROCEDURE RecShellSort (List : ListType ; ListLen : WholeNum) ;

  VAR Ct, Gap : WholeNum ;
      NoSwaps : BOOLEAN ;

  PROCEDURE Swap (VAR First , Second : Person) ;

    VAR Temp : Person ;

    BEGIN                                {Swap}
      Temp := First ;
      First := Second ;
      Second := Temp
    END ;                                {Swap}

  PROCEDURE ShowList (List : ListType ; TheLen : WholeNum) ;

    VAR Ct : WholeNum ;

    BEGIN                                {ShowList}
      FOR Ct := 1 TO TheLen DO           {show the list}
        BEGIN
          WITH List [Ct].Name DO
            WRITE (CONCAT (Last, ', ', First, ' ', MidInit,'.') : 40) ;
          WRITELN (' $', List[Ct].Income :1:2)
        END
    END ;                                {Showlist}

  BEGIN                                  {record Shell sort}
    ShowList (List, ListLen) ;           {Show old list}
    WRITELN ('Now sorting list-') ;
    Gap := (ListLen + 1) DIV 2 ;
    WHILE Gap >= 1 DO
      BEGIN                              {WHILE-DO loop}
        REPEAT
          NoSwaps := TRUE ;
          FOR Ct := 1 TO ListLen - Gap DO   {a pass through list}
            IF List [Ct].Income < List [Ct + Gap].Income
              THEN BEGIN                 {Swap elements}
                     Swap (List [Ct], List [Ct + Gap]) ;
                     NoSwaps := FALSE
                   END                   {Swap elements}
        UNTIL NoSwaps ;
        Gap := Gap DIV 2
      END ;                              {WHILE-DO loop}
    ShowList (List, ListLen)             {Show sorted list}
  END                                    {record Shell sort}
```

Original list

```
Gordon, David S.   $45000
Paulo, Frank K.    $78000
Pruitt, Lois A.    $89000
```

Sorted list

```
Pruitt, Lois A.    $89000
Paulo, Frank K.    $78000
Gordon, David S.   $45000
```

COMMENT

Order List from highest to lowest based on Income.

To overcome these problems, an *auxiliary list* that contains the indices of the records can be employed. Instead of sorting the list of records, the auxiliary list is sorted. In this approach to the problem, the list of records is a variable parameter (no extra memory is required for a copy of the list). AuxList of type `ARRAY [1 .. n] OF 1 .. n` (where n is the number of records) is to be sorted based on the Income field of the records. Here, the values being moved in the sort are numbers, not large data items like records. Also, the ordering of the original list is not altered. Once AuxList is sorted, it can then be used to send the desired information from the records in List to the screen in an ordered manner. The design for this approach is presented as follows:

Design:　*AuxSort (List , AuxList , ListLen)*
　　　　InitAuxlist
　　　　SortAuxList
　　　　WriteInfoToScreen

index　1　2　3
AuxList　| 1 | 2 | 3 |

Refinement of:　*InitAuxList*
　　　　FOR Ct : = 1 TO ListLen DO
　　　　　AuxList [Ct] : = Ct

index　　1　　2　　3

List	David	Frank	Lois
	S	K	A
	Gordon	Paulo	Pruitt
	45000	78000	89000

Refinement of:　*SortAuxList*　　　　　　　　　{use Shell sort}
　　　　Gap : = (ListLen + 1) DIV 2
　　　　WHILE Gap > = 1 DO
　　　　　REPEAT
　　　　　　NoSwaps : = TRUE
　　　　　　FOR Ct : = 1 TO ListLen − Gap DO
　　　　　　　IF List [AuxList [Ct]].Income < List [AuxList [Ct + Gap]].Income
　　　　　　　　THEN Swap (AuxList [Ct], AuxList [Ct + Gap])
　　　　　　　　　NoSwaps : = FALSE
　　　　　UNTIL NoSwaps
　　　　　Gap : = Gap DIV 2

index　1　2　3
AuxList　| 3 | 2 | 1 |

Refinement of:　*Swap (AuxList [Pt] , AuxList [Index])*
　　　　TempHold : = AuxList [Pt]
　　　　AuxList [Pt] : = AuxList [Index]
　　　　AuxList [Index] : = TempHold

Refinement of:　*WriteInfoToScreen*
　　　　FOR Ct : = 1 TO ListLen DO
　　　　　WITH List [AuxList [Ct]].Name DO
　　　　　　WRITE (CONCAT (Last,',', First,' ', MidInit,'.'))
　　　　　GOTOXY (50, Ct MOD 23)
　　　　　WRITELN (List [AuxList [Ct]].Income)
　　　　　IF Ct MOD 23 = 0　　　　　　　　　{hold for screen}
　　　　　　THEN WRITE ('Press RETURN to continue- ')
　　　　　　　READLN (Ans)
　　　　　　　CLRSCR

COMMENT
Once AuxList is ordered, based on the Income field of the records in List, it can be used to select the order in which the records are sent to the screen.

The design just given yields the Pascal procedure in Figure 8–15.

Figure 8–15

```
PROCEDURE AuxSort (VAR List : ListType ; VAR AuxList : NumList ;
                   ListLen : WholeNum) ;

  VAR Gap, Ct, Index : WholeNum ;
      NoSwaps : BOOLEAN ;

  PROCEDURE Swap (VAR FValue , SValue : WholeNum) ;

    VAR Temp : WholeNum ;

    BEGIN                                    {Swap}
      Temp := FValue ;
      FValue := SValue ;
      SValue := Temp
    END ;                                    {Swap}

  PROCEDURE WriteInfoToScreen (VAR List : ListType ;
                               VAR AuxList : NumList ;
                               ListLen : WholeNum) ;

    VAR Ct : WholeNum ;
        Ans : CHAR ;

    BEGIN                                    {WriteInfoToScreen}
      CLRSCR ;
      FOR Ct := 1 TO ListLen DO
        BEGIN                                {FOR-DO instruction}
          WITH List [AuxList [Ct]].Name DO
            WRITE (CONCAT (Last, ',', First, ' ', MidInit, '.')) ;
          GOTOXY (50 , Ct MOD 23) ;
          WRITELN ('$', List [AuxList [Ct]].Income : 1 : 2)
          IF Ct MOD 23 = 0
            THEN BEGIN                        {IF-THEN instruction}
                   WRITE ('Press RETURN to continue- ') ;
                   READLN (Ans) ;
                   CLRSCR
                 END                          {IF-THEN instruction}
        END                                   {FOR-DO instruction}
    END ;                                     {WriteInfoToScreen}
  BEGIN                                       {AuxSort}
    FOR Index := 1 TO ListLen DO              {initialize AuxList}
      AuxList [Index] := Index ;
    Gap := (ListLen + 1) DIV 2 ;
    WHILE Gap >= 1 DO                         {Shell sort}
      BEGIN                                   {WHILE-DO loop}
        REPEAT
          NoSwaps := TRUE ;
          FOR Ct := 1 TO (ListLen - Gap) DO   {a pass through list}
            IF List [AuxList[Ct]].Income < List [AuxList[Ct + Gap]].Income
              THEN BEGIN                       {Swap elements}
                     Swap (AuxList [Ct], AuxList [Ct + Gap]) ;
                     NoSwaps := FALSE
                   END                         {Swap elements}
        UNTIL NoSwaps ;
        Gap := Gap DIV 2
      END ;                                    {WHILE-DO loop}
    WriteInfoToScreen (List, AuxList , ListLen)
  END                                          {AuxSort}
```

COMMENT
Name and Income fields of List components are written to the screen based on order of the components in AuxList.

COMMENT
Compare Income field of List components. Order the components of AuxList.

DO IT NOW

1. Suppose List contained the following records:

1	2	3	4
Frank K Alverez 2914 Oak Street New Orleans Louisiana 26 25700	Sally M Homer Rt 11 Box 13 Lincoln Nebraska 42 31500	Ruth P James P.O. Box 8 Abilene Texas 29 47080	Walter W Whips 15 Water Way Walla Walla Washington 38 36000

Fill in the following chart for a walk through of the WHILE-DO instruction of AuxSort. The value passed for ListLen is 4.

```
Gap        AuxList
 2      1   2   3   4      {start of WHILE-DO}
 2      3   4   1   2      {after first pass through WHILE-DO loop}
 1      —   —   —   —      {after second pass through WHILE-DO loop}
```

2. Alter the procedure AuxSort to write to the screen the information from the Name field and Age field ordered from oldest to youngest.

DO IT NOW ANSWERS

1.
```
   Gap        AuxList
    2      1   2   3   4      {start WHILE-DO}
    2      3   4   1   2      {after first pass through WHILE-DO loop}
    1      3   4   2   1      {after second pass through WHILE-DO loop}
```
2. In the procedure main execution section of AuxSort, change
    List [...].Income to List [...].Age.
   In the procedure WriteInfoToScreen, change references to Income to Age.

Vocabulary

Page		
442	**Hierarchical record**	A record that has one or more fields of type RECORD.
442	**Nested record**	Same as hierarchical record.
443	**Path**	With nested records, the identifiers needed to access an inner field of the record. Example: For Customer of type RECORD with a field Name that has a field First, Customer.Name is a path to the field First.
448	**Shell sort**	A sort technique used for its simplicity of design and speed advantage over the insertion, selection, and bubble sorts.
442	**Tree structure**	Same as hierarchical record.
446	**WITH**	A Pascal instruction used to access the fields of a record. For example,

```
WITH Customer DO
  READ (Name)
```

replaces READ (Customer.Name).

Glad You Asked

Q I really do not understand how to make an assignment to a nested record. Is there a picture?

A Consider this assignment instruction picture:

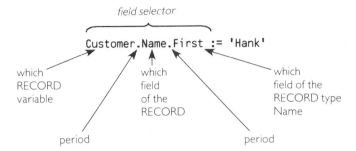

Q I was trying out the WITH instruction. I entered the following instructions in an attempt to fill an array of records:

```
WITH Customer [Index] DO
  FOR Index := 1 TO 5 DO
    BEGIN
      READLN (Name) ;
      READLN (Age)
    END ;
WITH Customer [Index] DO
  FOR Index := 1 TO 5 DO
    BEGIN
      WRITE (Name,' ') ;
      WRITELN (Age : 1)
    END
```

At first, I got repeated copies of the last record. I figured out that `Index` needed to be initialized. So I initialized `Index` with the instruction `Index := 1`. This time the program executed and I entered five records. However, only zeroes were output. What happened?

A I assume `Customer` was an array of records. Although `Index` varies from 1 to 5, the record identifier for the WITH instruction does not vary. In the first instruction,

```
WITH Customer [Index] DO
  FOR Index := 1 TO 5 DO
    BEGIN
      READLN (Name) ;
      READLN (Age)
    END ;
```

you assigned values to the fields (`Name` and `Age`) of record `Customer [1]` five times. Thus, record `Customer [1]` contained the last values you assigned. The other records were not initialized. In the instruction

```
WITH Customer [Index] DO
  FOR Index := 1 TO 5 DO
    BEGIN
      WRITE (Name, ' ') ;
      WRITELN (Age)
    END
```

there are several errors you could make. From the description you gave, the record that the WITH instruction processed was `Customer [6]` since after the FOR-DO loop `Index` contained 6. This record has not been initialized. Thus, the screen filled with whatever values might have been in the memory locations of the `Name` field of `Customer [6]`. The following instructions should accomplish what you want:

```
FOR Index := 1 TO 5 DO                {fill record fields}
   WITH Customer [Index] DO
      BEGIN
         READLN (Name) ;
         READLN (Age)
      END ;
FOR Index := 1 TO 5 DO                {write the record fields}
   WITH Customer [Index] DO
      BEGIN
         WRITE (Name , ' ') ;
         WRITELN (Age)
      END
```

Q Can the WITH instruction be nested?

A Yes. That is, for nested records like `Person` (see margin), the following is a valid instruction involving `Customer` of type `Person`:

```
WITH Customer DO
   WITH Name DO
      BEGIN
         READLN (First) ;
         READLN (MidInit) ;
         READLN (Last)
      END
```

Q What are variant records?

A They are records where the fields the record has can vary. The structure is a record with a fixed number of fields then a variant part. There is a tag field which is used to select one of several alternatives for the remaining fields of the record. The remaining fields are known as the variant part of the record. An example of this type of record is as follows.

```
TYPE Status = (Have, Out) ;
     Movie = RECORD
                   Title : STRING [40] ;
                   Stars : STRING [40] ;
                   CASE Status OF
                      Have : (Section : CHAR ;
                              Row : 1 .. 12) ;
                      Out : (Renter : STRING [40] ;
                             Phone : STRING [12] ;
                             DateDue : STRING [20])
             END
```

Here, the fixed fields are `Title` and `Stars`. The tag field is `Status`. The variant fields are `Section` and `Row` or `Renter`, `Phone`, and `DateDue`. Whether the fields are `Section` and `Row` or `Renter`, `Phone`, and `DateDue` depends on value assigned to `Status`.

TYPE Person

Customer

Name	First	John
	MidInit	G
	Last	Small
Address	Street	125 Boxwood Av.
	City	Helena
	State	Montana
Age		26
Income		31000

Section 8–2 Exercises

For problems 1 through 3, use the following TYPE and VAR sections:

```
TYPE Person = RECORD
                Name : STRING [30];
                Title : STRING [30]
             END ;
     Award = RECORD
                Album : Person ;
                MaleArtist : Person ;
                FemaleArtist : Person ;
                Group : Person
             END ;

VAR Grammy : Award ;
```

1. Write instructions to assign to the field `Grammy.Group` the value:

    The Beatles   A Hard Day's Night

2. Write instructions to assign to `Grammy` the value:

    Michael Jackson   Beat It
    Michael Jackson   Thriller
    Irene Cara   Flashdance
    Police   Every Breath You Take

3. Write instructions to output a value in `Grammy`.

4. Boot up Pascal; set the workfile to the file `SortRec.PAS` from the `Source` diskette. Enter the editor. Alter the program to sort the list based on the field `Age` (from youngest to oldest). The procedure `ShowList` should be modifed to reflect the alteration.

5. Boot up Pascal; set the workfile to the file `AuxSort.PAS` from the `Source` diskette. Enter the editor. Alter the program to sort the list (alphabetically) based on the field `AddRec.State`. The procedure `WriteInfoToScreen` should be modified to reflect the alteration.

6. Given the following TYPE and VAR sections:

```
TYPE Name = RECORD
                Common : STRING [40] ;
                Scientific : STRING [40]
             END ;
     Size = RECORD
                WingSpan : REAL ;
                AvWeight : REAL ;
                AvLength : REAL
             END ;
     Group = (Loon, Duck, Hawk, Wader, Owl) ;
     BirdRec = RECORD
                   Which : Name ;
                   Family : Group ;
                   Descript : Size
                END ;
     BirdList = ARRAY [1 .. MaxIndex] OF BirdRec ;
 VAR SightList : BirdList ;
```

Sample Execution

```
Enter common name for bird: Pintail
Not found.
Do you want to add bird to list? (Y/N): Y
Enter scientific name: Anas acuta tzitzihoa
Enter family: Duck
Enter weight (in pounds): 3
Enter wing span (in inches): 28
Enter length (in inches): 30
```

  a. Draw a diagram of the record `BirdRec`.
  b. Write a Pascal procedure that has as input `SightList` and its length. The procedure is to allow the user to enter a bird's common name. The procedure is to search the list for the name. If it is found, the procedure should output to the screen the information on the bird. If not found, the procedure should allow the user to add the information on the bird to the list.

Problems 7 through 10 refer to the following TYPE and VAR sections:

```
TYPE Property = RECORD
                    Kind : (Business, Residential, Farm, Undeveloped) ;
                    Address : STRING [50] ;
                    Value : REAL ;
                    Partners : STRING [80]
                END ;
     Paper = RECORD
                 Stocks : REAL ;
                 Bonds : REAL ;
                 Cash : REAL
             END ;
     Holdings = RECORD
                    Name : STRING [40] ;
                    Address : STRING [40] ;
                    RealEst : Property ;
                    Liquid : Paper
                END ;
     HoldingList = ARRAY [1 .. 20] OF Holdings ;

VAR Land : Property ;
    Person : Holdings ;
    Company : HoldingList ;
```

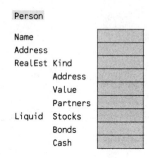

7. Insert *Valid* or *Invalid* for the following instructions (assume that instructions appear in the main execution section and valid variables have a defined value). If an instruction is invalid, state why it is invalid.

    _____ a. Holdings.Name := 'Marica Muskie'

    _____ b. Land := Person.RealEst

    _____ c. IF Person.Liquid.Bonds >= 100000
             THEN WRITE (Person.RealEst.Kind)

    _____ d. Company [12].Name := Person.Name

    _____ e. READ (Land.Kind)

8. Draw a tree diagram of the record type Holdings. What is the root of the tree? Identify each leaf of the tree.

9. Write a Pascal procedure SeeRec that has as input Company. The procedure is to allow the user to input a name, then see on the screen the component of Company associated with the name.

Sample Execution

```
Please enter name (Last, First): Skol, Lester
Skol, Lester
1920 West River Road Warrington

Business property: 3038 4th Avenue Midtown
                   Value: $1250000
                   Partners: Jones, Sanchez
Stocks: $21000
Bonds: $20000
Cash: $32000
```

10. Alter the procedure in problem 9 to allow the user to update the component of Company selected.

11. Define a record type `Flight` that has the following tree diagram:

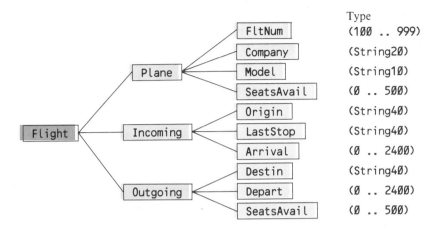

	Type
FltNum	(100 .. 999)
Company	(String20)
Model	(String10)
SeatsAvail	(0 .. 500)
Origin	(String40)
LastStop	(String40)
Arrival	(0 .. 2400)
Destin	(String40)
Depart	(0 .. 2400)
SeatsAvail	(0 .. 500)

Programming Problems

12. Define data type `FltList` an array with 500 components of type `Flight` (see problem 11). Declare variables `Today` (of type `FltList`) and `AFlight` (of type `Flight`). Write a Pascal procedure that has variable parameter `Today` and allows the user to input a flight number and to alter that component of `Today`. (Assume that `Today` contains a value ordered from highest flight number to lowest flight number. Also assume `BinarySearch` is a program procedure.)

13. Use the Shell sort discussed in this section to sort the list of records then write to the screen the information shown from `FltList` in problem 12. The list is to be ordered by arrival time.

14. Design a data structure to hold the following information:

Name	State	Mileage	Cities
I-4	Florida	132.10	Tampa, Lakeland, Orlando
I-5	California	797.00	San Diego, Los Angeles, Stockton, Sacramento, Red Bluff, Redding, Yreka
	Oregon	308.50	Ashland, Medford, Grants Pass, Roseburg, Eugene, Salem, Portland
	Washington	276.30	Vancouver, Kelso, Chehalis, Olympia, Tacoma, Seattle, Everett, Mount Vernon, Bellingham
⋮	⋮	⋮	⋮
I-65	Alabama	366.30	Mobile, Montgomery, Birmingham, Decatur, Athens
	Tennessee	121.40	Nashville
	Kentucky	137.60	Bowling Green, Elizabethtown, Louisville
	Indiana	262.08	Columbus, Indianapolis, Lebanon, Lafayette, Merrillville, Gary

Hint: Define `Road`, a record with fields `Name` and `StateList`, where each component of `StateList` is a record.

15. Write a Pascal procedure to operate on the data structure designed in problem 14. The procedure should allow the user to enter a state's name. The procedure is to write to the screen the total number of interstate highway miles in the state.

Sample Execution

```
Arrivals
Company    Flight Number    Time
Eastern    197              9:43 AM
Western    567              11:23 AM
TWA        671              4:12 PM
Delta      332              8:11 PM
  ⋮          ⋮
```

Sample Execution

```
Enter state name: Georgia
Interstate highway miles:
```

```
MetroList [n]

Identity City
         State
Feature  Population
         NumSchools
```

16. Write a Pascal program that allows the user to fill the list **MetroList** with records containing fields **Identity** and **Feature**. **Identity** has fields **City** and **State**, both of type STRING. **Feature** has fields **Population** of type REAL and **NumSchools** of type **Ø .. MAXINT**. Alter the insertion sort (see page 358) to fill the list based on the **Population** field from largest to smallest.

17. Write a Pascal program that allows the user to create a list of suspects in a crime. Each suspect should consist of a record with fields **Name**, **Physical**, **Occupation**, and **Alibi**. The **Name** field should have fields for real name and a list of up to four alias names. The **Physical** field should have fields **Sex**, **Weight**, **Height**, **Race**, **Markings**. The **Alibi** field should be of type BOOLEAN.

CHAPTER TEST

For problems 1 through 5, assume the following TYPE and VAR sections.

```
TYPE Leader = RECORD
                  Name : STRING [4Ø] ;
                  YearElected : 1776 .. 2ØØØ ;
                  AgeElected : 3Ø .. 1ØØ ;
                  Events : STRING [255]
              END ;

VAR President : Leader ;
    PresList : ARRAY [1 ..56] OF Leader
```

1. Which of the following is a variable of type RECORD?
   a. PresList **b.** President **c.** Name **d.** Leader.AgeElected

2. Which of the following is a field?
   a. PresList **b.** President **c.** Leader **d.** Name

3. Which of the following assigns a value to a field of the record?
   a. Leader.AgeElected := 69
   b. PresList [34] := Leader
   c. President.Events := 'Granada invaded'
   d. President := 'Ronald Wilson Reagan'

4. Complete the following FOR-DO instruction to count the number of presidents elected after age 65. (**MaxIndex** is a program constant whose value is the length of the list **PresList**.)

```
Number := Ø ;
FOR Ct := 1 TO MaxIndex DO
   BEGIN
      :
      :
   END
```

5. Write a list of instructions to assign to the 35th component in **PresList** the following information:

```
John Fitzgerald Kennedy
196Ø
43
Cuban missile crisis. Civil rights advancement. Space program expanded.
```

For problems 6 through 9, assume the following TYPE and VAR sections.

```
TYPE Pro = RECORD
                Name : STRING [40] ;
                School : STRING [40] ;
                Major : STRING [20]
            END ;
     Subject = RECORD
                  Title : STRING [40] ;
                  Number : 1000 .. 9999 ;
                  Hours : 1 .. 5 ;
                  Lab : BOOLEAN
                END ;
     Site = RECORD
              Building : STRING [40] ;
              Room : 1 .. 599
            END ;
     Class = RECORD
               Instructor : Pro ;
               Course : Subject ;
               Location : Site
             END ;

 VAR AClass : Class ;
     MyClasses : ARRAY [1 .. 6] OF Class
     TotalHrs : 0 .. 40 ;
```

6. Which of the following is an assignment to a field of `AClass`?
   a. `Class.Location.Room := 116`
   b. `Hours := 3`
   c. `AClass.Location := 'Milton'`
   d. `AClass.Course.Lab := TRUE`

7. Complete the instruction given here to compute the total number of hours taken. Assume that all the cells of `MyClasses` have been filled.

   ```
   Total Hrs := 0
   FOR Ct := 1 TO 6 DO
     WITH MyClasses [Ct] DO
        .
        .
        .
   ```

8. Draw a tree diagram of the RECORD-type `Class`.

9. Write a list of instructions to assign to `AClass` the following information: Calculus I (course number 1234) taught by James Desmond, a math major from Florida State University. The course is a required course for three credit hours without a lab and meets in the Baars Science Building, Room 487.

Programming Project

Project 8-1. The TEXT file `Books.TXT` contains lines like the following:

```
The Color Purple
Walker, Alice
1983
Fiction
```

That is, each group of four lines contains a book title, author, year published, and category. Write a Pascal program that allows the user to select from the following menu:

```
A. Fill book list from disk
B. See book list by author/title/category
C. Insert book in list
D. Delete a book from list
E. Save current list to disk
Q. Quit
Enter (A, B, C, D, E, Q=Quit):
```

If option **A** is selected, the program fills a list of records with the contents of the TEXT file in alphabetical order by title.

If option **B** is selected, the user selects from the menu:

```
A. See list alphabetically by author
B. See list alphabetically by title
C. Select category to see
```

If the user selects **A** or **B**, the list of records is presented as selected. *Hint:* Use the Shell sort with an auxiliary list to sort the list.
If the user selects option **C**, the user selects from the list
`A = fiction, B = nonfiction, C = advice and other.`

If option **C** is selected, the user can enter the information for the book and have it added to the list in its proper position.

Sample Execution

```
Please enter title: Bloom County
Please enter author: Breathed, Berke
Please enter year published: 1983
Select category:
A = Fiction
B = Nonfiction
C = advice and other
Enter A, B, or C: C
```

If option **D** is selected, the user can enter the title of a book and have it deleted from the list.

If option **E** is selected, the current list is saved to the TEXT file, replacing the old TEXT file.

Turn in your design and its refinements, a structured diagram of your design, and a copy of your program.

Project 8–2. The game of Boxes is played on a board similar to this one:

Players take turns connecting two dots. If a player connects two dots and completes a box, the player puts a letter in the box and gets another turn. The player with the most boxes containing his or her letter wins the game. Sample play:

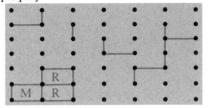

At this point, the player whose letter is M has one box and the player whose letter is R has two boxes.

Write a Pascal program to play the game Boxes. The program should start by getting the players' names and choice of letter (A...Z) to use on the board. Next, the screen should clear and the playing board should be presented.

To draw the board, you can use an asterisk for the dots. To space the dots on the screen, use the following design (where CtA and CtB are initialized to the top left screen values):

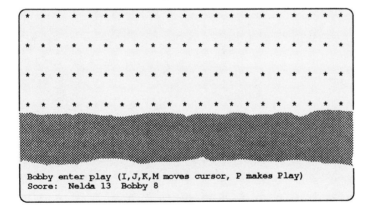

```
Bobby enter play (I,J,K,M moves cursor, P makes Play)
Score:  Nelda 13  Bobby 8
```

Design: WHILE CtA < = 21 DO
              WHILE CtB < = 80 DO
                 GOTOXY (CtB , CtA)
                 WRITE ('*')
                 CtB : = CtB + 3
              CtA : = CtA + 3

The player enters a play by moving the cursor to one of the two empty spaces between the asterisk characters and pressing the P key. When the P key is pressed, the two spaces fill with the asterisk character. When all four sides are filled, the player's letter is placed in the four open positions in the box. At this point, the score is updated and the player gets another turn. If no box is completed, the next player gets a turn.

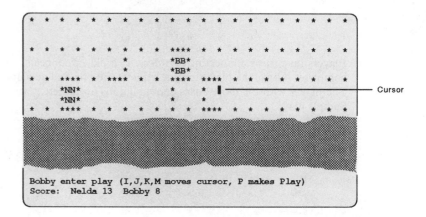

Cursor

```
*  *  *  *  *  *  *  *  *  *  *  *  *  *  *  *  *  *  *  *  *  *

*  *  *  *  *  *  *  *  ****  *  *  *  *  *  *  *  *  *  *  *
                    *      *BB*
                    *      *BB*
*  *  ****  *  ****  *  *  ****  *  *  *  *  *  *  *  *
   *NN*              *     *  █
   *NN*              *     *
*  *  ****  *  *  *  *  *  *  ****  *  *  *  *  *  *  *
```

```
Bobby enter play (I,J,K,M moves cursor, P makes Play)
Score:  Nelda 13  Bobby 8
```

In this illustration, if Bobby presses the P key, he will win the box. That is, his letter will be placed in the box, his score will be increased by one, and he will get another turn.

Turn in your design and its refinements, a structured diagram of your design, and a copy of your program.

Chapter Nine

Files

Introduction

In this chapter, you will learn about yet another data structure of the Pascal language, FILE OF. You have had some experience with this type of data structure when you studied TEXT files.

In the first section of this chapter, you will extend the idea of TEXT files to FILE OF INTEGER and FILE OF REAL. These data structures are known as "FILE OF simple types." In the second section, files whose components are of type ARRAY and type RECORD will be introduced. These files are known as "FILE OF structured types."

As with any data structure, access to the components is the first order of business. To access the components of FILE-type data, the Pascal procedures READ and WRITE are used. You will learn how to work with these procedures to access the components of a file. When you finish this chapter, you will be able to write a Pascal program that uses the data structure FILE OF.

```
PROGRAM Chapter9 ;
TYPE String20 = STRING [20] ;
     Person = RECORD
                  Who : String20 ;
                  Sex : BOOLEAN
              END ;
     IndexFile = FILE OF INTEGER ;              {page 466}
     FileType = FILE OF Person ;                {page 478}
     ListType = ARRAY [1 .. 300] OF INTEGER ;

VAR Index : INTEGER ;
    AList : ListType ;
    RecFile : FileType ;                        {page 478}
    IndiC : IndexFile ;                         {page 466}
PROCEDURE NewFile (VAR TheFile : FileType ;     {page 488}
                       TheList : ListType ;
                       ListLen : INTEGER) ;

  VAR ARecord : Person ;
      Ct : INTEGER ;
      SecFile : FileType ;
  BEGIN
    RESET (TheFile) ;
    ASSIGN (SecFile, 'TheOrder.DAT') ;
    REWRITE (SecFile) ;                         {page 468}
    FOR Ct := 1 TO ListLen DO
      BEGIN
        SEEK (TheFile, TheList [Ct]) ;          {page 470}
        READ (TheFile, ARecord) ;               {page 480}
        WRITE (SecFile, ARecord)                {page 478}
      END ;
    CLOSE (SecFile)                             {page 468}
  END ;
BEGIN            {main program}
  ASSIGN (IndiC, 'TheIndex.DAT') ;              {page 466}
  RESET (IndiC) ;                               {page 466}
  ASSIGN (RecFile, 'B:PeoRec.DAT') ;
  Index := 1 ;
  WHILE NOT EOF (IndiC) DO                      {page 467}
    BEGIN
      READ (IndiC, AList [Index]) ;             {page 467}
      Index := Index + 1
    END ;
  NewFile (RecFile, AList, FILESIZE (IndiC))    {page 472}
  CLOSE (IndiC) ;                               {page 468}
  CLOSE (RecFile)
END .            {main program}
```

FILE OF Simple Types

In this section, you will be introduced to the data structure FILE OF, including FILE OF INTEGER and FILE OF REAL. Like the data structure TEXT, this data structure is used for storing information external to the main memory. Access to the components of this data structure is via the Pascal reserved words READ and WRITE. You will learn how to use READ and WRITE to work with the data structure FILE OF. Additionally, you will study the built-in procedure SEEK. This procedure provides random access to the components of the data structure FILE OF.

A file is a sequence of components all of the same data type. Earlier, you worked with TEXT files whose components were of type CHAR. Pascal allows the components of a file to be any predefined type or user-defined type except FILE OF or TEXT. For example, you can define a data type to be a `FILE OF INTEGER` or a `FILE OF Color` (provided `Color` has been defined as a data type). The data type **FILE OF** is a data structure that provides a structuring for simpler data types in the form of a list. However, this list usually exists external to the computer's main memory on a magnetic disk (hard disk, diskette, etc.). Herein lies the power of this data structure. The memory space available in the computer's main memory is quite limited compared to the space available on a diskette. The main memory can have as little as 64,000 cells (and the Pascal operating system and program instructions reduce this space dramatically). Diskettes and hard disks can store from 360,000 characters on up.

9-1.1 The Contents of a File

Consider the following:

```
VAR NumFile : FILE OF INTEGER
```

This statement declares `NumFile` as a variable. The values this variable will reference are identifiers (names) of files. The **ASSIGN** instruction is used to assign the name of a file to the variable `InFile`. For example,

```
ASSIGN (NumFile , 'CBSData.DAT')
```

assigns to the file variable `NumFile` the file identifier `CBSData.DAT`. The components of this file will be of type INTEGER. To process the data stored in a file, the file must be opened (prepared for processing). This is accomplished for existing files by the instruction RESET.

When the file is opened with **RESET,** the file pointer is moved to the first component of the file (see Figure 9–1).

Figure 9–1   RESET (NumFile)

```
┌─────────────────────────────────────────────────┐
│ 5  43  −6  98  12  −15  3  1034  <end-of-file marker> │
└─────────────────────────────────────────────────┘
  ↑ File pointer
```

To access the components in the file, the Pascal instruction **READ** is used.

When READ (NumFile, Num) is executed, the component of the file (where the file pointer is) is assigned to the variable Num and the file pointer is advanced to the next component of the file (see Figure 9–2).

Figure 9–2

RESET (NumFile)

| 5 43 −6 98 12 −15 3 1Ø34 <end-of-file marker> |

↑ File pointer

READ (NumFile , Num)   Num is assigned 5

| 5 43 −6 98 12 −15 3 1Ø34 <end-of-file marker> |

↑ File pointer

Consider the Pascal program SeeNumFile in Figure 9–3. This program is used to write the contents of a FILE OF INTEGER to the screen.

Figure 9–3

```
PROGRAM SeeNumFile ;

VAR NumFile : FILE OF INTEGER ;
    Num : INTEGER ;

BEGIN
  ASSIGN (NumFile , 'CBSData.DAT') ;
  RESET (NumFile) ;               {open the file}
  WHILE NOT EOF (NumFile) DO
    BEGIN
      READ (NumFile , Num) ;      {read file component}
      WRITE (Num : 1, ' ')
    END ;
  CLOSE (NumFile)
END .
```

A FILE OF INTEGER is a sequence of integers. For the program SeeNumFile in Figure 9–3, RESET (NumFile) opens the file and moves the file pointer to the first component of NumFile provided the file CBSData.DAT exists and contains integers. The WHILE-DO instruction will execute the compound instruction as long as the end-of-file marker has not been reached. In the compound instruction

```
BEGIN
  READ (NumFile , Num) ;
  WRITE (Num : 1, ' ')
END
```

the instruction READ (NumFile , Num) will assign to Num the component pointed to by the file pointer, then move the pointer to the next component of the file. The instruction WRITE (Num : 1,' ') will write to the screen the value in Num (in a field of 1), then a blank space. Once the file pointer is at the end-of-file marker, the WHILE-DO loop is exited.

When the file is opened with RESET, the instruction RESET (NumFile) essentially says: *Go to the start of the file and place the file pointer at the first component.*

WARNING
If CBSData.DAT does *not* exist, a runtime error message is issued when RESET (NumFile) is executed. Also, ASSIGN should not be used with a file that is already in use (open).

COMMENT
If RESET is executed on a file that is in use (open), the file pointer is moved to the start of the file. The components of the file are not altered.

If the component pointed to is the end-of-file marker, then EOF is set to TRUE. If the instruction READ (NumFile , Num) is executed at this point, the value placed in Num is undefined and a Tried to read past EOF error message will be displayed.

COMMENT

Even though READ and WRITE are used to access the components of the data structure FILE OF, READLN and WRITELN are meaningless since there are no end-of-line markers in this data structure, only an end-of-file marker.

9–1.2 Building a Non-TEXT File

It is now time to look at how to construct a file whose components are values other than type CHAR. The key to accomplishing this task lies with the Pascal instructions **REWRITE** and **WRITE.** Suppose the programmer wants to construct a file whose components are real numbers. The program BuildFile in Figure 9–4 will accomplish the task.

Figure 9–4

```
PROGRAM BuildFile ;

VAR OutFile : FILE OF REAL ;
    InNum   : REAL ;
    Ch      : CHAR ;
    Count   : 1 .. MAXINT ;

BEGIN                                             {Main program}
  CLRSCR ;
  WRITE ('Ready to enter data (Y/N): ') ;
  READLN (Ch) ;
  IF Ch < > 'N'
    THEN
      BEGIN                                       {THEN instruction}
        ASSIGN (OutFile , 'XYData.DAT') ;
        REWRITE (OutFile) ;                       {Create the file XYData.DAT}
        Count := 1 ;
        REPEAT
          WRITE ('Enter value ', Count : 1 , ' : ') ;
          READLN (InNum) ;
          WRITE (OutFile , InNum) ;               {Place value in file}
          WRITE ('Enter Q to Quit, RETURN to continue ') ;
          READLN (Ch) ;
          Count := SUCC (Count)
        UNTIL Ch = 'Q' ;
        CLOSE (OutFile)
      END                                         {THEN instruction}
END .                                             {Main program}
```

Sample Execution

```
Ready to enter data (Y/N): Y
Enter value 1 : 17
Enter Q to Quit, RETURN to continue
Enter value 2 : 5.23
Enter Q to Quit, RETURN to continue
```

OutFile

| 17.0 | 5.23 | < end-of-file > |

↑ File pointer

WARNING

If a file exists on the disk named XYData.DAT, its contents will be destroyed (the file is cleaned out) when the instruction REWRITE (OutFile) is executed.

In the program in Figure 9–4, when the instruction REWRITE (OutFile) is executed, the system creates a file named XYData.DAT. The components of this file will be of type REAL since the file variable OutFile has stated type FILE OF REAL. The file pointer is placed at the start of the file (there are no components in the file; see Figure 9–5).

The key instructions in the program BuildFile in Figure 9–4 are READLN (InNum) and WRITE (OutFile , InNum). The instruction READLN (InNum) reads a string of characters from the keyboard. If the string can be converted to a REAL number, the number is assigned to the variable InNum. (If such a conversion cannot be made, a runtime error occurs.) The instruction WRITE (OutFile , InNum) places the value in the variable InNum in the file (see Figure 9–5).

The reserved words FILE OF can be used with any ordinal-type data and with REAL-type and STRING-type data. The following declaration is valid.

TYPE Day = (Monday , Tuesday , Wednesday , Thursday , Friday) ;

VAR NewDay : FILE OF Day ;

The components in the file NewDay are values of type Day.

COMMENT

Although FILE OF STRING is possible, a TEXT file accomplishes the task of storing STRING values. The advantage of using a TEXT file is that the components can be inspected by using an editor. The components from a FILE OF *cannot* be inspected, except from a Pascal program. However, in some situations a FILE OF STRING may be desired.

DO IT NOW

1. Write a Pascal program that will create a FILE OF WholeNums where WholeNums is of type 0 .. MAXINT. The program should also fill the file with the prime numbers less than 1000. Name the file Primes.DAT.
2. Use the file created in exercise 1 to write a Pascal program that allows the user to enter a counting number less than 1000 and outputs the prime divisors of the number.

DO IT NOW ANSWERS

```
1. PROGRAM BuildPrimes ;

   CONST Upper = 1000 ;

   TYPE WholeNum = 0 .. MAXINT ;

   VAR OutFile : FILE OF WholeNum ;
       Count : WholeNums ;

   FUNCTION PrimeNumCk (Num : WholeNum) : BOOLEAN ;

     VAR Ct : WholeNum ;
         Status : BOOLEAN ;

     BEGIN                              {PrimeNumCk}
       Ct := 2 ;
       Status := TRUE ;
       WHILE (Ct < Num) AND Status DO
         BEGIN                          {WHILE-DO}
           IF Num MOD CT = 0            {Look for divisor}
             THEN Status := FALSE ;
           Ct := SUCC (Ct)
         END ;                          {WHILE-DO}
       PrimeNumCk := Status
     END ;                              {PrimeNumCk}
```

Figure 9–5

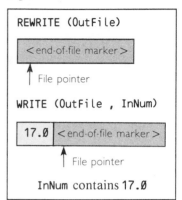

InNum contains 17.0

WARNING

If WRITE (OutFile , 13) is included in a program, the compiler will stop and issue an error message. The form of the WRITE instruction is WRITE (FileVar , Var). That is, the second parameter passed *must* be a variable identifier.

```
BEGIN                                              {BuildPrimes}
  ASSIGN (OutFile , 'Primes.DAT') ;
  REWRITE (OutFile) ;                              {Create file}
  Count := 2 ;
  WHILE Count < Upper DO
    BEGIN                                          {WHILE-DO}
      IF PrimeNumCk (Count)
        THEN WRITE (OutFile , Count) ;             {Send primes to file}
      Count := SUCC (Count)
    END ;                                          {WHILE-DO}
  CLOSE (OutFile)
END .                                              {BuildPrimes}
```

Primes.DAT

| 2 | 3 | 5 | 7 | 11 | < end-of-file > |

↑ File pointer

```
2. PROGRAM PrimeDivisors ;

   TYPE WholeNum = Ø .. MAXINT ;

   VAR InNum : WholeNum ;
       Ans : CHAR ;

   PROCEDURE GivePrimes (Num : WholeNum) ;

     VAR InFile : FILE OF WholeNum ;
         Factor : WholeNum ;

     BEGIN                                              {GivePrimes}
       WRITE ('Prime divisors of ' , Num : 1 , ' are: ') ;
       Factor := 1 ;
       ASSIGN (InFile , 'Primes.DAT') ;
       RESET (InFile) ;                                 {Open Primes}
       WHILE (NOT EOF (InFile)) AND (Factor <= Num) DO
         BEGIN                                          {WHILE-DO}
           READ (InFile , Factor) ;
           IF Num MOD Factor = Ø
             THEN WRITE (Factor : 1 , ' ')
         END ;                                          {WHILE-DO}
       CLOSE (InFile)                                   {ELSE instruction}
     END ;                                              {GivePrimes}

   BEGIN                                              {PrimeDivisors}
     REPEAT
       WRITE ('Please enter whole number: ') ;
       READLN (InNum) ;
       IF InNum > 1ØØØ
         THEN WRITELN ('Number too large! ')
         ELSE GivePrimes (InNum) ;
       WRITELN ;
       WRITE ('Do another number?(Y/N): ') ;
       READLN (Ans)
     UNTIL Ans = 'N'
   END .                                            {PrimeDivisors}
```

Sample Execution

```
Please enter whole number: 221
Prime divisors of 221 are: 13 17

Do another number?(Y/N): N
```

9-1.3 The SEEK Procedure

COMMENT
SEEK (InFile, Ø)
accomplishes the same thing as
RESET (InFile)
for an opened file.

In addition to the built-in procedures ASSIGN, RESET, REWRITE, READ, and WRITE, the Turbo Pascal system provides a built-in procedure known as **SEEK**. This procedure has as parameters a file identifier and a component number. The procedure places the file pointer at the component number. A typical call to this procedure would be as follows:

```
SEEK (InFile , Ø)
```

This call would result in the file pointer being placed at component Ø, the first component in the file. Consider the program UpdateNumFile presented in Figure 9-6. This program allows the user to specify a component of the file to be altered. If the component is found, a replacement value is entered by the user, then inserted in the file.

Figure 9-6

```
PROGRAM UpdateNumFile ;

VAR NumFile : FILE OF INTEGER ;
    Num, InNum : INTEGER ;
    Ct : Ø .. MAXINT ;                        {variable to keep up with file component #}
BEGIN
  WRITE ('Enter value in file to alter: ') ;
  READLN (Num) ;
  Ct := Ø ;                                   {Initialize Ct}
  ASSIGN (NumFile, 'Test.DAT') ;
  RESET (NumFile) ;                           {Open file}
  IF NOT EOF (NumFile)                        {File not empty}
    THEN READ (NumFile , InNum) ;
  WHILE (InNum < > Num) AND (NOT EOF (NumFile)) DO
    BEGIN
      READ (NumFile , InNum) ;                {Search file}
      Ct := Ct + 1                            {keep up with component number of file}
    END ;
  IF InNum < > Num
    THEN WRITE ('Value not found')
    ELSE BEGIN
           WRITE ('Enter replacement value: ') ;
           READLN (Num) ;
           SEEK (NumFile , Ct) ;              {move file pointer to component Ct}
           WRITE (NumFile , Num)
         END ;
  CLOSE (NumFile)
END .
```

Sample Execution

```
Enter value in file to alter: 23
Enter replacement value: -5
```

WARNING
SEEK only positions the file pointer. A READ must be executed to get the file component. A WRITE must be executed to place a component in the file.

After making a call to SEEK, a call to READ or WRITE should be made. Making successive calls to SEEK (without a call to READ or WRITE) will yield unreliable results. Essentially, SEEK provides for *random access* of the components of a file.

DO IT NOW

1. Write a Pascal procedure that has a variable parameter of type NumFile where NumFile = FILE OF INTEGER and value parameters are CompNum and Value. The procedure is to alter the file component in position CompNum to Value.
2. NYCFile is of type NumFile where NumFile = FILE OF REAL. NYCFile contains 25 components. Write a collection of instructions that writes to the screen the components in NYCFile in reverse order.

```
1. PROCEDURE AlterFileValue (VAR InFile : NumFile ;
                                 CompNum , Value : INTEGER) ;

     BEGIN                                           {AlterFileValue}
       RESET (InFile) ;
       SEEK (InFile , CompNum) ;
       WRITE (InFile , Value)
     END ;                                           {AlterFileValue}
2. FOR Ct := 24 DOWNTO 0 DO
     BEGIN
       SEEK (NYCFile, Ct) ;
       READ (NYCFile, InNum) ;
       WRITELN (InNum : 10)
     END
```

COMMENT

The 25 components of NYCFile are indexed from 0 to 24.

9-1.4 FILESIZE

In addition to the SEEK procedure just described, Turbo Pascal has a built-in function to make working with the FILE OF data structure easier. The function **FILESIZE** is used to find the number of components in a file. This function has a file variable as a parameter. The value returned by the function is the number of components in the file. Consider the following instruction:

```
IF FILESIZE (InFile) = 0
  THEN WRITELN ('File is empty.')
```

Another use of the function FILESIZE is to append (add to the end) a component to a file. Consider these instructions:

```
ASSIGN (InFile , 'Numbers.DAT') ;
RESET (InFile) ;
WRITE ('Enter number to add to the end of the file: ') ;
READLN (Num) ;
SEEK (InFile, FILESIZE (InFile)) ;
WRITE (InFile , Num) ;
CLOSE (InFile)
```

COMMENT

The APPEND procedure introduced for TEXT files in Chapter 5 will not accept a variable parameter of type FILE OF.

The function FILESIZE (InFile) returns the number of components in the file (0 if the file is empty). The instruction

```
SEEK (InFile, FILESIZE (InFile))
```

places the file pointer just beyond the last component in the file. The instruction WRITE (InFile , Num) is used to store in the file the value in Num.

9-1.5 Summary

To summarize this section, the following programming points should be emphasized:

1.
```
ASSIGN (InFile , 'Name.DAT') ;
RESET (InFile)
```

yields a runtime error message if 'Name.DAT' does not exist.

2. RESET (InFile) is used to move the file pointer to the start of an open file. If InFile has not been used in an ASSIGN instruction, an error occurs.

3. ```
   ASSIGN (InFile , 'Name.DAT') ;
   REWRITE (InFile)
   ```
   is used to create a new file named `'Name.DAT'`.

4. `REWRITE (InFile)` will destroy the contents of the file assigned to `InFile` if the file is an existing file.

5. SEEK simply positions the file pointer. A READ or WRITE must be executed to access the file component.

6. A quick way to place the file pointer at the end of a file is to use

   ```
   SEEK (InFile, FILESIZE (InFile))
   ```

7. To use SEEK, FILESIZE, READ, and WRITE on a file, the file must be open.

8. A file variable must be passed as a *variable* parameter to a module.

Vocabulary

Page

ASSIGN   A built-in Turbo Pascal procedure used to assign to a file variable the name of a file. Example: 466

```
ASSIGN (InFile , 'B:Numbers.DAT')
```

assigns to the variable `InFile` the file `Numbers.DAT` which is found on the diskette in drive `B:`.

FILE OF   Pascal reserved words used to declare a variable as an identifier of a file whose component type is given after the word `OF`. Example: 466

```
VAR NumFile : FILE OF INTEGER
```

declares `NumFile` as an identifier of a file whose components are integers.

FILESIZE   A built-in Turbo Pascal function used to find the number of components in a file. Example: 472

```
IF FILESIZE (InFile) = Ø
   THEN WRITELN ('File is empty!')
```

READ   A built-in Turbo Pascal procedure used to access a component of a file. The component of the file that the file pointer indicates is read and the file pointer is advanced to the next component. Example: 467

```
READ (MyFile , Age)
```

RESET   A built-in procedure used to open a file and to move the file pointer to the first component (component number 0) of a file. Example: 466

```
RESET (InFile)
```

REWRITE   A built-in procedure used to create a new file. Example: 468

```
REWRITE (InFile)
```

SEEK   A built-in Pascal procedure that has as parameters a file variable and a component number (from 0 to the number of components in the file minus 1). The procedure places the file pointer at the component number. Example: 470

```
SEEK (InFile, 2)
```

places the file pointer at the *third* component in `InFile`.
```

468   **WRITE**   A built-in Turbo Pascal procedure used to send a component to a file. A value is written to the file at the file pointer's position and the file pointer is advanced to the next component. Example:

```
WRITE (MyFile , Height)
```

Glad You Asked

Q   How many values can be placed in a file?

A   The answer to this question depends on how much space is available on the external storage device and the data type of the values. If a diskette is used with 360,000 (360K) bytes and if each component of the file was 6 bytes long, then approximately 60,000 values could be stored in the file.

Q   Can I have a FILE OF SET?

A   Yes. In fact, in the next section of this chapter, several more useful FILE OF data structures will be introduced. These files will have components of type ARRAY and RECORD. You cannot have FILE OF FILE OF.

Q   Why use FILE OF REAL? Can't data of type REAL be stored in a TEXT file?

A   Yes, data of type REAL can be stored in a TEXT file. However, the values are first transformed to character data. When the values are later entered back into a Pascal program another conversion is made from character data to a real number. Often a FILE OF REAL is used to avoid the inherent inaccuracy involved in these conversions. Also, by using SEEK the components can be accessed randomly. The only access possible for a TEXT file is sequential access.

Q   If the components in a FILE OF INTEGER are ordered, can I use the binary search to find a component in the file?

A   Yes. Through the use of SEEK a file can be worked with as if it were a one-dimensional array. The components of a file are indexed from zero to the number of components in the file minus one.

Q   What is the big difference between TEXT files and FILE OF (other than that SEEK and FILESIZE will not work with TEXT files, as I found out)?

A   The major difference has to do with the way data is stored on the disk. With a TEXT file, the data is stored in ASCII codes. With the FILE OF data structure, the data is stored in binary code (that is, a series of 0s and 1s). Also, the data structure FILE OF has a file header that is used to keep up with the components of the file. A TEXT file does not contain this header; thus, procedures like SEEK and FILESIZE do not work on TEXT files. With a TEXT file, either READ or WRITE is used to access the data, depending on how it was opened. With FILE OF both READ and WRITE can be used to access the data. With the FILE OF data structure READLN and WRITELN cannot be used since there are no end-of-line markers.

Section 9–1 Exercises

1. Which of the following is not a data structure?
   a. FILE OF INTEGER   **d.** CHAR
   b. ARRAY [1 .. 6] OF INTEGER **e.** SET OF CHAR
   c. TEXT

2. If RESET (InFile) is executed and the file assigned to InFile exists but is empty, then
   a. a runtime error occurs.
   b. the file pointer is moved to component 1.
   c. EOF (InFile) will return the value TRUE.
   d. the instruction WRITE (InFile, Value) will result in an error message if executed.

3. If RESET (InFile) is executed and the file assigned to InFile does not exist, describe what happens.

4. Discuss the differences between the data structures FILE OF INTEGER and TEXT.

5. Insert *True* for a true statement, *False* for a false statement.

_____ **a.** ASSIGN should not be used with a file that is in use (open).

_____ **b.** RESET can be executed at any time in a Turbo Pascal program.

_____ **c.** If a REWRITE instruction is executed and the file does not exist, a run time error message is issued.

_____ **d.** To place the file pointer at the first component of InFile, use SEEK (InFile, 1).

_____ **e.** If a file is opened with REWRITE, then FILESIZE will return the value 0.

_____ **f.** When a FILE OF data structure is defined, the number of components the data structure will hold is also defined.

_____ **g.** SEEK can only be used to move the file pointer to the end of the file.

_____ **h.** To access the components of a file, READ and WRITE are used.

_____ **i.** To see the contents of the data structure FILE OF, the editor is used.

_____ **j.** If RESET (InFile) is executed and the file assigned to InFile exists, then the instruction WRITE (InFile, Value) will replace component 0 with the value in the variable Value.

_____ **k.** If REWRITE (InFile) is executed, then the instruction READ (InFile, Value) will yield an error message.

_____ **l.** The instruction WRITE (InFile , 8) will yield an error message even if InFile is of type FILE OF INTEGER.

6. Suppose the variable NumFile is of type FILE OF INTEGER. The file 'Name.DAT' exists and appears as follows:

```
13  5  -18  12  6  0  234  21  9  9  -14  < end-of-file marker >
```

Assume the instruction ASSIGN (NumFile, 'Name.DAT') has been executed. Give the results of the following:

a.
```
RESET (NumFile) ;
READ (NumFile , Num) ;
WRITE (Num : 4)
```

b.
```
RESET (NumFile) ;
FOR Ct := 1 TO 3 DO
  BEGIN
    READ (NumFile , Num) ;
    WRITELN (Num)
  END
```

c.
```
RESET (NumFile) ;
FOR Ct := 1 TO 3 DO
  BEGIN
    RESET (NumFile) ;
    READ (NumFile , Num) ;
    WRITE (Num : 4)
  END
```

d.
```
REWRITE (NumFile) ;
FOR Ct := 1 TO 3 DO
  BEGIN
    READ (NumFile , Num) ;
    WRITE (Num : 4)
  END
```

7. For the following instructions, MyFile.DAT exists and is of type FILE OF INTEGER. InFile is a variable of type FILE OF INTEGER and ANumber is a variable of type INTEGER. Describe the error that will occur.

a.
```
ASSIGN (InFile , 'MyFile.DAT') ;
REWRITE (InFile) ;
READ (InFile , ANumber)
```

b.
```
ASSIGN (InFile , 'MyFile.DAT') ;
RESET (InFile) ;
SEEK (InFile, FILESIZE (InFile)) ;
READ (InFile , ANumber)
```

8. Compose the TYPE and VAR sections needed to read the values in the file named Color.DAT where the components of the file Color.DAT are of type Pastels and Pastels = (lime, lilac, rose, aquamarine).

9. Boot up Pascal; set the workfile to the file PriDemo.PAS from the Source diskette. Enter the editor. Alter the program so that it builds a file whose components are Fibonacci numbers (less than MAXINT) rather than prime numbers. The remainder

The Fibonacci numbers are 1,1,2,3,5,8,13,... Each number (after the first two) is the sum of the previous two numbers. That is, 13 is the sum of 5 and 8. The next number in the sequence would be 21 (the sum of 8 and 13).

of the program should be altered to allow the user to enter a number from 1 to MAXINT. The program should output whether or not the number is a Fibonacci number.

Sample Execution

```
Please enter number (1 .. 32766): 35
This number is not a Fibonacci number.
Press RETURN key to continue, enter Q to quit-
```

Sample Execution (Problem 11)

```
Which component number
would you like to see? 7
Component #7 is: -137
```

Sample Execution (Problem 12)

```
The files differ at component 3.
FileA component 3 is 5
FileB component 3 is 13

Continue comparison? (Y/N): Y

FileB ends at component 14.
```

Programming Problems

10. Suppose a FILE OF REAL has the name NBC.DAT. Write a Pascal program to find the average of the components of the file.

11. Suppose that KNumbers.DAT is the name of a FILE OF INTEGER. Write a Pascal program that allows the user to input index of the component of the file he or she would like to see. The output of the program is that component.

12. Suppose FileA.DAT and FileB.DAT are both FILE OF WholeNum where WholeNum is of type 0 .. MAXINT. Write a Pascal program to compare the corresponding components of the two files.

13. Suppose Num.DAT and ATT.DAT are both FILE OF REAL. Write a Pascal program that will add to (append) the components of Num.DAT the components of ATT.DAT.

14. Suppose Num2.DAT is a FILE OF INTEGER and that the components are ordered from smallest to largest. Write a Pascal program that allows the user to enter an integer from −MAXINT − 1 to MAXINT. The program will then insert that integer value in Num2.DAT at its proper place.

15. Alter the procedure BinarySearch to find a target in a file. The components in the file are ordered from smallest to largest. Assume the file is of type FILE OF WholeNum where WholeNum is of type 0 .. MAXINT.

16. Alter the insertion sort (page 357) to write a Pascal program that will allow the user to enter a list of integers from the keyboard in an unordered manner. The values are to be stored in a file as they are entered. The values in the file should be ordered from smallest to largest.

17. Suppose File17A.DAT contains a list of part numbers in the range 1001 .. 9999. These values are ordered from smallest to largest. File17B.DAT is of type FILE OF REAL and contains the prices for the parts in File17A.DAT. Write a Pascal program that allows the user to enter a part number. The program is to write the following to the screen:

    a. *input invalid,* if part number is out of range.

    b. *part not carried,* if part number not found in File17A.DAT.

    c. price of the part, if the part number is found in File17A.DAT.

Sample Execution

```
Enter part number (1001 .. 9999): 2318
Price is $2.78

Search for another part number?(Y/N):
```

FILE OF Structured Types

In the last section, the data structure FILE OF was introduced. FILE OF INTEGER, FILE OF REAL, etc. are known as FILE OF *simple types*. In this section, you will study the data structure FILE OF where the components of the file are structured data types: FILE OF ARRAY and FILE OF RECORD. These data structures are known as FILE OF *structured types*.

9-2.1 *Review*

In working with the data structure FILE OF, the instructions READ and WRITE are used to access components of the file. As a review, consider the following instructions to output the components of InFile to the screen:

```
VAR InFile : FILE OF INTEGER ;
    InNum : INTEGER ;

BEGIN
  ASSIGN (InFile , 'NumFile.DAT') ;
  RESET (InFile) ;                    {open the file}
  WHILE NOT EOF (InFile) DO
    BEGIN                             {process the file components}
      READ (InFile, InNum) ;
      WRITE (InNum : 8)
    END ;                             {process the file components}
  CLOSE (InFile)
END
```

9-2.2 *FILE OF Array*

In the data structure FILE OF, the components of the file can be any data type except FILE and TEXT. Thus, a file whose components are of type ARRAY is possible. Consider the following:

```
TYPE WholeNum = 0 .. 300 ;
     List = ARRAY [1 .. 100] OF WholeNum ;

VAR ListFile : FILE OF List ;
    InList : List ;
```

The components of the file, ListFile, will be array values. That is, each component of the file will be a list of values of type WholeNum indexed from 1 to 100. Suppose that the file named NumList.DAT of type FILE OF List exists on a disk. The following instructions would output the contents of the file to the screen.

```
BEGIN                                 {SeeFile}
  ASSIGN (ListFile, 'NumLists.DAT') ;
  RESET (ListFile) ;                  {open the file}
  WHILE NOT EOF (ListFile) DO
    BEGIN                             {WHILE-DO instruction}
      READ (ListFile, InList) ;
      FOR Ct := 1 TO 100 DO
        WRITE (InList [Ct] : 10) ;
      WRITELN
    END ;                             {WHILE-DO instruction}
  CLOSE (ListFile)
END                                   {SeeFile}
```

Since ListFile has components of type List, the components of the file are of type ARRAY [1 .. 100] OF INTEGER. The FOR-DO instruction is used to write the components of InList to the screen.

9-2.3 *Creating a File of Records*

A file is a collection of components that is typically stored external to the computer's main memory. A very important file type in Pascal is a FILE OF RECORD. Since a record often requires several memory locations, an external file is a natural place to store a list of records. The following program demonstrates building a file whose components are of type RECORD.

EXAMPLE

Write a Pascal program that allows the user to store on a disk data items that are records with fields for name, stock number, number in inventory, and price.

SOLUTION

See Figure 9-7.

Figure 9-7

InRec	
Name	Sears marble
StockNum	8913
Inventory	7
Price	25.87

```
PROGRAM BuildFile ;
TYPE Items = RECORD
                  Name : STRING [40] ;
                  StockNum : 1000 .. 9999 ;
                  Inventory : 0 .. MAXINT ;
                  Price : REAL
               END ;                          {record definition}
VAR Ans : CHAR ;
    InvFile : FILE OF Items ;
    InRec : Items ;
BEGIN                                         {Main program}
  ASSIGN (InvFile , 'PaintSto.DAT') ;
  REWRITE (InvFile) ;                         {Create new file}
  REPEAT
    WITH InRec DO
      BEGIN                                   {work with InRec}
        WRITE ('Enter name of item: ') ;
        READLN (Name) ;
        WRITE ('Enter stock # (1000 .. 9999): ') ;
        READLN (StockNum) ;
        WRITE ('Enter number in store: ') ;
        READLN (Inventory) ;
        WRITE ('Enter price of item: ') ;
        READLN (Price)
      END ;                                   {work with InRec}
    WRITE (InvFile, InRec) ;                  {send record to file}
    WRITELN ;                                 {send blank line to screen}
    WRITE ('Press RETURN to continue, enter Q to quit: ') ;
    READLN (Ans)
  UNTIL Ans IN ['Q' , 'q'] ;
  CLOSE (InvFile)
END .                                         {Main program}
```

In Figure 9-7, `InvFile` is declared a `FILE OF Items`. Thus, the file will have components that are records. As with all files, `WRITE` places the value in the file and advances the pointer to the next component of the file. After the user executes the program just given, there will be a file named `PaintSto.DAT` on the disk. A picture of the file is shown in Figure 9-8.

PaintSto.DAT   **Figure 9-8**

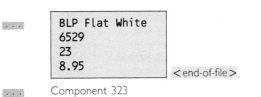

Old Dutch White	Sears Marble	....	BLP Flat White
1897	8913		6529
13	7		23
17.95	25.87		8.95	< end-of-file >

Component 0   Component 1   ....   Component 323

That is, the file is made up of components and each component is a record.

DO IT NOW

Write a Pascal program that will allow the user to enter a stock number. The program will then search the file `PaintSto.DAT` for the item with the input stock number and present the record on the screen.

DO IT NOW ANSWER

Since the search is of a file of records and the records are not ordered, a sequential (linear) search is the only search available. If the records had been entered or sorted based on the stock number field, then the binary search could be used. See the following program:

```
PROGRAM SearchFile ;

TYPE Stock = 1000 .. 9999 ;
     Items = RECORD
                Name : STRING [40] ;
                StockNum : Stock ;
                Inventory : 0 .. MAXINT ;
                Price : REAL
             END ;

VAR Ans : CHAR ;
    InRec : Items ;
    InvFile : FILE OF Items ;
    InvItem : Items ;
    StockID : Stock ;

PROCEDURE GiveData (ItemRec : Items) ;

  BEGIN                                          {GiveData}
    WRITE ('Item number ' , ItemRec.StockNum : 1, ' is: ') ;
    WRITELN (ItemRec.Name) ;
    WRITELN ('Number in store: ' , ItemRec.Inventory) ;
    WRITELN ('Price is: $' , ItemRec.Price:1:2)
  END ;                                          {GiveData}

BEGIN                                            {Main program}
  Ans := ' ' ;                                   {a blank}
  ASSIGN (InvFile, 'PaintSto.DAT') ;             {Open file}
```

```
                          WHILE Ans < > 'Q' DO
                            BEGIN                                              {WHILE-DO}
                              WRITE ('Enter stock number (1000 .. 9999): ') ;
                              READLN (StockID) ;
                              RESET (InvFile) ;                               {move pointer to start}
                              IF FILESIZE (InvFile) < > 0                     {file not empty}
                                THEN READ (InvFile , InvItem) ;
                              WHILE (NOT EOF (InvFile)) AND (InvItem.StockNum < > StockID) DO
                                READ (InvFile , InvItem) ;                    {Get next file component}
                              IF InvItem.StockNum = StockID
                                THEN GiveData (InvItem)
                                ELSE WRITELN ('Item not found in Paint Store') ;
                              WRITE ('Enter Q to Quit, press RETURN to continue: ') ;
                              READLN (Ans)
                            END ;                                             {WHILE-DO}
                          CLOSE (InvFile)
                        END .                                                 {main program}
```

COMMENT

When the instruction RESET (InvFile) in the program SearchFile is executed, the file pointer is set to the first component of the file. The function FILESIZE is used to protect against trying to READ from an empty file. The BOOLEAN expression

    (NOT EOF (InvFile)) AND (InvItem.StockNum < > StockID)

is the test for the WHILE-DO instruction. If the input number matches the StockNum field of the record then an exit is made from the WHILE-DO loop. Otherwise, another READ is performed on the file (that is, the next record is read into the variable InRec and the file pointer variable is advanced to the next record). When the file pointer reaches the end-of-file marker, NOT (EOF (Infile)) returns FALSE and an exit is made from the WHILE-DO instruction.

9-2.4 A Programming Example

As a second illustration of working with a FILE OF RECORDS data structure, consider the following example.

EXAMPLE

Valley Movies is a local store that rents VCR tapes. The manager wants to use a computer to aid in management of the tapes. The manager has decided that a record of each movie should be designed as follows:

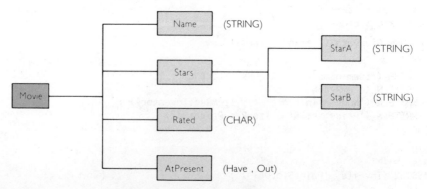

Write a Pascal program to create a file whose components are records of the type Movie. The file should be ordered alphabetically based on the name of the movie.

SOLUTION

To create a file of movie records whose components are ordered, first the records will be read into an array of records. The records can be sorted by the insertion sort as they are read in. After the movies are ordered in the array, the records can then be placed in a file.

MovieList [n]		
Name		Stakeout
Stars	StarA	R Dreyfuss
	StarB	E Estevez
Rated		R
AtPresent		Out

Design: GetRecord [1]
         WHILE MoreRecords DO
            GetRecord [n]
            InsertInList
            Increment n
         ASSIGN (MovieFile , 'Valley.DAT')
         REWRITE (MovieFile)   {create file}
         Write List to MovieFile
         CLOSE (MovieFile)

COMMENT

This design is a straightforward approach to the problem. However, for any sort, values must be moved about in the list. The values being moved are records. Thus, it will take time to move this size data item. A better approach to the problem is the following design, which uses a parallel array as a reference.

Design: n := 1
         WHILE MoreRecords DO   {fill record list}
            GetRecord [n]
            Increment n
         Initialize AuxList
         Sort AuxList based on RecordList
         ASSIGN (MovieFile, 'Valley.DAT')
         REWRITE (MovieFile)
         Write RecordList to MovieFile based on AuxList
         CLOSE (MovieFile)

COMMENT

In this design, the list of records is entered. An array of 1 .. n is then sorted based on the Name field of the RecordList. Here, the values being moved in the sort are numbers, not large data items like records. Once AuxList is sorted, it can then be used to send the records in RecordList to the file MovieFile in an ordered manner.

Refinement of: *InitAuxList*
           FOR Ct := 1 TO n DO
              AuxList [Ct] := Ct

Refinement of: *SortAuxList*   {use Selection sort}
           Pt := 1
           WHILE Pt <= n DO   {n is length of list}
              Search RecordList for smallest movie name (Index)
              IF AuxList [Pt] < > AuxList [Index]
                THEN Swap AuxList [Pt] with AuxList [Index]
              Pt := SUCC (Pt)

COMMENT
FindSmallest needs Pt so as to know where to start in the list. The procedure will return Index, the location of the smallest movie name in RecordList, from Pt to the end of the list.

COMMENT
Once AuxList is ordered, based on the Name field of the records in RecordList, it can be used to select the order in which the records are sent to the file MovieFile.

Refinement of: *FindSmallest (Pt, Index)*
Min : = RecordList [AuxList[Pt]].Name
Index : = Pt
FOR Ct : = Pt + 1 TO n DO
   IF RecordList [AuxList[Ct]].Name < Min
     THEN Min : = RecordList [AuxList[Ct]].Name
       Index : = Ct

Refinement of: *Swap (AuxList [Pt] , AuxList [Index])*
TempHold : = AuxList [Pt]
AuxList [Pt] : = AuxList [Index]
AuxList [Index] : = TempHold

Refinement of: *SendToFile*
FOR Ct : = 1 TO n DO
   WRITE (MovieFile , RecordList [AuxList [Ct]])

If RecordList contained the following values,

AuxList

RecordList
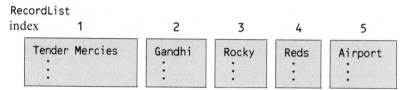

AuxList would be sorted to yield the value shown. Thus, the records would be sent to the file in the following order:
RecordList [5], RecordList [2], RecordList [4], RecordList [3], and RecordList [1]. That is, the order would be: *Airport, Gandhi, Reds, Rocky, Tender Mercies.*

After the design is tested, it is converted to the Pascal program in Figure 9–9.

Figure 9–9

```
PROGRAM BuildFile ;

CONST Max = 100 ;

TYPE Number = 1 .. Max ;
     State = (Have , Out) ;
     StarType = RECORD
                   StarA : STRING [30] ;
                   StarB : STRING [30]
                END ;
     Movie = RECORD
                Name : STRING [40] ;
                Stars : StarType ;
                Rated : CHAR ;
                AtPresent : State
             END ;
     MovieList = ARRAY [1 .. Max] OF Movie ;
     TempList = ARRAY [1 .. Max] OF Number ;

VAR n , Ct : Number ;
    Ans : CHAR ;
    RecordList : MovieList ;
    MovieFile : FILE OF Movie ;
    AuxList : TempList ;
```

Figure 9–9
Continued

```
PROCEDURE GetRecord (VAR Rental : Movie) ;

  VAR Ans : CHAR ;

  BEGIN                                      {GetRecord}
    WITH Rental DO
      BEGIN                                  {work with Rental record}
        WRITE ('Enter name of movie: ') ;
        READLN (Name) ;
        WRITE ('Enter star 1: ') ;
        READLN (Stars.StarA) ;
        WRITE ('Enter star 2: ') ;
        READLN (Stars.StarB) ;
        WRITE ('Enter rating (G, P, R, X, N): ') ;
        READLN (Rated) ;
        WRITE ('Is movie on shelf? (Y/N): ') ;
        READLN (Ans) ;
        IF (Ans = 'N') OR (Ans = 'n')
          THEN AtPresent := Out
          ELSE AtPresent := Have
      END                                    {work with Rental record}
  END ;                                      {GetRecord}
PROCEDURE SortAuxList (VAR RecordList : MovieList ;
                       VAR AuxList : TempList ;
                       n : Number) ;

  BEGIN                                      {SortAuxList}
    {Left as a Do It Now exercise}
  END ;                                      {SortAuxList}
BEGIN                                        {main program}
  n := 0 ;
  Ans := ' ' ;                               {A blank}
  WHILE NOT (Ans IN ['Q', 'q']) DO           {Fill Record List}
    BEGIN                                    {WHILE-DO}
      n := n + 1 ;
      GetRecord (RecordList [n]) ;
      WRITE ('Enter Q to quit, press RETURN to continue: ') ;
      READLN (Ans)
    END ;                                    {WHILE-DO}
  FOR Ct := 1 TO n DO                        {Initialize AuxList}
    AuxList [Ct] := Ct ;
  SortAuxList (RecordList , AuxList, n) ;
  ASSIGN (MovieFile , 'Valley.DAT') ;
  REWRITE (MovieFile) ;                      {Create file named Valley}
  FOR Ct := 1 TO n DO                        {send records to file}
    WRITE (MovieFile, RecordList [AuxList [Ct]]) ;
  CLOSE (MovieFile)
END .                                        {main program}
```

DO IT NOW

1. In Figure 9–9, RecordList is listed as a variable parameter for the procedure SortAuxList. RecordList will not be altered by SortAuxList. Why was it sent as a variable parameter?

2. Write the procedure `SortAuxList` for program `BuildFile` in Figure 9–9.

3. Suppose that after entering half of the movies, the user quits. Alter the program in Figure 9–9 to allow the user to add the other half of the movies to the file `Valley.DAT`.

DO IT NOW ANSWERS

1. To send a copy of a large data structure such as an array of records takes up too much memory. Thus, only the address of the data structure is sent (that is, a variable parameter is used rather than a value parameter).

2.
```
PROCEDURE SortAuxList (VAR RecordList : MovieList ;
                       VAR AuxList : TempList ;
                       n : Number) ;

  VAR Pt , Index : Number ;

  PROCEDURE FindSmallest (Start : Number ; AuxList : TempList ;
                          VAR FoundAt : Number ;
                          VAR RecordList : MovieList) ;

    VAR Min : STRING [40] ;
        Ct : Number ;

    BEGIN                                          {FindSmallest}
      Min := RecordList [AuxList [Start]].Name ;
      FoundAt := Start ;
      FOR Ct := Start + 1 TO n DO
        IF RecordList [AuxList [Ct]].Name < Min
          THEN BEGIN                               {THEN instruction}
                 Min := RecordList [AuxList [Ct]].Name ;
                 FoundAt := Ct
               END                                 {THEN instruction}
    END ;                                          {FindSmallest}

  PROCEDURE Swap (VAR FValue , SValue : Number) ;

    VAR Temp : Number ;

    BEGIN                                          {Swap}
      Temp := FValue ;
      FValue := SValue ;
      SValue := Temp
    END ;                                          {Swap}

  BEGIN                                            {SortAuxList}
    Pt := 1 ;
    Index := 1 ;
    WHILE Pt < n DO
      BEGIN                                        {WHILE-DO}
        FindSmallest (Pt, AuxList, Index, RecordList) ;
        IF AuxList [Pt] < > AuxList [Index]
          THEN Swap (AuxList [Pt] , AuxList [Index]) ;
        Pt := SUCC (Pt)
      END                                          {WHILE-DO}
  END ;                                            {SortAuxList}
```

3. After quitting, the file `Valley.DAT` will contain the first half of the movie records. Add the procedure `LoadFile` to the program `BuildFile`.

```
PROCEDURE LoadFile (VAR RecordList : MovieList ;
                    VAR n : Number) ;

  BEGIN                                            {LoadFile}
    ASSIGN (MovieFile, 'Valley.DAT') ;
    RESET (MovieFile) ;
    WHILE NOT EOF (MovieFile) DO
```

```
          BEGIN                                          {WHILE-DO}
            n := n + 1 ;
            READ (MovieFile , RecordList [n])
          END ;
        CLOSE (MovieFile)
      END ;                                              {LoadFile}
```

Insert a call to this procedure just after the instruction n := 0 in the main execution block. The procedure will fill RecordList with the previous records entered in Valley.DAT.

9-2.5 *Merge Sort for Files*

An alternative solution to exercise 3 of the last Do It Now is to perform a merge sort on two files. Suppose the program Buildfile has been executed twice to create the files Valley.DAT and Valley2.DAT. A merge sort of the two files could be done to create the file ValleyMv.DAT. A **merge sort** of files (see page 336 for a merge sort of arrays) means to create a third file, which contains the components of the original two files, in which the components are ordered in some fashion. In the movie records problem, the new file, ValleyMv.DAT will contain the records stored in Valley.DAT and Valley2.DAT and the records will be ordered alphabetically based on the Name field of the records.

A design for performing a merge sort on two files is as follows. The design assumes the records in the two files to be merged are ordered.

Figure 9–10

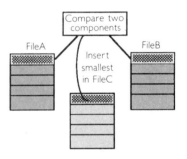

If component from FileB was smallest, READ next component from FileB

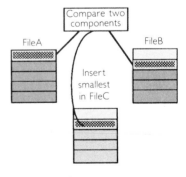

```
Design:   Open the existing files FileA and FileB
          Create the new file FileC
          Get the first component of FileA
          Get the first component of FileB
          Initialize CountA and CountB to 1
          WHILE CountA < = FILESIZE (FileA) AND CountB < = FILESIZE (FileB) DO
              IF FileA component < FileB component
                THEN WRITE FileA component to FileC
                     IF CountA < FILESIZE (FileA)
                       THEN READ next component of FileA
                     CountA : = CountA + 1
                ELSE WRITE FileB component to FileC
                     IF CountB < FILESIZE (FileC)
                       THEN READ next component of FileB
                     CountB : = CountB + 1
          WHILE CountA < = FILESIZE (FileA) DO          {finish out FileA if not finished}
              Send last component READ from FileA to FileC
              IF CountA < FILESIZE (FileA)
                THEN READ FileA component
              CountA : = CountA + 1
          WHILE CountB < = FILESIZE (FileB) DO          {finish out FileB if not finished}
              Send last component READ from FileB to FileC
              IF CountB < FILESIZE (FileB)
                THEN READ FileB component
              CountB : = CountB + 1
          CLOSE the files
```

See Figure 9–10 for a picture of the merge sort process. Notice the use of the function FILESIZE to protect from reading past the end-of-file marker. When the merge sort is finished, FileC will contain the components of FileA and FileB and the components will be ordered from smallest to largest.

Converting this design to a Pascal program yields the program `MergeSort` shown in Figure 9–11. In reading the Pascal program, remember that the Pascal program `BuildFile` has been executed to create the file `Valley2.DAT` which contains the second half of the movie records in alphabetical order by `Name` field.

Figure 9–11

```pascal
PROGRAM MergeSort ;

TYPE State = (Have , Out) ;
     StarType = RECORD
                     StarA : STRING [30] ;
                     StarB : STRING [30]
                 END ;
     Movie = RECORD
                Name : STRING [40] ;
                Stars : StarType ;
                Rated : CHAR ;
                AtPresent : State
             END ;

VAR Ans : CHAR ;
    MovieA, MovieB, MovieF : FILE OF Movie ;
    RecA , RecB : Movie ;
    ACt, BCt : INTEGER ;

BEGIN                                                     {main program}
  WRITE ('Ready to merge files Valley and Valley2. Press RETURN.') ;
  READLN (Ans) ;
  ASSIGN (MovieA , 'Valley.DAT') ;
  RESET (MovieA) ;
  ASSIGN (MovieB , 'Valley2.DAT') ;
  RESET (MovieB) ;
  ASSIGN (MovieF, 'ValleyMv.DAT') ;
  REWRITE (MovieF) ;                                      {create new file}
  READ (MovieA, RecA) ;
  READ (MovieB, RecB) ;
  ACt := 1 ;
  BCt := 1 ;
  WHILE (ACt <= FILESIZE (MovieA)) AND (BCt <= FILESIZE (MovieB)) DO
    BEGIN                                                 {WHILE-DO}
      IF RecA.Name < RecB.Name
        THEN BEGIN                                        {THEN instruction}
              WRITE (MovieF , RecA) ;
              IF ACt < FILESIZE (MovieA)
                THEN READ (MovieA , RecA) ;
              ACt := ACt + 1
            END                                           {THEN instruction}
        ELSE BEGIN                                        {ELSE instruction}
              WRITE (MovieF , RecB) ;
              IF BCt < FILESIZE (MovieB)
                THEN READ (MovieB , RecB) ;
              BCt := BCt + 1
            END                                           {ELSE instruction}
    END ;                                                 {WHILE-DO}
```

WARNING

If `MovieA` or `MovieB` is empty, a runtime error message is issued.

```
        WHILE ACt <= FILESIZE (MovieA) DO          {Finish MovieA file}
          BEGIN                                     {WHILE-DO}
            WRITE (MovieF , RecA) ;
            IF ACt < FILESIZE (MovieA)
              THEN READ (MovieA , RecA) ;
            ACt := ACt + 1
          END ;                                     {WHILE-DO}
        WHILE BCt <= FILESIZE (MovieB) DO           {Finish MovieB file}
          BEGIN                                     {WHILE-DO}
            WRITE (MovieF , RecB) ;
            IF BCt < FILESIZE (MovieB)
              THEN READ (MovieB , RecB) ;
            BCt := BCt + 1
          END ;                                     {WHILE-DO}
        CLOSE (MovieF) ;
        CLOSE (MovieA) ;
        CLOSE (MovieB)
      END .                                         {main program}
```

Figure 9–11

Continued

COMMENT

In Figure 9–11, the BOOLEAN expression `RecA.Name < RecB.Name` for the IF-THEN-ELSE compares the name fields of the records in the variables `RecA` and `RecB`. The files `Valley` and `Valley2` can be removed from the diskette by using the procedure **ERASE**. That is, after the `CLOSE` instructions in the main execution section, insert the instructions

```
    ERASE (MovieA) ;
    ERASE (MovieB)
```

Also, Turbo Pascal has a built-in procedure that can be used to rename a file. The file named `ValleyMv.DAT` could be renamed to `Valley.DAT` by using the instruction

```
    RENAME (MovieF , 'Valley.DAT')
```

As with ERASE and ASSIGN, RENAME should not be used with a file that is in use (opened but not yet closed).

Vocabulary

	Page
ERASE A built-in procedure in Turbo Pascal that erases (removes) the components of a file. The file's name is removed from the disk directory. Example:	487

```
    ERASE (InFile)
```

File of arrays A file data structure whose components are arrays.	477
File of records A file data structure whose components are records.	478
Merge sort The process of merging two data structures and ordering the components into a third data structure.	485
RENAME A built-in procedure in Turbo Pascal that can be used to change the name of a file. Example:	487

```
    RENAME (InFile , 'Movies.DAT')
```

Glad You Asked

Q I tested the program BuildFile using Movies and changed the value of the constant Max to 700. When I ran the program I got an error message: "Memory overflow." I suppose this means the computer's main memory wouldn't hold the array of records (RecordList) declared. Is there any way around this problem?

A First, Pascal is a teaching language designed to teach good programming habits. The learner should not be concerned about such everyday problems as limited memory. However, the problem you mentioned *is* an everyday problem to a programmer. One way around would be to read in part of the values, sort them, then place the values in a file. Repeat this process until all the values are entered. Once the values are in the different files, merge sort the files to create one file whose components are of type Movie.

Q Can I change one cell of a component in a file of list without loading in the entire list?

A No. If the components of the file are of type ARRAY OF, then the only access to the file is to a component of the file. Thus, you would have to read a component (a list). Alter the desired cell of the list, then write the altered component back to the file.

Q Can I assign the contents of one file to another file of the same type?

A No. Unlike other data structures, assignment of files is not allowed. That is, instructions like:

```
ASSIGN (FileA , 'MyData.DAT') ;
RESET (FileA) ;
ASSIGN (FileB , 'YourData.DAT') ;
RESET (FileB) ;
FileA := FileB
```

will yield an error message at compile time. Also, none of the relationals are allowed with files.

Q I keep getting an IO error message when I try to open a file. Is there a way around this?

A One way is to replace instructions like:

```
ASSIGN (InFile ,'MyFile.DAT') ;
RESET (InFile)
```

with a procedure like OpenFile as follows:

COMMENT
A variable of type FILE OF must be passed to a module as a variable parameter.

```
PROCEDURE OpenFile (VAR FileVar : FileType) ;

  VAR FName : STRING [13] ;
      OK : BOOLEAN ;

  BEGIN                                        {OpenFile}
    REPEAT
      WRITE ('Enter name of file to open: ') ;
      READLN (FName) ;
      {$I-}                                    {turn off IO checking}
      ASSIGN (FileVar , FName) ;
      RESET (FileVar) ;
      {$I+}                                    {turn back on IO checking}
      OK := (IORESULT = 0) ;
      IF NOT OK
        THEN WRITELN ('Sorry, file not found.')
    UNTIL OK                                   {success in opening file}
  END ;                                        {OpenFile}
```

A call to this procedure would be OpenFile (InFile). Also, FileType is defined in a TYPE section as FileType = FILE OF . . . where the ellipsis represents the components of the file. IORESULT is a predefined function which returns the value 0 if an error did not occur on the last IO operation (such as READ, RESET, etc.)

Q Can I READ a component of a file opened with REWRITE? That is, can I back up in a file that is being created? Or do I have to CLOSE the file, then reopen it with RESET, as you do with TEXT files?

A Yes, you can back up in a file being created and READ a previous entry. Of course, you must execute a SEEK instruction since the file pointer will be pointing to the end-of-file marker. To get back to the end of the file, use

```
SEEK (FileVar, FILESIZE (FileVar))
```

For example, the following instructions would create a file with components

1	2	3	4	5	23	7	8	9

```
VAR FileA : FILE OF INTEGER ;
    Ct : INTEGER ;

BEGIN
  ASSIGN (FileA , 'MyData.DAT') ;
  REWRITE (FileA) ;              {create file named MyData}
  FOR Ct := 1 To 9 DO
    WRITE (FileA , Ct) ;         {write some values to the file}
  SEEK (FileA , 5) ;            {move to component indexed 5}
  Ct := 23 ;
  WRITE (FileA , Ct) ;          {WRITE ( FileA , 23 ) yields an error}
  CLOSE (FileA)
END
```

Section 9–2 Exercises

For problems 1 through 5 use the following TYPE and VAR sections:

```
TYPE Number = Ø .. 25Ø ;
     NumList = ARRAY ['a' .. 'z'] OF Number ;
     FileType = FILE OF NumList ;

VAR FileComp : NumList ;
    ListComp : Number ;
    InFile : FileType
```

1. Which of the following is a valid Pascal instruction?
   a. READ (InFile)
   b. WRITE (FileComp)
   c. RESET (FileType)
   d. InFile := NumList [1]
   e. WRITE (InFile , FileComp)

2. Which of the following can be used to create 'MyLists.DAT', a file whose components are of type NumList?
   a. ASSIGN (InFile ,'MyLists.DAT') ;
      RESET (InFile)
   b. ASSIGN (InFile , 'MyLists.DAT') ;
      REWRITE (InFile)
   c. ASSIGN (MyLists , InFile) ;
      REWRITE (MyLists)
   d. ASSIGN (InFile , 'MyLists.DAT') ;
      OPEN (InFile)

3. Suppose the file 'MyLists.DAT' exists and has eight components of type NumList. If InFile has been assigned 'MyLists.DAT' and has also been RESET, which of the following will alter cell 'b' of the third component in the file?
   a. WRITE (InFile [3 , 'b'] , 23)
   b. SEEK (InFile , 3) ;
      WRITE (InFile ['b'] , 5)
   c. SEEK (InFile , 2) ;
      READ (InFile , FileComp) ;
      FileComp ['b'] := 17 ;
      WRITE (InFile , FileComp)
   d. SEEK (InFile , 2) ;
      READ (InFile , FileComp) ;
      FileComp ['b'] := 17 ;
      SEEK (InFile , 2) ;
      WRITE (InFile , FileComp)

4. Write a collection of Pascal instructions to change the value in the fourth cell of the first component of the file `'MyLists.DAT'` of type `FileType` to 7.

5. Write a collection of Pascal instructions to list to the screen the fifth component of the file `'MyLists.DAT'` of type `FileType`.

6. **a.** Declare CONST, TYPE, and VAR sections so as to declare the variable, `InTable`, of type `FILE OF Table`. `Table` is a two-dimensional array with `RowMax` rows and `ColMax` columns and components of type `Ø .. MAXINT`.

   b. Write a Pascal procedure that has a variable parameter `InTable`. The procedure is to allow the user to append a value to the file.

7. Given

```
TYPE Number = Ø .. 1ØØ ;
        Shooting = RECORD
                        AttShots : Number ;
                        Made : Number ;
                        AttFree : Number ;
                        FTMade : Number
                     END ;
        Member = RECORD
                    Name : STRING [4Ø] ;
                    Position : STRING [2Ø] ;
                    Height : STRING [8] ;
                    Perform : Shooting ;
                    Comment : STRING [255]
                 END ;
        Game = RECORD
                    School : STRING [4Ø] ;
                    Opponent : STRING [4Ø] ;
                    Players : ARRAY [1 .. 1Ø] OF Member ;
                    Comment : STRING [255]
                 END ;

VAR Scout : Game ;
       Reports : FILE OF Game ;
```

Suppose there is a file on a disk named `ScoutRpt.DAT` with components that are of type `Game`.

   a. Write instructions to output to the screen the shooting percent (Made / AttShot * 100) of the Madison team (one of the schools scouted).

   b. Write instructions to output the information on Sharon Kiler, who plays for the Flomaton team.

8. Boot up Pascal; set the workfile to the file `MovieMak.PAS` from the `Source` diskette. Enter the editor. Alter the program so that it allows the user to enter the name of the file to which the list of records is to be stored. Quit the editor and execute the program. Respond to the prompts by entering the movie data to fill four of the records. Respond to the filename prompt by entering the name `B:Valley.DAT`. Execute the program again to build a second file of records named `Valley2.DAT` on the diskette in disk drive `B`. Set the workfile to the file `MergeF.PAS` from the `Source` diskette. Enter the editor. Expand the program to write to the screen the names of the movies in the file created by merging the two existing files.

9. Write a Pascal program to create a file of records for library books. The records should have the fields `Title`, `Author`, `Reference` number.

10. A disk file named `KStLot.DAT` has components that are records for automobiles on the lot. Each record is of type `Car` (defined here). Write a Pascal program that will order the records based on ID number from smallest to largest.

```
TYPE Digits = 1ØØØ .. 9999 ;
     Car = RECORD
              IDNum : Digits ;
              Type : (New , Used) ;
              Model : STRING [4Ø] ;
              Price : REAL
           END ;
```

11. Write a Pascal program that will allow the user to delete a record from the file named `KStLot.DAT` or add a record to the file named `KStLot.DAT`. (See problem 10. Assume that file components are ordered by ID number from smallest to largest.)

12. Suppose a diskette contains the file named `Names.DAT` (a `FILE OF STRING`) and the file `Ages.DAT` (a `FILE OF Number` where `Number = Ø .. 12Ø`). There are 40 components in each file and they are matched (like parallel arrays). Write a Pascal program to create a file of records named `UCEmploy.DAT` where each component is a record with fields `Name` and `Age`.

13. Write a Pascal program to build a `FILE OF Elements` where `Elements` is as follows:

```
Elements = RECORD                          A. Add next record
             Name : STRING [2Ø] ;          B. See records entered so far
             Symbol : STRING [2] ;         C. Alter a record
             AtomicNumber : 1 .. 1Ø3 ;     Q. Quit
             Weight : REAL
           END                             Enter A, B, C, Q:
```

The program should build the file by allowing the user to select from the menu shown.
A typical value in one of the records is `Sodium Na 11 22.98977`.

14. Alter the procedure `SortAuxList` presented in this section (page 484) to use the Shell sort (page 448) rather than the selection sort.

CHAPTER TEST

1. Given `VAR InFile : FILE OF INTEGER`, which of the following is a valid Pascal instruction?
   a. `READ (InFile)`   **d.** `InFile := -5`
   b. `RESET (InFile)`   **e.** `SEEK (InFile)`
   c. `WRITE (InFile)`

2. Which of the following predefined Pascal procedures/functions is valid for `InFile` of type `FILE OF Person` where `Person` is of type `RECORD`?
   a. `EOLN (InFile)`   **d.** `SEEK (Person)`
   b. `WRITELN (InFile)`   **e.** `FILESIZE (InFile)`
   c. `READLN (InFile)`

3. Given this Pascal program:

```
PROGRAM Test9 ;

TYPE Number = Ø .. 3ØØ ;
     NumFile = FILE OF Number ;

VAR InFile , OutFile : NumFile ;
    NumA : Number ;

BEGIN
  ASSIGN ((InFile , 'MyFile.DAT') ;
  RESET (InFile) ;
  ASSIGN (OutFile , 'YourFile.DAT') ;
```

```
                    REWRITE (OutFile) ;
                    WHILE NOT EOF (InFile) DO
                      BEGIN
                        READ (InFile , NumA) ;
                        IF NumA >= 100
                          THEN WRITE (OutFile , NumA)
                      END ;
                    CLOSE (InFile) ;
                    CLOSE (OutFile)
                  END .
```

    a. Describe the contents of the file named `YourFile.DAT` after the execution of the program `Test9`.

    b. Alter the WHILE-DO instruction to also write to the screen the odd numbers in the file `'MyFile.DAT'`.

4. Complete the following Pascal program to add to the end of the file `'School234.DAT'` of type `RecFile` a record value input by the program user.

```
PROGRAM Chapter9 ;

TYPE MyRecord = RECORD
                   Name : STRING [40] ;
                   Age : INTEGER
                 END ;              {RECORD definition}
     RecFile = FILE OF MyRecord ;

VAR ...

BEGIN                               {Chapter9}
  .
  .
END .                               {Chapter9}
```

5. Complete this Pascal program so as to output to the screen the average value of each of the components of file `'RawBits.DAT'` of type `FileType`.

```
PROGRAM ChapTest ;

TYPE List = ARRAY [1 .. 50] OF INTEGER ;
     FileType = FILE OF List ;

VAR ListFile : FileType ;
    NumList : List ;

BEGIN
  .
  .
END .
```

Sample Execution

```
File: RawBits.DAT
Component 0 : Average = 17.3
Component 1 : Average = 10.7
```

Programming Project

Project 9. A file manager is a program that allows the user to create files and delete files. Once a file is created, the file manager allows the user to

    a. add and/or delete information within a file.

    b. update (modify) information within a file.

    c. search the file based on some criteria.

    d. sort information into some order.

    e. write file information to the printer.

Write a file manager dedicated to cities. The program should allow the user to create a FILE OF Cities where

```
Cities = RECORD
            Name : String20 ;
            State : String20 ;
            Population : REAL ;
            Unemployment : REAL ;
            PCIncome : WholeNum
         END
```

and String20 = STRING [20] and WholeNum = 0 .. MAXINT. The program should allow the user to select from the menu shown.

A. See list of cities
B. Add a record
C. Delete a record
D. Update (modify) a record
E. Search the file
F. Sort the records
G. Send output to printer
Q. Quit

If option A is selected, the Name field of the cities is listed.

If option B is selected, the user is allowed to add a record to the end of the list.

If option C is selected, the user enters the Name field of the record to be deleted and the record is deleted.

If option D is selected, the user enters the Name field of the record to be altered and is allowed to alter the record.

If option E is selected, the user is allowed to select the field to be searched. If one of the number fields is selected, the user is to enter a value and select Above or Below for the search. For example, suppose PCIncome is selected as the field.

Sample Execution

```
Enter value (0 .. 32000): 12000
Above or Below? (A/B): A
Cities with per capita income above 12000 are:
  Anaheim, California
  Anchorage, Alaska
  Boston, Massachusetts
  Chicago, Illinois
  Cleveland, Ohio
  Dallas, Texas
  Denver, Colorado
```

If option F is selected, the user selects the field on which to sort the records (the sort is from smallest to largest).

If option G is selected, the printer is activated for output when the user selects option A or option E.

Turn in a copy of your design and its refinement, a structured diagram, a copy of your program, a copy of the cities file (sorted by name), and a hard copy of three sample executions, one for option A after sorting by state, one for option E where search is based on the population field of more than 1,000,000, and one for option E where the search is based on the unemployment field of less than 7%.

Recursion and Pointers

Introduction

In this chapter, you will study a special programming technique known as recursion. Recursion involves a Pascal procedure or function calling itself and is often the natural way to solve a problem. It often provides a more readable alternative to repetition.

Also in this chapter, you will be introduced to a data structure called a linked list. This data structure is constructed by the programmer and is a list of unspecified length. To be able to construct this list, you have to learn to work with a new data type called a pointer data type. When you finish this chapter, you will be able to use recursion in a Pascal program and to construct a linked list data structure.

```
PROGRAM Chapter10 ;

TYPE RecMemLoc = ^Rec ;                                {page 512}
     Rec = RECORD
              Number : INTEGER ;
              Next : RecMemLoc ;                       {page 512}
           END ;

VAR Current, Last : RecMemLoc ;
    HeapTop : ^INTEGER ;                               {page 510}

PROCEDURE CreateList (VAR AHead : RecMemLoc) ;         {page 519}

  VAR Current, Last : RecMemLoc ;

  BEGIN
    AHead^.Next := NIL ;                               {page 510}
    Last := Head ;
    FOR Ct := 1 TO 10 DO
      BEGIN
        NEW (Current) ;
        Last^.Next := Current ;                        {page 514}
        Last := Current ;
        Current^.Number := RANDOM (20) ;               {page 512}
      END ;
    Last^.Next := NIL
  END ;

PROCEDURE SeeList (NumRec : RecMemLoc) ;               {page 517}

  BEGIN
    IF NumRec < > NIL
      THEN BEGIN              {Recursion}
             WRITE (NumRec^.Number : 5) ;
             SeeList (NumRec^.Next)                     {page 499}
           END
  END ;

BEGIN               {main program}
  MARK (HeapTop) ;                                     {page 522}
  NEW (Head) ;                                         {page 510}
  CreateList (Head) ;
  SeeList (Head) ;
  RELEASE (HeapTop)                                    {page 522}
END .              {main program}
```

Recursive Routines

In this section, a rather special programming technique known as **recursion** will be discussed. Essentially, recursion in programming means a procedure or function calling itself. This technique is very useful for several tasks in programming. One such task is a new sort routine known as the quicksort. In addition to recursion, the Pascal reserved word, FORWARD, will be discussed.

10–1.1 Recursive Definitions

A process is recursive if it repeats itself until some preset condition is met. Many concepts lend themselves to a recursive definition. Consider the whole numbers (0, 1, 2, 3, 4, . . .):

- The first element is 0.
- The nth element is the (nth − 1) element plus 1.

For example,

- The 5th element is the 4th element plus 1.
- The 4th element is the 3rd element plus 1.
- The 3rd element is the 2nd element plus 1.
- The 2nd element is the 1st element plus 1.
- The first element is 0.

- So, the 2nd element is 0 + 1 or 1.
- The 3rd element is 1 + 1 or 2.
- The 4th element is 2 + 1 or 3.
- The 5th element is 3 + 1 or 4.

The basic idea of a recursive definition is to define an ending case ("The first element is 0" in the example just given). After the ending case is defined, the remaining cases are defined in terms of the preceding cases ("The nth element is the nth − 1 element plus 1").

A famous recursive definition is that of the Fibonacci numbers:

- The first element is 1.
- The second element is 1.
- The nth element is the sum of the nth − 1 element and the nth − 2 element.

EXAMPLE

Find the fifth Fibonacci number.

SOLUTION

Using the notation F_5 for the fifth Fibonacci number and the recursive definition just presented,

$$F_5 = F_4 + F_3$$
$$F_4 = F_3 + F_2$$
$$F_3 = F_2 + F_1 \text{ which is } 1 + 1 \text{ which is } 2$$

Thus, F_4 is $2 + 1$ which is 3
F_5 is $3 + 2$ which is 5

PROGRAMMING POINT

The power of recursive definitions becomes apparent when you consider the formula for the nth Fibonacci number:

$$F_n = \frac{1}{\sqrt{5}} \left[\left(\frac{1 + \sqrt{5}}{2} \right)^n - \left(\frac{1 - \sqrt{5}}{2} \right)^n \right]$$

DO IT NOW

1. For the following recursive definition, find A_4 and A_5.

$$A_0 = 1$$
$$A_1 = 1$$
$$A_n = n * A_{n-1}$$

2. A triangular number *(T)* is a counting number that represents the total number of dots when the dots are stacked in a triangular pattern. For example:

```
                                        *
                              *        * *
                    *        * *      * * *
          *        * *      * * *    * * * *
 *       * *      * * *    * * * *  * * * * *

 1        3        6        10        15      and so forth
 T₁       T₂       T₃       T₄        T₅
```

Write a recursive definition for the triangular numbers.

10-1.2 Recursion in Programming

To introduce recursion in programming, we will first discuss the error situation. Consider the following example:

```
FUNCTION SumIt : INTEGER ;

VAR Count : 1 .. MAXINT ;

BEGIN
  Count := 1 ;
  WHILE Count < 10 DO
    BEGIN
      SumIt := SumIt + Count ;
      Count := SUCC (Count)
    END
END ;
```

A call to this function leads to a stack overflow error. The offending instruction is `SumIt := SumIt + Count`. When an attempt is made to execute this instruction, the function `SumIt` is called. In this second call to `SumIt`, `Count` (for this call) is assigned the value `1`; the WHILE-DO instruction is entered; an attempt is made to execute `SumIt := SumIt + Count`. Again a call is made to the function `SumIt`. The process continues until the stack overflow error is reported.

    Any time a call is made to the procedure or function, the value parameters and variables (local to the function or procedure called) are placed on a *stack*. A stack is an area of memory created when the program execution begins. See Figure 10–1.

DO IT NOW ANSWERS

1. $A_4 = 4 * A_3$
   $A_3 = 3 * A_2$
   $A_2 = 2 * A_1$
   $A_1 = 1.$
   Thus, $A_2 = 2 * 1$ which is 2
   $A_3 = 3 * 2$ which is 6
   $A_4 = 4 * 6$ which is 24
   $A_5 = 5 * A_4$
   $A_4 = 24$ (from the problem just solved)
   Thus, $A_5 = 5 * 24$ which is 120
2. $T_1 = 1$
   $T_n = n + T_{n-1}$

Figure 10-1

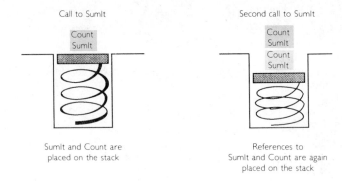

Call to SumIt

SumIt and Count are
placed on the stack

Second call to SumIt

References to
SumIt and Count are again
placed on the stack

If a procedure or function is called repeatedly, eventually this area of memory will fill up. At that point, the stack overflow error message is issued.

A stack picture is used in Figure 10-1 since the first item on the stack is the last item to come off the stack (think of the food trays in a cafeteria). This explains the way Count can be a program variable and a procedure variable. When the procedure is executing and a reference is made to Count, the stack is searched from the top down. The first occurrence of Count that is found is used. If Count is not declared locally to the procedure, then the program reference to Count is found and used.

To use recursion in programming, the basic form used is as follows:

```
PROCEDURE RecursiveForm ;            {or FUNCTION}

  BEGIN
    IF  <terminating case>
      THEN  <terminating task>
      ELSE BEGIN
               .
               .
               RecursiveForm
               .
               .
           END
  END
```

A nonmathematical example of recursion appears here:

```
PROCEDURE ReverseAlpha (Ch : CHAR) ;

  BEGIN
    IF Ch < 'z'
      THEN BEGIN
            Ch := SUCC (Ch) ;
            ReverseAlpha (Ch) ;
            WRITE (Ch)
          END

  END
```

A call to this procedure is

```
WRITELN ('Press RETURN to see example- ') ;
READLN ;
Ch := PRED ('a') ;
ReverseAlpha (Ch)
```

After writing `Press RETURN to see example-`, a call is made to the recursive procedure `ReverseAlpha`. The value sent, `PRED ('a')`, is less than `'z'`. Thus, the instruction `Ch := SUCC (Ch)` is executed (`Ch` is assigned the character `'a'`). The value placed on the stack is `'a'`. `ReverseAlpha` is called, and the next value placed on the stack is `'b'`. This process continues until the character `'z'` is placed on the stack. On the next call to `ReverseAlpha`, `Ch < 'z'` is `FALSE` and the call is completed. To complete the call that placed `'z'` on the stack, `WRITE (Ch)` is executed. Thus, the character `'z'` is written to the screen. Each call to `ReverseAlpha` is completed in this fashion.

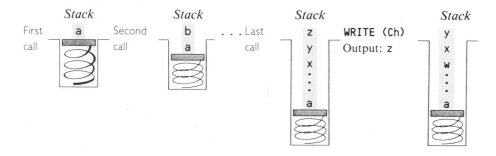

One of the easiest mathematical examples of a recursive procedure or function is that of summing the counting numbers from 1 to 100. First, the recursive definition is

$$S_1 = 1$$

$$S_n = S_{n-1} + n$$

Converting this recursive definition to a recursive procedure yields the following:

```
PROCEDURE RecursiveSum (Term : INTEGER ; VAR Sum : INTEGER) ;

  BEGIN
    IF Term = 1
      THEN Sum := 1
      ELSE BEGIN
             RecursiveSum (PRED (Term), Sum) ;
             Sum := Sum + Term
           END
  END ;
```

Consider the following calls to this procedure:

- `RecursiveSum (1 , Total):` This call is the **terminating case**. When the procedure `RecursiveSum` executes, `Term` is 1; thus, 1 is passed back to `Total`.
- `RecursiveSum (2 , Total):` When the procedure executes, `Term` is assigned the value 2. `Term = 1` is `FALSE`. `RecursiveSum` is called again. It is passed the value 1 and the variable `Sum`. Since `Term` is assigned the value 1, 1 is returned to `Sum`. Next, `Sum` is assigned the value `1 + 2` (the value passed back to `Sum` plus the value in `Term`). So the value 3 is returned to `Total`.
- `RecursiveSum (3 , Total):` When the procedure executes, `Term` is assigned the value 3 (see Figure 10-2).

Figure 10–2

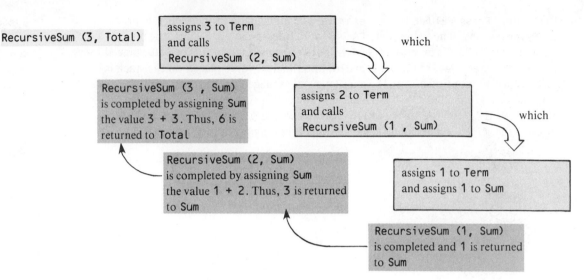

■ RecursiveSum (100, Total): When the procedure executes, Term is assigned the value 100. The recursion starts. Finally,
RecursiveSum (1, Sum)
is executed. The value 1 is passed back to Sum. The execution of
RecursiveSum (2, Sum)
is completed and 3 is passed back to Sum. The process continues until 4950 is passed back to Sum and the execution of
RecursiveSum (100, Total)
is completed by passing 5050 back to Total.

A recursive function to accomplish the task of finding the sum of the whole numbers from 1 to *n* would be as follows:

```
FUNCTION RecursiveSum (n : INTEGER) : INTEGER ;

  BEGIN
    IF n <= 1
      THEN RecursiveSum := 1
      ELSE RecursiveSum := RecursiveSum (n – 1) + n
  END
```

To understand this function, consider the following calls:

■ Total := RecursiveSum (1)   This is the terminating case. n <= 1 is TRUE. Thus, the value 1 is returned to Total.

■ Total := RecursiveSum (2)   When the function RecursiveSum (2) executes, n is assigned the value 2. The BOOLEAN expression n <= 1 is FALSE. Thus, RecursiveSum (1) is called. The value 1 is returned. The assignment instruction is completed and RecursiveSum is assigned the value 1 + 2. So the value 3 is returned to Total.

In general, the recursive calls are made until the terminating case is reached. Once this case is reached, the preceding call can be completed, and so forth all the way back to the instruction that started the recursion. After the recursive instruction's execution is completed, the instruction that follows it (if there is one) is executed.

DO IT NOW

1. In the procedure ReverseAlpha, what would be the effect of inserting the instruction WRITE (Ch) just before the recursive call to ReverseAlpha (see margin)?

2. For the following recursive function, where CountNum is of type 1 .. MAXINT,

```
FUNCTION WhatIsIt (n : CountNum) : CountNum ;

  BEGIN
    IF (n = 1) OR (n = 2)
      THEN WhatIsIt := 1
      ELSE WhatIsIt := WhatIsIt (n - 1) + WhatIsIt (n - 2) ;
  END ;
```

   a. Give the results of the call WRITE (WhatIsIt (2) : 5).
   b. Give the results of the call WRITE (WhatIsIt (4) : 5).

3. Complete the following function such that it will return the *n*th triangular number (see Do It Now exercise 2, page 497):

```
FUNCTION Triangular (n : CountNum) : CountNum ;

  BEGIN
    IF n = 1
      THEN Triangular := 1
      ELSE ...
```

```
IF Ch < 'z'
  THEN BEGIN
        Ch := SUCC (Ch) ;
        WRITE (Ch) ;
        ReverseAlpha (Ch) ;
        WRITE (Ch)
      END
```

DO IT NOW ANSWERS

1. abcdefghijklmnopqrstuvwxyzzyxwvutsrqponmlkjihgfedcba
2a. ▯▯▯▯1
 b. ▯▯▯▯3
3. ```
FUNCTION Triangular (n : CountNum) : CountNum ;

  BEGIN
    IF n = 1
      THEN Triangular := 1
      ELSE Triangular := Triangular (n - 1) + n
  END
```

## 10-1.3 Quicksort

A very fast sort technique for a list of length greater than 30 is the **quicksort**. This technique was developed by C.A.R. Hoare and is often expressed as a recursive procedure. The idea behind the quicksort technique is as follows:

1. Select the first component value of the array and call it the pivot point.
2. Partition (divide up) the list into LeftList (with values less than or equal to pivot point) and RightList (with values greater than pivot point).
3. Repeat this process on LeftList and RightList.

**COMMENT**
Any component of the array could be selected for the pivot point.

The process stops when a sublist has the length one. A picture of this process is shown in Figure 10–3.
```

Figure 10-3

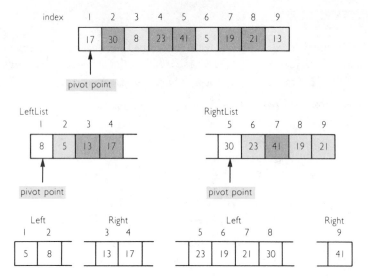

COMMENT

Recursion is a natural way to think of the quicksort technique. The list is divided into two sublists. This process is continued until the terminating case (the sublist has length one) is reached.

A recursive design for the quicksort technique would be as follows:

Design: Select pivot point   {usually component one}
           IF pivot point < > 0
              THEN BEGIN
                          Left := PivotPt + 1   {index of second component}
                          Right := Last   {index of last component}
                          REPEAT
                             WHILE List[Left] <= List[PivotPt] AND Left <= Right DO
                                Left := Left + 1
                             WHILE List[Right] > List[PivotPt] DO
                                Right := Right − 1
                             IF Right > Left
                                THEN Swap (List[Left] , List[Right])
                          UNTIL Left > Right
                          Swap (List [PivotPt] , List[Right])
                          QuickSort (List, First, Right − 1)
                          QuickSort (List, Right + 1 , Last)
                       END

COMMENT

SelectPivotPt will be written as a function that will be passed the values for Start and Finish. The function will return the desired pivot point (the leftmost element sent) or zero.

Refinement of: *SelectPivotPt (Start, Finish)*
                  IF Start >= Finish
                     THEN Pivot := 0
                     ELSE Pivot := Start

The array variable, List, must be passed as a variable parameter. If List is passed as a value parameter, the array values could fill up the stack, resulting in a stack overflow.

The conversion of the design for the quicksort technique to a Pascal procedure is presented in Figure 10-4.

Figure 10-4

```
PROCEDURE QuickSort (VAR List : ListType ; First , Last : SubScript) ;

  VAR PivotPt , Left , Right : SubScript ;

  FUNCTION Pivot (Start , Finish : SubScript) : SubScript ;

    BEGIN                                    {Pivot}
      IF Start >= Finish
        THEN Pivot := 0
        ELSE Pivot := Start
    END ;                                    {Pivot}

  PROCEDURE Swap (VAR First , Second : Component) ;

    VAR Temp : Component ;

    BEGIN                                    {Swap}
      Temp := First ;
      First := Second ;
      Second := Temp
    END ;                                    {Swap}

  BEGIN                                      {QuickSort}
    PivotPt := Pivot (First , Last) ;
    IF PivotPt < > 0
      THEN BEGIN                             {IF-THEN instruction}
            Left := PivotPt + 1 ;
            Right := Last ;
            REPEAT
              WHILE (List [Left] <= List [PivotPt]) AND (Left <= Right) DO
                Left := Left + 1 ;
              WHILE List [Right] > List [PivotPt] DO
                Right := Right - 1 ;
              IF Right > Left
                THEN Swap (List [Left] , List [Right])
            UNTIL Left > Right ;
            Swap (List [PivotPt] , List [Right]) ;
            QuickSort (List , First , Right - 1) ;
            QuickSort (List , Right + 1 , Last)
          END                                {IF-THEN instruction}
  END ;                                      {QuickSort}
```

For a list of length greater than 30, quicksort is more efficient than the insertion, selection, and bubble sorts. As you might imagine, the amount of time taken depends on how the list was arranged at the start of the sort. In terms of the average number of comparisons made the number is

List of 32 components

- 992 for the selection sort
- 486 for the bubble sort
- 243 for the insertion sort
- 224 for the quicksort

List of 1024 components

- 1,047,552 for the selection sort
- 553,776 for the bubble sort
- 261,888 for the insertion sort
- 14,336 for the quicksort

COMMENT

For lists that are close to ordered, the Shell sort is the fastest of the sorts discussed. For randomly ordered lists, the quicksort is the fastest.

Figure 10–5

```
PROCEDURE A ;

  BEGIN
    ...
    B ;
    ...
  END
```

```
PROCEDURE B ;

  BEGIN
    ...
    A ;
    ...
  END
```

10-1.4 FORWARD

The Pascal reserved word **FORWARD** will now be discussed. You should be aware of this word; however, it is not used in most programs.

A procedure or function cannot be used until it is declared. The compiler makes a list of identifiers (variables, constants, functions, procedures) as they are compiled. If an identifier appears in an instruction, the list is searched. If the identifier does not appear in the list, the error message "Undeclared identifier" is issued.

Suppose the following situation arises. PROCEDURE A calls PROCEDURE B and PROCEDURE B calls PROCEDURE A (as pictured in Figure 10–5). These two procedures cannot be compiled. Declaring PROCEDURE A first results in an error when the compiler attempts to compile the execution section of PROCEDURE A. Declaring PROCEDURE B first results in an error when the compiler attempts to compile the execution section of PROCEDURE B. (This is much like the saying: "You cannot get a job without experience. Of course, without a job you cannot get experience.") To avoid this dilemma, the word FORWARD is used.

Consider the program form shown in Figure 10–6. PROCEDURE A has been declared as a forward definition.

Figure 10–6

```
PROGRAM ..... ;

PROCEDURE A (parameter list) ; FORWARD ;      {forward definition}

PROCEDURE B (parameter list) ;

  BEGIN
    A ;
  END ;

PROCEDURE A ;                                  {parameter list as a comment}

  BEGIN
    B ;
  END ;

BEGIN                                          {Main program}
END.                                           {Main program}
```

Figure 10–7

```
PROGRAM ExampleForward ;

VAR Ch : CHAR ;

PROCEDURE DoAccounts ;

  BEGIN
  END ;

PROCEDURE PrintAccounts ;

  BEGIN
  END ;

BEGIN
  Menu
END .
```

As an illustration of how the reserved word FORWARD is used in a Pascal program, consider the following example.

EXAMPLE

Complete the Pascal program ExampleForward in Figure 10–7 by inserting the procedures Mover and Menu shown here.

```
PROCEDURE Mover (Ch : CHAR) ;

  BEGIN
    CASE Ch OF
      '1' : DoAccounts ;
      '2' : PrintAccounts
    ELSE Menu
    END
  END ;
```

```
PROCEDURE Menu ;

  BEGIN
    WRITELN ('1. Do Account') ;
    WRITELN ('2. Print Accounts') ;
    WRITE ('Please select (1,2): ') ;
    READLN (Ch) ;
    Mover (Ch)
  END ;
```

SOLUTION

See Figure 10–8.

Figure 10–8

```
PROGRAM ExampleForward ;

VAR Ch : CHAR ;

PROCEDURE DoAccounts ;

  BEGIN
  END ;

PROCEDURE PrintAccounts ;

  BEGIN
  END ;

PROCEDURE Mover (Ch : CHAR) ; FORWARD ;

PROCEDURE Menu ;

  BEGIN
    WRITELN ('1. Do Account') ;
    WRITELN ('2. Print Accounts') ;
    WRITE ('Please select (1,2): ') ;
    READLN (Ch) ;
    Mover (Ch)
  END ;

PROCEDURE Mover ;                        {parameter Ch : CHAR}

  BEGIN
    CASE Ch OF
      '1' : DoAccounts ;
      '2' : PrintAccounts
      ELSE Menu
    END
  END ;

BEGIN
  Menu
END .
```

COMMENT
As you can see in Figure 10–8, one of the procedures (**Menu** or **Mover**) had to be declared as a FORWARD definition.

Any time a procedure or function is declared as a forward definition, the entire header is written. Next, the word FORWARD is written. (Some programmers think of the word FORWARD as holding the place for the procedure's definition.) When the definition is made, only the procedure or function identifier is written. It is good documentation to write the parameters as a comment.

Vocabulary

504   **FORWARD**   A Pascal reserved word that is used to notify the compiler that the procedure (or function) will be defined later in the program. Typical use:

```
FUNCTION ExForward (VAR Num : INTEGER) : INTEGER ; FORWARD ;
```

When used, the entire header is written followed by a semicolon, the word FORWARD, and another semicolon. When the procedure or function is defined, only the identifier is listed in the header. The parameter list is usually listed as a comment.

501   **Quicksort**   An efficient method (compared to insertion, selection, and bubble sorts) of sorting a list of values.

496   **Recursion**   A programming technique whereby a procedure or function calls itself. If used improperly (no terminating situation) then a stack overflow error occurs. If used properly, then the Pascal program can mirror the programmer's thought process (in many situations).

498   **Terminating case**   A BOOLEAN expression that is used to halt a recursive procedure (or function) call. Typical use:

```
IF  < terminating case >
   THEN  < terminating instruction >
   ELSE BEGIN
       ...
       < Recursive call >
       ...
   END
```

Glad You Asked

Q Recursion is just plain silly! Can't all these things be done with iteration? And if so, doesn't recursion just make the program harder to read?

A I must confess that for the examples given at this introductory level, iteration would be as good as (if not better than) recursion. To test your claim, convert the quicksort routine to a procedure without using recursion.

Q What is meant by *exponential execution time*? I was reading another book on programming and the author stated that one of the dangers of using recursion was exponential execution time.

Figure 10–9

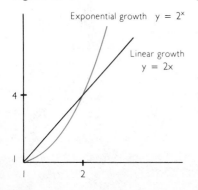

A Execution time usually refers to the amount of time it takes an instruction to execute. In order to execute, the instruction must call other instructions, which must call other instructions, and so forth. Therefore, the time to execute an instruction will increase. The term *exponential execution time* refers to the time increasing at an exponential rate. An exponential rate of growth is usually a very rapid rate of growth. For example, $Growth = 2x$ has a linear growth rate. $Growth = 2^x$ has an exponential growth rate. Compare the two for x increasing from 3 to 4. In the first case, *Growth* increases from 6 to 8 (or 2/6 or 33.3%). In the second case, *Growth* increases from 8 to 16 (or 8/8 or 100%). Compare the two for x increasing from 5 to 6. In the first case, *Growth* increases from 10 to 12 (or 2/10 or 20%). In the second case, *Growth* increases from 32 to 64 (or 32/32 or 100%). You can see that exponential growth is a much faster growth rate (see Figure 10–9). In some uses of recursion the amount of time needed to execute the recursive procedure grows at an exponential rate. The quicksort routine's execution is an example of exponential execution time. See the Towers of Hanoi problem (in the exercises for this section) for another example of exponential execution time.

Section 10–1 Exercises

1. For the recursive definition $F_1 = 3$
$$F_2 = 4$$
$$F_n = F_{n-2} + F_{n-1}$$
  a. $F_4 = $ ____ **b.** $F_5 = $ ____

2. For the recursive definition if $a \bmod b = 0$
  then $gcd\ (a, b) = b$
  else $gcd\ (a, b) = gcd\ (b, a \bmod b)$
  a. Find gcd (12, 18) **b.** Find gcd (15, 10)

3. For the series $1 + 1/2 + 1/3 + 1/4 + \ldots + 1/n$, complete the recursive definition for the sum.

    Sum (1) = ____
    Sum (n) = ____

4. For the following function, where `Whole` is of type `Ø .. MAXINT`,

    ```
    FUNCTION What (a , b : Whole) : Whole ;

      BEGIN
        IF b = 1
          THEN What := a
          ELSE What := What (a , PRED (b))
      END
    ```

    Give the output of `WRITE (What (3 , 2))`

5. Complete this procedure so that it will write to the screen the number input with its digits reversed. That is, `RevDigits (1345)` will output `5431`. (The data type `Whole` is of type `Ø .. MAXINT`.)

    ```
    PROCEDURE RevDigits (Num : Whole) ;

      BEGIN
        WRITE (Num MOD 1Ø) ;
        IF Num DIV 1Ø < > Ø
          THEN
            :
            :
            :
      END
    ```

6. Boot up Pascal; set the workfile to the file `RecurSam.PAS` from the `Source` diskette. Enter the editor. Alter the `DoPower` procedure of the program so that it allows the base to be entered as a number of type REAL. Further alter the procedure to allow the exponent to be entered as a value of type `-2Ø .. 2Ø`.

7. A computer game is to allow the user to enter a limit on correct guesses (n, an odd number) when a coin is to be flipped. For each flip, the user is to enter H or T. The game is to terminate when the user has won or lost n flips. Write a Pascal program for this game. Use recursion.

8. The game of Craps uses a pair of dice. The player rolls the dice and the sum of the numbers thrown is called the player's *point*.

    ```
    CASE point OF
      2, 3, 12 : player loses
      7 , 11 : player wins
      4, 5, 6, 8, 9, 10 : players rolls again
                    IF player rolls 7 or point
                      THEN {terminal case}
                      ELSE player rolls again
    END
    ```

Sample Execution

```
Enter limit: 3
Select (H= Heads or T= Tails) : H
Coin was Tails. You lose. Ø for 1.
Select (H= Heads or T= Tails) : T
Coin was Tails. You win. 1 for 2.
Select (H= Heads or T= Tails) : H
Coin was Heads. You win. 2 for 3.
Select (H= Heads or T= Tails) : H
Coin was Heads. You win. 3 for 4.

Want to play again? (Y/N): N
```

(continued)

For the case of 4, 5, 6, 8, 9, 10, the instruction can be written as `MakePoint (Point)`. A recursive procedure for `MakePoint` is

```
PROCEDURE MakePoint (VAR Point : DiceNum) ;

   VAR Roll : DiceNum ;

   BEGIN
     RollDice (Roll) ;
     WRITELN ('Throw of ', Roll , ' point is ', point) ;
     IF (Roll = 7) OR (Roll = Point)
       THEN BEGIN
              IF Roll = 7
                THEN WRITELN ('You lose!')
                ELSE WRITELN ('You made your point!')
            END
       ELSE MakePoint (Point)
   END
```

Using this recursive procedure, write a Pascal program to simulate the game Craps.

9. Pascal's triangle is often displayed as shown here:

```
    column
0  1  2  3  4  5  6
1                      row 0
1  1                   row 1
1  2  1                row 2
1  3  3  1             row 3
1  4  6  4  1          row 4
1  5 10 10  5  1       row 5
1  6 15 20 15  6  1    row 6
```

Using the notation $P(3, 2)$ to represent the entry in row 3 column 2, the value of $P(3, 2)$ is 3. In general, the value in $P(n, a)$ is defined as follows, where a is between zero and $n + 1$ inclusive:

> if $a = 0$ or $a = n + 1$
> then $P(n, a) = 1$
> else $P(n, a) = P(n-1, a-1) + P(n-1, a)$

Write a recursive function to return a value from Pascal's triangle.

Typical call: `Value := Pascal (9, 5)`

Programming Problems

10. A special game designed for this problem is called the "Put and Take Tango." The game starts with a bank of 100 points. The player rolls a die. If the number is odd, the player "takes" 10 times the die value from the bank (which is 100 points at the start of the game). If the number rolled is even, the player "puts" 10 times the die value in the bank. Write a Pascal program to simulate the game of Put and Take Tango. The game should continue until the bank is empty or the player has lost 1000 points.

Sample Execution

```
Welcome to Put and Take Tango. Press RETURN to start rolling.
Bank is 100 points. Roll 1 is a 2. You put 20. Your winnings: -70
Bank is 120 points. Roll 2 is a 5. You take 50. Your winnings: -20
Bank is 70 points. Roll 3 is a 1. You take 10. Your winnings: -10
```

11. The Towers of Hanoi is a game of three pegs and *n* disks. The object is to move the disks from the start peg to the end peg, observing the rules:
    1. Only one disk can be moved at a time.
    2. A larger disk cannot be placed on a smaller disk (see Figure 10–10.)

    Write a Pascal program that will output the directions for solving the puzzle.

Figure 10–10

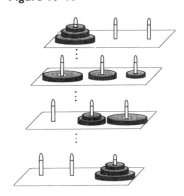

Design: Get NumDisk
         Hanoi (NumDisk , 1 , 3)

Refinement of: *Hanoi (NumDisk, StartPost, EndPost)*
                FreePost : = 6 − StartPost − EndPost
                IF NumDisk < > 1
                  THEN Hanoi (NumDisk − 1 , StartPost , FreePost)
                WRITELN ('Move disk ' , NumDisk ,
                        ' from post ' , StartPost ,
                        ' to post ' , EndPost)
                IF NumDisk < > 1
                  THEN Hanoi (NumDisk − 1 , FreePost , EndPost)

  a. Walk through this design for NumDisk = 1. Give output.
  b. Walk through this design for NumDisk = 2. Give output.
  c. Convert the design to a Pascal program.
  d. Make a table of NumDisk versus number of times Hanoi is executed.
  e. The original puzzle supposedly contained 64 gold disks. If it takes one second to move one disk, how long would it take to solve the puzzle? (This is an example of exponential execution time.)

12. Boot up Pascal; set the workfile to the file Quick.PAS from the Source diskette. Enter the editor. Alter the program so that it fills the list with a collection of random numbers (rather than a collection of names).

13. Write a Pascal program named CompareQ that will allow the user to input a value for ListLen from 10 to 2000. The program will then create a value for List of type ARRAY [1 .. 2000] OF INTEGER. List is to be initialized with the values from ListLen down to 1. The output of the program is to be the number of comparisons for the quicksort procedure to sort List from smallest to largest and the number of comparisons for the Shell sort procedure to sort List from smallest to largest.

Sample Execution

```
Please enter length of List: 100
QuickSort requires 4950 comparisons to sort List.
ShellSort requires 1094 comparisons to sort List.

Press RETURN to do another comparison. Enter Q to quit.
```

14. Alter the program CompareQ in problem 13 to initialize List with random numbers from 1 to ListLen.

Section 10–2

Pointer Data Type

In the last section, you learned about using recursion routines in Pascal programs. In this section, you will work with a data structure called a linked list. To build this data structure, you must learn how to work with a new data type called a pointer type. Also, you will need to learn how to use the built-in procedures NEW, MARK, and RELEASE.

10-2.1 Dynamic Data Structures

An array is a data structure commonly used in solving problems on the computer. But a major weakness of this data structure is its fixed length. When a variable is declared and its type is stated as an array, the array's length (number of components) is also stated. This length cannot be altered while the instructions of the program are being executed. One way around this problem is to use a file data structure. However, the time required to access the components of a file is slow compared to the access time for the components of an array.

The Pascal language provides a method of constructing a list in memory of arbitrary length. That is, the length of the list is determined by the demands of the program. This type of data structure is referred to as a **dynamic data structure** (as opposed to a static data structure such as an array). One example of a dynamic data structure is a **linked list**. This data structure is constructed by the programmer; it is not built in. The components of a linked list are linked (joined) together by the programmer. To accomplish this, a new data type known as a **pointer** data type must be used.

10-2.2 Pointers

A variable is a location in memory in which data of the type stated for the variable is stored. The variable is said to hold or reference the value stored in the memory location. A variable whose type is pointer is used to store an address of a memory location; that is, it references (or points to) a memory location. To declare a variable and state its type as a pointer type, the following declaration form is employed:

```
VAR MemLoc : ^INTEGER
```

This declaration declares `MemLoc` a variable and states its type as a pointer type. The value that `MemLoc` will hold is a memory address and at this memory address a value of type INTEGER will be stored.

`MemLoc`, like all variables, is undefined until it is initialized. To initialize a variable of type pointer, the built-in procedure **NEW** is used. For example, the instruction

```
NEW (MemLoc)
```

results in the assignment to the variable `MemLoc` of a memory address. This memory address is assigned by the Pascal system and is *not* available to the programmer. To gain access to the memory location (whose address is stored in `MemLoc`), the programmer uses the identifier `MemLoc^`. For example,

```
MemLoc^ := -17
```

assigns to the memory location (whose address is stored in `MemLoc`) the value `-17`.

In addition to the built-in procedure NEW, the Pascal language contains a predefined constant NIL. The constant **NIL** is used to allow a variable of type pointer to point to (reference) nothing. For example, the assignment instruction

```
MemLoc := NIL
```

results in the assignment to the variable `MemLoc` of a predefined value representing no memory location.

COMMENT

The reserved word NIL is unique in Pascal in that it can be assigned to any variable of type pointer. It allows a variable of type pointer to be defined without referencing a memory location.

To better your understanding of variables of type pointer and the reserved words NEW and NIL, consider the following VAR section and instructions.

```
VAR ChMemLoc : ^CHAR ;

BEGIN
  NEW (ChMemLoc) ;
  READ (ChMemLoc^) ;
  IF ChMemLoc^ >= 'E'
    THEN WRITE (ChMemLoc^)
    ELSE ChMemLoc := NIL
END
```

Before executing the compound instruction, a location in memory is assigned to the identifier ChMemLoc. The value in this location is undefined until it is initialized. Once the instruction NEW (ChMemLoc) is executed, a value is assigned to the memory location referenced by ChMemLoc. This value is the address of a location in memory. See Figure 10–11 where MemAdd1 represents memory address created by the NEW procedure.

Figure 10–11

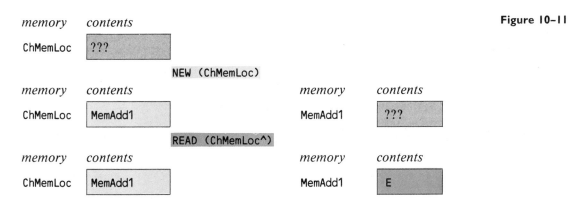

Figure 10–12

In Figure 10–11, the value in memory location MemAdd1 (whose address is stored in ChMemLoc) is undefined until it is initialized. The instruction READ (ChMemLoc^) is used to assign a value to the memory location referenced by ChMemLoc. If the program user enters the value E, that value is assigned to ChMemLoc^. Next, the IF-THEN-ELSE instruction executes. Since the expression ChMemLoc^ >= 'E' has value TRUE, the instruction WRITE (ChMemLoc^) is executed. If the user had entered the value C, the ELSE instruction of the IF-THEN-ELSE would execute. The results would be as pictured in Figure 10–12.

In Figure 10–12, ChMemLoc now references (points to) no memory location. However, the location in memory that contains the character value still exists. The memory location is *not* available to the system to use for other purposes. Later, you will see how to use MARK and RELEASE to reclaim this memory location for other uses.

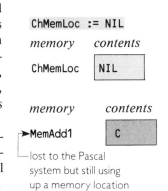

ChMemLoc := NIL

lost to the Pascal system but still using up a memory location

DO IT NOW

1. For

```
VAR MemLocA : ^REAL ;
    MemLocB : ^CHAR ;
```

   a. Write instruction(s) to assign a value to `MemLocA`.
   b. Write instruction(s) to assign a value to `MemLocB^`.

2. Construct a VAR section that will declare `Num` a variable and state its type as pointer. The memory location referenced by `Num` is to hold data of type INTEGER.

10-2.3 Pointers and Structured Data Types

To declare a pointer type where the location in memory is to hold a structured type (such as an array or record), a TYPE section is used. For example, to declare a pointer type where the memory location will hold a value of type RECORD, the following could be used

```
TYPE Rec = RECORD
             Name : STRING [40] ;
             Age : 12 .. 99
           END ;
     RecMemLoc = ^Rec ;

VAR Person : RecMemLoc ;
```

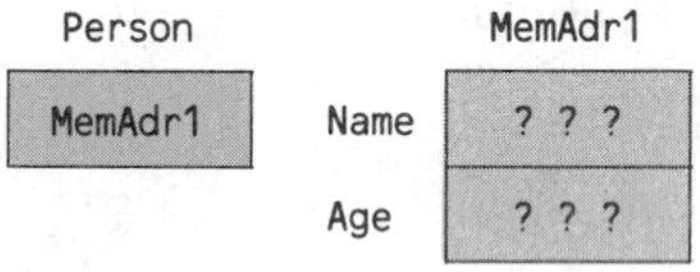
Person
MemAdr1
MemAdr1
Name
? ? ?
Age
? ? ?

To assign a value to the variable `Person`, the following could be used:

```
NEW (Person)
```

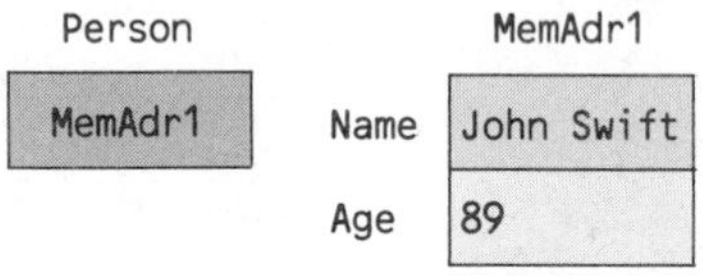
Person
MemAdr1
MemAdr1
Name
John Swift
Age
89

To assign a value to the memory location referenced by `Person`, the following could be used:

```
Person^.Name := 'John Swift' ;
Person^.Age := 89
```

COMMENT

The Pascal system maintains different arrangements of memory. One arrangement mentioned earlier was a **stack**. This arrangement is used to store identifiers of the program by the compiler. The arrangement is a first-in, last-out type of arrangement (like a stack of plates). Another arrangement of memory used is a **heap**. In a heap arrangement the components are "thrown in a pile." Values stored in the memory address referenced by variables of type pointer are said to be stored in the heap area of memory.

A commonly used variable of type pointer is one whose memory location holds a value of type RECORD. In fact, one of the fields of this RECORD is itself of type pointer. To declare such an item, a TYPE section and VAR section similar to the following is used:

```
TYPE RecMemLoc = ^Rec ;
     Rec = RECORD
             Name : STRING [40] ;
             Next : RecMemLoc
           END ;

VAR Person : RecMemLoc ;
```

DO IT NOW ANSWERS

1a. The instruction `NEW (MemLocA)` will assign a value to the variable `MemLocA`.

b. The following instructions will assign a value to `MemLocB^`.

```
NEW (MemLocB) ;
READ (MemLocB^)
```

2. `VAR Num : ^INTEGER`

COMMENT

You should notice something strange about this TYPE section. The declaration of `RecMemLoc` makes a reference to `Rec` before `Rec` has been defined. This is a special case of a general Pascal rule that an identifier must be defined before it can be used. If you failed to define `Rec` after listing `RecMemLoc = ^Rec`, the compiler would stop the compilation with an error message.

To assign a value to the variable `Person`, the following could be used:

```
NEW (Person)
```

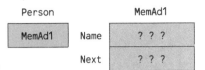

To assign a value to the memory address referenced by `Person`, the following could be used:

```
Person^.Name := 'Benny Franklin' ;
NEW (Person^.Next)
```

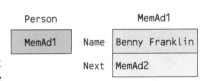

A variable of type pointer is quite limited. It can be assigned the value NIL and it can be assigned a memory address via the procedure NEW. Two variables of type pointer that reference memory locations of the same type can be compared for equality and inequality. These variables can also be assigned to each other.

10-2.4 *Linked Lists*

One use of variables of type pointer is to create dynamic (changeable) data structures. One such structure is a **linked list**. A linked list is composed by the programmer through the use of variables of type pointer. The value in the memory address referenced by the variable is of type RECORD. One or more of the fields of this record are of type pointer. Consider the TYPE section and VAR section presented here.

```
TYPE RecMemLoc = ^Rec ;
     REC = RECORD
              Name : STRING [40] ;
              Next : RecMemLoc
           END ;

VAR Person : RecMemLoc ;
```

Additionally, consider the following instructions, and the picture in Figure 10–13.

```
NEW (Person) ;
READLN (Person^.Name) ;
NEW (Person^.Next) ;
READLN (Person^.Next^.Name) ;
NEW (Person^.Next^.Next)
```

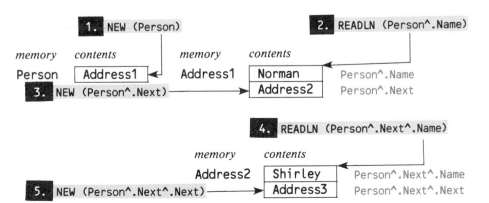

Figure 10–13

These instructions build a list of records with each record linked to the next record by a field of the record. The process is often pictured as shown in Figure 10–14.

Figure 10–14

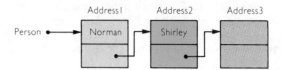

Of course, a much better method of linking the records can be devised. Consider the procedure shown in Figure 10–15.

Figure 10–15

```
PROCEDURE CreateList (VAR Person : RecMemLoc) ;

  VAR Current , Last : RecMemLoc ;
      Ans : CHAR ;

  BEGIN                                    {CreateList}
    NEW (Person) ;
    WRITE ('Please enter first name on list: ') ;
    READLN (Person^.Name) ;
    Person^.Next := NIL ;
    Last := Person ;
    WRITE ('Enter another  name for list?(Y/N) : ') ;
    READLN (Ans);
    WHILE (Ans < > 'N') OR (Ans < > 'n') DO
      BEGIN
        NEW (Current) ;
        Last^.Next := Current ;
        Last := Current ;
        WRITE ('Enter person''s name: ') ;
        READLN (Current^.Name) ;
        WRITE ('Enter another name for list?(Y/N): ') ;
        READLN (Ans)
      END ;
    Last^.Next := NIL
  END ;                                    {CreateList}
```

A picture of the procedure given in Figure 10–15 would be as shown in Figures 10–16 and 10–17.

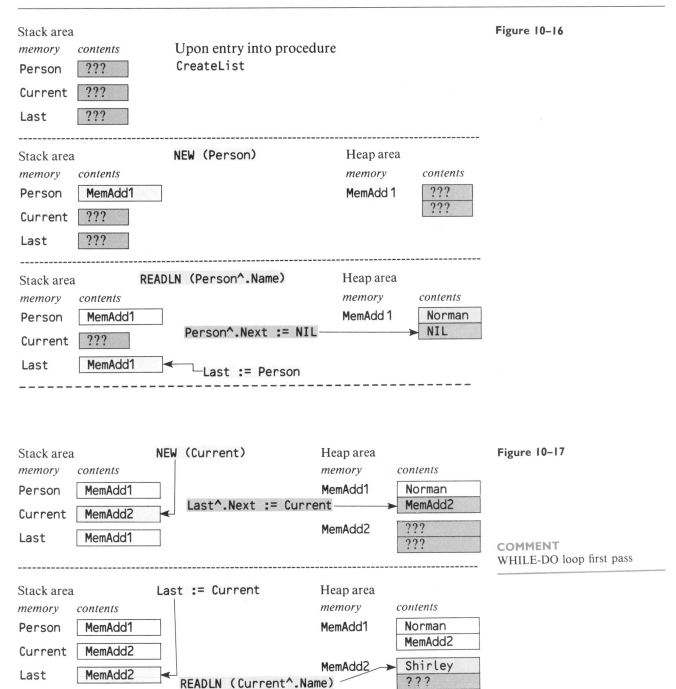

Figure 10–16

Upon entry into procedure CreateList

Figure 10–17

COMMENT
WHILE-DO loop first pass

Figure 10–18

Stack area   NEW (Current)   Heap area

memory	contents
Person	MemAdd1
Current	MemAdd3
Last	MemAdd2

memory	contents
MemAdd1	Norman
	MemAdd2
MemAdd2	Shirley
	???
MemAdd3	???
	???

Stack area   Last^.Next := Current   Heap area

memory	contents
Person	MemAdd1
Current	MemAdd3
Last	MemAdd2

memory	contents
MemAdd1	Norman
	MemAdd2
MemAdd2	Shirley
	MemAdd3
MemAdd3	???
	???

Stack area   Last := Current   Heap area

memory	contents
Person	MemAdd1
Current	MemAdd3
Last	MemAdd3

memory	contents
MemAdd1	Norman
	MemAdd2
MemAdd2	Shirley
	MemAdd3
MemAdd3	Robin
	???

READLN (Current^.Name)

The second pass through the WHILE-DO loop appears as shown in Figure 10–18. Notice how the heap area of memory grows (is dynamic) while the stack area of memory remains constant (is static).

Once the WHILE-DO loop is exited in procedure `CreateList`, the instruction `Last^.Next := NIL` is executed. The step-by-step picture shown in Figures 10–16, 10–17, and 10–18 is often represented as shown in Figure 10–19.

Figure 10–19

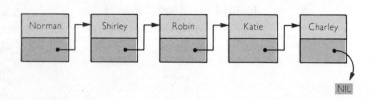

As you can see in Figure 10–19, each record in the list is linked to the next record in the list. The link is accomplished by the `Next` field of the record pointing to the location in memory where the next record is stored.

Without knowledge of where the first record is located in memory the entire list is useless. Do you know where to find this memory location? It is contained in the variable `Person`. To write the list to the screen, the following procedure could be used:

```
PROCEDURE WriteList (Person : RecMemLoc) ;
   BEGIN                              {WriteList}
     IF Person < > NIL
       THEN REPEAT
              WRITELN (Person^.Name) ;
              Person := Person^.Next
            UNTIL Person = NIL
   END ;                              {WriteList}
```

A recursive procedure to accomplish this task would be as shown here:

```
PROCEDURE WriteList (Person : RecMemLoc) ;
   BEGIN
     IF Person < > NIL
       THEN BEGIN
              WRITELN (Person^.Name) ;
              WriteList (Person^.Next)
            END
   END ;
```

COMMENT

Care must be taken not to attempt to access the fields of `Person^` when `Person` is undefined or contains the value `NIL`. Also, notice that `Person` is sent as a value parameter. If the original value in `Person` is lost, the linked list is lost!

DO IT NOW

1. Expand the procedure `CreateList` such that the variable `Person` has fields `Address` of type `String80` and `Age` of type `WholeNum` (where `String80 = STRING [80]` and `WholeNum = 0 .. 103`).
2. What would be the results of switching the instructions `WRITELN (Person^.Name)` and `WriteList` in the recursive procedure `WriteList`?

DO IT NOW ANSWERS

```
1. PROCEDURE CreateList (VAR Person : RecMemLoc) ;
      VAR Current , Last : RecMemLoc ;
          Ans : CHAR ;
```

```
PROCEDURE FillData (VAR RecItem : RecMemLoc) ;

  BEGIN                                         {FillData}
    WRITE ('Please enter name: ') ;
    READLN (RecItem^.Name) ;
    WRITE ('Please enter address: ') ;
    READLN (RecItem^.Address) ;
    WRITE ('Enter age: ') ;
    READLN (RecItem^.Age)
  END ;                                         {FillData}
BEGIN                                           {CreateList}
  NEW (Person) ;
  FillData (Person) ;
  Person^.Next := NIL ;
  Last := Person ;
  WRITE ('Enter another name for list?(Y/N) : ') ;
  READLN (Ans) ;
  WHILE (Ans < > 'N') OR (Ans < > 'n') DO
    BEGIN
      NEW (Current) ;
      Last^.Next := Current ;
      Last := Current ;
      FillData (Current) ;
      WRITE ('Enter another name for list?(Y/N) : ') ;
      READLN (Ans)
    END ;
  Last^.Next := NIL
END ;                                           {CreateList}
```

2. The procedure **WriteList** would be called recursively until the end of the list is reached. On each call, the address of the next record is placed on the stack (the address in **Person** is on bottom, the address in **Person^.Next** is next on the stack and so forth). When **NIL** is reached, the last call is completed (nothing happens). The next to the last call is completed by writing the name in the **Name** field to the screen. Thus, the names in the list are written in reverse order.

```
PROCEDURE WriteList (Person : RecMemLoc) ;

  BEGIN
    IF Person < > NIL
      THEN BEGIN
             WriteList (Person^.Next) ;
             WRITELN (Person^.Name)
           END
  END ;
```

10-2.5 *Maintenance of a Linked List*

You have already seen how pointer data types are defined, how to build a linked list, and how to move through a linked list. It is now time to discuss maintenance of a linked list: how to delete a record, how to insert a record, and how to dispose of a linked list.

Header Record A **header record** is a record in a linked list that contains the address of the head of the linked list. Linked lists with a header record are easier to maintain. To create such a linked list, the procedure **CreateList** in Figure 10–20 can be used.

Figure 10-20

```
PROCEDURE CreateList (VAR Head : RecMemLoc) ;

  VAR Current, Last : RecMemLoc ;
      Ans : CHAR ;

  BEGIN                                        {CreateList}
    NEW (Head) ;
    Head^.Next := NIL ;
    Last := Head ;
    WRITE ('Ready to create linked list?(Y/N): ') ;
    READLN (Ans) ;
    WHILE (Ans < > 'N') OR (Ans < > 'n') DO
      BEGIN
        NEW (Current) ;
        Last^.Next := Current ;
        Last := Current ;
        WRITELN ('Please enter name: ') ;
        READLN (Current^.Name) ;
        WRITE ('Enter another name for list?(Y/N): ') ;
        READLN (Ans)
      END ;
    Last^.Next := NIL
  END ;                                        {CreateList}
```

A picture of a linked list with a header record is shown in Figure 10–21.

Figure 10-21

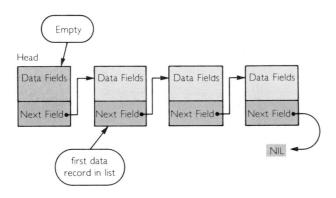

COMMENT

The header record (**Head** in Figure 10–21) sometimes contains information about the linked list and its data fields. Its field of type pointer (**Head^.Next**) contains the address of the first data record in the linked list. On the first pass through the WHILE-DO, **Last^.Next** is assigned the address stored in **Current**. On this pass, **Last** contains the memory address stored in **Head**. Thus, **Head^.Next** is assigned the memory address stored in **Current** (the first data record in the list).

Insert a Record A major advantage of using a header record occurs when a new record is to be inserted in a linked list. A procedure for accomplishing an insertion is shown in Figure 10–22.

Figure 10–22

```
PROCEDURE InsertNext (VAR Previous : RecMemLoc ;
                          Name : String30) ;

  VAR Current : RecMemLoc ;

  BEGIN                                         {InsertNext}
    NEW (Current) ;
    Current^.Name := Name ;
    Current^.Next := Previous^.Next ;           {Save end of list}
    Previous^.Next := Current                   {connect two list}
  END ;                                         {InsertNext}
```

A call to the procedure in Figure 10–22 would be set up as follows:

```
       .
       .                {create linked list with header record}
       .
WRITE ('Enter name to add to linked list: ') ;
READLN (Name) ;
Previous := Head ;
Finished := FALSE ;
WHILE (Previous^.Next < > NIL) AND NOT Finished DO   {search for insertion spot}
  BEGIN                                               {Search}
    Current := Previous^.Next ;
    IF Current.Name > Name
      THEN Finished := TRUE
      ELSE Previous := Current
  END ;                                               {Search}
InsertNext (Previous , Name) ;
       .
       .
       .
```

A picture of the procedure `InsertNext` is shown in Figure 10–23.

Figure 10–23

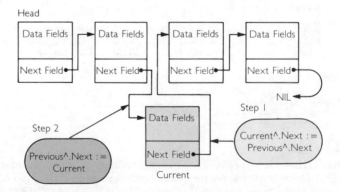

Suppose the record to be inserted is to be placed first in the list. Without a header record, this is a messy operation. With a header record, `Previous` contains the address stored in `Head`. Thus, Step 1 in Figure 10–23 links `Current` (the record to be inserted) to the rest of the list. Step 2 assigns to `Previous^.Next` the address stored in `Current` (the memory address of the first record in the list). But `Previous` contains the address stored in `Head`. Thus, `Head^.Next` contains the address stored in `Current` (the memory address of the first record in the list).

Delete a Record A procedure to delete a record from a linked list is presented in Figure 10–24.

Figure 10–24

```
PROCEDURE DeleteNext (VAR Previous : RecMemLoc) ;

  VAR Current : RecMemLoc ;

  BEGIN                                    {DeleteNext}
    IF Previous^.Next < > NIL              {Previous not last record in list}
      THEN
        BEGIN                              {delete the next record}
          Current := Previous^.Next ;      {save address of end of list}
          Previous^.Next := Current^.Next  {cut current out of list}
        END                                {delete the next record}
  END ;                                    {DeleteNext}
```

A picture of the procedure `DeleteNext` is shown in Figure 10–25.

Figure 10–25

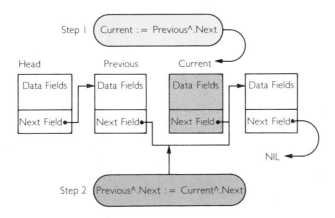

A call to the procedure `DeleteNext` could be set up as follows:

```
       .
       .       {create linked list with header record etc.}
       .
WRITE ('Enter name to be deleted: ') ;
READLN (Name) ;
Previous := Head^.Next ;
Current := Previous^.Next ;
WHILE Current < > NIL DO                  {search for record to delete}
  IF Name < Current^.Name
    THEN BEGIN                            {move Current and Previous down list}
           Previous := Current ;          {move Previous down list}
           Current := Current^.Next ;     {move to next record}
         END ;                            {move Current and Previous down list}
IF Previous^.Next = NIL
  THEN WRITELN ('Sorry name not found in linked list.')
  ELSE DeleteNext (Previous) ;
       .
       .
       .
```

Dispose of a List The last maintenance activity to consider is how to dispose of a linked list. One idea behind the use of a linked list data structure is to conserve memory. That is, rather than declaring an array data structure to handle any situation (usually an array with many components), a linked list is used. Once an array data structure is declared, it must remain for the execution of the program (it is static). With a linked list data structure, once its job is completed, the memory used is given back to the system for other uses. To accomplish this, the linked list is removed by disposing of each component of the list.

To dispose of a linked list, the built-in procedures MARK and RELEASE can be employed. Before calling `CreateList`, the procedure **MARK** is called. This procedure marks the start address of the heap area of memory used for the list. The procedure MARK has a parameter of type `^INTEGER`. A typical call to MARK is as follows:

```
MARK (HeapTop)
```

where `HeapTop` is a variable of type `^INTEGER`. A typical use of the procedures MARK and RELEASE is

```
BEGIN
  MARK (HeapTop) ;
  NEW (Head) ;
  CreateList (Head) ;
     .
     .
     .
  RELEASE (HeapTop) ;
     .
     .
     .
END
```

The call to the procedure MARK stores the address of the heap memory area (at that particular point in the program) in the identifier `HeapTop`. The call to procedure **RELEASE** gives back to the system the memory locations in the heap area, starting at the address in `HeapTop`. Thus, the above instructions dispose of the linked list created by `CreateList`.

DO IT NOW

1. In the procedure `InsertNext`, why was `Previous` sent as a value parameter rather than a variable parameter?
2. Write a Pascal procedure to delete the record sent (not the next record after the record sent) from a linked list of records with a header record `Head`. The procedure header should be as shown here:

   ```
   PROCEDURE Delete (Component : RecMemLoc) ;
   ```

3. Draw a picture of the stack and heap memory areas for the procedure `CreateList` where a header record is used.

DO IT NOW ANSWERS

1. The value in `Previous` is not being altered. The value being altered is `Previous^.Next`.
2. If the only parameter sent is `Component` (the record to be deleted), such a procedure cannot be written. There would be no way to link the end of the list to the front of the list after the deletion was made. `Component` contains the pointer to the next record after `Component`. However, without the pointer field of the record before `Component`, the link cannot be made.

3. A picture would be as follows:

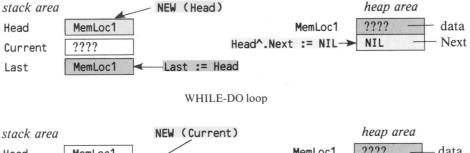

WHILE-DO loop

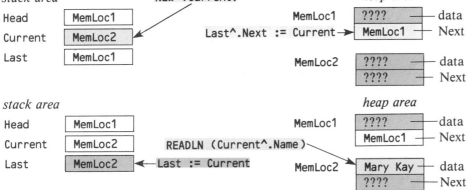

When the WHILE-DO loop is exited, the `Next` field of the last record is assigned the value NIL.

10-2.6 Binary Trees

A linked list is a linear data structure. To move through the list, you must move from one component to the next component (much like TEXT files). A nonlinear data structure can also be constructed using pointers. One such nonlinear data structure is a **binary tree**. A binary tree is very useful in programs requiring a search of a data structure. Consider Figure 10–26, which shows a binary tree of a collection of names.

Figure 10–26

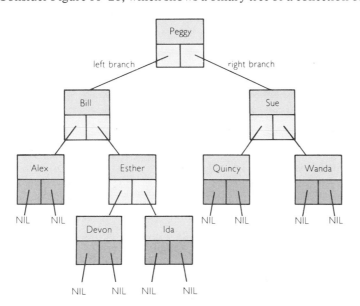

Although it might appear that there is no order to the data, it is organized alphabetically. To read the data in a binary tree, the secret is left branch-center-right branch. This approach is to continue (recursively) until a branch is NIL.

In the binary tree in Figure 10–26, move down the left branch (find the record containing Bill). To read this record, use left branch-center-right branch. Move down the left branch (find the record containing Alex). To read this record, use left branch-center-right branch. This time, left branch is NIL. Thus, the *first name* is `Alex`. Also, the right branch is NIL. So the left branch of Bill is finished. The center is Bill. Thus, the *second name* is `Bill`. The right branch of Bill yields the record containing Esther. Using left branch-center-right branch, the record with center Devon is found. This record has left branch NIL. Thus, the *third name* is `Devon`. The left branch of Esther is finished. So, the *fourth name* is `Esther`. The right branch of Esther yields the record with center Ida. This record has left branch NIL. So, the *fifth name* is `Ida`. The right branch of the Ida record is NIL. The Ida record is finished. The Esther record is finished. The Bill record is finished. The left branch of the Peggy record is finished. Thus, the *sixth name* is `Peggy`. Next, the right branch of the Peggy record is done. Reading the right branch of the Peggy record yields the rest of the alphabetically ordered data. Figure 10–27shows the path taken.

Figure 10–27

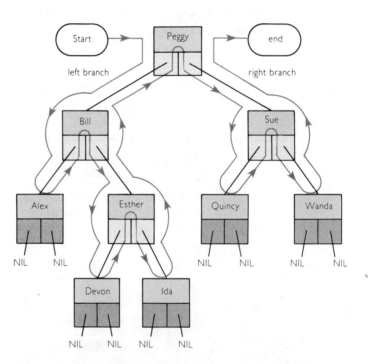

The power of a binary tree lies in searching for a name in the data structure. Suppose the name Ida is sought. `Ida` is less than `Peggy`, so the left branch is taken. `Ida` is greater than `Bill`, so the right branch is taken. `Ida` is greater than `Esther`, so the right branch is taken. `Ida` is found. It took four comparisons to find `Ida`. Had the names been entered in a linked list in alphabetical order, six comparisons would be required to find `Ida`.

The arrangement of this binary tree depends on how the names were entered. The first name entered was Peggy. However, it is impossible to know whether Bill or Sue was entered next. Had the names been entered in a different order, a different binary tree would have been produced.

To build a binary tree data structure, a TYPE section and a VAR section similar to the following are used:

```
TYPE RecMemLoc = ^Rec ;
     Rec = RECORD
              Name : STRING [30] ;
              Left : RecMemLoc ;
              Right : RecMemLoc
           END ;
VAR Center, Current : RecMemLoc ;
```

A design to build a binary tree structure is as follows:

Design: NEW (Center)
         WRITE ('Enter first name: ')
         READLN (Center^.Name)
         Center^.Left : = NIL
         Center^.Right : = NIL
         WRITE ('Enter more names?(Y/N): ')
         READLN (Ans)
         WHILE (Ans < > 'N') OR (Ans < > 'n') DO
             Current : = Center
             WRITE ('Enter name: ')
             READLN (Name)
             FindSlot
             InsertName
             WRITE ('Enter another name?(Y/N): ')
             READLN (Ans)

Refinement of: *FindSlot*
         EndOfBranch : = (Current^.Left = NIL) AND (Current^.Right = NIL)
         WHILE NOT EndOfBranch DO
             IF Name < Current^.Name
                THEN IF Current^.Left < > NIL
                        THEN Current : = Current^.Left
                        ELSE EndOfBranch : = TRUE
                ELSE IF Current^.Right < > NIL
                        THEN Current : = Current^.Right
                        ELSE EndOfBranch : = TRUE
             IF NOT EndOfBranch
                THEN EndOfBranch : = (Current^.Left = NIL) AND (Current^.Right = NIL)

COMMENT
FindSlot will need variable parameter Current. It will return the record in the binary tree where the new record needs to be inserted.

Refinement of: *InsertName*
         NEW (Branch)
         Branch^.Name : = Name
         Branch^.Left : = NIL
         Branch^.Right : = NIL
         IF Name < Current^.Name
            THEN Current^.Left : = Branch
            ELSE Current^.Right : = Branch

COMMENT
InsertName will need the value parameter Current.

DO IT NOW

1. Walk through the design just given and its refinements for the entry of the names Kelly, Garian, Mark, and Zelda.
2. Convert the design to build a binary tree (page 525) to a Pascal program.

DO IT NOW ANSWERS

1. When `Kelly` is entered, `Kelly` becomes the `Center`. At this point, the binary tree appears as shown.

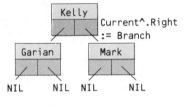

Next, the WHILE-DO instruction executes. The user enters the name `Garian`. `FindSlot` is called and is sent `Current` (which contains the same address as `Center`). Since `EndOfList` is `TRUE`, the WHILE-DO is not entered and the value in `Current` is not changed. The instruction `InsertName` executes. A new branch is created. `Branch^.Name` is assigned the value `Garian` and its two pointer fields are assigned NIL. `Current^.Left` is assigned `Branch` (the link is made). Now the tree appears as shown.

On the next pass through the WHILE-DO loop, the name `Mark` is entered. The instruction `FindSlot` is executed. `EndOfList` is evaluated as `FALSE`. Thus, the WHILE-DO loop is entered. The ELSE part of the IF-THEN-ELSE instruction is executed. Since the expression `Current^.Right = NIL` is true, the ELSE part of the nested IF-THEN-ELSE instruction is executed. So `EndOfBranch` is assigned the value `TRUE`. The WHILE-DO loop is exited. The value in `Current` is not altered. The instruction `InsertName` is executed. The tree now appears as shown.

On the next pass through the WHILE-DO loop, the name `Zelda` is entered. When the instruction `FindSlot` is executed, the WHILE-DO loop is entered. The ELSE part of the IF-THEN-ELSE instruction is executed. The THEN part of the nested IF-THEN-ELSE instruction is executed. `Current` is assigned the value in `Current^.Right` (the Mark record). When the IF-THEN instruction is executed, `EndOfBranch` is assigned the value `TRUE`. The WHILE-DO loop is exited. The value returned in `Current` is the location of the Mark record. The `InsertName` instruction executes. Since `Zelda` is greater than `Mark`, a new `Branch` is created and assigned to the field `Current^.Right`. The final binary tree appears as shown.

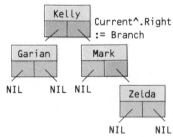

2.
```pascal
PROGRAM BinaryTree ;

TYPE String30 = STRING [30] ;
     RecMemLoc = ^Rec ;
     Rec = RECORD
               Name : String30 ;
               Left : RecMemLoc ;
               Right : RecMemLoc
           END ;

VAR Center , Current : RecMemLoc ;
    Name : String30 ;
    Ans : CHAR ;

PROCEDURE FindSlot (VAR Current : RecMemLoc ;
                    Name : String30) ;

VAR EndOfBranch : BOOLEAN ;

BEGIN                                           {FindSlot}
  EndOfBranch := (Current^.Left = NIL) AND (Current^.Right = NIL) ;
  WHILE NOT EndOfBranch DO
    BEGIN                                       {Search}
      IF Name < Current^.Name
        THEN IF Current^.Left < > NIL
                THEN Current := Current^.Left
                ELSE EndOfBranch := TRUE
        ELSE IF Current^.Right < > NIL
                THEN Current := Current^.Right
                ELSE EndOfBranch := TRUE ;
```

```
            IF NOT EndOfBranch
              THEN EndOfBranch := (Current^.Left = NIL) AND (Current^.Right = NIL)
        END                                        {search}
      END ;                                        {FindSlot}
  PROCEDURE InsertName (Current : RecMemLoc ;
                        Name : String30) ;

    VAR Branch : RecMemLoc ;
    BEGIN                                          {InsertName}
      NEW (Branch) ;
      Branch^.Name := Name;
      Branch^.Left := NIL ;
      Branch^.Right := NIL ;
      IF Name < Current^.Name
        THEN Current^.Left := Branch
        ELSE Current^.Right := Branch
    END ;                                          {InsertName}
  BEGIN                                            {BinaryTree}
    WRITE ('Enter first name: ') ;
    READLN (Name) ;
    NEW (Center) ;
    Center^.Name := Name ;
    Center^.Left := NIL ;
    Center^.Right := NIL ;
    WRITE ('Enter another name?(Y/N): ') ;
    READLN (Ans) ;
    WHILE (Ans < > 'N') AND (Ans < > 'n') DO
      BEGIN
        WRITE ('Enter name: ') ;
        READLN (Name) ;
        Current := Center ;
        FindSlot (Current , Name) ;
        InsertName (Current , Name) ;
        WRITE ('Enter another name?(Y/N): ') ;
        READLN (Ans)
      END
  END .                                            {Binarytree}
```

Vocabulary

	Page
Binary tree A nonlinear data structure constructed by using variables of type pointer. The components of the tree are records that have two pointer fields, one for a left branch and one for a right branch.	523
Dynamic data structure A data structure constructed by the programmer. Its length is not fixed; it can vary while the instructions of the program execute.	510
Header record A record in a linked list that contains the address of the head of the linked list.	518
Heap A memory arrangement without any particular order (as in objects thrown in a pile or heap). This memory arrangement is the way the Pascal system handles variables of type pointer.	512
Linked list A particular type of a dynamic data structure, typically made up of a list of records of which at least one field is of type pointer (used to form the link to the next record in the list).	513

522 **MARK** A predefined Pascal procedure used to store the memory address of the system's current position in the heap area of memory. The procedure has a variable parameter of type ^INTEGER. Example:

    MARK (HeapTop)

510 **NEW** A predefined Pascal procedure that has as a parameter a variable of type pointer. The procedure assigns a memory location to the variable of type pointer. Example:

    NEW (MemoryLoc)

510 **NIL** A predefined constant used to initialize a variable of type pointer to reference no memory location (yet the variable is defined). Example:

    MemoryLoc := NIL

510 **Pointer type** A variable whose content is a memory address in which a value of a defined data type is stored. Example:

    MemoryLoc : ^REAL

522 **RELEASE** A predefined Pascal procedure used to return to the system memory locations in the heap area. The procedure has a parameter of type ^INTEGER. Example:

    RELEASE (HeapTop)

512 **Stack** A memory arrangement in which values are stored on a first-in, last-out (FILO) basis. Typical uses of this memory arrangement are in handling recursion and compilation.

Glad You Asked

Q I really don't see the advantage of a linked list over an ARRAY OF RECORD data structure.

A Each data structure has its purpose. Linked lists are mainly used in situations where the data is constantly changing. In these situations, linked lists do have an advantage when items must be added or deleted. Additionally, linked lists only take up the amount of memory needed by the situation. With the ARRAY data structure, the amount of memory used is predetermined.

Q In the VAR sections you keep defining Head, Current, and Last to be of type RecMemLoc. Why aren't they defined to be of type Rec? I thought the linked list was made up of records.

A Given

```
TYPE RecMemLoc = ^Rec ;
     Rec = RECORD
             Name : STRING [30] ;
             Next : RecMemLoc
           END ;
```

the variables Head, Current, and Last were defined as type RecMemLoc. The memory locations these variables hold are of type RECORD. It is these records that are the components of the linked list. The variables given here are used to build the list.

Q In the routine to delete a record from a linked list, you said the component to be deleted could not be passed as a parameter. That is, a procedure header like

    PROCEDURE Delete (Component : RecMemLoc) ;

would not work. Would it work if Head was also passed as a parameter?

A Yes. If the value for **Head** was passed, then the address of the previous record could be found. Thus, the front of the list could be linked to the end of the list after the deletion is made.

Q Can I do a binary search on a linked list?

A No. A binary search depends on knowing the length of the list. Remember, you start in the middle of the list, then move to the top half or bottom half. In general, the length of (number of components in) a linked list is not known. Even if the length is known, there is no way to jump about in the list. To get from one component to the next, the link must be followed. (Think about trying to move backwards in a linked list.) For this reason, a linked list is called a linear data structure.

Q How can I save the values in a linked list? Is there such a thing as a FILE OF Linked List?

A A linked list is not a data type in the sense of an array. There is no FILE OF Linked List. Often a linked list is of no value after the execution of the program. However, there are times when you would want to save the components of the list. To accomplish this, use a TYPE section and VAR section similar to these:

```
TYPE DataFields = RECORD
                      Name : STRING [30] ;
                      Age : 0 .. 115 ;
                      Insurance : BOOLEAN
                  END ;
     RecMemLoc = ^Rec ;
     Rec = RECORD
             Data : DataFields ;
             Next : RecMemLoc
           END ;

VAR Head , Current , Last : RecMemLoc ;
    OutFile : FILE OF DataFields
```

Now, as the linked list is transversed, each record in the list can be sent to the file. You would use **WRITE (OutFile , Current^.Data)**

Q What happens if a linked list gets too long?

A When a request for a new memory location is made and no more memory is available, a heap/stack collision will occur. Sometimes this will result in an error message. However, such a collision often results in the system having to be rebooted. Turbo Pascal provides the predefined function MEMAVAIL to avoid this situation.

Q Do I have to use a header record?

A No. A header record makes working with a linked list easier but it is not required.

Q What does the predefined procedure DISPOSE do?

A With MARK and RELEASE all memory locations in the heap are given back to the system from the marked location forward. DISPOSE is used to give back a single location. If DISPOSE is used, then MARK and RELEASE should not be used.

Section 10–2 Exercises

For problems 1 through 4, use the following VAR section:

```
VAR MemLocA : ^CHAR ;
    MemLocB : ^CHAR ;
```

1. Which of the following assigns a value to **MemLocA**?
    a. NEW (MemLocA)
    b. MemLocA := 2304
    c. MemLocA^ := 'B'
    d. RELEASE (MemLocA^)

2. Which of the following assigns a value to `MemLocA^`?

   a. `MemLocA^ := NIL`   **c.** `READ (MemLocA^)`

   b. `NEW (MemLocA^)`   **d.** `READ (MemLocA)`

3. If the instruction `NEW (MemLocB)` has been executed, which of the following is a valid Pascal instruction?

   a. `WRITE (MemLocB^)`   **c.** `MemLocB^ := NIL`

   b. `MemLocB^ := 'M'`   **d.** `MARK (MemLocB^)`

```
VAR MemLocA : ^CHAR ;
    MemLocB : ^CHAR ;
```

4. Suppose the following instructions have been executed:

```
NEW (MemLocA) ;
MemLocB := MemLocA ;
MemLocB^ := 'Z' ;
WRITE (MemLocA^)
```

The output will be

   a. an error, since `MemLocA^` has not been assigned a value.

   b. the character `Z` since both `MemLocA` and `MemLocB` point to the same memory location.

   c. an error, since `MemLocB` has not been initialized via `NEW`.

   d. whatever "trash" that might be in memory location `MemLocA`.

5. Insert *True* for a true statement. Insert *False* for a false statement. (Assume that the variable `MemLocA` is of type pointer.)

   _____ **a.** If `NEW (MemLocA)` is executed and followed immediately by `MemLocA := NIL`, there is no change in the status of pointer variable `MemLocA`.

   _____ **b.** `MemLocA := NIL` can be executed even if `NEW (MemLocA)` has not been executed.

   _____ **c.** To construct a linked list, a header record must be used.

   _____ **d.** A linked list is an example of a dynamic data structure.

   _____ **e.** A linked list is a built-in data type.

   _____ **f.** To dispose of a linked list, simply RELEASE the first component of the list.

6. Given the following Pascal program,

   a. Draw a picture of the linked list *before* executing `Swap (Head)`.

   b. Draw a picture of the linked list *after* executing `Swap (Head)`.

   c. In the call to `Swap`, replace `Head` with `Head^.Next`. Draw a picture of the linked list after executing `Swap (Head^.Next)`.

```
PROGRAM StackExample ;

TYPE RecMemLoc = ^Rec ;
     Rec = RECORD
                Number : INTEGER ;
                Next : RecMemLoc
           END ;

VAR Head , Current , Last : RecMemLoc ;
    Ct : 1 .. 5 ;

PROCEDURE Swap (Head : RecMemLoc) ;

  VAR Top , Hold , EndOfList : RecMemLoc ;

  BEGIN                                        {Swap}
    Top := Head^.Next ;
    Hold := Top^.Next ;
    EndOfList := Hold^.Next ;
    Head^.Next := Hold ;
    Hold^.Next := Top ;
    Top^.Next := EndOfList
  END ;                                        {Swap}
```

CHAPTER TEST

1. A procedure that calls itself is known as a _____ procedure.

2. If a recursive function has no terminating case (calls itself over and over without a stopping condition), then
   a. the system stops the execution after 1024 repeats.
   b. the function cannot be compiled.
   c. the program enters an endless loop.
   d. the program execution stops with a stack overflow message.

3. Given the function `Chapter11`,

```
FUNCTION Chapter11 (Number : INTEGER): INTEGER ;

  BEGIN
    IF Number < 3
      THEN Chapter11 := 1
      ELSE Number := Chapter11 (Number - 3) + 3
  END ;
```

the output of `WRITE (Chapter11 (9))` is _____.

4. To declare `Number` a variable and state its type as pointer to an `INTEGER`, which of the following would be used?
   a. `NEW (Number)`
   b. `VAR Number : ^INTEGER`
   c. `VAR Number : INTEGER^`
   d. `VAR Number : Pointer to INTEGER`

5. If `MemLoc` is of type `^CHAR`, which of the following is a valid instruction?
   a. `NEW (MemLoc)`
   b. `MemLoc^ := NIL`
   c. `MemLoc := 'M'`
   d. `NEW (MemLoc^)`

6. Insert *True* for a true statement. Insert *False* for a false statement.
   _____ a. A linked list must have a header record.
   _____ b. The pointer field of each component of a linked list contains the value of the memory location of the next component in the list.
   _____ c. The length of a linked list is stated in the VAR section.
   _____ d. A linked list is an example of a static data structure.
   _____ e. Each component in a linked list consists of a collection of data fields and exactly one field of type pointer.
   _____ f. To save a linked list to a file you must declare a file variable of type FILE OF Linked List.

7. Given

```
TYPE ItemPtr = ^Item ;
     Item = RECORD
                Name : STRING [30] ;
                SeatNum : 1 .. 30 ;
                Next : ItemPtr
            END ;

VAR Head , Current , Last : ItemPtr ;
```

discuss the errors in the following.
   a. `IF Head = NIL`
      `  THEN WRITELN ('The list is empty.')`
   b. `NEW (Current) ;`
      `IF Current^.Name = 'John'`
      `  THEN WRITELN ('John is in the list.')`

```
BEGIN                                    {main}
  NEW (Head) ;
  Last := Head ;
  FOR Ct := 1 TO 5 DO
    BEGIN                                {build linked list}
      NEW (Current) ;
      Last^.Next := Current ;
      Current^.Number := Ct ;
      Last := Current
    END ;                                {build linked list}
  Last^.Next := NIL ;
  Swap (Head)
END .                                    {main}
```

7. Write a procedure named `Duplicate` to be inserted in the program `StackExample` in problem 6. The procedure is to have the value parameter `Head` and is to duplicate the first data record in the list.

8. Boot up Pascal; set the workfile to the file `LinkedLi.PAS` from the `Source` diskette. Run the program instructions. Test the program options. The `Delete` option does not function properly. Enter the editor and debug the program.
   Hint: In the case selection for C, replace the `FindSlot` call with the procedure call

   `Search (Name, Head, Previous, Found)`

   and the IF-THEN-ELSE instruction with

   ```
   IF Found
      THEN DeleteNext (Previous)
      ELSE WRITELN ('Sorry, name not found in list.')
   ```

   Write the procedure `Search`.

For problems 9, 10, and 11 use the TYPE section and VAR section shown here.

```
TYPE String30 = STRING [30] ;
     WholeNum = 0 .. 108 ;
     DataFields = RECORD
                     Name : String30 ;
                     Age : WholeNum
                  END ;
     RecMemLoc = ^Rec ;
     Rec = RECORD
              Data : DataFields ;
              Next : RecMemLoc
           END ;

VAR Head , Current , Last : RecMemLoc ;
```

9. Write a Pascal procedure similar to `CreateList` (presented in this section) that allows the user to create a linked list by entering from the keyboard the `Name` and `Age` of each component in the list.

10. Write a Pascal procedure similar to `CreateList` (presented in this section) that creates a linked list by reading in the components from the file named `LinkFile.DAT` (a file of type `FILE OF DataFields`).

11. Alter the Pascal procedure in problem 9 to create an ordered linked list. The components are of type `RecMemLoc` and the list should be ordered by `Age` from youngest to oldest.

Programming Problems

12. Write a Pascal program to create a linked list with records whose data fields are `Suit` and `Value` where

```
Suit = (diamonds, clubs, hearts, spades)
Value = (two, three, four, five, six, seven, eight, nine, ten,
         jack, queen, king, ace)
```

13. Expand your program in problem 10 to create a duplicate linked list.

14. Continue the expansion of your program in problems 12 and 13 to deal a five-card hand from the duplicate linked list by randomly selecting a card from the list. As a card is dealt, the component of the linked list should be deleted.

15. Julia is giving a bridal shower for a friend. She has asked the guests to sign in by entering their name and a description of their gift on her personal computer. Write a Pascal program that allows this input and builds a linked list. The program should also (a) identify gifts (and who gave them) that are duplicates and (b) identify the fifth and fifteenth arrivals as winners of the door prizes.

16. A *queue* (also known as a first-in, first-out or FIFO data structure) is a linked list that allows insertions only at the end and deletions only at the front of the list. A typical example of a queue would be at a doctor's office. Patients arrive and sign in. The first patient in sees the doctor and is the first patient out. Write a Pascal program to simulate the receptionist's job. A possible design is as follows:

Mr. Ages, the doctor will see you now.

```
Create header record
REPEAT
    NumA := RANDOM (4)
    IF NumA > 1
      THEN add a new patient to end of list
    NumB := RANDOM (4)
    IF NumB > 2
      THEN delete patient at top of list
    WriteList
    Check to see if user wants to quit
UNTIL user ready to quit
```

17. Suppose the files `FileA` and `FileB` are both of type `FILE OF String30` where `String30 = STRING [30]`. The components of the files are in alphabetical order. Write a Pascal program to read the components of `FileA` into a linked list and the components of `FileB` into a linked list. The program then should merge sort the two linked lists, write the merged list to screen, and save the merged list back to `FileC` of type `FILE OF String30`.

18. A stack (also known as a first-in, last-out or FILO data structure) is a linked list in which components can only be inserted and deleted from the top of the list (the `Head^.Next` component or first data record of the list). Write a Pascal program that builds a stack from a string of characters entered from the keyboard. Once the initial stack is built, the program should allow the user to select from the menu shown.

```
A. Pop element off the stack
B. Push element on the stack
C. Duplicate top element on stack
D. Rotate top two stack elements
E. See stack
Q. Quit
Enter (A, B, C, D, E, Q):
```

If option `A` is selected, the first component of the linked list is deleted.

If option `B` is selected, the user enters a character and the character is inserted as the first component in the linked list.

If option `C` is selected, the value of the first component is inserted as the first component in the linked list.

If option `D` is selected, the first component is deleted, then inserted as the second component in the list.

If option `E` is selected, the components of the stack are written to the screen.

The program should start like the one below:

```
Enter string of characters to built stack: Michel
```

19. A doubly linked list is a linked list in which each component has two fields of type pointer. One field points to the next component in the linked list, the other points to the previous component in the linked list. The TYPE section and VAR section shown here could be used to build a doubly linked list, in which the components are of type `String40`.

```
TYPE String40 = STRING [40] ;
     RecMemLoc = ^Rec ;
     Rec = RECORD
               Name : String40 ;
               Next : RecMemLoc ;
               Back : RecMemLoc
           END ;

VAR Head, Current, Last : RecMemLoc ;
```

Write a Pascal program to build a doubly linked list. The `Back` field of the first data component should be set to `NIL`. The `Next` field of the last data component should be set to `NIL`. To test the construction, write a procedure to print the list forward, then backward.

20. Expand your program from problem 19 to allow the user to enter a name. The doubly linked list should be searched for the name. If found, the previous and next names (if they exist) in the list should be written to the screen.

21. Boot up Pascal; set the workfile to the file `BTree.PAS` from the `Source` diskette. Enter the editor. Alter the program so that it builds a binary tree of 30 random numbers (0 .. 99) rather than a binary tree of names.

22. A procedure to search a binary tree of names for a target name is essentially the `FindSlot` procedure in the program `BinaryTree` (presented in this section). Alter the program to carry on a dialogue similar to the one here after the binary tree is built.

Sample Execution

```
Enter another name?(Y/N): N

Would you like to search for a name?(Y/N): Y
Please enter name: Nelda
The name Nelda is not in the binary tree.
Do you want to add the name?(Y/N): Y
```

23. Write a Pascal procedure `WriteTree` to insert into the program `BinaryTree` that will write to the screen the names in the binary tree in alphabetical order. A design for a recursive procedure `WriteTree` is as follows:

```
Current := Center
If Center <> NIL
  Then WriteTree (Current^.Left)
       WRITELN (Current^.Name)
       WriteTree (Current^.Right)
```

A call to the procedure would be `WriteTree (Center)`

c. Suppose a linked list has been successfully created with a header record `Head` and the following instructions are to search the list for a name in the variable `Target`.

```
Current := Head^.Next ;
WHILE (Current < > NIL) AND (Current^.Name < > Target) DO
  Current := Current^.Next ;
IF Current^.Next < > NIL
  THEN WRITELN (Target, ' is not in the list.')
  ELSE WRITELN (Target, ' has been found.')
```

8. Using the TYPE section and VAR section in problem 7, write a Pascal program to create a linked list. The data for the components of the list originates from passengers making reservations for a flight. The data is to be entered from the keyboard in the order that the passengers show up.

9. Write a procedure to be inserted in the program in problem 8. The procedure is to check the status of a seat. If the seat is taken, the passenger's name should be returned. Otherwise, the word *empty* should be returned.

Programming Project

Project 10. The game of TAS is played with a deck of 52 cards as listed here:

Deck = '001111222222222333334444444555556666667777888888999'

The deck is shuffled and five cards are dealt to each player. Next, a two-card goal is dealt.

Sample Execution

```
Tonia, your hand is: 2 3 6 1 4
Alex, your hand is: 7 7 1 5 2
Goal is: 29
Tonia, enter your expression:
6*4 + 2*3 - 1        Correct!    Points = 14
Alex, enter your expression:
15*2 - 7/7           Correct!    Points = 16
Alex wins the hand.
Score is: Tonia = 53  Alex = 51     Game = 100
Press RETURN for next hand
```

Each player takes the five cards and constructs an arithmetic expression whose value equals the goal dealt. Any of the four arithmetic operations (+ , − , *, /) are allowed. Only one-digit and two-digit numbers are allowed. Parentheses are *not* allowed. The points for an arithmetic expression are awarded as follows:

A one-digit number is worth one point.
A two-digit number is worth four points.
A + operation is worth one point.
A − operation is worth two points.
A * operation is worth three points.
A / operation is worth four points.

Order-of-operation rules are followed in evaluating the expressions. Only whole-number arithmetic is allowed. That is, an expression like 5/2 + 1/2 for a goal of 3 is not allowed.

Write a Pascal program that allows two players to play the game TAS on the computer. The game should start by allowing the players to enter their names (up to eight letters) and the number of points in the game (50, 100, or 200).

Your program should use two linked lists: one for the numbers in the expression and one for the operations in the expression. For example, the expression 15*2 − 7/7 would yield the linked lists shown here:

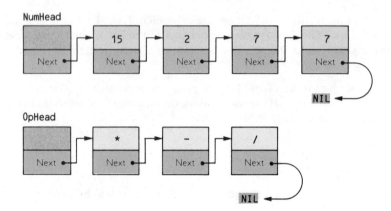

A possible design to evaluate an expression after the linked lists are formed is as follows:

```
REPEAT
    Check OpList component for a * or a / operation
    IF found
      THEN replace corresponding NumList component with
            (NumList component) Op (Next NumList component).
            Delete the OpList component,
            Delete the next NumList component.
UNTIL end of OpList
```

Make another pass through `OpList` similar to that just shown for + and − operations. `OpList` should be empty after this pass. `NumList` should contain one component, the value of the expression.

Turn in a copy of your design and its refinements, a structured diagram, and a copy of your program.

Extra credit:
Discuss the difficulties involved in programming the computer to play this game.

Appendix A: Turbo Pascal Tutorials

The Turbo System

In this tutorial, you will learn how to boot up Pascal and move about the Turbo Pascal system. Also, you will learn about the operating system.

This tutorial assumes the following:

1. You have a working copy of (a diskette containing) Turbo Pascal (IBM version). The diskette should contain the MS-DOS operating system (or a compatible operating system) and the Turbo Pascal system files.
2. You have a formatted diskette. (See page A-16 if you need to format a diskette.)

COMMENT
The Source diskette can be used as the formatted diskette.

Figure A–I

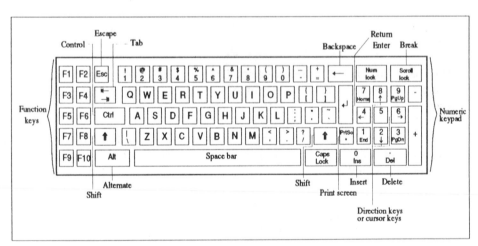

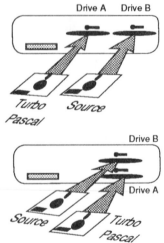

Boot Up Pascal

COMMENT
IBM keyboards and the keyboards of IBM compatibles vary in the placement of the keys.

Insert the diskette containing Turbo Pascal in disk drive A. Insert the data (formatted) diskette in disk drive B (see Figure A–1). Turn on the computer. After some disk drive activity, the copyright notice for the operating system is presented. Also presented is a prompt to enter the current date.

```
Current date is Tue 1-01-1980
Enter new date:
```

To enter the date September 1, 1988 type **09-01-88** and press the **RETURN** key. Next, you are presented a prompt to enter the current time. To enter a time of 2:32 PM, type **14:32** and press the **RETURN** key. After entering the date and time, you will see the prompt for the operating system: **A>**. Type **TURBO**, then press the **RETURN** key. After some disk drive activity, the screen clears. The screen now displays the version number of Turbo Pascal with which you are working. Also, this screen presents the following question:

```
Include error messages (Y/N)?
```

Respond to this question by pressing the **Y** key. That is, yes, you do want to include the error messages.

After some disk drive activity as the error messages are loaded in, the screen clears and you are presented the Turbo Pascal main menu (as shown in Figure A-2).

Figure A-2

```
Logged drive: A
Active directory: \

Work file :
Main file :

Edit   Compile     Run     Save

Dir    Quit      compiler  Options

Text :      0 bytes
Free :  62024 bytes

>
```

This screen is your menu for selecting applications in the Turbo Pascal system. The Turbo prompt, **>**, appears at the bottom of the screen (the operating system prompt is **A>**).

DIR To obtain a feeling for this screen and for the process of selecting from this menu, press the **D** key. This key selects the **Directory** application. You are presented the following prompt:

```
Dir mask:
```

Press the **RETURN** key. The screen clears and you are shown a listing of all the files on the diskette in disk drive A. The listing should appear similar to the one in Figure A-3.

Figure A-3

```
Dir mask:
COMMAND.COM    READ.ME     TURBO.COM    TURBO.MSG    GRAPH.P
GRAPH.BIN      LISTER.PAS  CMDLIN.PAS

32k bytes free
>
```

Press the RETURN key and you are returned to the main menu of the Turbo Pascal system. To see the list of diskette files on disk drive B, from the Turbo Pascal main menu press the D key for directory application. Respond to the prompt:

    Dir mask:

by typing B:, then pressing the RETURN key. The screen clears and you are shown the diskette files on disk drive B. Press the RETURN key and you are returned to the Turbo Pascal main menu.

Edit The next application selection to experience from the main menu is the *edit* application. To select this application, press the E key. You are presented the prompt:

    Work file name:

This prompt is an invitation to enter the name of a TEXT file on which you would like to work (edit). For this walk through of the Turbo Pascal system, respond to this prompt by typing MyFile, then pressing the RETURN key. The screen clears and you enter the editor with an empty page. The screen should now appear as shown in Figure A-4.

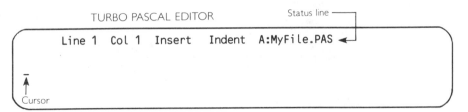

Figure A-4

The line at the top of the screen is called the *status line*. This line reads as follows:

1. You are at line 1 and you are at column 1 of line 1.
2. You are in the Insert mode (that is, what you type in is added to any existing text).
3. You are in the Indent mode (that is, once you indent a line, the indention is held to the next line).
4. The file you are working on (editing) is named MyFile.PAS. (Although you indicated the name MyFile, the extension .PAS was added automatically by the Turbo Pascal system.)

RETURN
Or
ENTER key

To obtain a feeling for the editor, type the following material (press the RETURN key at the end of each line). As you type in the characters, notice how the status line changes. Also notice how the indentation is held once it is made. To return to the original margin, use the backspace key.

```
Research indicates that a breakfast high
   in protein (30% plus) improves the
   performance of learners. Thus, I guess
it is eggs for breakfast!
```

At this point, you have inserted four lines of text (observe the status line). To show off the power of the Turbo Pascal editor, you will now *delete* (remove) the material you inserted above. To do this,

1. Move the cursor to the start of the file by using Ctrl-Q R that is, hold down the key labeled Ctrl, press the Q key (in the top left corner of the screen observe ^Q and the cursor), then press the R key.

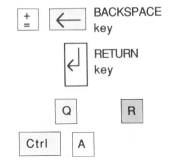

BACKSPACE
key

RETURN
key

COMMENT
The cursor should now be under the R in the first line of the material. Also, the status line should now indicate this by showing:
Line 1 Col 1.

2. Delete the first line by using `Ctrl-Y` (that is, hold down the `Ctrl` key and press the Y key).
3. Repeat step 2 until all the material is gone.

You should now have a clean workspace. In Tutorial 2, a much more detailed explanation of how to use the editor will be presented. For now, you need only obtain a *feeling* for the Turbo Pascal editor.

A First Program

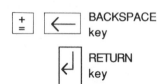

BACKSPACE
key

RETURN
key

It is now time to insert your first Pascal program. Type the following demonstration Pascal program. At the end of each line, press the `RETURN` key. To return to the original margin, use the `BACKSPACE` key. It is not important that you understand the meaning of the program lines at this time. Be very careful to include all punctuation marks. If you make a mistake, use the `BACKSPACE` key to back over the text and correct the mistake by retyping.

COMMENT
After typing a line, check the line before pressing the `RETURN` key. If you spot an error use the `BACKSPACE` key to back up and correct the error.

```
PROGRAM DemoOne ;

VAR Count : INTEGER;
    Name : STRING [80] ;

BEGIN
  WRITE ('Please enter your name: ') ;
  READLN (Name) ;
  FOR Count := 1 TO 10 DO
    WRITELN ('Hello ', Name)
END .
```

Quitting the Editor It is now time to quit (leave) the editor and return to the Turbo Pascal main menu. To accomplish this, use `Ctrl-K D`. That is, hold down the `Ctrl` key, press the K key (the characters `^K` should appear at the top left of the screen); next, press the D key. You are presented the Turbo Pascal prompt, `>`. Press the RETURN key and the Turbo Pascal main menu appears on the screen.

WARNING
Save your work to save hours of work!

Save The material you entered while in the editor is held in *memory* only. That is, if you now had a power failure, the material would be lost. To avoid this untimely demise of your work, employ the *Save* application. To select the *Save* application, press the S key. You are presented the message:

    Saving A: MyFile.PAS

After some disk drive activity (the file `MyFile.PAS` being saved to the diskette in drive A), you are back at the Turbo Pascal main menu.

COMMENT
You might like to use the `Directory` application now to see that the file `MyFile.PAS` really is on the diskette in drive A. From the main menu, press the D key. Respond to the mask prompt by pressing the `RETURN` key. After observing the listing of the files on the diskette in drive A, press the `RETURN` key to return to the Turbo Pascal main menu.

Compiler

The next application to experience from the Turbo Pascal main menu is the *Compile* application. The text you entered while in the editor was a valid Pascal program. The compiler is used to convert this text into code that can be executed by the computer's CPU. There are two ways to select the compiler. For this walk through, the method used is the *Run* application. Press the R key. You will see the message:

```
Running ......
```

Actually, the Turbo Pascal system *Run* application first uses the compiler to convert the copy of MyFile.PAS, which is in memory, to code. Next, the system executes this code.

If everything goes well, the screen should clear and present the prompt:

```
Please enter your name:
```

Respond to this prompt by typing your name, then pressing the RETURN key. The program instructions then print the message:

```
Hello Rab Cika
```

(or whatever name you entered) ten times. After execution, you are presented the prompt >. Press the RETURN key and you are returned to the Turbo Pascal main menu.

If everything *did not go well*, you are presented an error message similar to the following:

```
Error 1: ';' expected. Press <ESC>.
```

Press the key marked ESC and you are returned to the Turbo Pascal editor. In actual practice, you would now fix only the error. In this demonstration do the following,

1. Use the approach just demonstrated to clean out the workspace (that is, use the keystrokes Ctrl-Q R to jump to the top of the file, then use Ctrl-Y to delete the lines of the program).
2. Retype the program DemoOne.
3. Quit the editor (Ctrl-K D).
4. *Save* the program.
5. *Run* the program.

After the program executes, press the RETURN key and you are returned to the Turbo Pascal main menu.

The Operating System

The Turbo Pascal system for the IBM computer and compatibles operates under the MS-DOS or PC-DOS operating system. Remember, when you first booted up the system, you got the system prompt, A>. It is now time to return to the operating system to do some work with the files on the diskettes.

Figure A–5

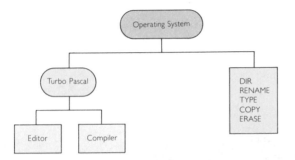

To return to the operating system from the Turbo Pascal main menu, press the Q key. If you did not save the material entered while in the editor, you are given the message and prompt:

> Workfile A: MYFILE.PAS not saved. Save (Y/N)?

If you get this message, press Y for yes. The file will be saved to the diskette in disk drive A.

You should now see the operating system prompt, A>. There are five applications to be considered from the operating system (see Figure A–5). The first of these is DIR.

DIR DIR is short for directory. A directory provides you with a listing of the names of the files on a disk. This is helpful when you cannot remember the name of a file. To experience this application, type

> DIR A:

COMMENT
Responding to the DIR: prompt with B:/P will pause the listing. Entering B:/W will yield a wide form of the directory listing.

then press the RETURN key. After some disk drive activity, the names of the files on the diskette in disk drive A are listed on the screen and the operating system prompt returns. To see the list of file names on the diskette in disk drive B, type DIR B:, then press the RETURN key. The list of file names appears, then the operating system prompt returns.

RENAME The next operating system application to experience is *RENAME*. This application allows you to change the name of a file on the disk. Type

```
                                      ┌─── one blank space
  RENAME MyFile.PAS PasDemo.TXT
```

then press the RETURN key. After some disk drive activity, the operating system prompt returns. Now, type DIR A: and press the RETURN key. As you can see, the file MyFile.PAS has been renamed to PasDemo.TXT.

WARNING
Using TYPE with a non-TEXT file (a file *not* created in the Turbo Pascal editor, for now) will result in "trash" being written to the screen.

TYPE The next operating system application to experience is *TYPE*, which allows you to see the contents of a TEXT file. Type

```
              ┌─── one blank space
  TYPE PasDemo.TXT
```

then press the RETURN key. After some disk drive activity, the contents of the file PasDemo.TXT are written to the screen. The operating system prompt is returned.

COMMENT
To see the contents of a TEXT file named on the diskette in drive B, enter the name of the file as B: . . . (where the ellipsis represents the name of the file). If the name entered is *not* on the diskette, the operating system responds by writing a message similar to File not found

A major use of the *TYPE* application is to list the contents of a TEXT file to the printer. To accomplish this,

1. The printer must be connected to the computer, turned on, and ready (on-line).
2. Type the following:

```
              ┌─── one blank space
  TYPE PasDemo.TXT >PRN
```

then press the RETURN key. The contents of the TEXT file PasDemo.TXT is written to the printer (that is, a *hard copy* is made).

If the printer is not ready to print, you get a message similar to the following:

```
Write fault error writing device PRN
Abort , Retry , Ignore?
```

You can press the **A** key and return to operating system prompt. Or, you can get the printer to a ready state then press the **R** key to retry outputting the material to the printer.

COPY The *COPY* application is used to copy files from the diskette in one disk drive to the diskette in the other disk drive. The **COPY** application is also used to make a copy of a file under a different name on the same diskette. To experience this application, you will now send a copy of the file **PasDemo.TXT**, which is on the diskette in disk drive A, to the diskette in disk drive B. To accomplish this,

                                                    ── one blank space

1. Type COPY⌐A:PasDemo.TXT⌐B:PasDemo.TXT

2. Press the **RETURN** key.

After some disk drive activity, the operating system prompt **A>** returns. To see the results of these actions, type **DIR B:** and press the **RETURN** key. You are presented a listing of the file names that are on the diskette in disk drive B. One of these names should be **PasDemo.TXT**.

ERASE The last application of the operating system to experience is the *ERASE* application. This application is used to *erase a file*. To experience this application, you will now erase the file **PasDemo.TXT** on the diskette in disk drive A. To accomplish this, type

                            ── one blank space

      ERASE⌐A:PasDemo.TXT

then press the **RETURN** key. After some disk drive activity, the prompt for the operating system is presented. To see the results of this action, type **DIR** and press the **RETURN** key. You are presented a list of the file names on the diskette in disk drive A. The file **PasDemo.TXT** should be missing from this list.

This concludes the walk through of the Turbo Pascal system and the operating system.

Soon you will be designing solutions to problems, then converting the solution design to the Pascal language. Once this is accomplished, you will use the Turbo Pascal system to enter the Pascal program to the computer, convert the text to code, and execute the code. You will use the operating system to manipulate the files created in this process. The following description relates a typical experience with the Turbo Pascal system and the operating system.

  1. Boot up the system. The operating system prompt (**A>**) is displayed.

  2. Enter the Turbo Pascal system (type **TURBO**, press **RETURN** key).

  3. From the Turbo main menu, select the editor by pressing the **E** key.

  4. Respond to the prompt **Work file name:** by entering the name you want for your file.

  5. Insert the material of your Pascal program.

  6. Quit the editor by using **Ctrl-K D**.

  7. Save the text entered in the editor to diskette by pressing **S** for *Save*.

  8. From the Turbo Pascal main menu, select *Run* by pressing the **R** key.

  9. If your program compiles, observe the output. Otherwise, reenter the editor and fix the errors. Return to step 6.

10. If the output of your program is as desired, quit the Turbo system by pressing the Q key. Otherwise, return to the design stage.

11. From the operating system, use the *TYPE* application to produce a hard copy of your program.

Exercise

Take the first Pascal program on page 13 and follow the 11 steps just presented. In step 4, enter B:APSAMPLE. When you finish, you should have a copy of the program APascalSample on the diskette in disk drive B. Also, you should have a hard copy (printout from the printer) of the program APascalSample.

Tutorial 2

The Turbo Editor

In this tutorial, you will learn how to use the Turbo Pascal editor. You will learn how to insert material and delete material. You will also learn how to move the cursor about in the material you have inserted. Additionally, you will gain additional experience with the Turbo Pascal system.

Boot Up Pascal

Insert the diskette containing Turbo Pascal in disk drive A. Insert the data diskette in disk drive B. Turn on the computer. After some disk drive activity, you will see the prompt for the operating system: A>. Type TURBO, then press the RETURN key. After some disk drive activity, the screen clears. The screen now displays the version number of Turbo Pascal with which you are working. Also, this screen presents the question:

```
Include  error  messages  (Y/N)?
```

Respond to this question by pressing the Y key. That is, yes, you do want to include the error messages.

After some disk drive activity (the error messages are loaded in), the screen clears and you are presented the Turbo Pascal main menu, as shown in Figure A–6.

Figure A–6

```
Logged drive: A
Active directory: \

Work file :
Main file :

Edit  Compile     Run     Save

Dir   Quit     compiler  Options

Text:      Ø bytes
Free:  63485 bytes

>
```

Work File An additional feature of the main menu is the work file designator. To experience this feature, press the W key. You are presented the prompt:

```
Work file name:
```

Respond to this prompt by typing **B:PasDemo.TXT**, then pressing the **RETURN** key. You should see the message **Loading B:PasDemo.TXT**. You are returned to the Turbo Pascal prompt, **>**.

COMMENT

If this file does not exist, you will also see the message:

```
New File
```

This means the work file has been created and named **B:PasDemo.TXT** and the workspace is clean (contains no text material).

Press the **RETURN** key to return to the Turbo Pascal main menu.

It is now time to enter the Turbo Pascal editor. To do this, press the E key. The screen clears and the editor status line appears. Also, the contents of the file **B:PasDemo.TXT** appear under the status line. Your screen should now appear as shown below. The editor cursor is on the **P** in the word **PROGRAM**.

```
        Line 1  Col 1  Insert Indent   B:PasDemo.TXT

PROGRAM DemoOne ;

VAR Count : INTEGER ;
    Name : STRING [80] ;

BEGIN
  WRITE ('Please enter your name: ');
  READLN (Name) ;
  FOR Count := 1 TO 10 DO
    WRITELN ('Hello ', Name)
END .
```

Moving Commands

One of the first skills to develop with the editor is learning how to move the cursor. You are now at the start of the file.

To jump to the end of the file, use **Ctrl-Q C**. That is, hold down the **Ctrl** key and press the Q key. Next, press the C key. The cursor should jump to the space immediately after the period at the end of the text material.

To jump to the start of the file, use **Ctrl-Q R**. That is, hold down the **Ctrl** key and press the Q key. Next, press the R key. The cursor should jump to the start of the file (the letter **P** in the word **PROGRAM**).

The four keys pictured in Figure A–7 represent the kernel of the moving commands. To experience these commands, do the following.

1. Use **right arrow** key to move the cursor to the right four spaces.
2. Use **down arrow** key to move the cursor down six lines.
3. Use **left arrow** key to move the cursor to the left two spaces.
4. Use **up arrow** key to move the cursor up two lines.

Figure A-7

Up one line

Left one space — Right one space

Down one line

COMMENT

You can also use the control key to move the cursor. See Figure A–8.

Figure A-8

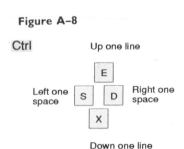

Ctrl   Up one line

Left one space   Right one space

Down one line

COMMENT
The **HOME** key jumps the cursor to the start of the line. The **END** key jumps the cursor to the end of the line.

Take some additional time at this point to play with moving the cursor using the commands just described. Also, play with using the jumps (`Ctrl-Q R` and `Ctrl-Q C`). It is essential that you learn how to move the cursor about in the text file.

COMMENT
Several other moving commands are available in the Turbo Pascal editor. Two important ones are PAGE UP and PAGE DOWN. However, the file now in the editor is too short to see the effect of these commands.

Pg Up key (`Ctrl-R`) moves the cursor *up* one page.
Pg Dn key (`Ctrl-C`) moves the cursor *down* one page.

Insert and Delete

The default mode for the Turbo Pascal editor is insert. That is, when you enter the editor, anything you type is inserted, wherever the cursor is located. To see the effect of this mode, use the moving commands to move the cursor to the line:

        WRITELN ('Hello ', Name)

and to the space after the word `Hello`. The cursor should be located as shown (where ▌ represents the cursor):

        WRITELN ('Hello▌', Name)

Now, type the characters:

        . How are you?

The line should now appear as:

        WRITELN ('Hello. How are you?▌', Name)

Notice how the rest of the text material on the line moves over to accept the insertion.

The other mode of insert is the exchange mode. To see this mode, use the **INSERT** key. Notice the status line. The word `Insert` has been replaced by the word `Overwrite`. To see the effect of this mode for insert, move the cursor to the period after the word `Hello` (use the `left arrow` key).

        WRITELN ('Hello▌ How are you? ', Name)

Now, type the character `!`. The period was *exchanged* for the exclamation mark.

        WRITELN ('Hello!▌How are you? ', Name)

Use the `Insert` key to return to the normal (default) mode for insert. Notice that the status line replaces the word `Overwrite` with the word `Insert`.

The normal method of deleting material in the editor is to move the cursor to a point to the right of the material and use the **BACKSPACE** key. To see this method of deleting, move the cursor (use the `right arrow` key) to the space after the character `?`.

        WRITELN ('Hello! How are you?▌', Name)

Now, press the **BACKSPACE** key until the cursor is just to the right of the character `!`.

        WRITELN ('Hello!▌', Name)

The other major methods of deleting material are

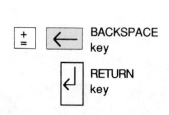

BACKSPACE key

RETURN key

1. Ctrl-Y deletes the entire line on which the cursor is located (use this method with *caution*).
2. Ctrl-Q Y deletes from the cursor to the end of the line.
3. Ctrl-T deletes the word to the right of the cursor.

A Walk Through

The following is a typical experience with the editor and the Turbo Pascal system. This experience will create an error in the program DemoOne. When you attempt to compile this altered version, the error will be caught by the compiler. You will then return to the editor and fix the error.

1. Start by moving the cursor to the space to the right of the word BEGIN.
2. Use the BACKSPACE key to delete the word BEGIN.
3. Use Ctrl-K D to quit the editor (press the RETURN key to see the main menu).
4. From the Turbo Pascal main menu, select the *Run* application (press the R key). At the bottom of the screen, you should see:

```
>

Compiling
  7 lines

Error 2: ':' expected. Press < ESC >
```

As expected, the missing BEGIN resulted in an error.

5. Press the ESC key. You are returned to the editor. The cursor is in the text material at a point *after* the place where the error occurred.
6. You now want to insert the word BEGIN. To do this, move the cursor up one line (use the up arrow key) and over to the left margin (use the HOME key).
7. Type the word BEGIN
8. Use Ctrl-K D to quit the editor (press the RETURN key to see the main menu).
9. Press the R key to select the Run application. At the bottom of your screen, you should see lines similar to the following:

```
>

Compiling
  11 lines

Code:        000A paragraphs (   160 bytes),...
Free:        0008 paragraphs (   128 bytes),...
Stack/Heap: 4824 paragraphs (295488 bytes)

Running
Please enter your name:
```

10. The key word in these lines is Running. That is, your program has compiled and is now executing. The last line is the prompt from the program DemoOne for the user to enter a name. Type a name and press the RETURN key. The program responds by writing the message

```
Hello! Jack Butler
```

(or whatever name you entered) ten times. The Turbo Pascal prompt (>) appears at the bottom of the screen. Press the RETURN key and the Turbo Pascal main menu appears.

11. Press the `Q` key to quit the Turbo Pascal system. You get the message:

    `WorkFile B:PASDEMO.TXT not saved. Save (Y/N)?`

    When you altered the contents of this file in the editor, the Turbo Pascal system picked up this change. If you press `Y` for yes, the altered version is saved (the old version becomes a backup file: `B:PASDEMO.BAK`). If you press `N` for no, the altered version is lost. Press the `Y` key. The exit from the Turbo Pascal system is completed and you are now in the operating system.

    This completes the demonstration of the Turbo Pascal editor.

Exercises

1. Enter the Turbo Pascal system. Select the file `B:PasDemo.TXT` as your work file. Enter the editor. *Jump* to the end of the file. *Delete* the period. *Quit* the editor. Attempt to *Run* the altered version. Reenter the editor. Fix the error. Quit the editor. *Run* the fixed version.

2. From the Turbo Pascal main menu, select `W` to name the work file. Type the name `B:MyProgram.TXT` and press the `RETURN` key. Enter the editor. Type in the following material:

```
PROGRAM Trial ;

VAR Name : STRING [4Ø] ;

BEGIN
  WRITE ('This is Pascal. Who are you? ') ;
  READLN (Name)
  WRITELN ;
  WRITELN (Name , ' I hope you will enjoy this course!') ;
  WRITELN ('Au revoir.')
END .
```

    Quit the editor. From the main menu, select *Save*. Next, select *Run*. The compilation should stop with an error. Return to the editor and fix the error (insert a semicolon after the line `READLN (Name)`). Quit the editor; select *Save*, then *Run* from the main menu. After the program executes, quit the Pascal system. From the operating system, obtain a hard copy of the text file `MyProgra.TXT`. Also, delete (erase) this file from the diskette in disk drive B.

Quick Reference Guide to the Turbo Pascal System

The parts of the Turbo Pascal System that we are concerned with are the main menu, the editor status line, and the operating system prompt, which are shown in Figure A-9. In general, the route followed through the system is the following:

(a) TURBO PASCAL MAIN MENU

```
Logged drive: A
Active directory: \

Work file:
Main file:

Edit  Compile    Run    Save
Dir   Quit    compiler  Options

Text:      Ø bytes
Free:   61818 bytes

>
```

(b) TURBO PASCAL EDITOR STATUS LINE

```
Line  1  Col  1   Insert   Indent   A:MyFile.PAS
—
```

(c) OPERATING SYSTEM PROMPT

```
A>
```

1. Start at the operating system prompt. Type `Turbo` and press the `RETURN` key.
2. From the version number/copyright screen respond to the error message query by pressing the `Y` key.
3. From the Turbo Pascal main menu, press the `W` key to select the workfile.
4. Enter the desired name for the workfile (example: `B:MyFile.TXT`).
5. Press the `E` key to select the Turbo Pascal editor.
6. Type in (insert) the text of your program, then use `Ctrl-K D` to exit the editor (press any key for Turbo Pascal main menu).
7. From the main menu, press the `S` key to *Save* the material entered while in the editor to the file specified as the workfile.
8. From the Pascal command line, press the `R` key to compile the program and execute the code generated by the compiler.
9. After execution, return to the Turbo Pascal main menu by pressing the `RETURN` key.

The following is a list of tasks frequently carried out.

1. *To start (boot up Pascal):*
   a. Insert the diskette containing Turbo Pascal and the operating system in disk drive A.
   b. Insert the data (or programs) diskette in disk drive B.
   c. Turn on the computer.
   d. The operating system prompt (`A>`) should be present. Type `Turbo`, then press the `RETURN` key. Respond to the error messages prompt by pressing the `Y` key. The Turbo Pascal main menu should be present.
2. *To see a list of the file names on a diskette:*
   a. From the Turbo Pascal main menu, press the `D` key for `Directory`.
   b. Respond to the prompt `Dir mask:` by entering the drive (`A:` or `B:`) that contains the diskette for which you want the directory listing.
   c. Press the `RETURN` key to see the Turbo Pascal main menu.

COMMENT

If a file extension (like `.TXT`) is not present, the Turbo System automatically adds the `.PAS` extension.

COMMENT

Any changes made in the editor are stored in main memory only. To save the changes, from the main menu press the `S` key. The existing file is renamed with the `.BAK` file extension.

WARNING

Once material is deleted it cannot be recovered!

  BACKSPACE key

 RETURN key

COMMENT

To move through the text *quickly*, use `Pg Dn` key for next page *down*; use `Pg Up` for next page *up*. Use the `END` key to *jump* to the end of a line. Use the `HOME` key to *jump* to the start of a line.

3. *To get a clean workspace:*
   a. From the Turbo Pascal main menu, press the `W` key for `Workfile`.
   b. Type the name you wish the file to have (example: `B:MyFile.TXT`).
   c. If there is a file present on the diskette in the disk drive specified with the name entered, that file will be loaded into the editor. Otherwise, a new file is created and the workspace is clean.

4. *To enter new program text:*
   a. Get a clean workspace (see number 3).
   b. From the Turbo Pascal main menu, press the `E` key for editor.
   c. Type in the text of your program.
   d. Use `Ctrl-K D` to quit the editor.
   e. Press the `RETURN` key for the Turbo Pascal main menu.
   f. From the Turbo Pascal main menu, press the `S` key for *Save*.

5. *To add material to the current workfile:*
   a. From the Turbo Pascal main menu, press the `E` key to enter the editor.
   b. Move the cursor to the point of insertion:
      (1) Use the `down arrow` key or `Ctrl-X` to move the text *down* one line.
      (2) Use the `up arrow` key or `Ctrl-E` to move the text *up* one line.
      (3) Use the `right arrow` key or `Ctrl-D` to move one space to the *right*.
      (4) Use the `left arrow` key or `Ctrl-S` to move one space to the *left*.
   c. Once at the point of insertion, type in the material to be added.
   d. If the insert mode is set, the material will be inserted. If the overwrite mode is set, the typed material will overwrite the existing material. To change from one mode to the other mode (toggle), use the `INSERT` key or `Ctrl-V`.
   e. Use `Ctrl-K D` to quit the editor (press the `RETURN` key for the Turbo Pascal main menu).

6. *To remove material from the current workfile:*
   a. Enter the editor and move the cursor to a point just beyond the point of deletion by using the moving commands (see number 5).
   b. Press the `BACKSPACE` key to delete a character. Use `Ctrl-Y` to delete the entire line the cursor is on.

COMMENT

If you really mess up, use `Ctrl-K D` to quit the editor. From the Turbo Pascal main menu, press `W` for `Workfile`. Answer the save prompt by pressing the `N` key, for *no*. Set the workfile to the last saved version of the TEXT file.

7. *To make a correction to the workfile:*
   a. From the editor command line, move to the point where the correction is to be made (use moving commands).
   b. Delete material if needed (see number 6).
   c. Insert new material if needed (see number 5).

8. *To get to the beginning or end of a text file quickly:*
   a. Use `Ctrl-Q C` to *jump* to the *end* of the text file.
   b. Use `Ctrl-Q R` to *jump* to the *beginning* of the text file.

9. *To adjust text for indentation:*
   a. Use moving commands (or the `HOME` key) to move the cursor to the start of the line where the indentation needs to be altered.
   b. Use the space bar to insert blank spaces for the correct indentation.
   or:
   a. Use the moving commands to move the cursor to the first word in the line where indentation needs to be altered.
   b. Use the `BACKSPACE` key to remove spaces for the correct indentation.

10. *To exit the editor:*
Use `Ctrl-K D` (press the `RETURN` key to see the Turbo Pascal main menu).

COMMENT
It is a good idea to *save* any changes made in the editor.

11. *To load a text file from a disk into the editor:*
    a. From the Turbo Pascal main menu, press the `W` key for `Workfile`.
    b. Respond to the prompt `Work file name:` by entering the disk drive, then the name of the text file you desire to load into the editor. Example:

        `B:Program2.TXT`

    c. Press the `E` key to select the editor.
12. *To compile a program in the workfile:*
From the Turbo Pascal main menu, press `C` for *Compile*. (Any errors in the program involving spelling, punctuation, or undefined words will stop the compilation of the program. At this point, press the `ESC` key to enter the editor and fix the error.)

COMMENT
The code resulting from this compilation is held in *memory* only.

13. *To execute the code of a program in the workfile:*
First compile the text file (see number 12), then from the Turbo Pascal main menu press the `R` key for *Run*.

COMMENT
`Run` always compiles then executes the program text in the editor. If the text is already compiled, the code is executed.

14. *To run a program that is in the workfile:*
From the Turbo Pascal main menu, press the `R` key for *Run*. The *Run* application compiles, then executes the program in the workfile. The code resulting from the compilation is held in memory only.
15. *To compile a program to a file on the diskette:*
    a. Press the `W` key to select the `Workfile`.
    b. Enter the name of the text file you desire to compile to a file. Example:

        `B:MyFile.PAS`

    c. From the Turbo Pascal main menu, press the `O` key to select

        `compiler Options`

    d. From the menu presented, press the `C` key to select

        `compile to a COM file`

    e. Press the `Q` key to quit the `compiler Options` menu.
    f. From the Turbo Pascal command line, press the `C` key to select *Compile*.
    g. The text in the workfile will be compiled and stored in a file named the same as the workfile specified, except the extension will be `COM`. Example:

        `B:MyFile.COM`

    h. From the Turbo Pascal main menu, press the `O` key to select `compiler Options`.
    i. Press the `M` key to set the compiler options back to `Memory`. Press the `Q` key to quit the `compiler Options` menu.
16. *To run a program that is in a COM file on a diskette:*
    a. Exit Turbo Pascal (from the Turbo Pascal main menu press the `Q` key for `Quit`) to the operating system.
    b. From the operating system prompt `A>` type the name of the file and press the `RETURN` key. Example:
    Type `Program1` (the name of the COM file), then press the `RETURN` key.

17. *To remove a file from a diskette:*
    a. Exit Turbo Pascal (from the Turbo Pascal main menu, press the Q key for Quit) to the operating system.
    b. From the operating system cursor (A>) type: ERASE *file name.*
    c. Press the RETURN key.
       Example: Type ERASE B:MyFile.PAS, then press the RETURN key.

18. *To print a text file on the printer (operating system method):*
    a. Exit Turbo Pascal (from the Turbo Pascal main menu, press the Q key for Quit) to the operating system.
    b. From the operating system cursor A>, type TYPE, then file name, then >PRN. For example, type TYPE B:MyFile.PAS >PRN then press the RETURN key to send the contents of MyFile to the printer.

COMMENT
To use this application, a printer must be connected to the computer. The printer must be turned on and ready.

19. *To print a text file on the printer (Turbo Pascal method):*
    If your version of Turbo Pascal contains a file named Lister.PAS, you can obtain a hard copy of a TEXT file as follows:
    a. Press W for WorkFile. Enter Lister.PAS
    b. Press R for *Run.* Respond to the prompt:

       Enter filename:

    by entering the name of the TEXT file you would like to send to the printer.

20. *To copy a file from one diskette to another diskette:*
    a. Exit Turbo Pascal (from the Turbo Pascal main menu, press the Q key for Quit) to the operating system.
    b. From the operating system cursor A>, type

       COPY A:PasDemo.TXT B:PasDemo.TXT ⎤— one blank space

       Press the RETURN key. General form is:

       COPY *file name of source file* ⎤ *name of destination file* — one blank space

COMMENT
You will need a *formatted* diskette.

21. *To make a backup copy of a diskette:*
    a. Exit Turbo Pascal (from the Turbo Pascal main menu, press the Q key for Quit) to the operating system.
    b. From the operating system prompt (A>), type

       COPY A:*.* B: — one blank space

       Press the RETURN key (all the files on the diskette in disk drive A will be copied to the diskette in disk drive B).

COMMENT
The diskette in drive B can now be used for a Turbo Pascal data diskette.

22. *To create a formatted diskette:*
    Have the diskette that is to be formatted ready.
    a. Place diskette to be formatted in disk drive B.
    b. From the operating system prompt (A>) type FORMAT B: and press the RETURN key.
    c. After some disk drive activity, the prompt

       Format another (Y/N)?

    is presented. Type N and press RETURN to return to the operating system.

Appendix B: Language Summary

Reserved Words

These words have special meaning to the Turbo Pascal language; therefore, they cannot be used as identifiers composed by the programmer.

ABSOLUTE	DOWNTO	GOTO	NOT	RECORD	TO
AND	ELSE	IF	OF	REPEAT	TYPE
ARRAY	END	IN	OR	SET	UNTIL
BEGIN	EXTERNAL	INLINE	OVERLAY	SHL	VAR
CASE	FILE	LABEL	PACKED	SHR	WHILE
CONST	FOR	MOD	PROCEDURE	STRING	WITH
DIV	FORWARD	NIL	PROGRAM	THEN	XOR
DO	FUNCTION				

Constants
FALSE, TRUE, MAXINT, PI, NIL

Simple data types
Predefined: BOOLEAN, CHAR, INTEGER, REAL
User-defined simple (enumerated) data types
Subrange data types

Data Structures
Predefined: STRING, TEXT
User-defined: SET, ARRAY, RECORD, FILE

Predefined TEXT Files
INPUT, OUTPUT

Predefined Procedures
Input/output: READ, READLN, WRITE, WRITELN, LST
Screen: GOTOXY, CLRSCR, CLREOL, WINDOW
Strings: DELETE, INSERT, STR, VAL
Files: RESET, REWRITE, CLOSE, SEEK
Pointer: NEW, MARK, RELEASE, DISPOSE
Other: RANDOMIZE

Predefined Functions
Arithmetic: ABS, ARCTAN, SIN, COS, EXP, FRAC,
        INT, LN, SQR, SQRT, ROUND, TRUNC
Strings: CONCAT, COPY, LENGTH, POS
Files: EOLN, EOF, IORESULT, FILESIZE, FILEPOS
Other: ORD, CHR, SUCC, PRED, ODD, RANDOM, FRAC,
        UPCASE

Input/Output Device Names
CON:, TRM:, KBD:, LST:

Assignment
Use assignment operator: :=

Relationals
=, < >, >, >=, <, <=, IN

Operators
NOT
*, /, DIV, MOD , AND
+, - , OR

Control Instructions
Decision control: IF-THEN-ELSE, IF-THEN,
                CASE-OF-ELSE-END
Repetition control: WHILE-DO, REPEAT-UNTIL,
                FOR-DO
Procedures and functions

Program Sections and Their Order
Program header
CONST section
TYPE section
VAR section
PROCEDURE and/or FUNCTION blocks
Execution section

Appendix C: ISO Standard Pascal

This appendix is designed to illustrate the major differences between the Pascal implementation presented in this textbook and ISO (International Standards Organization) Standard Pascal. Standard Pascal was developed with the additional aim (beyond readability and structuring of programs) of portability of programs. Portability deals with moving a program written on one computer to another computer.

The Program Header

In Standard Pascal, external files used for input and output must be listed in the program header. For example:

```
PROGRAM GradeReports (INPUT , OUTPUT) ;
```

and

```
PROGRAM UpKeep (INPUT , OUTPUT , Items) ;
```

INPUT and OUTPUT are predefined files and are not declared in the program VAR section. Other files listed in the header are declared and their type stated in the program VAR section.

Strings

Strings are a major area of difference between Standard Pascal and the version of Pascal presented in this textbook. In Standard Pascal STRING is *not* a predefined type (it must be defined in a type section). The identifier *String* is usually listed in the TYPE section in Standard Pascal as follows:

```
TYPE String = PACKED ARRAY [1 .. 10] OF CHAR ;

VAR WordA , WordB : String ;
```

Here, the identifier String is a user-defined type. The word PACKED is a predefined procedure used to conserve computer memory. Some major differences now arise.

Consider the following:

```
WordA := 'Hello'
```

This assignment is *invalid*. A valid assignment would be

```
WordA := 'Hello□□□□□'
```

where □ represents a blank (often called a padding blank).

The word PACKED in the declaration of String results in some other oddities (compared to the material presented in this textbook). To read a value into a variable (WordA) of type String (as declared previously), the following instruction could be used:

```
FOR Count := 1 TO 10 DO
  BEGIN
    READ (Ch) ;
    WordA [Count] := Ch
  END ;
```

An instruction like READ (WordA [Count]) is invalid because a component of a PACKED ARRAY cannot be passed as a parameter. Also,

```
READLN (WordA)
```

is not a good idea because the program user might enter more characters than the components declared for WordA. However,

```
READLN (InFile , WordA)
```

would be fine because since the programmer would know the data structure InFile. Of course, InFile would be of type FILE OF String.

To output a value in WordA, the WRITELN procedure can be employed. Unlike arrays, the value in a PACKED ARRAY can be printed directly without the need to use subscripts. Thus, WRITELN (WordA) is a valid instruction in Standard Pascal.

Also, unlike other structured types, variables of type

```
PACKED ARRAY [1 .. n] OF CHAR
```

can be used with the relationals: $<>$, $>$, $>=$, $<$, $<=$. For example,

```
IF WordA > WordB
  THEN WRITELN (WordA)
  ELSE WRITELN (WordB)
```

is a valid instruction in Standard Pascal.

Of course, since STRING is not implemented in Standard Pascal the built-in procedures and functions for values of type STRING presented in this textbook must be written by the programmer in Standard Pascal.

Files

The next major area of difference between the Pascal implementation in the textbook materials and Standard Pascal is with files. As mentioned earlier, any external file used in a Standard Pascal program must be listed in the program header. Also, any external files other than INPUT and OUTPUT are declared in the program VAR section. A typical Standard Pascal program which works with files follows:

```
PROGRAM GradeReport (INPUT , OUTPUT , Grades) ;

VAR Grades : FILE OF INTEGER ;
    Count, Sum, Average : INTEGER ;

BEGIN
  RESET (Grades) ;                       {Open existing file}
  Sum := Ø ;                             {Initialize sum}
  Count := Ø ;                           {Initialize count}
  WHILE NOT EOF (Grades) DO
    BEGIN
      Sum := Sum + Grades^ ;             {RESET does a GET}
      Count := Count + 1 ;               {Keep up with number of values}
      GET (Grades)                       {Get next component of file}
    END ;
  IF Count >= 1
    THEN WRITELN ('Average is: ', Sum / Count : 1 : 3)
    ELSE WRITELN ('Grades file was empty');
  CLOSE (Grades)                         {Close file}
END .
```

As you can see, the method of opening the file `Grades` via `RESET (Grades)` is different from Turbo Pascal. The assignment occurs in the program header. Also, in ISO Standard Pascal the compound instruction for the WHILE-DO could have been written as follows (provided `Value` is declared and of type INTEGER):

```
BEGIN
  READ (Grades , Value) ;
  Sum := Sum + Value ;
  Count := Count + 1
END
```

That is, `READ` and `WRITE` can be used with non-TEXT files. Finally, file access is *sequential* only. That is, `SEEK` (thus, random access of files) is not defined (allowed) in Standard Pascal.

Other Differences

Other differences between Turbo Pascal and ISO Standard Pascal are as follows.

1. CASE statements in Standard Pascal do not allow the ELSE option. Also, if the expression for the CASE instruction does not match one of the selections an error results.
2. Standard Pascal does not allow compiler options.
3. Standard Pascal uses PAGE rather than CLRSCR to clear the screen. Standard Pascal does have the procedures CLREOL and WINDOW.
4. Standard Pascal does not have the procedure RANDOMIZE nor the function RANDOM.
5. Standard Pascal does not have the procedures MARK and RELEASE.

ISO Language Summary

Reserved Words in ISO Standard Pascal

AND	DO	FORWARD	MOD	PROCEDURE	TO
ARRAY	DOWNTO	FUNCTION	NIL	PROGRAM	TYPE
BEGIN	ELSE	GOTO	NOT	RECORD	UNTIL
CASE	END	IF	OF	REPEAT	VAR
CONST	FILE	IN	OR	SET	WHILE
DIV	FOR	LABEL	PACKED	THEN	WITH

Simple Data Types
Predefined: BOOLEAN, CHAR, INTEGER, REAL
User defined: *enumerated, subrange*

Data Structures
Predefined: TEXT
User-defined: SET, ARRAY, RECORD, FILE, PACKED ARRAY

Predefined Procedures
Input/Output: READ, READLN, WRITE, WRITELN
Files: RESET, REWRITE, CLOSE, GET, PUT
Screen: PAGE
Pointer: NEW, DISPOSE
Other: PACK, UNPACK

Predefined Functions
Arithmetic: ABS, ARCTAN, SIN, COS, EXP, LN, SQR, SQRT, ROUND, TRUNC
Files: EOLN, EOF
Other: ORD, CHR, SUCC, PRED, ODD

Appendix D: Graphics

Graphics has become a valid topic in computer science and is increasing in importance. Because a majority of programs require output to the screen, an attractive screen is important to software development. Since this topic is immense and is specific to each machine, only an introduction will be presented in this book. To do this unit, you need to know the material through Chapter 3.

Graphics I

Graphics starts with a *high-resolution* screen. Up to this point, you have worked with a TEXT screen. That is, a screen made up of 80 columns and 25 rows. The TEXT screen is designed to handle characters and numbers. To display lines and points, you must switch to a high-resolution screen. The high-resolution screen is 640 pixels (picture elements or points) wide by 200 pixels long. See Figure D–1.

COMMENT
Your system must have graphics capabilities for you to do this material.

Figure D–1

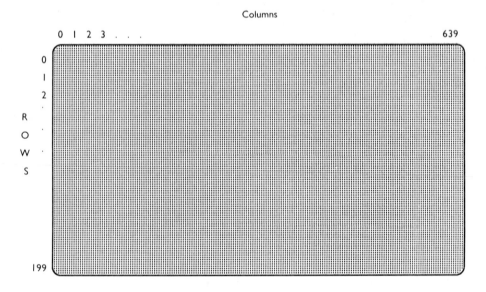

HIRES

To switch to the high-resolution screen, the built-in Pascal instruction HIRES is used. When this instruction is executed, the screen is cleared, the background is black, and the material placed on the screen is white.

To plot a pixel on the high-resolution screen, the built-in instruction PLOT is used. The general form of this instruction is

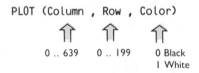

Consider the following instructions:

```
HIRES ;
WRITE ('Hello') ;
PLOT (30, 50, 1) ;
WRITE ('Bye')
```

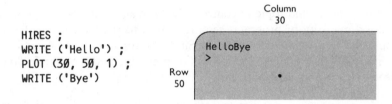

Another object (other than a point) that can be placed on this screen is a *line*. To accomplish this, the built-in instruction DRAW is used. The general form of this instruction is

```
DRAW (StartCol, StartRow, EndCol, EndRow, Color)
```
```
         0 .. 639   0 .. 199   0 .. 639   0 .. 199   0 Black
                                                     1 White
```

Consider the following instructions:

```
HIRES ;
DRAW (20,30,150,120,1) ;
WRITE ('Line')
```

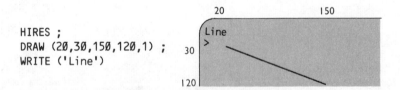

The instruction DRAW (20, 30, 150, 120, 1) draws a line starting at column 20 and row 30 and ending at column 150 and row 120, using the color white.

As an example of a program using graphics, consider the following example.

EXAMPLE

Write a Pascal program that draws a 50 by 50 square on the screen with top left vertex at column 30 and row 40. The word Square should be written to right of the drawing.

SOLUTION

```
PROGRAM GrSquare ;

BEGIN
  HIRES ;
  DRAW (30, 40, 80, 40, 1) ;        {Do top of square}
  DRAW (80, 40, 80, 90, 1) ;        {Do left side of square}
  DRAW (80, 90, 30, 90, 1) ;        {Do bottom of square}
  DRAW (30, 90, 30, 40, 1) ;        {Do right side of square}
  GOTOXY (12, 6) ;                  {Position cursor}
  WRITE ('Square')
END .
```

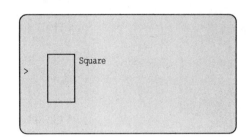

COMMENT

The position of the cursor for writing the word **Square** was computed by thinking of a character as an 8 by 8 square. That is, the top right corner of the square was at column 80 and row 40. Since 80 **DIV** 8 is 10, column 12 was used to position the cursor to the right of the figure. Also, 40 **DIV** 8 is 5. Thus, row 6 was selected to align with the top of the figure.

As you can see from the sample execution, there is some distortion. In reality, a pixel (picture element) is 1 dot wide by 2 dots long. Thus, to achieve a shape that looks like a square, you replace the 80 by 130 in the previous program. That is, the instruction to draw the top side becomes

```
DRAW (30, 40, 130, 40, 1)
```

Also, to position of the cursor to write the word **Square**, you use **GOTOXY (18, 6)**. Since 130 **DIV** 8 is 16, 18 is used to clear the right side of the square drawn (see sample execution).

From the sample execution you can see that the Pascal prompt is at column 1 and row 7. This is *not* a very good way to end a program involving the high-resolution screen. The screen should be returned to TEXT mode. This can be accomplished by using the built-in instruction TEXTMODE. However, this instruction also clears the screen. An improved method of ending the program would be as shown in Figure D–2.

COMMENT

The ratio of the width of a pixel to its length is called the *aspect ratio*. This ratio is different for different monitors. Thus, there could be some slight differences in your screen and the ones displayed in these materials.

Figure D–2

```
PROGRAM GrSquare ;

BEGIN
  HIRES ;
  DRAW (30, 40, 130, 40, 1) ;       {Do top of square}
  DRAW (130, 40, 130, 90, 1) ;      {Do left side of square}
  DRAW (130, 90, 30, 90, 1) ;       {Do bottom of square}
  DRAW (30, 90, 30, 40, 1) ;        {Do right side of square}
  GOTOXY (18, 6) ;                  {Position cursor}
  WRITE ('Square') ;
  GOTOXY (1, 24) ;
  WRITE ('Press any key to quit- ') ;
  REPEAT
     {Do nothing}
  UNTIL KEYPRESSED ;                {Wait for user to press a key}
  TEXTMODE
END .
```

COMMENT

The built-in function KEYPRESSED scans the keyboard. If a key has been pressed, the BOOLEAN value TRUE is returned. If no key was pressed, the function KEYPRESSED returns the value FALSE. Thus, the REPEAT-UNTIL instruction will execute until the user presses a key on the keyboard. Once this occurs an exit is made from the loop and the instruction TEXTMODE is executed. That is, the screen is cleared and the TEXT screen appears.

Color

The background for the high-resolution screen is always black. The material placed on the screen can be in a color other than white. The instruction to set the color of the material placed on the high-resolution screen is HIRESCOLOR. The general form of this instruction is

    HIRESCOLOR (ColorNumber)

where the parameter ColorNumber is a value from 0 to 15. The list of colors is shown in Table D–1.

Table D–I

ColorNumber	Color	ColorNumber	Color
0	Black	8	DarkGray
1	Blue	9	LightBlue
2	Green	10	LightGreen
3	Cyan	11	LightCyan
4	Red	12	LightRed
5	Magenta	13	LightMagenta
6	Brown	14	Yellow
7	LightGray	15	White

COMMENT

Cyan is a blue and magenta is a purple.

Thus, inserting the instruction HIRESCOLOR (4) in the program GrSquare would result in all the material on the screen being in Red. Only one color is allowed for the high-resolution screen. Additionally, the color word can be used in place of the color number. That is, you could write

    HIRESCOLOR (RED)

To increase your understanding of high-resolution graphics, study the program Moire in Figure D–3.

The FOR-DO loops draw a collection of lines starting at the center of the screen (320,100) and radiating to the edge of the screen. These lines produce an interesting design known as a *moire* (a watered or wavy pattern). After the design is drawn, the message

    Press any key to quit–

is written at the bottom of the screen. Next, the REPEAT-UNTIL loop is entered. The instructions repeated cause the material on the screen to switch from one color to the next, then pause (the timing loop). These instructions will be repeated until the user presses a key on the keyboard. Once the user presses a key, an exit is made from the loop and the instruction TEXTMODE is executed. That is, the screen is cleared and the TEXT screen appears.

```
PROGRAM Moire ;

VAR Ct : INTEGER ;

BEGIN
  HIRES ;
  HIRESCOLOR (GREEN) ;                    {objects in Green}
  FOR Ct := 0 TO 50 DO                    {Right section}
    DRAW (320, 100, 640, 4*Ct, 1) ;
  FOR Ct := 0 TO 80 DO                    {Bottom section}
    DRAW (320, 100, 640 - 8*Ct, 200, 1) ;
  FOR Ct := 0 TO 50 DO                    {Left section}
    DRAW (320, 100, 0, 200 - 4*Ct, 1) ;
  FOR Ct := 0 TO 80 DO                    {Top section}
    DRAW (320, 100, 8*Ct, 0, 1) ;
  GOTOXY (1, 24) ;
  WRITE ('Press any key to quit- ') ;
  REPEAT
    HIRESCOLOR (Ct MOD 15 + 1) ;          {Color number from 1 to 15}
    Ct := Ct + 1 ;
    FOR Time := 1 TO MAXINT DO            {Pause}
      {Nothing}
  UNTIL KEYPRESSED ;
  TEXTMODE
END .
```

Figure D–3

Moire patterns

BarGraph Update

To conclude this first session on graphics, the program BarGraph from Chapter 3, page 159 will be updated to include high-resolution graphics. The program BarGraph used a bar of asterisks (*) to indicate the sales for a given year. A much better bar graph could be drawn using a rectangle to indicate the sales for a given year. To achieve this, the instruction DRAW is used.

Consider the layout for a given rectangle in the program (see Figure D–4).

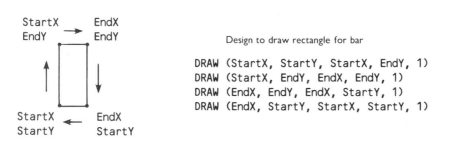

Figure D–4

Design to draw rectangle for bar

```
DRAW (StartX, StartY, StartX, EndY, 1)
DRAW (StartX, EndY, EndX, EndY, 1)
DRAW (EndX, EndY, EndX, StartY, 1)
DRAW (EndX, StartY, StartX, StartY, 1)
```

In Figure D–4 StartX changes with each bar to be drawn. To assign a value to StartX the assignment instruction

```
StartX := 32*(Year - 1) + 1
```

can be used. This instruction starts each bar 32 pixels or 4 characters from the start of the last bar. StartY is assigned the value 176 (character row 22). EndX is assigned the value EndX + 32 because each bar is to be 32 pixels wide. EndY changes with the amount of sales for the year. EndY can be assigned a value by using the assignment instruction

```
EndY := 176 - 8*AmtOfSales
```

The program BarGraph altered to include high-resolution graphics is shown in Figure D–5.

Figure D–5

Sample Execution

```
PROGRAM BarGraphics ;

VAR NumOfYears, Sales, Year, AmtOfSales : INTEGER ;
    Ch : CHAR ;
    StartX, StartY, EndX, EndY : INTEGER ;

BEGIN
  WRITE ('For how many years is graph? (2 .. 9): ') ;
  READLN (NumOfYears) ;
  HIRES ;
  HIRESCOLOR (GREEN) ;
  WRITE ('Enter sales for the year  : ') ;
  FOR Year := 1 TO NumOfYears DO
    BEGIN
      GOTOXY (25, 1) ;
      WRITE (Year) ;
      GOTOXY (29, 1) ;
      WRITE ('    ') ;                      {CLREOL does not work in HIRES}
      GOTOXY (29, 1) ;
      READLN (AmtOfSales) ;
      GOTOXY (4*(Year - 1) + 3, 25) ;
      WRITE (Year) ;
      StartX := 32*(Year - 1) + 1 ;
      StartY := 176 ;
      EndX := StartX + 32 ;
      EndY := 176 - 8*AmtOfSales ;
      DRAW (StartX, StartY, StartX, EndY, 1) ;     {Left side}
      DRAW (StartX, EndY, EndX, EndY, 1) ;         {Top side}
      DRAW (EndX, EndY, EndX, StartY, 1) ;         {Right side}
      DRAW (EndX, StartY, StartX, StartY, 1) ;     {Bottom side}
      GOTOXY (EndX DIV 8 - 2 , EndY DIV 8) ;
      WRITE (AmtOfSales)
    END  ;
  GOTOXY (1, 1) ;
  WRITE ('Press RETURN to quit-          ') ;
  READLN (Ch) ;
  TEXTMODE
END .
```

In Figure D–5, the instructions

```
GOTOXY (EndX DIV 8 - 2 , EndY DIV 8) ;
WRITE (AmtOfSales)
```

write the sales for the year above the bar drawn for a given year.

Exercises

1. Which of the following changes the screen to the high-resolution screen?
   a. GRAPHMODE   **b.** TEXTMODE   **c.** HIGHRES   **d.** HIRES   **e.** GRAPHICS
2. Which of the following plots a point at column 35 row 68?
   a. DRAW (35, 68)   **b.** PLOT (35,68,1)   **c.** DOT (35,68)   **d.** PLOT (35,68)
3. The high-resolution screen is _____ pixels wide and _____ pixels long. The background color is _____ and the color of the material placed on the screen can be set by using the instruction _____.
4. Insert *True* for a true statement, *False* for a false statement.
   _____ **a.** The instruction KEYPRESSED reads a character from the keyboard.
   _____ **b.** To change back to the text screen, the instruction TEXTMODE is used.
   _____ **c.** The instruction PLOT (35, 87, Ø) erases the pixel at column 35 and row 87.
   _____ **d.** Before a program using the high-resolution screen is finished, the program should switch back to the text screen.
   _____ **e.** Characters cannot be placed on the high-resolution screen.
   _____ **f.** To draw a line on the high-resolution screen, the instruction LINE is used.
   _____ **g.** The instruction HIRESCOLOR (PINK) is a valid instruction.
   _____ **h.** The instruction GOTOXY will not work with the high-resolution screen.
   _____ **i.** The instruction CLREOL will not work with the high-resolution screen.
5. Write a Pascal program that draws a 90 by 20 rectangle whose lower left corner is at column 50 row 140 and whose color is light blue.
6. Set the workfile to MOIRE.PAS from the Source diskette.
   a. Alter the Pascal program Moire to first draw a horizontal line at each row that is a multiple of 5 (that is, row 5, 10, 15, etc.).
   b. Further alter the program Moire to draw horizontal lines at each column that is a multiple of 5.
   c. Further alter the program where the drawing of the radiating lines are drawn in color 0 (black).
7. Set the workfile to BARGRAF.PAS from the Source diskette. Rewrite the program BarGraphics such that the bars (rectangles) are drawn horizontally.
8. Write a Pascal program that allows the program user to do graphics from the keyboard. That is, when the user presses the M key, a line 10 pixels long is drawn. When the user presses the T key, the direction in which the line is drawn changes (see design). When the user presses the E key, the screen is erased and the cursor is moved to the center of the screen.

Design: Switch to high-resolution screen
          Write prompt at row 25
          Col : = 320
          Row : = 100
          REPEAT
            READ (KBD,Ch)
            CASE Ch OF
            'M','m' : DRAW (Col, Row, Col + X, Row + Y, 1)
                   Col : = Col + X
                   Row : = Row + Y
            'T','t' : Dir : = (Dir + 1) MOD 8
                   CASE Dir OF
                   0 : X : = 20
                      Y : = 0
                   1 : X : = 14
                      Y : = −7

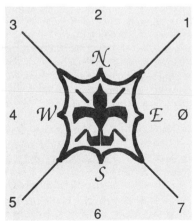

(Continued)

COMMENT
Insert the compiler directive
{$B–} to defeat the buffered
input feature of Turbo Pascal.
This will allow the READ instruc-
tion to terminate without the
RETURN key being pressed.

```
                              2 : X := 0
                                  Y := – 10
                              3 : X := – 14
                                  Y := – 7
                                    :
                                    :
                             END
          'E','e'  : CLEARSCREEN
                     Col := 320
                     Row := 100
          UNTIL Ch = 'Q'
```

Graphics 2

In the last unit, you were introduced to the essentials of graphics in Turbo Pascal. In this unit, you will work with a collection of modules stored in the file GRAPH.P. These modules include instructions for drawing circles and arcs, painting the screen and regions on the screen, and performing TurtleGraphics. This section requires knowledge of control instructions and modules.

GRAPHCOLORMODE

Before exploring the procedures in the file GRAPH.P, a new graphics mode needs to be discussed. This graphics mode is a medium-resolution color mode and is entered using the built-in procedure GRAPHCOLORMODE. The screen in this mode is 320 pixels wide and 200 pixels high with the top left corner of column 0 row 0. In this mode, a pixel is 1 by 1 (as opposed to 1 by 2 in the mode HIRES). Also, this graphics mode allows for four colors on the screen (as opposed to two colors in HIRES).

The colors selected are determined by use of the built-in procedure PALETTE. This procedure has the form

        PALETTE (PalValue)

where PalValue is one of the values 0, 1, 2, or 3. The colors for the different values are shown in Table D–2.

Table D–2

COMMENT
Cyan is a blue and Magenta is a
purple.

PalValue	Colors			
0	0 = Black	1 = Green	2 = Red	3 = Brown
1	0 = Black	1 = Cyan	2 = Magenta	3 = LightGray
2	0 = Black	1 = LightGreen	2 = LightRed	3 = Yellow
3	0 = Black	1 = LightCyan	2 = LightMagenta	3 = White

GRAPH.P

Turbo Pascal provides a file containing a collection of graphics routines. To use these routines, the programmer must include the compiler directive

        {$I GRAPH.P}

at the start of the program (usually inserted immediately after the program header).

Three of the routines included when the file `GRAPH.P` is used are FILLSCREEN, CIRCLE, and ARC. These procedures are summarized as follows.

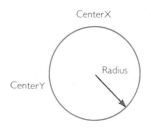

FILLSCREEN (color value)

This procedure fills the screen with a color where value is indicated by either `0`, `1`, `2`, or `3`. The actual color used is determined by the palette used.

CIRCLE (CenterX, CenterY, Radius, ColorNumber)

This procedure draws a circle centered at column `CenterX`, row `CenterY` of radius `Radius` in the color `ColorNumber`. The value in `ColorNumber` is one of the values `0`, `1`, `2`, or `3`.

ARC (StartX, StartY, Angle, Radius, ColorNumber)

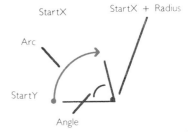

This procedure draws an arc (part of a circle) that starts at column `StartX`, row `StartY`. The part of the circle drawn is determined by the value in `Angle`. The value 90 yields a quarter-circle, the value 180 yields a half-circle, and so forth. The value in `Radius` determines the radius of the circle from which the arc is derived. The circle is centered at column `StartX + Radius`, row `StartY`. Thus, if the value in `Radius` is negative, the arc is drawn to the left. The value in `ColorNumber` is one of the values `0`, `1`, `2`, or `3`.

As a demonstration of the procedures just described, consider the program in Figure D–6.

```
PROGRAM GrafDemo ;

{$I GRAPH.P}

VAR Ans : CHAR ;

BEGIN
  GRAPHCOLORMODE ;
  PALETTE (2) ;                    {Black, Green, Red, Yellow}
  FILLSCREEN (1) ;                 {Green}
  CIRCLE (160, 100, 50, 0) ;       {Draw circle in black}
  ARC (160, 100, 90, 50, 2) ;      {Draw quarter-circle in red}
  ARC (160, 100, 180, -50, 3) ;    {Draw semicircle to left in yellow}
  GOTOXY (1,25) ;
  WRITE ('Press ENTER to quit-') ;
  READLN (Ans) ;
  TEXTMODE
END .
```

Figure D–6

TurtleGraphics

The file `GRAPH.P` contains a collection of modules that allow drawings to be done in TurtleGraphics. With TurtleGraphics, a turtle is placed at the center of the screen, heading up. The turtle can move, turn, and leave a trail of its movement. In many situations, this is a natural approach to graphics. The screen for the turtle can be the high-resolution screen or the medium-resolution color screen. In either case, the center of the screen is column 0 row 0. The top left corner becomes column − 159 row 100 (in medium resolution). Some of the essential procedures and functions included in the file `GRAPH.P` are as follows.

COMMENT
The idea of this type of graphics was devised by S. Papert at MIT.

- HOME Sends turtle to the center of screen (0,0) and sets its heading to 0 (up).
- PENDOWN Sets turtle to draw line when it is moved.
- PENUP Sets turtle *not* to draw line when it is moved.
- FORWD (*Value*) Moves the turtle forward the *value* pixels. The direction moved depends on the turtle's heading.
- TURNLEFT (*Angle*) Alters the turtle's heading by subtracting the value in *Angle* to the turtle's heading. Turns turtle to left or counterclockwise.
- TURNRIGHT (*Angle*) Alters the turtle's heading by adding the value in *Angle* from the turtle's heading. Turns turtle to right or clockwise.
- SETHEADING (*Value*) Sets the turtle's heading to determine the direction the turtle will move. The value 0 indicates up, the value 90 indicates right, the value 180 indicates down, and the value 270 indicates left. The value can be any integer from 0 to 359. If the value is outside the range, it is converted to a value in the range (uses MOD 360).
- SETPOSITION (*XValue, YValue*) Relocates the turtle to column *XValue* and row *YValue* where column 0 and row 0 indicate center of screen.
- XCOR Returns the turtle's current column location.
- YCOR Returns the turtle's current row location.
- HEADING Returns the turtle's current heading.

As an example of using TurtleGraphics, consider the program in Figure D–7 for drawing a right triangle.

Figure D–7

```
PROGRAM TurtleDemo ;

VAR ANS : CHAR ;

BEGIN
  GRAPHCOLORMODE ;
  PALETTE (3) ;                      {black, blue, purple, white}
  HOME ;
  FORWD (50) ;                       {Draw left side}
  TURNRIGHT (135) ;
  FORWD (71) ;                       {Draw longest side—hypotenuse}
  TURNRIGHT (135) ;
  FORWD (50) ;                       {Draw bottom side}
  TURNRIGHT (90) ;                   {Make state-transparent}
  GOTOXY (1,25) ;
  WRITE ('Press RETURN  to quit-') ;
  READLN (Ans)
END .
```

To demonstrate the power of TurtleGraphics, procedure usage, and the Turbo Pascal system, do the following hands-on experiment.

EXPERIMENT

Set the workfile to the file TDemo.PAS from the Source diskette. Execute the program to observe its output. Enter the editor.

1. Move the cursor down the program to the blank line before the program execution section. Insert a blank line, the line

        VAR Ct : INTEGER ;

   and another blank line.

2. Move the cursor to the start of the line

```
    FORWD (50) ;                    {Do left side}
```

Press the **F7** key to mark the start of the block.
Move the cursor to the end of the line (use the **END** key)

```
    TURNRIGHT (90) ;                {Make state-transparent}
```

Press the **F8** key to mark the end of the block.
3. Move to the blank line before the program execution section. Insert a blank line. Insert the lines

```
    PROCEDURE DoTriangle ;

      BEGIN

      END ;
```

Insert a another blank line to separate the procedure block from the program execution section.
4. Move the cursor to the blank line between the **BEGIN** and **END** of the procedure execution section. Use **Ctrl-K V** to move the marked block. Adjust the indentation.
5. Move the cursor to the blank line in the program execution section. Insert the following lines:

```
    FOR Ct := 1 TO 20 DO
      BEGIN
        DoTriangle ;
        TURNLEFT (18)
      END ;
```

6. Quit the editor, then execute the altered program.
7. Enter the editor. Move the cursor to the end instruction (in the procedure **DoTriangle**)

```
    TURNRIGHT (90)
```

Insert a semicolon, then press the **RETURN** key. Insert the instruction

```
    FORWD (10)
```

8. Quit the editor, then execute the altered program.
9. Save the altered program to the file **TDemo.PAS** on the **Source** diskette.

A Better Circle

The built-in circle and arc procedures of Turbo Pascal are quite limited. The circle procedure draws a circle about a given point. It is often desirable to have the circle start at the turtle's location. The arc procedure only draws an arc up to the right or up to the left. There is no way to draw an arc in a direction desired by the programmer. We will now contruct a circle using the turtle (later an arc using the turtle will be constructed). Consider the following procedure:

```
PROCEDURE TCircle (Size : INTEGER) ;

  VAR Ct : INTEGER ;

  BEGIN
    FOR Ct := 1 TO 36 DO
      BEGIN
        TURNLEFT (5) ;
        FORWD (Size) ;
        TURNLEFT (5)
      END
  END ;                        {TCircle}
```

This procedure will draw a circle starting at the turtle's present location, moving to the left. To see an example of the use of this procedure, set the workfile to the file `Circles.PAS` from the `Source` diskette. Execute the program commands. After the program has completed its execution, enter the editor. Notice the slight alteration in the procedure `TCircle`. The relationship between the number of times the loop's instruction is executed and the turn amount is as follows: the product should yield 360 (a full circle). Page down (use `Pg Dn` key) the program. The first FOR-DO loop in the program's execution section draws the nine circles output by the `Circles.PAS` program.

Painting Regions

In the program `Circles.PAS` the series of FOR-DO loops that contains the instruction FILLSHAPE paints the various regions of the design produced. The built-in procedure FILLSHAPE is used to paint an enclosed region on the screen. The general form of the instruction is

```
FILLSHAPE (XLocation, YLocation, Color, BorderColor)
```

The values for `XLocation` and `YLocation` are *not* computed on the turtle coordinate system. These values are based on normal screen coordinates (where column 0 row 0 is the name of the top left corner of the screen). For this reason, a translation is performed. When the turtle is at home (the center of the screen), the `XLocation` for FILLSHAPE is `160` and the `YLocation` for FILLSHAPE is `100`. The value for color is `0`, `1`, `2`, or `3`. The value for `BorderColor` is the color number of the border enclosing the shape to be painted. Also notice that the FORWD instruction is passed a negative value. This results in the turtle moving backward.

Translation from turtle coordinates to screen coordinates.

```
XCOR + 160
100 - YCOR
```

Figure D-8

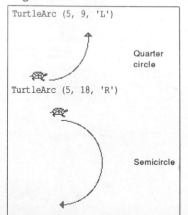

```
TurtleArc (5, 9, 'L')
```
Quarter circle

```
TurtleArc (5, 18, 'R')
```
Semicircle

A Better Arc

If the procedure `TCircle` is altered by inserting a second parameter for the amount of circle to be drawn, then a procedure is developed to draw an arc. If the procedure is further altered by adding a parameter for direction, the arc can be drawn to the left or to the right (see Figure D–8). To see such an alteration, load the file `TARC.PAS` from the `Source` diskette. Execute the program. After playing with various options, quit the program and enter the editor.

As an experiment with arcs, delete the REPEAT-UNTIL instruction in the program execution section of the program TurtleArcs. Insert the following instructions:

```
FOR Ct := 1 TO 36 DO
  BEGIN
    TurtleArc (5,9,'R') ;
    TurtleArc (5,9,'L') ;
    TURNLEFT (90) ;
    TurtleArc (5,9,'L') ;
    TurtleArc (5,9,'R') ;
    HOME ;
    TURNRIGHT (10*Ct)
  END ;
GOTOXY (1,24) ;
WRITE ('Press RETURN- ') ;
READLN (Ch) ;
```

COMMENT
To delete the instructions, use F7 to mark the start and F8 to mark the end. Use Ctrl-K Y to delete the block.

Insert the program variable Ct of type INTEGER in the program VAR section. Quit the editor and execute the altered instructions.

Spirals

The designs that use spirals are some of the most pleasing in graphics. Consider the Pascal program Spirals in Figure D-9.

Figure D-9

```
PROGRAM Spirals ;

{$I GRAPH.P} ;

VAR Dist, Ang : INTEGER ;

BEGIN
  WRITE ('Please enter length (1 .. 50): ') ;
  READLN (Dist) ;
  WRITE ('Please enter angle (5 .. 355): ') ;
  READLN (Ang) ;
  GRAPHCOLORMODE ;
  PALETTE (3) ;
  FILLSCREEN (3) ;
  SETPENCOLOR (2) ;
  PENDOWN ;
  WHILE NOT KEYPRESSED DO
    BEGIN
      FORWD (Dist) ;
      TURNLEFT (Ang) ;
      Dist := Dist + 5
    END
END .
```

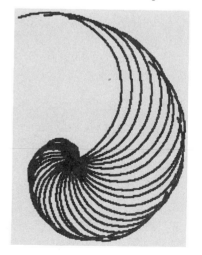

Arc Design

The program `Spirals` in Figure D–9 allows the user to assign the values to the variables `Dist` and `Ang`. The control instruction

```
WHILE NOT KEYPRESSED DO
  BEGIN
    MOVE (Dist) ;
    TURN (Ang) ;
    Dist := Dist + 5
  END
```

has a BOOLEAN expression, `NOT KEYPRESSED`. The BOOLEAN valued function KEYPRESSED returns the value `TRUE` if a key on the keyboard is pressed. Thus, the BOOLEAN expression `NOT KEYPRESSED` has a value `TRUE` while the user has not pressed a key. Therefore, the compound instruction

```
BEGIN
  MOVE (Dist) ;
  TURN (Ang) ;
  Dist := Dist + 5
END
```

will be executed while the user does not press a key (to stop the execution, the user presses a key).

The designs in Figure D–10 were produced by the program `Spirals`. The assignments to the variables `Dist` and `Ang` are listed with the design.

Figure D–10

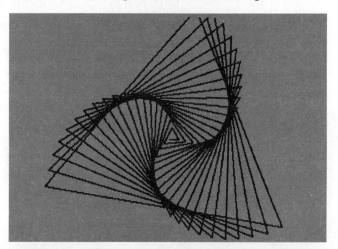

Dist 1Ø
Ang 175

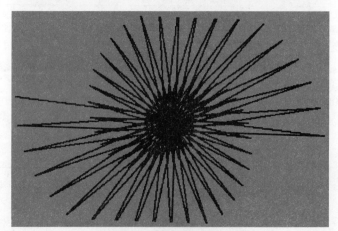

Dist 1Ø
Ang 122

Load the program `Spirals.PAS` from the `Source` diskette. Execute the program and experiment with drawing spirals using TurtleGraphics.

Exercises

1a. Using the procedure `Arc` presented in this section, write a Pascal program to draw the following snake design.

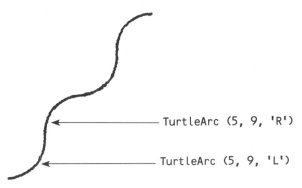

TurtleArc (5, 9, 'R')

TurtleArc (5, 9, 'L')

b. Convert the program in part a to a procedure `Snake`. Use the procedure `Snake` and the following design to write a Pascal program to create the `SunSnake` as shown.

Design: Home
         FOR Count : = 1 TO 36 DO
             Snake
             Rotate 150 degrees

2. Graphics provides a very useful technique of finding the area measure of a region. This technique is known as the *Monte Carlo* method. The method relates the area of a region to the probability of a randomly selected point being in the region. Consider the following region:

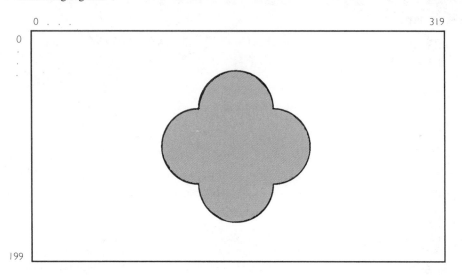

Write a Pascal program to find the area of a region based on the following design. The design requires the regular graphics function GETDOTCOLOR. This function has input two numbers (the *x* and *y* coordinates of a screen location). The function has as output the color number of the location.

Design: Get number of trials from user   {Suggest 200}
         GraphColorMode
         DrawShape   {Four overlapping circles}
         PaintShape (Green)
         While Total < Trials DO
             PickPoint   {0 < = x < 320 and 0 < = y < 200}
             IF PointInRegion   {Use GETDOTCOLOR}
                THEN Hit : = Hit + 1
             Total : = Total + 1
             PlotPoint (Red)   {Show user the process}
         Compute Probability   {Hit / Total}
         Area : = Probability *(320*200) {Medium resolution}
         TextMode
         Report Area

COMMENT
To draw a shape, you could use the instruction:

```
FOR Ct := 1 TO 4 DO
  BEGIN
    TCircle (3) ;
    TURNLEFT (90)
  END
```

Graphics 3

Up to this point, you have seen high-resolution graphics, medium-resolution color graphics, and TurtleGraphics. In this section, you will see some examples of programs that employ graphics. The first example is a game called Pebbles. It makes use of graphics and one-dimensional arrays. The second example is the game called LifeGo. It makes use of graphics and two-dimensional arrays. The last example is a demonstration of graphic patterns that can be created by the use of recursion.

Pebbles

The game of Pebbles is an old game of African and/or Arabic origin. It is known by many names, one of which is Wari. The game of Pebbles provides an excellent example of parallel arrays. The board for the Pebbles game appears in Figure D–11.

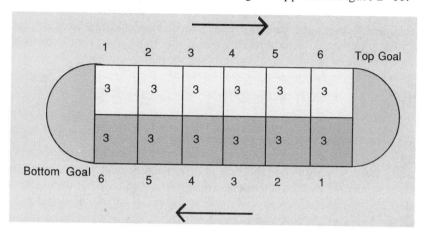

The goal of the game is to win as many of the 36 pebbles as possible. The pebbles are won by getting them into your goal area. This can be accomplished in one of two ways:

1. Placing a pebble in your goal during a regular move.
2. Placing a pebble in an open (empty) square (and collecting the pebbles in the opposite square).

A move in Pebbles consists of picking up all the pebbles in a square on *your* side of the board. The pebbles are then distributed (one at a time) to the squares to your left (including your goal area). If the number of pebbles moved is such that the distribution goes beyond your goal area, the distribution is continued to your opponent's squares. The game is over when all the pebbles have been moved to the goal areas. The winner is the player with the most pebbles.

To see a Pascal program for the game Pebbles, set the workfile to `Pebbles.PAS` from the `Source` diskette. Execute the program. The design for the program is an follows:

```
Design:    Get Player Info
           InitVariables
           REPEAT
               Set board
               Set Player to Top
               WHILE Pebbles on board DO
                   Get PlayerMove
                   Execute Move
                   Update board
                   SwitchPlayers
               Write ('Play another game?(Y/N): ')
               READLN (Ans)
           UNTIL Ans = 'N'
```

Life

The game LifeGo is a hybrid of one of the earliest games known (the Chinese game of Go) and a computer simulation known as Life (developed by John Conway). The simulation Life is performed on an *m* by *n* board. In the development that follows, an 8 by 8 board (checker or chessboard) will be used. The simulation Life starts by requesting the user to place organisms on the board. After the organisms are placed, the computer takes over to determine the fate of the organisms. That is, the computer views each of the 64 cells on the board and determines

1. if the organism in that cell will live.
2. if the organism in that cell will die.
3. if an empty cell will come to life.

These determinations are based on the following rules.

- Rule 1: If a cell is empty and has exactly three neighbors, it will come to life.
- Rule 2: If an organism has zero or one neighbors, it will die of loneliness.
- Rule 3: If an organism has four or more neighbors, it will die of overcrowding.
- Rule 4: If an organism has two or three neighbors, it will live.

Consider the starting board shown in Figure D–12.

Figure D–12

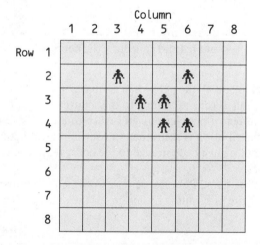

In Figure D–12, the player has placed organisms at Board [2,3], Board [2,6], Board [3,4], Board [3,5], Board [4,5], and Board [4,6]. Now the computer determines the next generation. All births and deaths occur at the same time. Thus, the computer scans the board, flagging each empty cell for birth or not and each organism for death or not. The births and deaths are implemented and the next generation is produced. Such a scan for the board in Figure D–12 is depicted in Figure D–13.

Column
1 2 3 4 5 6 7 8

Row 1–8 grid (8×8)

* = birth
X = death

As Figure D-13 shows, the organism at Board [3,5] has four or more neighbors. Thus, it is marked for death. The organisms at Board [2,3] and Board [2,6] have only one neighbor. Thus, they are marked for death. The empty cells at Board [4,4], Board [2,4], and Board [2,5] each have exactly three neighbors. Thus, they are marked for birth. The next generation is as shown in Figure D-14.

Column
1 2 3 4 5 6 7 8

Row 1–8 grid (8×8)

To see a Pascal program that performs the simulation Life, set the workfile to `Life.PAS` from the `Source` diskette. In this program, two new procedures from the file `GRAPH.P` are introduced. These procedures are GETPIC and PUTPIC. The procedure GETPIC has the form

```
GETPIC (Variable, StartX, StartY, EndX, EndY)
```

where `StartX,StartY` is the top left corner of a picture and `EndX`, `EndY` is the lower right corner of the picture. `Variable` is usually of type

```
ARRAY [1 .. n] OF CHAR
```

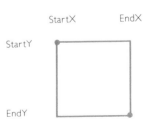

The value for *n* is computed as follows:

$$(\text{EndX} - \text{StartX}) \text{ DIV } 4*(\text{EndY} - \text{StartY})*2 + 6$$

Thus, for a shape from (20,50) to (30,70) the value of *n* would be

$$(30 - 20) \text{ DIV } 4*(70 - 50)*2 + 6 \text{ or } 86$$

The procedure PUTPIC is used to draw the picture captured by the procedure GETPIC. It has the form

```
PUTPIC (Variable, XLoc, YLoc)
```

XLoc

YLoc

where XLoc and YLoc are the bottom left corner of the location where the picture is placed on the screen. All coordinates are based on the screen coordinates, where 0,0 is the top left corner of the screen.

LifeGo

The two-player game LifeGo is based on the simulation Life. Each player has a token organism. Three organisms for each player are placed at random in the center of the board. Players take turns placing an organism on the board. The next generation is produced by the computer, following the rules of Life. If a cell is empty and has three neighbors, it will come to life. The new organism born is of the species for which the neighbors are in the majority. To see the game LifeGo, set the workfile to LifeGo.PAS from the Source diskette. Execute the program instructions.

Graphic Designs

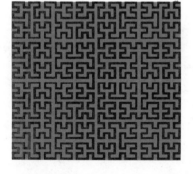

A demonstration of graphics using recursive procedures is available on the Source diskette. Set the workfile to the file DesignRe.PAS from the Source diskette. Compile, then execute the program instructions. The program starts by presenting a menu lising various graphic designs using recursive modules (a procedure or function that calls itself).

The first option draws a picture of a tree. The procedure to accomplish this option employs the instruction FORWARD. The procedure demonstrates mutually recursive procedures. Procedures of this nature call each other. The second option draws a lace pattern on the screen. The third option draws a fractal curve called a snowflake. The final option draws a space-filling curve. Two versions (Hilbert and Sierpinski) of these curves are presented.

Exercises

1. Alter the game Pebbles such that the computer will become one of the players. Develop, then implement, a strategy for the computer to use. As an extension of this problem, test your computer strategy against the strategy developed by another member of your class.

2. Alter the simulation of Life to insert organisms of a sex (male or female). Alter the rule for birth to the following:

   > *An empty cell with exactly two neighbors, one male and one female, will come to life (sex of organism born is randomly determined).*

   As an extension, allow the user to enter the probability of a birth being female.

3. Research the recursive design known as a Dragon curve. Add this option to the menu in the program RecursiveDesigns (found in the file DesignRe.PAS on the Source diskette).

Quick Guide to Turbo Graphics

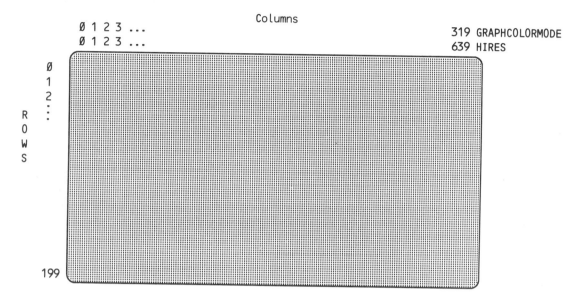

```
                          Columns
    0 1 2 3 ...                                    319 GRAPHCOLORMODE
    0 1 2 3 ...                                    639 HIRES
0
1
2
:
R
O
W
S

199
```

HIRESCOLOR/GRAPHBACKGROUND

0	Black	8	DarkGray
1	Blue	9	LightBlue
2	Green	10	LightGreen
3	Cyan	11	LightCyan
4	Red	12	LightRed
5	Magenta	13	LightMagenta
6	Brown	14	Yellow
7	LightGray	15	White

PALETTE

ColorNum	Palette Number			
	0	1	2	3
0	Black	Black	Black	Black
1	Green	Blue	Green	Blue
2	Red	Purple	LightRed	LightPurple
3	Brown	Gray	Yellow	White

In Screen Coordinates

```
PLOT (X,Y,ColorNum)
DRAW (X1,Y1,X2,Y2,ColorNum)
ARC (X,Y, Angle, Radius, ColorNum)
CIRCLE (X,Y, Radius, ColorNum)
GETPIC (VarName, X1,Y1,X2,Y2)
PUTPIC (VarName,X,Y)
FILLSCREEN (ColorNum)
FILLSHAPE (X,Y, FillColor,BorderColor)
CLEARSCREEN
```

Function

```
GETDOTCOLOR (X,Y)
```

In Turtle Coordinates

```
FORWD (Distance)
TURNLEFT (AngleAmt)
TURNRIGHT (AngleAmt)
SETPOSITION (X,Y)
SETHEADING (Angle)
HOME
PENDOWN
PENUP
SETPENCOLOR (ColorNum)
```

Functions

```
XCOR
YCOR
HEADING
```

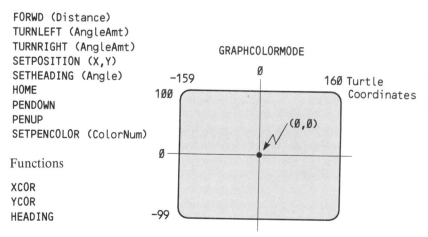

```
                    GRAPHCOLORMODE
                          0
            -159                    160 Turtle
            100                         Coordinates

                            (0,0)

             0

            -99
```

Appendix E: ASCII Table

ASCII stands for American Standard Code for Information Interchange. These codes are used with the functions ORD, CHR, and comparisons of CHAR and STRING data. Values 0 through 31 are not printable and are not listed in this table.

Dec	Hex	Char	Dec	Hex	Char	Dec	Hex	Char
32	20	SP	64	40	@	96	60	`
33	21	!	65	41	A	97	61	a
34	22	"	66	42	B	98	62	b
35	23	#	67	43	C	99	63	c
36	24	$	68	44	D	100	64	d
37	25	%	69	45	E	101	65	e
38	26	&	70	46	F	102	66	f
39	27	'	71	47	G	103	67	g
40	28	(	72	48	H	104	68	h
41	29	)	73	49	I	105	69	i
42	2A	*	74	4A	J	106	6A	j
43	2B	+	75	4B	K	107	6B	k
44	2C	,	76	4C	L	108	6C	l
45	2D	–	77	4D	M	109	6D	m
46	2E	.	78	4E	N	110	6E	n
47	2F	/	79	4F	O	111	6F	o
48	30	0	80	50	P	112	70	p
49	31	1	81	51	Q	113	71	q
50	32	2	82	52	R	114	72	r
51	33	3	83	53	S	115	73	s
52	34	4	84	54	T	116	74	t
53	35	5	85	55	U	117	75	u
54	36	6	86	56	V	118	76	v
55	37	7	87	57	W	119	77	w
56	38	8	88	58	X	120	78	x
57	39	9	89	59	Y	121	79	y
58	3A	:	90	5A	Z	122	7A	z
59	3B	;	91	5B	[	123	7B	{
60	3C	<	92	5C	\	124	7C		
61	3D	=	93	5D	]	125	7D	}
62	3E	>	94	5E	^	126	7E	~
63	3F	?	95	5F	__	127	7F	DEL

COMMENT

SP means blank space and DEL means DELETE key. Also, 7 is the code for BELL and 13 (0D in Hex) is CR, the RETURN key.

Extended ASCII Table

ASCII Value	Character	ASCII Value	Character	ASCII Value	Character	ASCII Value	Character	ASCII Value	Character	ASCII Value	Character
000	(null)	043	+	086	V	129	ü	172	¼	214	╓
001	☺	044	,	087	W	130	é	173	¡	215	╫
002	●	045	-	088	X	131	â	174	«	216	╪
003	♥	046	.	089	Y	132	ä	175	»	217	┘
004	♦	047	/	090	Z	133	à	176	░	218	┌
005	♣	048	0	091	[	134	å	177	▒	219	█
006	♣	049	1	092	\	135	ç	178	▓	220	▄
007	(beep)	050	2	093	]	136	e	179	│	221	▌
008	◘	051	3	094	∧	137	ë	180	┤	222	▐
009	(tab)	052	4	095	—	138	è	181	╡	223	▀
010	(line feed)	053	5	096	'	139	ï	182	╢	224	α
011	(home)	054	6	097	a	140	î	183	╖	225	β
012	(form feed)	055	7	098	b	141	ì	184	╕	226	Γ
013	(carriage return)	056	8	099	c	142	Ä	185	╣	227	π
014	♫	057	9	100	d	143	Å	186	║	228	Σ
015	☼	058	:	101	e	144	É	187	╗	229	ϑ
016	►	059	;	102	f	145	æ	188	╝	230	µ
017	◄	060	<	103	g	146	Æ	189	╜	231	τ
018	↕	061	=	104	h	147	o	190	╛	232	○
019	‼	062	>	105	i	148	ö	191	┐	233	Θ
020	¶	063	?	106	j	149	ò	192	└	234	Ω
021	§	064	@	107	k	150	û	193	┴	235	δ
022	▬	065	A	108	l	151	ù	194	┬	236	∞
023	↨	066	B	109	m	152	ÿ	195	├	237	Ø
024	↑	067	C	110	n	153	Ö	196	─	238	∈
025	↓	068	D	111	o	154	Ü	197	┼	239	∩
026	→	069	E	112	p	155	¢	198	╞	240	≡
027	←	070	F	113	q	156	£	199	╟	241	±
028	(cursor right)	071	G	114	r	157	¥	200	╚	242	≥
029	(cursor left)	072	H	115	s	158	Pt	201	╔	243	≤
030	(cursor up)	073	I	116	t	159	ƒ	202	╩	244	⌠
031	(cursor down)	074	J	117	u	160	á	203	╦	245	⌡
032	(space)	075	K	118	v	161	í	204	╠	246	÷
033	!	076	L	119	w	162	ó	205	═	247	≈
034	"	077	M	120	x	163	ú	206	╬	248	°
035	#	078	N	121	y	164	ñ	207	╧	249	•
036	$	079	O	122	z	165	Ñ	208	╨	250	·
037	%	080	P	123	{	166	a	209	╤	251	√
038	&	081	Q	124	¦	167	o	210	╥	252	ⁿ
039	'	082	R	125	}	168	¿	211	╙	253	²
040	(	083	S	126	~	169	⌐	212	╘	254	■
041	)	084	T	127	⌂	170	¬	213	╒	255	(blank 'FF')
042	*	085	U	128	Ç	171	½				

Index